HAMPTON-BROWN

HIGH POINT

SUCCESS IN LANGUAGE • LITERATURE • CONTENT

Teacher's Edition

ALFREDO SCHIFINI
DEBORAH SHORT
JOSEFINA VILLAMIL TINAJERO

HAMPTON-BROWN

Hampton-Brown
P.O. Box 223220
Carmel, California 93922
1-800-333-3510

Printed in the United States of America
0-7362-0902-6
 02 03 04 05 06 07 08 09 10 9 8 7 6 5 4 3

ACKNOWLEDGMENTS
Every effort has been made to secure permission, but if any omissions have been made, please let us know. We gratefully acknowledge permission to reprint the following material:

Children's Book Press: "George Littlechild" and "Nancy Hom" from *Just Like Me.* Pages 9–10 copyright © 1997 by Nancy Hom; pages 11–12 copyright © 1997 by George Littlechild. Overall book project copyright © 1997 by Harriet Rohmer. "I Honor My Ancestors" by Stephen Von Mason, "I Honor My Father and Mother" by Enrique Chagoya, "I Honor My Grandmother" by Helen Zughaib from *Honoring Our Ancestors*. Pages 6–7 copyright © 1999 by Enrique Chagoya; pages 22–23 copyright © 1999 by Stephen Von Mason; pages 30–31 copyright © 1999 by Helen Zughaib. Overall book project copyright © 1999 by Harriet Rohmer. All reprinted with permission of the publisher, Children's Book Press, San Francisco, California.

Acknowledgments continued on page T391

Contents

Program Authors

Outstanding authors, experts in second-language acquisition, literacy, and content, turn research into practice for your classroom!

Dr. Alfredo Schifini assists schools across the nation and internationally in developing comprehensive ESL programs. He has worked as a high school ESL teacher, elementary reading specialist, and school administrator. Dr. Schifini directs the Southern California Professional Development Institute for teachers of ELD. Through an arrangement with Cal Poly at Pomona, he also serves as program consultant to two large teacher-training efforts in the area of reading for struggling older students. His research interests include literacy development for older second-language learners and the integration of language and content-area instruction.

CURRICULUM REVIEWERS

Tedi Armet
Fort Bend Independent School District
Sugar Land, Texas

Suzanne Barton
International Newcomer Academy
Fort Worth Independent School District
Fort Worth, Texas

Maggie Brookshire
Emerald Middle School
Cajon Valley Unified School District
El Cajon, California

Raina Cannard
Elk Grove Unified School District
El Cajon, California

Lily Dam
Dallas Independent School District
Dallas, Texas

Judy Doss
Burbank High School
Burbank Unified School District
Burbank, California

Rossana Font-Carrasco
Paul W. Bell Middle School
Miami-Dade County School District 5
Miami, Florida

Jillian Friedman
Howard Middle School
Orange County Public Schools
Orlando, Florida

Vivian Kahn
Halsey Intermediate School 296
Community School District 32
New York, New York

Suzanne Lee
Josiah Quincy School
Boston, Massachusetts

Mary McBride
Monroe Middle School
Inglewood Unified School District
Los Angeles, California

Carolyn McGavock
Rafael Cordero Bilingual Academy, Junior
High School 45
Community School District 4
New York, New York

Dr. Deborah Short is a division director at the Center for Applied Linguistics (CAL) in Washington, D.C. She has worked as a teacher, trainer, researcher, and curriculum/materials developer. Her work at CAL has concentrated on the integration of language learning with content-area instruction. Through several national projects, she has conducted research and has provided professional development and technical assistance to local and state education agencies across the United States. She currently directs the ESL Standards and Assessment Project for TESOL.

Dr. Josefina Villamil Tinajero specializes in staff development and school–university partnership programs, and consulted with school districts in the U.S. to design ESL, bilingual, literacy, and bi-literacy programs. She has served on state and national advisory committees for standards development, including English as a New Language Advisory Panel of the National Board of Professional Teaching Standards. She is currently Professor of Education and Associate Dean at the University of Texas at El Paso, and was President of the National Association for Bilingual Education, 1997–2000.

Juan Carlos Méndez
Community School District 9
Bronx, New York

Cynthia Nelson-Mosca
Cicero School District 99
Cicero, Illinois

Kim-Anh Nguyen
Franklin McKinley School District
San Jose, California

Ellie Paiewonsky
Technical Assistance Center of Nassau
Board of Cooperative Educational Services
Massapequa Park, New York

Jeanne Perrin
Boston Public Schools
Boston, Massachusetts

Becky Peurifoy
Rockwall Independent School District
Rockwall, Texas

Marjorie Rosenberg
Montgomery County Public Schools
Rockville, Maryland

Harriet Rudnit
Grades 6–8
Lincoln Hall Middle School
Lincolnwood, Illinois

Olga Ryzhikov
Forest Oak Middle School
Montgomery County, Maryland

Dr. Wageh Saad, Ed.D.
Dearborn Public Schools
Dearborn, Michigan

Gilbert Socas
West Miami Middle School
Miami-Dade County Public Schools
Miami, Florida

HIGH POINT

Standards-Based with Specialized Instructional Strategies

The Basics

Motivates
Struggling Readers and English Learners

➤ High interest, multicultural selections

➤ Significant themes

➤ Real-world appeal

➤ Engaging activities

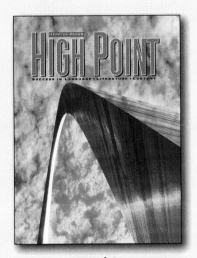

Level A

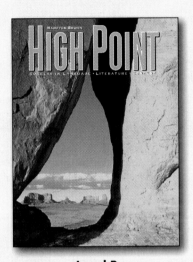

Level B

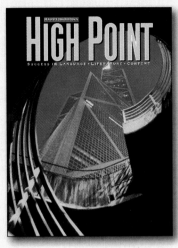

Level C

Closes Gaps in Language and Literacy

➤ Extensive vocabulary development and skills practice

➤ Complete learning to read strand

➤ Direct instruction in reading strategies

➤ Abundant use of expository text

➤ Comprehensive grammar instruction

➤ Fully supported Writing Projects

Equips Teachers for Effective Instruction

➤ Multi-level teaching strategies to address diverse needs

➤ Full array of assessment to diagnose, plan instruction, and measure progress

➤ Varied teaching tools—from transparencies to technology to tapes and theme books!

➤ Family newsletters in 7 languages to increase home involvement

Components

Integrated content across components creates a rich and contextualized learning environment. The variety of instructional tools keeps students engaged.

RESOURCES FOR STANDARDS-BASED INSTRUCTION		The Basics	LEVEL A	LEVEL B	LEVEL C
Student Books	Literature selected especially for struggling readers and English learners, instructional activities, and useful Handbooks all in one place **The Basics** **Level A** **Level B** **Level C**	•	•	•	•
The Basics Bookshelf	18 read-aloud Theme Books for building basic vocabulary and language patterns and for developing concepts of print, listening comprehension, and knowledge of text structures	•	•	•	•
Language Tapes/CDs	Recordings of songs, poems, stories, interviews, and speeches to develop vocabulary and language		•	•	•
Selection Tapes/CDs	Readings of the Student Book selections at Levels A–C and of the Theme Books in The Basics Bookshelf	•	•	•	•
Instructional Overheads	For group instruction in grammar skills, reading strategies, and the writing process	•	•	•	•
Reading Basics	Transparencies to teach phonics and word structure plus teacher scripts, letter tiles for word building, and word tiles for high frequency word instruction.	•			

RESOURCES FOR STANDARDS-BASED INSTRUCTION		The Basics	LEVEL A	LEVEL B	LEVEL C
Practice Books	Student workbooks for skills practice The Basics · Level A · Level B · Level C	•	•	•	•
Teacher's Resource Books	Reproducible activity sheets that match the instructional overheads at Levels A–C and offer handwriting practice at The Basics, as well as family newsletters in seven languages	•	•	•	•
Diagnosis and Placement Inventory	Group-administered test for placing students into the appropriate *High Point* level based on reading and writing skills, along with a Teacher's Edition	•	•	•	•
Assessment Handbooks	A complete array of assessment tools including Language Acquisition Assessments, Selection Tests, Unit Tests, Writing Assessments, and Peer- and Self-Assessments The Basics · Level A · Level B · Level C	•	•	•	•
CD-ROM Technology	*Inspiration* Visual Learning software for making graphic organizers and mind maps	•	•	•	•
Theme Libraries	10 books per level coordinated with unit themes and targeted to beginning, intermediate, and advanced levels		•	•	•
Teacher's Edition	Your complete resource for planning and instruction The Basics · Level A · Level B · Level C	•	•	•	•

Motivational, Real-World Content

For The Basics, 18 themes with related read-aloud Theme Books motivate students as they build a foundation in vocabulary, English structures, and early literacy skills.

LEVEL

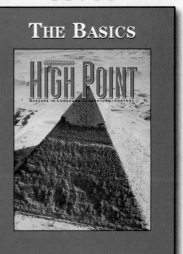

UNIT 1	Glad to Meet You!	UNIT 7	Pack Your Bags!	UNIT 13	Past and Present
UNIT 2	Set the Table	UNIT 8	Friend to Friend	UNIT 14	Tell Me More
UNIT 3	On the Job	UNIT 9	Let's Celebrate!	UNIT 15	Personal Best
UNIT 4	Numbers Count	UNIT 10	Here to Help	UNIT 16	This Land is Our Land
UNIT 5	City Sights	UNIT 11	Make a Difference!	UNIT 17	Harvest Time
UNIT 6	Welcome Home!	UNIT 12	Our Living Planet	UNIT 18	Superstars

Relevant, Curriculum-Connected Themes

At Levels A–C, significant themes speak to issues of interest for students, connect to middle school content, and offer instructional choices for teachers.

LEVEL **A**

LEVEL **B**

LEVEL **C**

	LEVEL A	LEVEL B	LEVEL C
UNIT 1	Identity	Communication	Personal Expression
UNIT 2	Cooperation	Belonging	Discoveries
UNIT 3	Relationships	Dreams and Decisions	Conflict and Resolution
UNIT 4	Community	Continuity and Change	Choices
UNIT 5	Traditions	Challenges	Triumphs

Standards-Based Instruction for All Students

*Curriculum Standards provide the foundation for **High Point**. Carefully selected readings and specially designed lessons with Multi-Level Strategies ensure standards-based instruction for struggling readers and English learners!*

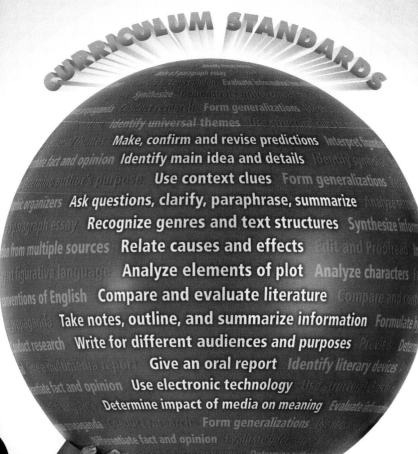

CURRICULUM STANDARDS

Make, confirm and revise predictions
Identify main idea and details
Use context clues
Ask questions, clarify, paraphrase, summarize
Recognize genres and text structures
Relate causes and effects
Analyze elements of plot
Compare and evaluate literature
Take notes, outline, and summarize information
Write for different audiences and purposes
Give an oral report
Use electronic technology
Determine impact of media on meaning

DIFFERENTIATED INSTRUCTION FOR EACH STANDARD

Multi-Level Strategies
ACTIVITY OPTIONS FOR ANALYZING ELEMENTS OF PLOT

BEGINNING Read the myth aloud, pausing after each event to clarify meaning. Have students sketch the event. Select and save one sketch per event. After reading, draw a rising-and-falling action map. Review the myth as you place the sketches on the map. Create a group sentence about each step in the plot: *A conflict happens when Hades steals Demeter's daughter.*

INTERMEDIATE Read the myth aloud or play its recording. Pause after key events to elicit steps in the plot: *What is the conflict about?* Work as a group to record events on the rising-and-falling action map on **Transparency 72**. After reading, partners retell the myth to each other.

ADVANCED As partners read the myth or listen to its recording, have them complete the plot diagram on **Master 72**. After reading, students retell the myth to each other. Then have students change an event and revise the plot diagram before telling the story again to see how events in the plot affect the final outcome.

Complete Skills Coverage

The **High Point** Scope and Sequence covers the full range of skills English learners need for academic success.

SCOPE AND SEQUENCE	The Basics	LEVEL A	LEVEL B	LEVEL C
Language Development and Communication	•	•	•	•
Language Functions	•	•	•	•
Language Patterns and Structures	•	•	•	•
Concepts and Vocabulary	•	•	•	•
Reading	•	•	•	•
Learning to Read: concepts of print, phonemic awareness, phonics, decoding, and word recognition	•			
Reading Strategies	•	•	•	•
Comprehension	•	•	•	•
Literary Analysis and Appreciation		•	•	•
Speaking, Listening, Viewing, Representing	•	•	•	•
Cognitive Academic Skills	•	•	•	•
Learning Strategies	•	•	•	•
Critical Thinking	•	•	•	•
Research Skills	•	•	•	•
Writing	•	•	•	•
Handwriting	•			
Writing Modes and Forms	•	•	•	•
Writing Process	•	•	•	•
Writer's Craft		•	•	•
Grammar, Usage, Mechanics, Spelling	•	•	•	•
Technology / Media		•	•	•
Cultural Perspectives	•	•	•	•

Assessment To Inform Instruction

High Point includes a comprehensive array of assessment tools to place students at the appropriate level, to monitor students' progress, and to assess mastery of the Language Arts standards.

DIAGNOSIS AND PLACEMENT

Diagnosis and Placement Inventory
This group-administered test places students into the appropriate *High Point* level based on reading and writing skills. A Teacher's Edition contains additional diagnostic tools, including reading fluency assessments, and provides guidance on administering the test, scoring, and interpreting results.

PROGRESS MONITORING AND SUMMATIVE EVALUATION

These assessments appear in the Assessment Handbook for each level.

Language Acquisition Assessment
Identifies Performance Assessment opportunities in each unit and offers scoring rubrics to monitor the student's progress through the stages of language proficiency.

Selection Tests
At Levels A–C, multiple-choice items and short-answer questions measure mastery of the reading strategies and the vocabulary, comprehension, and language arts skills taught with each reading selection.

Unit Tests in Standardized Test Format
The multiple-choice sections of these tests for all levels measure students' cumulative understanding of skills and language. Writing Prompts for all levels measure progress in writing skills and fluency. At Levels A–C, the Read, Think, and Explain sections offer open-ended items to measure strategies and comprehension.

Writing Assessment
A Writing Progress Checklist is used to evaluate writing in The Basics. At Levels A–C, scoring rubrics offer guidance in evaluating students' work for the Writing Project in each unit. These rubrics assist teachers in assessing how students might score on a similar task if it were encountered on a standardized test by looking at content, form, and written conventions.

Self-Assessment and Peer-Assessment Forms
Students use these forms to evaluate their work and offer feedback to their classmates.

Portfolio Evaluation Form
Students and teachers use this form to evaluate progress shown by the work collected in the portfolio.

Diagnosis and Placement Inventory

Student Test   Teacher's Edition

Assessment Handbooks

The Basics   Level A

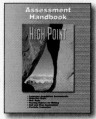

Level B   Level C

PROGRAM GUIDE FOR
Assessment and Instruction

HIGH POINT

Program Guide for Assessment and Instruction

Program Goals and Organization

High Point offers standards-based instruction in reading and language arts. The program is carefully designed for English learners and struggling readers to accelerate their growth in language and literacy.

Four overlapping levels proceed on a continuum from The Basics, a beginning language and literacy level, to Level C, the most advanced level. From Level C, students move to study in mainstream materials.

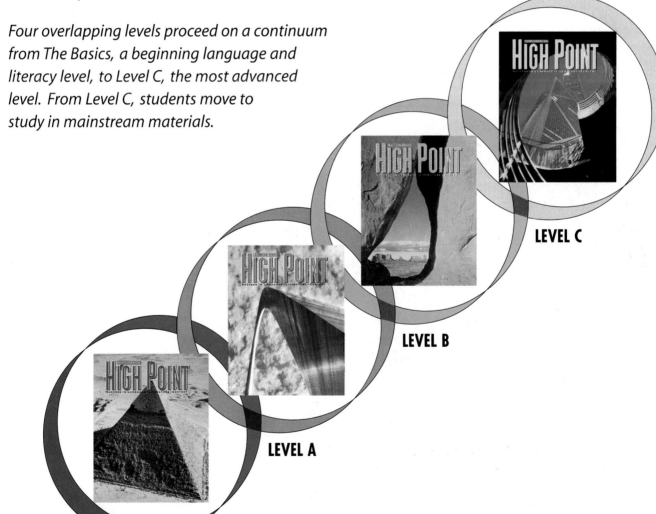

LEVEL C

LEVEL B

LEVEL A

THE BASICS

Identifying Students Who Need *High Point*

INITIAL IDENTIFICATION

High Point addresses the needs of struggling readers and English learners. To identify students who should study in *High Point*, consider information from assessments, such as the following:

- Standardized tests measure student performance in relation to a national norm. These tests report a student's percentile rank. Students scoring below the percentile rank set by your district, generally the 25th percentile, need the intervention program.

- Other tests report a student's reading level. Students whose reading level is two or more years below their grade level need the intervention program.

- A reading fluency measure, such as Edformation's *Standard Benchmark Reading Fluency Assessment Passages* available through Hampton-Brown, can also be used to determine reading level. Start by giving the student the fluency measure for the grade two years lower than the student's actual grade. If the number of words read correctly per minute by the student is lower than the mean for that grade level, the student should receive the intervention program.

- For English learners, districts are required to give a test that measures language proficiency level. Use the information from this test to identify students who need English language development.

The students identified for instruction in *High Point* come from a variety of backgrounds and educational experiences. Some have not yet learned to decode or have basic decoding skills but have not yet learned to apply them to multisyllabic words. Others possess decoding skills, but need to learn about text structures and the strategies of reading so that they can access grade-level materials and be successful in academic tasks.

Some English learners bring a solid educational foundation from their native country. In their home language they have developed academic skills that are on a par with their native English-speaking counterparts. Even if these students are literate in a language with a non-Roman alphabet and have the challenge of a new written code to crack, they already bring many of the skills and experiences they need to succeed in a structured academic setting.

Other English learners come from a patchwork of academic and life experiences. War, epidemics, natural disasters, or economic conditions may have caused students and their families to relocate within their home country or in other countries even before arriving in the U.S. School attendance may have been sporadic, with acquisition of skills and content more random than systematic. Limited academic experiences and the lack of formal literacy skills create special challenges for these students and their teachers.

High Point will help you meet these challenges. The Basics level teaches students how to decode and comprehend text up to a third-grade level. The direct, spiraling instruction in text structures, reading strategies and comprehension skills in Levels A–C builds reading power, moving students to a sixth grade reading level. Coupled with the reading instruction is a complete language development strand to support English learners as well as struggling readers who may also need to broaden their vocabularies and to gain facility with the structures of English.

> **Correct placement is crucial to students' success in the program.**

DIAGNOSIS AND PLACEMENT

Correct placement is crucial to students' success in the program. The *Diagnosis and Placement Inventory* that accompanies *High Point* provides for six placement points into the materials. Students who need decoding skills will begin in The Basics level. See page 17 for the scope and sequence of decoding skills and the three placement points:

1. Non-readers and newly-arrived English learners will be placed at the beginning of the level.

2. Students with some literacy skills will be placed before the work on long vowels begins in Unit 5.

3. Students who can decode but still need to learn to apply their skills to multisyllabic words will be placed at Unit 14.

Students who have mastered decoding skills will be placed at the beginning of Level A, Level B, or Level C according to their reading level and the array of skills mastered on the *Diagnosis and Placement Inventory*.

Placement Points in *High Point*

The *Diagnosis and Placement Inventory* surveys students' reading and writing skills to present a student profile of strengths and weaknesses and place students into *High Point*. Students who are reading severely below grade level are likely to place in The Basics level because they need the phonics and decoding skills shown below. These are listed for the purpose of clarifying the placement points. The Basics level, like Levels A–C, contains a balance of skills in vocabulary development, reading comprehension, writing strategies and applications, and written and oral English conventions. The Student Profile that is generated from the administration of the *Diagnosis and Placement Inventory* presents a picture of where students stand in all these skills areas.

		THE BASICS Reading/Lexile Levels: Grades 1-3
Placement Point 1	LAKESIDE SCHOOL	Letters and Sounds
	UNIT 1	Short Vowels
	UNIT 2	Short Vowels and Digraphs
	UNIT 3	Short Vowels, Digraphs, and Double Consonants
	UNIT 4	Blends and Digraphs
Placement Point 2	UNIT 5	Long Vowels, Word Patterns, and Multisyllabic Words
	UNIT 6	Long Vowels and Word Patterns
	UNIT 7	Long Vowels and Word Patterns
	UNIT 8	Inflections
	UNIT 9	Inflections
	UNIT 10	Long Vowels
	UNIT 11	*R*-controlled Vowels
	UNIT 12	Multisyllabic Words
	UNIT 13	Words with *y*
Placement Point 3	UNIT 14	Diphthongs and Variant Vowels
	UNIT 15	Variant Vowels and Consonants
	UNIT 16	Multisyllabic Words
	UNIT 17	Multisyllabic Words (Suffixes and Prefixes)
	UNIT 18	Multisyllabic Words
Placement Point 4		**LEVEL A** Reading/Lexile Level: Grade 4
Placement Point 5		**LEVEL B** Reading/Lexile Level: Grade 5
Placement Point 6		**LEVEL C** Reading/Lexile Level: Grade 6

Assessment to Inform Instruction

ASSESSMENT TOOLS

High Point offers a comprehensive array of assessment tools to inform instruction. These tools will help you place students into the program, monitor their progress, and evaluate their achievement both in language acquisition and in the language arts standards. These tools and the spiraling curriculum work together to ensure that students receive the instruction they need to accelerate their growth in language and literacy.

Assessment Tool	Description	Entry Level and Placement	Progress Monitoring	Summative Evaluation
Standard Benchmark Reading Fluency Assessment Passages	Three graded and equivalent passages are provided for each grade and are designed for administration at the beginning, middle, and end of the year. Administration of the passages identifies the student's fluency rate measured in words read correctly per minute (wcpm). This fluency rate can be compared to normative performance in order to identify students who need instruction in *High Point* or to assess their progress and achievement. Passages are available for license and downloading at www.edformation.com/hampton-brown .	✔	✔	✔
Diagnosis and Placement Inventory	This inventory surveys the skills taught in each level. It provides for six placement points into the program and gives a picture of the student's strengths and weaknesses in specific skills areas.	✔		
Language Acquisition Assessments	These assessments identify opportunities in each unit for performance assessments in which you can evaluate how well students demonstrate the language functions and structures targeted in the unit.		✔	
Decoding Progress Checks	At The Basics level, these word lists can be used on a weekly basis to monitor attainment of the targeted phonics skills.		✔	
Selection Tests	At Levels A–C, twenty tests, one per main selection, measure students' progress in reading strategies and vocabulary, comprehension, and language arts skills taught with the main selection.		✔	

Assessment Tool	Description	Entry Level and Placement	Progress Monitoring	Summative Evaluation
Standard Progress Monitoring Reading Fluency Assessment Passages	Weekly graded and equivalent passages are provided for each grade. By measuring the number of words read correctly on the passages across several weeks, you can monitor a student's progress and plan effective instruction. Passages are available for license and downloading at www.edformation.com/hampton-brown .		✔	
Writing Assessments	At Levels A–C, these assessments, one per unit, provide rubrics and scoring guidelines for evaluating a student's writing in the mode and form targeted in each unit's writing project.		✔	
Writing Checklist / Writing Progress and Conference Form	These forms can be used to evaluate any writing done by the students and to hold writing conferences.		✔	
Self-Assessment Forms	These forms enable students to evaluate their own work.		✔	
Peer-Assessment Form	This form provides a vehicle for peer feedback on a variety of student work.		✔	
Portfolio Evaluation Form	This form serves as a record of both teacher- and student-selected samples in the portfolio and provides for summarizing performance.		✔	
Unit Tests	These tests, one for every three units at The Basics level and one for every unit at Levels A, B, or C, measure students' achievement.			✔
Student-Profile: Year-End	This form organizes information obtained from both formal and informal assessment and provides a permanent record of performance.			✔

Reading Instruction in *High Point*

Learning to Read in The Basics

In each unit, students learn high frequency words, phonics skills, and decoding strategies, then apply them in decodable text.

1 **The Basics** introduces 266 high frequency words. Students see them, hear them, say them, spell them, and use them in word work activities to help commit them to memory. They then read the words in context to develop automatic recognition.

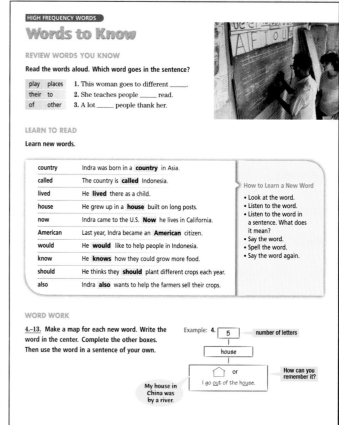

High Frequency
Word Instruction
from Unit 11
of The Basics
Student Book

Practice

*The **Reading Practice Book** and additional reinforcement activities in the Teacher's Edition provide sufficient repetitions to build skills mastery.*

High Frequency Word
Practice in the Reading
Practice Book

HIGH FREQUENCY WORDS
Words to Know
READ AND WRITE
Read each word. Then write it.

1. now _____ 2. would _____ 3. also _____
4. called _____ 5. should _____ 6. know _____
7. lived _____ 8. house _____ 9. country _____
10. American _____

WORD WORK
Read each sentence. Find the new words in the box.
Write the words on the lines.

11. These 2 words rhyme.
    would   should

12. This word is the opposite of **later**.
    _____

13. This word rhymes with **show**.
    _____

14. This word rhymes with **cow**.
    _____

15. This word has the word **so** in it.
    _____

16. This word means almost the same as **home**.
    _____

17. These 2 words are past tense verbs.
    _____ _____

18. This word always begins with a capital letter.
    _____

19. These 2 words have a silent l.
    _____ _____

20. These 2 words have 2 syllables.

2 **Transparencies** help you build the meaning of words used in decoding activities, introduce phonics skills, model decoding strategies, and direct the guided practice. **Teacher Scripts** are in the Teacher's Edition and in a separate booklet to facilitate instruction at the overhead.

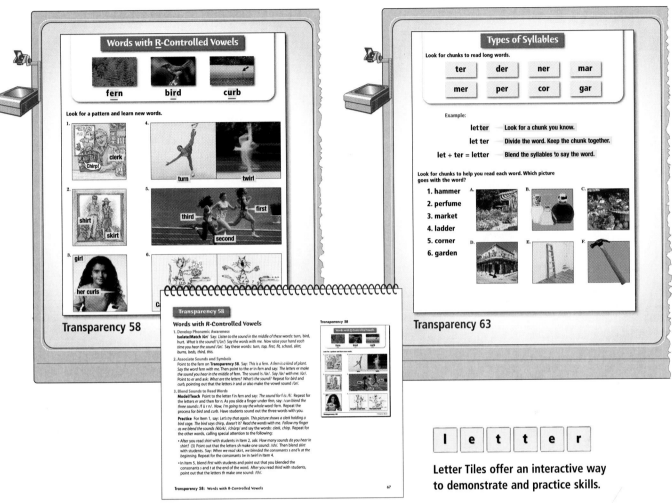

Transparency 58

Transparency 63

Teacher Scripts

Letter Tiles offer an interactive way to demonstrate and practice skills.

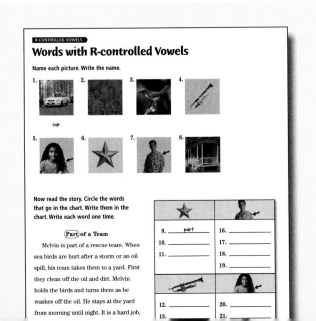

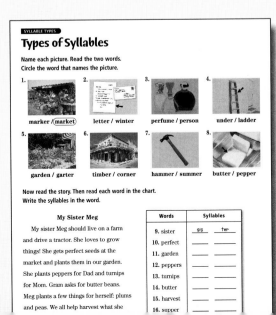

Phonics Practice and Decodable Text in the Reading Practice Book

Learning to Read in The Basics, continued

❸ Next, in the Student Book, students review the skills, try the decoding strategy on their own, read decodable text, spell words with the new phonetic element, and participate in hands-on activities that anchor their understanding of the new skill.

Reading and Spelling Pages from Unit 11 of The Basics Student Book

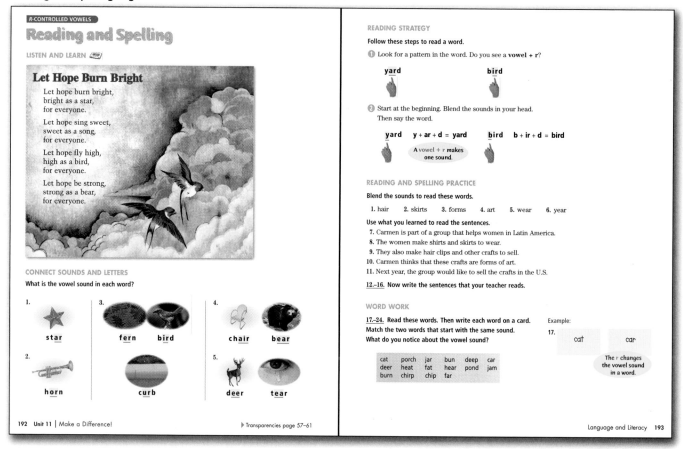

Practice

*The **Reading Practice Book** offers plenty of opportunities to read decodable text and build reading fluency.*

Unit 11 Decodable Book (made from pages of the Reading Practice Book)

4 Students then apply phonics skills and read the pretaught high frequency words as they read and respond to a decodable selection.

Read on Your Own Pages from Unit 11 of The Basics Student Book

COMPREHENSION: CLASSIFY INFORMATION

Read on Your Own

Nadja Halilbegovich is from Bosnia.

Hafsat Abiola is from Nigeria.

Craig Kielburger is from Canada.

Kids Are Helping Kids

Kids can help other kids in important ways. Nadja, Hafsat, and Craig show us how.

Nadja helped kids in Bosnia. When Nadja was a girl, ethnic groups in Bosnia started a war. Kids lived in fear. A lot of them were hurt. Nadja started a radio show. She sang on the air to give children courage. She also published two books. They tell how hard it is to live through a war. She hopes her books will help end fighting in the world.

Hafsat helps kids in Nigeria. She formed a group called KIND. The group teaches children their rights. It shows kids how to be leaders. KIND also helps women and children get fair treatment.

Craig was 12 years old when he read that many kids were made to work in hard jobs for no pay. People treated them very badly. He had to help these kids. He formed a group called Free the Children. Now, his group speaks out for children's rights in 27 countries.

194 Unit 11 | Make a Difference!

CHECK YOUR UNDERSTANDING

1.–3. Copy the chart and then complete it.

Who Helped Others?	Where?	What Group of People Did He or She Help?	How?
1. Nadja Halilbegovich	Bosnia	children	She published two books. She started a radio show.

EXPAND YOUR VOCABULARY

4.–6. Tell a partner about each person on page 194. Use information from your chart and some of these words and phrases.

brings hope	fair treatment	hard jobs
sang on the air	rights	formed a group
war	published	Free the Children

Example: 4. Nadja published two books.
The books tell about the war in Bosnia.

WRITE ABOUT PEOPLE ✎

7. Choose one of the kids from page 194 or another person you know. Tell how the person makes a difference.

Example: 7. Craig helps kids who were made to work in hard jobs. He formed a group called Free the Children.

Language and Literacy 195

COMPREHENSION

Build Reading Fluency

Read the article. Stop when the timer goes off. Mark your score.
Then try it again two more times on different days.

Another Kid Helps Kids

Kimmie Weeks started making a difference when he was 10. The year was 1991. His country, Liberia, was at war. Many homes and schools were destroyed. Hundreds of children had no food. Many were sick. The fighting was so bad, children were trained to be soldiers. No one seemed to know what to do. Kimmie felt he had to help.

He and other kids started cleaning the streets. They picked up bricks, stones, and other trash left after the fighting. Then he started speaking on the radio. He said that children should not fight in war. His speeches helped. In 1996, Liberia stopped training children to fight.

Kimmie is now a young man. He is still helping the children of his country. He raises money to open more schools. Today, many children have better lives thanks to Kimmie Weeks.

Timed Passage for Reading Fluency from Unit 11 of the Reading Practice Book

	Day 1	Day 2	Day 3
Total Words Read in One Minute			

Building Reading Power in Levels A–C

Once students have learned to decode in The Basics, they build reading power through the increasingly more difficult selections in Levels A–C.

Within and across levels:

- Reading level advances
- Length of selections increases
- Text density builds
- Picture/text correspondence decreases
- Vocabulary and concept loads progress
- Sentence structure and verb tenses increase in complexity

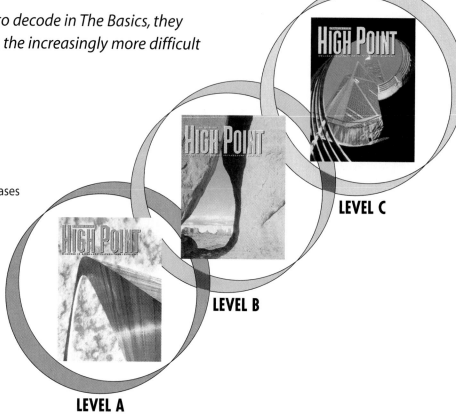

LEVEL C

LEVEL B

LEVEL A

Level A

THE WORLD TODAY

Today, our common resources are being used up.

*T*oday the world is much like that village. Now our commons are our parks, **reserves**, and **natural resources**, and the waters and air of the whole world. Today we have almost the same problem that the villagers had.

Today each fisherman tries to catch as many fish as he can from the common sea. This way, the fisherman has more fish to sell—**in the short run**. But soon there are fewer and fewer fish. This is not good for the fish, the sea, or for the people.

Today each **lumber company** wants to cut down as many trees as it can, to sell for wood, paper, and **fuel**. The more trees the lumber company cuts down, the more money it makes—in the short run. But after cutting down so many trees, there are fewer and fewer **forests**. This is not good for the trees, or for the **forest creatures**, or the forest **soil**.

BEFORE YOU MOVE ON...

1. **Vocabulary** *In the short run* means "now." What do you think *in the long run* means?
2. **Details** The villagers almost used up all the grass on the commons. List two resources that we are in danger of using up today.
3. **Cause and Effect** What would happen if we used all the fish and trees now?

reserves land that is saved for a special reason
in the short run now, at the present time
lumber company company that cuts down trees for use in making products
fuel something used to give heat and power
forest creatures animals that live in the woods
soil dirt, ground, earth

Today each fisherman tries to catch as many fish as he can.

This is not good for the fish, the sea or for the people.

Today each lumber company wants to cut down as many trees as it can.

This is not good for the trees, or the forest creatures, or the forest soil.

Level B

THE SILENT YEARS

The twins' parents discover that Suzy and Neshy are deaf. They all learn sign language so everyone in the family can communicate with each other.

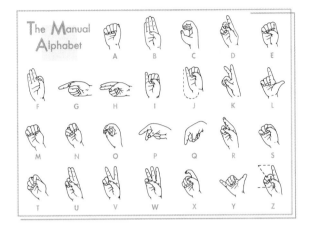

The Manual Alphabet

Early on they knew they were different from other children, because they were the only ones who shared a face. "They loved that about themselves," says Maria Aguayo, mother of Neshmayda and Suzette. "They had a way of communicating that no one else understood. One of them would point at something or make some noise and the other would go and get what she wanted." Two kids **cavorting through** a happy world of their own, experiencing life's surprises as one—in other words, twins.

But Suzy and Neshy were different for a much greater reason—they were born **deaf**.

---

cavorting through having fun in

deaf without the ability to hear

160 Unit 3 | Dreams and Decisions

"We did not know it for their first two-and-a-half years," says Maria, who **contracted** German measles during her first **trimester**. The technology in her native Puerto Rico was not as **advanced** as it is today, so her twins' deafness was not **diagnosed** until they were nearly three. "And when we first discovered they were deaf, I did not want to believe it. It was a mother's denial."

Maria soon accepted her daughters' **condition**, and as soon as she and her husband, Joaquin, heard about the Gallaudet school for the deaf in Washington, D.C., they moved their family and enrolled the twins,

then five years old. "We all learned **sign language** so we could communicate with the girls," says Maria. "We started to talk about all the things that had happened to them in their first five years. I learned all these things that I had not known. For instance, Suzette had once been with her grandmother and **wound up** in the emergency room **getting stitches**. Her grandmother didn't know how she got hurt. Suzy later told me that she had fallen, that she was scared, that she wanted me there with her in the hospital **so badly**. When I discovered these things, I cried and cried."

Suzette (left) and Neshmayda (right) at age six. The twins are wearing hearing aids strapped to their chests as they enjoy a day at Baltimore's Inner Harbor.

BEFORE YOU MOVE ON...

1. **Inference** What do you think helped the twins form their own way of communicating?

2. **Cause and Effect** What caused the twins' deafness, and why did it take so long to diagnose?

3. **Prediction** Do you think the twins will remain close as they grow up? Why or why not?

---

contracted got, caught

trimester three months of being pregnant

diagnosed discovered by doctors

sign language a way to communicate with our hands

wound up in the end was

getting stitches having her cut or wound closed by sewing

so badly so much

Twins 161

Level C

CINQUÉ PLEADS FOR FREEDOM

Instead of Africa, the *Amistad* arrives in America. The Africans remain prisoners until Cinqué and his ally, John Adams, win their freedom in court.

But they had **claimed victory** too soon. Cinqué ordered the Spaniards to steer the ship toward the rising sun. They obeyed and sailed the ship east toward Africa during the day, but then at night turned the ship around and sailed northwest toward North America.

For two months the ship **pitched** back and forth across the Atlantic Ocean. Eight more Africans died during that time—some from their battle wounds, some from food poisoning, and some from starvation.

Then on August 27, 1839, the *Amistad* was **escorted** by an American ship into the harbor of New London, Connecticut. Weary, hungry, and hopelessly lost, Cinqué and the others were forced to come ashore.

An American naval lieutenant saw the possibility for quick **profits** in the Africans. But this was the North, and a group of whites and free blacks **campaigning against** the **institution of slavery** was gaining popularity. They called themselves **abolitionists**, and they took on Cinqué and the other Africans as their most important **case**.

The Africans were sent to prison in New Haven, Connecticut, until a decision could be made.

The abolitionists managed to find a translator, and Cinqué told his story in a U.S. court. He was only twenty-five years old, but his experience on the *Amistad* had given him the confidence of a much older man.

The courtroom was crowded, and many were moved by Cinqué's **impassioned words**.

"I am not here to argue the case against slavery," Cinqué said, "though I will say it is a sin against man and God. I am here to argue the facts. The **indisputable**, international law is that the stealing of slaves from Africa is now **illegal**."

"The men who kidnapped us, who beat and tortured us, were—and are—guilty of this crime," Cinqué continued.

"We are a peaceful people. We regret the loss of life caused by our **mutiny**. But we are not savages. We took over the ship to save our lives. We have done no wrong. Allow us to go home."

The weekend before the judge made his decision, Cinqué and his companions waited in the New Haven jail, their hearts filled with fear and hope. The judge held the power to make the Africans slaves or to set them free. On Monday morning, January 13, 1840, they worried no longer. He had decided they should be returned home.

They were free.

"We have done no wrong."

But as Cinqué was soon to learn, the passage to freedom was as winding as the *Amistad*'s journey across the sea. President Martin Van Buren, concerned that freeing the Mende would enrage southern slave holders, ordered the district attorney to **file an appeal** so the case would be heard in the U.S. Supreme Court. And because of this, Cinqué gained his greatest American **ally**: former president John Quincy Adams.

Having heard about the mutineers, Adams came out of **retirement** to argue Cinqué's case. He was seventy-two years old. It had been more than thirty years since he had argued a case in a courtroom, and the thought of bearing the responsibility for this one worried the elderly statesman deeply.

But inspired by Cinqué, whom many of the abolitionists had begun to refer to as the Black Prince, Adams tirelessly prepared his **defense**. In court he spoke on behalf of the Mende for eight and a half hours. Sweat poured from his brow, and his voice filled the packed courtroom as he presented his case.

---

claimed victory thought they won

pitched rocked

escorted guided, led, accompanied

profits earned money, income

campaigning against trying to convince others to stop

institution of slavery tradition of keeping slaves

impassioned words speech full of emotion

indisputable not-to-be-questioned

mutiny fight to take over the ship

file an appeal request a new trial

ally friend, supporter

retirement the private life he had since he quit working

170 Unit 3 Conflict and Resolution

Amistad Rising 171

Explicit Skills Instruction

Instructional Overheads allow the teacher to present instruction explicitly.

TEXT FEATURES

This Overhead explains how to read for information. The Teacher's Edition tells the teacher how to model the skill and conduct guided practice. Students then apply the skill immediately as they read the article in the Student Book.

HOW TO READ FOR INFORMATION

Directions: Use these strategies when you look at photos, maps, and diagrams.

Much of San Francisco was in ruins after the 1906 earthquake.

Photos and Captions

1. Look at the photo. Ask yourself: What does it show?

2. Read the caption. Think about how it explains the photo.

California's San Andreas Fault

Maps

1. Use the compass rose to see which direction is north, south, east, and west on the map.

2. Use the legend to find out what symbols on the map mean.

3. Use the scale of miles to estimate distance.

4. Read titles or captions, to help you understand what the map shows.

When plates move against each other, pressure is created.

Diagrams

1. Look at the picture.

2. Read the labels, captions, and other text.

3. Describe what you see. Explain what the picture shows in your own words.

Transparency 68 Level A, Unit 4 | Community   © Hampton-Brown

Level A Instructional Overhead

Level A Student Book

Hurricane in the Caribbean, 1998

MONDAY, SEPTEMBER 21, 1998

Hurricane Georges Hits Puerto Rico

Hurricane Georges slammed into the island of Puerto Rico at around 6 p.m. today. Winds **reached** over 115 miles per hour. Airplanes flipped over like toys. Trees were **uprooted** and flew through the air like missiles. Over 80 percent of the island is without electricity. Seventy percent of all homes are without water.

Inside a Hurricane

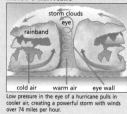

storm clouds
eye
rainband
cold air   warm air   eye wall

Low pressure in the eye of a hurricane pulls in cooler air, creating a powerful storm with winds over 74 miles per hour.

UNITED STATES
Gulf of Mexico
Atlantic Ocean
CUBA
Mexico
DOMINICAN REPUBLIC
Jamaica
HAITI
Caribbean Sea
PUERTO RICO
Central America
MILES

The path of Hurricane Georges

TUESDAY, SEPTEMBER 22, 1998

Georges Blasts Dominican Republic— Rescue Efforts Begin

Hurricane Georges spreads its destruction to the Dominican Republic. **Mudslides** and **flooding** kill over 200 people. More than 100,000 people are left **homeless**.

Meanwhile, rescue workers bring aid to Puerto Rico. More than 20,000 people **crowd into shelters** in San Juan and other cities.

FRIDAY, SEPTEMBER 25, 1998

Hurricane Relief Underway

Rescue workers in the Dominican Republic and Haiti **struggle** to bring food, water, and shelter to people. House

after house **lies in ruins** or without a roof.

"There's no water. There's no power. There is nothing," says Domingo Osvaldo Fortuna as he fills a plastic jug with water from the garbage-filled Ozama River in Santo Domingo.

Aid from the United States begins to arrive. A French cargo plane brings **relief workers**, food, and medicine. Sixty-three firefighters from New York help to search for survivors.

SUNDAY, SEPTEMBER 27, 1998

Hurricane Continues— Tons of Food On the Way

Tons of food and supplies begin to arrive in the Dominican Republic and Haiti. Volunteers fly in with tons of bottled water and enough **plastic sheeting** to repair 15,000 houses. Members of the U.S. military carry aid to towns **cut off by** flooding and mudslides.

Although it will take weeks or even years for the islands to **repair** the **damage**, **recovery** has slowly begun.

▶ **POINT-BY-POINT**

HOW COMMUNITIES RESPOND TO DISASTERS

After a Hurricane:

- Emergency shelters are set up for people who are left homeless.
- Rescue workers bring food, water, and medicine to disaster victims.
- Rescue workers search for survivors.
- The international community sends aid to help victims recover and rebuild.

BEFORE YOU MOVE ON...

1. **Vocabulary** What words or phrases describe the strength of the hurricane?
2. **Cause and Effect** What problems did the hurricane cause?
3. **Details** How did other countries help the people on the islands?

---

reached got as fast as
uprooted pulled from the ground
Mudslides Rushing rivers of mud and rain

flooding water overflowing the banks of rivers
homeless without homes, with nowhere to live
crowd into are pushed together in

lies in ruins sits on the ground in pieces
Tons Several thousands of pounds
plastic sheeting waterproof covering

cut off by unable to have contact with the outside world because of
repair fix, correct

246 **Unit 4** | Community

When Disaster Strikes **247**

TEXT STRUCTURES

This Overhead outlines the structures of different kinds of text and the corresponding reading strategies. The Teacher's Edition tells the teacher how to model the strategies and conduct guided practice. Students immediately apply the strategies to paired selections about ancient China, one fictional and one informational.

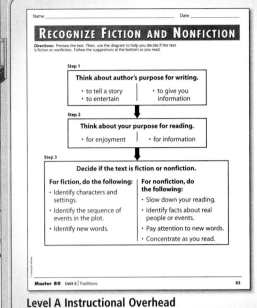

Name _____ Date _____

RECOGNIZE FICTION AND NONFICTION

Directions: Preview the text. Then, use the diagram to help you decide if the text is fiction or nonfiction. Follow the suggestions at the bottom as you read.

Step 1

Think about author's purpose for writing.

- to tell a story
- to entertain
- to give you information

Step 2

Think about your purpose for reading.

- for enjoyment
- for information

Step 3

Decide if the text is fiction or nonfiction.

For fiction, do the following:
- Identify characters and settings.
- Identify the sequence of events in the plot.
- Identify new words.

For nonfiction, do the following:
- Slow down your reading.
- Identify facts about real people or events.
- Pay attention to new words.
- Concentrate as you read.

Master 80 Unit 5 | Traditions   83

Level A Instructional Overhead

Level A Student Book: Fiction and Nonfiction

HOW THE Ox Star FELL FROM Heaven

by Lily Toy Hong

This ancient Chinese story tells about a message that gets mixed up. It also explains why people use oxen to help grow crops for food.

In the beginning, [...]
on Earth. They could o[...]
the heavens, among th[...]
with the Emperor of Al[...]
his Imperial Palace.

Clothed in robes of the finest **silk**, they **reclined** on **billowy** clouds. They never had to work, and their lives were easy.

Life on Earth was hard, especially hard since oxen did not live here. Farmers had no **beast of burden** to help with the planting of vegetables and rice in the spring, or with the gathering of **crops** at **harvest time**.

People were always tired and hungry. They **labored** from **sunup** to **sundown**, yet they could never finish all their work.

Because there was so little food, they sometimes went three, four, even five days without **one single meal**.

the heavens the sky
silk soft, shiny cloth
reclined leaned back, rested
billowy soft and fluffy
beast of burden animal used for heavy work
one single meal one meal to eat, anything to eat

BEFORE YOU MOVE ON...

1. **Details** What made life on Earth difficult for the farmers?
2. **Comparisons** How were the lives of the oxen and the humans different?
3. **Prediction** This story describes what life was like "in the beginning." How do you think the story may change by the end?

Ancient China during the Zhou Dynasty, 1050 BCE–256 CE

GOBI DESERT

HIMALAYAS

MODERN CHINA

A Peasant's Life in ANCIENT CHINA

an article by Shirleyann Costigan

Life was never easy for the peasant farmers of ancient China. They worked the earth, planted, and **harvested** the crops by hand. It was slow, **backbreaking** work. Around 700 BCE, many farmers began to use oxen or water buffalo to pull the plows and seed the fields. **Food production increased**. Everyone ate better. Life got a little easier, but not by much.

Most peasants lived in small villages near the **manor houses** of their **lords**. Their small huts were made of **packed earth** with dirt floors. Peasants rented the land they lived and

In ancient China, the lords and scholars

Emperor
the Son of Heaven

Lords & Scholars
rulers of the land

Knights
protectors of the land

CLASSES OF SOCIETY IN ANCIENT CHINA, 700 BCE

There were three classes of people under the Emperor of ancient China. The people of each class had a place to fill in the Chinese order of life. The order rarely changed.

Peasant farmers worked from sunup to sundo[...] all year long. They also had to work on roads and canals that ran through the countryside.

 Rice

Peasants grew their own food, as well as food for the ruling classes. Rice, soybeans, and millet were all common crops.

 Soybeans

 Millet

Spiraling Instruction

*Instruction in **High Point** spirals across the levels and is tailored to students' increasing literacy and language skills.*

Level A

This level introduces self-monitoring strategies. Teachers use the Instructional Overhead to model the strategy and conduct guided practice. Students then use a simple Note-Taking Chart to apply the strategy as they read.

ASK QUESTIONS AND CLARIFY

Directions: Read a paragraph. Write questions about what you read. Reread the paragraph and try to answer your questions. Write the answers.

All About Dogs

The dog is a favorite pet. All over the world people like to own dogs.

Dogs can learn many skills. They can protect cattle and sheep. They can hunt. They can even help guide blind people.

For thousands of years, humans and dogs have been partners. They count on and take care of each other. Dogs have even been called our "best friend."

Questions	Answers

Transparency 28 Level A, Unit 2 | Cooperation   © Hampton-Brown

Level A Instructional Overhead

A DOG YOU CAN COUNT ON

from *A Guide Dog Puppy Grows Up*
by Caroline Arnold

It takes a lot of training to be a guide dog for the blind. That's because guide dog owners really count on their furry friends. This article shows how they learn to work together.

Stacy will teach Moe how to work with his new guide dog.

When Moe Enguillado **arrives** to begin his **guide dog** training, Stacy Burrow **greets** him. She is one of his **instructors**. Moe is excited about getting a dog. At the same time, he is a little **worried** about everything he will have to learn.

Stacy knows the dogs very well. Each dog has its own **personality**. After meeting the new students, Stacy carefully **matches each person with** one of the dogs.

Level A Student Book

Name _____   Date _____

NOTE-TAKING CHART

Directions: After you read each paragraph, stop to ask questions. Write your questions. Reread to find information. Write your answers or your best guess.

A Dog You Can Count On

Page	Your Questions	Your Answers
Page 96		
Page 97		
Page 98		

**Level A
Note-Taking Chart**

Levels B and C

These levels show the spiraling instruction. The Instructional Overhead introduces new aspects of the self-monitoring strategy—summarizing and predicting. Students use more advanced Note-Taking Charts as they read.

HOW TO MONITOR YOUR READING

Directions: Read the passage. Then read and answer the questions in the chart below. Try to think of other questions that would help you understand the reading better.

Wednesday, July 8, 1942

Dearest Kitty,

It seems like years since Sunday morning. So much has happened. It's as if the whole world had suddenly turned upside down. But as you can see, Kitty, I'm still alive, and that's the main thing, Father says. I'm alive all right, but don't ask where or how. You probably don't understand a word I'm saying, so I'll begin by telling you what happened Sunday afternoon.

Clarify	Ask Questions
What words need more explanation?	What questions did I have while I was reading?
Summarize	**Predict**
What does the author want us to remember from this reading?	What will the next section of the reading be about?

Transparency 66 Level B, Unit 4 | Continuity and Change   © Hampton-Brown

Level B Instructional Overhead

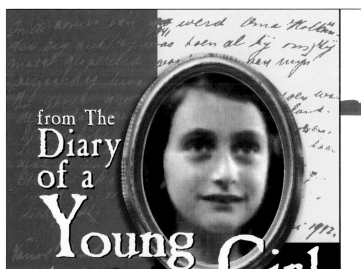

from The **Diary of a Young Girl**

BY ANNE FRANK

he will be taken away to a concentration camp.

WEDNESDAY, JULY 8, 1942

Dearest Kitty,

It seems like years since Sunday morning. So much has happened it's as if the whole world had suddenly turned upside down. But as you can see, Kitty, I'm still alive, and that's the **main thing**, Father says. I'm alive all right, but don't ask where or how. You probably don't understand a word I'm saying, so I'll begin by telling you what happened Sunday afternoon.

At three o'clock (Hello* had left but was supposed to come back later), the doorbell rang. I didn't hear it, since I was out on the balcony, lazily reading in the sun. A little while later Margot appeared in the kitchen doorway looking very **agitated**. "Father has received a **call-up notice** from **the SS**," she whispered. "Mother has gone to see Mr. van Daan." (Mr. van Daan is Father's **business partner** and a good friend.)

I was **stunned**. A call-up: everyone knows what that means. **Visions** of concentration camps and lonely **cells** raced through my head. How could we let Father go to such a fate? "Of course he's not going," declared Margot as we waited for Mother in the living room. "Mother's gone to Mr. van Daan to ask whether we can move to our hiding place tomorrow. The van Daans are going with us. There will be seven of us altogether." Silence. We couldn't speak. The thought of Father off visiting someone in the Jewish Hospital and completely **unaware of** what was happening, the long wait for Mother, the heat, the **suspense**—all this **reduced us to silence**.

cells rooms in a prison
unaware of not knowing
suspense fear, tension
reduced us to silence made us unable to speak

Level B Student Book

Name _____   Date _____

HOW TO MONITOR YOUR READING

Directions: Use the four strategies on this chart to monitor your reading. Fill in the boxes as you read each section of the selection.

Clarify	Ask Questions
• One of the words I wasn't sure about was	• One question I had as I read was: _____
• What other word can be used in place of _____	• What am I thinking as I read? _____
Summarize	**Predict**
• What is the main event in this section? _____	• What will the next section be about? _____
• What does the author want me to remember? _____	• How does my own experience help me make predictions?

Level C Note-Taking Chart

Extensive Practice

After reading, the Respond activities provide followup to the pretaught strategies and ensure ample skills practice.

Theme Book for Listening Comprehension and Main Idea Practice in The Basics

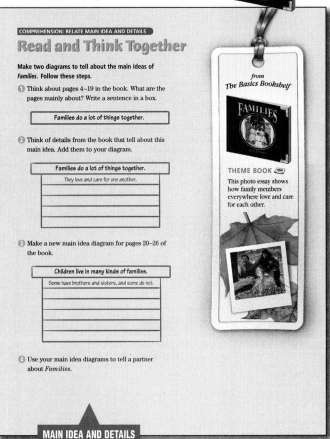

COMPREHENSION: RELATE MAIN IDEA AND DETAILS

Read and Think Together

Make two diagrams to tell about the main ideas of *Families*. Follow these steps.

1. Think about pages 4–19 in the book. What are the pages mainly about? Write a sentence in a box.

> Families do a lot of things together.

2. Think of details from the book that tell about this main idea. Add them to your diagram.

> Families do a lot of things together.
> They love and care for one another.

3. Make a new main idea diagram for pages 20–26 of the book.

> Children live in many kinds of families.
> Some have brothers and sisters, and some do not.

4. Use your main idea diagrams to tell a partner about *Families*.

MAIN IDEA AND DETAILS
The Basics

from The Basics Bookshelf

FAMILIES

THEME BOOK

This photo essay shows how family members everywhere love and care for each other.

Reading Selection and Main Idea Practice in Level A

Respond to the Autobiography
Check Your Understanding

SUM IT UP

Relate Main Ideas and Details Study the tree diagram for pages 144–145 of "My Best Friend." Then make diagrams for Parts 2 and 3.

Tree Diagram for Part 1

Main Idea	Details
Lillie and Lessie were best friends	They liked to play together.
	They visited each other.
	They made frog houses together.
	They liked to talk and talk.

Write a Paragraph Use the tree diagram for Part 1 to write your paragraph. Follow these steps:

- Write a **topic sentence** to tell the main idea.
- Write details to support the main idea.
- Write a **concluding sentence** to sum up your paragraph.

> Lessie and Lillie were best friends. They liked to play together. They visited each other every chance they got. They made frog houses together. They liked to talk and talk. They had fun being best friends.

Now write paragraphs for Parts 2 and 3. Use your tree diagrams for ideas.

THINK IT OVER

Discuss Talk about these questions with a partner.

1. **Opinion** Would Lessie be a good friend? Why or why not?
2. **Author's Purpose** Why do you think Lessie wrote her autobiography?
3. **Comparisons** How would Lillie and Lessie's story be different if they grew up today? How would it be the same?
4. **Personal Experience** Do you have your life all planned out, like Lessie and Lillie did? Explain.

EXPRESS YOURSELF
► EXPRESS LIKES AND DISLIKES

Think about the qualities you like and dislike in a best friend. Share your ideas with the class. Then make a large class T-chart. Write the qualities that most people said.

MAIN IDEA AND DETAILS
Level A

My **Best** Friend

Practice

Level A

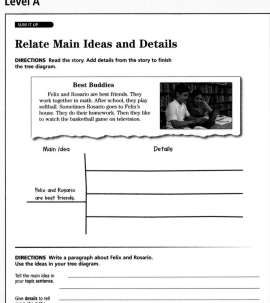

SUM IT UP

Relate Main Ideas and Details

DIRECTIONS Read the story. Add details from the story to finish the tree diagram.

Best Buddies

Felix and Rosario are best friends. They work together in math. After school, they play softball. Sometimes Rosario goes to Felix's house. They do their homework. Then they like to watch the basketball game on television.

Main Idea	Details
Felix and Rosario are best friends.	

DIRECTIONS Write a paragraph about Felix and Rosario. Use the ideas in your tree diagram.

Tell the main idea in your topic sentence. _____

Give details to tell more about the _____

Main Idea Practice in the Reading Practice Book

Reading Selection and
Main Idea Practice in Level B

Respond to the Essay
Check Your Understanding

SUM IT UP

Relate Main Ideas and Details Make a main idea diagram for each section of the essay.

Main Idea Diagram

> Topic: Diego Rivera's Murals
>
> Main Idea: Rivera's murals celebrate the people and history of Mexico.
>
> Detail: His paintings show workers and people fighting for their rights.
> Detail: Rivera used ancient wall paintings for inspiration.

Write a Paragraph Use the main idea diagram to write a paragraph. A paragraph is a group of sentences that all tell about the same idea. One sentence gives the **main idea** of the paragraph. The other sentences give details that support the main idea.

Example:

Diego Rivera's Murals

　Diego Rivera painted walls to celebrate Mexico's history. He painted people hard at work. He also painted people fighting for their rights. Rivera got some of his inspiration from ancient murals of Teotihuacán.

THINK IT OVER

Discuss and Write Talk about these questions with a partner. Write the answers.

1. **Cause and Effect** Why have people in the past and in the present created talking walls? Why are they important?

2. **Comparison** How do you think viewers feel about each of the talking walls in the essay? How are each of their messages similar?

3. **Conclusions** If you were a painter or architect, how would you represent the people of the U.S. in a mural? Why?

4. **Judgments** Imagine that you could leave a message on the fence of someone whom you admire. Whose fence would it be? Explain what tribute you would write and why.

EXPRESS YOURSELF 　EXPRESS OPINIONS

Tell a group about your favorite wall from the essay. Give three reasons that tell why you like that wall. Think about the way it looks, how it makes you feel, and the message it gives.

**MAIN IDEA AND DETAILS
Level B**

Reading Selection and
Main Idea Practice in Level C

Respond to the Photo Essay
Check Your Understanding

SUM IT UP

Relate Main Idea and Details Share your details for one section with your group. What is the main idea? Complete a chart to share with the class.

Main Idea and Details Chart

> Section Title: ___Curtain Up!___
>
> Main Idea:
> This section describes what it is like to watch the opening of The Lion King play.
>
> Detail: The performance starts in New York City a little after 8 o'clock.
> Detail: The Lion King is a stage musical about a young lion.
> Detail: Actors dressed in fantastic masks and costumes play the animals.

Write a Summary With your class, brainstorm several main idea statements for the entire selection. Take a vote for the best one. Then list details that support your main idea. Cross out the unimportant details.

Example:

Important detail: The Lion King is a stage musical about a young lion.

Unimportant detail: It starts a little after 8 o'clock.

Use the important details that remain on your list to write a summary of "The Lion King Goes to Broadway."

THINK IT OVER

Discuss and Write Talk about these questions with a partner. Write the answers.

1. **Analyze Information** Why did Julie Taymor feel it was important to show the actors' faces?

2. **Paraphrase** Tell a partner what a photo essay is like.

3. **Personal Experience** What creative ideas have you had? How have you accomplished them?

EXPRESS YOURSELF ▸DESCRIBE

Look at the photographs in the selection. Choose an animal costume and describe it to your partner. Include details about its size, how it is made, how it is worn, and how it moves. What makes this costume like the animal it represents?

**MAIN IDEA AND DETAILS
Level C**

Level B

SUM IT UP

Relate Main Ideas and Details

DIRECTIONS Complete the main idea diagram for each topic from "Talking Walls." Then write two paragraphs on a separate sheet of paper. Tell about one topic in each paragraph.

> Topic: The Vietnam Veterans Memorial
>
> Main Idea:
>
> Detail:
> Detail:

> Topic: Pablo Neruda's Gate
>
> Main Idea:
>
> Detail:
> Detail:

Level C

SUM IT UP

Relate Main Idea and Details

DIRECTIONS Read the article Rafael wrote for his school newspaper. Then complete the main idea and details chart.

A Great Stage Show!

　The Lion King was much better as a stage play than as a movie. Seeing the live production was an experience I won't forget.

　When you see real actors dressed in elaborate costumes, it really captures your imagination. A movie just can't match that. Julie Taymor, who has worked on other Broadway productions, was the main designer. She and her team did a great job creating the amazing costumes.

　The sets and the lighting were also wonderful. I thought the atmosphere of Africa was better in the stage play than in the movie. There were some great special effects, too. For instance, when the lake dried up, I had to remind myself that it was a trick of the eye.

　Seeing the actors in person, instead of on a movie screen, was thrilling. Watching them on stage, I really thought they were jungle creatures. They trotted, slithered, and glided across the stage like real-life animals.

　The costumes, the sets, the lighting, and the performances made the stage play great. It was more exciting than any movie I have ever seen.

Main Idea and Details Chart

> Main Idea:
>
> Detail:
> Detail:
> Detail:

DIRECTIONS Write a summary of the article. Use information from the chart.

Language Development in *High Point*

Natural Language Models

Each theme begins with a song, poem, chant, story, or speech on tape. These interactive, motivational experiences spark language, model specific language functions or structures, and provide context for developing vocabulary and grammar skills.

The Basics

The Basics Student Book and Tape

SONG

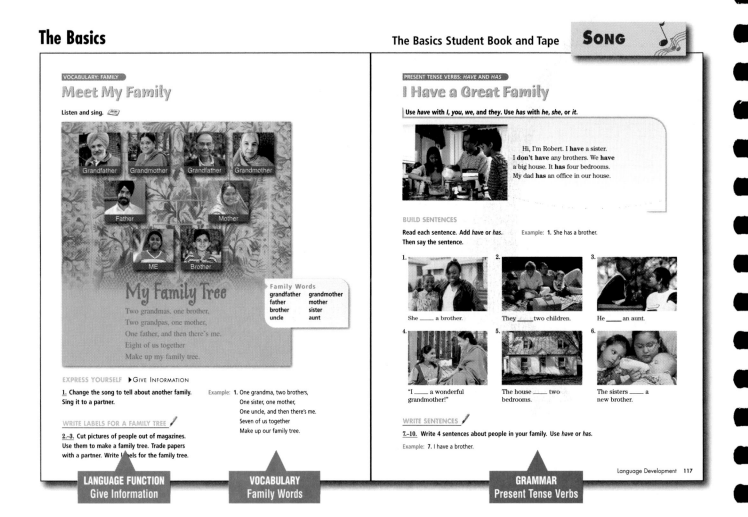

LANGUAGE FUNCTION
Give Information

VOCABULARY
Family Words

GRAMMAR
Present Tense Verbs

Build Language and Vocabulary
DESCRIBE

Listen to this rap about the gods and goddesses of ancient Greece.

ZEUS AND HERA

ATHENA

ARES

APHRODITE

GAIA

CHAOS

CRONUS

The Mount Olympus Rap

In the beginning there was one great abyss,
  and Chaos formed the earth and heaven out of this.
Then Earth Mother Gaia had her babies like mad.
  The twelve giant Titans were the children she had.
One Titan named Cronus was the father of Zeus.
  His five other children were soon on the loose.
Mount Olympus was home to the family of gods.
  They sometimes got along, but were often at odds.
After Zeus married Hera, life was never a bore.
  She had a son, Ares, the god of war.
Wise Athena was also a charmer.
  She protected Greek cities and wore a suit of armor.
Aphrodite was the goddess of love and flowers.
  The countryside bloomed because of her powers.
Today, we tell stories of these gods from the past.
  As long as we remember them, they'll last and last.

—*Anne Miranda*

266 Unit 5 | Traditions

**LANGUAGE FUNCTION
Describe**

MAKE A CHARACTER CHART

Work with the group to list all the characters in the poem on a chart. Also record what each character did. Follow this model:

Name	What Character Did	
Chaos	formed earth and heaven	
Gaia	had the 12 Titans	

BUILD YOUR VOCABULARY

Describing Words Look at the pictures of the gods and goddesses on page 266. Think of a word to describe each one, or choose one from the **Word Bank**. Add a third column to your chart. In it, write a word to describe each character:

Name	What Character Did	What Character Was Like
Chaos	formed earth and heaven	powerful
Gaia	had the 12 Titans	strong

Word Bank
beautiful
big
dark
fierce
powerful
strong
tall
ugly

**VOCABULARY
Describing
Words**

USE LANGUAGE STRUCTURES ▶ COMPLETE SENTENCES

Writing: Describe Greek Gods Choose a Greek god or goddess. Use the information from the character chart to write two complete sentences. Tell what the god or goddess did, and what he or she was like. Be sure each sentence includes a subject and a predicate.

Example:
Athena protected Greek cities. She was powerful.

**GRAMMAR
Complete
Sentences**

Build Language and Vocabulary 267

Level B

Level B Student Book and Tape **STORY**

Build Language and Vocabulary
TELL A STORY

Listen to this tale from Vietnam about a rooster who learns what matters most to him.

The Rooster and the Jewel
A VIETNAMESE TALE

144 Unit 3 | Dreams and Decisions

**LANGUAGE FUNCTION
Tell a Story**

MAKE A STORY MAP

Work with a group to plan a story about something that matters most to you. Choose the object or event. Then fill out a story map to name the characters, tell the setting, and outline the events in the plot.

Characters	Setting

Beginning

Middle

Ending

BUILD YOUR VOCABULARY

Descriptive Words Think of words you will use to describe the story's characters and setting. Collect them in the charts.

Character	What is the character like?	What does the character do?	How, when, and where does the character do things?
Yolanda	young smart	She skates. She seems to fly.	quickly before dark through the park

Setting	What can you see?	What can you hear?	What can you smell?	What can you taste?	What can you touch?
an afternoon in a park	trees lake	birds traffic	smoke food cooking	hamburger	earth grass

**VOCABULARY
Describing Words
Story Elements**

USE LANGUAGE STRUCTURES
▶ ADJECTIVES, ADVERBS, AND PREPOSITIONAL PHRASES

Speaking: Tell a Story Use your story map and the descriptive words in your charts to tell your story. Divide the story into parts so that each member of your group will have a part to tell.

Example:
Yolanda **quickly** gathered her skates and went **to the park**. She wanted to skate all **around the lake before dark**. She seemed to fly **through the park**, but then made a **sudden** stop. There **in the trees** she saw flames and smelled smoke. . . .

**GRAMMAR
Adjectives
Adverbs
Prepositions**

Build Language and Vocabulary 145

Systematic Grammar Instruction

The Instructional Overhead for Build Language and Vocabulary introduces the grammar skill. Followup lessons build skills in a logical sequence.

ADD DETAILS TO SENTENCES

You can add adjectives, adverbs, or prepositional phrases to a sentence to make it more interesting.

A squirrel scrambles.

A red squirrel scrambles quickly across the garden.
adjective   adverb   prepositional phrase

1. An **adjective** describes a noun or pronoun.

   The **huge** barn has a **blue** door. It is **full** of animals.

2. An **adverb** tells "how," "where," or "when." Adverbs usually tell more about a verb.

   We pet the bull **carefully**. The chickens live **outside**.

3. A prepositional phrase also tells "where" or "when." It starts with a **preposition** and ends with a noun or pronoun.

   The pigs live **across** the barnyard.
   prepositional phrase

Try It!

Add details to these sentences. Use adjectives, adverbs, and prepositional phrases.

1. The rooster ran home.   3. The chicks found nothing to eat.
2. I lost the jewel.   4. I saw the animals.

Instructional Overhead

Level B Student Book: Unit 3

Build Language and Vocabulary
TELL A STORY

Listen to this tale from Vietnam about a rooster who learns what matters most to him.

The Rooster and the Jewel
A VIETNAMESE TALE

MAKE A STORY

Work with a group
to you. Choose th
the characters, tel

BUILD YOUR VO

Descriptive Words Think of words you will use to describe the story's characters and setting. Collect them in the charts.

Character	What is the character like?	What does the character do?	How, when, and where does the character do things?
Yolanda	young smart	She skates. She seems to fly.	quickly before dark through the park

Setting	What can you see?	What can you hear?	What can you smell?	What can you taste?	What can you touch?
an afternoon in a park	trees lake	birds traffic	smoke food cooking	hamburger	earth grass

GRAMMAR INTRODUCTION
Adjectives
Adverbs
Prepositions

USE LANGUAGE STRUCTURES
▶ ADJECTIVES, ADVERBS, AND PREPOSITIONAL PHRASES

Speaking: Tell a Story Use your story map and the descriptive words in your charts to tell your story. Divide the story into parts so that each member of your group will have a part to tell.

Example:
Yolanda **quickly** gathered her skates and went **to the park**. She wanted to skate all **around the lake before dark**. She seemed to fly **through the park**, but then made a **sudden** stop. There **in the trees** she saw flames and smelled smoke. . . .

144   Unit 3 | Dreams and Decisions

Build Language and Vocabulary   145

Practice

*Abundant practice for each grammar skill in the **Language Practice Book** helps students master the complexities of English and transfer skills to writing.*

Grammar Practice in the Language Practice Book, Level B Unit 3

BUILD LANGUAGE AND VOCABULARY

An Interesting Story

Vietnamese potbellied pigs grow to about 100 pounds in weight. They live to between 12 and 17 years of age.

Adding Details to Sentences
There are many ways to add details to sentences.
Use an **adjective** to describe a noun or pronoun.
   The potbellied pig has white fur.
Use an **adverb** to tell how, where, or when.
   The pig looks up eagerly.
Use a prepositional phrase to add details like where, when, or for what purpose.
   My friend adopts the pig as a pet.

DIRECTIONS Rewrite each sentence. Make it more interesting. Add adjectives, adverbs, and prepositional phrases from the boxes, or add some of your own.

1. My friend Tan adopted a Vietnamese potbellied pig.

   My good friend Tan generously adopted a spotted

   Vietnamese potbellied pig.

2. One day, Tan's pig noticed a smell.

3. The pig dug.

4. The sofa was destroyed.

5. Tan says, "I recommend you learn about pigs."

Adjectives	
tasty	potbellied
lovely	hungry
good	domestic
pudgy	beautiful
naughty	spotted
delicious	wonderful

Adverbs	
busily	strongly
quickly	generously
inside	almost
nearly	always

Prepositional Phrases
with his nose
for a treat
before adopting one
within seconds

Level B Student Book: Unit 3

Level B Student Book: Unit 3

Respond to the Story, continued
Language Arts and Literature

▶ GRAMMAR IN CONTEXT

USE ADJECTIVES

Learn About Adjectives An adjective is a word that describes, or tells about, a noun.

Adjectives can tell how many or how much.

Yenna waited **four** years.
Yenna had **little** interest in marrying.

Adjectives can tell which one.

Yenna shook out the **first** shirt.

Adjectives can tell what something is like.

The ginger was **fragrant** and **moist**.
The **young** man asked Yenna to marry him.

Proper adjectives come from proper nouns. They begin with a capital letter.

Chang was from China. He was **Chinese**.

Add Adjectives Expand these sentences with adjectives.

1. Yenna sewed with _____ needles and _____ thread.
2. The _____ man held the _____ ginger in his _____ hand.

Practice Write this paragraph. Add an adjective in each blank.

The _____ streets of Chinatown are interesting to see. There are _____ buildings. Some have _____ walls and _____ windows. One building has a _____ tower with _____ roof.

▶ WRITING/SPEAKING

WRITE AN OUTCOME

Think of the new endings to the story you discussed with your group in the Sum It Up activity on page 155. How would the characters' actions change in order to cause a new outcome? Would their goals also change? Make a chart to organize your ideas. Then write the new outcome.

1. **Complete a Chart** Fill in a new Goal-and-Outcome Chart like the one you made on page 155.

2. **Write a Draft** Write the main events of the beginning, middle, and end of the new story. Include dialogue that shows what the characters' goals are.

3. **Edit Your Work** Add, change, or take out text to make your story more interesting. Do the characters have believable goals? What is the final outcome? Finally, check for correct spelling, punctuation, and grammar.

4. **Read and Discuss** Read your work in a group. Discuss the goals and actions that caused the new outcomes.

For more about the **writing process**, see Handbook pages 408–413.

GRAMMAR REVIEW
Adjectives

Respond to the Article, continued
Language Arts and Literature

▶ GRAMMAR IN CONTEXT

USE ADJECTIVES THAT COMPARE

Learn About Comparative Adjectives A comparative adjective compares two things. To make the comparison, add **–er** to the adjective and use the word **than**.

Neshy's hair is **longer than** Suzy's.

If the adjective is a long word, use **more** or **less**.

Neshy is **more independent than** Suzy.

Learn About Superlative Adjectives A superlative adjective compares three or more things. Add **–est** to the adjective. Use **the** before the adjective.

Suzy is **the fastest** runner in her class.

If the adjective is long, use **the most** or **the least**.

The most important thing to the twins is staying in touch.

Practice Write these sentences. Use the correct form of the adjective in parentheses.

1. Some hearing-impaired people have a (great) hearing loss than others do.

2. Gallaudet is perhaps the (fine) school in the world for hearing-impaired students.

3. When they learned sign language, the twins were (confident) than before.

4. The (difficult) time of all came after the twins were separated.

▶ TECHNOLOGY/MEDIA
▶ WRITING

WRITE TO A TWIN

With a partner, take the roles of Suzy and Neshy. Pretend that you have been apart for one month. Write a series of letters or e-mails to each other.

1. **Choose a Topic** Here are some possible topics for your first letters:
   • future dreams or plans
   • life in your new city or home
   • an upcoming visit
   • family and friends

2. **Start the Series** One partner writes the first letter or e-mail. The other partner reads it and writes back. Write several more letters or e-mails back and forth.

3. **Check Your Work** Check your work before sending it to your "twin." Check for correct spelling and punctuation.

For more about e-mail, see Handbook page 382.

SEQUENTIAL GRAMMAR SKILL
Comparative Adjectives

GRAMMAR: ADJECTIVES

Historic Letters

DIRECTIONS Work with a small group. Read the article. Circle the adjectives. Write each adjective in the correct column of the chart.

In 1850, a boat sailed into the (crowded) harbor in San Francisco. On the boat were Louise Clappe, her husband, and her two sisters. They had come all the way from (central) Massachusetts. Leaving his wife in San Francisco, Dr. Fayette Clappe traveled to a rough camp in the Sierras to open a medical practice. Eventually, Louise joined him.

Over fifteen months, Louise wrote twenty-three letters from the camps. Her first letter describes her wild journey to the camp. The letters describe a distant time in American history. They tell about the French and Spanish miners and people from around the world. They describe the steep mountains, the brilliant river, and the crude buildings.

Louise wrote her last letter in November, 1852. After that, she returned to San Francisco and taught school for twenty-four years. She died in New Jersey in 1906.

Adjectives
An **adjective** describes a noun or pronoun. Adjectives can tell how many, how much, which one, or what something is like.
    The second letter describes the important rooms in the **grand** Empire Hotel.
A **proper adjective** comes from a proper noun.
    The letters bring **American** history to life.

How Many/ How Much	Which One	What Something Is Like	Proper Adjectives
1. _____	5. central	9. crowded	16. _____
2. _____	6. _____	10. _____	17. _____
3. _____	7. _____	11. _____	18. _____
4. _____	8. _____	12. _____	
		13. _____	
		14. _____	
		15. _____	

GRAMMAR: ADJECTIVES THAT COMPARE

Family Comparisons

Whitewater rafting is a thrilling adventure for many.

Adjectives That Compare
A **comparative adjective** compares two things.
    My sister is **quieter** than I am.
    She is **less sociable** than me, too.
A **superlative adjective** compares three or more things.
    I am the **friendliest** person in the family.
    I am the **most sociable** person in my home!
Use **-er** and **-est** for most two-syllable adjectives. Use **less / more** and **least / most** for words with three or more syllables.

DIRECTIONS Complete each sentence. Write the correct form of the adjective in parentheses.

1. Jayesh is _____more adventurous_____ than his twin brother, Kuval. (**adventurous**)

2. He wants to raft down the _____ river in the West. (**wild**)

3. He wants to climb the _____ peak on the continent. (**high**)

4. Jayesh is _____ than Kuval. (**studious**)

5. Kuval is _____ than his brother. (**calm**)

6. To Kuval, drawing is the _____ thing in the world! (**exciting**)

DIRECTIONS Write sentences to compare people you know. Use the correct forms of the adjectives in the box or some of your own.

7. My sister is less confident than I am.

8. _____

9. _____

10.

creative
independent
tidy
nice
confident
funny
strong

More Practice on Adjectives in the Language Practice Book, Level B Unit 3

Writing Instruction in *High Point*

Fundamentals of Writing

The Basics level addresses the fundamentals of writing—from sentences to an expository paragraph.

The Basics Student Book

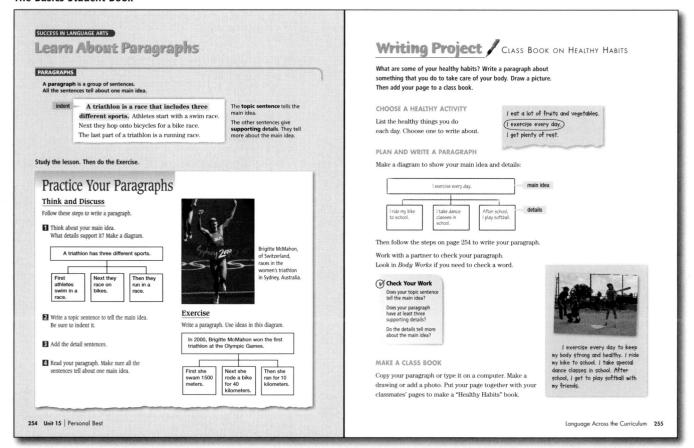

SUCCESS IN LANGUAGE ARTS

Learn About Paragraphs

PARAGRAPHS

A **paragraph** is a group of sentences. All the sentences tell about one main idea.

indent → **A triathlon is a race that includes three different sports.** Athletes start with a swim race. Next they hop onto bicycles for a bike race. The last part of a triathlon is a running race.

The **topic sentence** tells the main idea.

The other sentences give **supporting details**. They tell more about the main idea.

Study the lesson. Then do the Exercise.

Practice Your Paragraphs

Think and Discuss

Follow these steps to write a paragraph.

1. Think about your main idea. What details support it? Make a diagram.

| A triathlon has three different sports. |
| First athletes swim in a race. | Next they race on bikes. | Then they run in a race. |

2. Write a topic sentence to tell the main idea. Be sure to indent it.

3. Add the detail sentences.

4. Read your paragraph. Make sure all the sentences tell about one main idea.

Brigitte McMahon, of Switzerland, races in the women's triathlon in Sydney, Australia.

Exercise

Write a paragraph. Use ideas in this diagram.

| In 2000, Brigitte McMahon won the first triathlon at the Olympic Games. |
| First she swam 1500 meters. | Next she rode a bike for 40 kilometers. | Then she ran for 10 kilometers. |

Writing Project ✏ CLASS BOOK ON HEALTHY HABITS

What are some of your healthy habits? Write a paragraph about something that you do to take care of your body. Draw a picture. Then add your page to a class book.

CHOOSE A HEALTHY ACTIVITY

List the healthy things you do each day. Choose one to write about.

I eat a lot of fruits and vegetables.
I exercise every day.
I get plenty of rest.

PLAN AND WRITE A PARAGRAPH

Make a diagram to show your main idea and details:

| I exercise every day. | → main idea |
| I ride my bike to school. | I take dance classes in school. | After school, I play softball. | → details |

Then follow the steps on page 254 to write your paragraph.

Work with a partner to check your paragraph. Look in *Body Works* if you need to check a word.

☑ **Check Your Work**
Does your topic sentence tell the main idea?
Does your paragraph have at least three supporting details?
Do the details tell more about the main idea?

MAKE A CLASS BOOK

Copy your paragraph or type it on a computer. Make a drawing or add a photo. Put your page together with your classmates' pages to make a "Healthy Habits" book.

I exercise every day to keep my body strong and healthy. I ride my bike to school. I take special dance classes in school. After school, I get to play softball with my friends.

Writing Support

Writing instruction is scaffolded to ensure success.

Drafting Support

The Basics

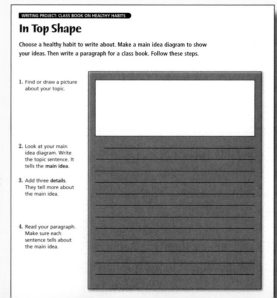

WRITING PROJECT: CLASS BOOK ON HEALTHY HABITS

In Top Shape

Choose a healthy habit to write about. Make a main idea diagram to show your ideas. Then write a paragraph for a class book. Follow these steps.

1. Find or draw a picture about your topic.

2. Look at your main idea diagram. Write the topic sentence. It tells the **main idea**.

3. Add three **details**. They tell more about the main idea.

4. Read your paragraph. Make sure each sentence tells about the main idea.

Writing Strategies and Applications

Writing Projects in each unit give experience with the modes and forms of writing represented in the standards and assessed on standardized tests.

THE WRITING PROCESS AT LEVELS A–C

- Students first study the writing mode through professional and student models and explore ways to organize their writing.

Level B Student Book: Unit 3 Writing Project

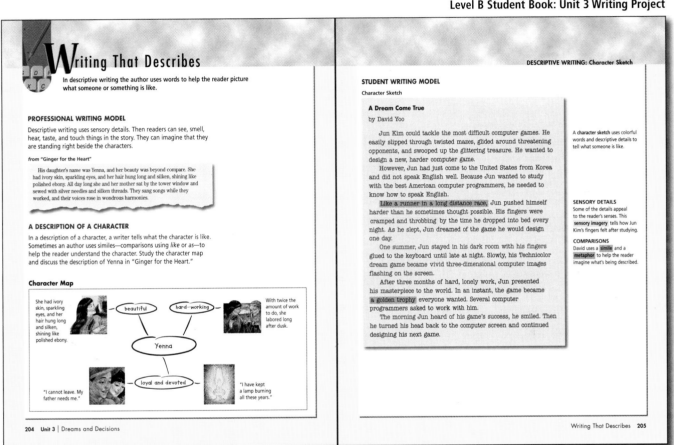

Support for Studying Writing Models

Writing Strategies and Applications, continued

THE WRITING PROCESS AT LEVELS A–C

- Next, students are guided step-by-step through the entire writing process with visual support.

- The Reflect and Evaluate features challenge students to self-assess so they can continually improve their writing.

- The Writer's Craft teaches such skills as word choice and elaboration to help students shape their writing. Language models illustrate quality differences.

Level B Student Book: Unit 3 Writing Project

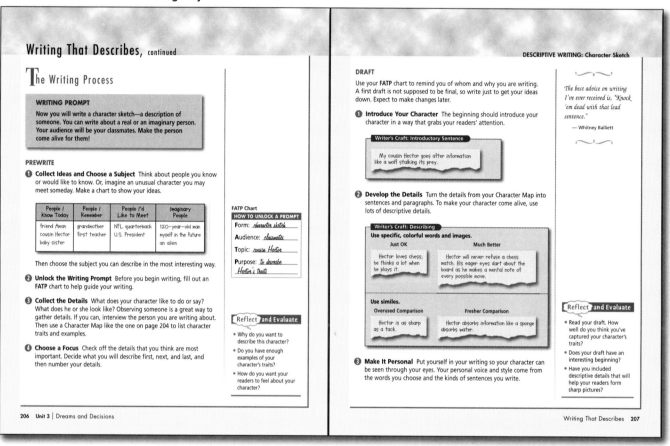

Writing That Describes, continued

The Writing Process

WRITING PROMPT

Now you will write a character sketch—a description of someone. You can write about a real or an imaginary person. Your audience will be your classmates. Make the person come alive for them!

PREWRITE

1 **Collect Ideas and Choose a Subject** Think about people you know or would like to know. Or, imagine an unusual character you may meet someday. Make a chart to show your ideas.

People I Know Today	People I Remember	People I'd Like to Meet	Imaginary People
friend Aman cousin Hector baby sister	grandmother first teacher	NFL quarterback U.S. President	120-year-old man myself in the future an alien

Then choose the subject you can describe in the most interesting way.

2 **Unlock the Writing Prompt** Before you begin writing, fill out an FATP chart to help guide your writing.

3 **Collect the Details** What does your character like to do or say? What does he or she look like? Observing someone is a great way to gather details. If you can, interview the person you are writing about. Then use a Character Map like the one on page 204 to list character traits and examples.

4 **Choose a Focus** Check off the details that you think are most important. Decide what you will describe first, next, and last, and then number your details.

FATP Chart
HOW TO UNLOCK A PROMPT
Form: *character sketch*
Audience: *classmates*
Topic: *cousin Hector*
Purpose: *to describe Hector's traits*

Reflect and Evaluate
- Why do you want to describe this character?
- Do you have enough examples of your character's traits?
- How do you want your readers to feel about your character?

206 Unit 3 | Dreams and Decisions

DESCRIPTIVE WRITING: Character Sketch

DRAFT

Use your FATP chart to remind you of whom and why you are writing. A first draft is not supposed to be final, so write just to get your ideas down. Expect to make changes later.

1 **Introduce Your Character** The beginning should introduce your character in a way that grabs your readers' attention.

Writer's Craft: Introductory Sentence
My cousin Hector goes after information like a wolf stalking its prey.

2 **Develop the Details** Turn the details from your Character Map into sentences and paragraphs. To make your character come alive, use lots of descriptive details.

Writer's Craft: Describing
Use specific, colorful words and images.

Just OK	Much Better
Hector loves chess; he thinks a lot when he plays it.	Hector will never refuse a chess match. His eager eyes dart about the board as he makes a mental note of every possible move.

Use similes.

Overused Comparison	Fresher Comparison
Hector is as sharp as a tack.	Hector absorbs information like a sponge absorbs water.

3 **Make It Personal** Put yourself in your writing so your character can be seen through your eyes. Your personal voice and style come from the words you choose and the kinds of sentences you write.

The best advice on writing I've ever received is, "Knock 'em dead with that lead sentence."
— Whitney Balliett

Reflect and Evaluate
- Read your draft. How well do you think you've captured your character's traits?
- Does your draft have an interesting beginning?
- Have you included descriptive details that will help your readers form sharp pictures?

Writing That Describes 207

Level B

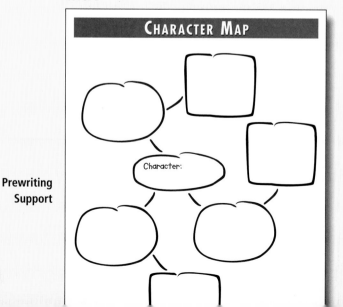

CHARACTER MAP

Character:

Prewriting Support

Level B

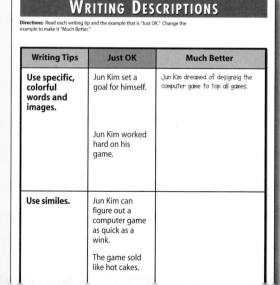

WRITING DESCRIPTIONS

Directions: Read each writing tip and the example that is "Just OK." Change the example to make it "Much Better."

Writing Tips	Just OK	Much Better
Use specific, colorful words and images.	Jun Kim set a goal for himself.	Jun Kim dreamed of designing the computer game to top all games.
	Jun Kim worked hard on his game.	
Use similes.	Jun Kim can figure out a computer game as quick as a wink.	
	The game sold like hot cakes.	

Writer's Craft Support

THE WRITING PROCESS AT LEVELS A–C

- Revising strategies model language for effective participation in peer conferences.
- Technology features help students learn to write and revise their work on the computer.

- Grammar in context relates the unit's grammar focus to the writing.

Level B Student Book: Unit 3 Writing Project

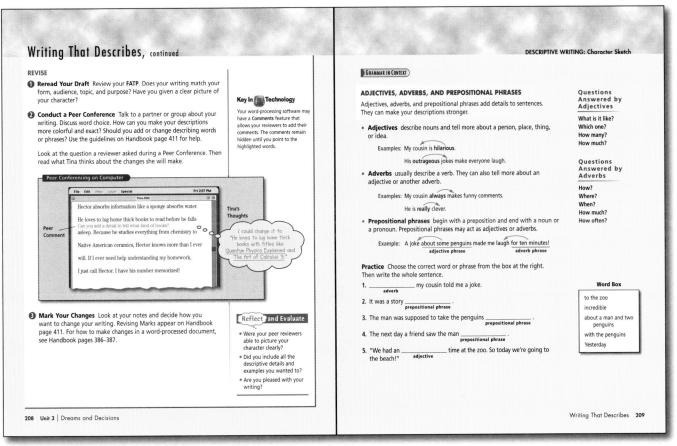

Writing That Describes, continued

REVISE

1 Reread Your Draft Review your **FATP**. Does your writing match your form, audience, topic, and purpose? Have you given a clear picture of your character?

2 Conduct a Peer Conference Talk to a partner or group about your writing. Discuss word choice. How can you make your descriptions more colorful and exact? Should you add or change describing words or phrases? Use the guidelines on Handbook page 411 for help.

Look at the question a reviewer asked during a Peer Conference. Then read what Tina thinks about the changes she will make.

Key In to Technology

Your word-processing software may have a **Comments** feature that allows your reviewers to add their comments. The comments remain hidden until you point to the highlighted words.

Peer Conferencing on Computer

> Hector absorbs information like a sponge absorbs water.
>
> He loves to lug home thick books to read before he falls
>
> Can you add a detail to tell what kind of books?
> asleep. Because he studies everything from chemistry to
>
> Native American ceramics, Hector knows more than I ever
>
> will. If I ever need help understanding my homework,
>
> I just call Hector. I have his number memorized!

Peer Comment

Tina's Thoughts

> I could change it to "He loves to lug home thick books with titles like Quantum Physics Explained and The Art of Calculus 3."

3 Mark Your Changes Look at your notes and decide how you want to change your writing. Revising Marks appear on Handbook page 411. For how to make changes in a word-processed document, see Handbook pages 386–387.

Reflect and Evaluate

- Were your peer reviewers able to picture your character clearly?
- Did you include all the descriptive details and examples you wanted to?
- Are you pleased with your writing?

208   Unit 3 | Dreams and Decisions

DESCRIPTIVE WRITING: Character Sketch

GRAMMAR IN CONTEXT

ADJECTIVES, ADVERBS, AND PREPOSITIONAL PHRASES

Adjectives, adverbs, and prepositional phrases add details to sentences. They can make your descriptions stronger.

- **Adjectives** describe nouns and tell more about a person, place, thing, or idea.

    Examples: My cousin is **hilarious**.

    His **outrageous** jokes make everyone laugh.

- **Adverbs** usually describe a verb. They can also tell more about an adjective or another adverb.

    Examples: My cousin **always** makes funny comments.

    He is **really** clever.

- **Prepositional phrases** begin with a preposition and end with a noun or a pronoun. Prepositional phrases may act as adjectives or adverbs.

    Example: A joke **about some penguins** made me laugh **for ten minutes**!
    adjective phrase   adverb phrase

Practice Choose the correct word or phrase from the box at the right. Then write the whole sentence.

1. _____ my cousin told me a joke.
   adverb

2. It was a story _____ .
   prepositional phrase

3. The man was supposed to take the penguins _____ .
   prepositional phrase

4. The next day a friend saw the man _____ .
   prepositional phrase

5. "We had an _____ time at the zoo. So today we're going to the beach!"
   adjective

Questions Answered by Adjectives

What is it like?
Which one?
How many?
How much?

Questions Answered by Adverbs

How?
Where?
When?
How much?
How often?

Word Box

to the zoo
incredible
about a man and two penguins
with the penguins
Yesterday

Writing That Describes   209

Level B

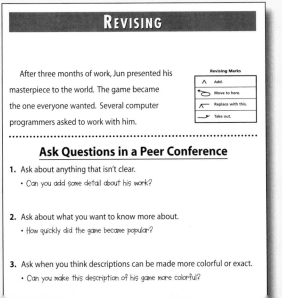

REVISING

> After three months of work, Jun presented his masterpiece to the world. The game became the one everyone wanted. Several computer programmers asked to work with him.

Revising Marks

∧	Add.
⟲	Move to here.
⟋	Replace with this.
⟿	Take out.

Ask Questions in a Peer Conference

1. Ask about anything that isn't clear.
   - Can you add some detail about his work?

2. Ask about what you want to know more about.
   - How quickly did the game became popular?

3. Ask when you think descriptions can be made more colorful or exact.
   - Can you make this description of his game more colorful?

Revising Support

Writing Strategies and Applications, continued

THE WRITING PROCESS IN LEVELS A–C

- Editing and proofreading strategies help students achieve accuracy in written conventions.
- Technology features help students edit and publish work on the computer.

Level B Student Book: Unit 3 Writing Project

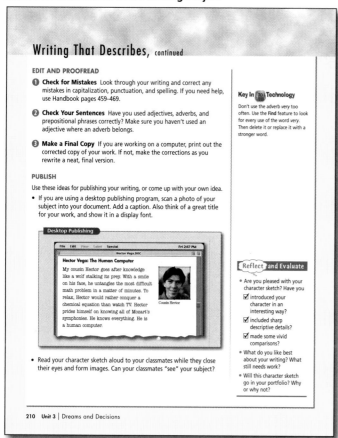

Writing That Describes, continued

EDIT AND PROOFREAD

1. **Check for Mistakes** Look through your writing and correct any mistakes in capitalization, punctuation, and spelling. If you need help, use Handbook pages 459–469.

2. **Check Your Sentences** Have you used adjectives, adverbs, and prepositional phrases correctly? Make sure you haven't used an adjective where an adverb belongs.

3. **Make a Final Copy** If you are working on a computer, print out the corrected copy of your work. If not, make the corrections as you rewrite a neat, final version.

PUBLISH

Use these ideas for publishing your writing, or come up with your own idea.

- If you are using a desktop publishing program, scan a photo of your subject into your document. Add a caption. Also think of a great title for your work, and show it in a display font.

Key In Technology

Don't use the adverb *very* too often. Use the **Find** feature to look for every use of the word *very*. Then delete it or replace it with a stronger word.

Desktop Publishing

File   Edit   Place   Label   Special   Fri 2:57 PM

Hector Vega.DOC

Hector Vega: The Human Computer

My cousin Hector goes after knowledge like a wolf stalking its prey. With a smile on his face, he untangles the most difficult math problem in a matter of minutes. To relax, Hector would rather conquer a chemical equation than watch TV. Hector prides himself on knowing all of Mozart's symphonies. He knows everything. He is a human computer.

Cousin Hector

Reflect and Evaluate

- Are you pleased with your character sketch? Have you
  ☑ introduced your character in an interesting way?
  ☑ included sharp descriptive details?
  ☑ made some vivid comparisons?
- What do you like best about your writing? What still needs work?
- Will this character sketch go in your portfolio? Why or why not?

- Read your character sketch aloud to your classmates while they close their eyes and form images. Can your classmates "see" your subject?

210   Unit 3 | Dreams and Decisions

Practice in Written Conventions

Editing and Proofreading Support

Level B

EDITING AND PROOFREADING

Directions: Read each sentence. Check for errors in capitalization, spelling, and punctuation. Use the Proofreading Marks to correct the mistakes

1. However, Jun had just come to the United states from Korea and did not speak English well?

2. One summer, jun stayed in his dark room with his fingers glud to the keyboard until late at night.

3. The Morning Jun heard of his game's success, he smiled.

Proofreading Marks

∧	Add.
⋏	Add a comma.
⊙	Add a period.
≡	Capitalize.
/	Make lowercase.
⟋	Take out.
¶	Indent.

Directions: Read the paragraph. Check for errors in capitalization, spelling, and punctuation. Check whether adjectives and adverbs are used correctly. Use the Proofreading Marks to correct the mistakes.

Like a runner in a long distance race, Jun pushed himself hard than he sometimes thot possible. His fingers were cramped and throbbing by the time he dropped into bed all night as he slept, Jun dreamed of the game he would design one day.

Written Conventions

Handbooks at each level support students in applying the written conventions of English.

Grammar Support in Handbook

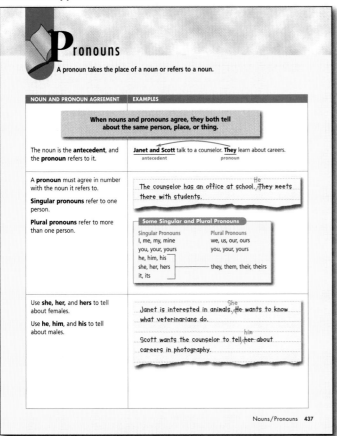

Pronouns

A pronoun takes the place of a noun or refers to a noun.

NOUN AND PRONOUN AGREEMENT	EXAMPLES
When nouns and pronouns agree, they both tell about the same person, place, or thing.	
The noun is the **antecedent**, and the **pronoun** refers to it.	Janet and Scott talk to a counselor. They learn about careers. antecedent — pronoun
A **pronoun** must agree in number with the noun it refers to. **Singular pronouns** refer to one person. **Plural pronouns** refer to more than one person.	The counselor has an office at school. ~~They~~ He meets there with students.
	Some Singular and Plural Pronouns Singular Pronouns: I, me, my, mine / you, your, yours / he, him, his / she, her, hers / it, its Plural Pronouns: we, us, our, ours / you, your, yours / they, them, their, theirs
Use **she, her,** and **hers** to tell about females. Use **he, him,** and **his** to tell about males.	Janet is interested in animals. ~~He~~ She wants to know what veterinarians do. Scott wants the counselor to tell ~~her~~ him about careers in photography.

Nouns/Pronouns **437**

Punctuation Support in Handbook

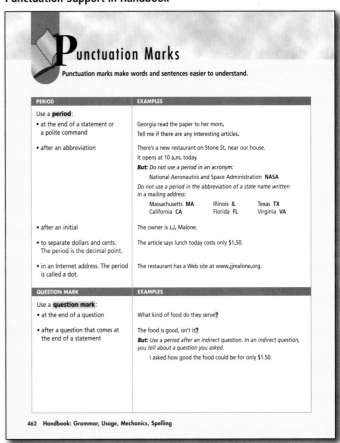

Punctuation Marks

Punctuation marks make words and sentences easier to understand.

PERIOD	EXAMPLES
Use a **period**:	
• at the end of a statement or a polite command	Georgia read the paper to her mom. Tell me if there are any interesting articles.
• after an abbreviation	There's a new restaurant on Stone St. near our house. It opens at 10 a.m. today. ***But:*** *Do not use a period in an acronym:* National Aeronautics and Space Administration **NASA** *Do not use a period in the abbreviation of a state name written in a mailing address:* Massachusetts **MA** Illinois **IL** Texas **TX** California **CA** Florida **FL** Virginia **VA**
• after an initial	The owner is J.J. Malone.
• to separate dollars and cents. The period is the decimal point.	The article says lunch today costs only $1.50.
• in an Internet address. The period is called a dot.	The restaurant has a Web site at www.jjmalone.org.

QUESTION MARK	EXAMPLES
Use a **question mark**:	
• at the end of a question	What kind of food do they serve?
• after a question that comes at the end of a statement	The food is good, isn't it? ***But:*** *Use a period after an indirect question. In an indirect question, you tell about a question you asked.* I asked how good the food could be for only $1.50.

462 Handbook: Grammar, Usage, Mechanics, Spelling

Level A

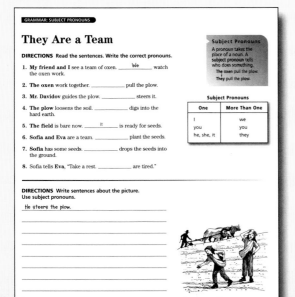

GRAMMAR: SUBJECT PRONOUNS

They Are a Team

DIRECTIONS Read the sentences. Write the correct pronouns.

1. **My friend and I** see a team of oxen. __We__ watch the oxen work.
2. **The oxen** work together. _____ pull the plow.
3. **Mr. Davidov** guides the plow. _____ steers it.
4. **The plow** loosens the soil. _____ digs into the hard earth.
5. **The field** is bare now. __It__ is ready for seeds.
6. **Sofia and Eva** are a team. _____ plant the seeds.
7. **Sofia** has some seeds. _____ drops the seeds into the ground.
8. Sofia tells **Eva**, "Take a rest. _____ are tired."

Subject Pronouns
A pronoun takes the place of a noun. A subject pronoun tells who does something.
The oxen pull the plow.
They pull the plow.

Subject Pronouns

One	More Than One
I	we
you	you
he, she, it	they

DIRECTIONS Write sentences about the picture. Use subject pronouns.

He steers the plow.
_____
_____
_____
_____
_____

Level A

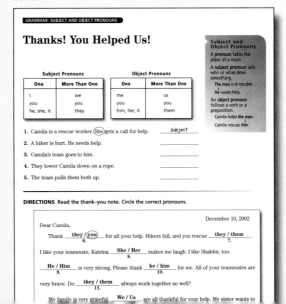

GRAMMAR: SUBJECT AND OBJECT PRONOUNS

Thanks! You Helped Us!

Subject Pronouns

One	More Than One
I	we
you	you
he, she, it	they

Object Pronouns

One	More Than One
me	us
you	you
him, her, it	them

Subject and Object Pronouns
A pronoun takes the place of a noun.
A subject pronoun tells who or what does something.
The man is in trouble.
He needs help.
An object pronoun follows a verb or a preposition.
Camila helps the man.
Camila rescues him.

1. Camila is a rescue worker. She gets a call for help. __subject__
2. A hiker is hurt. He needs help. _____
3. Camila's team goes to him. _____
4. They lower Camila down on a rope. _____
5. The team pulls them both up. _____

DIRECTIONS Read the thank-you note. Circle the correct pronouns.

December 10, 2002

Dear Camila,

Thank __they / (you)__ for all your help. Hikers fall, and you rescue __they / them__ .
          6.   7.

I like your teammate, Katrina. __She / Her__ makes me laugh. I like Shabbir, too.
                                              8.

__He / Him__ is very strong. Please thank __he / him__ for me. All of your teammates are
      9.   10.

very brave. Do __they / them__ always work together so well?
                        11.

My family is very grateful. __We / Us__ are all thankful for your help. My sister wants to

Extensive Pronoun Practice in the Practice Books

Pacing Options

High Point is a flexible program whose pacing can be adjusted to one-hour, two-hour, or three-hour sessions.

The Basics

This level of *High Point* contains 18 units and an optional unit called Lakeside School. See page T10e of The Basics Teacher's Edition for the recommended pacing of Lakeside School.

3-HOUR INTERVENTION PACING
In this model, each unit takes one week. (Number of lessons in a unit varies from 13 to 16.)

UNIT 11	Day 1	Day 2	Day 3	Day 4	Day 5
Language Development (1 hour)	Lesson 1 Introduce the Unit Lesson 2 Vocabulary or Grammar Lesson	Lessons 3–4 Vocabulary or Grammar Lessons	Lesson 5 Vocabulary or Grammar Lesson Lesson 12 Content Area Connection	Lesson 13 Writing Project	Lesson 13 (cont.) Writing Project
Language and Literacy (2 hours)	Lesson 6 The Basics Bookshelf: Theme Book Read-Alouds	Lesson 8 High Frequency Words Lesson 9 (Part 1) Phonemic Awareness and Phonics	Lesson 7 The Basics Bookshelf: Theme Book Comprehension and Retelling Lesson 9 (Part 2) Phonemic Awareness and Phonics	Lesson 10 Reading and Spelling with Practice in Decodable Text	Lesson 11 Independent Reading (decodable text), Comprehension, and Reading Fluency

DAILY PERIOD PACING
In this model, each unit takes about two weeks to complete.

UNIT 11 (Week 1)	Day 1	Day 2	Day 3	Day 4	Day 5
Language Development and Literacy (1 hour)	Lesson 1 Introduce the Unit Lesson 2 Vocabulary or Grammar Lesson	Lessons 3–4 Vocabulary or Grammar Lessons	Lesson 5 Vocabulary or Grammar Lesson Lesson 6 The Basics Bookshelf: Theme Book Read-Alouds	Lesson 7 The Basics Bookshelf: Theme Book Comprehension and Retelling	Lesson 8 High Frequency Words Lesson 9 (Part 1) Phonemic Awareness and Phonics

UNIT 11 (Week 2)	Day 6	Day 7	Day 8	Day 9	Day 10
Language Development and Literacy (1 hour)	Lesson 9 (Part 2) Phonemic Awareness and Phonics	Lesson 10 Reading and Spelling with Practice in Decodable Text	Lesson 11 Independent Reading (decodable text), Comprehension, and Reading Fluency	Lesson 12 Content Area Connection Lesson 13 Writing Project	Lesson 13 (cont.) Writing Project

BLOCK SCHEDULE PACING
In this model, two or three sessions occur each week, so each unit takes about two weeks.

UNIT 11	Session 1	Session 2	Session 3	Session 4	Session 5	Session 6
Language Development (1 hour)	Lesson 1 Introduce the Unit Lesson 2 Vocabulary or Grammar Lesson	Lessons 3–4 Vocabulary or Grammar Lessons	Lesson 5 Vocabulary or Grammar Lesson	Lesson 12 Language Across the Curriculum	Lesson 13 Writing Project	Lesson 13 (cont.) Writing Project
Language and Literacy (1 to 1 1/2 hours)	Lesson 6 The Basics Bookshelf: Theme Book Read-Alouds	Lesson 7 The Basics Bookshelf: Theme Book Comprehension and Retelling Lesson 8 High Frequency Words	Lesson 9 (Part 1) Phonemic Awareness and Phonics	Lesson 9 (Part 2) Phonemic Awareness and Phonics	Lesson 10 Reading and Spelling with Practice in Decodable Text	Lesson 11 Independent Reading (decodable text), Comprehension, and Reading Fluency

Levels A–C

Levels A–C of **High Point** each contain 5 units. Each unit contains 2 themes.

3-HOUR INTERVENTION PACING

In this model, each unit takes approximately 3 weeks. (Number of lessons per theme varies.)

LEVEL A, UNIT 1	Day 1	Day 2	Day 3	Day 4	Day 5
THEME 1	**THEME 1** **Lesson 1** • Introduce the Theme **Lesson 2** • Build Language and Vocabulary	**Lesson 3** Prepare to Read • Vocabulary • Reading Strategy **Lessons 4–5** Read the Selection	**Lesson 6** Respond to the Selection • Check Your Understanding activities **Lesson 7** Respond to the Selection • Language Arts and Literature activities	**Lesson 8** Respond to the Selection • Content Area Connections **Conduct Grammar Minilesson**	**Lesson 9** Build Language and Vocabulary **Lesson 10** Prepare to Read • Vocabulary • Reading Strategy

LEVEL A, UNIT 1	Day 6	Day 7	Day 8	Day 9	Day 10
THEME 1 and THEME 2	**Lessons 11–12** Read the Selection **Lesson 13** Respond to the Selection • Check Your Understanding activities	**Lesson 14** Respond to the Selection • Language Arts and Literature activities **Conduct Grammar Minilesson**	**Lesson 15** Respond to the Selection • Content Area Connections **Conduct Research Skills Minilesson**	**THEME 2** **Lesson 1** • Introduce the Theme **Lesson 2** Build Language and Vocabulary **Lesson 3** Prepare to Read • Vocabulary • Reading Strategy	**Lessons 4–5** Read the Selection **Lesson 6** Respond to the Selection • Check Your Understanding activities **Conduct Grammar Minilesson**

LEVEL A, UNIT 1	Day 11	Day 12	Day 13	Day 14	Day 15
THEME 2	**Lesson 7** Respond to the Selection • Language Arts and Content Area Connections **Conduct Grammar Minilesson**	**Lesson 8** Build Language and Vocabulary **Lesson 9** Prepare to Read • Vocabulary • Reading Strategy **Lessons 10–11** Read the Selection	**Lesson 12** Respond to the Selection • Check Your Understanding activities **Lesson 13** Respond to the Selection • Language Arts and Literature	**Lesson 14** Respond to the Selection • Content Area Connections **Conduct Grammar Minilesson**	**Lesson 15** Prepare to Read • Vocabulary • Reading Strategy **Lesson 16** Read and Respond to the Poem **Unit Debrief and Assessment**
Writing Project		Study Writing Models Write Together	Prewrite Draft	Revise Grammar in Context	Edit and Proofread Publish

The intervention program will last two years for the student who places at the beginning of The Basics.

YEAR 1 33–36 weeks	The Basics	18-21 weeks
	Level A	15 weeks
YEAR 2 30 weeks	Level B	15 weeks
	Level C	15 weeks

DAILY PERIOD PACING

In this model, each unit takes 6-7 weeks to complete. The Activity Planners at the start of each unit in the Levels A–C Teacher's Editions show how to divide the units into daily periods. In general, each lesson takes about a day and the Writing Project is spread across the last week of each unit.

BLOCK SCHEDULE OR 2-HOUR SESSION PACING

In this model, two or three block schedule sessions occur each week such that each unit takes 6-7 weeks to complete. The Activity Planners at the start of each unit in the Levels A–C Teacher's Editions show how to divide the units into block schedule sessions. In general, two lessons can be completed per session and the Writing Project is spread across the last two weeks of the unit.

Practice Book Contents and Homework Opportunities

- **Homework Opportunity**

LESSON PLANS FOR
Units 1-5

Contents for Your Teacher's Edition

UNIT 1 — Unique You

Contents for Your Teacher's Edition, continued

UNIT 2 UNITED, WE STAND

Making Connections

Contents for Your Teacher's Edition, continued

UNIT 4 Communities Count

Resources

For Success in Language, Literature, and Content

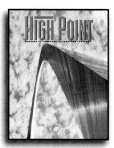

Student Book pages 8–65

For Skills Practice

Practice Book
pages 1–31

For Planning and Instruction

Teacher's Edition
pages T8a–T65

For Vocabulary and Language Development

Language Tape Side A
Language CD Tracks 1 and 2

For Audio Walk-Throughs and Selection Readings

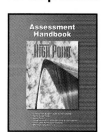

Selection Tape 1
Selection CD 1

For Technology Support

Inspiration
Visual Learning Software
with Graphic Organizers

For Classroom Activities

Transparencies or Masters 1–19

For Home-School Connections

High Point Newsletters 1 and 2

For Comprehensive Assessment

Language Acquisition Assessment,
Selection Tests, Unit Test, Writing
Assessment, Self-Assessment

In the Theme Library

Grandfather's Journey
by Allen Say

Just Like Me
edited by Harriet Rohmer

From *The Basics Bookshelf*

▶ *Good News*

▶ *What Is It?*

▶ *I Make Pictures Move*

Theme-related books with
simple text for including
newcomers

A VERY
Unique You

Curiosity: The Food of the Heart, David Diaz, digital illustration, Copyright © 1999.

EVERY HUMAN BEING IS UNIQUE. NO TWO HAVE THE SAME GENETIC MAKEUP, THE SAME LIKES, DREAMS, OR FEELINGS ABOUT THE WORLD. STUDENTS, IN THE PROCESS OF DISCOVERING THEIR UNIQUENESS, LEARN IN THIS UNIT THAT IDENTITY IS A BLEND OF ONE'S INTERESTS, THOUGHTS, AND ACTIONS.

THEME 1 Discover Yourself

Students read about others who continue to discover new things about themselves, their dreams, and their goals.

THEME 2 Many Kinds of Smart

Students examine the different ways they learn and express themselves.

THEME 1: Discover Yourself

PACING SUGGESTIONS		
LESSONS	45–55 MINUTE PERIODS	BLOCK SCHEDULE SESSIONS
1	1 period	1 session
2–8	7 periods	3 sessions
9–15	6 periods	3 sessions

LESSONS
1

THEME 1 OPENER			▶ pages T10–T11
Function Engage in Discussion	**Learning Strategy** Make a Comparison Chart	**Vocabulary** Describing Words	**Critical Thinking** Make Comparisons

2–8

Discovery by John Y. Wang   POEM ▶ pages T14–T21

BUILD LANGUAGE AND VOCABULARY pages T12–T13	**Function** ⊕ Describe People	**Learning Strategy** Classify Words	**Vocabulary** People Words	**Patterns and Structures** ⊕ Present Tense Verbs; ⊕ Adjectives

PREPARE TO READ page T14	**READ THE SELECTION** pages T15–T18		**RESPOND** pages T19–T21		
Activate Prior Knowledge Make a Circle Graph	**Pre-Reading Strategies** Preview and Predict	📁 **Grammar Minilesson:** ⊕ Present Tense Verbs	**CHECK YOUR UNDERSTANDING**	**LANGUAGE ARTS AND LITERATURE**	**CONTENT AREA CONNECTIONS**
Vocabulary ⊕ Relate Words	Set Purpose		**Critical Thinking and Comprehension** Sum It Up: ⊕ Classify Ideas; Write Sentences	**Grammar in Context and Vocabulary** ⊕ Use Verbs Use Character Traits	**Science and Technology/Media** Research a Scientist
Reading Strategy ⊕ Classify Ideas	**Strategy Focus** ⊕ Classify Ideas		Think It Over: Discuss	**Literary Analysis and Writing/Speaking** Write a Free-Verse Poem	
	Comprehension Before you Move On: Think and Discuss		**Function** Express Yourself: Describe		

9–15

Could I Ask You a Question? by Gilbert Socas   INTERVIEW ▶ pages T24–T31

BUILD LANGUAGE AND VOCABULARY pages T22–T23	**Function** ⊕ Ask and Answer Questions	**Learning Strategy** Predict and Listen	**Vocabulary** Question Words	**Patterns and Structures** ⊕ Questions

PREPARE TO READ page T24	**READ THE SELECTION** pages T25–T28		**RESPOND** pages T29–T31		
Activate Prior Knowledge Make a Word Web	**Pre-Reading Strategies** Preview and Relate to Personal Experience	📁 **Grammar Minilesson:** Nouns	**CHECK YOUR UNDERSTANDING**	**LANGUAGE ARTS AND LITERATURE**	**LANGUAGE ARTS AND CONTENT AREA CONNECTIONS**
Vocabulary ⊕ Use New Words in Context	Set Purpose		**Critical Thinking and Comprehension** Sum It Up: ⊕ Make Comparisons; Draw Conclusions	**Grammar in Context** Ask Questions	**Social Studies** Explore Geography
Reading Strategy ⊕ Make Comparisons	**Strategy Focus** ⊕ Make Comparisons		Think It Over: Discuss	**Writing and Speaking/Listening** Conduct an Interview	**Writing** Study a News Story
	Comprehension Before You Move On: Think and Discuss		**Function** Express Yourself: Ask and Answer Questions		

THEME 2: Many Kinds of Smart

LESSONS

1

THEME 2 OPENER ▶ *pages T32–T33*

Function	Learning Strategy	Vocabulary	Critical Thinking
Engage in Discussion	Make a T-Chart	Words about Identity	Draw Conclusions

2–7

Many People, Many Intelligences by Joanne Ryder
SCIENCE ARTICLE ▶ *pages T36–T43*

BUILD LANGUAGE AND VOCABULARY pages T34–T35

Function	Learning Strategy	Vocabulary	Patterns and Structures
T Give Information	Relate to Personal Experience	Brain Power Words	T Present Tense Verbs

PREPARE TO READ page T36

Activate Prior Knowledge
Make a Bar Graph

Vocabulary T
Use New Words in Context

Reading Strategy T
Make and Confirm Predictions

READ THE SELECTION pages T37–T41

Pre-Reading Strategies
Preview and Predict

Set Purpose

Strategy Focus T
Make Predictions

Vocabulary
Use New Words in Context

Comprehension
Before You Move On:
Think and Discuss

Grammar Minilessons:
T Present Tense Verbs

Articles

RESPOND pages T42–T43

CHECK YOUR UNDERSTANDING

Critical Thinking and Comprehension
Sum It Up:
T Confirm Predictions;
Ask Questions

Think It Over: Discuss

Function
Express Yourself:
Give Information

LANGUAGE ARTS AND CONTENT AREA CONNECTIONS

Vocabulary
Match Jobs and Skills

Mathematics
Graph Intelligence Types

8–14

Art Smart by Nancy Hom and George Littlechild
SELF-PORTRAITS ▶ *pages T46–T54*

BUILD LANGUAGE AND VOCABULARY pages T44–T45

Function	Learning Strategy	Vocabulary	Patterns and Structures
T Describe Things	Make Observations	Colors, Sizes, Shapes	T Adjectives

PREPARE TO READ page T46

Activate Prior Knowledge
Tell About a Picture

Vocabulary T
Use New Words in Context

Reading Strategy T
Relate Cause and Effect

READ THE SELECTION pages T47–T51

Pre-Reading Strategies
Preview and Predict

Set Purpose

Strategy Focus T
Relate Cause and Effect

Vocabulary
Use New Words in Context

Comprehension
Before You Move On:
Think and Discuss

Grammar Minilessons:
Adjectives

Proper Adjectives

RESPOND pages T52–T54

CHECK YOUR UNDERSTANDING

Critical Thinking and Comprehension
Sum It Up:
T Relate Cause and Effect

Think It Over: Discuss

Function
Express Yourself: Describe and Give Information

LANGUAGE ARTS AND LITERATURE

Grammar in Context
T Use Nouns

Writing/Representing
Create a Portrait Gallery

CONTENT AREA CONNECTIONS

Mathematics and Fine Arts
Identify Geometric Shapes

Viewing/Speaking and Technology/Media
Research a Portrait Artist

15–16

Just Me by Margaret Hillert
POEM ▶ *pages T55–T57*

PREPARE TO READ page T55

Activate Prior Knowledge
Talk It Over

Vocabulary
Use New Words in Context

Literary Analysis
Rhyme

READ THE POEM page T56

Pre-Reading Strategies
Set Purpose

Strategy Focus
Use Text Features in Poetry (rhyme)

RESPOND page T57

Critical Thinking and Comprehension
Think It Over: Discuss

Function
Express Yourself: Read Aloud a Poem

BUILD WRITING SKILLS

WRITING THAT DESCRIBES DESCRIPTIVE: POETRY ▶ *pages T58–T64*

Writing Mode/Form	Writing Process T	Writer's Craft	Grammar in Context	Reflect and Evaluate
T Descriptive	Prewrite; Draft; Revise; Edit and Proofread; Publish	T Word Choice	T Subject-Verb Agreement	Self-Assessment
Poetry				

T = Assessed on **Unit 1 Test**   T = Assessed on **Unit 1 Language Acquisition Assessment**

THEME 1: Discover Yourself

MORE RESOURCES

Grandfather's Journey
by Allen Say
I In this Caldecott medal-winner, Say looks at his grandfather's life in two countries. This helps him understand his own identity. (Available from Hampton-Brown)

People
by Peter Spier
B I An award-winning author/illustrator looks at similarities and differences in people all over the world. (Bantam Doubleday Dell)

Weslandia
by Paul Fleischman
A An award-winning author tells the story of a boy who finds happiness when he creates his own unique identity. (Candlewick Press)

Children Just Like Me
by Barnabas and Anabel Kindersley
B This photo-filled cultural survey shows the world from the points of view of individual children and their families. (Dorling Kindersley)

Isn't My Name Magical?: Sister and Brother Poems
by James Berry
I A poetry and picture book about family, identity, and friendship. (Simon & Schuster)

In My Own Voice: Multicultural Poets on Identity
I A Multicultural poets read their own poetry and discuss their sources of inspiration. Includes examples of fine art and musical selections. (Sunburst)
Multimedia CD-ROM

THEME 2: Many Kinds of Smart

MORE RESOURCES

Just Like Me
edited by Harriet Rohmer
I Fourteen artists use words and pictures to tell about their lives. (Available from Hampton-Brown)

My Name is Georgia
by Jeanette Winter
B The story of a girl who is not afraid to be herself and who grows up to become a famous artist. (Silver Whistle)

Eye on the Wild: A Story About Ansel Adams
by Julie Dunlap
A The true story of a boy who doesn't like school but loves to learn. He also loves nature and becomes a nature photographer. (Carolrhoda Books)

The Straight Line Wonder
by Mem Fox
B I In a world of straight lines, one line decides to go curvy. At first he is rejected, but his unconventional talents are eventually accepted. (Mondo)

With Open Eyes: Images from the Art Institute of Chicago
by Allen Say
B I A tour through the collections of the Art Institute of Chicago highlights many kinds of artwork. A game reinforces the meaning of each image. (Interactive Solutions) **CD-ROM**

TesselMania! Deluxe
I A This program provides the tools to combine geometry and art in the tradition of the "tesselations," or interlocking figures, created by the artist M. C. Escher. (MECC) **CD-ROM**

ONGOING, INFORMAL ASSESSMENT

Check for understanding and achieve closure for every lesson with the targeted questions and activities in the **Close and Assess** boxes in your Teacher's Edition.

INDIVIDUAL AND GROUP-ADMINISTERED TESTS

The **Assessment Handbook** includes these comprehensive assessment tools for Unit 1:

▶ **Selection Tests**
Test students' mastery of reading strategies and the vocabulary, comprehension, and language arts skills taught with each main selection of Unit 1.

▶ **Unit Test in Standardized Test Format**
The multiple-choice sections of this test measure students' cumulative understanding of the skills and language developed in Unit 1. A Writing Prompt measures progress in writing skills and fluency. The Read, Think, and Explain section offers open-ended items to measure strategies and comprehension.

▶ **Language Acquisition Assessment**
To verify students' ability to use the vocabulary and grammar structures taught in Unit 1, conduct these performance assessments.

SELF- AND PEER-ASSESSMENT

Students use the Unit 1 Self-Assessment Form in the **Assessment Handbook** to evaluate their own work and develop learning strategies appropriate to their needs. Students offer feedback to their classmates with the Peer-Assessment Form.

WRITING ASSESSMENT / PORTFOLIO OPPORTUNITIES

You can evaluate students' writing using the rubrics and scoring guidelines provided in the **Assessment Handbook**. Then collaborate with students to choose work for their portfolios.

UNIT 1 ASSESSMENT OPPORTUNITIES	Assessment Handbook Pages
Unit 1 Language Acquisition Assessment	1–2
Selection Tests	
Discovery	3–4
Could I Ask You a Question?	5–6
Many People, Many Intelligences	7–8
Art Smart	9–10
Unit 1 Writing Assessment	11
Unit 1 Self-Assessment Form	12
Unit 1 Test	13–20
Peer-Assessment Form	101
Portfolio Evaluation Form	103

Curiosity: The Food of the Heart, David Díaz, digital illustration, Copyright © 1999.

8

OBJECTIVES

Function: Engage in Discussion

Concepts and Vocabulary: Identity—*unique, discover, dreams, goals;* Color Words; Foods; Character Traits; Values

Viewing: Interpret a Visual Image

Critical Thinking and Learning Strategies: Make Comparisons; Preview; Build Background; Use Graphic Organizers (mind map)

INTRODUCE UNIT CONCEPT

1 View *Curiosity: The Food of the Heart* Read the unit title and define unique as "one-of-a-kind." Ask: *What makes a person unique?* Then read the activity. Go over each part of the artist's picture and ask: *What makes this artist unique?*

2 Make Identity Pictures and Build Vocabulary Have students make their four-part pictures. Display them and work together as a class to build lists of vocabulary words that go with students' pictures. Record the words on **Transparency 1**.

> Use the Vocabulary Options in the **Multi-Level Strategies** to work with all proficiency levels.

REACHING ALL STUDENTS

Transparency 1 / Master 1

WORDS ABOUT US			
Our Favorite Colors	Our Favorite Foods	Words that Describe Us	What's Important to Us

Transparency 1 Level A, Unit 1 | Identity   © Hampton-Brown

Multi-Level Strategies
VOCABULARY BUILDING OPTIONS

BEGINNING Ask students to name the colors and foods in the identity pictures. Ask questions with yes/no or one-word answers: *Is the sky blue in this picture? Does Jenna like pizza or salad?* Repeat each answer as a complete sentence, emphasizing the key word as you write it: *Yes, the sky is **blue**.*

INTERMEDIATE Ask students to collect the words that their classmates chose to describe themselves. Use follow-up questions to expand language: *Is Jake really funny? How does he make his friends laugh? Did you know Louise was artistic? Tell me about her artwork.*

ADVANCED Encourage students to provide vocabulary words that go with the values, beliefs, and ideas they have shown in the last part of their pictures. Ask: *What is important to Juan? How does he show this in his picture? What is important to you? Can you explain why you feel this way?*

A VERY Unique You

In this picture, the artist shows parts of his identity: his favorite colors, his favorite food, a word that describes him, and something that is important to him. Make a four-part picture for yourself. Compare pictures with your classmates. Is your picture exactly like any other? What did you learn about people being unique?

THEME 1
Discover Yourself
As we grow older, we discover new things about ourselves, our dreams, and our goals.

THEME 2
Many Kinds of Smart
We have our own special ways of learning and expressing ourselves.

9

UNIT 1 Mind Map

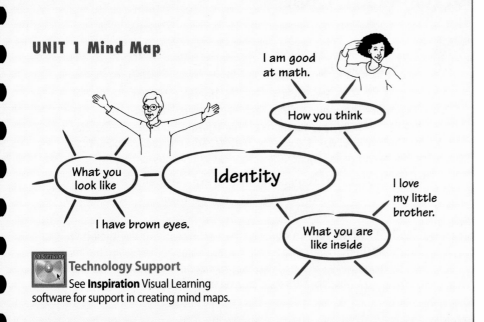

- I am good at math.
- How you think
- What you look like
- Identity
- I have brown eyes.
- I love my little brother.
- What you are like inside

Technology Support
See **Inspiration** Visual Learning software for support in creating mind maps.

---

3 Compare Pictures and Discuss Identity Discuss answers to these questions:

- Is your picture like any other?
- What did you learn about people being unique?

Summarize: *A person's identity is what he or she is like. The way we look and act, what we like, how we think, and what we care about all go together to make up our identity. Each of us has a unique identity.*

PREVIEW UNIT THEMES

4 Preview Theme 1: Discover Yourself Read aloud the theme title and the theme statement. Define *discover* as "learn something new." Offer examples of *dreams* (what we hope will happen) and *goals* (plans we make for the future). Then ask: *Do you have a goal? Is it the same one you had at age 10?*

Invite students to look over pages 10–31. Discuss photos that show examples of hopes and dreams.

5 Preview Theme 2: Many Kinds of Smart Read the theme title and statement. Explain that people can learn and be smart in different ways. Then leaf through pages 32–57, previewing the photo collage of "smart people" on page 32.

6 Create a Mind Map Begin a class mind map on Identity, and have students start a personal map in their notebooks or in the **Practice Book**. Students should write at least one sentence for each part of the map. Provide sentence frames (*I am _____; I have _____.*) for beginners. More advanced learners can use these category names: *Physical, Mental, Emotional.* Have students add to the map as they move through the unit.

▶ **Practice Book** page 1

CLOSE AND ASSESS

Ask students what this unit will be about. (identity; being unique) Then ask: *Can identity ever change?* (Yes. New experiences can bring new discoveries.)

INTRODUCE THEME 1

OBJECTIVES

Functions: Engage in Discussion; Role-Play

Concepts and Vocabulary: Describing Words

Viewing: Respond to a Photograph; Interpret a Visual Image

Learning Strategies: Relate to Personal Experience; Use Graphic Organizers (chart)

Critical Thinking: ⊕ Make Comparisons; Generate Ideas

TAP PRIOR KNOWLEDGE

1 Discuss Identity Ask: *What can you say about yourself? What words tell about, or describe, you?* Show the completed **Transparency 1** (see page T8) to remind students what they already know how to say about themselves. Tell students they will *discover*, or find out, more ways to describe themselves in this theme.

VIEW, DISCUSS, AND ROLE-PLAY

2 Compare Parts of a Photograph After students view the photo, make a chart to compare the two images of the girl. Help students see that the image in the mirror shows the girl's dream for the future. Ask: *What does this girl see in the mirror? Is this image real? What is she thinking about?*

Real	In the Mirror
girl with school books	girl is older
wears school clothes	wears cap and gown
is happening now	is happening in the future

3 Role-Play a Dream for the Future Have students personalize the photo in a role-play that shows a dream they have for themselves.

▮ Use the Role-Play Options in the **Multi-Level Strategies** to help all students participate.

10 Unit 1 | Identity

REACHING ALL STUDENTS

▮ Multi-Level Strategies
ROLE-PLAY OPTIONS

BEGINNING Provide a mirror as a prop. Ask students to use the mirror to introduce themselves. Offer sentence starters, such as: *I see...* , *I am...* , *I have...* . Pass out photographs from magazines to prompt students' ideas about the future. Ask: *Do you see [a pilot] in the mirror?* Use gestures to clarify meaning and encourage students to do the same.

INTERMEDIATE Encourage students to expand upon the mirror introductions and to ask one another questions. *Suki, you see a teacher. What do you want to teach?*

ADVANCED Give students notice so they can prepare their own props. Ask them to describe and act out the dream they see in the mirror. Say: *What job will you have? Tell what you do and what you like best about your work. Tell about the other dreams you have for the future.*

THEME 1

Discover Yourself

- What words describe the way you look?
  What words describe the way you are?

- What do you want to find out about yourself?
  How can you learn more about yourself?

- What kind of person do you want to become?
  How can knowing about yourself help you now
  and later?

THEME-RELATED BOOKS

Grandfather's Journey
by Allen Say

In this Caldecott Medal-winner,
Say looks at his grandfather's life
in two countries. This helps him
understand his own identity.

`BEGINNING`

People
by Peter Spier

An award-winning author/
illustrator looks at similarities
and differences among people
all over the world.

`INTERMEDIATE`

Weslandia
by Paul Fleischman

An award-winning author tells
the story of a boy who finds
happiness when he creates his
own unique identity.

`ADVANCED`

11

DISCUSS THE GUIDING QUESTIONS

4 Set the Theme Some key points to
develop during the discussion are:

- There are many ways to describe, or
  tell about, ourselves. Words about
  color, size, and shape can tell about
  the way we look. Words about
  feelings and ideas can describe the
  way we are.

- It is important to discover, or find
  out, the many things that make us
  unique. We need to take a good
  look at what we do and how we
  act. We can also ask others what
  they see when they look at us.
  This can help us to learn more
  about ourselves.

- As we grow older, we learn new
  things about ourselves and others.
  We may decide to change how we
  look and how we are. In order to
  change, we must first know who we
  are now. Then we can decide what
  we want to add to the picture we
  see in the mirror.

  Form groups and use the
  Multi-Level Strategies so all
  students can participate.

CLOSE AND ASSESS

Sketch out a graphic organizer that is the
outline of a head. Ask students to draw or
write something inside the head that
describes their identity.

Multi-Level Strategies
GROUPING GUIDELINES

`BEGINNING` Work on vocabulary development with these students.
Ask them to use the words from **Transparency 1** (see page T8) to describe
themselves and their classmates as they answer the questions. Model
complete sentences to help students place their describing words in context.
Continue to add new words to the lists, and help students to set up personal
vocabulary notebooks to track the words.

`INTERMEDIATE` / `ADVANCED` Have Advanced students work with
Intermediate students in small groups to discuss the essential questions.
Then have students make a T-chart in
their notebooks and summarize their
answers. Have students date their charts
and return to them at the end of the unit
to see what they would add or change.

What I Know About Myself	What I Want to Learn

Grandfather's Journey
by Allen Say

Invite students to read this book and
consider its theme—that discovering
more about your family can help you
understand your identity. People
who leave their home country and
begin new lives elsewhere have
many things to discover. Ask
students to consider how the theme
of this story may apply to John Wang
in "Discovery" or Téssely in "Could I
Ask You a Question?" Ask: *Do you feel
this theme applies to your own life?*

BUILD LANGUAGE AND VOCABULARY

START WITH A COMMON EXPERIENCE

1 Listen to a Poem
Play "Outside and In" on
the **Language Tape/CD** or
read aloud the poem. Use
illustrations, exaggerated gestures,
and role-play to support meaning.
Define *secret* using poem text:
"something they don't know." Point
out that we can learn about people
by seeing what they are like outside.
Work with students to list what the
girl is like outside. Ask: *What are
some things we can't find out about
people from the outside? What about
people's feelings and ideas?* Then play
the tape again and ask students to
point to illustrations that show
outside traits.

Tape 1A

CD 1
Track 1

2 Recite a Poem Have students recite
the poem several times.

▌ Use the Reciting Options in the
▌ **Multi-Level Strategies** so that all
▌ students can participate.

3 Model How to Describe Use the
following Think Aloud to help
students learn to describe people.

How to Describe People

• Tell what someone looks like:
  You have curly hair.

• Tell more: *The ribbon in your
  hair is pretty.*

• Tell what someone is like inside:
  You are so kind.

Build Language and Vocabulary
DESCRIBE PEOPLE

Listen to the poem. Then say it as a group.

Outside and In

Sometimes people tell me,

"You are graceful on the stage!"

"Your voice is smooth and silky."

"You are clever for your age!"

But I have a secret—

There is something they don't know.

I'm more than what I do,

How I act, and what I show.

Those things are on the outside.

They're what everyone can see.

But there is even more to love

Deep down inside of me!

—Daphne Liu

REACHING ALL STUDENTS

Multi-Level Strategies
RECITING OPTIONS

BEGINNING Assign each of the spoken lines in the first stanza to a
small group. Ask them to choose a gesture to accompany their line, and to
present it as part of a class recitation.

INTERMEDIATE / **ADVANCED** Assign the second and third stanzas
to mixed-ability groups. Suggest that groups recite the poem using a call
and response pattern. For example: One student, acting as leader, calls out a
line from the poem—*There is something they don't know.* The group responds
with an original line—*Like my insides!* The leader calls out the next line of
the poem—*I'm more than what I do.* The group responds with a line of their
own—*I have feelings!* Ask students to create responses and recite their
stanzas with expression.

MAKE A WORD CHART

Make a chart like this one. Write words about the girl from the poem in the chart.

What the Girl Does	What She Is Like
dances	graceful

BUILD YOUR VOCABULARY

People Words Work with a group to think of more words about people. Write the words in your chart. Keep adding new words to this chart. You will find many words about people in this unit.

USE LANGUAGE STRUCTURES ▶ PRESENT TENSE VERBS; ADJECTIVES

Speaking: Describe an Interesting Person Work with the class to make up a new poem about an interesting person or a character in a story.

- Think of words that tell what the person is like on the outside: how he or she looks and acts, and what he or she does.
- Then think of words that tell what the person is like on the inside.
- Follow this pattern to make up a new poem.

Example:

> **Outside and In**
>
> On the outside,   On the inside,
> he is a cowboy,   he is funny,
> he rides a pig,   he likes to dream,
> and he swats flies.   he's a surprise!

Build Language and Vocabulary **13**

CONDUCT THE ACTIVITIES

4 Make a Word Chart Have students work with a partner to classify the words.

5 Build Your Vocabulary: People Words Remind students to place new words under the heading that makes the most sense.

6 Use Language Structures: Present Tense Verbs; Adjectives Teach the verbs, using the examples on **Transparency 2**. Invite a student to role-play the dialogue in the examples with you. Small groups of students can also act out different feelings (sad, tired, angry, etc.) and describe them using *I am...*, *She is...*, *We are...*, *You are...*, and *They are....* Then have students complete the sentences in Try It!

Speaking: Describe an Interesting Person Conduct the activity at the bottom of page 13. Have students use their Word Charts to add describing words to the poem.

Use the Speaking Activity Options in the **Multi-Level Strategies** to adjust instruction.

▶ **Practice Book** page 2

CLOSE AND ASSESS

Ask students to list three words that describe people. Then have them complete this sentence: *You are a _____ person.*

Multi-Level Strategies
SPEAKING ACTIVITY OPTIONS

BEGINNING Place students in charge of creating word cards about the person the new poem will describe. Have them write the words on cardboard strips after they are presented and modeled. They can take turns holding up word cards for the class to say as they recite.

INTERMEDIATE / ADVANCED Have students make up one or more additional poems on their own. Encourage them to do research in order to choose appropriate words to describe the subject of their poem. They can also write their poem and illustrate it for a classroom display.

Transparency 2 / Master 2

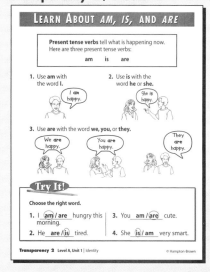

Build Language and Vocabulary **T13**

PREPARE TO READ

OBJECTIVES

THINK ABOUT WHAT YOU KNOW
Concepts and Vocabulary:
Math—*circle graph, percent*

Reading and Learning Strategies:
Activate Prior Knowledge; Use Graphic
Organizers (circle graph)

LEARN KEY VOCABULARY **T**

Vocabulary Strategy: Relate Words

LEARN TO CLASSIFY IDEAS
Reading Strategy: **T**Classify

THINK ABOUT WHAT YOU KNOW

1 Make a Circle Graph Demonstrate
how to make a circle graph. Have
students refer to the lists of
describing words in their notebooks
to complete the graphs. They can
then use the information in their
graphs to complete this sentence: *I
am* [happy] *for about* [50 %] *of the day.*

LEARN KEY VOCABULARY

2 Relate Words Read each vocabulary
word and its defining sentence aloud.

▌ Use the Vocabulary Options in
Multi-Level Strategies to clarify
meaning for all proficiency levels.

After students understand the
meanings of the key vocabulary
words, conduct the chart activity.

▶ **Practice Book** page 3

LEARN TO CLASSIFY IDEAS

3 Model How to Classify Ideas Define
classify. Then model the process with
the steps in the box. For guided
practice, conduct the activity on
Transparency 3.

CLOSE AND ASSESS

Ask students: *What do you do when you
classify?* (put things in a group)

Discovery **P**repare to Read Poetry

poem
by John Y. Wang

THINK ABOUT WHAT YOU KNOW

Make a Circle Graph What words describe you?
Show what you are like on a circle graph.

character Your **character**
is what you are really like.

discover When you
discover something, you learn
about it for the first time.

intelligent You are
intelligent if you are smart.

irresponsible People who
are **irresponsible** do not do
what they say they will do.

irritable You are **irritable**
when you get upset easily.

lazy A **lazy** person does not
want to work or do anything.

merits Someone's good
points are called **merits**.

optimistic You are
optimistic when you are
cheerful and hopeful.

positive You are **positive**
when you are sure that things
will work out well.

shortcomings Someone's
bad points are called
shortcomings.

LEARN KEY VOCABULARY

Relate Words Study the new words. Work with a group to make a
chart. Write the new vocabulary words where they belong.

Discover Your Character

Merits	Shortcomings
intelligent	lazy
optimistic	irresponsible
positive	irritable

LEARN TO CLASSIFY IDEAS

When you **classify** things, you put them in a group. Classifying
ideas helps you remember what you read.

READING STRATEGY
How to Classify Ideas
1. Look for ideas that are about the same
   thing. Put them in the same group.
2. Give the group a name that tells how
   the ideas are alike.

FEELINGS

Now read "Discovery." Stop after each page to classify the ideas.

14   **Unit 1** | Identity

REACHING ALL STUDENTS

▌ **Multi-Level Strategies**
VOCABULARY OPTIONS

BEGINNING / **INTERMEDIATE**
Act out or show photos that illustrate
the vocabulary words. Smile and act
cheerful for *optimistic;* frown and look
annoyed for *irritable;* throw a piece of
paper on the ground for *irresponsible.*
Write *Merits are good; Shortcomings are
not good.* Elicit examples before
students make the Word Chart.

ADVANCED Ask students to
rewrite the sentence for each
vocabulary word, replacing the word
with a synonym they find in a thesaurus.

Transparency 3 / Master 3

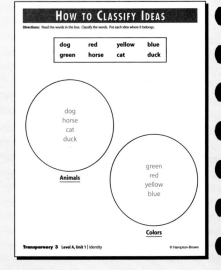

HOW TO CLASSIFY IDEAS

Directions: Read the words in the box. Classify the words. Put each idea where it belongs.

| dog | red | yellow | blue |
| green | horse | cat | duck |

dog
horse
cat
duck

Animals

green
red
yellow
blue

Colors

Transparency 3 Level A, Unit 1 | Identity   © Hampton-Brown

Discovery

by John Y. Wang

MANY TEENAGERS WANT TO FIND OUT THINGS ABOUT THEMSELVES AND THEIR WORLD. HERE IS WHAT ONE TEENAGER WANTS TO DISCOVER.

15

OBJECTIVES

Listening: Listen to a Preview
Reading Strategies: Preview; Predict

INTRODUCE THE SELECTION

4 Preview and Predict Read the title, author, and introduction to the poem on page 15 with students. Talk about the photos and illustrations on page 15. Ask: *What do you think John wants to discover?* Next, have students page through the poem, looking at the pictures and reading the words in large type. Remind students that they have seen many of these words before. Review the meanings of the words as necessary.

5 Audio Walk-Through Play the Audio Walk-Through for "Discovery" on the **Selection Tape/CD** to give students the overall idea of the story.

Tape 1A
CD 1
Track 1

Discovery
by John Y. Wang

Theme Connection This poem tells what one boy thinks about his own identity.

Selection Summary When John Y. Wang was a teenager, he went to school near Boston, Massachusetts. His class talked about the theme of *discovery,* and John wrote this poem. In it, he describes himself. He tells how he is unique. He also tells what he hopes to discover about himself as time goes on.

THE BASICS ▶ BOOKSHELF

■ *Good News* by Suzy Blackaby

Exciting news travels to each member of this family via phone, fax, and e-mail, but the reader doesn't learn what the news is until the end of the story. *Good News* introduces basic communication vocabulary while the patterned text and realistic visuals provide support for beginning English learners.

For Lesson Plans: See the Teacher's Guide for *The Basics Bookshelf*.

OBJECTIVES

Function: Read a Poem

Concepts and Vocabulary: Hobbies; Character Traits

Grammar: ⊕ Present Tense Verbs

Listening: Listen to a Poem

Reading and Learning Strategies: Set a Purpose for Reading; ⊕ Classify; Use Graphic Organizers (T-chart); Relate to Personal Experience

Comprehension: Identify Details

SET PURPOSE

1 Say: *Look for details that show what one teenager wants to discover.*

READ AND THINK

2 Strategy Focus: Classify
Have students classify ideas in a T-chart during the reading process.

▌ Choose Reading Options in the **Multi-Level Strategies** to tailor the reading to proficiency levels.

The recording of "Discovery" on the **Selection Tape/CD** offers an oral language model and the opportunity to build reading fluency.

Red annotations offer opportunities to clarify meaning and check for understanding

I like to **discover.**

I love to discover. **Restate:** I like to find out.

I want to discover. I like to learn.

I want to discover everything.

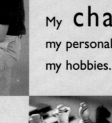

I want to discover the cure for AIDS.

I want to discover the

whole world.

Ask: Can John really discover "the whole world? **Restate:** I think John means he wants to see and do as much as he can.

Above all, I want to discover myself.

I want to discover what kind of man I am:

My **character,** **Give examples:** happy, quiet, helpful.

my personality,

my hobbies.

cure for AIDS way to stop a sickness that often kills people

my personality the things I do or say that make me different from everyone else

hobbies favorite things to do

BEFORE YOU MOVE ON...

1. **Details** What does John Y. Wang want to discover?

2. **Vocabulary** Think about your hobbies. Make a list of them.

REACHING ALL STUDENTS

Transparency 4 / Master 4

T-CHART FOR CLASSIFYING IDEAS

Directions: Look for ideas as you read the poem. Classify the ideas in this chart.

Discovery

Things John Knows About Himself	Things John Wants to Discover
1.	1.
2.	2.
3.	3.
4.	4.
5.	5.
6.	6.

Transparency 4 Level A, Unit 1 | Identity   © Hampton-Brown

▌ **Multi-Level Strategies**

READING OPTIONS FOR LESSONS 4-5

BEGINNING Read aloud the poem one stanza at a time. Use the pictures and the red annotations on the facsimile pages to clarify meaning. Play the recording of "Discovery" on the **Selection Tape/CD**, and ask students to chime in. Record the appropriate details on **Transparency 4** as a group.

INTERMEDIATE Read each page of the poem aloud, or play its recording on the **Selection Tape/CD**. Record appropriate details on **Transparency 4** as a group, discussing what should be placed in each column of the chart and why.

ADVANCED Have these students read the selection on their own, referring to the dictionary or thesaurus for the meanings of unfamiliar words or phrases. Distribute copies of **Master 4** for students to complete independently and then discuss with a partner.

I discover more about myself every day.

Up to now, I have discovered

I am this kind of person:

I am **intelligent.**

I am **optimistic.**

I am **positive.**

Define up to now: in the time that came before now. Have students practice a similar phrase: Up to now, I have learned …

Also, I am **lazy.**

I am **irresponsible.**

I am **irritable.**

Have students classify the describing words on this page as positive or negative.

BEFORE YOU MOVE ON...

1. **Vocabulary** Make a list of words about John. Now make a list of words about yourself.

2. **Personal Experience** What are you like? Finish this sentence: *I am ___ .*

Discovery **17**

---

3 Answers to "Before You Move On"

page 16

1. **Details** John wants to discover a cure for AIDS. He wants to discover the whole world. He wants to discover what kind of man he is.

2. **Vocabulary** Some possible hobbies are playing chess, collecting shells, or making model airplanes.

page 17

1. **Vocabulary** Lists about John include *intelligent, optimistic, positive, lazy, irresponsible, irritable.* Lists about students will vary.

2. **Personal Experience** Answers will vary, but must include a descriptive adjective.

CLOSE AND ASSESS

Check for accuracy: Do the details in the first column of the T-chart tell what John knows about himself? Do the details in the second column of the T-chart tell what John wants to discover about himself?

Grammar Minilesson

▶ **PRESENT TENSE VERBS**

TEACH Read the first three sentences in the poem. Then say: *The verbs like, love, and* want *tell about something that is happening now or that is always happening. They are in the present tense.*

Rewrite the sentences using *John* as the subject:

> John like<u>s</u> to discover.
>
> John love<u>s</u> to discover.
>
> John want<u>s</u> to discover

Point out the *s* at the end of the verb and say: *When we talk about something one other person does, the verb ends in* s.

PRACTICE Write these sentence starters:

> *I like. . .*
>
> *I love. . .*
>
> *I want. . .*

Ask students to finish each sentence and trade with a partner. The partner should rewrite the sentences using the person's name and adding an *s* to the verb. Partners should then compare their sentences.

▶ **Practice Book** page 4

Vocabulary
CONTRACTIONS

Have pairs of students practice restating the verses on page 17 by using the contraction *I'm* in place of *I am.* Then have students restate the verses using *You are* and *you're, He is* and *He's,* and *She is* and *She's.* Finally, encourage more advanced students to rewrite the verses on this page using contractions and the synonyms they discovered for the Key Vocabulary in the activity on page T14.

OBJECTIVES

Function: Read a Poem
Listening: Listen to a Poem
Reading and Learning Strategies:
Set a Purpose for Reading; Predict;
Ⓣ Classify; Use Graphic
Organizers (T-chart)
Comprehension: Make Judgments

SET PURPOSE

1 Say: *Look for the details that show John's goals for the future.*

READ AND THINK

Tape 1A
CD 1
Track 2

2 Strategy Focus: Classify
Involve students in reading page 18.

See the **Multi-Level Strategies** on page T16 to tailor the reading experience to all proficiency levels.

CHECK COMPREHENSION

3 Answers to "Before You Move On"

1. Prediction Answers will vary, but may include *doctor* or *scientist*.

2. Judgments Answers will vary.

CLOSE AND ASSESS

Ask students to name one of John's merits and one of his shortcomings.

These discoveries are very helpful to me.

I know what my **merits** are.

I will keep them going.

I know what my

shortcomings are.

I can plan how to correct them.

I will keep on discovering.

Use visuals: Have students point to the picture that shows a merit. Have them point to one that shows a shortcoming.

I will discover more about myself.

I like to discover.

I love to **discover.**

BEFORE YOU MOVE ON...

1. Prediction What job do you think John will have? Why?

2. Judgments Is it a good idea to "keep on discovering?" Why or why not?

to correct them to change them in a way that is better

keep on go on

18 **Unit 1** | Identity

ABOUT THE AUTHOR

John Y. Wang went to Charlestown High School in Boston, Massachusetts. His poem was published in 1993 in a book of poems written by students on the topic of "discovery."

REACHING ALL STUDENTS

HOME CONNECTION

What's New–An Interview Send home a copy of the *High Point Newsletter 1* in the **Teacher's Resource Book**. (See pages 97–103.) In this home activity, students interview a family member to learn what he or she has discovered about life in the United States. Record class discoveries on a T-chart with these headings: *Most Surprising Discoveries* and *Happiest Discoveries*. Discuss class findings.

Language Development
EXPRESS SOCIAL COURTESIES

Teach greetings and daily social language, such as *Hi, my name is.... How are you today? I'm fine, thanks.* For practice, assign partners, and arrange the pairs into two circles. Each time you say "Time for a visit," the inner circle of pairs should rotate to the right. The partners take turns introducing themselves and one another to the new pair they are facing. Provide index cards with a variety of social expressions that students may use.

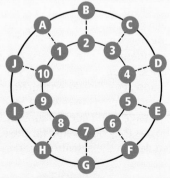

**Cooperative Learning Structure:
Inside-Outside Circle**

Respond to the Poem
Check Your Understanding

SUM IT UP

Classify Ideas How does John describe himself? Copy this chart. Add ideas from the poem.

Things John Knows About Himself	Things John Wants to Discover
He is intelligent.	He wants to discover what kind of man he is.
He is optimistic, lazy, positive, irresponsible, and irritable.	John wants to discover: • the cure for AIDS, • more about his character and personality.

Write Sentences Tell what John is like. Tell what he wants to discover.

Example:

John is intelligent.
He wants to discover the cure for AIDS.

THINK IT OVER

Discuss Talk about these questions with a partner.

1. **Comparisons** How are you like John? How are you different?

2. **Opinion** Would John be a good friend? Why or why not?

3. **Personal Experience** How did the poem make you feel?

4. **Prediction** What do you think John will do in the future?

EXPRESS YOURSELF ▶ DESCRIBE PEOPLE

Tell a partner about yourself. Listen to your partner. Then tell the class what you learned about each other.

Example:

Veronica is smart.
Her favorite class is science.
She likes computers.

✓ **LANGUAGE ACQUISITION ASSESSMENT**
See page 1 of the Assessment Handbook.

Discovery 19

Multi-Level Strategies
SUM IT UP OPTIONS

BEGINNING Work with students in groups to write sentences. Provide sentence frames: *John is _____ . John wants to _____ .* When several sentences have been written, invite students to read them aloud round-robin style.

INTERMEDIATE / ADVANCED Have students work with partners to share the ideas from the T-charts they have completed. Encourage them to write as many new present tense sentences as they can about what John knows and what he wants to discover.

OBJECTIVES

SUM IT UP
Function: Write
Reading and Learning Strategies:
❶ Classify; Use Graphic Organizers (T-chart)
Writing: Sentences

THINK IT OVER
Function: Engage in Discussion
Critical Thinking and Comprehension:
❶ Make Comparisons; Express Opinions; Relate to Personal Experience;
❶ Make Predictions

EXPRESS YOURSELF
Function: ❶ Describe People

CHECK YOUR UNDERSTANDING

1 **Sum It Up** Annotations in the T-chart show possible answers. Suggest that students use the verb *is* in the first sentence. For the second sentence, remind them that John is one person. Words that tell what John does must end in *s* (e.g., *wants*).

▶ **Practice Book** page 5

2 **Think It Over** Possible answers are:

1. **Comparisons** Students should compare John's traits, such as optimistic and lazy, with their own merits and shortcomings.

2. **Opinion** Students may say that they would like John for a friend because he is honest or curious. Ask students to give a reason.

3. **Personal Experience** Answers will vary.

4. **Prediction** Students may say that John will discover a cure or become interested in a hobby.

3 **Express Yourself** Prompt the use of describing words and present tense verbs *is, wants,* and *likes*.

CLOSE AND ASSESS

Ask students to classify ideas in a T-chart headed: What I Know About Myself and What I Want to Discover.

Discovery **T19**

RESPOND

ASSESSMENT
Selection Test 1 on page 3 of the Assessment Handbook tests students' mastery of the reading strategies and the vocabulary, comprehension, and language arts skills taught with this selection.

OBJECTIVES

VERBS AND CHARACTER TRAITS
Concepts and Vocabulary:
Character Traits
Grammar: ❶ Present Tense Verbs
Critical Thinking and Learning
Strategy: ❶ Make Comparisons;
Use Graphic Organizers (Venn diagram)
Writing: Sentences

FREE-VERSE POEM
Function: Express Feelings; Write
Concepts and Vocabulary:
Character Traits
Speaking and Listening:
Read a Poem; Listen to a Poem
Literary Analysis and Writing:
Free-Verse Poem

LANGUAGE ARTS AND LITERATURE

1 Use Verbs and Character Traits
Sample answers to the Practice items are:

1. am; friendly

2. is; brave / is; thoughtful

3. are; active / are; smart

▶ **Practice Book** page 6

2 Write a Free-Verse Poem To provide support, share an innovation:

> I love to *discover*.
> I want to discover *a new planet*.
> Up to now, I have discovered
> I am this kind of person:
> I am *brave*.
> I am *hardworking*.
> I love to discover.

To help students offer positive feedback, offer these models:

> I like your ideas.
> Your poem uses clear words.
> Your poem is interesting.

CLOSE AND ASSESS

Students can refer to their practice papers or poems to give examples of sentences that describe character.

Respond to the Poem, continued

Language Arts and Literature

▶ GRAMMAR IN CONTEXT
▶ VOCABULARY

USE VERBS AND CHARACTER TRAITS

Learn About Verbs *Am*, *is*, and *are* are verbs.

• Use **am** with the word *I*.

   I **am** intelligent.

• Use **is** with the words *he* or *she*.

   He **is** optimistic. She **is** lazy.

• Use **are** with the words *we*, *you*, or *they*.

   We **are** irritable. You **are** positive.
   They **are** irresponsible.

Compare Character Traits Words that describe people are **character traits**. Work with a partner. Compare your character traits.

Venn Diagram

Practice Write sentences. Use the verbs *am*, *is*, and *are*. Add character traits that describe you and your partner.

Example:
I **am** careful. Keisha **is** brave. We both **are** active.

▶ LITERARY ANALYSIS
▶ WRITING/SPEAKING

WRITE A FREE-VERSE POEM

"Discovery" is a free-verse poem. A **free-verse poem** does not rhyme or have a regular rhythm.

❶ **Create a Discovery Poem** Copy the poetry frame. Then add words that tell about you.

Poetry Frame

> I love to _____ .
> I want to discover a _____.
> Up to now, I have discovered I am this kind
> of person:
> I am _____.
> I am _____.
> I love to discover.

❷ **Share Your Poem** Read your poem to a group. Listen to the other poems. Tell each other what you like about the poems.

REACHING ALL STUDENTS

Multi-Level Strategies
WRITING OPTIONS FOR FREE-VERSE POEMS

BEGINNING Ask yes/no questions and questions with one-word answers to prepare for creating a poem. Model drawing three boxes and filling each one with a picture that shows a character trait or a goal. Students can dictate a caption for each picture. Leave a space in each caption for them to write a sight word: *I*, *am*, *like*, *love*, or *want*.

INTERMEDIATE Have students fill in a cluster web with the word *I* in the center circle and the words *am*, *love to*, and *want to discover* in three branching circles. They can use the web to plan ideas before writing the poem.

ADVANCED Students can participate in written peer conferencing. After reading a partner's poem, each peer writes one positive thing and asks one question or offers one suggestion for improvement. The writer chooses suggestions to include in a revision.

Content Area Connections

> SCIENCE
> TECHNOLOGY/MEDIA

RESEARCH A SCIENTIST

Scientists make discoveries in areas like medicine, electronics, and farming. Study a scientist like:

- George Washington Carver
- Marie Curie
- Galileo Galilei
- Robert Goddard

❶ Find Information Look for a book about the scientist, ask a science teacher, or search the Internet. Take notes.

Use the scientist's name as a key word for your search. These on-line encyclopedias may be helpful, but remember that new sites appear every day!

INTERNET

INFORMATION ON-LINE

Web Sites:
➤ On-line Encyclopedias
- www.encarta.msn.com
- www.britannica.com

❷ Create Your Poster Write about the scientist. Then add art that shows the scientist or something about his or her discovery.

❸ Share Your Poster Tell why the discovery is important. Explain how you found the information.

George
Washington
Carver

George Washington Carver was a famous botanist. He lived from 1864 to 1943. He made many discoveries about the peanut.

Learn how to do **research**.
See Handbook pages 366–370.
Learn to use the **Internet** on pages 364–365.

Research Skills

▶ **USING ALPHABETICAL ORDER**

TEACH Write a few students' names, circle the first letter, and prompt students to arrange them in alphabetical order. Then write *hand, help, hot*. Circle the second letter in each and explain that when words begin with the same letter, you use the second letter to alphabetize them. Write *let, lead, lemon*. Circle the third letter in each. Ask students to place the words in alphabetical order.

PRACTICE Make three sets of index cards using the lists below. Give each set to a different group. Have them arrange the cards in alphabetical order.

List 1: biology, chemistry, physics, astronomy, agriculture

List 2: Carver, Crick, Curie, Clark, Campbell

List 3: evaporation, elements, ether, echo, egret

▶ **Practice Book** page 7

RESPOND

| OBJECTIVES |

RESEARCH A SCIENTIST

Function: ❶ Give Information

Learning Strategies, Critical Thinking, and Research Skills: Locate Resources; Gather Information; Take Notes; Generate Ideas

Technology/Media: Use the Internet

Representing and Writing: Research Poster

CONTENT AREA CONNECTIONS

1 Research a Scientist Facts about the scientists in the activity are:

Scientist	Discovery	Why It Was Important
George Washington Carver	Over 300 uses for peanuts	Helped modernize agriculture
Marie Curie	Radium and polonium	Used in research about radioactivity
Galileo Galilei	Law of gravity; improved telescope	Used in modern astronomy and physics
James Watson and Francis Crick	Molecular structure of DNA	Revolutionized medical research
Robert Goddard	Liquid-fueled rockets	Facilitated modern space travel

For Multi-Level Strategies: Create heterogeneous groups to work on the poster project. Encourage Beginners to help draw the background or the picture of the scientist. Give them sentence starters for the poster text: *I am _____. I discovered _____.* More Advanced students may enjoy creating companion Biography Cards about scientists and their discoveries.

▶ **Practice Book** pages 8–9

| CLOSE AND ASSESS |

Have students role-play the scientists they studied, using the information on their posters to introduce themselves. More advanced students may describe how their discoveries made them feel.

BUILD LANGUAGE AND VOCABULARY

OBJECTIVES

Function: Listen Actively;
🅣 Ask and Answer Questions

Concepts and Vocabulary:
Question Words

Patterns and Structures: 🅣 Questions

Speaking: Interview

Viewing: Respond to a Photograph;
Interpret a Visual Image

**Critical Thinking and Learning
Strategies:** Make Inferences; Formulate
Predictions, Questions; Use Graphic
Organizers (five Ws chart)

START WITH A COMMON EXPERIENCE

1 View and Interpret View the
photograph, encouraging students
to identify objects that reflect Anna's
interests, such as the trumpet on the
music stand and the tennis racket.
Ask questions to prompt
interpretation of the photograph.

> Use the Questioning Techniques
> in the **Multi-Level Strategies** to
> include all proficiency levels.

**2 Model How to Ask and Answer
Questions** Use the following Think
Aloud to help students learn to ask
questions.

How to Ask Questions

- Ask about a person: *Who is the
girl in the photograph?*

- Ask about a place: *Where are the
people standing?*

- Ask about a thing: *What is on the
music stand?*

- Ask about a time: *When do you
think Anna plays tennis?*

- Ask about reasons: *Why is the
woman interviewing Anna?*

Then model giving answers to the
above questions and others students
have. Read aloud the interviewer's
question and ask students to start
thinking about how they would
answer it.

Build Language and Vocabulary
ASK AND ANSWER QUESTIONS

Look at this photograph. Read the interviewer's question.

Anna, imagine yourself ten years from now. What will you be doing?

REACHING ALL STUDENTS

Multi-Level Strategies
QUESTIONING TECHNIQUES

BEGINNING Ask yes/no questions, either/or questions, or questions
with one-word answers: *Is Anna talking to her mother? Are Anna and the
interviewer in the kitchen or in her room? Is the trumpet shiny? What color is
the interviewer's shirt? Is Anna's shirt plain or striped?*

INTERMEDIATE Have students talk about the photo in pairs. Then ask
questions that call for some inference or opinion: *What sports does Anna
play? What other activities does Anna like? Does Anna's room look messy to
you? How do you think Anna feels about being interviewed?*

ADVANCED Invite students to speculate beyond the specifics of the
photograph. *What interests do you think Anna will have in ten years? Will her
interests be the same ones she has now, or will they be different? Why do you
think this?*

PREDICT AND LISTEN

How do you think Anna will answer the question on page 22? Look at Anna's room for clues. Explain your answer.

Now listen to the interview and find out what Anna said.

BUILD YOUR VOCABULARY

Question Words This picture shows six question words you can use to ask a question. Here are examples of questions for Anna:

Who is your favorite singer?
What do you do after school?
When do you practice?
Where do you go to school?
How did you learn to play the trumpet?
Why did you choose the trumpet?

Now, make a list of questions you want to ask Anna.

USE LANGUAGE STRUCTURES ▸ QUESTIONS

Speaking: Conduct an Interview Work with a partner. Use your list of questions for Anna. Think about Anna's answers. Then:

- Practice your interview. One of you will be the interviewer and ask the questions. The other will be Anna.
- Present your interview to the class.

> **Example:**
> Interviewer: When did you begin to play the trumpet?
> Anna: I began in 5th grade.

Build Language and Vocabulary **23**

CONDUCT THE ACTIVITIES

3 Predict and Listen
Encourage students to make a prediction about Anna's answer to the question. Then have them listen to the interview on Track 2, or read the script on page T381.

Tape 1A / CD 1 Track 2

4 Build Your Vocabulary: Question Words Read the introduction on page 23. Then teach the question words, using the explanations on **Transparency 5**. Read aloud each numbered item on the transparency, using the examples on page 23 to illustrate the concepts. Work with students to create their lists of questions for Anna.

5 Use Language Structures: Questions Model the proper intonation for questions before students work on their interviews.

Speaking: Conduct an Interview Conduct the activity at the bottom of page 23. Have students use their lists of questions for ideas.

> Use the Speaking Activity Options in the **Multi-Level Strategies** to adjust instruction.

▸ **Practice Book** page 10

CLOSE AND ASSESS

Ask students to tell when they use each of the six question words presented.

Multi-Level Strategies
SPEAKING ACTIVITY OPTIONS

BEGINNING / ADVANCED Pair Beginning students with more Advanced learners. Assign the Advanced student as the Interviewer, the Beginning student as Anna. The Interviewer should choose questions that have one-word or short answers, and help Anna practice her responses.

INTERMEDIATE Have partners collaborate on choosing from among the questions they developed in Build Your Vocabulary. They can then choose roles and practice conducting the interview. Later, partners reverse roles and conduct the interview again.

Transparency 5 / Master 5

LEARN ABOUT QUESTIONS

Use a **question** to ask for information.
What games do you like to play?

Try It!

1. Use **Who** to ask about a person.

2. Use **What** to ask about an action or a thing.

3. Use **When** to ask about time.

4. Use **Where** to ask about a place.

5. Use **Why** to ask about reasons.

6. Use **How** to ask in what way.

Transparency 5 Level A, Unit 1 | Identity   © Hampton-Brown

Build Language and Vocabulary **T23**

PREPARE TO READ

OBJECTIVES

THINK ABOUT WHAT YOU KNOW

Concepts and Vocabulary: Interviews

Reading and Learning Strategies: Activate Prior Knowledge; Use Graphic Organizers (word web)

LEARN KEY VOCABULARY 🅣

Vocabulary Strategy: Use New Words In Context

LEARN TO MAKE COMPARISONS

Reading Strategy: 🅣 Make Comparisons

THINK ABOUT WHAT YOU KNOW

1 Make a Word Web Demonstrate how to make a word web. Possible entries for word web: *Interviewer: takes notes, asks questions, uses tape recorder. Subject: gives information, answers questions, talks about life.*

LEARN KEY VOCABULARY

2 Use New Words in Context Read each vocabulary word and its defining sentence aloud. Use each word in a sentence. Then conduct the activity.

▌ Use the Vocabulary Options in **Multi-Level Strategies** to adjust instruction for all proficiency levels.

▶ **Practice Book** page 11

LEARN TO MAKE COMPARISONS

3 Model How to Make Comparisons Define *comparisons*. Demonstrate the steps in the box with **Transparency 6**:

• Read aloud the paragraph.

• As you read each statement about Javier, ask a volunteer to provide information to complete the statement in column 2.

• Elicit discussion about whether the statements in columns 1 and 2 are similar or different.

CLOSE AND ASSESS

Ask students: *What do you do when you make comparisons?* (identify how things are alike and different)

Could I Ask You a **Question**❓

interview
by Gilbert Socas

Prepare to Read

THINK ABOUT WHAT YOU KNOW

Make a Word Web What happens during an interview? Show your ideas in a web.

word web: asks questions → interviewer — subject — interview

adapt
When you **adapt** to something new, you change to get used to it.

culture
People's **culture** includes their art, customs, beliefs, food, music, and clothing.

enjoy
When you **enjoy** something, you like it.

felt
When we **feel**, we can be happy, sad, scared, and so on. **Felt** is the past tense of *feel*.

island
An **island** is land that has water on all sides.

miss
When you **miss** something, you feel sad because it is not there.

situation
A **situation** is something that happens.

strange
Something is **strange** when it is different from what people are used to.

LEARN KEY VOCABULARY

Use New Words in Context Study the new words. Then write each sentence. Add the correct word.

1. I moved to here from the ___(island / situation)___ of Taiwan.

2. I was sad and began to ___(miss / enjoy)___ my friends in Taiwan.

3. Then I started to ___(felt / adapt)___ to my new life.

4. Now I know more about the ___(culture / strange)___ of the U.S.

LEARN TO MAKE COMPARISONS

You make **comparisons** to see how things are the same and how they are different.

READING STRATEGY

How to Make Comparisons

1. When you read about a person, think about what the person says or does.

2. Ask yourself: Does the person act or think the same way I do? How is the person different from me?

3. Ask yourself: How would I feel or act in the same situation?

Now read "Could I Ask You a Question?" Take notes about how you and Téssely are the same and different.

24 **Unit 1** | Identity

REACHING ALL STUDENTS

Multi-Level Strategies

VOCABULARY OPTIONS

BEGINNING / INTERMEDIATE

Act out or show pictures that illustrate the vocabulary words. Use the map on page 26 for *island*; look sad for *miss*; look happy for *enjoy*. Use the photo of dancers on page 73 to help students understand how costumes, dances, and traditions are part of a *culture*.

ADVANCED Have students use two of the words in the same sentence.

Transparency 6 / Master 6

HOW TO MAKE COMPARISONS

Directions: Read about Javier. Think about how you and Javier are alike. Think about how you are different. Fill in the chart.

Adapting to Life in Los Angeles

Javier moved to Los Angeles one month ago. Javier misses his friends and his home in Costa Rica. At school he is making new friends. He plays on the school soccer team.

All About Javier	All About _____
Javier lives in Los Angeles now.	I live in
He comes from Costa Rica.	I come from
Javier misses his friends and home.	I miss
Javier plays soccer.	I play
	Answers will vary depending on each student's experiences.

Transparency 6 Level A, Unit 1 | Identity   © Hampton-Brown

Could I Ask You a Question?

by Gilbert Socas

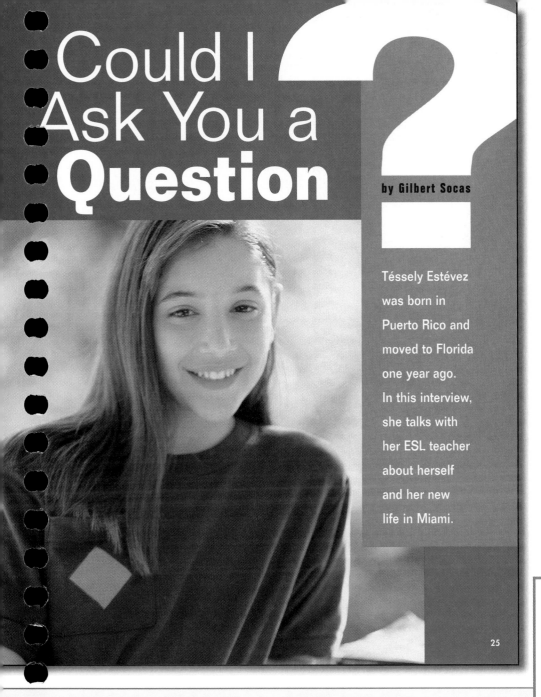

Téssely Estévez was born in Puerto Rico and moved to Florida one year ago. In this interview, she talks with her ESL teacher about herself and her new life in Miami.

25

READ THE SELECTION

OBJECTIVES

Listening: Listen to a Preview
Reading Strategies: Preview; Relate to Personal Experience; Use Text Features (typographical clues)

INTRODUCE THE SELECTION

4 **Preview and Relate to Personal Experience** Read the title and introduction. Ask: *What kinds of questions do you think Mr. Socas will ask Téssely? How will her answers compare to answers you would give?*

5 **Use Text Features** Direct students to look at the names in boldface type followed by a colon. Tell them these words show who is speaking in the interview. Ask students to point out any question words they notice.

6 **Audio Walk-Through**
Play the Audio Walk-Through for "Could I Ask You a Question?" on the **Selection Tape/CD** to give students the overall idea of the selection.

Tape 1A
CD 1 Track 3

Could I Ask You A Question?
by Gilbert Socas

Theme Connection This selection examines how one young girl from Puerto Rico adapts to her new life in Miami and learns more about her identity.

Selection Summary This interview explores the uncertainties and new experiences of sixth grader Téssely Estévez during her first year in the United States. She recounts the things she misses about her homeland, Puerto Rico, and describes her new experiences in the United States.

Background Puerto Rico is an island in the Caribbean and a commonwealth of the United States.

OBJECTIVES

Function: Read a Selection
Grammar: Nouns
Listening: Listen to a Selection
Reading and Learning Strategies: Set a Purpose for Reading; ❶ Make Comparisons; Use Graphic Organizers (T-chart); Relate to Personal Experience
Comprehension: Identify Details

SET PURPOSE

1 Say: *Look for details that show how one middle-school student has adapted to life in a new country.*

READ AND THINK

2 **Strategy Focus: Make Comparisons** Have students look for details about Téssely's life in Miami and add them to the T-chart during the reading process.

Tape 1A
CD 1
Track 4

Choose Reading Options in **Multi-Level Strategies** to tailor the reading to proficiency levels.

The recording of "Could I Ask You a Question?" on the **Selection Tape/CD** offers an oral language model and the opportunity to build reading fluency.

Téssely lives in Miami with her brother, sister, mother, grandmother, and great-grandmother. Téssely says, "My great-grandmother is 90, but she's very lively!"

Red annotations offer opportunities to clarify meaning and check for understanding.

Meet Téssely Estévez

Mr. Socas: Téssely, how do you like middle school in Miami? Use visuals: Point out Miami on the map. Explain that it is a city in Florida.

Téssely: In fifth grade, I **felt** good because I was one of the big kids. Now, I feel like a little kid in a school full of big kids. I'm getting used to it now. I **adapt** well to new **situations**.

Puerto Rico is about 1,000 miles off the Florida coast (shown at the left). It is a commonwealth of the United States. English and Spanish are the official languages of Puerto Rico.

26　Unit 1　Identity

REACHING ALL STUDENTS

Transparency 7 / Master 7

T-CHART FOR MAKING COMPARISONS

Directions: Look for details about Téssely. Write the details in the T-chart. Write details about yourself in the chart, too.

Could I Ask You a Question?

All About Téssely	All About _____

Transparency 7　Level A, Unit 1 | Identity　© Hampton-Brown

Multi-Level Strategies
READING OPTIONS FOR LESSONS 11–12

BEGINNING Read the interview aloud or play its recording on the **Selection Tape/CD**. Use the photos and the red annotations on the facsimile pages to clarify meaning. Pause after each question and response. Work with the group to record appropriate details about Téssely in column 1 of **Transparency 7**, vocalizing as you write.

INTERMEDIATE / **ADVANCED** Have partners with varying proficiency levels read the interview. One student should take the role of the interviewer, the other the role of Téssely. Suggest that they refer to a dictionary for the meaning of unfamiliar words. Distribute copies of **Master 7** for students to complete independently and discuss with a partner.

The *coquí* is a tiny frog from Puerto Rico. It lives in forests like Toro Negro, shown here with its beautiful waterfall.

Mr. Socas: So, was it easy to adapt to life in the United States?

Téssely: I feel **strange** sometimes. Some things are **the same** here, because Puerto Rico is part of the United States, but the **culture** is different. **Use visuals:** Pause to point out Puerto Rico on the map.

Mr. Socas: What do you **miss** about Puerto Rico?

Téssely: I remember the beautiful mountains and **waterfalls**. The sky at night was so full of stars. I really miss that.

BEFORE YOU MOVE ON...

1. **Details** What are some of the things from Puerto Rico that Téssely misses?
2. **Personal Experience** Do you adapt well to new situations? Think of some examples.

the same the way they were in Puerto Rico
waterfalls places where rivers go over the edge of a hill or mountain

Could I Ask You a Question? **27**

CHECK COMPREHENSION

3 Answers to "Before You Move On"

1. **Details** Téssely misses the beautiful mountains and waterfalls, as well as the nights full of stars.

2. **Personal Experience** Students should support their answers with examples, such as: *I adapt well to new experiences. When I came to my new school in the United States, I was nervous at first. But then I made friends and started to fit in.*

CLOSE AND ASSESS

Check for accuracy: Do the details in the first column of the T-chart describe Téssely's life in Miami?

Vocabulary
FEELINGS

Point out to students that many of the verbs on pages 26–27 tell how Téssely is feeling or what she is thinking. In pairs, have students use *I like, I feel, I felt, I adapt,* and *I miss* to write complete sentences that tell how they've adapted to life in the United States. Pairs share their sentences with the class.

Grammar Minilesson

▶ NOUNS

TEACH Read the question and answer on page 26. Then say: *The words Téssely, school, Miami, kid, and situations are nouns. Nouns name people, places, and things.*

Create a three-column chart with the headings *People, Places,* and *Things.* Work with students to classify words.

People	Places	Things
Téssely	school	situations
kid	Miami	

PRACTICE Ask students to identify nouns in the questions and answers on page 27, and record the words for their reference. Then ask partners or small groups to create category charts similar to the one in Teach in order to classify each noun as naming a person, place, or thing. Ask more advanced students to also categorize the nouns in the photo captions. Have groups compare their charts.

▶ **Practice Book** page 12

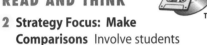

OBJECTIVES

Function: Read a Selection
Listening: Listen to a Selection
Reading and Learning Strategies:
Set a Purpose for Reading;
❶ Make Comparisons; Use Graphic
Organizers (T-chart); Relate to
Personal Experience
Comprehension: Form Opinions;
Identify Details

SET PURPOSE

1 Say: *Find details about life in Miami.*

READ AND THINK

Tape 1A
CD 1
Track 4

2 **Strategy Focus: Make
Comparisons** Involve students
in reading page 28.

> See the **Multi-Level Strategies**
> on page T26 to tailor the reading
> experience to proficiency levels.

CHECK COMPREHENSION

3 **Answers to "Before You Move On"**

1. Opinion Answers will vary.

2. Details She would chat on-line.

3. Personal Experience Students
should give reasons.

CLOSE AND ASSESS

Ask: *How are you and Téssely alike?*

Téssely works on a computer at
the West Miami Middle School
computer lab in Miami, Florida.

Mr. Socas: What do you **enjoy** about
life in Miami?

Téssely: I like the fact that we speak
English. I love languages. In school,
I like my French class **best**. That
language is kind of **weird**, and I
guess I like strange things.
Clarify: *Weird* and *strange* are synonyms and
mean the same thing: *different* or *unusual.*

Mr. Socas: If you could have anything
you want, what would it be?

Téssely: I would love to have a
computer of my own so that I could
chat on-line with my **Boricua** friends
from the **island**!

BEFORE YOU MOVE ON...

1. Opinion Do you think new languages are
strange or weird? Why?

2. Details What would Téssely do if she had her
own computer?

3. Personal Experience Which class do you
like best? Why?

---

best the most; better than all the other classes
weird strange, different, unusual
chat on-line send and receive messages on a
computer using the Internet
Boricua Puerto Rican

ABOUT THE INTERVIEWER

Gilbert Socas has been a teacher
for 20 years. He loves teaching ESL
classes because the students remind
him of himself when he came to the
United States. Mr. Socas was born
in Cuba. He has lived in the United
States for 34 years. He has published two books of
poetry in Spanish and is now writing a children's book
about young immigrants.

Ask: Where was Mr. Socas born? How long
has he lived in the United States?

28 **Unit 1** | Identity

REACHING ALL STUDENTS

INTERNET

LANGUAGE ARTS CONNECTION

Have students log on to a classroom
exchange program. Have students
formulate three questions, use them to
interview peers from other countries, and
share their results.

Web Sites
Web sites undergo frequent changes, but
here are some you may want to suggest:

www.epals.com
www.kidlink.org

CULTURAL PERSPECTIVES

Materials: multicultural artwork or artifacts,
or pictures of artifacts

World Cultures: Artwork Collect
artwork or photos of artwork from a
variety of countries. Pieces could
include murals, paintings, pottery,
textiles, weavings, and jewelry. Display
each photo or piece and have students
note the materials used, the colors, and
any design or motif. Have students
create a chart to compare features of
artwork from different cultures.

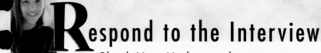

Respond to the Interview
Check Your Understanding

SUM IT UP

Compare Experiences Copy the chart. Add information about Téssely and yourself.

Possible answers:

All About Téssely	All About _____
Téssely was born in Puerto Rico. She lives in Florida. She adapts well to new situations. She misses the beauty of Puerto Rico. She loves to learn languages. She wants her own computer.	Answers will vary.

Draw Conclusions Work with a partner. Ask and answer questions like these:

Question: How are you and Téssely the same?

Answer: We both adapt well to new things.

Question: How are you and Téssely different?

Answer: Téssely likes to learn French, but I like to learn Spanish.

THINK IT OVER

Discuss Talk about these questions with a partner.

1. **Character's Point of View** How does Téssely feel about the changes in her life?

2. **Opinion** What are some of Téssely's merits?

3. **Personal Experience** What change did you make this year?

EXPRESS YOURSELF
▶ ASK AND ANSWER QUESTIONS

Role-play an interview with a partner. One person asks questions. The other person answers as the character. Choose one of these ideas:

• Mr. Socas interviews Téssely again.

• Téssely interviews Mr. Socas.

• Mr. Socas interviews John Wang, the author of "Discovery."

• Mr. Socas interviews Téssely in five years.

✓ LANGUAGE ACQUISITION ASSESSMENT
See page 1 of the Assessment Handbook.

Could I Ask You a Question? **29**

Multi-Level Strategies
SUM IT UP OPTIONS

BEGINNING Work with students to complete the chart. To help students express a comparison, provide these sentence frames:

> We both _____. Téssely _____, but I _____.

Write some of the students' sentences on sentence strips, cut them apart, and have students reassemble them.

INTERMEDIATE / **ADVANCED** Have students conduct mock interviews. Encourage them to ask a variety of present tense questions and answer them in ways that show how they are like Téssely and how they are different.

OBJECTIVES

SUM IT UP

Function: Write

Reading and Learning Strategies:
❶ Make Comparisons; Use Graphic Organizers (T-chart)

Critical Thinking: Draw Conclusions

THINK IT OVER

Function: Engage in Discussion

Critical Thinking and Comprehension: Identify Character's Point of View; Formulate Questions; Relate to Personal Experience

EXPRESS YOURSELF

Function: ❶ Ask and Answer Questions

Speaking and Listening: Role-Play

CHECK YOUR UNDERSTANDING

1 **Sum It Up** Have students compare the first item listed for Téssely with the first item they've written for themselves. They note whether it is the same or different and then continue comparing items.

▶ **Practice Book** page 13

2 **Think It Over** Possible answers are:

1. **Character's Point of View** Students might describe Téssely's sadness to leave Puerto Rico or her happiness about life in America.

2. **Opinion** Students might mention Téssely's positive outlook on life, her appreciation of beauty, and her adaptability.

3. **Personal Experience** Answers will vary.

3 **Express Yourself** Remind students that the interviewer poses questions and the subject responds. Suggest that students use verbs such as *like, feel, enjoy, miss,* and *adapt* in their interviews.

CLOSE AND ASSESS

Ask students to describe something that is different in Téssely's life since she moved to Miami.

RESPOND

OBJECTIVES

ASK QUESTIONS
Function: ❶ Ask and Answer Questions
Grammar: Questions; Statements
Writing: Questions

CONDUCT AN INTERVIEW
Function: ❶ Ask and Answer Questions; Write
Speaking and Listening: Interview
Critical Thinking: Formulate Questions
Writing: Questions

LANGUAGE ARTS AND LITERATURE

1 **Ask Questions** Annotations show answers to the Practice items.

▶ **Practice Book** page 14

2 **Conduct an Interview** To help students get started, suggest that they:

- First think about what they would like to know about the person they are interviewing.

- List four or five of these things and use them to formulate their questions.

- Use the questions in the selection as models for their own questions.

CLOSE AND ASSESS

Distribute index cards for students to use as exit slips. Have each student write an interview question to ask you as they leave the classroom. Return the slips with answers during the next class.

✓ **ASSESSMENT**
Selection Test 2 on page 5 of the Assessment Handbook tests students' mastery of the reading strategies and the vocabulary, comprehension, and language arts skills taught with this selection.

Respond to the Interview, continued

Language Arts and Literature

GRAMMAR IN CONTEXT

ASK QUESTIONS

Learn About Statements and Questions
Make a **statement** to tell something. Ask a **question** to find out something. Some questions begin with *Are, Can,* and *Do.*

Statements	Questions
They are in 6th grade.	**Are** they in 6th grade?
You can speak French.	**Can** you speak French?
I need a computer.	**Do** I need a computer?

Make Up Questions Copy the chart. Then ask your friends questions that start with *Are, Can,* or *Do.* Finish the questions with words in the chart. Write the names of the classmates who answer "yes."

Are you...	Can you...	Do you...
positive *Ramon*	ride a bike	read every day
on a sports team	play an instrument	help at home
lazy	speak 3 languages	want to go to college

Practice Copy the statements. Then write them as questions using *Are, Can,* or *Do.*

1. I study for tests.   Do I study for tests?

2. She can play soccer.   Can she play soccer?

3. You are a good singer.   Are you a good singer?

WRITING
SPEAKING/LISTENING

CONDUCT AN INTERVIEW

When you **conduct an interview,** you ask someone questions. Find someone to interview. Then follow these steps.

❶ **Write Your Questions** Look at Mr. Socas's questions. Write four or five questions like these. Leave room for the answers.

❷ **Ask the Questions** Write down what the person says. Say "thank you" when you are finished.

❸ **Share Your Work** Read your interview to the class. Listen while others read their interviews.

Review **questions**. See Handbook page 402.
Learn how to **listen** and **discuss** on pages 373–374.

REACHING ALL STUDENTS

Multi-Level Strategies
PRACTICE OPTIONS FOR ASKING QUESTIONS

BEGINNING Help students formulate questions by giving them more examples. Write:

I can play soccer.	*Can you play soccer?*
I am in 6th grade.	*Are you in 6th grade?*
I like to go to the movies.	*Do you like to go to the movies?*

Have students suggest other statements. Work with students to turn the statements into questions.

INTERMEDIATE / ADVANCED Call on students to pose their own interview questions using the words *can, are,* and *do.* Students write three questions using these words, use the questions to interview a partner, and then role-play their interviews for the rest of the class.

Language Arts and Content Area Connections

▶ SOCIAL STUDIES

EXPLORE GEOGRAPHY

Compare Puerto Rico and Miami Research Puerto Rico and Miami, Florida. Tell how they are the same and different.

❶ Gather Information Use books, an atlas, an encyclopedia, or the Internet to research both places. Take notes.

❷ Organize Your Information Compare the two places.

Venn Diagram

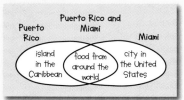

Puerto Rico and Miami

Puerto Rico — island in the Caribbean

food from around the world

Miami — city in the United States

❸ Share Your Diagram Tell your class what you learned about both places.

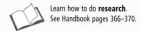

Learn how to do **research**.
See Handbook pages 366–370.

▶ WRITING

STUDY A NEWS STORY

Sometimes writers conduct interviews to get information for a news story. Work with a partner. Study news stories in magazines or newspapers.

Find Quotations Look for a news story with quotations. A **quotation** shows the exact words a person said.

> ### STUDENTS WIN CONTEST
> Three Miami students won tickets to the Orange Bowl this week. They won a school writing contest.
> **"The Orange Bowl is a great football game,"** said Julie Cata, one winner.
> **"It is played every New Year's Day in Miami,"** added her friend Mei Wen.
> **"They worked hard,"** said their teacher. **"That is why they won."**

Write Questions List the quotations you found. Think about what questions the writer asked. Write each question by the quotation.

Quotation: "The Orange Bowl is a great football game."

Question: What is the Orange Bowl?

Research Skills

▶ USING A MAP

TEACH Display a wall map of North America that shows the Caribbean. Write the geographic terms *country, continent, ocean, island, river, lake, city,* and *state*. Have students identify the United States and tell them it is a *country*. Use the map to define the other terms. Then point out the compass rose and the arrows pointing north, east, south, and west. Model how to use the compass rose to indicate direction: *Canada is north of the United States. Miami is south of New York City.*

PRACTICE Have students copy the geographic terms on self-stick notes and use them to label examples on the map. Also label the place where they live. Students then tell which direction they would travel to go from where they live to one of the other places they have labeled.

▶ **Practice Book** page 15

RESPOND

OBJECTIVES

EXPLORE GEOGRAPHY

Function: ❶ Give Information

Concepts and Vocabulary:
Geography—*country, continent, ocean;* Directions—*north, south, east, west*

Learning Strategies, Critical Thinking, and Research Skills:
Gather Information; Take Notes; Organize and Synthesize Information; ❶ Make Comparisons; Use a Map

Representing and Writing:
Venn Diagram

STUDY A NEWS ARTICLE

Function: Write

Critical Thinking: Formulate Questions

Writing: Questions

LANGUAGE ARTS AND CONTENT AREA CONNECTIONS

1 Explore Geography Some facts about the two places are:

Puerto Rico: an island in the West Indies; tropical climate; geography includes rugged mountains, beaches, lakes; coffee and tourism are major industries; Spanish is the predominant language.

Miami, Florida: a large city in Florida; tropical climate; geography includes beaches, swamp areas; tourism is a major industry; English is the predominant language.

▶ **Practice Book** page 16

2 Study a News Story Suggest that students use the words *Are you, Can you, Do you, What, When, Why, Where, Who,* and *How* to formulate their questions.

▶ **Practice Book** page 17

CLOSE AND ASSESS

Have students work in heterogeneous groups to create a sentence telling what they learned in the lesson. Then have each group share their responses with the class.

INTRODUCE THEME 2

> **OBJECTIVES**
>
> **Function:** Engage in Discussion
> **Concepts and Vocabulary:** Identity; Careers; Multiple Intelligences
> **Viewing:** Respond to Photographs
> **Learning Strategies:** Relate to Personal Experience; Use Graphic Organizers (T-chart)
> **Critical Thinking:** Generate Ideas; Draw Conclusions

TAP PRIOR KNOWLEDGE

1 **Define "Smart"** Invite students to draw a head in profile. Ask: *What does "smart" mean? How can people be smart in different ways?* Have partners brainstorm and record their ideas inside the head. As students share their ideas, record them in the left side of a T-chart (see below).

VIEW AND DISCUSS

2 **Identify Intelligences** Clarify the career labels for Cisneros, Chávez, and Einstein, whose pictures do not show what they do. Fill out the "Examples" column in the T-chart with students.

Kinds of Smart	Examples
Word	Cisneros
Music	Estefan
Math	Einstein
Movement	Sosa
Art	Hom
On-Your-Own (know yourself well)	Halilbegovich
Face-to-Face (work well with others)	Chávez

> Use the Discussion Prompts in the **Multi-Level Strategies** to help all students participate.

3 **A Special Kind of Smart** Point out that all the people in the photographs share a special skill with words. Ask: *Can you guess what they have in common?* (They all learned English as a second language.)

Sammy Sosa, baseball player

Nancy Hom, artist

Sandra Cisneros, author

Albert Einstein, physicist

Gloria Estefan, singer

Nadja Halilbegovich, writer

César Chávez, labor leader

32 Unit 1 | Identity

REACHING ALL STUDENTS

Multi-Level Strategies
DISCUSSION PROMPTS

BEGINNING Ask students concrete questions about the photographs: *What is Nancy Hom doing?* (painting a picture). *What is she using?* (a paint brush). Then pose questions about the abilities of the people in the photos: *Is Sosa clumsy or graceful? Does he use music or movement in his work?*

INTERMEDIATE Have students work in pairs to complete the T-chart. Ask them to explain each choice in two sentences: *A singer uses music. Gloria Estefan is smart in music.* Then have them add other people they know to the chart.

ADVANCED After students complete the T-chart, ask them to expand the concept of many kinds of smart by thinking about the combinations of intelligence each person might have. Have each student write a short paragraph about the multiple intelligences of one of the people on page 32.

THEME 2

Many Kinds of Smart

- How do you express yourself? Can you sing or dance? Do you like to draw or write?

- What do you do well? What is hard for you? How could you get better at the things that are hard for you?

- Every person is good at something different. Why is that important for our world?

THEME-RELATED BOOKS

My Name is Georgia
by Jeanette Winter

The story of a girl who is not afraid to be herself and who grows up to become a famous artist.

`BEGINNING`

Just Like Me
edited by Harriet Rohmer

Fourteen artists use words and pictures to tell about their lives.

`INTERMEDIATE`

**Eye on the Wild:
A Story About Ansel Adams**
by Julie Dunlap

The true story of a boy who doesn't like school but loves to learn. He also loves nature and becomes a nature photographer.

`ADVANCED`

33

DISCUSS THE GUIDING QUESTIONS

4 **Set the Theme** Some key points to develop during the discussion are:

- People express themselves in different ways. We can identify our particular modes of expression by looking at our talents and the activities we enjoy.

- While we all have natural abilities, we also know that certain things are difficult for us. It is important to work on these areas and not to avoid them. We can ask friends who are talented in these areas to help us improve. We can help them in return.

- Our world is made up of many different kinds of people with different kinds of talents. This diversity allows us to learn from one another. It also means that everyone has a valuable talent of his or her own to contribute. It makes the world a richer place.

▮ Form groups and use the **Multi-Level Strategies** so all students can participate.

CLOSE AND ASSESS

Ask students to tell something they learned about the "many kinds of smart" from this lesson.

Multi-Level Strategies
GROUPING GUIDELINES

`BEGINNING` To help students build understanding of each type of intelligence, conduct role-plays. Use word webs to record concepts.

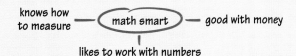

knows how to measure — (math smart) — good with money

likes to work with numbers

`INTERMEDIATE` Have students work in a group to evaluate their own kinds of intelligences. They can ask questions to learn about people with intelligences different from their own, and can share suggestions for improving.

`ADVANCED` Have pairs of students interview each other about their intelligences, using the guiding questions. Students should take notes on their partner's responses, then report back to the class on what they learned.

THEME LIBRARY

▮ *Just Like Me*
edited by Harriet Rohmer

Encourage students to read this book to see what they learn about the artists' identities from their words and their images. Encourage students to notice the different styles and techniques used by the various artists, as well as the different influences that affected each. Encourage students to articulate what they like about their favorite written and graphic portraits or to indicate the style they might use to represent themselves.

OBJECTIVES

Function: ❶ Give Information

Concepts and Vocabulary:
Words About Intelligence

Patterns and Structures:
❶ Present Tense Verbs

Speaking: Report

Critical Thinking and Learning Strategies: Classify; Relate to Personal Experience; Use Graphic Organizers (concept map)

START WITH A COMMON EXPERIENCE

1 Explore Interests Remind students that different people have different interests and abilities, and each person is good at something different. Work through the list on page 34, asking students to think about which items describe their own interests and abilities. Then have students choose and copy the sentences that describe them best.

▌ Use the **Multi-Level Strategies** to help students take the Brain Power test.

2 Model How to Give Information Use the following Think Aloud to help students learn to give information.

▌ **How to Give Information**

• Tell a detail: *I like to play soccer.*

• Tell another detail: *I am a fast runner.*

• State the main point: *I am good at sports.*

Build Language and Vocabulary
GIVE INFORMATION

Read these sentences. They describe different ways that people use their brain power. In your notebook, copy the sentences that describe you best.

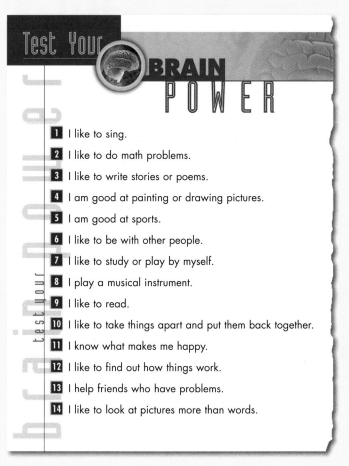

Test Your BRAIN POWER

1 I like to sing.

2 I like to do math problems.

3 I like to write stories or poems.

4 I am good at painting or drawing pictures.

5 I am good at sports.

6 I like to be with other people.

7 I like to study or play by myself.

8 I play a musical instrument.

9 I like to read.

10 I like to take things apart and put them back together.

11 I know what makes me happy.

12 I like to find out how things work.

13 I help friends who have problems.

14 I like to look at pictures more than words.

REACHING ALL STUDENTS

▌ **Multi-Level Strategies**
OPTIONS FOR BRAIN POWER TEST

BEGINNING Use acting, pantomime, and realia to help students understand the descriptions in the list. Engage volunteers to pantomime with you for items 6 and 13.

INTERMEDIATE Read each sentence aloud. For each item, ask students to stand if the description fits them and repeat the sentence chorally.

ADVANCED Ask students to rewrite the sentences that apply to them, replacing the general terms (*sports,* for example) with more specific words (*basketball*).

LEARN ABOUT YOUR BRAIN POWER

Which sentences did you write in your notebook? Check this list. It will tell you what kind of brain power you have.

Talk with some classmates. Ask questions to find out about their brain power.

Examples:
How do you use your musical brain power?
How many kinds of brain power do you have?
What sports do you play?

If you chose:	You have:
1 and 8	Musical Brain Power
2 and 12	Math Brain Power
3 and 9	Word Brain Power
4 and 14	Artistic Brain Power
5 and 10	Movement Brain Power
6 and 13	Face-to-Face Brain Power
7 and 11	On-Your-Own Brain Power

BUILD YOUR VOCABULARY

Brain Power Words Work with a group to make a mind map about one type of brain power.

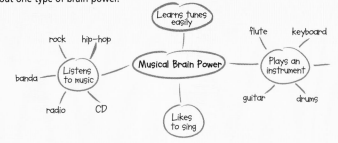

USE LANGUAGE STRUCTURES ▶ PRESENT TENSE VERBS

Speaking: Give a Report Work with a partner or a group. Choose someone you know or a person shown on page 32. Tell what kind of brain power that person has. Give an example of how the person uses it. You can use words from the **Word Bank**.

Examples:
Gloria Estefan has musical brain power. She sings.
Sasha has artistic brain power. He draws.

Word Bank

dances
draws
paints
plays an instrument
reads
sings
works with numbers
writes

Build Language and Vocabulary **35**

Multi-Level Strategies
SPEAKING ACTIVITY OPTIONS

BEGINNING Place students in charge of creating word cards about the person the sentences will describe. Have them write the words on cardboard strips. They can take turns holding up a word when the partner or group presents the report.

INTERMEDIATE These students can expand the second sentence that is part of each example. For instance, *She sings* might be expanded to *She sings pop songs.*

ADVANCED Have these students make up additional sentences telling about the person in their report. If they are reporting on a real person, encourage them to do research in order to include additional information about the subject. Remind them to use present tense verbs correctly.

CONDUCT THE ACTIVITIES

3 Learn About Your Brain Power Pair beginning speakers with more fluent partners to ask questions of classmates.

4 Build Your Vocabulary: Brain Power Words Suggest that students choose a category, brainstorm lists of words related to that category, and then organize their lists into a mind map.

5 Use Language Structures: Present Tense Verbs Present the skill, using the definition and examples on **Transparency 8**. Point out the *s* at the end of verbs used with third-person singular subjects, and say: *When we talk about something one other person, place, or thing does, the verb must end in* s. Then have students complete the sentences in Try It!

Speaking: Give a Report Conduct the activity at the bottom of page 35. Suggest that students use the Word Bank for ideas.

▌ Use the Speaking Activity Options in the **Multi-Level Strategies** to adjust instruction.

▶ **Practice Book** page 18

CLOSE AND ASSESS

Ask students to list three verbs that tell what one other person does. Then have them complete these sentences: *Elena _____. Ricki _____.*

Transparency 8 / Master 8

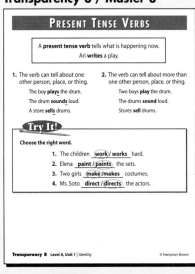

Build Language and Vocabulary **T35**

PREPARE TO READ

OBJECTIVES

THINK ABOUT WHAT YOU KNOW

Concepts and Vocabulary:
Multiple Intelligences

Reading and Learning Strategies:
Activate Prior Knowledge; Use Graphic Organizers (bar graph, prediction chart)

LEARN KEY VOCABULARY ⊤

Vocabulary Strategy:
Use New Words in Context

LEARN TO MAKE PREDICTIONS

Reading Strategy: ⊤ Make Predictions

THINK ABOUT WHAT YOU KNOW

1 Make a Bar Graph Tally the results of the quiz from page 34. On a bar graph, record the number of students who report having each type of intelligence. Summarize what the graph reveals: _____ *people in our class have* _____ *intelligence.*

LEARN KEY VOCABULARY

2 Use New Words in Context Read each vocabulary word and its defining sentence aloud, then use each word in a sentence.

When students understand the meaning of the vocabulary words, conduct the index card activity.

▌ Use the Vocabulary Options in **Multi-Level Strategies** to include all proficiency levels.

▶ **Practice Book** page 19

LEARN TO MAKE PREDICTIONS

3 Model How to Make and Check Predictions Define *prediction* as "a good guess." Demonstrate the steps in the box with **Transparency 9**. Distribute **Master 9** so students can record their predictions before reading. Then ask students to make one or more predictions of their own.

CLOSE AND ASSESS

Ask: *Why is it helpful to make predictions before reading?* (It helps you focus and prepare for reading.)

Ma**n**y
PEOPLE,
Many Intelligences

Prepare to Read

science article
by Joanne Ryder

THINK ABOUT WHAT YOU KNOW

Make a Bar Graph Show the kinds of intelligence people in your class have. Then discuss your graphs.

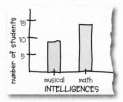

brain power Your brain power helps you think, feel, learn, remember, and move.

figure out When you figure out something, you learn how to do it.

improve When you improve, you get better at something.

intelligence The ability to think, understand, learn, and express yourself is called **intelligence**.

Possible answers to the vocabulary activity:
• My brain has brain power.
• My brain has intelligence.
• My brain can improve.
• My brain can figure out new things.

LEARN KEY VOCABULARY

Use New Words in Context Study the new words. Make sentence-starter cards that say *My brain has* and *My brain can*. Then write each new word on a card. Use the cards to make sentences.

My brain has

intelligence

LEARN TO MAKE PREDICTIONS

You **predict** before you read. A **prediction** tells what you think you will learn.

READING STRATEGY

How to Make and Check Predictions

1. Look at the pictures and headings in the article.
2. Think about what you will learn. Write your predictions.
3. Read the article.
4. Check your predictions. Were they correct?

Make a prediction chart for "Many People, Many Intelligences." Then read the article to see if your predictions were right.

REACHING ALL STUDENTS

▌ **Multi-Level Strategies**
VOCABULARY OPTIONS

BEGINNING / **INTERMEDIATE**

Make sure students see that *kinds of smart, intelligence,* and *brain power* refer to the same thing. Have students work in heterogeneous pairs to form sentences with the cards. Explain that the first sentence starter must be followed by a noun, and the second must be followed by a verb.

ADVANCED Have students work on their own to form sentences with the cards and write a paragraph that begins with one of the new sentences.

Transparency 9 / Master 9

HOW TO MAKE & CHECK PREDICTIONS

Directions: Read the statements. Predict if the statement is true or false. Mark your answer in column 1. After you read the selection, reread the statements and mark your answers in column 3. Were your predictions correct?

Prediction Chart

Before You Read	Statements About *Many People, Many Intelligences*	After You Read
	1. Each person has only one kind of intelligence.	F
	2. There are six kinds of intelligence.	F
	3. People who run have math intelligence.	F
	4. People can strengthen their intelligences.	T

Transparency 9 Level A, Unit 1 | Identity   © Hampton-Brown

MANY PEOPLE
Many Intelligences
by Joanne Ryder

There are many kinds of brain power and many ways to put it to work. Learn more about the types of intelligence that you already have and those you want to improve.

37

INTRODUCE THE SELECTION

4 **Preview and Predict** Read aloud the title, author, and introduction to the article. Discuss the photograph. Ask: *What is happening in the photograph? Describe what each student is doing.* (The students are preparing to put on a play. One student is painting the scenery….) Next, have students page through the selection, looking at the photos and the main headings. Ask students whether they want to change any of their predictions based on this preview.

5 **Audio Walk-Through** Play the Audio Walk-Through for "Many People, Many Intelligences" on the **Selection Tape/CD** to give students the overall idea of the story.

Tape 1B
CD 1
Track 5

Many People, Many Intelligences
by Joanne Ryder

Theme Connection This selection looks at the seven intelligences and how they affect each person's unique identity.

Selection Summary The introduction on page 37 of the student book offers a summary of the selection.

Author Awards Joanne Ryder received the American Nature Study Society's Award for her outstanding nature books for children.

THE BASICS BOOKSHELF

■ *What Is It?* by Shirleyann Costigan

In this humorous book, a rock from outer space is passed from person to person until it's transformed into something quite unexpected. Along the way students learn basic vocabulary related to careers. The picture support and patterned text promote language acquisition for beginning English learners.

For Lesson Plans: See the Teacher's Guide for *The Basics Bookshelf*.

OBJECTIVES

Function: Read a Selection
Concepts and Vocabulary:
Drama—*play, sets, actors*
Grammar: ❶ Present Tense Verbs
Listening: Listen to a Selection
Reading and Learning Strategies:
Set a Purpose for Reading;
❶ Make Predictions
Comprehension: Identify Details;
Make Inferences

SET PURPOSE

1 Say: *Find out how the intelligences
are used by people putting
on a play.*

READ AND THINK

Tape 1B
CD 1
Track 6

**2 Strategy Focus: Make
Predictions** As students read the
selection, have them look for
information that confirms their
predictions.

> Choose Reading Options in the
> **Multi-Level Strategies** to tailor
> the reading to proficiency levels.

The recording of "Many People, Many
Intelligences" on the **Selection
Tape/CD** offers an oral language
model and the opportunity to build
reading fluency.

What Special Intelligence Do You Have?

Red annotations offer
opportunities to clarify
meaning and check for
understanding.

It takes many people and many kinds of **intelligence**
to **put on a play**.

Some people write the words.

Clarify: The words in a play tell the
actors what to do and say.

Some **make the sets**.

Build background: Clarify
play, sets, and *actor*. Take
students to the auditorium
to teach related drama
words: *stage, curtain*.

Others are actors and singers.

Some work best alone. Others
help everyone to work well
together.

Encourage elaboration: Name some
ways that people help each other work
well together.

put on a play act out a story for
people to see
make the sets make the pictures and
decorations that go on a stage for a play

REACHING ALL STUDENTS

HOME CONNECTION

Family Intelligences Send home a
copy of *High Point Newsletter 2* in the
Teacher's Resource Book. (See pages
104–110.) In this home activity,
students interview a family member
to find out about the dominant
intelligences of other members of the
family. They will model their questions
after those in the chart on page 39.
Students compare the information to
their own intelligences to discover
patterns in the family. Findings can be
reported to the class.

Multi-Level Strategies
READING OPTIONS FOR LESSONS 4–5

BEGINNING Read the article aloud, or play its recording on the
Selection Tape/CD. Use the pictures, icons, and the red annotations on the
facsimile pages to clarify meaning. After each section, work together to
identify and take notes on information related to students' predictions.

INTERMEDIATE Read the article aloud, or play its recording on the
Selection Tape/CD, pausing to clarify meaning. Then, have students work in
pairs to skim the article, identifying and taking notes on information related
to their predictions.

ADVANCED Have students read the article on their own, referring to a
dictionary for the meaning of unfamiliar words. Students should identify and
take notes on information related to their predictions, then compare and
discuss their findings with a partner.

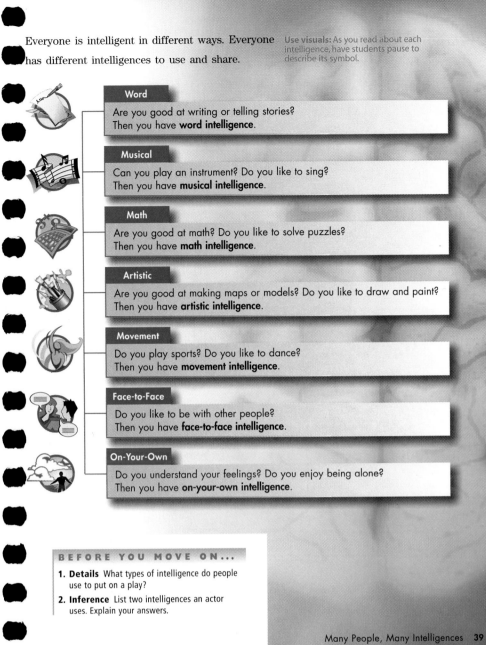

Everyone is intelligent in different ways. Everyone has different intelligences to use and share.

Use visuals: As you read about each intelligence, have students pause to describe its symbol.

Word
Are you good at writing or telling stories? Then you have **word intelligence**.

Musical
Can you play an instrument? Do you like to sing? Then you have **musical intelligence**.

Math
Are you good at math? Do you like to solve puzzles? Then you have **math intelligence**.

Artistic
Are you good at making maps or models? Do you like to draw and paint? Then you have **artistic intelligence**.

Movement
Do you play sports? Do you like to dance? Then you have **movement intelligence**.

Face-to-Face
Do you like to be with other people? Then you have **face-to-face intelligence**.

On-Your-Own
Do you understand your feelings? Do you enjoy being alone? Then you have **on-your-own intelligence**.

BEFORE YOU MOVE ON...

1. **Details** What types of intelligence do people use to put on a play?
2. **Inference** List two intelligences an actor uses. Explain your answers.

Many People, Many Intelligences **39**

CHECK COMPREHENSION

3 Answers to "Before You Move On"

1. **Details** People use word, artistic, face-to-face, and on-your-own intelligences to put on a play. Students may also infer that movement and musical intelligences are used.

2. **Inference** Actors use word intelligence to learn and speak their lines. They use face-to-face intelligence to communicate with one another while rehearsing and performing. They use movement intelligence as they move around the stage during the play. They may use musical intelligence if they are performing in a musical.

CLOSE AND ASSESS

Have each student draw and label an icon for one of his or her kinds of intelligence.

INTERNET

SOCIAL STUDIES CONNECTION

Have students search the Internet for information about the famous people pictured on page 32. Students should try to find information on how these people use their particular intelligence and what impact they have had on the world. Students should then use key words to search for more people who represent each intelligence.

Key Word Search

singer	painter	mathematician
writer	musician	dancer
athlete		

Grammar Minilesson

▶ **PRESENT TENSE VERBS**

TEACH Read the captions for the first two photos on page 38. Say: *The words* write *and* make *are action verbs. These words tell what people do. They tell about something that is happening now. They are in the present tense.*

Rewrite the sentences using *Juan* as the subject of the first sentence and *Lia* as the subject of the second. Point out the *s* at the end of each verb. Remind students: *When we tell what one person does, we add* s *to the verb.*

PRACTICE Write these sentence starters:

I write...

I make...

I help...

Ask students to finish each sentence and trade papers with a partner. The partner should rewrite the sentences using the other person's name and adding an *s* to the verb. Have students explain why they added the *s*.

▶ **Practice Book** page 20

Many People, Many Intelligences **T39**

SET PURPOSE

1 Say: *Look for the ways that math intelligence is used in different kinds of work.*

READ AND THINK

Tape 1B
CD 1
Track 6

2 Strategy Focus: Make Predictions Involve students in reading pages 40–41.

> See the **Multi-Level Strategies** on page T38 to tailor the reading experience to all proficiency levels.

Intelligences Go to Work!

Every job uses one or more of the intelligences. Here are some ways people use math **brain power** in their jobs:

• When cashiers **figure out** how to make change, they use math intelligence.

Define *cashier*: Cashiers work at stores or restaurants. They add up what customers buy, take money, and make change.

• When carpenters measure boards, they use math intelligence.

Clarify: Carpenters build furniture with wood. They need to measure boards exactly so everything fits.

Corn
Average wholesale prices
Cartons of 2 dozen

$6.25 $6.50

Clarify: The value of a farmer's crop is the amount of money people will pay for it.

• When farmers **estimate** the value of their crops, they use math intelligence.

estimate make a good guess about
distance how far away something is
angles the direction the ball must travel

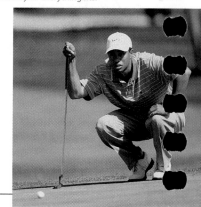

• When professional golfers estimate **distance** and **angles**, they use math intelligence.

Clarify: Use a ruler to clarify the meaning of distance. Make a drawing to explain angles.

40   Unit 1 | Identity

REACHING ALL STUDENTS

Vocabulary
CAREER WORDS

Refer students to pages 73–76 or other selections that show pictures of people engaged in various kinds of work. Have students work in pairs to choose and discuss a picture and to brainstorm a list of additional activities associated with the profession shown. Pairs discuss the intelligence to which each of the activities is linked. Students decide which intelligence is most important to succeeding in this profession and explain each decision to the class.

Learning Styles
INTELLIGENCES PROJECT

Ask students to form groups according to their dominant intelligence. Each group conducts a study of the city they live in. Reports vary according to each group's strength:

• **Visual Learners** Students gather pictures and paint murals of the city.

• **Auditory Learners** Students compose a song about the city.

• **Kinesthetic Learners** Students perform a role-play about events in the city's history.

Exercise Your Intelligence
Pause to repeat the seven intelligences.

You may have one or two intelligences you use most often.

But everyone has some of each of the seven intelligences.

You use them everyday—in and out of school.

How many intelligences do you use when you:

Encourage elaboration: Ask students to name the intelligences they use for these activities.

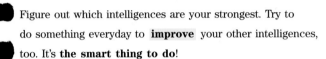

- read a magazine?
- play soccer?
- talk with a friend?
- dance to music on the radio?
- go shopping?

Figure out which intelligences are your strongest. Try to do something everyday to **improve** your other intelligences, too. It's **the smart thing to do**!

BEFORE YOU MOVE ON...

1. **Inference** You use your word intelligence to write at school. What other intelligences do you use at school?

2. **Personal Experience** Which of the seven intelligences is your strongest? Which would you like to improve?

3. **Opinion** Do you think it is a good idea to use all your intelligences? Why?

....

the smart thing to do a good idea

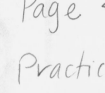

ABOUT THE AUTHOR

Joanne Ryder has strong word intelligence. Sh... has written more than 50 books for children! When she was 10, Joanne discovered the joy o... painting pictures with words. Her father helpe... her discover the world of nature. As a writer, Joanne likes to combine her love of words wit... her love of nature. Joanne received the Ameri... Nature Study Society's Award for her outstand... nature books for children.

Many People, Many Intelligences **41**

[handwritten note:] Page 412- Nouns
Practice pg 21

REVIEW KEY VOCABULARY

3 Use New Words in Context Have students use the vocabulary words to write sentences about their individual intelligences. Encourage them to give specific examples.

CHECK COMPREHENSION

4 Answers to "Before You Move On"

1. **Inference** Students may mention any of the intelligences; ask them to support their answers.

2. **Personal Experience** Ask students to suggest ways to improve a weaker intelligence.

3. **Opinion** A possible answer is that using all your intelligences helps ...

Vocabulary
WORD SORT

For each group of four students, prepare a set of index cards: one names each intelligence and another gives an example of that intelligence: *musical intelligence; listens to country music.* Cards are distributed around the group and read aloud, one at a time. The group selects one word and discusses which example it matches. When all members agree, the matched pair of cards is put aside. Continue until all cards are matched.

Grammar Minilesson

▶ **ARTICLES**

TEACH Reread the bulleted list on page 41 with students. Explain that words like *a* in "read a magazine" and *the* in "on the radio" help identify nouns. Present *an* as another word that signals a noun. Then use Handbook page 412 to teach these rules:

- Use **a** and **an** to talk about one thing in a general way. Use **a** before a noun that begins with a consonant. Use **an** before a noun that begins with a vowel.

  a game   *an interest*

- Use **the** to talk about one specific thing.

  the soccer game

PRACTICE Have students choose *a, an,* or *the* to finish each sentence.

1. The carpenter measures (a, the) long board before cutting it.

2. He marks where to cut (the, an) board.

3. Some boards are cut at (a, an) angle.

▶ **Practice Book** page 21

RESPOND

SUM IT UP

Function: ❶ Ask Questions

Reading and Learning Strategies:
❶ Confirm Predictions

Writing: Questions

THINK IT OVER

Function: Engage in Discussion

Reading and Learning Strategies:
Paraphrase; Relate to Personal Experience

Critical Thinking and Comprehension:
Make Inferences; Form Opinions

EXPRESS YOURSELF

Function: ❶ Give Information

Critical Thinking: Analyze Information

CHECK YOUR UNDERSTANDING

1 Sum It Up Correct statements are:

1. Each person has more than one kind of intelligence.

2. There are seven kinds of intelligence.

3. People who run have movement intelligence.

4. People can strengthen their intelligences.

▶ **Practice Book** page 22

2 Think It Over Possible answers are:

1. **Inference** You can tell by looking at what people do.

2. **Paraphrase** Answers will vary.

3. **Opinion** Answers will vary but should show an awareness of the concept of multiple intelligences.

4. **Personal Experience** I can choose hobbies and jobs that use my strongest intelligences.

3 Express Yourself Invite the class to share their observations on their classmates' dominant intelligence.

CLOSE AND ASSESS

On the Mind Map on page T9, have students add details about their intelligences to the "How You Think" part of the web.

Respond to the Article
Check Your Understanding

SUM IT UP

Check Predictions Read the predictions you made about the article.

Before You Read	Statements About "Many People, Many Intelligences"	After You Read
F	1. Each person only has one kind of intelligence.	F
T	2. There are six kinds of intelligence.	F
F	3. People who run have math intelligence.	F
F	4. People can strengthen their intelligences.	T

Write each sentence on an index card. Correct the false statements.

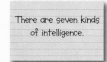

There are seven kinds of intelligence.

Ask Questions Use the back of the card. Write questions you still have about intelligences. Read your questions to the class. Think of a way to find answers.

How can I improve my intelligences?

THINK IT OVER

Discuss Talk about these questions with a partner.

1. **Inference** How can you tell the kind of intelligence a person has?

2. **Paraphrase** Tell something you learned about intelligences. Use your own words.

3. **Opinion** Can you say that someone is not intelligent? Explain your answer.

4. **Personal Experience** How can knowing your intelligences help you?

EXPRESS YOURSELF ▶ GIVE INFORMATION

Tell your partner three things you like to do. Describe the intelligences you have. Use sentences like these:

I like to read. I have word intelligence.

Then your partner will tell the class about you:

Juana likes to read. She has word intelligence.

✓ LANGUAGE ACQUISITION ASSESSMENT
See page 2 of the Assessment Handbook.

REACHING ALL STUDENTS

Multi-Level Strategies
SUM IT UP OPTIONS

BEGINNING Work with students to make the false statements true, referring to the notes made while reading. Help students identify the sentences that present main ideas and the one that presents a detail. Help them formulate questions.

INTERMEDIATE Students work together to correct the false statements. Pairs then write a short summary using the sentences on the index cards and other key points in the reading. Provide students with frames: *This article was about _____. The most important points were _____.*

ADVANCED Students work on their own to correct the false statements. They can elaborate on the sentences to write a one-paragraph summary of the article. Students then choose a question to answer using appropriate resources.

Language Arts and Content Area Connections

> **VOCABULARY**

MATCH JOBS AND SKILLS

The people on page 40 use their intelligences for their jobs. Find jobs that use your strongest intelligences.

Find Out About Jobs and Skills Think of a job you would like to do. Then list the skills used in the job. A **skill** is the ability to do something well. You can look for information in a book in the library, or talk to someone who has that job.

Make a Tree Diagram Show the job and the skills. Show the intelligence you need for each skill. Share your information with the class.

Tree Diagram

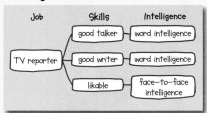

> **MATHEMATICS**

GRAPH INTELLIGENCE TYPES

A **circle graph** shows all of the parts of a whole thing. Use a circle graph to show the intelligences in your class.

1 Gather Information Write the strongest intelligence for each student in your class.

2 Use the Formula Find the percentages for each type of intelligence.

$$\frac{\text{number of students with math intelligence}}{\text{number of students in your class}} \times 100 = \text{\% with math intelligence}$$

Example:

$$\frac{\text{5 students have math intelligence}}{\text{25 students in my class}} \times 100 = 20\% \text{ math intelligence}$$

3 Draw a Circle Graph Make a section for each percentage. Label each part.

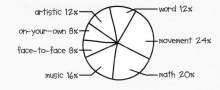

Many People, Many Intelligences **43**

Multi-Level Strategies

ACTIVITY OPTIONS FOR JOB/SKILL MATCH

Materials: career photos/illustrations

BEGINNING / **INTERMEDIATE** Work with the group to teach names of professions and to elicit information about skills and intelligences: *A person who plans how to build a house is called an architect. An architect has to measure. What intelligence does that use? Yes, math intelligence.* Reword labels in the tree diagram. Beginning students can choose their favorite profession to present to the class. Intermediate students can write sentences about their favorite job.

ADVANCED Have partners research their chosen profession. One student performs the library research, while the other interviews a person who works in the profession. Invite students to present their findings. Have them conclude with an evaluation of whether, based upon what they learned, they have the right intelligences for the profession and why.

OBJECTIVES

MATCH JOBS AND SKILLS

Concepts and Vocabulary: Careers— *teacher, mechanic, doctor, reporter*

Learning Strategies, Critical Thinking, and Research Skills: Gather Information; ❶ Classify; Use Graphic Organizers (tree diagram)

GRAPH INTELLIGENCE TYPES

Function: ❶ Give Information

Concepts and Vocabulary: Math—*calculate, percentage, graph*

Critical Thinking and Research Skills: Gather Information; Analyze Information

Representing and Writing: Circle Graph

LANGUAGE ARTS AND CONTENT AREA CONNECTIONS

1 Match Jobs and Skills Brainstorm a list of jobs and classify them under broad headings, such as *health care, business, education.* Assign heterogeneous pairs or groups to work on the tree diagrams.

▶ **Practice Book** page 23

2 Graph Intelligence Types Preview mathematical terms:

- **graph:** A diagram that shows differences in quantities.

- **calculate:** Using addition, subtraction, multiplication, or division to solve problems. Illustrate with simple calculations.

- **percentage:** An amount of something expressed by what part of 100 it is. Explain that 100 percent is the total amount of something. Use everyday examples, such as test scores, daily attendance, etc., to illustrate.

CLOSE AND ASSESS

As they leave the classroom, have students restate a fact they learned.

BUILD LANGUAGE AND VOCABULARY

OBJECTIVES

Function: ❶ Describe Things

Concepts and Vocabulary: Color, Size, and Shape Words

Patterns and Structures: ❶ Adjectives

Speaking: Describing Game

Viewing: Describe a Painting

Learning Strategies: Use Graphic Organizers (category chart); Make Observations

Critical Thinking: Classify; Formulate Questions; Draw Conclusions

START WITH A COMMON EXPERIENCE

1 **View and Describe** View the painting, encouraging students to describe the colors and shapes they see. Then model how to give an effective description:

> **How to Describe**
>
> • Name a shape: *triangle*
>
> • Tell what it looks like: *It has three sides that meet at points.*
>
> • Tell more: *It is bright red, and its sides are straight.*

2 **Discuss the Painting** Engage students in a discussion about the painting, encouraging them to use their imaginations to tell what they think it represents. You may wish to explain that the painting's title, *Vendredi*, is the French word for *Friday*. Through the discussion, develop the idea that each of us sees things in different ways.

> Use the Discussion Prompts in the **Multi-Level Strategies** to include students at all proficiency levels.

Build Language and Vocabulary
DESCRIBE THINGS

View this painting. Describe what you see.

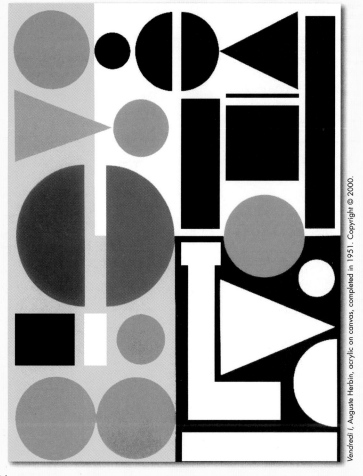

Vendredi I, Auguste Herbin, acrylic on canvas, completed in 1951. Copyright © 2000.

REACHING ALL STUDENTS

Multi-Level Strategies
DISCUSSION PROMPTS

BEGINNING Ask about shapes in the painting: *What is this red shape called? Can you find a black one? Show me the smallest rectangle.*

INTERMEDIATE Point out possible changes in viewpoint to prompt comments from these students: *What might the painting make you think of if you were looking down from high in the air?* (a city, fields)

ADVANCED Ask these students to make observations about the painting that go beyond the geometric shapes: *The artist titled his painting* Friday. *What happens on Friday that does not happen on any other day? What do you think Friday means to the artist? What would a painting of yours named* Friday *look like?*

SEARCH FOR SHAPES

The painting on page 44 has a lot of colorful forms called *geometric shapes*. Draw some of the shapes in your notebook. Work with a group to label the shapes.

BUILD YOUR VOCABULARY

Color, Size, and Shape Words Start a chart like this one in your notebook. Work with the class to describe each of the geometric shapes.

GEOMETRIC SHAPE	Number of Sides	Number of Corners	Type of Line	Color	Size
RECTANGLE ▪	4 (2 long, 2 short)	4	straight	black	big
CIRCLE ●	0	0	curved	red	medium

USE LANGUAGE STRUCTURES ▶ADJECTIVES

Speaking: Play a Describing Game Form two teams, Team A and Team B.

- Team A chooses a shape in the painting.
- Team B asks three yes or no questions about the shape. Use words from the **Word Bank**.

  Examples:
  Is your shape big?
  Does it have three corners?
  Is it black?

- Team B tries to guess the shape.
- The team with the most correct guesses wins.

Word Bank

big
corners
curved
dark
light
medium
round
sides
small
straight

CONDUCT THE ACTIVITIES

3 Search for Shapes Have students work in groups to label the shapes. As an aid, list the names of the geometric shapes pictured.

4 Build Your Vocabulary: Color, Size, and Shape Words Work with the class to complete the chart for each of the remaining geometric shapes in the painting.

5 Use Language Structures: Adjectives Present adjectives, using the definition and examples on **Transparency 10**. Invite students to give additional examples for each numbered category. Then have students complete the sentences in Try It!

Speaking: Play a Describing Game Conduct the activity at the bottom of page 45. Suggest that students use the Word Bank to help them create their questions. Have teams reverse roles after each game.

▌ Use the Speaking Activity Options in the **Multi-Level Strategies** to adjust instruction.

▶ **Practice Book** page 24

CLOSE AND ASSESS

Ask students to list three words that describe things. Then have them complete this sentence: *A rectangle has _____ sides and _____ corners.*

Multi-Level Strategies
SPEAKING ACTIVITY OPTIONS

BEGINNING To help students form questions, suggest that they refer to their shape chart for words to describe each shape.

INTERMEDIATE Students can use the Word Bank and their shape charts to assist them in formulating questions.

ADVANCED Encourage Team A students to choose less simple geometric shapes in the painting, such as a semi-circle or the L-shape. Team B students should adapt their questioning accordingly.

Transparency 10 / Master 10

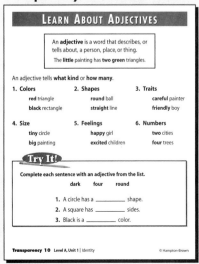

LEARN ABOUT ADJECTIVES

An **adjective** is a word that describes, or tells about, a person, place, or thing.
The **little** painting has **two green** triangles.

An adjective tells **what kind** or **how many**.

1. Colors	2. Shapes	3. Traits
red triangle	**round** ball	**careful** painter
black rectangle	**straight** line	**friendly** boy

4. Size	5. Feelings	6. Numbers
tiny circle	**happy** girl	**two** cities
big painting	**excited** children	**four** trees

Try It!

Complete each sentence with an adjective from the list.

     dark   four   round

1. A circle has a _____ shape.
2. A square has _____ sides.
3. Black is a _____ color.

Transparency 10 Level A, Unit 1 | Identity   © Hampton-Brown

PREPARE TO READ

OBJECTIVES

THINK ABOUT WHAT YOU KNOW

Reading Strategy:
Activate Prior Knowledge

Viewing: Respond to a Photograph

LEARN KEY VOCABULARY ⊕

Vocabulary Strategy:
Use New Words in Context

LEARN TO RELATE CAUSE AND EFFECT

Reading Strategy: ⊕ Relate Cause
and Effect

THINK ABOUT WHAT YOU KNOW

1 Tell About a Picture Model the
activity by bringing in a photograph
of your own. Encourage students to
ask additional questions.

LEARN KEY VOCABULARY

2 Use New Words in Context Read
each vocabulary word and its
defining sentence aloud. Then
complete the sentences as a group.

▌ Use the Vocabulary Options in
Multi-Level Strategies to tailor
the activity to proficiency levels.

▶ **Practice Book** page 25

LEARN TO RELATE CAUSES AND EFFECTS

**3 Model How to Relate Causes and
Effects** Define *cause* and *effect*.
Demonstrate how to relate causes
and effects with **Transparency 11**:

• Read the first paragraph. Point out
the last sentence as an effect, and
ask volunteers to state the cause
(she was in an accident).

• In the last paragraph, point out
because as a signal word for cause.

• Point out the signal words in the
practice sentences. Have students
suggest ways to complete
each sentence.

CLOSE AND ASSESS

Ask students: *What words can signal a
cause?* (since, because)

ArtSmart **P**repare to Read

self-portraits
by Nancy Hom
and George Littlechild

THINK ABOUT WHAT YOU KNOW

Tell About a Picture Bring a favorite photograph of yourself to class.
Show the picture and answer the questions:

• What are you doing in the picture? Where was it taken?

• What does the picture tell about you? What doesn't it show?

accept When you **accept**
something, you like it the way
it is.

decide When you **decide**,
you make up your mind about
something.

express You **express**
when you show or to tell
something.

feature A **feature** is part
of your face.

portrait A **portrait** is a
picture of a person.

LEARN KEY VOCABULARY

Use New Words in Context Study the new words. Then write the
sentences. Choose the correct word to complete each sentence.

1. I want to paint a ____(feature /(portrait)____ of myself.

2. I can ____((decide)/ accept)____ to use pencils or paints.

3. I can draw each ____(portrait /(feature)____ , like my nose and eyes.

4. A picture is a way to ____((express)/ decide)____ my ideas.

5. I hope that my teacher will ____(decide /(accept)____ my picture.

LEARN TO RELATE CAUSES AND EFFECTS

A **cause** is why something happens. An **effect** is what happens. When you
relate causes and effects, you can understand why things happen.

> **READING STRATEGY**
>
> **How to Relate Causes and Effects**
>
> 1. Read the story or article.
> 2. Look for something that happened. It is the effect.
> 3. Ask yourself, "Why did that happen?" Your answer is
>   the cause.

Read "Art Smart." Look for causes and effects.

REACHING ALL STUDENTS

▌ **Multi-Level Strategies**
VOCABULARY OPTIONS

BEGINNING Show *portraits* on
pages 48 and 50. Point to the *features*
on your face as you name them.
Role-play *accepting* something.

INTERMEDIATE Students work in
triads to role-play *decide, accept*, and
express. Use Think Alouds for the
sentences: *A portrait is a picture, so
portrait is correct.*

ADVANCED Have students write
about a classmate's photograph, using
vocabulary words.

Transparency 11 / Master 11

HOW TO RELATE CAUSES AND EFFECTS

Directions: Read the passage. Find examples of cause and effect. Then complete
the two sentences below. Write an effect and a cause.

A Famous Mexican Artist

Frida Kahlo was born in Mexico in 1907. When she was a girl,
she wanted to be a doctor. When she was 18, Frida was in a bus
accident. She had to stay in bed for one month.
Staying in bed was not fun. There was nothing to do. Since
she couldn't do much else, Frida began to paint.
Frida created 55 self-portraits during her life. She always
painted herself in traditional clothing because she wanted to
show her love for her country. Frida also used bright colors to
express her moods.

1. Since she was in an accident, Frida ____had to stay in bed____
____for a month.____

2. Frida used bright colors because ____they helped her____
____express her moods.____

Transparency 11 Level A, Unit 1 | Identity   © Hampton-Brown

ArtSmart

by Nancy Hom and George Littlechild

Self-portraits are pictures that artists make of themselves. In this selection, two artists use their artistic and word intelligences to present self-portraits.

47

OBJECTIVES

Listening: Listen to a Preview
Reading Strategies: Preview; Predict

INTRODUCE THE SELECTION

4 **Preview and Predict** Read aloud the title, authors, and introduction to the selection. Initiate a discussion about the illustration. Ask: *What do you think "Art Smart" is about?* Next, invite students to page through the selection, studying the illustrations. Have students point out any describing words they notice.

5 **Audio Walk-Through** Play the Audio Walk-Through for "Art Smart" on the **Selection Tape/CD** to give students the overall idea of the selection.

Tape 1B
CD 1
Track 7

Art Smart
by Nancy Hom and George Littlechild

Theme Connection This selection tells how two artists use their artwork to express their identities.

Selection Summary The introduction on page 47 of the student book offers a summary of the selection.

🟩 THE BASICS ▨ BOOKSHELF

■ *I Make Pictures Move* by Daphne Liu

He starts with a line or a squiggle. He fills in the shapes with color. Using the tools of his trade, an animator artist shows how he makes pictures move. This story, which is also a flip book, teaches basic vocabulary related to food, shapes, and colors. Pictures and simple patterned text also support language acquisition.

For Lesson Plans: See the Teacher's Guide for *The Basics Bookshelf*.

OBJECTIVES

Function: Read a Selection
Vocabulary Strategy: Relate Words
Grammar: ⊙ Adjectives
Listening: Listen to a Selection
Reading and Learning Strategies: Set a Purpose for Reading; Use Graphic Organizers (chart); ⊙ Relate Cause and Effect
Comprehension: Identify Details
Literary Analysis: Evaluate Impact of Author's Culture on Literature

SET PURPOSE

1 Ask: *What can we learn about Nancy Hom from her self-portrait?*

READ AND THINK

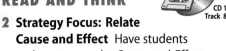

Tape 1B

CD 1
Track 8

2 Strategy Focus: Relate Cause and Effect Have students make notes on the Cause-and-Effect Chart during the reading process.

> Choose Reading Options in the **Multi-Level Strategies** to tailor the reading to proficiency levels.

The recording of "Art Smart" on the **Selection Tape/CD** offers an oral language model and the opportunity to build reading fluency.

Red annotations offer opportunities to clarify meaning and check for understanding.

A Self-Portrait
by Nancy Hom

Self-Portrait, Nancy Hom. Copyright © 1997.

Clarify: This is a self-portrait of Nancy Hom. She painted this picture of herself.

48 Unit 1 | Identity

REACHING ALL STUDENTS

Transparency 12 / Master 12

CAUSE-AND-EFFECT CHART

Directions: Look for causes and effects as you read the selection. List them on this chart.

Art Smart

Causes	Effects
• Nancy likes to draw flat shapes.	• Nancy's art is simple.
• Nancy is strong.	• Nancy uses bold colors and patterns.
• Nancy comes from China.	• Nancy's portrait has bamboo from China.
• George had features like his Indian mother.	• When George was young, people knew he was Indian.
• As George got older, he looked more like his white father.	• People weren't sure about George's race.
• No one told him he was mixed-blood.	• George was confused about his identity.
• George's looks change with his mood.	• George made four self-portraits.

Transparency 12 Level A, Unit 1 | Identity   © Hampton-Brown

Multi-Level Strategies
READING OPTIONS FOR LESSONS 10–11

BEGINNING Read the selection aloud, two sentences at a time. Use the red annotations on the facsimile pages to clarify meaning. Pause to prompt students to identify causes and effects. Vocalize as you record information on **Transparency 12**.

INTERMEDIATE Have partners read the selection, referring to the Glossary or a dictionary for the meaning of unfamiliar words or phrases. Distribute copies of **Master 12** for students to complete and discuss with classmates. Encourage students to contribute to the group discussion of the selection.

ADVANCED Have students read the selection, referring to the Glossary or a dictionary as needed. Then distribute copies of **Master 12** for them to complete. Challenge students to write responses, thoughts, and summary statements about the selection in a Reflection Log.

I like to draw flat shapes that fit together like jigsaw puzzles. My artwork is very simple and graceful, with curves like the edges of clouds. I am like that—soft, gentle, quiet, but strong at the same time. I **express** my strength through **bold** colors and **patterns**. This **portrait** has leaves of **bamboo** in it because bamboo also comes from China. It is strong, but it can bend when it needs to, just like me. **Ask:** Where does Nancy come from?

Clarify: Jigsaw puzzles are made with pieces that fit together to show a bigger picture; have students view puzzle pieces on page 122.

BEFORE YOU MOVE ON...

1. Details What plant does the artist say she is like? How are they alike?

2. Vocabulary Make a list of the words Nancy used to describe her painting.

---

bold strong; clear and easy to see
patterns colors or shapes that repeat
bamboo a tall plant with long, stiff stems

ABOUT THE AUTH

Nancy Hom is an artist, mother, designer, Executive Director of Kearny Street Works Asian American arts organization. She wa Toisan, China, in 1949. She grew up in Nev City and now lives in San Francisco, Califor

Art

Practice pg 26

CHECK COMPREHENSION

3 Answers to "Before You Move On"

1. Details Nancy is like bamboo. They are both strong, but can bend as needed.

2. Vocabulary Answers will vary, but may include *simple, graceful, curves, bold colors and patterns.*

ABOUT THE AUTHOR

4 Evaluate Literature: Author's Culture Remind students that this author/artist has made a point of explaining how her cultural background affects her work and her personality. Read aloud About the Author. Ask: *How does Nancy Hom's culture affect her artwork and writing?*

CLOSE AND ASSESS

Have students share their charts. Check
ause

Vocabulary
MULTIPLE-MEANING WORDS

Tell students that some words have more than one meaning. Write: *Nancy Hom draws flat shapes. Another artist might shape clay into a pot.* Point out and discuss other words from the selection that have multiple meanings: *features, dash, works, looks.* Have pairs of students write sentences that use the different meanings and share them with the class.

Grammar Minilesson

▶ ADJECTIVES

TEACH Read the first three sentences in the text. Then say: *The words flat, simple, graceful, soft, gentle, quiet, and strong are adjectives. They describe, or tell about, nouns.*

Tell students that some adjectives point out *which one* is meant. Use concrete examples to explain the meaning of *this, that, these,* and *those.* Use gestures to show that the words *this* and *these* go with close objects, while *that* and *those* are used to describe objects that are farther away.

PRACTICE Place one book and a group of pencils near students. At a distance place a different book and another group of like objects, such as index cards. Ask pairs of students to write sentences that describe the objects in two different ways. Offer as an example: *These pencils are yellow.* You may wish to provide a word bank for students.

| this | these | yellow |
| that | those | thin |

▶ Practice Book page 26

Art Smart **T49**

Function: Read a Selection

Vocabulary Strategy:
Use New Words in Context

Grammar: Proper Adjectives

Listening: Listen to a Selection

Reading and Learning Strategies:
Set a Purpose for Reading;
Use Graphic Organizers (chart);
⊕ Relate Cause and Effect; Relate to
Personal Experience

Comprehension: Identify Author's
Purpose; Make an Inference

Literary Analysis: Evaluate Impact of
Author's Culture on Literature

SET PURPOSE

1 Invite students to study George
Littlechild's self-portrait. Say: *Look for
ways that this artist expresses his
personality in his art.*

READ AND THINK

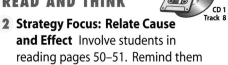

Tape 1B

CD 1
Track 8

**2 Strategy Focus: Relate Cause
and Effect** Involve students in
reading pages 50–51. Remind them
to add information about George
Littlechild to the Cause/Effect Chart
as they read.

> See the **Multi-Level Strategies** on
> page T48 to tailor the reading
> experience to all proficiency levels.

A SELF-PORTRAIT
by George Littlechild

Use visuals: Point to the illustration and ask
who made the self-portrait.

Self-Portrait, George Littlechild. Copyright © 1997.

REACHING ALL STUDENTS

Language Development
DESCRIBE

Have students use classroom resources
or the Internet to browse through the
work of a number of artists. Ask them
to select a piece of art that they really
love and describe it, using vocabulary
words from this selection and vivid
describing words. To plan the
description, suggest they create a word
web to trap words about colors, shapes,
and the feelings the art suggests. Then
have them show the picture and tell
classmates about it.

A WORLD OF LANGUAGES

English/Spanish Cognates Point out to students whose first language
is Spanish that they already know many words in the selection.

PAGE 47	PAGE 49	PAGE 51
art arte	**simple** simple	**Indian** indio
artists artistas	**curves** curvas	**exotic** exótica
artistic artístico	**quiet** quieto	**Spanish** español
intelligences inteligencias	**express** expresar	**Italian** italiano
present presentar	**colors** colores	**Portuguese** portugués
	bamboo bambú	**family** familia
	China China	**confused** confuso
		accept aceptar
		decided decidido

See page T373 for English/Spanish cognates in the other selections in *High Point*.

Clarify: Indians and First Nations are people whose ancestors were the first people to live on the continent of North America.

When I was a boy, people knew I was Indian (or First Nations, as we say in Canada) because I had the **features** of my Indian mother. As I got older, people weren't sure anymore. "You sure are **exotic** looking," they told me. "Are you Spanish? Italian? Portuguese?" I was looking more like my white father. But since both of my parents were dead and I was living with my Dutch **foster family**, I was very confused about who I was. No one ever told me then that I was **mixed-blood**.

Sometimes I look Indian now, but sometimes I don't. My looks change according to my **mood**. That's why I've made these four different self-portraits. It took me many years to **accept** my features. Then one day I **decided** that I had to love myself the way I am. I'm a rainbow man, with a half of this and a quarter of that, and a **dash of a mixture of everything**!

Restate: It took George many years to feel okay about the way he looks.

BEFORE YOU MOVE ON...

1. **Motive** Why did George paint four self-portraits instead of one?
2. **Inference** George wrote about his different moods. Look at his four pictures. Write words that tell how he felt in each picture.
3. **Personal Experience** George describes himself as a "dash of a mixture of everything." What are you like? Do you have a little bit of many cultures, or just one?

exotic different and interesting
foster family family who took care of me
mixed-blood a child who has parents of different races
mood feelings
dash of a mixture of everything little bit of many things mixed together

ABOUT THE AUTHOR

George Littlechild is a painter, printmaker, and mixed-media artist whose works are exhibited in galleries and museums throughout the world. He is a member of the Plains Cree Nation of Canada. George was born in Edmonton, Alberta, in 1958. He now lives in Vancouver, British Columbia.

Art Smart **51**

REVIEW KEY VOCABULARY

3 **Use New Words in Context** Have partners create picture dictionary entries for two vocabulary words, using the definitions on page 46 and original art. As a class, select the drawing that best expresses the meaning of each word.

CHECK COMPREHENSION

4 **Answers to "Before You Move On"**

1. **Motive** George wanted to express how his looks change according to his mood.
2. **Inference** Answers include: *proud, confused, angry, happy.*
3. **Personal Experience** Answers should describe students' cultural heritage.

ABOUT THE AUTHOR

5 **Evaluate Literature: Author's Culture** Remind students that this author/artist came to accept being a "rainbow man." Ask: *How does having a mixed cultural heritage contribute to this artist's imagination?*

CLOSE AND ASSESS

Have students use the mind map on page T9 as a model to create a mind map for Nancy Hom or George Littlechild.

COMMUNITY CONNECTION

Museum Visit Visit an art museum or have a local artist or art teacher visit the class to share information about the different media artists use. Then challenge students to use only classroom materials to create a piece of art that expresses their personality.

Grammar Minilesson

▶ **PROPER ADJECTIVES**

TEACH Draw students' attention to this sentence: *"Are you Spanish? Italian? Portuguese?"* Identify the words *Spanish, Italian,* and *Portuguese* as adjectives.

Review that names of particular persons, places, or things are called proper nouns and begin with a capital letter. Write *Spain–Spanish, Italy–Italian,* and *Portugal–Portuguese.* Explain that adjectives that come from proper nouns are called proper adjectives. They begin with a capital letter.

PRACTICE Write pairs of sentences:

John was born in _____.
He is _____.

Anna was born in _____.
She is _____.

Students finish sentences with the name of a country and a proper adjective. Provide lists of countries and nationalities. They can also complete a sentence to describe their own heritage:

I was born in _____. I am _____.

▶ **Practice Book** page 27

OBJECTIVES

SUM IT UP

Function: Write

Reading and Learning Strategies:
Use Graphic Organizers (chart);
🅣 Relate Cause and Effect

Writing: Sentences

THINK IT OVER

Function: Engage in Discussion

Critical Thinking and Comprehension:
Make Inferences; 🅣 Make Comparisons;
Make Judgments; Form Opinions

EXPRESS YOURSELF

Function: 🅣 Describe;
🅣 Give Information

CHECK YOUR UNDERSTANDING

1 **Sum It Up** Annotations on the
Cause-and-Effect Chart show
possible answers. As a follow-up,
remind students that *because* and
since can signal a cause-effect
relationship, and that causes and
effects can sometimes be inferred.

▶ **Practice Book** page 28

2 **Think It Over** Possible answers are:

1. Inference Nancy and George
express their cultures, moods, and
ideas in their portraits.

2. Comparisons Both self-portraits
use bright colors. Nancy made
one and George made four.

3. Judgment Answers will vary.
Students might say they feel
George Littlechild's portrait tells
more about him because it offers
four views.

4. Opinion Answers will vary.

3 **Express Yourself** Prompt students
to use describing words and to
elaborate on their reasons for
choosing specific items.

CLOSE AND ASSESS

Ask students to offer a good excuse for
being late to school that includes a cause
and effect.

T52 Unit 1 | Identity

Respond to the Self-Portraits
Check Your Understanding

SUM IT UP

Relate Causes and Effects Copy and complete
these charts.

A Self-Portrait by Nancy Hom

Causes	Effects
Nancy likes to draw flat shapes.	Nancy's art is simple.
Nancy is strong.	Nancy uses bold colors and patterns.
Nancy comes from China.	Nancy's portrait has bamboo from China.

A Self-Portrait by George Littlechild

Causes	Effects
George had features like his Indian mother.	When George was young, people knew he was Indian.
As George got older, he looked more like his white father.	People weren't sure about George's race.
No one told him he was mixed-blood.	George was confused about his identity.
George's looks change with his mood.	George made four self-portraits.

Write Sentences Tell about Nancy or George.
Write a sentence that gives a cause and an
effect. Use the word *because*.

Example:
Nancy showed bamboo leaves in her portrait
because she is from China.

THINK IT OVER

Discuss Talk about these questions with
a partner.

1. Inference What do Nancy and George express
in their paintings?

2. Comparisons How are the self-portraits the
same? How are they different?

3. Judgment Which self-portrait describes the
artist the best? Explain your answer.

4. Opinion Which artist would you like to meet?
Why?

EXPRESS YOURSELF

▶ DESCRIBE AND GIVE INFORMATION

Nancy and George added things to their self-
portraits that tell about them. Nancy painted
bamboo leaves. They show her Chinese culture.
Think about something that describes you. Share
it with the class and tell how it is like you.

✓ **LANGUAGE ACQUISITION ASSESSMENT**
See page 2 of the Assessment Handbook.

REACHING ALL STUDENTS

Multi-Level Strategies
SUM IT UP OPTIONS

BEGINNING Work with students to write sentences with *because*.
Provide these sentence frames: *Nancy painted bamboo because _____.*
George made four self-portraits because _____.

INTERMEDIATE Have students work in pairs to write sentences that sum
up the selection and that relate cause and effect. Challenge students to
use the thesaurus to find interesting describing words to include in their
summary sentences.

ADVANCED Have students review what they have written in their
Reflection Logs. Using information from the logs, challenge them to write
sentences that sum up the selection and relate cause and effect.

ASSESSMENT
Selection Test 4 on page 9 of the Assessment Handbook tests students'
mastery of the reading strategies and the vocabulary, comprehension,
and language arts skills taught with this selection.

Language Arts and Literature

GRAMMAR IN CONTEXT

USE NOUNS IN THE SUBJECT

Learn About Nouns A **noun** is the name of a person, place, or thing. A **common noun** names any person, place, or thing. A **proper noun** names one particular person, place, or thing. Proper nouns begin with capital letters.

Common Nouns	Proper Nouns
girl, doctor	Hannah, Dr. Chen
city, lake	St. Louis, Lake Erie
building, dog	Sears Tower, Lassie

- A **noun** can appear anywhere in a sentence.

  The **painter** puts her **brushes** in the **box**.

- A **noun** is often the subject of a sentence. The subject tells whom or what the sentence is about.

  The painter puts her brushes in the box.

  The box is on the table.

Practice Copy this paragraph. Add a noun to form the subject of each sentence. Then circle all the nouns in the paragraph. List the ones that are proper nouns.

___Ricky___ was born in the Philippines. His ___family___ moved to the United States last year. Now, ___science___ is Ricky's favorite class. handball is his favorite sport. ___Karen___ is Ricky's best friend.

Answers will vary. Sample answers:
common nouns: family, year, science, class, sport, handball, friend
proper nouns: Ricky, the Philippines, United States, Karen

WRITING/REPRESENTING

CREATE A PORTRAIT GALLERY

Make your own self-portrait. Then write about it.

❶ **Create a Self-Portrait** Draw yourself, take a photograph, or use pictures from magazines. Add things that tell about you.

❷ **Write a Description** Tell about your self-portrait. Describe what you are doing and the things you show.

❸ **Share Your Work** Put up your poster. Go on a tour of the gallery and look at the class portraits.

 Learn how to improve your writing in the **writer's craft**. See Handbook pages 390–401.

Art Smart **53**

OBJECTIVES

CREATE A NOUNS IN THE SUBJECT
Grammar: ❶ Common and Proper Nouns

CREATE A PORTRAIT GALLERY
Function: ❶ Describe; Express Feelings; Write
Viewing: Interpret a Visual Image
Critical Thinking: Generate Ideas
Writing: Description

LANGUAGE ARTS AND LITERATURE

1 Use Nouns in the Subject See annotations for possible answers to the Practice items.

▶ Practice Book page 29

2 Create a Portrait Gallery Help students brainstorm a list of things that can be expressed in the self-portrait, such as nationalities, hobbies, favorite colors, and musical groups.

Encourage students to plan their descriptions by jotting down ideas from the brainstorm session.

▶ Practice Book page 30

CLOSE AND ASSESS

Ask: *How well does your self-portrait express your feelings and interests? What nouns and adjectives did you use in your description?*

Multi-Level Strategies
OPTIONS FOR CREATING PORTRAITS

BEGINNING Have students review their Identity mind maps to help them generate ideas before beginning to draw and write. Have students add information about things they like and dislike. After students create their self-portraits, have them label the elements of their picture and write several sentences using this frame: *I made a _____ because _____.*

INTERMEDIATE To generate ideas, have students review and expand their Identity mind maps, adding likes, dislikes, interests, and feelings. Invite them to write sentences using *because* to describe their portraits.

ADVANCED Students review and expand their Identity mind maps to include additional likes, dislikes, interests, and feelings. Challenge them to write a paragraph explaining their choice of elements in the portrait. Remind them to use *since* and *because* in their paragraphs to reflect cause and effect.

RESPOND

IDENTIFY GEOMETRIC SHAPES

Function: ❶ Describe

Concepts and Vocabulary: Shapes—
geometric, circle, rectangle, square, triangle

Reading and Learning Strategies:
Visualize; ❶ Make Comparisons

RESEARCH A PORTRAIT ARTIST

Function: ❶ Give Information

Speaking: Oral Report

**Learning Strategies and Research
Skills:** Gather Information; Take Notes;
Organize Information

Technology/Media: Use the Internet

Representing and Writing:
Research Report

CONTENT AREA CONNECTIONS

1 Identify Geometric Shapes As a
follow-up to this activity, have
students search for shapes in
buildings, street signs, and other
features of the community.
Encourage them to draw these
shapes and write captions: *A yield
sign is a triangle.* Add these shape
drawings to a word/concept wall.

2 Research a Portrait Artist Provide
background information in the form
of art books from the school library
before sending students to the
Internet. Discuss the names of artists
and the countries they are from.
Offer some guiding questions:

- *What kind of artwork does this
  artist do?*

- *What is it about the artwork that
  I like?*

- *Do I wish that I could do artwork
  like this?*

▶ **Practice Book** page 31

CLOSE AND ASSESS

Ask: *What did you learn about artists from
this lesson?* (Answers will vary, but should
mention that artists use geometric shapes
in their work, or should give information
about a specific artist.)

Respond to the Self-Portraits, continued

Content Area Connections

> MATHEMATICS
> FINE ARTS

IDENTIFY GEOMETRIC SHAPES

A **geometric shape** is a form made of straight
lines or curves. Find geometric shapes in the
self-portraits.

❶ **Learn Geometric Shapes** These are some
geometric shapes.

circle rectangle square triangle

❷ **Chart Geometric Shapes** Copy the chart.
Mark the shapes you can find in each portrait.
Add information about your own self-portrait.

Artist	◯	▯	▢	△
N. Hom	X	X		X
G. Littlechild	X		X	X
Me				

❸ **Share Your List** Work with a small group.
Describe the shapes you found. Point to the
shapes on the self-portraits.

> VIEWING/SPEAKING
> TECHNOLOGY/MEDIA

RESEARCH A PORTRAIT ARTIST

Give an oral report about an artist like:

Rembrandt   Pablo Picasso

Vincent Van Gogh   Norman Rockwell

Find Information Use encyclopedias, books, or
the Internet. Take notes about the artist's life
and work. Try these Web sites, but remember
that new sites appear every day! Use the artist's
name as a key word.

INTERNET

INFORMATION ON-LINE

Web Sites:
➤ **Artists and Museums**
- library.thinkquest.org/17142
- metalab.unc.edu/wm

Give a Presentation Tell about your artist and
show a painting or self-portrait. Explain what
you like about the art.

Learn how to give an **oral presentation**.
See Handbook pages 374–376.

REACHING ALL STUDENTS

Multi-Level Strategies

OPTIONS FOR RESEARCHING A PORTRAIT ARTIST

Materials: index cards

BEGINNING Have students use index cards to organize their research.
Title the notecards: *The Artist's Work, About the Artist's Life, What I Like About
the Art.* Tell students to use these cards to take notes on key points. Model
for students, using Nancy Hom or George Littlechild.

INTERMEDIATE / **ADVANCED** To help organize students'
notetaking and reading, encourage them to create a K-W-L chart. In the first
column, they write what they know about the artist they have chosen. In the
second column they write simple questions they hope to answer. They
record what they learn from their research in the last column. Tell students
that it is important to determine how well their presentation matches the
needs of the audience. If students have selected an artist whose work is
familiar to the class, challenge them to present fresh ideas and images.

Just Me Prepare to Read Poetry

poem
by Margaret Hillert

OBJECTIVES

THINK ABOUT WHAT YOU KNOW
Reading Strategy:
Activate Prior Knowledge

LEARN KEY VOCABULARY ❶
Vocabulary Strategy:
Use New Words in Context

LEARN TO READ A RHYMING POEM
Reading Strategy:
Use Text Features in Poetry
Literary Analysis: Rhyme

THINK ABOUT WHAT YOU KNOW

Talk It Over Tell about a problem you had with someone. What did the other person think? Do people always see things the same way?

LEARN KEY VOCABULARY

Use New Words in Context Read the vocabulary words. Write new sentences that tell about you.

handwritten notes in left margin:
I — subject
me — object pronoun
my — possessive
myself — reflexive

All About Me

I can taste _____.	My eyes see _____.	I hear myself _____.
a salty peanut some sweet grapes	the blue sky green grass	sing a song talk loudly

LEARN TO READ A RHYMING POEM

When words **rhyme**, they have the same ending sounds. In a **rhyming poem**, the last words in some of the lines of the poem rhyme.

READING STRATEGY
How to Read a Rhyming Poem
1. Look at the end of each line. Which lines rhyme?
2. Read the poem out loud. Listen for rhyming words.
3. Picture what the poet says.
4. Read the poem again. Do you understand it? If not, read it again.

Read "Just Me." Listen for the rhyming words. Think about what the poem means.

Just Me **55**

THINK ABOUT WHAT YOU KNOW

1 **Talk It Over** Group students to discuss differences of opinion. Assign a recorder to write down answers. Reconvene to discuss group responses.

LEARN KEY VOCABULARY

2 **Use New Words in Context** Read aloud each vocabulary word and offer several examples of its use in context. Then work together to complete the chart.

▌ Use the Vocabulary Options in **Multi-Level Strategies** to help all students participate.

LEARN TO READ A RHYMING POEM

3 **Model How to Read a Rhyming Poem** Say: *When you hear the same sounds at the end of two or more words, we say they rhyme.* Demonstrate how to read a rhyming poem with **Transparency 13**.

• Read the first poem. Have students discuss the rhyme scheme.

• Have students choose rhyming words from the word bank to complete the second poem.

• Read the poem aloud, emphasizing the rhyme scheme.

CLOSE AND ASSESS

Ask: *How can you tell if a poem rhymes?* (Say aloud the words at the end of the lines to see if they have the same sounds.)

Multi-Level Strategies

VOCABULARY OPTIONS

BEGINNING As you work with the group, present images of concrete items that appeal to the senses (popcorn, music, a photograph) to prompt responses to complete the "All About Me" chart.

INTERMEDIATE / ADVANCED As you work with the group, ask students to use several descriptive words to complete the sentences on the chart. *I can taste [a juicy, green pickle]. I can see [a huge, dark cloud].* Invite them to share their responses with the class.

Transparency 13 / Master 13

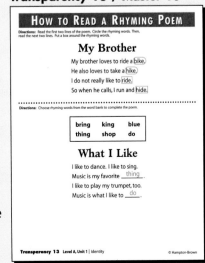

HOW TO READ A RHYMING POEM

Directions: Read the first two lines of the poem. Circle the rhyming words. Then, read the next two lines. Put a box around the rhyming words.

My Brother

My brother loves to ride a bike.
He also loves to take a hike.
I do not really like to ride.
So when he calls, I run and hide.

Directions: Choose rhyming words from the word bank to complete the poem.

bring	king	blue
thing	shop	do

What I Like

I like to dance. I like to sing.
Music is my favorite ___thing___.
I like to play my trumpet, too.
Music is what I like to ___do___.

Transparency 13 Level A, Unit 1 | Identity   © Hampton-Brown

Just Me **T55**

Just Me

Nobody sees what I can see,

For back of my eyes there is only me.

And nobody knows how my thoughts begin,

For there's only myself inside my skin.

—Margaret Hillert

back of my eyes in my mind
inside my skin inside me

56   Unit 1 | Identity

OBJECTIVES

Function: Read a Poem
Listening: Listen to a Poem
Reading Strategy: Set a Purpose for Listening; Use Text Features in Poetry
Literary Analysis: Rhyme; Rhyme Scheme

SET PURPOSE

1 Read aloud the title and invite students to look at the photo. Set the purpose for listening to the poem: *What is the poet saying about identity?*

LISTEN AND READ

Tape 1B
CD 1
Track 9

2 Strategy Focus: Use Text Features in Poetry Play "Just Me" on the **Selection Tape/CD**. Then play or read the poem again, pausing after each line to clarify meaning. Next, have pairs practice reading the poem aloud. Invite volunteers to signal each time they hear a rhyming word.

Choose Activity Options in the **Multi-Level Strategies** to tailor instruction to proficiency levels.

REACHING ALL STUDENTS

Multi-Level Strategies
ACTIVITY OPTIONS

BEGINNING Have students listen to the recording of "Just Me" on the **Selection Tape/CD**. Point out the *aabb* rhyme scheme. Pairs can practice reading the poem aloud, emphasizing the rhyming words by standing, turning, or raising their arms when they reach those words.

INTERMEDIATE / **ADVANCED** Read the poem aloud. Pause to clarify meaning. Define *rhyme scheme* (the pattern of rhyme). Group students to find the rhyme scheme of "Just Me" and to practice reading the poem aloud. Encourage individuals to write poems about themselves, using words they added to the chart on page 55. Have them incorporate the *aabb* rhyme scheme.

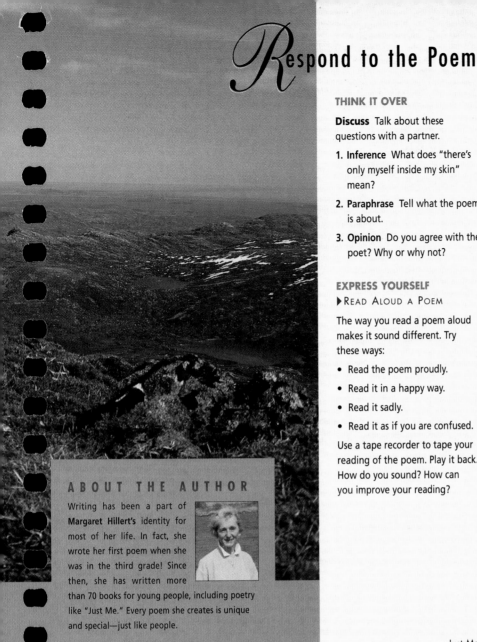

Respond to the Poem

THINK IT OVER

Discuss Talk about these questions with a partner.

1. **Inference** What does "there's only myself inside my skin" mean?

2. **Paraphrase** Tell what the poem is about.

3. **Opinion** Do you agree with the poet? Why or why not?

EXPRESS YOURSELF

▶ READ ALOUD A POEM

The way you read a poem aloud makes it sound different. Try these ways:

• Read the poem proudly.

• Read it in a happy way.

• Read it sadly.

• Read it as if you are confused.

Use a tape recorder to tape your reading of the poem. Play it back. How do you sound? How can you improve your reading?

ABOUT THE AUTHOR

Writing has been a part of **Margaret Hillert's** identity for most of her life. In fact, she wrote her first poem when she was in the third grade! Since then, she has written more than 70 books for young people, including poetry like "Just Me." Every poem she creates is unique and special—just like people.

Just Me **57**

Vocabulary
SENSORY WORDS

Demonstrate to students that everyone senses things in a unique way. Ask students to create the chart below using phrases that appeal to the five senses. Invite them to go outside for five minutes to complete the chart. Instruct them to do this on their own, without talking to anyone. When students return, have them share responses aloud as you create a comprehensive chart. Point out that the wide variety of responses shows that each person experiences life in a unique way.

What do I experience?

I see...	I hear...	I smell...	I touch...	I taste...
	kids playing		a dry leaf	

OBJECTIVES

THINK IT OVER
Function: Engage in Discussion
Reading Strategy: Paraphrase
Critical Thinking and Comprehension: Make Inferences; Form Opinions
EXPRESS YOURSELF
Speaking and Listening: Recite; Listen Actively
ABOUT THE AUTHOR
Literary Analysis: Respond to Literature

THINK IT OVER

3 Possible answers are:

1. **Inference** No one else can be me. No one sees things the same way that I see them.

2. **Paraphrase** The poem says that no one else is exactly like me. I have a unique identity. I'm the only one who can understand what goes on inside my mind.

3. **Opinion** Answers will vary.

EXPRESS YOURSELF

4 **Read Aloud a Poem** Tell students that careful preparation will ensure a good outcome. First, invite them to "get in the mood" they selected. Ask: *What do you say or how do you act when you feel this way?*

ABOUT THE AUTHOR

5 **Respond to Literature** After reading About the Author, remind students of poet Margaret Hillert's main message. (No one sees things the same way that I see them.) Encourage students to think about a time when they felt the same way. Have them do a quickwrite or draw an illustration to express that experience.

CLOSE AND ASSESS

Have students select the line from the poem that means the most to them. Ask: *Which line did you choose? Why?*

Just Me **T57**

OBJECTIVES

Function: Engage in Discussion
Viewing: Interpret a Visual Image
Critical Thinking: Classify
Writing: ❶ Descriptive (poem)

INTRODUCE WRITING THAT DESCRIBES

1 Discuss Descriptive Writing Read the introduction. Ask: *How can we "paint a picture" of this room in writing? What colorful details should we include?* Restate students' ideas in simple sentences.

2 Study the Models Ask: *What details in the poem describe John Wang?* Then make a chart of details students identify in Nancy Hom's work.

Writing	Portrait
soft	✻
strong, but can bend	✂

Use the Options for Studying Writing in the **Multi-Level Strategies** to adjust instruction.

CLOSE AND ASSESS

Ask students to agree on a summary sentence that defines descriptive writing.

Writing That Describes

A description paints a picture with words. The writer uses colorful details to help you "see" what someone or something is like.

WRITING MODELS

Look at the poem "Discovery." What words does John Wang use to describe himself?

from "Discovery"

> I discover more about myself every day.
> Up to now, I have discovered
> I am this kind of person:
> I am **intelligent.**
> I am **optimistic.**
> I am **positive.**

Look at Nancy Hom's description and portrait. They both show what she is like.

from "Art Smart"

> My artwork is very simple and graceful, with curves like the edges of clouds. I am like that—soft, gentle, quiet, but strong at the same time. I express my strength through bold colors and patterns. The portrait has leaves of bamboo in it because bamboo also comes from China. It is strong, but it can bend when it needs to, just like me.

A Self-Portrait by Nancy Hom

REACHING ALL STUDENTS

Multi-Level Strategies

OPTIONS FOR STUDYING DESCRIPTIVE WRITING

BEGINNING Define descriptive details as "words that tell how someone or something looks, feels, and acts." Help students paraphrase or restate the descriptive words in John Wang's poem, for example: *Intelligent means John is smart.* Ask them to find descriptive details in Nancy Hom's writing, and paraphrase or sketch them for the chart.

INTERMEDIATE In Nancy Hom's writing, focus on *I express my strength through bold colors and patterns.* Ask: *How do these words paint a picture of what Nancy Hom is like?*

ADVANCED Point out the comparisons in Hom's writing: *artwork... with curves like the edges of clouds; bamboo... strong, but it can bend when it needs to, just like me.* Encourage discussion of how the images paint a picture in words. Students can illustrate the comparisons to show what they mean.

Write Together

WRITING PROMPT

First write a class poem for someone in your school. Describe that person.

Plan the Poem Your poem will have five lines. Each line will answer one question. Here is a way you can plan the poem:

Line 1	**Who?**	Name of the person
Line 2	**What?**	What the person likes to do
Line 3	**Where?**	Where the person does the activity
Line 4	**When?**	When the person does the activity
Line 5	**Why?**	Why the person does the activity

2 Brainstorm Ideas Fill in a 5Ws chart. Look at the two examples.

3 Write the Poem Turn your answers into sentences for the poem.

STUDENT WRITING MODELS

Model 1

Nancy Hom
paints beautiful pictures
in San Francisco
every day.
She uses bright colors to show things she likes.

A good description uses colorful verbs and adjectives.

Model 2

Nancy Hom
loves the tall bamboo from China.
She paints it in her pictures
whenever she can
because it is strong like she is.

5Ws Chart

Who?	Nancy Hom
What?	draws pictures
Where?	in San Francisco
When?	every day
Why?	to show things she likes

5Ws Chart

Who?	Nancy Hom
What?	loves to paint bamboo
Where?	from China
When?	as often as she can
Why?	because it is strong like she is

Transparency 14 / Master 14

5WS CHART

Directions: Think about your topic. Answer each question.

Who? _____

What? _____

Where? _____

When? _____

Why? _____
_____
_____

Transparency 14 Level A, Unit 1 | Identity   © Hampton-Brown

Transparency 15 / Master 15

FEATURES OF DESCRIPTIVE WRITING

Directions: Read each Student Writing Model. Compare it to the features of the descriptive poem. Check the box if the model has the feature. Write the details.

A Descriptive Poem... _Model 1_

describes **someone** or **something**	☑ describes a person, Nancy Hom
give **details**, such as	
• what	☑ paints beautiful pictures, uses bright colors
• where	☑ San Francisco
• when	☑ every day
• why	☑ to show things she likes
• includes **colorful verbs** and **adjectives**	☑ paints; beautiful, bright

Transparency 15 Level A, Unit 1 | Identity   © Hampton-Brown

OBJECTIVES

Function: Write
Learning Strategies and Critical Thinking: Plan; Generate Ideas; Interact with Peers; Analyze and Evaluate Information
Writing: Class Poem

WRITE TOGETHER

Discuss the Writing Prompt First define *writing prompt* as "an instruction that tells you what kind of writing to do." Then read the prompt and ask volunteers to tell

- what kind of writing the class will do together (poem)
- what or whom the poem will be about (a person in our school)
- what the poem will do (describe the person).

Plan the Poem Work with students to choose a person they know and like as their subject. Go over the explanation of what will go on each line, and study the sample charts. Then fill out the 5Ws Chart on **Transparency 14** for the class poem.

Analyze and Evaluate Descriptions Display **Transparency 15**. Guide students in analyzing and evaluating the models against the features.

If students have difficulty finding a feature, have them look back at the sample 5Ws chart for the poem. The organization there may help them discover the feature.

Write the Class Poem Help students turn the answers on their 5Ws chart into a poem. Guide students in choosing colorful verbs and adjectives to express their ideas.

CLOSE AND ASSESS

Distribute copies of **Master 15** and have students work with partners or in small groups to analyze and evaluate your class poem against the features.

OBJECTIVES

PREWRITE

Function: Write

Learning Strategies and Critical Thinking: Plan; Generate Ideas; Interact with Peers; Organize Ideas; Self-Assess

Representing: Web; Chart

Writing: ❶ Writing Process

WRITE ON YOUR OWN

Read the prompt together. Have volunteers tell what kind of writing they will do, whom the poem should be about, and what the poem should do.

For more about the Writing Process, refer students to Handbook pages 382–389.

PREWRITE

Say: *Prewrite means "to make a plan before you write."* Students should first think of people they can write about. Then they will choose one person and plan the poem on a 5Ws chart.

▌ Use the Prewriting Support in the **Multi-Level Strategies** to tailor this stage to proficiency levels.

CLOSE AND ASSESS

Have partners answer the questions in Think About Your Writing.

Writing That Describes, continued

Write on Your Own

WRITING PROMPT

Now write your own poem for your classmates to read. Describe a friend or someone in your family.

PREWRITE

❶ **Choose a Person to Describe** Think about people you know. Write their names in a word web.

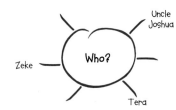

Uncle Joshua

Zeke

Who?

Tera

Choose one person to write about. This person is your **topic**.

❷ **Get Organized** Make a 5Ws chart about your topic.

5Ws Chart

Who?	Tera
What?	likes music
Where?	in her room
When?	all the time
Why?	makes her feel happy

To Get 💡 Ideas...

Try making a list. Name someone
- who makes you laugh
- likes the same things you do
- you admire or want to be like
- who does something unusual.

Think About Your Writing

- Are you happy with your topic?
- Do you have enough details to write about? Add more details if you need to.

Transparency 16 / Master 16

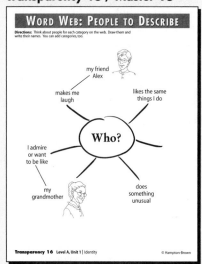

WORD WEB: PEOPLE TO DESCRIBE

Directions: Think about people for each category on the web. Draw them and write their names. You can add categories, too.

my friend Alex

makes me laugh

likes the same things I do

Who?

I admire or want to be like

my grandmother

does something unusual

Transparency 16 Level A, Unit 1 | Identity   © Hampton-Brown

Multi-Level Strategies

PREWRITING SUPPORT

BEGINNING **Transparency 16** lists the categories from "To Get Ideas." For each category, model listing people students know, drawing them and/or writing their names. Then distribute copies of **Master 16** and have students draw people on their webs. Assist them in writing the names. Next, have students circle the one person they will write about. Finally, guide them in filling out a 5Ws chart on copies of **Master 14**. (See page T59.)

INTERMEDIATE / ADVANCED Have partners brainstorm people for each category on **Master 16**. Encourage them to add categories and list people for those, too. Have students choose one person and fill out a 5Ws chart on **Master 14**. (See page T59.)

DRAFT

① Write Your Poem Use your notes to write sentences and phrases.

② Choose the Best Details Study these examples.

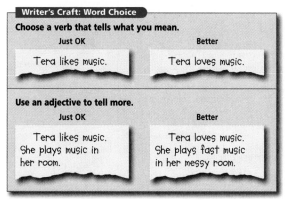

Writer's Craft: Word Choice

Choose a verb that tells what you mean.

Just OK	Better
Tera likes music.	Tera loves music.

Use an adjective to tell more.

Just OK	Better
Tera likes music. She plays music in her room.	Tera loves music. She plays fast music in her messy room.

Choose some words from these lists to help you say just what you mean.

Verbs

likes	laughs	moves	talks
enjoys	smiles	walks	shouts
appreciates	grins	runs	mumbles
loves	giggles	races	whispers
treasures	chuckles	dances	yells
		leaps	
		twirls	

Adjectives

pretty	good	big	strong
attractive	fine	large	tough
lovely	wonderful	huge	powerful
beautiful	super	enormous	mighty
gorgeous	excellent	gigantic	
	first-rate		

Painting is silent poetry, and poetry is painting that speaks.

— Simonedes, a poet in ancient Greece

Think About Your Writing

- Read your draft. Do you like the way it sounds?
- Did you choose the best details?

DRAFT

Function: ❶ Describe; Write

Learning Strategies and Critical Thinking: Generate Ideas; Self-Assess

Writer's Craft: ❶ Word Choice

Writing: ❶ Writing Process

DRAFT

Say: *When you draft, you write to get your ideas on paper. Do not worry about making your writing perfect.*

Study the Writer's Craft to help students include effective details in their writing. Read the examples and ask volunteers to point out the changes. Talk about why the new sentences are better.

Go over the word lists together. Use the words in sentences or act out the synonyms in each column to clarify meaning.

■ Use the Drafting Support in the **Multi-Level Strategies** to tailor this stage to proficiency levels.

For more about the Writer's Craft, refer students to Handbook pages 390–401.

CLOSE AND ASSESS

Have small groups discuss the questions in Think About Your Writing while you work with those who may need more support in assessing their drafts.

Multi-Level Strategies

DRAFTING SUPPORT

BEGINNING To draft their poems, students may need you to write the lines they dictate. If so, vocalize each word as you write it. Help students turn the lines of the 5Ws Chart, one at a time, into the lines of the poem. As students work, encourage them to use words from the lists on page 61.

INTERMEDIATE / ADVANCED Students can work with a partner to apply the Writer's Craft skill as they create the "Better" examples on **Master 17**. They should look up in a thesaurus the verbs and adjectives in the word lists on page 61 to find additional words to use in their writing. Have them record these words in the Word File.

Transparency 17 / Master 17

WRITING: WORD CHOICE

Directions: Read each writing tip and the example that is "Just Okay." Change the example to make it "Better."

Writing Tips	Just Okay	Better
Choose a verb that tells what you mean.	My sister went to South America.	My sister traveled to South America. My sister flew to South America.
Use an adjective to tell more.	She visited places.	She visited beautiful places. She visited exciting places.

Word File Directions: List colorful verbs and adjectives you can use in your writing.

Verbs	Adjectives

Transparency 17 Level A, Unit 1 | Identity   © Hampton-Brown

REVISE

Function: Write; Engage in Discussion

Learning Strategies and Critical Thinking: Generate Ideas; Review; Clarify; Interact with Peers; Self-Assess

Listening and Speaking: Peer-Conferencing

Technology and Media: Use Word-Processing Software

Writing: ❶ Writing Process

REVISE

Say: *When you revise, you decide on changes to make your writing clearer and more interesting.* Have students read their poems and think about possible changes.

Next, model how to participate in a peer conference. Also model how to make revisions. Then conduct peer conferences and have students revise their writing. If students are writing on a computer, demonstrate the revising steps illustrated on page 62.

▌ Use the Peer Conference Support in the **Multi-Level Strategies** to model how to evaluate and revise writing.

CLOSE AND ASSESS

Have peers discuss the questions in Think About Your Writing.

Writing That Describes, continued

REVISE

❶ **Read Your Poem** How does it sound?

❷ **Share Your Poem** Have your teacher or a friend read your poem. Ask:
- What do you like best about my poem?
- Did I give a good picture of the person?
- Do I need more colorful verbs or adjectives?

❸ **Make Your Changes** Think about the answers to your questions. Then make changes to your poem. Use the revising marks.

Sample of a Revised Line

dances   steady
Ricky ̶m̶o̶v̶e̶s̶ to the beat.

If you are on a computer, make changes like this.

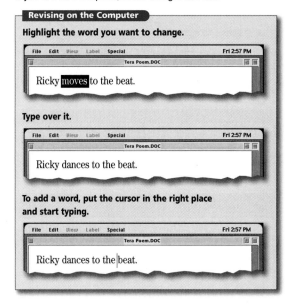

Revising on the Computer

Highlight the word you want to change.

| File | Edit | View | Label | Special | Fri 2:57 PM |

Tera Poem.DOC

Ricky [moves] to the beat.

Type over it.

| File | Edit | View | Label | Special | Fri 2:57 PM |

Tera Poem.DOC

Ricky dances to the beat.

To add a word, put the cursor in the right place and start typing.

| File | Edit | View | Label | Special | Fri 2:57 PM |

Tera Poem.DOC

Ricky dances to the|beat.

Revising Marks

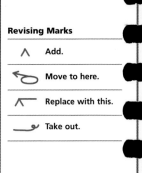

∧   Add.

↩   Move to here.

⤳   Replace with this.

⤶   Take out.

Think About Your Writing
- What words or details did you change?
- Did you make your poem better?

Transparency 18 / Master 18

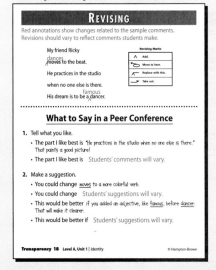

REVISING

Red annotations show changes related to the sample comments. Revisions should vary to reflect comments students make.

My friend Ricky
dances
̶m̶o̶v̶e̶s̶ to the beat.
He practices in the studio
when no one else is there.
famous
His dream is to be a dancer.

Revising Marks
∧ Add.
↩ Move to here.
⤳ Replace with this.
⤶ Take out.

What to Say in a Peer Conference

1. Tell what you like.
   - The part I like best is "He practices in the studio when no one else is there." That paints a good picture!
   - The part I like best is _____ Students' comments will vary.

2. Make a suggestion.
   - You could change _moves_ to a more colorful verb.
   - You could change _____ Students' suggestions will vary.
   - This would be better if you added an adjective, like _famous_, before _dancer_. That will make it clearer.
   - This would be better if _____ Students' suggestions will vary.

Transparency 18 Level A, Unit 1 | Identity   © Hampton-Brown

▌ # Multi-Level Strategies
PEER CONFERENCE SUPPORT

BEGINNING Display **Transparency 18**. Read the poem and support comprehension as needed: act out moving to a beat, sketch someone dancing alone, and/or paraphrase the ideas. Then model how to participate in a peer conference, noting that students should first tell what they like and then make suggestions. Use the sentence starters to develop appropriate language, and have volunteers dictate ways to complete each sentence. Then model how to revise the poem, based on the comments.

INTERMEDIATE / ADVANCED Distribute copies of **Master 18**. Read the poem. Use the sample comments to model how to participate in a peer conference. Have students write more comments of each type and share suggestions with the class. Students can then make revisions to the poem, based on the comments, and compare their changes.

GRAMMAR IN CONTEXT

SUBJECTS AND VERBS THAT AGREE

Every sentence has a subject and a verb. The subject and the verb must agree, or tell about the same number of people, places, or things.

> **Examples:** Tera **sing**s. Tera and Ricky **sing**.

Study these examples.

Tera

One	More Than One
I **love** music.	We **love** music.
You **love** music.	You **love** music.
Tera **love**s music.	The friends **love** music.
Ricky **love**s music.	They **love** music
The cat **love**s music.	The cats **love** music.

Tera and Ricky

- When you tell about **one other person or thing**, add **s** at the end of the verb.

  > **Examples:** Tera **love**s popular music.
  > This song **make**s her very happy.

- When you tell about **more than one other person or thing**, do <u>not</u> add **s** at the end of the verb.

  > **Examples:** Tera's friends **sing**, too.
  > They all **dance** to the music.

- When you tell about **yourself** or speak directly to another person, do <u>not</u> add **s** at the end of the verb.

  > **Examples:** I **listen** to music.
  > You **like** music, too.

Practice Write each sentence. Use the correct verb.
1. The Beetle Bug Boys ___play / plays___ great music.
2. I ___collect / collects___ tapes by the group.
3. My sister ___know / knows___ all the songs.
4. Sometimes we ___sing / sings___ along.
5. Then my parents ___cover / covers___ their ears!

Writing That Describes **63**

OBJECTIVES

GRAMMAR IN CONTEXT
Grammar: ① Subject-Verb Agreement

GRAMMAR IN CONTEXT

1 Teach Subject-Verb Agreement
Read the introduction and review the meaning of subject and verb: The subject of a sentence tells whom or what the sentence is about. The verb tells what the subject is, has, or does. Identify the subjects and verbs in the examples. Use the photos to focus students on the difference between singular and plural subjects. Read the rest of the rules aloud and discuss the examples. Then conduct the cooperative learning activity below.

2 Answers to Practice Items

1. play

2. collect

3. knows

4. sing

5. cover

CLOSE AND ASSESS

Assign students different third-person subjects, some singular, some plural. Ask them to write their subject with the form of the verb *smile* that agrees.

Cooperative Learning

FOR LANGUAGE DEVELOPMENT:
Subject-Verb Agreement

Match Subjects and Verbs Assign a verb to each of four groups: *write, run, sit, grin*. Display a chart of subjects: *I, we, Nancy Hom, Nancy Hom and John Wang, The poet, The poets*.

Groups should copy the chart and add the correct forms of their verb. In Think Time, individuals figure out which verb form to use. In Talk Time, groups agree on what to write. For Share Time, call on a different number to read the entry for each subject.

Debrief the Skill Ask: *What ending did you add to the verb that goes with Nancy Hom? When do you use the verb without that ending?*

Debrief the Cooperative Process
Have students reflect on how the activity worked out: *Did your group always agree on what the verb should be? If not, how did you decide what to write?*

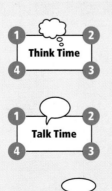

Cooperative Learning Structure:
Numbered Heads

Build Writing Skills **T63**

✓ **WRITING ASSESSMENT**
Use the Writing Rubric on page 12 of the Assessment
Handbook to evaluate this writing assignment.

BUILD WRITING SKILLS

OBJECTIVES

EDIT AND PROOFREAD

Learning Strategies and Critical Thinking: Review; Clarify; Self-Assess
Writing: ⊤ Writing Process

PUBLISH

Learning Strategies and Critical Thinking: Interact with Peers; Self-Assess; Make Decisions
Speaking: Read Aloud
Technology and Media: Use E-Mail
Writing: ⊤ Writing Process

EDIT AND PROOFREAD

Say: *When you edit, look for errors in spelling, capitalization, and punctuation. Then correct the errors and proofread, or check, your final copy.* Use **Transparency 19** to model the process.

PUBLISH

Say: *When you publish your writing, you put it in a form to be shared.* Have students choose from the publishing suggestions on page 64.

▌ Use the Editing and Publishing Support in the **Multi-Level Strategies** to adjust instruction.

CLOSE AND ASSESS

Have groups discuss the questions in Think About Your Writing. Monitor how students complete the checklist.

Writing That Describes, continued

EDIT AND PROOFREAD

① **Proofread Your Poem** Did you use a capital letter for the person's name? When you find a mistake, correct it. Use the Proofreading Marks.

② **Check Your Verbs** Do your subjects and verbs agree?

③ **Make a Final Copy** If you are working on a computer, print out the corrected copy of your work. If not, rewrite it and make the corrections you marked.

PUBLISH

Here are some ways to share your writing.

• Print your poem. Add a picture.

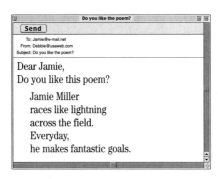

Debbi
cheers for the team
in the gym
every Friday.
She is an energetic person.

• Read your poem aloud. Don't tell the person's name. Can your classmates guess who it is?

• E-mail your poem to the person.

> **Do you like the poem?**
> **Send**
> To: Jamie@e-mail.net
> From: Debbie@usaweb.com
> Subject: Do you like the poem?
>
> Dear Jamie,
> Do you like this poem?
>
> Jamie Miller
> races like lightning
> across the field.
> Everyday,
> he makes fantastic goals.

Proofreading Marks

∧	Add.
⋏	Add a comma.
⊙	Add a period.
≡	Capitalize.
╱	Make lowercase.
⤴	Take out.
¶	Indent.

Think About Your Writing

• Do you like your poem?
  ☑ Does it describe a person?
  ☑ Does it tell who, what, where, when, and why?
  ☑ Are there colorful verbs and adjectives?
  ☑ Do the subjects and verbs agree?
• What do you like best about your poem? What do you like the least?
• Will this poem go in your portfolio? Why or why not?

REACHING ALL STUDENTS

Transparency 19 / Master 19

EDITING AND PROOFREADING

Directions: Read the poem. Check for errors in capitalization, spelling, and punctuation. Make sure the subjects and verbs agree. Correct the mistakes. Use the Proofreading Marks.

Jamie miller
races like litning
across the field.
Everyday,
he make fantastic goals.

Proofreading Marks

∧	Add.
⋏	Add a comma.
⊙	Add a period.
≡	Capitalize.
╱	Make lowercase.
⤴	Take out.
¶	Indent.

Transparency 19 Level A, Unit 1 | Identity   © Hampton-Brown

Multi-Level Strategies

EDITING AND PUBLISHING SUPPORT

BEGINNING Model finding and correcting errors in the poem on **Transparency 19**. After marking the edits, have students write out the corrected poem. For publishing, offer students who want to read their poem to the class a chance to practice with you first.

INTERMEDIATE Guide students in finding and correcting the errors in the poem on **Transparency 19**. For publishing, encourage students to practice their speaking skills by reading their poem to the group, in addition to publishing it in whatever other way they choose.

ADVANCED Distribute copies of **Master 19** and have students work on finding and correcting the errors individually or with partners. Have this group compile a book of class poems. They can write a short preface, telling about the class and the process they followed to write the poems.

Debrief A VERY Unique You

✓ **ASSESSMENT**
The Unit 1 Test on page 13 of the Assessment Handbook measures students' progress in reading, language arts, literary study, and writing.

1 Look Back at the Unit

Find Key Ideas In this unit, you read selections about unique people.

Discovery — **Could I Ask You a Question?** — **Many People, Many Intelligences** — **Art Smart**

Additional forms in the Assessment Handbook allow for
• Self Assessment on page 12
• Peer Assessment on page 101
• Portfolio Evaluation on page 103

Work with a group. Copy an important quote from each selection onto index cards. Trade cards with another group. Then talk about each quote. What does it say about identity?

2 Show What You Know

Sum It All Up Add important ideas about identity to the mind map. Share what you learned with a partner.

Reflect and Evaluate Write sentences to tell:
• what you learned about yourself
• what you learned about others

Put these sentences in your portfolio. Add work that shows what you learned about identity.

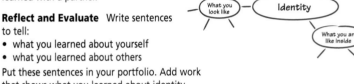

How you think

What you look like — **Identity**

What you are like inside

3 Make Connections

To Your School Make a class mural. Allow space for each student to show something unique and personal.

DEBRIEF UNIT 1

OBJECTIVES

Function: Engage in Discussion; Express Opinions

Learning Strategies and Critical Thinking: Interact with Peers; Generate Ideas; Make Judgments; Summarize; Self-Assess; Evaluate Information; Use Graphic Organizers (mind map)

Literary Analysis: Respond to Literature; Compare and Evaluate Literature

EXPLORE "A VERY UNIQUE YOU"

1 **Look Back at the Unit** Discuss criteria for choosing key quotes, for example: *Do they help me think about identity in new ways?* Then begin the Cooperative Learning Activity.

2 **Show What You Know** Encourage students to choose work that helped them understand their own identity.

3 **Make Connections** Together, plan the mural's organization, e.g. individual spots unified by a title.

CLOSE AND ASSESS

Have students tell you the most important thing they learned in the unit.

Cooperative Learning

FOR CRITICAL THINKING:
Relate to Personal Experience

Take Roles After discussing the criteria for choosing quotes, organize students into groups. Review the responsibilities of each role: Supervisor, Recorder, Reporter, and Checker.

Discuss Quotes Encourage students to consider how the ideas of the four quotes add up to a description of identity. Have each group's Reporter present that description to the class.

Debrief the Content Have students discuss what they learned about identity from the presentations. Help them begin by modeling your response: *I discovered that the way in which we learn is part of our identity.*

Debrief the Cooperative Process Ask students what they learned from the group activity: *Was the Checker able to find good quotes? If not, how did other group members help out?*

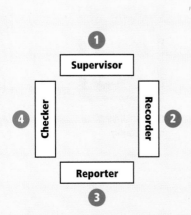

Roles for Cooperative Groups

Resources

For Success in Language, Literature, and Content

Student Book pages 66–121

For Skills Practice

Practice Book
pages 32–61

For Planning and Instruction

Teacher's Edition
pages T66a–T121

For Vocabulary and Language Development

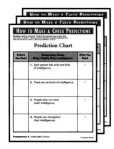

Language Tape Side A
Language CD Tracks 3 and 4

For Audio Walk-Throughs and Selection Readings

Selection Tape 2
Selection CD 2

For Technology Support

Inspiration
Visual Learning Software
with Graphic Organizers

For Classroom Activities

Transparencies or Masters 20–38

For Home-School Connections

High Point Newsletters 3 and 4

For Comprehensive Assessment

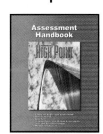

Language Acquisition Assessment,
Selection Tests, Unit Test, Writing
Assessment, Self-Assessment

In the Theme Library

Seven Blind Mice
by Ed Young

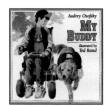

My Buddy
by Audrey Osofsky

From *The Basics Bookshelf*

▶ *A Year Without Rain*

▶ *Families*

▶ *More Than a Meal*

Theme-related books with
simple text for including
newcomers

UNITED, WE STAND

Ringling Brothers: Astounding Feat of Ernest Clark. Circus poster. Copyright ©1910.

EVERY DAY, EACH PERSON'S SURVIVAL DEPENDS ON TRUST, RESPONSIBILITY, AND COOPERATION. THIS UNIT INVITES STUDENTS, WHO ARE LEARNING TO BALANCE DEPENDENCE AND INDEPENDENCE IN THEIR OWN LIVES, TO EXPLORE THE RESULTS OF COOPERATION AND THE IMPORTANCE OF DEPENDABILITY.

THEME **1** **Pulling Together**

Students discover what can be accomplished through teamwork.

THEME **2** **Count on Me**

Students learn about people whose lives have depended on being able to count on others.

THEME 1: Pulling Together

LESSONS

1

THEME 1 OPENER			▶ pages T68–T69
Function Engage in Discussion	**Learning Strategy** Make a Data Chart	**Vocabulary** Words About Cooperation	**Critical Thinking** Relate to Personal Experience

2–8   *Teamwork* by Ann Morris   PHOTO-ESSAY ▶ pages T72–T79

BUILD LANGUAGE AND VOCABULARY pages T70–T71	**Function** ⊤ Engage in Discussion	**Learning Strategy** Listen and Represent Information	**Vocabulary** Pronouns	**Patterns and Structures** ⊤ Pronouns

PREPARE TO READ page T72	READ THE SELECTION pages T73–T76		RESPOND pages T77–T79		
Activate Prior Knowledge Role-Play	**Pre-Reading Strategies** Preview and Predict	📁 **Grammar Minilesson:** Count and Noncount Nouns	**CHECK YOUR UNDERSTANDING**	**LANGUAGE ARTS AND LITERATURE**	**CONTENT AREA CONNECTIONS**
Vocabulary ⊤ Use New Words in Context	Identify Genre: Photo-Essay Set Purpose		**Critical Thinking and Comprehension** Sum It Up: ⊤ Identify Main Ideas; ⊤ Add Details to a Paragraph	**Grammar in Context** ⊤ Use Subject Pronouns **Speaking/Listening** Play "Finish My Sentence"	**Social Studies** Make a Government Team Chart **Science** Study Wildlife Teams
Reading Strategy ⊤ Identify Main Ideas	**Strategy Focus** ⊤ Identify Main Ideas **Comprehension** Before You Move On: Think and Discuss		Think It Over: Discuss **Function** Express Yourself: Make Requests, Give and Accept Suggestions		

9–14   *Together, We Dream* by Francisco X. Alarcón   POEMS ▶ pages T82–T89

BUILD LANGUAGE AND VOCABULARY pages T80–T81	**Function** ⊤ Describe Events	**Learning Strategy** Listen and Take Notes	**Vocabulary** Pronouns	**Patterns and Structures** ⊤ Pronouns; Prepositions

PREPARE TO READ page T82	READ THE SELECTION pages T83–T87		RESPOND pages T88–T89	
Activate Prior Knowledge Match Dreams	**Pre-Reading Strategies** Preview and Predict Set Purpose	📁 **Grammar Minilesson:** Plural Nouns	**CHECK YOUR UNDERSTANDING**	**LANGUAGE ARTS AND LITERATURE**
Vocabulary ⊤ Use New Words in Context	**Strategy Focus** Visualize	📁 **Literary Analysis Minilesson:** Simile	**Critical Thinking and Comprehension** Sum It Up: Visualize; Make Comparisons	**Grammar in Context** Use Prepositional Phrases **Speaking/Listening** Memorize and Recite Poetry
Reading Strategy Visualize	**Comprehension** Before You Move On: Think and Discuss		Think It Over: Discuss **Function** Express Yourself: Describe Events	**Representing/ Speaking** Create a Multimedia Photo-Essay

THEME 2: Count on Me

PACING SUGGESTIONS

LESSONS	45–55 MINUTE PERIODS	BLOCK SCHEDULE SESSIONS
1	1 period	
2–8	7 periods	4 sessions
9–15	6 periods	3 sessions

LESSONS 1

THEME 2 OPENER ▶ *pages T90–T91*

Function	Learning Strategy	Vocabulary	Critical Thinking
Engage in Discussion	Make a Chart	Words About Cooperation	Generate Ideas

2–8

A Dog You Can Count On by Caroline Arnold ARTICLE ▶ *pages T94–T101*

BUILD LANGUAGE AND VOCABULARY pages T92–T93	Function ⊤ Give Directions	Learning Strategy Interact with Peers	Vocabulary Pronouns	Patterns and Structures ⊤ Commands; ⊤ Pronouns

PREPARE TO READ
page T94

Activate Prior Knowledge
Make a Class Web

Vocabulary ⊤
Relate Words

Reading Strategy ⊤
Ask Questions and Clarify

READ THE SELECTION
pages T95–T98

Pre-Reading Strategies
Preview and Predict

Set Purpose

Strategy Focus ⊤
Ask Questions and Clarify

Comprehension
Before You Move On:
Think and Discuss

📁 **Grammar Minilesson:** ⊤
Possessive Pronouns

RESPOND
pages T99–T101

CHECK YOUR UNDERSTANDING

Critical Thinking and Comprehension
Sum It Up:
⊤ Identify Steps in a Process;
⊤ Make a Prediction

Think It Over: Discuss

Function
Express Yourself: Ask and Answer Questions

LANGUAGE ARTS AND LITERATURE

Grammar in Context ⊤
Use Object Pronouns

Writing
Write a Thank-You Letter

CONTENT AREA CONNECTIONS

Science
Study Human and Animal Teams

Science and Technology/Media
Research Blindness

9–15

A Mountain Rescue by James Ramsey Ullman STORY ▶ *pages T104–T113*

BUILD LANGUAGE AND VOCABULARY pages T102–T103	Function ⊤ Ask for and Give Information	Learning Strategy Brainstorm and Represent Information	Vocabulary Survival Words	Patterns and Structures ⊤ Questions; Statements

PREPARE TO READ
page T104

Activate Prior Knowledge
Talk It Over

Vocabulary ⊤
Use New Words in Context

Reading Strategy ⊤
Identify Problems and Solutions

READ THE SELECTION
pages T105–T110

Pre-Reading Strategies
Preview and Predict

Set Purpose

Strategy Focus ⊤
Identify Problems and Solutions

Self-Monitoring and Comprehension
Visualize

Before You Move On:
Think and Discuss

📁 **Grammar Minilessons:**
Reflexive Pronouns

Possessive Nouns

RESPOND
pages T111–T113

CHECK YOUR UNDERSTANDING

Critical Thinking and Comprehension
Sum It Up:
⊤ Identify Problems and Solutions;
Summarize

Think It Over: Discuss

Function
Express Yourself:
Ask for and Give Information

LANGUAGE ARTS AND LITERATURE

Grammar in Context ⊤
Use Subject and Object Pronouns

Writing/Speaking
Extend the Story

CONTENT AREA CONNECTIONS

Social Studies
Explore Geography (map, fact sheet)

Social Studies and Technology/Media
Compare Mountains

BUILD WRITING SKILLS

WRITING THAT INFORMS AND EXPLAINS EXPOSITORY: SUMMARY ▶ *pages T114–T120*

Writing Mode/Form ⊤ Expository	Writing Process ⊤	Writer's Craft ⊤	Grammar in Context ⊤	Reflect and Evaluate
Summary	Prewrite Draft Revise Edit and Proofread Publish	Word Choice	Pronouns	Self-Assessment

⊤ = Assessed on **Unit 2 Test**   ⊤ = Assessed on **Unit 2 Language Acquisition Assessment**

THEME 1: Pulling Together

MORE RESOURCES

Seven Blind Mice
by Ed Young
B In this award-winning book, seven blind mice must work together to solve a riddle. (Available from Hampton-Brown)

Raising Yoder's Barn
by Jane Yolen
I When lightning strikes Yoder's barn, the whole Amish community comes to help. (Little, Brown & Co.)

All for the Better: A Story of El Barrio
by Nicholasa Mohr
A An award-winning author tells the story of how a young girl shows her community the importance of working together. (Steck-Vaughn)

Ant Cities
by Arthur Dorros
B This easy to read book uses text and illustrations to explain the interdependent community of ants. (Ty Crowell Co.)

The Three Musketeers
by Alexandre Dumas (abridged by Joan Cameron)
I An adaptation of the classic story of teamwork, friendship, and loyalty. (Ladybird Books)

Sounder
I **A** This beautifully written film recounts the difficulties faced by an African American family in rural Louisiana during the depression and how the family pulls together in order to survive. **Film/Video**

THEME 2: Count on Me

MORE RESOURCES

My Buddy
by Audrey Osofsky
I A boy who uses a wheelchair counts on Buddy, his service dog, to help him in many ways. Buddy even goes to school! (Available from Hampton-Brown)

It's Mine!
by Leo Lionni
B In this fable, three selfish frogs learn an important lesson after they count on each other to survive a frightening storm. (Dragonfly)

Rikki-Tikki-Tavi
by Rudyard Kipling, adapted and illustrated by Jerry Pinkney
A In this version of a classic story, a mongoose saves the family that saved its life. (William Morrow & Co.)

Ten True Animal Rescues
by Jeanne Betancourt
I **A** Ten stories about animals who saved the lives of their owners or complete strangers. (Little Apple)

Julie of the Wolves
by Jean Craighead George
A An Eskimo girl stranded on the Alaskan tundra depends on her culture and a wolf pack to survive. (HarperCollins)

Black Stallion
B **I** **A** Mickey Rooney stars in this classic tale of a boy and a wild horse. Together they survive a shipwreck, forge bonds of friendship and go on to exciting adventures. **Film/Video**

ONGOING, INFORMAL ASSESSMENT

Check for understanding and achieve closure for every lesson with the targeted questions and activities in the **Close and Assess** boxes in your Teacher's Edition.

INDIVIDUAL AND GROUP-ADMINISTERED TESTS

The **Assessment Handbook** includes these comprehensive assessment tools for Unit 2:

▶ **Selection Tests**
Test students' mastery of reading strategies and the vocabulary, comprehension, and language arts skills taught with each main selection of Unit 2.

▶ **Unit Test in Standardized Test Format**
The multiple-choice sections of this test measure students' cumulative understanding of the skills and language developed in Unit 2. A Writing Prompt measures progress in writing skills and fluency. The Read, Think, and Explain section offers open-ended items to measure strategies and comprehension.

▶ **Language Acquisition Assessment**
To verify students' ability to use the vocabulary and grammar structures taught in Unit 2, conduct these performance assessments.

UNIT 2 ASSESSMENT OPPORTUNITIES	Assessment Handbook Pages
Unit 2 Language Acquisition Assessment	21–22
Selection Tests	
Teamwork	23–24
Together, We Dream	25–26
A Dog You Can Count On	27–28
A Mountain Rescue	29–30
Unit 2 Writing Assessment	31
Unit 2 Self-Assessment Form	32
Unit 2 Test	33–40
Peer-Assessment Form	101
Portfolio Evaluation Form	103

SELF- AND PEER-ASSESSMENT

Students use the Unit 2 Self-Assessment Form in the **Assessment Handbook** to evaluate their own work and develop learning strategies appropriate to their needs. Students offer feedback to their classmates with the Peer-Assessment Form.

WRITING ASSESSMENT / PORTFOLIO OPPORTUNITIES

You can evaluate students' writing using the rubrics and scoring guidelines provided in the **Assessment Handbook**. Then collaborate with students to choose work for their portfolios.

OBJECTIVES

Function: Engage in Discussion
Concepts and Vocabulary:
Cooperation—*depend on, count on, cooperate, teamwork*
Viewing: Interpret a Visual Image
Learning Strategies and Critical Thinking: Preview; Build Background; Activate Prior Knowledge; Use Graphic Organizers (mind map)

INTRODUCE UNIT CONCEPT

1 **View the Circus Poster** Read the unit title and the text on the poster. Ask: *Why do the trapeze artists need to cooperate?* Elicit that they must cooperate to prevent a fall.

2 **Practice Cooperating and Build Vocabulary** Have students try the cooperation activity, and then discuss the importance of cooperation in daily life. Tell students: *When you cooperate with someone, you work together to do something. When you depend on someone, you cannot do something unless someone else helps.* Brainstorm situations where people cooperate with and depend on one another; record ideas on **Transparency 20**.

▌ Use the Vocabulary Options in the **Multi-Level Strategies** to work with all proficiency levels.

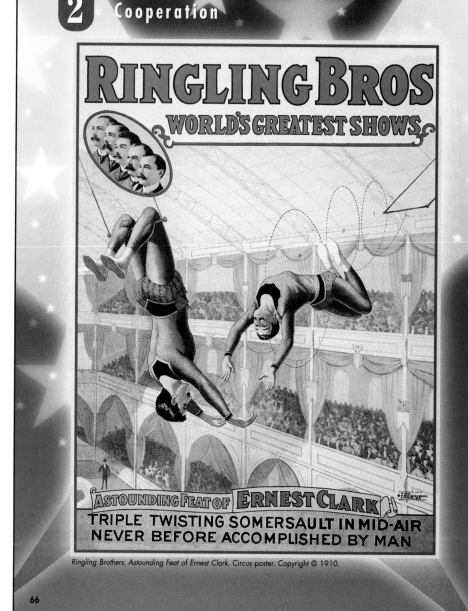

UNIT
2 Cooperation

RINGLING BROS
WORLD'S GREATEST SHOWS

ASTOUNDING FEAT OF ERNEST CLARK
TRIPLE TWISTING SOMERSAULT IN MID-AIR
NEVER BEFORE ACCOMPLISHED BY MAN

Ringling Brothers: Astounding Feat of Ernest Clark. Circus poster. Copyright © 1910.

66

REACHING ALL STUDENTS

Transparency 20 / Master 20

HOW WE COOPERATE			
Directions: List the ways you cooperate with others. Then list the ways you depend on others. Choose one of the ways. Talk about your idea with a partner.			
We Cooperate with Others		**We Depend on Others**	
Who?	How?	Who?	How?

Transparency 20 Level A, Unit 2 | Cooperation   © Hampton-Brown

Multi-Level Strategies
VOCABULARY BUILDING OPTIONS

BEGINNING To help students understand the difference between *cooperating with* and *depending on,* use the example of an infant: *An infant cannot cooperate with her parents, but she depends on them to take care of her.* As you build **Transparency 20**, use prompts to elicit information: *Who do you depend on in your family? Do you depend on your parents for food? How do you cooperate at school?* etc.

INTERMEDIATE Work with students to expand language, using ideas collected on **Transparency 20**. Ask: *How do you depend on others? How do you help at home? How do you cooperate on group projects at school?*

ADVANCED Ask students to discuss whether the trapeze artists cooperate, depend on each other, or both. Have them write a paragraph to explain their answer.

UNITED, WE STAND

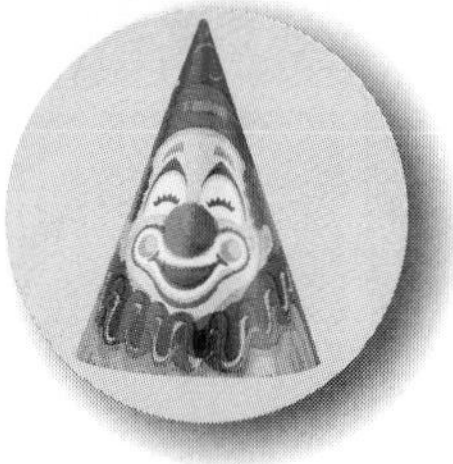

The acrobats in this poster depend on each other for their safety. What is it like to count on someone else? Try this: With a partner, sit back-to-back and link elbows. Now work together to stand. What happens if one partner doesn't cooperate? How does it feel to depend on someone else?

THEME 1 **Pulling Together**
When people pull together to get the job done, that's called teamwork.

THEME 2 **Count on Me**
Sometimes, our lives depend on being able to count on others.

67

UNIT 2 Mind Map

Cooperation

Looks Like	Sounds Like	Feels Like
playing on a team	offering to help	you are not alone
sitting around a table together	discussing a project	people can count on you

Technology Support
See **Inspiration** Visual Learning software for support in creating mind maps.

3 Discuss Cooperation Discuss answers to these questions:

- What happened when you sat back-to-back with your partner and tried to get up?
- How does it feel when you need to depend on another?
- What happens when you are not able to depend on another?

Summarize: *In day-to-day life, we need to depend on others in many ways. We need to cooperate with others and be dependable and trustworthy ourselves.*

PREVIEW UNIT THEMES

4 Preview Theme 1: Pulling Together Read aloud the theme title and the theme statement. Define *teamwork* as "people working together for the same goal."

Invite students to look over pages 68–89. Discuss photographs and illustrations that show examples of cooperation and teamwork.

5 Preview Theme 2: Count on Me Read the theme title and statement. Tell students they will learn how important it can be to depend and count on others. Invite them to look over pages 90–113 to find examples that show that sometimes your life depends on others.

6 Create a Mind Map Begin a class mind map on *Cooperation* and have students start a personal map in their notebooks or in the **Practice Book**. As you work through the unit, encourage students to continue to add to their mind maps.

▶ **Practice Book** page 32

CLOSE AND ASSESS

Ask:

- *What will this unit be about?* (cooperation)
- *What are some ways we cooperate with others?* (helping at home; working in groups at school)
- *What happens when we do not cooperate with others?* (It feels bad; it is more difficult to get things done.)

INTRODUCE THEME 1

OBJECTIVES

Function: ❶ Engage in Discussion
Concepts and Vocabulary:
Cooperation—*teammates, teamwork*
Viewing: Respond to a Photograph
**Learning Strategies and Critical
Thinking:** Preview; Build Background;
Relate to Personal Experience;
Use Graphic Organizers (data chart);
Draw Conclusions; Generate Ideas

TAP PRIOR KNOWLEDGE

1 *Teamwork* **Twenty Questions**
Remind students that *teamwork*
means "pulling together as a group
to accomplish a goal." Have small
groups choose an activity requiring
teamwork. Then groups take turns
answering classmates' questions: *Do
you pass a ball in this activity? Is this a
game you play outdoors?*

VIEW AND DISCUSS

2 **Draw Conclusions** Have students
look at the photograph on page 68.
Ask: *Is teamwork important in
basketball? Why?* Ask students to
identify activities they enjoy.
Record responses on a chart. Prompt
students to draw conclusions from
the data, for example: *Some activities
are done alone, while others
require teamwork.*

Activity	How Many People?	Team?
softball	9	Yes
chess	2	Sometimes
play guitar	1	No

3 **Identify Team Member Roles** Have
students work in small groups to
choose any of the kinds of teams
pictured on pages 66–76. The groups
should identify and discuss the
distinct roles performed by each
member of the team.

> Use the Activity Options in the
> **Multi-Level Strategies** to work
> with all proficiency levels.

68 Unit 2 | Cooperation

REACHING ALL STUDENTS

Multi-Level Strategies
ACTIVITY OPTIONS

BEGINNING Have students draw a picture to illustrate the role of each
team member in the team they have chosen. Provide sentence frames to
help students express these roles: *This person is called a _____. It is his/her
job to _____. He/She is important because _____.*

INTERMEDIATE Have students discuss the individual roles of the members
of their chosen group. Each student should then be assigned one of these
roles to act out in a group role-play to be performed in front of the class.

ADVANCED Have students do research to learn about the individual
roles of the members of the team they have chosen. Have students present
their findings in a short oral report. Encourage them to include an
explanation of how the roles are interrelated and what would happen to the
team without any one of its members.

Pulling Together

- How do teammates work together to get a job done?

- Why is it important for every team member to do his or her part?

- When is working as a team easier than working alone?

THEME-RELATED BOOKS

Seven Blind Mice
by Ed Young

In this award-winning book, seven blind mice must work together to solve a riddle.

BEGINNING

Raising Yoder's Barn
by Jane Yolen

When lightning strikes Yoder's barn, the whole Amish community comes to help.

INTERMEDIATE

NOVEL

**All for the Better:
A Story of El Barrio**
by Nicholasa Mohr

An award-winning author tells the story of how a young girl shows her community the importance of working together.

ADVANCED

69

DISCUSS THE GUIDING QUESTIONS

4 Set the Theme Some key points to develop during the discussion are:

- Teams work together toward a common goal. Members rely on one another but also work to compensate for any weaknesses of other players. Each player does his or her job with an understanding of how it affects the rest of the team.

- Teams are structured in such a way that each player fulfills a certain need on the team. Each part is necessary for the team to function effectively.

- There are tasks that no one person can do alone; they require the participation of several people. Often, these tasks are complex, and the necessary skills might be represented by several people. This is especially true when there are actions that must be performed simultaneously.

▐ Form groups and use the **Multi-Level Strategies** so all students can participate.

CLOSE AND ASSESS

Have students draw a picture of an object representing a particular team sport, then write a word or words inside the object about teamwork.

Multi-Level Strategies

GROUPING GUIDELINES

BEGINNING To help students focus on the guiding questions, choose examples from the words and ideas students suggested for **Transparency 20**. (See page T66.) Ask: *How do teammates work together in ESL class?* Restate student responses in complete sentences: *We study new words together*, etc.

INTERMEDIATE / **ADVANCED** Have students work in groups to answer the guiding questions. Then, invite groups to choose one question and write a paragraph to elaborate on the answers.

■ *Seven Blind Mice* by Ed Young

The selections in Theme 1 of Unit 2 include a nonfiction photo-essay and a collection of poems. *Seven Blind Mice* is a fable. Ask students to compare how the theme of cooperation or pulling together is conveyed in each of these literary forms. Ask: *What do you learn about working together when you read a photo-essay? What do you learn when you read about teamwork in poems or a fable? Which do you prefer? Why?*

BUILD LANGUAGE AND VOCABULARY

OBJECTIVES

Function: ❶ Engage in Discussion; Listen Actively

Concepts and Vocabulary: Pronouns

Patterns and Structures: ❶ Pronouns

Speaking: Discussion

Viewing: Respond to a Photograph; Interpret Visual Information

Learning Strategies: Use Graphic Organizers (word web, category chart)

Critical Thinking: Draw Conclusions; Classify

START WITH A COMMON EXPERIENCE

1 View and Describe View the photograph, encouraging students to describe the various elements they see. Read the saying with them, and ask them to think about how it relates to the photograph.

2 Explain How to Engage in a Discussion Read Handbook page 373 with students to review guidelines for successful group discussions. Summarize the key points:

How to Engage in Discussion

• Wait to be recognized to make comments and ask questions.

• Listen while others speak.

• Focus on the topic of discussion.

• Respect other opinions.

3 Discuss the Saying You may want to use a roundtable cooperative technique to discuss the saying. Have students number off within a group. Ask: *What do you think the saying means?* Each student contributes ideas in turn, going around the table in the numbered order.

▌ Use the Questioning Techniques in the **Multi-Level Strategies** to involve all students.

Build Language and Vocabulary
ENGAGE IN DISCUSSION

Study the photographs and read the saying. What do you think it means?

Many hands make light work.

—*Traditional saying*

REACHING ALL STUDENTS

Multi-Level Strategies
QUESTIONING TECHNIQUES

BEGINNING   Act out trying to do something by yourself, such as move a piece of furniture or lift a heavy weight. Then have several students join you in the task. Ask: *Could I move the desk myself? Which was easier for me, working alone or working with help?* Summarize: *When I worked with other people, the job was easier.*

INTERMEDIATE   Have students identify the value to the farmers of building a barn together. *How long might it take for one man to build a barn by himself? How long do you think it takes for a group of people to build a barn? What can the group do that one person alone cannot do?*

ADVANCED   Encourage students to give examples from their lives when other people's help made a task easier. *How did you feel when the job was done? How do you think the people in the photo felt when they finished?*

LISTEN TO A DESCRIPTION

Listen to a description of the picture on page 70. Then listen again for all the words that name people. Make a web.

men

Males — People — Females

carpenter

women

BUILD YOUR VOCABULARY

Pronouns You can use the words in the chart to tell who does something.

In your web, replace the words that name people with pronouns from the chart.

Subject Pronouns

One Person	More Than One Person	Examples
I	We	I listen to the tape. We listen to the tape.
you	you	You look at the picture.
he, she, it	they	He works hard. They work hard.

USE LANGUAGE STRUCTURES ▶ PRONOUNS

Speaking: Draw and Discuss Draw a picture to illustrate one of these traditional sayings. They tell about people working together.
- Two heads are better than one.
- There is strength in numbers.

Form a group with others who illustrated the same saying. Discuss the saying and your pictures. Use pronouns.

Example:
The friends are working on a hard math problem. **He** is dividing and **she** is subtracting. **They** work together to solve the problem.

Build Language and Vocabulary **71**

CONDUCT THE ACTIVITIES

4 Listen to a Description Tape 1A / CD 1 Track 3
Play the **Language Tape/CD** or read aloud the script on page T381. Have students create word webs. Invite them to share and compare their webs.

5 Build Your Vocabulary: Pronouns
Present the skill, using the definition and examples in **Transparency 21**. Stress that *I*, *he*, *she*, and *it* are used for one person, place, or thing; *we* and *they* are used for more than one; and *you* refers to both one and more than one person. Then have students complete the sentences in Try It!

6 Use Language Structures: Pronouns Remind students to use what they have learned about pronouns.

Speaking: Draw and Discuss Conduct the activity. Remind students to follow the Discussion Guidelines on page 373 in the Handbook.

Use the Speaking Activity Options in the **Multi-Level Strategies** to adjust instruction.

▶ **Practice Book** page 33

CLOSE AND ASSESS

Have students work in Think, Pair, Share or small buzz groups to come up with one sentence that summarizes what they learned in the lesson. Each group dictates a sentence for you to write.

Multi-Level Strategies
SPEAKING ACTIVITY OPTIONS

BEGINNING / INTERMEDIATE Let Beginning students work with more fluent partners to create oral descriptions of their pictures. Within a group, students ask each other questions about how their pictures relate to the saying. Encourage students to use pronouns to refer to the people pictured: *Who is this? What is she doing? How are they helping each other?*

ADVANCED After working on the activity, have students work in pairs to create their own sayings about people working together. Have them draw a new illustration and label it with their saying.

Transparency 21 / Master 21

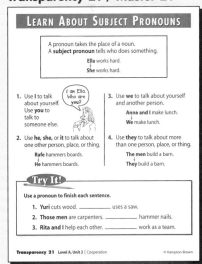

LEARN ABOUT SUBJECT PRONOUNS

A pronoun takes the place of a noun.
A **subject pronoun** tells who does something.

Ella works hard.
She works hard.

1. Use **I** to talk about yourself. Use **you** to talk to someone else. *I am Ella. Who are you?*

2. Use **he, she,** or **it** to talk about one other person, place, or thing.
   Rafe hammers boards.
   He hammers boards.

3. Use **we** to talk about yourself and another person.
   Anna and I make lunch.
   We make lunch.

4. Use **they** to talk about more than one person, place, or thing.
   The men build a barn.
   They build a barn.

Try It!

Use a pronoun to finish each sentence.

1. **Yuri** cuts wood. _____ uses a saw.
2. Those **men** are carpenters. _____ hammer nails.
3. **Rita and I** help each other. _____ work as a team.

Transparency 21 Level A, Unit 2 | Cooperation   © Hampton-Brown

Build Language and Vocabulary **T71**

PREPARE TO READ

OBJECTIVES

THINK ABOUT WHAT YOU KNOW
Reading and Learning Strategies:
Activate Prior Knowledge;
Relate to Personal Experience

LEARN KEY VOCABULARY 🟢
Vocabulary Strategy: Use New Words
in Context

LEARN TO IDENTIFY MAIN IDEAS
Reading Strategy: 🟢 Identify Main Ideas

THINK ABOUT WHAT YOU KNOW

1 **Role-Play** Give groups a few moments to brainstorm. Remind them that they can use activities mentioned during the theme introduction.

LEARN KEY VOCABULARY

2 **Use New Words in Context** Read aloud the key vocabulary words and defining sentences. Then conduct the sentence-writing activity.

▌ Use the Vocabulary Options in **Multi-Level Strategies** to tailor instruction to proficiency levels.

▶ **Practice Book** page 34

LEARN TO IDENTIFY MAIN IDEAS

3 **Model How to Identify Main Ideas** Define *main ideas* and *key words.* Demonstrate the steps in the box with **Transparency 22**:

- Read aloud the text. Record key words on **Transparency 22**.

- Work with students to use the key words to identify the most important idea. Tell students this is the main idea.

CLOSE AND ASSESS

Ask students to vote on the best response to this question: *How do you identify main ideas?* (look for key words)

TEAMWORK **P**repare to Read

photo-essay
by Ann Morris

THINK ABOUT WHAT YOU KNOW

Role-Play Work with a group. Act out a job that is easier when people work together. Can your classmates guess what it is?

LEARN KEY VOCABULARY

Use New Words in Context Study the new words. Work with a partner to write sentences about team members. Use the new words.

> • Team members care for each other.
> • They cooperate to get a job done.

care for People can **care for** each other by loving and helping each other.

cooperate You **cooperate** when you work together.

depend on You **depend on** things or people that you need.

member A **member** is someone who is part of a group.

plan You **plan** when you think about how to do something before you do it.

proud You feel **proud** when you are happy about something you did well.

solve problems When you **solve problems**, you find answers.

team A **team** is a group that works together.

Possible answers to the vocabulary activity:
· Team members depend on each other.
· They plan what to do.
· They are proud of their work.
· They solve problems together.

LEARN TO IDENTIFY MAIN IDEAS

Key words tell about the most important ideas in a selection. Look for key words as you read. They will help you understand the **main ideas**.

READING STRATEGY
How to Identify Main Ideas

1. Read one part of the selection. Write two or three key words.
2. Look at the key words. Ask yourself: What is the most important idea?
3. Write the main idea.
4. Repeat the steps as you read.

Now read "Teamwork." Find key words that tell the main ideas of the photo-essay.

REACHING ALL STUDENTS

▌ **Multi-Level Strategies**
VOCABULARY OPTIONS

BEGINNING / **INTERMEDIATE** Have students form two teams. Give each group a set of cards with key vocabulary and cards with definitions. Have the two teams compete to see who can match the words and definition first. Then, ask yes/no questions: *Were you a member of a team? Did team members cooperate? Were you able to solve problems? Were you proud to win?* Encourage students to answer in complete sentences, using the new words.

ADVANCED Have students brainstorm and list some things that team members do and then use these ideas to write the sentences.

Transparency 22 / Master 22

HOW TO IDENTIFY MAIN IDEAS

Directions: Read the sentences. Identify the key words and the important ideas. Record your ideas on the chart below.

Every member of a team has a special job to do. That's how people work in teams. Honeybees work that way, too.
The queen bee's job is to lay eggs. The job of the drone bees is to mate with the queen. The other bees in the hive are all workers.
There are more workers than any other type of bee in the hive. Some work outside in the field, and some work inside the hive.

Key Words	Important Ideas
every member of a team, special job, honeybees	Honeybees do special jobs on teams.
queen lays eggs, drones mate with queen, rest are workers	The queen lays eggs, the drones mate with the queen, and the other bees are workers.
most bees are workers, work outside, work inside	Most of the bees are workers. They can work inside or outside the hive.

Transparency 22 Level A, Unit 2 | Cooperation © Hampton-

TEAMWORK
by Ann Morris

In this photo-essay, Ann Morris shows how people all over the world work together to get things done.

73

INTRODUCE THE SELECTION

4 Preview and Predict Read with students the title, author, and introduction to the photo-essay on page 73. Discuss the photos and then look through the selection. Ask: *What do you think this selection will be about?*

5 Identify Genre: Photo-Essay Tell students that when a writer offers personal ideas about a topic, it is called an essay. An essay heavily illustrated with photographs is called a photo-essay. Discuss reasons an author might choose to use photos to help deliver the message.

6 Audio Walk-Through Play the Audio Walk-Through for "Teamwork" on the **Selection Tape/CD** to give students the overall idea of the story.

Tape 2A
CD 2
Track 1

Teamwork
by Ann Morris

Theme Connection This photo-essay explores the ways in which a variety of teams pull together to solve problems and accomplish goals.

Selection Summary and Awards This selection looks at teams in a variety of contexts—from sports teams to teams of animals, and from the teams that work together on the job to those that cooperate at home. *Teamwork* by Ann Morris has won the NCSS Notable Book (1995), the Child Study Association Award (1994), and the ALA Notable Award (1992).

THE BASICS BOOKSHELF

■ *A Year Without Rain* by Evelyn Stone

This story, set in ancient China, tells how a community pools its resources so all can eat in a time of drought. Beautiful art supports the patterned text, "The children come first . . . Each gives one bowl of rice. The monks come second . . . " and so on. The sequential presentation of numerals and ordinals increase access to number vocabulary for beginning English learners.

For Lesson Plans: See the Teacher's Guide for *The Basics Bookshelf*.

Teamwork **T73**

OBJECTIVES

Function: Read a Selection
Concepts and Vocabulary: Cooperation
Grammar: Count and Noncount Nouns
Listening: Listen to a Selection
Viewing: Respond to Photographs
Reading and Learning Strategies:
Set a Purpose for Reading;
❶ Identify Main Ideas;
Use Graphic Organizers (T-chart)
Comprehension: Identify Details;
Relate to Personal Experience

SET PURPOSE

1 Say: *Read to find out about different kinds of teams arou~~nd~~...*

READ AND T...

2 Strategy Focu...
Main Ideas A...
have them iden...
important ideas...
on **Transparenc...**

> Choose Readi...
> **Multi-Level S...**
> the reading to...

The recording of "...
Selection Tape/CD...
language model an...
to build reading flue...

[handwritten note:] Note taking chart — "A gear w/o rain

Red annotations offer opportunities to clarify meaning and check for understanding.

A **team** is a group that works together or plays together.

Team **members cooperate** to **get the job done.** That's called *teamwork.*

A team can be just a few or a team can be many.

Even animals can work in teams.

Use visuals: Pause to look at the photos. Ask students to point out the team of animals.

get the job done do something together, finish the work

74 Unit 2 | Cooperation

REACHING ALL STUDENTS

Transparency 23 / Master 23

NOTE-TAKING CHART

Directions: Identify the key words on each page. Then look at your key words and decide what the important ideas for that section are. Record what you find for each page on the chart.

Teamwork

Page	Key Words	Important Ideas
Page 74		
Page 75		
Page 76		

Transparency 23 Level A, Unit 2 | Cooperation   © Hampton-Brown

Multi-Level Strategies
READING OPTIONS FOR LESSONS 4–5

BEGINNING As you read the selection aloud with students, pause after each sentence or group of sentences to clarify meaning. Prompt use of photos: *Show a picture of a group that plays together. What are they doing?* After reading through each page, ask: *What are the important ideas on this page?* Work with students to distinguish important ideas from details, and record information on **Transparency 23**, vocalizing as you write. You may need to provide the key words on the chart and prompt students to provide the main ideas.

INTERMEDIATE / **ADVANCED** Have students read in heterogeneous pairs, with partners reading every other sentence. On a second reading, have students work together to identify key words and main ideas to record on **Master 23**.

Some teams wear **uniforms**.
Others do not.

Teams **plan** together to make things
come out right. Team members
depend on one another. Team
members are **proud** of one another.

> **Restate depend on:** Team members need one another.

Each team member is
part of a whole.

> **Encourage elaboration:** Describe the teams in the photos.

Teamwork makes
the job easier.
Teamwork gets
the job done.

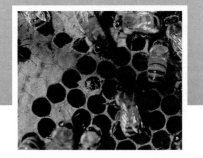

BEFORE YOU MOVE ON...

1. **Viewing/Details** Which teams are wearing uniforms? Which are not?
2. **Personal Experience** Think of a team that you are a part of. Tell a partner about your team.
3. **Viewing/Vocabulary** Look at a picture of one of the teams. Describe how the team members cooperate to do their job.

---

uniforms a set of matching clothing
come out right happen in the way they were planned

Teamwork **75**

CHECK COMPREHENSION

3 Answers to "Before You Move On"

1. **Viewing/Details** The crew team, the firefighters, and the team cleaning up the oil spill are wearing uniforms; others are wearing clothing appropriate for the tasks they are doing.

2. **Personal Experience** Answers will vary. Encourage students to elaborate.

3. **Viewing/Vocabulary** Choices of photograph and response will vary but students should point out how each member performs a specific role as a contribution to the team.

CLOSE AND ASSESS

Have students collaborate in groups of three to formulate and state an important idea about teams.

HOME CONNECTION

Family Teamwork Send home a copy of *High Point Newsletter 3* in the **Teacher's Resource Book**. (See pages 111–117.) In this home activity, students develop a plan for a family activity that can be done as a team. They then enlist the help of family members to implement the plan. After family members discuss how the plan worked, students share information about their plan and its implementation with the class.

Grammar Minilesson

▶ **COUNT AND NONCOUNT NOUNS**

TEACH Read the last two lines of text on page 75. Say: *The words* teamwork *and* job *are both nouns. Some nouns, like* job, *name things that can be counted. Other nouns, like* teamwork, *name things that can't be counted, such as ideas. Nouns that can't be counted have only one form for "one" and "more than one."* See Handbook pages 410–411. Begin lists:

> Nouns That Can Be Counted
>
> job—jobs   uniform—uniforms
>
> Nouns That Cannot Be Counted
>
> teamwork   pride

PRACTICE Ask students to look at the photos on pages 74–75. Guide a discussion of the photos, aimed at eliciting both count and noncount nouns. Extend the concept of noncount nouns to sports *(basketball)*, activities *(fishing)*, food *(rice)*, and category nouns *(time)*.

Ask partners or small groups to create their own lists of count and noncount nouns. Invite students to share their lists.

▶ **Practice Book** page 35

Teamwork **T75**

READ PAGE 76

OBJECTIVES

Function: Read a Selection

Listening: Listen to a Selection

Reading and Learning Strategies:
Set a Purpose for Reading;
T Identify Main Ideas;
Use Graphic Organizers (T-chart)

Comprehension: Identify Details; Classify

SET PURPOSE

1 Say: *Find out about other teams.*

READ AND THINK

Tape 2A

CD 2
Track 2

2 Strategy Focus: Identify Main Ideas Involve students in reading page 76.

> See the **Multi-Level Strategies** on page T74 to tailor the reading to all proficiency levels.

CHECK COMPREHENSION

3 Answers to "Before You Move On"

1. Vocabulary It is the biggest and most important team.

2. Details They help one another, solve problems, and make peace.

3. Categorizing Answers will vary.

CLOSE AND ASSESS

Ask for one key word from the story that supports a main idea.

Restate: Members of a family are the best team. They work together, play together, and take care of one another.

The best team of all is the family— working together, playing together, **caring for** one another.

And the biggest and most important team is the *world's* family—all the world's **nations** working together to help one another, to **solve problems**, to make peace.

Restate: Nations or countries around the world are members of the world's family.

nations countries

BEFORE YOU MOVE ON...

1. Vocabulary The author describes the family team as *the best team.* How does she describe the world's family?

2. Details What are some ways that the world's nations work together?

3. Categorizing Write a list of teams that work together. Write a list of teams that play together.

ABOUT THE AUTHOR

Ann Morris says she wrote *Teamwork* because "teamwork in school and in life is so important." Ann works with a team of editors, artists, photographers, and others to get her books published. She respects rescue workers who work together to help people in trouble. She also admires teams of people who put on ballets and operas.

76 Unit 2 | Cooperation

REACHING ALL STUDENTS

Cooperative Learning

FOR A RESEARCH PROJECT:
Teams

Define Roles Teach students about roles that will help them complete a report about a specific kind of team. The roles should include facilitator, materials monitor, writer, illustrator, and reporter. Define responsibilities.

Plan a Report Students can work as a class to brainstorm kinds of teams. Each group should then choose one to research and decide on the form of their report. They can choose from posters, collages, oral reports, or

written reports. Groups should then assign roles to each member.

Prepare and Present a Report Instruct students to collect materials, gather and organize information, write and illustrate the report, and then present the report to the class.

Debrief the Cooperative Process Have students share what they learned from the specific roles they took. Ask: *How could you improve the group process next time?*

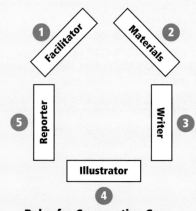

Roles for Cooperative Groups

Respond to the Photo-Essay
Check Your Understanding

✓ LANGUAGE ACQUISITION ASSESSMENT
See page 21 of the Assessment Handbook.

SUM IT UP

Identify Main Ideas Complete a chart of key words and important ideas from "Teamwork."

Page	Key Words	Important Ideas
74	a team, works, plays, members cooperate, get the job done	Teams cooperate in work or play to get a job done.
75	uniforms, plan, depend on, proud, part of whole, job	Team members plan together and depend on each other to do a good job.
76	best team is family, biggest is world, solve problems	The best team is the family. The biggest team is the nations of the world.

Add Details to a Paragraph What are the most important ideas of the photo-essay? Work with your class to finish this paragraph:

> This photo-essay is about teams. Teams cooperate. They work together to get a job done. Teams also _____
> _____
> _____ .

THINK IT OVER

Discuss Talk about these questions with a partner.

1. **Theme** What is an important lesson you learned from "Teamwork"?

2. **Personal Experience** What are some teams at your school?

3. **Opinion** Do you like to work alone or with a team? Explain your answer.

EXPRESS YOURSELF

▶ MAKE REQUESTS,
  GIVE AND ACCEPT SUGGESTIONS

When you make a **request**, you ask for something. When you give a **suggestion**, you tell an idea or opinion. Pretend that you and a partner are drawing a map. Practice making requests and giving suggestions politely. Use these sentence starters:

Make Requests	Make Suggestions	Accept Suggestions
May I please	Maybe you could	Thank you for
Would you please	It might be better if	Yes, I agree that

Examples:
- **May I please** use the ruler?
- **It might be better if** you used a red pen.
- **Thank you for** your ideas.

Teamwork **77**

Multi-Level Strategies
SUM IT UP OPTIONS

BEGINNING Work with students to review the key words and important ideas recorded on **Transparency 23**. Then, guide the group in using the important ideas to formulate a summary paragraph. Have volunteers read the paragraph aloud for the class.

INTERMEDIATE / **ADVANCED** Have partners use the important ideas they recorded on **Master 23** to complete the summary paragraph. Invite them to read their paragraphs to the class.

OBJECTIVES

SUM IT UP
Function: Write
Reading and Learning Strategies:
➊ Identify Main Ideas, Details

THINK IT OVER
Function: ➊ Engage in Discussion
Critical Thinking and Comprehension:
Form Opinions; Relate to Personal Experience
Literary Analysis: Theme

EXPRESS YOURSELF
Function: Make Requests; Give and Accept Suggestions
Speaking and Listening: Role-Play

CHECK YOUR UNDERSTANDING

1 **Sum It Up** Invite volunteers to read the important ideas from **Transparency 23/Master 23** before students complete the paragraph.

▶ **Practice Book** page 36

2 **Think It Over** Possible answers are:

   1. **Theme** Answers will vary but should convey a message such as: *Working in teams helps people get jobs done.*

   2. **Personal Experience** Answers will vary.

   3. **Opinion** Opinions should be supported by examples.

3 **Express Yourself** Put the sentence starters on strips and have students sort them into categories (making a request, making a suggestion, accepting a suggestion). Have students work in three groups to complete each phrase. Help students to see how these expressions can change the tone of what we say.

CLOSE AND ASSESS

Ask: *How would you tell a friend about what you have learned in this lesson?*

RESPOND

OBJECTIVES

SUBJECT PRONOUNS

Grammar: ❶ Subject Pronouns
Learning Strategies:
Use Graphic Organizers (chart)
Writing: Sentences

PLAY "FINISH MY SENTENCE"

Function: Write
Learning Strategy: Interact with Peers;
Use Graphic Organizers (class chart)
Writing: Sentences

LANGUAGE ARTS AND LITERATURE

1 Use Subject Pronouns See annotations for answers to Practice items.

▶ **Practice Book** page 37

2 Play "Finish My Sentence" Provide some examples of how students might complete their sentences. To give support, you might want to:

• Suggest students use pictures from the selection and ideas from the unit mind map and theme opener activities to generate information about teams.

• Model how students can work with partners to complete the sentences.

CLOSE AND ASSESS

Have students circle all the subject pronouns in the sentences they wrote for the "Finish My Sentence" activity.

✓ **ASSESSMENT**
Selection Test 5 on page 23 of the Assessment Handbook tests students' mastery of the reading strategies and the vocabulary, comprehension, and language arts skills taught with this selection.

Respond to the Photo-Essay, continued
Language Arts and Literature

GRAMMAR IN CONTEXT

USE SUBJECT PRONOUNS

Learn About Subject Pronouns A pronoun takes the place of a **noun**. A subject pronoun is used in the subject of a sentence. It tells who or what is doing something.

The **girls** are a team. They work together.

• Use **I** to tell about yourself. Use **you** to say something directly to another person or persons.

I will wait. You can go first.

• Use **he** to tell about a male. Use **she** to tell about a female. Use **it** for a place or thing.

Joe needs help. He calls a friend.
Irene answers. She helps.
The box is full. It is heavy.

• Use **we** and **they** to tell about more than one person.

Rob and I call. We can help.
Jon and Nia call. They will help, too.

Practice Rewrite the sentences. Use subject pronouns in place of the underlined words.

1. Gabriel is a member of a team.   He
2. Rita and Carrie play together.   They
3. The men carry a basket.   They
4. Susan puts out fires.   She

SPEAKING/LISTENING

PLAY "FINISH MY SENTENCE"

Work with a partner to make sentences about different kinds of teams. Use this sentence frame:

It takes _____ people on a team to _____.

❶ Start a Sentence One partner fills in the first blank with a number.

❷ Finish the Sentence The other partner names an activity for that number of people.

Example:
Partner 1: It takes   four   people on a team
Partner 2: to   have a relay race   .

❸ Change Roles Take turns filling in new numbers and teams. Then share your ideas with the class.

 Learn how to be a good **listener**. See Handbook pages 373–374.

REACHING ALL STUDENTS

❙ Multi-Level Strategies

OPTIONS FOR PLAYING "FINISH MY SENTENCE"

BEGINNING Begin the activity by handing out numeral cards and a series of activities, such as *jump rope, play tag, play a softball game*. Review the cards with students, helping them with words related to numerals and activities. Then have them complete the sentences.

INTERMEDIATE / **ADVANCED** Have pairs follow the three steps to complete the activity, recording how each student completes the sentence. When pairs are finished, the group comes together to record their results on a chart to share with the class.

Content Area Connections

SOCIAL STUDIES

MAKE A GOVERNMENT TEAM CHART

The United States government has many teams that work together. Learn about teams like:

- the Supreme Court
- the Senate
- the House of Representatives
- the President's Cabinet

1 Find Information Use the government section in the white pages of a telephone directory. Choose a team from the city, county, state, or federal government. Then use social studies books, encyclopedias, or the Internet to find information. Take notes about each team you find.

2 Organize Your Ideas Use your notes to complete a chart like this:

Government Teams

Team	Members Are Called	Number of Members	What the Team Does
Supreme Court	Justices	9	makes decisions about laws

SCIENCE

STUDY WILDLIFE TEAMS

Some wild animals and insects live and work in teams. Work with a group to write a report about one kind of wildlife. Choose animals like:

ants	bees	wolves
lions	gorillas	whales

1 Find Information Use print or electronic encyclopedias, science books, or the Internet. Take notes about your team.

2 Write a Report Use your notes to write sentences about how the wildlife team works together. Add pictures of the team at work.

3 Share Your Report Tell about the team. Show your pictures.

A team of ants carries leaves to its nest.

Teamwork **79**

Research Skills

▶ **TAKE NOTES**

TEACH Ask students where they could find out about wildlife teams. Explain that taking notes can help them organize and remember information.

Tell students to use a separate card for each reference source. Provide an example of a 4" x 6" index card.

PRACTICE Have students begin their research, using this model.

Topic: Wildlife Teams: The Honey Bee
Card Number: 1
Subtopic: How Bees Work as Teams
Reference Source: The Internet
Location: www.honey.com/kids
Notes: 1) social insects
2) division of labor in the colony

▶ **Practice Book** page 38

OBJECTIVES

GOVERNMENT TEAMS

Function: ❶ Give information

Concepts and Vocabulary: Government

Learning Strategies and Research Skills: Locate Resources; Gather and Organize Information; Take Notes

Representing: Chart

WILDLIFE TEAMS

Function: ❶ Give Information; Write

Concepts and Vocabulary: Animals

Learning Strategies and Research Skills: Gather and Organize Information; Take Notes; Use Visuals

Writing: Report

CONTENT AREA CONNECTIONS

1 Make a Government Team Chart Prepare students by providing the following explanations of terms:

House of Representatives: A group of elected officials from each state, who draft and pass laws.

Senate: A group composed of two senators from each state, who debate issues and pass laws.

Supreme Court: The highest court in the U.S.

President's Cabinet: A group of advisors to the president.

Encourage students to develop a diagram to support their chart.

2 Study Wildlife Teams Teach content area vocabulary by displaying illustrations of the animals in the chart. Have students identify and classify each animal as either a mammal or an insect. Have them discuss the habitat of each animal and draw a picture of each animal in its habitat. Provide phrases used to refer to these animals collectively, such as: a *pod* of whales, a *colony* of ants or bees, and a *pride* of lions.

▶ **Practice Book** page 39

CLOSE AND ASSESS

Ask students to create a chart showing the key words and most important ideas of one of their activities.

BUILD LANGUAGE AND VOCABULARY

OBJECTIVES

Function: ❶ Describe Events; Listen Actively

Concepts and Vocabulary: Location Words

Patterns and Structures: ❶ Pronouns; Prepositions

Speaking: Describing Game

Viewing: Interpret Visual Information

Learning Strategy: Use Graphic Organizers (category chart)

Critical Thinking: Relate Steps in a Process

START WITH A COMMON EXPERIENCE

1 View and Listen Play the **Language Tape/CD** or read aloud the script on page T381 while students view the painting on page 80. Use the painting to develop meaning for the activities that are described in the recording. Then play the recording again and ask students to point to the parts of the painting that match each description.

Tape 1A
CD 1
Track 4

2 Model How to Describe Use the following Think Aloud to help students learn to describe events.

> **How to Describe Events**
>
> • Tell about an action. *(Mother spreads cornmeal dough.)*
>
> • Tell how. *(Mother spreads cornmeal dough with a spoon.)*
>
> • Tell where. *(Mother spreads cornmeal dough with a spoon onto a cornhusk.)*

Encourage students to try their hands at describing parts of the picture.

▌ Use the Describing Options in the **Multi-Level Strategies** to include students at all proficiency levels.

Build Language and Vocabulary
DESCRIBE EVENTS

View the painting. The family works together to make tamales.
Listen to a description of what the family does.

Making Tamales/La tamalada, Carmen Lomas Garza, Acrylic. Copyright © 1990.

80 Unit 2 | Cooperation

REACHING ALL STUDENTS

Multi-Level Strategies
DESCRIBING OPTIONS

BEGINNING Ask students to point out actions being performed in the painting. Ask questions with yes-no or one-word answers: *Is the mother spreading dough? Is the grandmother folding the cornhusks? How many girls are taking cornhusks out of the water?*

INTERMEDIATE Ask students to list the action words, or verbs, used on the audio recording. Use follow-up questions to expand language: *What do the cornhusks look like before they are rolled and folded? What do they look like afterward?*

ADVANCED Encourage students to describe events in the picture that are not included in the audio recording. Ask: *How would you describe what the man in the doorway is doing? Why do you think he isn't helping to make the tamales? What do you think he might do next?*

LISTEN FOR LOCATION WORDS

🔊 Listen to the recording again. Listen for phrases that begin with these words, called **prepositions**. Write the phrases.

Location Words

1. into _____	7. with _____
2. of _____	8. on _____
3. from _____	9. with _____
4. into _____	10. to _____
5. on _____	11. into _____
6. over _____	12. from _____

Compare charts with a classmate. Listen to the recording again if you need to.

BUILD YOUR VOCABULARY

Pronouns You can use these words to show who owns something.

Which person in the picture are these sentences about?

- She has a green bowl in her hands.
- He has a red handkerchief in his pocket.
- They have spoons in their hands.

Possessive Pronouns

One Person	More Than One Person
my	our
your	your
his, her, its	their

USE LANGUAGE STRUCTURES ▶ PRONOUNS AND PREPOSITIONS

Speaking: Describe Events and People Form two teams to play "I Spy." Team 1 chooses someone or something in the picture on page 80. They give three clues that include a possessive pronoun and a preposition. Team 2 guesses.

Example:

Team 1: I spy someone. **His** sweater is brown, **his** hands are **on the table**, and you can't see **his** feet.

CONDUCT THE ACTIVITIES

3 **Listen for Location Words** Have students work with a partner or in a group to list prepositional phrases. Students should listen to the audio recording as many times as necessary to complete their charts.

4 **Build Your Vocabulary: Pronouns** Teach the skill using the definition and examples on **Transparency 24**. Remind students that pronouns that show who owns something take the place of nouns that show who owns something. Then have students complete the sentences in Try It!

5 **Use Language Structures: Pronouns and Prepositions** Point out prepositions used in the example sentences on **Transparency 24**, and explain that prepositions often show location, direction, and time.

Speaking: Describe Events and People Conduct the activity at the bottom of page 81. After each round, have teams reverse roles.

▌ Use the Speaking Activity Options in the **Multi-Level Strategies** to adjust instruction.

▶ **Practice Book** page 40

CLOSE AND ASSESS

Ask students to list three examples of pronouns that show who owns something. Then have them write a sentence for each pronoun.

▌ Multi-Level Strategies
SPEAKING ACTIVITY OPTIONS

BEGINNING Encourage these students to participate by selecting the person or thing in the picture for the team to describe. They can offer one-word suggestions for the description.

INTERMEDIATE Encourage students to create more detailed descriptions of the chosen person or thing: *His back is bent over the pot. There is a bandanna in his pocket.*

ADVANCED Challenge students to use prepositions to give multiple location clues in the same sentence. For instance: *I spy something. It is on the wall, near the table, over the family.*

Transparency 24 / Master 24

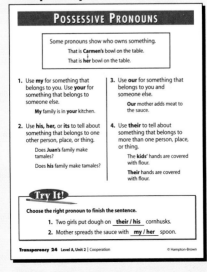

POSSESSIVE PRONOUNS

Some pronouns show who owns something.
That is **Carmen's** bowl on the table.
That is **her** bowl on the table.

1. Use **my** for something that belongs to you. Use **your** for something that belongs to someone else.
   My family is in **your** kitchen.

2. Use **his, her,** or **its** to tell about something that belongs to one other person, place, or thing.
   Does **Juan's** family make tamales?
   Does **his** family make tamales?

3. Use **our** for something that belongs to you and someone else.
   Our mother adds meat to the sauce.

4. Use **their** to tell about something that belongs to more than one person, place, or thing.
   The **kids'** hands are covered with flour.
   Their hands are covered with flour.

Try It!

Choose the right pronoun to finish the sentence.
1. Two girls put dough on **their / his** cornhusks.
2. Mother spreads the sauce with **my / her** spoon.

Transparency 24 Level A, Unit 2 | Cooperation   © Hampton-Brown

Build Language and Vocabulary **T81**

OBJECTIVES

THINK ABOUT WHAT YOU KNOW
Reading Strategy:
Relate to Personal Experience

LEARN KEY VOCABULARY ⊤
Vocabulary Strategy:
Use New Words in Context

LEARN TO VISUALIZE
Reading Strategy: Visualize

THINK ABOUT WHAT YOU KNOW

1 Match Dreams After students find classmates who share similar dreams, encourage each buzz group to discuss why that dream is important to them.

LEARN KEY VOCABULARY

2 Use New Words in Context Read each vocabulary word and its definition aloud. Have students rely on context to answer the questions in the activity.

Use the Vocabulary Options in **Multi-Level Strategies** to work with all proficiency levels.

▶ **Practice Book** page 41

LEARN TO VISUALIZE

3 Model How to Visualize Define *visualize* as *"making a picture in your mind."* Begin the activity on **Transparency 25**:

• Have students visualize as you read the poem.

• Reread and pause after each stanza to circle key words (stanza 1: *oldest, homes;* stanza 2: *New Mexico;* stanza 3: *built, out of the Earth*).

• Have students describe how their mental pictures changed as they heard new key words.

CLOSE AND ASSESS

Ask students: *What do you do when you visualize?* (You make pictures in your mind.)

Together, we DREAM
poems
by Francisco X. Alarcón

Prepare to Read Poetry

THINK ABOUT WHAT YOU KNOW

Match Dreams A dream is a goal that you have for the future. What is your dream? Write it down or draw a picture of it on a card. Then find a classmate who has a dream like yours.

---

adobe An **adobe** is a brick made of mud and straw that dries in the sun.

bar A **bar** is a solid object that is longer than it is wide.

entire Something is **entire** when it is complete or whole.

gather When people **gather**, they come together.

layer A **layer** is one thickness of something.

plaster When you **plaster** a wall, you cover it with material to protect it.

reality The way things really are is called **reality**.

require When you **require** something, you need it.

tend When you **tend** something, you take care of it.

weathered Something is **weathered** when it is changed by wind, sun, and rain.

Answers to the vocabulary activity:
1. mud and straw
2–5. Answers will vary.

LEARN KEY VOCABULARY

Use New Words in Context Study the new words. Work with a partner to answer the questions. Explain your answers.

1. What is a **bar** of **adobe** made of?

2. Why do you need to **plaster** a new **layer** on a **weathered** house?

3. Why is it better when an **entire** family can **gather** to help?

4. What tools do you **require** when you **tend** a garden?

5. How can you make a dream become **reality**?

LEARN TO VISUALIZE

When you **visualize**, you see a picture in your mind. Visualizing helps you enjoy the feeling of a poem.

READING STRATEGY
How to Visualize
1. Read the entire collection of poems to get the feeling.
2. Go back and read each poem slowly. Look for clear, colorful words.
3. Use the words to make pictures in your mind.

Now read "Together, We Dream." Try to visualize what the poet describes.

REACHING ALL STUDENTS

Multi-Level Strategies
VOCABULARY OPTIONS

BEGINNING / INTERMEDIATE

Describe your actions as you pantomime *gather, plaster* (use an imaginary trowel to scoop plaster and smooth it on a wall), and *tend*. Use the illustration on page 84 to point out *adobe* and *bar*. Use objects to clarify the meaning of *entire* and *layer*. Then, work with students to read and answer the questions.

ADVANCED After students answer the questions, have them write sentences that include two of the vocabulary words.

Transparency 25 / Master 25

HOW TO VISUALIZE

Directions: Listen to these stanzas from a poem. Listen to key words and phrases. Then draw a picture that shows what you see in your mind.

from **Adobes**
by Francisco X. Alarcón

some of	still	were built
the oldest	standing	right out
homes	in New Mexico	of the Earth

Transparency 25 Level A, Unit 2 | Cooperation   © Hampton-Brown

like some
big chocolate
bars

every few
years entire
families

their
neighbors
and friends

would gather
before the rains
to plaster

Restate: before the
rainy season

the weathered
outside adobe
walls

with a new
layer of mud
and straw

adobes—
like people—
require

lots of
attention
and love

Restate: Adobes and
people need lots of
attention and love.

BEFORE YOU MOVE ON...

1. **Details** What are adobes made of?
2. **Inference** Why do adobe walls need new plaster "before the rains"?
3. **Opinion** Do you agree with the poet that people "require lots of attention and love"?

attention care

Together, We Dream **85**

3 Answers to "Before You Move On"

1. **Details** Adobes are made of mud and straw, which are dried by the sun.

2. **Inference** The plaster helps to keep the adobe walls from being washed away by rain.

3. **Opinion** Student responses will vary.

CLOSE AND ASSESS

Have students tell how visualizing helped them to appreciate the poem. Ask: *What visual images did you "see" in your mind?* Have students share the pictures they drew.

CULTURAL PERSPECTIVES

World Cultures: Housing Have students conduct research on how houses are constructed in different climates, as a result of the different kinds of materials available. Have them download, cut out, or draw pictures and write captions explaining why the houses are built the way they are in the country or countries they studied.

Literary Analysis Minilesson

▶ **SIMILE**

TEACH In the poem "Adobes," point out the lines that describe adobes lying in the sun "like some big chocolate bars." Tell students that similes are comparisons that use the words *like* or *as*. Ask volunteers why the poet might have used this simile. (Adobes are bar-shaped and brown.)

Offer other, more common similes. Ask: *What does it mean to "swim like a fish" or "be as slow as a snail"?* (swim well; move slowly)

PRACTICE Invite students to talk about how comparisons that use similes can help a reader visualize and better understand the poet's message. Ask students to find a simile in the poem "Family Garden" on page 86. *(garden that smiles like the sun)*

▶ **Practice Book** page 42

Function: Read Poems
Grammar: Plural Nouns
Concepts and Vocabulary:
Figurative Language
Listening: Listen to Poems
Reading and Learning Strategies:
Set a Purpose for Reading; Visualize;
Use Graphic Organizers (chart)
Comprehension: Identify Details
Literary Analysis: Figurative Language;
Mood and Tone; Evaluate Impact of
Author's Background on Meaning

SET PURPOSE

1 Say: *Listen to find out how the author expresses the importance of people working together.*

READ AND THINK

Tape 2A

CD 2
Track 3

2 Strategy Focus: Visualize
Involve students in listening to and reading the poems on pages 86–87. As students listen, have them visualize the characters, setting, and action of the poems, and record key words and images on **Master 26**.

> See the **Multi-Level Strategies** on page T84 to tailor the reading experience to all proficiency levels.

FAMILY GARDEN

in the backyard
of our home
there is a garden

all in our family
do our share
to tend it

Restate: Everyone in our family works together to take care of it.

Mami loves
to plant and trim
rosebushes

Abuelita keeps
her *yerbabuena*
in a small plot

more than anything
Papi likes
to water everything

the lemon tree
the *calabacitas*
the vegetable rows

and the tomatoes
my sisters grow
every spring

my brothers and I
in turn weed out
and cut the grass

Restate: My brothers and I take turns weeding and cutting the grass.

even our puppy
has learned
to plant bones

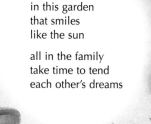

in this garden
that smiles
like the sun

all in the family
take time to tend
each other's dreams

Mami Mom (in Spanish)
Abuelita Grandma (in Spanish)
yerbabuena mint plant (in Spanish)
plot area of ground for planting

Papi Dad (in Spanish)
calabacitas zucchini squash (in Spanish)
weed out pull out the unwanted plants

REACHING ALL STUDENTS

Vocabulary
SENSORY WORDS

Ask students to describe everything they can about vegetables, using only their sense of sight. (If possible, bring in a variety of vegetables.) Begin by presenting the name of a vegetable and showing a picture of it. Have students describe the vegetable with increasingly detailed descriptions. Record student ideas on a chart. Then provide real samples of the vegetable and have students add to their descriptions, using their other senses: taste, smell, sound, and touch. Have students record their ideas on a chart.

A WORLD  OF LANGUAGES

Multicultural Proverbs Although proverbs are not often used in everyday speech in English, they are in other languages and countries. Invite students to discuss the meaning of the following proverbs related to teamwork. Ask: *How do proverbs help you learn about other cultures?*

PROVERB	ORIGIN
When spider webs unite, they can tie up a lion.	Ethiopia
Many hands make light work.	"The Proverbs of John Heywood" (1546)
A single arrow is easily broken; a bundle of ten is not.	Japan

COLLECTIVE DREAM

a dream
we dream
alone

reality
we dream
together

Encourage elaboration: Name some dreams you have by yourself and some that you share with others.

BEFORE YOU MOVE ON...

1. **Details** How does each member of the family help with the garden?
2. **Figurative Language** Reread "Collective Dream" and the last three lines in "Family Garden." What reality did the people in "Family Garden" dream together?
3. **Mood** How do these poems make you feel?

Collective Dream Dream that belongs to everyone in a group

ABOUT THE POET

Francisco X. Alarcón was born in California, but he grew up in Jalisco, Mexico. One of his best memories about growing up is working in the family garden. "I believe my parents kept this garden for two reasons. One was to have a steady supply of vegetables. The other was to teach me, my five brothers, and two sisters to work together as a team." Today, Francisco X. Alarcón works as a professor and a writer. His work has won many awards.

CHECK COMPREHENSION

3 Answers to "Before You Move On"

1. **Details** Each family member has a different responsibility: Mami tends roses; Papi likes to water everything; brothers weed and cut grass; sisters grow tomatoes; Abuelita grows mint.

2. **Figurative Language** The family dreamed of having a garden and worked together to make their dream a reality.

3. **Mood** Responses will vary. Encourage students to elaborate.

ABOUT THE POET

4 Evaluate Impact of Author's Background on Meaning Read aloud About the Poet. Ask students to identify information about Alarcón's background. Ask: *How does it contribute to the meaning of the poems when you know that Alarcón grew up in Mexico? That his family had a garden?*

CLOSE AND ASSESS

Have students work together with partners to answer these questions: *What did you learn by reading these three poems? How did you use visualization to help you understand the poems' meaning?* Then ask students to share what they discussed.

Grammar Minilesson

▶ REGULAR PLURALS

TEACH Ask students to name the things in "Family Garden" that the family grows. List singular and plural nouns in different columns. Then say: *The words* rosebushes, rows, *and* tomatoes *are plural nouns. They name more than one thing.*

Use these and other words in the poems to teach rules for forming plurals. See Handbook page 410.

PRACTICE Ask partners or small groups to see how many nouns they can find in the three poems. Students should list the words in two columns, **One** and **More Than One**. Let students compare their lists.

Make three columns on the board, headed *s, es,* and *y to i + es*. Invite students to take turns listing in the correct columns the plural nouns they found.

▶ **Practice Book** page 43

Language Development

ASK FOR AND GIVE INFORMATION

Have students work in pairs. One partner names a member of the team in "Family Garden," while the other tells what that family member did to help the garden flourish. Then the partners switch roles. Students can follow these same procedures to discuss the teamwork in the poem "Adobes" (pages 84–85).

RESPOND

OBJECTIVES

SUM IT UP

Critical Thinking, Reading, and Learning Strategies: Visualize; Make Comparisons; Use Graphic Organizers (chart)

THINK IT OVER

Function: ❶ Engage in Discussion
Critical Thinking and Comprehension: Make Inferences; Make Judgments; Form Opinions
Literary Analysis: Figurative Language

EXPRESS YOURSELF

Function: ❶ Describe Events
Speaking and Listening: Interview

CHECK YOUR UNDERSTANDING

1 Sum It Up Have students share what they recorded on their charts. When finished, ask students to tell what they learned from sharing ideas with others.

▶ **Practice Book** page 44

2 Think It Over Possible answers are:

1. Figurative Language The garden is as bright, cheerful, and warm as the sun.

2. Inference Adobe houses are made from mud and straw. Some are still standing because they have many layers that have been weathered over hundreds of years.

3. Judgment Answers will vary. Encourage elaboration.

4. Personal Experience Answers will vary. Encourage students to give reasons for their choices.

3 Express Yourself Have students share what they found by asking questions of partners.

CLOSE AND ASSESS

Ask students to return to the unit mind map (see page T67) and add new ideas to it. Encourage them to use sensory words.

Respond to the Poems
Check Your Understanding

SUM IT UP

Visualize Copy and complete this chart. Write the title of each poem. Write words from the poem that helped you make pictures in your mind. Then draw what you pictured.

Poem	Key Words	Picture
"Adobes"	oldest homes, New Mexico, built out of the Earth	

Make Comparisons Show your chart to a group. Are your key words and pictures the same? What things look different? Talk about how different pictures can come from the same words.

THINK IT OVER

Discuss Talk about these questions with a partner.

1. **Figurative Language** What does the poet mean when he says that the family garden *smiles like the sun*?

2. **Inference** What did you learn about adobe houses from the poems? Why are some old adobe houses still standing?

3. **Judgment** The poet says that it takes more than one person to make a dream a reality. Is this true? Why or why not?

4. **Personal Experience** Which poem do you like the best? Why?

EXPRESS YOURSELF ▶ DESCRIBE EVENTS

Tell a partner about a time you were on a team. Your partner will ask questions to find out more about the team event. Use questions like these:

- How many people were on the team?
- What did each member do?
- How did working as a team make the job easier?

✓ **LANGUAGE ACQUISITION ASSESSMENT** See page 21 of the Assessment Handbook.

88 Unit 2 | Cooperation

REACHING ALL STUDENTS

Multi-Level Strategies
SUM IT UP OPTIONS

BEGINNING Remind students of what they learned about visualizing. Ask students to identify highly visual concept words or phrases from the story (*spread out for the sun to dry* or *like some big chocolate bars*), and tell how these words were useful. Use frames to capture students' use of visualization: *When I read the words _____, I can see _____ in my mind.* Help students compare their drawings.

INTERMEDIATE / ADVANCED Have students discuss why a word or phrase (*home, entire families, puppy, dream*) generates one mental image in one person's mind but a different mental image in another's. Then, have students work in pairs to record comparisons. Provide sentence starters: *When I hear the word* rains, *I see _____. When my partner hears the word* rains, *he visualizes _____.*

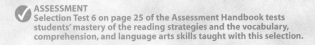

ASSESSMENT
Selection Test 6 on page 25 of the Assessment Handbook tests
students' mastery of the reading strategies and the vocabulary,
comprehension, and language arts skills taught with this selection.

Language Arts and Literature

▶ GRAMMAR IN CONTEXT

USE PREPOSITIONAL PHRASES

Learn About Prepositions A **preposition** is a short word like *to, on,* or *with.* It is the first word in a **prepositional phrase.** The last word in the phrase is often a noun.

Prepositional phrases add details to a sentence. They may tell about:

- location: **in** the garden
- direction: **into** the ground
- time: **before** the rains

Find Prepositional Phrases Reread the poems. Talk with a partner about how the prepositional phrases help you visualize the poems.

Practice Copy the poetry frame. Study the prepositions. Then complete the prepositional phrases to show location, direction, and time.
Answers will vary.

The flowers in my garden

Turn their faces to the sun .

They bloom from morning to evening

And rise up from the ground .

▶ SPEAKING/LISTENING

MEMORIZE AND RECITE POETRY

When you **memorize** and **recite** a poem, you say it aloud without looking at the words. Work with a team to memorize and recite "Adobes" or "Family Garden":

- Decide which lines each member will memorize.
- Practice reciting the poem together. Think about the meaning and feeling of the words as you say them.
- Then recite your poem for the class.

▶ REPRESENTING/SPEAKING

CREATE A MULTIMEDIA PHOTO-ESSAY

In a school, many people share the dream of learning. Take photos or make a video of people as they do things like:

| study in the library | work on projects |
| do experiments | use computers |

Present your photo-essay to the class. Tell what your pictures show.

Learn how to create a **multimedia presentation**. See Handbook pages 362–363.

Together, We Dream **89**

Multi-Level Strategies
WRITING OPTIONS FOR CREATING A PHOTO-ESSAY

BEGINNING Go on a walk with students, modeling language to describe learning activities that are encountered. If possible, use an instant camera so that events can be captured immediately, or discuss the events as they are happening. Once students have recorded ideas through photographs or video, use this material to develop language for writing captions or the "voiceovers" for video.

INTERMEDIATE / **ADVANCED** To give students some ideas for possible approaches to the activity, you might want to have photo-essay books and videos available for students to peruse before they begin their project. Provide an opportunity for students to share what they have done. Utilize student work to develop and expand language with students of all proficiency levels.

RESPOND

OBJECTIVES

PREPOSITIONAL PHRASES
Function: Write
Grammar: Prepositions
MEMORIZE AND RECITE POETRY
Function: Recite; Listen Actively
Learning Strategies: Interact with Peers
Speaking and Listening: Choral Reading
CREATE A MULTIMEDIA PHOTO-ESSAY
Learning Strategies:
Gather Information
Technology/Media:
Select Appropriate Media
Representing/Speaking:
Photo-Essay; Captions

LANGUAGE ARTS AND LITERATURE

1 **Use Prepositional Phrases** Annotations on the Practice exercises show possible answers.

▶ **Practice Book** page 45

2 **Memorize and Recite Poetry** Have students divide up the poem, each taking a short segment to recite. Suggest that students use a tape recorder. Model for students how to express feeling as they recite.

3 **Create a Multimedia Photo-Essay** Conduct a walk with students and point out environments at school in which learning takes place—at a library; in a computer lab; at recess, when learning a new game. On the return from the walk, develop a concept web in which students identify what they saw.

CLOSE AND ASSESS

Ask students to write something they learned on an exit slip to hand in before leaving class.

INTRODUCE THEME 2

OBJECTIVES

Functions: ❶ Engage in Discussion

Concepts and Vocabulary:
Cooperation—*count on, rely on, survive, people, animals, better, mountain climb, rappel, trust*

Viewing: Respond to a Photograph

Learning Strategies and Critical Thinking: Preview; Build Background; Activate Prior Knowledge; Use Graphic Organizers (chart); Generate Ideas

TAP PRIOR KNOWLEDGE

1 **Quickwrite for *Count on Me*** Ask students to do a quickwrite about a time they counted on someone or someone counted on them. Share student stories. Conclude by asking: *How does it feel to count on someone? How do you think it feels when others count on us?*

VIEW AND DISCUSS

2 **Discuss the Photograph** Say: *Sometimes, being able to count on someone can make a difference between life and death.* Prompt students to discuss how the climber counts on his partner for his survival. Use the example of the man at the top to point out that often partners do not count on each other in the same way. Elicit situations where we count on others for survival and for other needs; record ideas in a chart.

We Count on People:

To Survive	For Other Things
mom & dad (food, house, clothing)	
farmers (to grow our food)	

Use the Activity Options in the **Multi-Level Strategies** to include all proficiency levels.

90 · Unit 2 | Cooperation

REACHING ALL STUDENTS

Multi-Level Strategies

ACTIVITY OPTIONS

BEGINNING Brainstorm with students about times they counted on others or others counted on them. Offer language support and modeling: *We count on our friends to listen to us. We count on the bus driver to get us to school safely. My brother counts on me to _____.* Ask students to draw a picture of a time they counted on someone or someone counted on them. Write captions based on student dictation to describe each event.

INTERMEDIATE / ADVANCED Ask students to illustrate their quickwrites or ideas from the chart in the form of cartoon panels. Have them take turns retelling the story of what happened, using the illustrations for visual support. Combine the illustrations into a class book entitled, "We Count on Each Other."

THEME 2

Count on Me

- In what ways do people count on other people to survive?

- In what ways do people and animals count on each other to survive?

- How are our lives made better when we have others that we can count on?

THEME-RELATED BOOKS

It's Mine!
by Leo Lionni

In this fable, three selfish frogs learn an important lesson after they count on each other to survive a frightening storm.

BEGINNING

My Buddy
by Audrey Osofsky

A boy who uses a wheelchair counts on Buddy, his Service Dog, to help him in many ways. Buddy even goes to school!

INTERMEDIATE

Rikki-Tikki-Tavi
by Rudyard Kipling, adapted and illustrated by Jerry Pinkney

In this version of a classic story, a mongoose saves the family that saved its life.

ADVANCED

91

DISCUSS THE GUIDING QUESTIONS

3 Set the Theme Some key points to develop during the discussion are:

- People count on doctors and nurses to care for their health. Police officers and fire fighters count on one another's support to keep them safe. It is important to respect those who risk their lives for the safety and survival of others.

- Some people count on animals to help them do work, as on a farm. Blind people count on guide dogs to help them to get around. Rescue dogs find people who are lost. Pets and other working animals rely on people to feed, shelter, and care for them.

- People can help one another when someone is not well. When people are there to listen to our problems, we feel less alone. It can be scary not to have support when we need it.

■ Form groups and use the **Multi-Level Strategies** so all students can participate.

CLOSE AND ASSESS

Have each student complete the following sentences: *I can count on _____ when I need _____. _____ can count on me when _____.*

Multi-Level Strategies
GROUPING GUIDELINES

BEGINNING Rephrase questions to elicit yes/no responses: *Is the climber counting on the person at the top to stay alive? Do our pets count on us? Do we count on our pets?* etc. Point out words with similar meanings, for example, *count on, depend on, rely on, stay alive,* and *survive.*

INTERMEDIATE / ADVANCED Have Advanced students work with Intermediate students in small groups to answer the questions. Have groups create one chart that shows how people count on people, and another to show how animals and people count on one another. Have students agree on a group statement in response to the third question.

THEME LIBRARY

■ **My Buddy** by Audrey Osofsky
After students read this book, encourage them to write a review that includes a simple rating (such as 1–5 stars, etc.) and a summary. Students may wish to compare the human/animal teams in *My Buddy* and "A Dog You Can Count On." If students have not started a reading log, encourage them to set up a chart with columns for title, author, date read, and genre (fiction or nonfiction). They may also wish to include a rating and summary.

OBJECTIVES

Function: ⓣ Give Directions

Concepts and Vocabulary:
Direction Words

Patterns and Structures:
ⓣ Commands; ⓣ Pronouns

Speaking: Directions Game

Learning Strategies: Interact with Peers;
Use Graphic Organizers (category chart)

Critical Thinking: Draw Conclusions;
Relate to Personal Experience

START WITH A COMMON EXPERIENCE

1 Build Background Tell students that
Helen Keller became blind and deaf
as the result of a childhood illness.
She was unable to communicate until
her teacher, Anne Sullivan, taught
her sign language. Explain that Helen
Keller went on to complete college
and became famous for her many
accomplishments.

2 Discuss the Quotation Guide
students to speculate on what Helen
Keller meant. *(Working as a group,
people can accomplish far more than
one person working alone.)*

▊ Use the Discussion Prompts in the
Multi-Level Strategies to involve
all proficiency levels.

3 Model How to Give Directions
Point out that when we work with
other people, we sometimes have to
give directions. Use the following
Think Aloud to model the skill.

How to Give Directions

• Tell the first thing to do.
(Go to the board.)

• Tell the next step. Use a time order
word. *(Now pick up the chalk.)*

• Tell another step. Use another
time order word. *(Next, write
your name.)*

• Tell the last thing to do. *(Go back
to your seat.)*

Build Language and Vocabulary
GIVE DIRECTIONS

View this photograph and read the quote. How do people
with special needs count on others?

Helen Keller uses a
special alphabet to
communicate with
her teacher, Anne
Sullivan. Helen uses
her hands to speak
to her.

**Alone we can do so little,
together we can do so much.**

—*Helen Keller*

REACHING ALL STUDENTS

▊ **Multi-Level Strategies**
DISCUSSION PROMPTS

BEGINNING Ask for information shown in the photograph: *Where is
Anne Sullivan's left hand?* Restate the answer as you write it: *under Helen
Keller's hand.* Help Beginning students grasp the concept of communicating
through signs that are felt, not seen.

INTERMEDIATE Prompt comment from students with more open-ended
questions: *How did Helen Keller communicate with other people?* (through
Anne Sullivan) *How do you think she expressed her needs before she learned
sign language?*

ADVANCED Invite students to make observations that go beyond the
information provided: *How do you think Helen Keller's life changed when Anne
Sullivan became her teacher? How might Helen Keller's experiences have
changed the lives of other people who were both blind and deaf?*

TAKE A TRUST WALK

Work with a partner. Learn what it is like to count on someone else. One partner will be the guide. The other will keep his or her eyes closed. The guide leads the partner around the room or outside. The guide gives directions: *Walk forward. Stop. Turn left. Go up one step.*, etc. Then, partners can trade places. Discuss what you learned about teamwork and trust.

BUILD YOUR VOCABULARY

Pronouns You can use the words in this chart after a verb or a preposition.

Object Pronouns

One Person	More Than One Person	Examples
me	us	Listen to me. Walk toward us.
you	you	I will guide you.
him, her, it	them	Walk around her. Step over it. Don't trip on them.

Tell the group some of the directions you gave your partner in your "Trust Walk." Use object pronouns.

USE LANGUAGE STRUCTURES ▶ COMMANDS, PRONOUNS

Speaking: Play a Directions Game Form a line of eight to ten people. Choose a leader to give commands. Each command must use an object pronoun. The goal of the game is to move an eraser from the beginning to the end of the line. Try not to repeat any directions. Give everyone a turn as leader.

Examples:
Pass the eraser around **her**.
Throw the eraser over **them**.
Give it to **him**.

✓ **LANGUAGE ACQUISITION ASSESSMENT**
See page 22 of the Assessment Handbook.

Build Language and Vocabulary **93**

CONDUCT THE ACTIVITIES

4 Take a Trust Walk After partners have performed the activity, conduct a group discussion on what they learned from it.

5 Build Your Vocabulary: Pronouns Present the skill, using the definition and examples on **Transparency 27**. If necessary, remind students that prepositions are words that often show direction, location, and time. Then have students complete the sentences in Try It!

6 Use Language Structures: Commands, Pronouns Explain that a command tells someone to do something. Help students identify the sentences on **Transparency 27** that are commands.

Speaking: Play a Directions Game Conduct the activity at the bottom of page 93. Suggest that students refer to the chart in Build Your Vocabulary if they need help remembering object pronouns.

Use the Speaking Activity Options in the **Multi-Level Strategies** to adjust instruction.

▶ **Practice Book** page 46

CLOSE AND ASSESS

Ask students to list three pronouns that come after a verb or a preposition. Then have them write a sentence for each pronoun.

Multi-Level Strategies
SPEAKING ACTIVITY OPTIONS

BEGINNING Prepare a chart that students can refer to during the game. Provide simple sketches illustrating prepositions that show direction and location. You might include the following, among others:

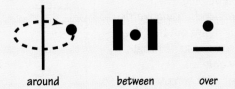

| around | between | over |

INTERMEDIATE / ADVANCED Encourage students to use directions with multiple steps; for example: *Hold the eraser in back of you and pass it to him.*

Transparency 27 / Master 27

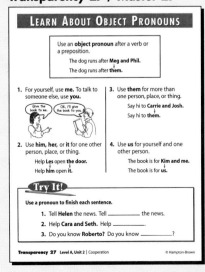

LEARN ABOUT OBJECT PRONOUNS

Use an **object pronoun** after a verb or a preposition.
The dog runs after **Meg and Phil**.
The dog runs after **them**.

1. For yourself, use **me**. To talk to someone else, use **you**.
   Give the book to me. / OK, I'll give the book to you.

2. Use **him, her,** or **it** for one other person, place, or thing.
   Help **Les** open the door.
   Help **him** open **it**.

3. Use **them** for more than one person, place, or thing.
   Say hi to **Carrie and Josh**.
   Say hi to **them**.

4. Use **us** for yourself and one other person.
   The book is for **Kim and me**.
   The book is for **us**.

Try It!
Use a pronoun to finish each sentence.
1. Tell **Helen** the news. Tell _____ the news.
2. Help **Cara and Seth**. Help _____.
3. Do you know **Roberto**? Do you know _____?

Transparency 27 Level A, Unit 2 | Cooperation   © Hampton-Brown

Build Language and Vocabulary **T93**

OBJECTIVES

THINK ABOUT WHAT YOU KNOW

Reading and Learning Strategies:
Activate Prior Knowledge;
Relate to Personal Experience;
Use Graphic Organizers (word web)

LEARN KEY VOCABULARY ✪

Vocabulary Strategy: Relate Words

LEARN TO ASK QUESTIONS AND CLARIFY

Reading Strategy:
✪ Ask Questions; ✪ Clarify

THINK ABOUT WHAT YOU KNOW

1 Make a Class Web Record ideas on the word web and have students elaborate on the work these animals do.

LEARN KEY VOCABULARY

2 Relate Words Read each vocabulary word and its defining sentence aloud. Then conduct the matching activity.

▎ Use the Vocabulary Options in **Multi-Level Strategies** to tailor instruction to proficiency levels.

▶ **Practice Book** page 47

LEARN TO ASK QUESTIONS AND CLARIFY

3 Model How to Ask Questions and Clarify Define *clarify: When you clarify, you get information to answer questions you have.* Model the steps in the box with **Transparency 28:**

• Read the first paragraph aloud and use a Think Aloud approach as you record one or two questions. Then, reread the paragraph and propose answers to the questions, using the annotations on the facsimile.

• Work through the other paragraphs, recording students' questions and answers on the transparency.

CLOSE AND ASSESS

Ask: *How does asking questions help us as we read?*

A DOG YOU CAN COUNT ON

article
by Caroline Arnold

Prepare to Read

THINK ABOUT WHAT YOU KNOW

Make a Class Web How do people and animals work together as teams? Show some examples on a word web.

teams — people ride horses

LEARN KEY VOCABULARY

blind A **blind** person is someone who cannot see.

command A **command** is an order; it tells what to do.

count on When you **count on** someone, you need that person to help you.

guide dog A **guide dog** is trained to help a person who cannot see.

instructor An **instructor** is a teacher.

partner A **partner** is a person or animal who works with you.

personality Your **personality** is the way you act or what you are like.

skill A **skill** is the ability to do something well.

take care of When you **take care of** something, you give it your time and attention.

training When you get **training**, someone teaches you how to do something.

Relate Words Study the new words. Then write sentences. Use a beginning from column 1 and an ending from column 2.

Beginning
1. A **guide dog** must learn how to D
2. A guide dog has special **skills** and B
3. Dogs must learn to obey E
4. An **instructor** gives the A
5. You can **count on** a guide dog C

Ending
A. **training** to the team.
B. a gentle **personality**.
C. to be a helpful **partner**.
D. take care of a **blind** person.
E. every **command**.

LEARN TO ASK QUESTIONS AND CLARIFY

As you read, you can stop to **ask questions**. This can help you **clarify**, or check your understanding of the main ideas, before you read on.

READING STRATEGY

How to Ask Questions and Clarify

1. Read one part of the article with a partner.
2. Stop at the end of the section. Ask each other questions about what you read.
3. If something is not clear, go back and read that part again. Help each other understand the article.

As you read "A Dog You Can Count On," stop often to ask questions. Make sure you understand each part before you continue.

REACHING ALL STUDENTS

▎ **Multi-Level Strategies**

VOCABULARY OPTIONS

BEGINNING Use the photographs in the selection to clarify meaning for *instructor, blind, guide dogs, partner,* and *training.* Demonstrate *commands,* using words like *come, sit, stay.* Point out that, like people, dogs have *personalities* that make them lively or quiet.

INTERMEDIATE / ADVANCED

Ask students to use key vocabulary words to describe the photographs. Then have them write original captions and read them for the class.

Transparency 28 / Master 28

ASK QUESTIONS AND CLARIFY

Directions: Read a paragraph. Write questions about what you read. Reread the paragraph and try to answer your questions. Write the answers.

All About Dogs

The dog is a favorite pet. All over the world people like to own dogs.

Dogs can learn many skills. They can protect cattle and sheep. They can hunt. They can even help guide blind people. For thousands of years, humans and dogs have been partners. They count on and take care of each other. Dogs have even been called our "best friend."

Questions	Answers
What is a pet? What does favorite mean?	A pet is an animal that people own. Since people everywhere have dogs, favorite must mean "something you like."
What are skills?	Skills are like jobs.
What does cattle mean?	It must be an animal, maybe cows.
What does guide mean?	Dogs help blind people; guide must be a way to help.

Transparency 28 Level A, Unit 2 | Cooperation   © Hampton-Brown

A DOG YOU CAN COUNT ON

from *A Guide Dog Puppy Grows Up*
by Caroline Arnold

It takes a lot of training to be a guide dog for the blind. That's because guide dog owners really count on their furry friends. This article shows how they learn to work together.

95

INTRODUCE THE SELECTION

4 **Preview and Predict** Read the title, author, and introduction to the article on page 95 with students. Ask: *What can you tell about this article from the photograph?* (It will be about how people and dogs get along and count on one another. You can tell because the boy is petting the dog.) Then have students page through the selection. Ask: *What questions do you have about guide dogs?*

5 **Audio Walk-Through** Play the Audio Walk-Through for "A Dog You Can Count On" on the **Selection Tape/CD** to give students the overall idea of the story.

Tape 2B
CD 2
Track 4

A Dog You Can Count On
by Caroline Arnold

Theme Connection This selection explores another aspect of cooperation by showing how teams of people and animals count on one another.

Selection Summary The introduction on page 95 of the student book offers a summary of the selection.

Author Awards Author Caroline Arnold has won many awards. She has received the NSTA/CBC Outstanding Science Tradebooks Award six times. The Southern California Council on Literature for Children awarded her work Outstanding Nonfiction and Outstanding Body of Work in 1994. Her work has received the ALA Notable Book Award in 1989, 1987, and 1985.

OBJECTIVES

Function: Read a Selection

Grammar: ❶ Possessive Pronouns

Listening: Listen to a Selection

Reading and Learning Strategies: Set a Purpose for Reading; ❶ Ask Questions; ❶ Clarify; Use Graphic Organizers (T-chart); Use Text Features (captions); Relate to Personal Experience

Comprehension: Predict; Make an Inference

SET PURPOSE

1 Say: *Listen to find out how guide dogs and blind people learn to work together.*

READ AND THINK

Tape 2B
CD 2
Track 5

2 Strategy Focus: Ask Questions and Clarify As students read, have them ask questions and clarify meaning on **Transparency 29/Master 29**.

▌ Choose Reading Options in the **Multi-Level Strategies** to tailor the reading to proficiency levels.

The recording of "A Dog You Can Count On" on the **Selection Tape/CD** offers an oral language model and the opportunity to build reading fluency.

This is the Guide Dog Training Center in San Rafael, California. Hundreds of guide dogs are trained here each year.

Red annotations offer opportunities to clarify meaning and check for understanding.

Clarify: Guide dog training teaches guide dog owners and their dogs how to work as a team.

When Moe Enguillado **arrives** to begin his **guide dog** training, Stacy Burrow **greets** him. She is one of his **instructors**. Moe is excited about getting a dog. At the same time, he is a little **worried** about everything he will have to learn.

Stacy knows the dogs very well. Each dog has its own **personality**. After meeting the new students, Stacy carefully **matches each person with** one of the dogs.

Stacy will teach Moe how to work with his new guide dog.

arrives gets to the place he is going
greets says hello to
worried scared, concerned
matches each person with finds a person who is like each

96 Unit 2 | Cooperation

REACHING ALL STUDENTS

Transparency 29 / Master 29

NOTE-TAKING CHART

Directions: After you read each paragraph, stop to ask questions. Write your questions. Reread to find information. Write your answers or your best guess.

A Dog You Can Count On

Page	Your Questions	Your Answers
Page 96		
Page 97		
Page 98		

Transparency 29 Level A, Unit 2 | Cooperation   © Hampton-Brown

---

▌ ## Multi-Level Strategies
READING OPTIONS FOR LESSONS 4–5

BEGINNING Before reading, build or review key selection concepts by prompting students to talk about the photographs: *This is a school for guide dogs. Who do you think she is?* etc. Read through the selection or play its recording on the **Selection Tape/CD**. Then read it aloud one paragraph at a time. Pause and prompt students to ask questions for you to record on **Transparency 29**. Reread each paragraph and prompt students to formulate answers or hypotheses about new words and ideas: *Do you think* excited *and* worried *mean the same thing?* etc. Restate key ideas after each section.

INTERMEDIATE / ADVANCED First read the selection together, using the red annotations on the facsimile pages to clarify meaning. Then have students read the selection with a partner, each partner reading a paragraph, while the other asks questions to clarify. Students may use **Master 29** to record their thoughts during the paired reading.

Moe Enguillado meets Aria, his new guide dog.

"Hello, Moe," says Stacy. "Here's Aria. I **picked** her **especially** for you because you both have **lively** personalities." **Pose choices:** Is Aria Moe's instructor or his new guide dog?

Moe **scratches** Aria under the chin. "Hello, Aria," Moe says. "I can't wait to **get to know you better**. We're going to have fun together."

"Yes," says Stacy. "It won't be easy at first. But, one month from now, you two are going to be a **real** team."

Ask: What commands are Moe and Aria practicing in the pictures?

Aria sits by Moe's side when he gives the command, "Sit."

Aria stands by Moe's side when he gives the command, "Heel."

BEFORE YOU MOVE ON...

1. **Personal Experience** What kind of dog would match your personality?
2. **Inference** Would you describe Moe Enguillado and Aria as *active* or *quiet*?
3. **Prediction** What do you think Moe and Aria will be able to do after one month of training?

---

picked chose
especially just, only
lively fun, active, busy
scratches rubs, pets
get to know you better learn more about what you are like
real true

A Dog You Can Count On **97**

CHECK COMPREHENSION

3 Answers to "Before You Move On"

1. **Personal Experience** Answers will vary. Students may say they would like a shy dog, a curious dog, a fun-loving dog, or a wild dog.

2. **Inference** They are described as *lively; active* is similar to *lively*.

3. **Prediction** Answers may vary but students might say they will be able to work together as a team.

CLOSE AND ASSESS

Ask students to share two questions they wrote on **Transparency 29/Master 29**.

Social Studies Connection
INFLUENTIAL PEOPLE

Have students watch a video about Helen Keller. Then have students conduct research about other distinguished blind people, such as Louis Braille; musicians Stevie Wonder, Andrea Bocelli, or José Feliciano; or athletes such as mountain-climber Erik Weinhenmayer. In their reports, have students focus on how each of these people has depended on others. Point out that sighted people have counted on them for the rich contributions they have made in many fields.

Grammar Minilesson

▶ POSSESSIVE PRONOUNS

TEACH Using possessive pronouns, ask questions about the photos on these pages, such as: *What color is his guide dog? What is the dog doing with its tail?* Then say: *The words his, her, its, their, and our tell who or what something belongs to. They take the place of a person's name or another noun that shows that something is owned.*

Illustrate the substitution of a possessive pronoun:

| Enrique's dog | his dog |
| the dog's tail | its tail |

PRACTICE Write these sentences. Have students rewrite the sentences, substituting a possessive pronoun for the underlined words.

1. Stacy told Moe Stacy's name.
2. She told Moe Aria would be Moe's new guide dog.
3. Moe scratched the dog under the dog's chin.
4. All the children loved the children's new guide dogs.

▶ **Practice Book** page 48

OBJECTIVES

Function: Read a Selection

Listening: Listen to a Selection

Reading and Learning Strategies: Set a Purpose for Reading; 🔵 Ask Questions; 🔵 Clarify; Use Graphic Organizers (T-chart); Use Text Features (captions)

Comprehension: Identify Details; 🔵 Predict

SET PURPOSE

1 Say: *Read to find out how Moe and Aria learn to work as a team.*

READ AND THINK

Tape 2B
CD 2
Track 5

2 **Strategy Focus: Ask Questions and Clarify** Involve students in reading page 98.

See the **Multi-Level Strategies** on Page T96 to tailor the reading experience to all proficiency levels.

CHECK COMPREHENSION

3 **Answers to "Before You Move On"**

1. Details They learn to use stairs and elevators, give commands, etc.

2. Prediction Answers will vary.

CLOSE AND ASSESS

Have each student ask a clarifying question.

They learn how to go around barriers,

ELEVATOR

into and out of elevators,

and up and down stairs.

Use visuals: Point out barriers in the first picture.

Blind students must learn how to work with their dogs and how to **take care of** them. They learn how to go around **barriers**, into and out of elevators, and up and down stairs. They **enter** offices, grocery stores, and banks. The instructors help the students learn the kind of **skills** and **commands** they will need when they go home with their dogs.

Finally, after four weeks of hard work, the students and their dog **partners** finish their **training**.

As each day goes by, Moe and Aria will **continue to learn** from each other, and they can **look forward to** many happy years together.

Clarify: Aria will need Moe to take care of her, too. She will need food and water and lots of love.

BEFORE YOU MOVE ON...

1. Details What are some of the things students must learn during their training?

2. Prediction How will Moe count on Aria in the years to come?

---

barriers things used to block off an open space for walking

enter go inside

continue to learn keep on learning

look forward to plan to have

98 Unit 2 | Cooperation

ABOUT THE AUTHOR

Caroline Arnold says, "Like many writers of children's books, I began when my children were small." This probably explains why she likes to write for young readers. Some of her books—such as *Why Do We Have Rules?* and *Who Keeps Us Safe?*—explain how people depend on each other in daily life. Caroline Arnold also is the author of the award-winning book, *Saving the Peregrine Falcon*.

REACHING ALL STUDENTS

Language Development
GIVE AND FOLLOW DIRECTIONS

Have pairs of students give one another commands. One student will act as the guide while the other will follow the commands that are given. For example, students might say: *Walk to the flag, pick up the book, and bring it to me. Put the book by my right foot.* Have students switch roles. When finished, have students discuss what it was like to both give and follow directions. Have them talk about other examples of giving and following directions.

Vocabulary
WORDS ABOUT MOVEMENT AND TASKS

Explain that our world is set up for sighted people and that blind people face challenges sighted people never even think about. Have students make a two-column chart and sort words and phrases about challenging tasks and obstacles the blind encounter.

Obstacles To Movement	Challenging Tasks
Curbs	Dialing a telephone
Fences	Matching clothes

HOME CONNECTION

People I Count On Send home a copy of *High Point Newsletter 4* in the **Teacher's Resource Book**. (See pages 118–124.) In this home activity, students keep a log to track the things they count on a family member for over the course of one week. Have students compile and discuss the results in class at the end of the week. Students should then write a thank you card to this person, expressing their appreciation.

Respond to the Article
Check Your Understanding

SUM IT UP

Identify Steps in a Process Put these events from the article in order. Then make a storyboard with a picture and sentence in each box.

- Moe and Aria go home together.
- Moe goes to the training center.
- Moe and Aria learn skills.
- Stacy chooses Aria to be Moe's partner.

Moe goes to the training center.

Make a Prediction What do you think will happen to Moe and his guide dog? Show your ideas on a new paper. Then share your finished storyboard with a partner.

THINK IT OVER

Discuss Talk about these questions with a partner.

1. **Summary** How do Aria and Moe help each other?

2. **Inference** What special personality does a guide dog need to have?

3. **Comparison** How are guide dogs like pets? How are they different?

4. **Personal Experience** Describe a time that someone helped you do something. How did you feel?

EXPRESS YOURSELF
▶ ASK AND ANSWER QUESTIONS

Play "Hot Seat." One student plays Moe. The class asks Moe questions. The student answers questions as if he or she is Moe.

Choose another student to sit in the "hot seat" and play Stacy.

A Dog You Can Count On **99**

Multi-Level Strategies
SUM IT UP OPTIONS

BEGINNING Do a retelling of the selection with students to help them identify the order in which events happened. Track events, using numerals and signal words to identify what happened first, second, and so on. Point out how the photographs can help represent the order of events. Develop the storyboard as a group.

INTERMEDIATE / **ADVANCED** Have students work independently to complete their storyboards and then have them share their work with a partner. Encourage them to include as many details as possible. You might want to pair them with students of beginning proficiency as they talk through their drawings. Compile all the predictions students make and write a class prediction: *Most people in our class think that Moe and Aria will _____.*

RESPOND

OBJECTIVES

SUM IT UP
Functions: Write; ❶ Give Information
Reading and Learning Strategies:
❶ Identify Steps in a Process;
Use Graphic Organizers (storyboard);
❶ Make Predictions
THINK IT OVER
Function: ❶ Engage in Discussion
Critical Thinking and Comprehension:
Summarize; Make an Inference;
Make Comparisons;
Relate to Personal Experience
EXPRESS YOURSELF
Function: Ask and Answer Questions
Speaking and Listening: Role-Play

CHECK YOUR UNDERSTANDING

1 **Sum It Up** Explain that a storyboard is similar to a comic strip in the way it uses pictures to tell a story.

▶ **Practice Book** page 49

2 **Think It Over** Possible answers are:

1. **Summary** Aria guides Moe. Moe feeds Aria and keeps her healthy. They give each other companionship.

2. **Inference** A guide dog needs to be intelligent, obedient, healthy, strong, and calm.

3. **Comparison** They are like pets because they are companions, but their responsibilities make them different.

4. **Personal Experience** Answers will vary. Encourage students to elaborate on their responses.

3 **Express Yourself** Suggest questions students might ask.

CLOSE AND ASSESS

Have students write a quiz question related to this selection.

ASSESSMENT
Selection Test 7 on page 27 of the Assessment Handbook tests students' mastery of the reading strategies and the vocabulary, comprehension, and language arts skills taught with this selection.

OBJECTIVES

OBJECT PRONOUNS

Grammar: ❶ Object Pronouns

THANK-YOU LETTER

Functions: Express Feelings; Write

Concepts and Vocabulary: Thank-You Letter—*heading, greeting, body, closing, signature*

Writing: Thank-You Letter

LANGUAGE ARTS AND LITERATURE

1 Use Object Pronouns See annotations for answers to Practice items.

▶ **Practice Book** page 50

2 Write a Thank-You Letter To support students, provide samples of thank-you letters, some written by hand on note cards and some typed. Ask students to identify times they might write a thank-you note and record their responses.

listening to my problem

helping me today

Thank you for...

the gift

being kind and thoughtful

▶ **Practice Book** page 51

CLOSE AND ASSESS

Have students identify the object pronouns they used in their thank-you letters by circling or underlining them. Display student letters.

Respond to the Article, continued

Language Arts and Literature

GRAMMAR IN CONTEXT

USE OBJECT PRONOUNS

Learn About Object Pronouns A pronoun takes the place of a **noun**. An **object pronoun** comes after a verb or words like *to*, *for*, or *from*.

> A trainer takes the **dogs** to **mom**.
>
> A trainer takes **them** to **her**.

• Use **me** to tell about yourself. Use **you** to say something directly to another person.

> Stacy taught **me**. I can teach **you**.

• Use **him** to tell about a male. Use **her** to tell about a female. Use **it** for a place or thing.

> I see **Abraham**. I call **him**.
>
> We look for **Karen**. We want to see **her**.
>
> She brings the **dog**. We play with **it**.

• Use **us** and **them** to talk about more than one person.

> Henry calls **Eva and me**. He talks to **us**.
>
> Here are **Pam and David**. We can ask **them**.

Practice Rewrite the sentences. Use object pronouns in place of the underlined words.

1. Stacy welcomed <u>Mike and Jane</u>.   them

2. Stacy gave <u>Mike</u> a gentle dog.   him

3. Stacy gave <u>Jane</u> a lively dog.   her

4. The children walked <u>their dogs</u>.   them

WRITING

WRITE A THANK-YOU LETTER

Pretend you are Moe or his instructor. Write a thank-you letter. Here are some ideas:

• Moe thanks Stacy for training Aria.

• Moe thanks Stacy for her instruction.

• Stacy thanks Moe for coming to the center.

❶ **Write the Heading** Include an address and today's date.

❷ **Write the Greeting** Write *Dear* and the person's name.

❸ **Write the Body** Say "thank you" and tell how you feel.

❹ **Write the Closing and the Signature** Write a closing like *Sincerely, Yours truly,* or *Your friend*. Then sign your name.

Heading

Greeting

Body

Closing and Signature

> 350 Los Ranchitos Rd.
> San Rafael, CA 94903
> November 5, 2002
>
> Dear Moe,
>   Thank you for giving Aria a good home. You and Aria are a great team. I think you two will be very happy together!
>
>   Your friend,
>   Stacy

REACHING ALL STUDENTS

Multi-Level Strategies

WRITING OPTIONS FOR THANK-YOU LETTERS

BEGINNING Brainstorm appropriate words to use to thank someone for a special favor, a kind deed, or a gift. List words and phrases, such as: *Thank you so much... I really appreciate... Your kindness....* Have students act out dialogues in which someone has been kind to them in some way. Then work together to compose the thank-you letter from Moe or his instructor, concentrating on using the correct form.

INTERMEDIATE Have students work in pairs to compose the thank-you letter from Moe or his instructor. Then encourage the pair to write a response to the letter.

ADVANCED Have students form pairs. One partner will be Moe and the other Stacy. Have students write thank-you letters to each other, and then respond to the letters.

Content Area Connections

SCIENCE

STUDY HUMAN AND ANIMAL TEAMS

Work with a group. Research one human and animal team from a category below:

- **entertainment**—films, the circus
- **transportation**—sled dogs, wagons
- **farming**—teams of horses or oxen
- **rescue work**—snow and earthquake rescue

1 **Find Information** Use library books, science and social studies textbooks, or the Internet. Take notes about how animals and humans work together.

2 **Share Information** Make a class chart. List human and animal teams. Tell how they work together.

3 **Make a Generalization** A generalization is a statement you can make after studying many examples. Make a generalization about human and animal teams.

SCIENCE

TECHNOLOGY/MEDIA

RESEARCH BLINDNESS

Work with a team to learn about blindness. Research a topic like:

- **famous people**—Helen Keller, Louis Braille
- **causes of blindness**—diseases, injuries
- **services for the blind**—guide dogs, Braille

1 **Find Information** Use the library or the Internet. Try these Web sites, but remember that new sites appear every day! Use your topic as a key word.

INTERNET

INFORMATION ON-LINE

Web Sites:
➤ Blindness
  - www.keystoneblind.org
  - www.nfb.org/kids.htm
  - tqjunior.thinkquest.org/5852
  - www.guidedogs.com

2 **Give an Oral Presentation** Work with your group to tell what you learned.

Learn how to do **research**. See Handbook pages 366–370. Learn how to use the **Internet** on pages 364–365.

A Dog You Can Count On **101**

Multimedia Presentation Skills

▶ **USING THE INTERNET TO LOCATE RESOURCES**

Plan the Course of Action
Direct students to identify questions to answer in their report, for example, on services for the blind: *Is training available to learn the Braille alphabet? What kinds of organizations provide information about and for the blind?* They can begin a K-W-L chart.

Identify Resources Lead students through the Web sites noted on the student page. You might want to

lead students directly to:

http://www.blind.net or
http://www.blind.net/bg100000.htm

Tell students to keep a list of their resources to cite in their report.

Evaluate Once students have identified useful Web sites, have them go back to their original questions to see if they have been answered.

▶ **Practice Book** page 52

RESPOND

OBJECTIVES

HUMAN AND ANIMAL TEAMS
Function: ❶ Give Information
Learning Strategies and Research Skills: Locate Resources; Gather and Organize Information; Take Notes
Critical Thinking: Form Generalizations
Representing: Class T-Chart

RESEARCH BLINDNESS
Function: ❶ Give Information
Learning Strategies and Research Skills: Choose and Narrow a Topic; Gather and Synthesize Information; Use Visuals
Speaking: Oral Report
Technology/Media: Use the Internet; Multimedia Presentation

CONTENT AREA CONNECTIONS

1 **Study Human and Animal Teams** To develop vocabulary, provide pictures that represent each of the categories.

2 **Research Blindness** After students complete their research, have them discuss what they learned about blindness. You might want to bring out the following points to support what students have discovered:

- **Famous People:** People who are blind can accomplish a great deal, as evidenced by achievements of famous blind people.

- **Causes of Blindness:** About 750,000 people in the U.S. are blind. Causes include cataracts, diabetic retinopathy, glaucoma, macular degeneration, and retinitis pigmentosa, or "night blindness," as well as eye injuries.

- **Services for the Blind:** Develop vocabulary related to adaptive technology equipment, guide dogs, the Braille alphabet, employment, and rehabilitation.

CLOSE AND ASSESS

Invite students to share their reports with the class. Ask: *What did you learn from this lesson that has increased your understanding of cooperation?*

A Dog You Can Count On **T101**

BUILD LANGUAGE AND VOCABULARY

START WITH A COMMON EXPERIENCE

1 **View and Discuss** View the photographs, inviting students to describe what is happening in the scenes. Ask questions designed to elicit information about the ways people are working together in the rescue.

> Use the Questioning Techniques in the **Multi-Level Strategies** to help all students participate.

2 **Model How to Ask For and Give Information** Use the following Think Aloud to model sharing information.

> **How to Ask For and Give Information**
>
> • Decide what you want to know: *How the person in the crevasse will get rescued.*
>
> • Use a question word that asks for that information: *How will they rescue the person trapped in the crevasse?*
>
> • To answer, think about the facts: *The people have long ropes.*
>
> • Give your answer: *They will lower the ropes to the trapped person and pull on them to get the person out.*

Build Language and Vocabulary
ASK FOR AND GIVE INFORMATION

View the photos. How are people counting on each other in the rescue scenes?

REACHING ALL STUDENTS

Multi-Level Strategies
QUESTIONING TECHNIQUES

BEGINNING Ask questions about the scene that will result in short answers. Then expand the answer for students. *What are the people doing? Yes, they are pulling on ropes. They are trying to rescue the person who fell in the crevasse.*

INTERMEDIATE Encourage students to speculate on the feelings of both the rescuers and the person being rescued. Ask: *How do you think the rescuers felt when they saved the person? How do you think the person felt?*

ADVANCED Elicit ideas about motives: *What kinds of people do you think take part in rescues like the one pictured? What would make a person place his or her own life in danger in order to save someone else's life?*

MAKE RESCUE PICTURES

The pictures on page 102 show a snow rescue. What are other situations where people can be rescued? Brainstorm ideas with your class. Record them on a web. Then choose one rescue situation to draw. Share your picture with the group

BUILD YOUR VOCABULARY

Survival Words To **survive** means to stay alive. Make a chart like this one. List the things people need to survive. Add your own ideas.

What People Need

shelter	water	food
house	to drink	fruit
tent	to wash	meat
apartment		

USE LANGUAGE STRUCTURES ▶ QUESTIONS AND STATEMENTS

Speaking: Ask and Answer Questions Work with a partner. Take turns asking and answering questions about survival. Use the ideas from your chart.

> Example:
> Question: What kind of shelter do people need to survive?
> Answer: People need a house or tent.

CONDUCT THE ACTIVITIES

3 Make Rescue Pictures Have students work individually and then share their pictures and ideas with a group.

4 Build Your Vocabulary: Survival Words Encourage students to expand the chart to include additional categories that could aid a person's survival.

5 Use Language Structures: Questions and Statements Present the skill, using the definitions and examples on **Transparency 30**. For item 3, you may want to present additional options for framing a question; for example: *What does everyone need? Who needs clean air?* Then have students turn the statements in Try It! into questions.

Speaking: Ask and Answer Questions Conduct the activity at the bottom of page 103. Help students use their charts for ideas.

▌ Use the Speaking Activity Options in the **Multi-Level Strategies** to adjust instruction.

▶ **Practice Book** page 53

CLOSE AND ASSESS

Have students tell how a statement and a question are different. Then ask them to create a question and a statement about something they learned in this lesson.

Multi-Level Strategies
SPEAKING ACTIVITY OPTIONS

BEGINNING Students use their charts to compose simple questions by placing the words in the appropriate order. Students may provide one-word answers to the questions.

INTERMEDIATE / **ADVANCED** Encourage students to go beyond the information in the charts when composing questions and answering them. Suggest that students expand their statements with information from their own experience and knowledge.

Transparency 30 / Master 30

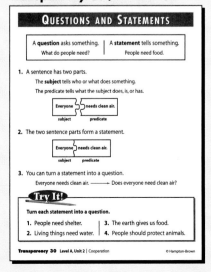

PREPARE TO READ

OBJECTIVES

THINK ABOUT WHAT YOU KNOW
Reading Strategy:
Activate Prior Knowledge
Speaking and Listening: Role-Play

LEARN KEY VOCABULARY ⊕
Vocabulary Strategy:
Use New Words in Context

LEARN ABOUT PROBLEMS AND SOLUTIONS
Reading Strategy:
⊕ Identify Problems and Solutions

THINK ABOUT WHAT YOU KNOW

1 Talk It Over Encourage students to think of rescues in many different contexts.

LEARN KEY VOCABULARY

2 Use New Words in Context Read each vocabulary word and its defining sentence aloud. Clarify meaning; then conduct the activity.

> Use the Vocabulary Options in **Multi-Level Strategies** to tailor the activity to all proficiency levels.

▶ **Practice Book** page 54

LEARN ABOUT PROBLEMS AND SOLUTIONS

3 Model How to Identify Problems and Solutions Define *problem* and *solution*. Demonstrate the steps in the box with **Transparency 31**:

- After reading and viewing the first two panels, ask students to state what the problem is in this story. Record their ideas in the chart.

- After reading and viewing the last two panels, ask students to describe the story events; record them in the chart.

- Ask: *How was the problem in this story solved?* Record this information to complete the chart.

CLOSE AND ASSESS

Ask students why a writer would include problems and solutions in a story (to create curiosity and suspense for the reader).

A MOUNTAIN
RESCUE
story
by James Ramsey Ullman

Prepare to Read

THINK ABOUT WHAT YOU KNOW

Talk It Over Tell your class about a rescue you have seen or heard about.

---

answer You **answer** when you say or do something after you hear a question or a statement.

brave A **brave** person does not show fear in a difficult situation.

climb When you **climb**, you move yourself up with your hands and feet.

hold on When you **hold on** to something, you do not let go of it.

lower When you **lower** something, you move it downward.

pull When you **pull** something, you move it toward yourself.

remove You **remove** something when you take it away.

silence When everything is quiet, there is **silence**.

tighten When you **tighten** the way you hold something, you grab it harder.

weight A **weight** is something heavy.

LEARN KEY VOCABULARY

Use New Words in Context Study the new words. Act out the action words in a group. Draw pictures of the other words. Then work together to write a sentence for each word.

LEARN ABOUT PROBLEMS AND SOLUTIONS

In some stories, a character has a **problem**. The **solution** is what the character does to solve the problem. When you find the problem and solution in a story, it helps you understand the most important events.

> ### READING STRATEGY
> **How to Identify Problems and Solutions**
> 1. Read the beginning of the story.
> 2. Ask yourself: What problem does the main character need to solve?
> 3. Find the events that lead to the solution.
> 4. Finish reading the story. Ask yourself: How was the problem solved?

Now read "A Mountain Rescue." Look for the problem at the beginning of the story and the solution at the end.

REACHING ALL STUDENTS

▌ **Multi-Level Strategies**
VOCABULARY OPTIONS

BEGINNING / **INTERMEDIATE**
Have students draw a picture of a mountain-climbing scene and act it out. Narrate and model gestures: *You are climbing a mountain. There is a heavy weight on your back. You must be brave to get to the top. There is someone at the top who will pull you up with a rope. Hold on to the rope. Tighten your hands around the rope.*

ADVANCED Have students work together to write and act out a dialogue about a mountain-climbing experience.

Transparency 31 / Master 31

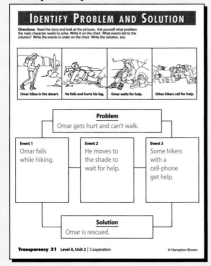

IDENTIFY PROBLEM AND SOLUTION

Directions: Read the story and look at the pictures. Ask yourself what problem the main character needs to solve. Write it on the chart. What events led to the solution? Write the events in order on the chart. Write the solution, too.

Omar hikes in the desert.	He falls and hurts his leg.	Omar waits for help.	Other hikers call for help.

Problem
Omar gets hurt and can't walk.

Event 1
Omar falls while hiking.

Event 2
He moves to the shade to wait for help.

Event 3
Some hikers with a cell-phone get help.

Solution
Omar is rescued.

Transparency 31 Level A, Unit 2 | Cooperation   © Hampton-Brown

A MOUNTAIN RESCUE

from *Banner in the Sky* • by James Ramsey Ullman

Sometimes counting on another person makes the difference between life and death. Sixteen-year-old Rudi Matt is alone on a snow-covered mountain in the Alps. Suddenly, he hears a cry for help. Can a boy save a man's life?

105

OBJECTIVES

Listening: Listen to a Preview
Reading Strategies: Preview; Predict

INTRODUCE THE SELECTION

4 Preview and Predict Read with students the title, author, and introduction to the story on page 105. Talk about the picture on the page. Then have them look through the selection and talk about the pictures. Ask: *What do you think the problem will be in this story? What ideas do you have about the solution?*

5 Audio Walk-Through
Play the Audio Walk-Through for "A Mountain Rescue" on the **Selection Tape/CD** to give students the overall idea of the story.

Tape 2B
CD 2
Track 6

A Mountain Rescue
by James Ramsey Ullman

Theme Connection This selection explores how counting on another person—sometimes even a total stranger—can mean the difference between life and death.

Selection Summary and Awards
"A Mountain Rescue" by James Ramsey Ullman comes from his 1955 Newbery Honor Book, *Banner in the Sky*. It describes a young man's rescue of a famous mountaineer who has fallen into an Alpine crevasse. Mr. Ullman writes with authority on the subject of mountaineering: he was a member of the first American team to scale Mt. Everest. Set in the Alps, *Banner in the Sky* includes details based on the original ascent of the Matterhorn. The book was also named an ALA Notable Children's Book.

OBJECTIVES
Function: Read a Selection
Grammar: Reflexive Pronouns
Listening: Listen to a Selection
Reading and Learning Strategies: Set a Purpose for Reading; ❶ Identify Problems and Solutions; Use Graphic Organizers (problem-solution chart)
Comprehension: Identify Details; Make an Inference; ❶ Predict

SET PURPOSE

1 Read aloud the introduction to the story. Say: *Listen to find out the problem that Rudi needs to solve.*

READ AND THINK

Tape 2B
CD 2
Track 7

2 Strategy Focus: Identify Problems and Solutions Involve students in reading pages 106–107. Use **Transparency 32/Master 32** to track the story problem, events, and solution.

> Choose Reading Options in the **Multi-Level Strategies** to tailor the reading to proficiency levels.

The recording of "A Mountain Rescue" on the **Selection Tape/CD** offers an oral language model and the opportunity to build reading fluency.

1

DANGER ON A MOUNTAIN

Rudi finds a man who has fallen down a crack in the ice. Together, they try to think of a way to pull the man up.

Red annotations offer opportunities to clarify meaning and check for understanding.

The **crevasse** was six feet **wide** at the top. But Rudi could not tell how **deep** it was. **Role-Play:** Have student partners act out the two characters' dialogue.

"Hello!" Rudi called. "Hello—"

A **voice** answered from below.

"How far down are you?"

"About twenty feet, I guess."

"How long have you been there?"

"About three hours."

Rudi looked up and down the crevasse. He was thinking **desperately** of what he could do.

"Do you have a rope?" asked the voice.

"No."

"You'll have to get help."

---

crevasse deep crack in the ice
wide long from side to side
deep far down from the top
voice sound made by a person
desperately wildly, hopelessly

REACHING ALL STUDENTS

Transparency 32 / Master 32

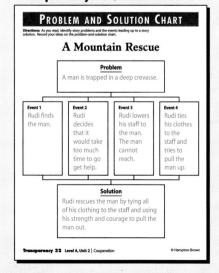

PROBLEM AND SOLUTION CHART

Directions: As you read, identify story problems and the events leading up to a story solution. Record your ideas on the problem-and-solution chart.

A Mountain Rescue

| **Problem** |
| A man is trapped in a deep crevasse. |

| **Event 1** | **Event 2** | **Event 3** | **Event 4** |
| Rudi finds the man. | Rudi decides that it would take too much time to go get help. | Rudi lowers his staff to the man. The man cannot reach. | Rudi ties his clothes to the staff and tries to pull the man up. |

| **Solution** |
| Rudi rescues the man by tying all of his clothing to the staff and using his strength and courage to pull the man out. |

Transparency 32 Level A, Unit 2 | Cooperation   © Hampton-Brown

---

> ## Multi-Level Strategies
> **READING OPTIONS FOR LESSONS 11–12**

BEGINNING Read the selection aloud, using red annotations and illustrations to clarify meaning. Use prompts to elicit information about the problem and the story events: *What is the problem Rudi must solve?* Record student responses on **Transparency 32**, vocalizing as you write.

INTERMEDIATE Students listen to the recording of the story on the **Selection Tape/CD**. Then they work in small groups to reread the story and discuss the story problem, events, and solution. Each student records information on **Master 32**. Groups can compare their charts.

ADVANCED Have students read the selection silently. Then, partners can work together to discuss the story problem, events, and solution and record their information on **Master 32**. Have students take turns pointing out portions of text that support the information they record.

Rudi didn't answer. To get down to town would take two hours. To **climb** back up would take three. By that time the man would be frozen to death.

"No," said Rudi, "it would take too long." **Clarify:** Rudi figured out how long it would take him to go for help.

There was another **silence**. "I'll think of something," Rudi cried. "I'll think of *something!*"

"Don't **lose your head**," the voice said.

The voice was as quiet as ever. Rudi didn't know who the man was, but he knew he was a **brave** man.

Use text features: Point out the italic type. Read the sentence with emphasis on the word *something*.

BEFORE YOU MOVE ON...

1. **Details** Why didn't Rudi go to town for help?
2. **Inference** Why did Rudi think that the man was brave?
3. **Prediction** What do you think Rudi will do to help the man?

---

lose your head do something silly or crazy

A Mountain Rescue **107**

---

3 Answers to "Before You Move On"

1. **Details** Rudi didn't go to town for help because it was too far away. The man needed help quickly because he could freeze to death.

2. **Inference** Rudi thought the man was brave because he remained calm despite the danger.

3. **Prediction** Answers will vary. Suggestions should be supported by details from the story.

CLOSE AND ASSESS

Ask students: *What do you think is the problem in the story?* (The man is stuck in a deep crevasse.) *How might someone go about solving this problem?* (They might go for help or they might figure out a way to bring the man to safety.)

Vocabulary
MEASUREMENT TERMS

Materials: ruler, yardstick, measuring tape

Point out to students the use of words denoting measurement, for example, *six feet, wide, deep, three hours*. Work with students to develop vocabulary related to measurement, such as *inch, foot, yard, measure, long*. Use a ruler, yardstick, and measuring tape to compare units of measure and what they are used to describe. Have students measure classroom objects using new vocabulary. Then, have them measure out twenty feet by six feet to show the depth and width of the crevasse in the story.

Grammar Minilesson

▶ **REFLEXIVE PRONOUNS**

TEACH Ask: *Can Rudi save the man by himself?* Explain that *himself* is a special type of pronoun. Say: *When you talk about yourself or another person twice in a sentence, use pronouns that end in **-self** or **-selves**.*

One	More than One
myself	ourselves
yourself	yourselves
himself	
herself	themselves
itself	

PRACTICE Write the chart of reflexive pronouns for students to refer to. Then write these cloze sentences. Have students add a reflexive pronoun to finish each sentence.

1. I heard Rudi's story _____.
2. The man could not save _____.
3. We would have helped the man _____ if we had been there.
4. Rudi's staff was not long enough _____ to reach the man.

▶ **Practice Book** page 55

A Mountain Rescue **T107**

READ PAGES 108–109

OBJECTIVES

Function: Read a Selection
Grammar: Possessive Nouns
Listening: Listen to a Selection
Reading and Learning Strategies:
Set a Purpose for Reading;
🟕 Identify Problems and Solutions;
Use Graphic Organizers (problem-solution chart); Visualize

SET PURPOSE

1 Summarize with students what has happened in the story so far. Then say: *Read to find out what Rudi does to help the man.*

READ AND THINK

Tape 2B
CD 2
Track 7

2 Strategy Focus: Identify Problems and Solutions Involve students in identifying story events as they read pages 108–110.

> See the **Multi-Level Strategies** on page T106 to tailor the reading experience to all proficiency levels.

2
THE RESCUE

Rudi makes a long rope by tying his clothes to his staff. He and the man work together to pull the man to safety.

Restate: Lying flat on the ice, he pushed his walking stick down into the crack as far as he could reach.

Rudi drew in a long, slow breath. Lying flat on the **glacier**, he **lowered** the **staff** as far as it would go.

"Can you see it?" he asked

"See what?" said the man.

Obviously he couldn't. Rudi **removed** his jacket and tied it to the staff.

Then, Rudi took his shirt and tied one sleeve to the sleeve of the jacket. As he lay down, the ice **bit into** his **bare** chest.

"Can you reach it?"

"I **can't make it**," said the voice. It was **fainter** than before.

Ask: Why do you think the voice was quieter than before?

....
glacier large area of ice
staff long walking stick
Obviously Clearly, It was clear that
bit into hurt, cut painfully into

bare uncovered
can't make it can't reach it
fainter quieter, harder to hear

108   **Unit 2** │ Cooperation

REACHING ALL STUDENTS

Language Development
GIVE DIRECTIONS

Have students work in pairs, one partner taking the role of the man, the other the role of Rudi. Then have them role-play the story, giving each other directions to help achieve the rescue. For example, students might say: *Tie something else to the jacket; grab the trouser leg; or, grab my hand.*

Vocabulary
CLOTHING

Ask students to look at illustrations and describe items of clothing they see: *hat, boots, glove, scarf.* Discuss the kinds of clothing one wears in various seasons in various parts of the world. You might want to start a chart:

Clothing All Year Round

winter	spring	summer	fall
jacket hat			

"Wait," said Rudi. He took off his **trousers**. He tied a trouser-leg to the sleeve of the shirt. Then, he lowered the staff and clothes like a **fishing line**.

"Can you reach it now?" he called.

"Yes," the voice answered. "You won't be able to hold me. I'll **pull** you in."

"No you won't."

The pull came. His hands **tightened** on the staff until the **knuckles showed white**. He could hear **scraping** below. The man was **clawing** his boots against the ice-wall.

It seemed like hours. Then at last a head **appeared**.

The climber was close now. But Rudi could **hold on** no longer. His hands were opening. It was all over.

Clarify: Rudi didn't think he could rescue the man after all.

Ask: Did Rudi hold on for hours? How long do you think it really took for the man to climb up the ice-wall?

---

trousers pants
fishing line string used to catch fish
knuckles showed white skin over his bones turned white from squeezing

scraping a scratching noise
clawing scratching and climbing with
appeared came into sight, could be seen

A Mountain Rescue **109**

MONITOR YOUR READING

3 Visualize Tell students this story has many descriptive details that can help them imagine the scene as if it were a movie. As students read or listen, ask them to make a mental picture of the snow, the cold, the colors of the clothing. Then have them listen for the sounds of Rudi and the man talking, the scraping sound of the man's boots on the ice-wall. They might also try to imagine the feelings and thoughts of both Rudi and the man.

Science Connection
EARTH SCIENCE

Have students research how glaciers and crevasses are formed using library resources or the Internet, for example, www.asf.alaska.edu:2222. Invite students to share any stories they have about seeing a glacier or crevasse and what it was like. Volunteers can report on what they found through their research. Encourage students to make models or illustrations of glaciers and how they are formed.

Grammar Minilesson

▶ **POSSESSIVE NOUNS**

TEACH Write this sentence: *The man could not see Rudi's staff.* Then say: *The word* Rudi's *shows that Rudi owns something. The staff belongs to Rudi. A word like* Rudi's *is called a possessive noun.*

Point out the **'s** on *Rudi's* and explain that we add an apostrophe and an *s* to nouns that name one person, place, or thing. Say: *With nouns that name more than one person, place, or thing that end in s, add just an apostrophe.* Provide examples.

the boy's shirt   the boys' shirts

the hiker's staff   the hikers' staffs

PRACTICE Have students choose the correct possessive noun to finish each sentence.

1. The ice bit into (Rudi's/Rudis') bare chest.

2. The (mans'/man's) voice was growing fainter.

3. The (trousers'/trouser's) legs were long enough to reach the man.

4. The two (boots'/boot's) soles scraped the ice.

▶ **Practice Book** page 56

A Mountain Rescue **T109**

READ PAGE 110

CHECK COMPREHENSION

4 Answers to "Before You Move On"

1. **Details** Rudi used a staff and his own clothing to help the man.

2. **Inference** He was surprised to find that such a young person could save him.

3. **Character** Rudi is resourceful, courageous, and cares for others.

ABOUT THE AUTHOR

5 Evaluate Literature: Author's Background Point out that the author wrote this story based on his own experiences. Have students read aloud About the Author. Ask: *Do you think this kind of incident could really happen? Why do you think the experiences seem so real?*

CLOSE AND ASSESS

Ask: *What was the most difficult problem in the story?*

Restate: The man made it to the top and climbed out of the crevasse.

And then it *was* over. The **weight** was gone. The man was beside Rudi, turning to him, **staring** at him.

"Why—you're just a boy!" he said in **astonishment**.

BEFORE YOU MOVE ON...

1. **Details** What did Rudi use to help the man?
2. **Inference** Why was the man surprised when he reached the top?
3. **Character** What does this story tell you about Rudi? What is he like?

....
staring looking with wide open eyes
astonishment surprise, amazement

**ABOUT
THE
AUTHOR**

James Ramsey Ullman was a newspaper reporter, a writer, and a mountain climber. He also was part of the first American team to climb Mount Everest. Mr. Ullman used many of his own experiences to help him write his Newbery Honor Book, *Banner in the Sky*. "A Mountain Rescue" comes from that novel.

REACHING ALL STUDENTS

Cooperative Learning

**FOR LANGUAGE DEVELOPMENT:
Give Information**

Identify Teams Form heterogeneous teams of 3 or 4. Assign each team member a number from 1–4. Then ask:

- How do you think the man got stuck in the crevasse?
- How long do you think it took for Rudi to save the man?
- How do you think Rudi felt when he could not hold on any longer?
- What tells you that Rudi was brave, smart, and caring?

Group members agree on how to answer each question.

Share Responses Choose a question and call a number between 1–4. Students assigned that number take turns presenting their group's response.

Debrief the Content Ask students to share insights they gained.

Debrief the Cooperative Process Have students evaluate the process of agreeing in a group.

Think Time

Talk Time

Share 2's Time

**Cooperative Learning Structure:
Numbered Heads**

Respond to the Story
Check Your Understanding

SUM IT UP

Identify Problems and Solutions Copy and complete this chart. Show Rudi's problem and the events that led to the solution.

Problem-and-Solution Chart

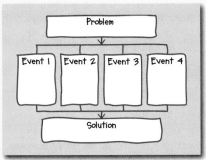

Summarize Use your chart to retell the story. Copy and complete this summary.

> Rudi had to _____.
> First he _____.
> Then Rudi _____.
> The man helped by _____.
> They worked together to _____.
> In the end _____.

THINK IT OVER

Discuss Talk about these questions with a partner.

1. **Character's Feelings** How did Rudi feel when he found the man trapped in the crevasse?

2. **Opinion** Was it a good idea for Rudi to try to help the man by himself? Explain.

3. **Details** What did the man do to help with the rescue?

4. **Personal Experience** Have you ever helped someone in need? What happened? How did you feel?

EXPRESS YOURSELF
▶ ASK FOR AND GIVE INFORMATION

Work with a partner. Take turns asking questions about details in the story. For example:

- How wide was the crevasse at the top?
- How far down was the man?
- How long was the man trapped?

✓ **LANGUAGE ACQUISITION ASSESSMENT**
See page 22 of the Assessment Handbook.

A Mountain Rescue 111

Multi-Level Strategies
SUM IT UP OPTIONS

BEGINNING Work with students to retell the story. Use the problem-solution chart to provide support for students. Write the sentence frames on separate strips. As a group, agree on how to complete each sentence. Then have students hold the strips and narrate the story, one strip at a time, while classmates act it out.

INTERMEDIATE Verify that groups completed the problem-and-solution chart accurately. Have groups work to complete the sentence frames. Have groups share their completed sentences.

ADVANCED These students can work independently to complete sentence frames. Using the frames and the completed problem-and-solution chart, have students write a paragraph to retell the story. Students share their versions of the story with the class.

OBJECTIVES

SUM IT UP
Reading and Learning Strategies:
❶ Identify Problems and Solutions; Use Graphic Organizers (problem-solution chart); Summarize

THINK IT OVER
Function: ❶ Engage in Discussion
Critical Thinking and Comprehension:
Identify Character's Feelings;
Identify Details; Form Opinions;
Relate to Personal Experience

EXPRESS YOURSELF
Function: ❶ Ask For and Give Information
Speaking and Listening: Interview

CHECK YOUR UNDERSTANDING

1 **Sum It Up** Refer to annotations on **Transparency 32** (see page T106) for possible chart entries.

▶ **Practice Book** page 57

2 **Think It Over** Possible answers are:

1. **Character's Feelings** Rudi felt frightened and alone.

2. **Opinion** Answers may vary. Encourage elaboration.

3. **Details** The man clawed against the ice-wall with his boots to take some weight off the rope as he lifted himself up.

4. **Personal Experience** Answers will vary. Encourage elaboration.

3 **Express Yourself** Prompt the use of measurement vocabulary in students' questions and responses.

CLOSE AND ASSESS

Have students give a one- or two-sentence review of this selection, including whether they recommend it to others.

RESPOND

OBJECTIVES

SUBJECT AND OBJECT PRONOUNS

Grammar: ❶ Subject and Object Pronouns

EXTEND THE STORY

Functions: Tell a Story; Write

Critical Thinking and Learning Strategies: Use Graphic Organizers (web, list); Interact with Peers; Make Comparisons

Writing: Story Ending

LANGUAGE ARTS AND LITERATURE

1 Use Subject and Object Pronouns See annotations for answers to the Practice items.

▶ **Practice Book** page 58

2 Extend the Story Give students time to brainstorm events that might have happened after the man was rescued. Suggest that pairs record their ideas in a web or list. Remind students to:

• Visualize the scene before writing.

• Present story events in a logical order.

• Choose clear and vivid words.

CLOSE AND ASSESS

Have students tell how they decided what their new story should be about in their story extensions.

 ✔ **ASSESSMENT**
Selection Test 8 on page 29 of the Assessment Handbook tests students' mastery of the reading strategies and the vocabulary, comprehension, and language arts skills taught with this selection.

Respond to the Story, continued
Language Arts and Literature

GRAMMAR IN CONTEXT

USE SUBJECT AND OBJECT PRONOUNS

Learn about Subject and Object Pronouns A **pronoun** is word that takes the place of a noun. Use a **subject pronoun** in the subject of a sentence. Use an **object pronoun** after a preposition or a verb.

Subject Pronouns	Object Pronouns
I	me
you	you
he, she, it	him, her, it
we	us
you	you
they	them

Use Subject and Object Pronouns Work with a partner. Retell "A Mountain Rescue." Use correct pronouns.

Example:
Rudi heard a man call for help. **He** found **him** trapped in the crevasse.
"**I** have to help **him,**" Rudi thought.

Practice Rewrite the sentences. Use pronouns in place of the underlined words.

1. <u>Rudi</u> tied his clothes to make a rope.   He

2. The man climbed toward <u>Rudi</u>.   him

3. <u>The time</u> seemed like hours.   It

4. "We did it!" <u>Rudi and the man</u> shouted.   they

WRITING/SPEAKING

EXTEND THE STORY

Work with a partner to **extend**, or add to, the story. Tell what happened after Rudi saved the man.

❶ **Write Your Ideas** How will you and your partner extend the story? Will you write about how the man thanks Rudi? Will you tell how they work together to get off the mountain? Write the new events clearly and in order.

❷ **Edit Your Work** Trade papers with another group. Make sure that the events are clear and in order. Check for the correct pronouns. Then make a better final draft.

❸ **Share Your Work** Join other pairs of students. Read the stories aloud. Then compare the endings.

 Learn how to improve your writing in the **writer's craft**. See Handbook pages 390–401. Review **pronouns** on pages 414–416.

REACHING ALL STUDENTS

Multi-Level Strategies
OPTIONS FOR EXTENDING THE STORY

BEGINNING   Discuss the story ending with students and brainstorm possible story extensions: *Did Rudi save the man's life? How do you think the man will thank Rudi? Do you think they will continue climbing the mountain together, or turn back to town?* List group ideas. Then, have the group choose one story extension. Work with students to write a sequence of events for the new ending. Students can share their extension with the rest of the class.

INTERMEDIATE / **ADVANCED**   Have students discuss the ending of the story as a group. As students begin writing an extension to the story, prompt them to elaborate with details: *Why do Rudi and the man decide to hike together down to town? What do Rudi and the man encounter as they hike back down the mountain? Does the man feel weak from being stuck in the crevasse?* Have students turn their events into a dialogue and present it.

Content Area Connections

SOCIAL STUDIES

EXPLORE GEOGRAPHY

Learn About the Alps "A Mountain Rescue" takes place in the Alpine Mountains of Switzerland. The **Alps** are mountains that run across several countries in Europe including:

France	Germany	Switzerland
Italy	Austria	Bosnia & Herzegovina
Croatia	Slovenia	Yugoslavia

Create a Map Draw and label the countries the Alps pass through. Then show the path of the mountain range. Label the tallest mountains like Mont Blanc, Piz Bernina, and the Matterhorn.

Make a Fact Sheet Find facts about the Alps. Then answer these questions to display with your map.

- How many miles long are the Alps?
- How many miles wide are they?
- How tall are the highest mountains?

SOCIAL STUDIES
TECHNOLOGY/MEDIA

COMPARE MOUNTAINS

The **Seven Summits** are the tallest mountains on each continent. Work with a group to study a mountain below:

Aconcagua	Elbrus	Puncak Jaya
Kilimanjaro	Everest	Vinson Massif
McKinley		

Find Information Use encyclopedias, atlases, or the Internet. Take notes about the mountain's location, height, and when it was first climbed.

Try these Web sites, but remember that new sites appear every day! Use the mountain's name as a key word.

INTERNET

INFORMATION ON-LINE

Web Sites:
➤ **Mountains**
  - www.eblast.com
  - www.peakware.com

Combine Information Make a class chart to compare the seven mountains your class studied.

 Learn how to make a **chart**. See Handbook pages 340–341.

A Mountain Rescue **113**

Research Skills

▶ MAP SKILLS

TEACH Display a map of Europe or a map of the world. Begin by having students identify any places on the map that are familiar to them. Label places students identify. As they note places, say, for example: *This location is just north of Italy; This location is surrounded by the Alps.* Point out to students the legend and scale bar on the map. Model how to use the scale bar to measure distances.

PRACTICE Have small groups choose several place names from a map and write them on index cards. Then have students exchange index cards, challenging their classmates to find the locations. Encourage groups to ask questions using geographical terms: *Is it north or south of Mount Kilimanjaro? Is it in Italy or Switzerland?* Have students report on their success rates.

▶ **Practice Book** page 59

OBJECTIVES

EXPLORE GEOGRAPHY

Function: ❶ Give Information

Learning Strategies, Critical Thinking, and Research Skills: Set Goals; Generate Ideas; Gather and Organize Information; Take Notes; Use a Map

Writing: Fact Sheet

COMPARE MOUNTAINS

Functions: ❶ Give Information; ❶ Describe

Learning Strategies, Critical Thinking, and Research Skills: Set Goals; Generate Ideas; Gather and Organize Information; Take Notes; Use a Map; Use an Atlas; Make Comparisons

Technology/Media: Use the Internet

Representing: Class Chart

CONTENT AREA CONNECTIONS

1 Explore Geography Provide a map or atlas to show students the Alps. Students can work together to make a map of the Alps and the surrounding countries.

▶ **Practice Book** page 60

2 Compare Mountains Facts about the seven summits are:

Mountain and Continent	Height	First scaled
Mt. Everest; Asia	29,028 ft	1953
Aconcagua; S. America	22,834 ft	1897
Mt. McKinley (Denali); N. America	20,320 ft	1913
Mt. Kilimanjaro; Africa	19,340 ft	1889
Mt. Elbrus; Europe	18,150 ft	1868
Puncak Jaya; Australia/Oceania	16,500 ft	1962
Vinson Massif; Antarctica	16,066 ft	1966

▶ **Practice Book** page 61

CLOSE AND ASSESS

Ask students to write a test item about mountains based upon either activity.

A Mountain Rescue **T113**

INTRODUCE WRITING THAT INFORMS AND EXPLAINS

1 Discuss Expository Writing Read the introduction. Ask: *How can we give information about our school in writing? What details should we include?* Restate students' ideas.

2 Study the Models Make a chart of information students got from the sentences and from the photographs.

Sentences	Photographs
team	carry things
just a few	cleaning up oil spill

▌ Use the Options for Studying Writing in the **Multi-Level Strategies** to adjust instruction.

CLOSE AND ASSESS

Ask students to agree on a summary sentence that defines expository writing.

Writing That Informs and Explains

Expository writing gives information about an idea or event. The writer includes important details to help explain the information.

WRITING MODEL

Look at these sentences and photographs from "Teamwork." What words give you information about teamwork? How do the photographs help explain the information?

from "Teamwork"

Team members cooperate
to get the job done.
That's called teamwork.

A team can be just a few . . .
or a team can be many.

Even animals can
work in teams.

REACHING ALL STUDENTS

▌ Multi-Level Strategies
OPTIONS FOR STUDYING EXPOSITORY WRITING

BEGINNING Explain that the details in expository writing usually tell about ideas or things that happen. Help students paraphrase details in the sentences in the model, for example: *A team is a group of people.* Ask them to find expository details in the photographs, and paraphrase or sketch them for the chart.

INTERMEDIATE Have students associate the photographs and sentences. Ask: *Which photos show a few team members? Which shows many? How are the man and the oxen a team?*

ADVANCED Point out the team aspect of each photo. Ask: *What is the team doing in this photo? How would this work be harder if the team members did not cooperate?* Encourage a discussion of how the photos support the text in giving information about teamwork.

Write Together

WRITING PROMPT

First think about an activity your class did as a team. Make a chart about it with your class. Then use the chart to write a summary.

1 **Plan the Chart and Summary** The chart will show
- **What** we did
- **Why** we did it
- **When** we did it
- **Where** we did it
- **How** we did it
- **How** we felt about it

2 **Brainstorm Ideas** Fill in the chart. Look at the example.

3 **Write the Summary** Use the chart to write a summary.

STUDENT WRITING MODEL

Our class had a beach cleanup to make Seaside Park cleaner and safer. We went to the beach on Friday afternoon. We divided the class into teams, and each person got a job to do. Then we picked up empty soda cans and old crumpled papers. Finally we loaded up five big bags of garbage. We were proud of our work. We were excited to tell our friends and family about it.

The events follow a logical order. **Time order words** show the steps.

Details help to make the story more interesting.

Experience Chart

What we did _beach cleanup_
Why we did it _to make the beach a cleaner, safer place_
When we did it _Friday afternoon_
Where we did it _Seaside Park_
How we did it _on teams, each person had a job_
How we felt about it _____ _proud, excited to tell others_

Transparency 33 / Master 33

EXPERIENCE CHART

What we did _____
Why we did it _____
When we did it _____
Where we did it _____
How we did it _____
How we felt about it _____

Transparency 33 Level A, Unit 2 | Cooperation   © Hampton-Brown

Transparency 34 / Master 34

FEATURES OF EXPOSITORY WRITING

Directions: Read the Student Writing Model. Compare it to the features of a summary. Check the box if the model has the feature. Write the details.

A Summary of an Event. . . _Our Beach Cleanup_

tells the important ideas about the **event**	☑ Our class cleaned up Seaside Park.
gives details, such as	
• **what** you did	☑ clean up the beach
• **why** you did it	☑ to make the park cleaner and safer
• **when** you did it	☑ Friday afternoon
• **where** you did it	☑ Seaside Park
• **how** you did it	☑ divided the class into teams
• **how** you felt	☑ proud, excited
tells what happened in the **correct order**	☑ 1) went to beach, 2) divided into teams, 3) picked up garbage, 4) loaded up garbage bags

Transparency 34 Level A, Unit 2 | Cooperation   © Hampton-Brown

---

OBJECTIVES

Function: Write
Learning Strategies and Critical Thinking: Plan; Generate Ideas; Interact with Peers; Analyze and Evaluate Information
Writing: Class Summary

WRITE TOGETHER

Discuss the Writing Prompt Remind students that a *writing prompt* is an instruction that tells you what kind of writing to do. Then read the prompt and ask volunteers to tell

- what kind of writing the class will do together (summary)
- what the summary will be about (a class activity)
- what the summary will do (describe what the class did and tell how the class felt about the activity).

Plan the Summary Work with students to choose an activity. Go over the explanation of what will go on each line, and study the sample charts. Then fill out the Experience Chart on **Transparency 33** for the class summary.

Analyze and Evaluate Summaries Display **Transparency 34**. Guide students in analyzing and evaluating the model against the features.

If students have difficulty finding a feature, have them look back at the sample experience chart for the activity. The organization there may help them discover the feature.

Write the Class Summary Help students turn the answers on their experience chart into a summary. Guide students in using sequence words to tell the events in order.

CLOSE AND ASSESS

Distribute copies of **Master 34** and have students work with partners or in small groups to analyze and evaluate your class summary against the features.

PREWRITE

Function: Write

Learning Strategies and Critical Thinking: Plan; Generate Ideas; Interact with Peers; Organize Ideas; Self-Assess

Representing: Flow Chart; Chart

Writing: ❶ Writing Process

WRITE ON YOUR OWN

Read the prompt together. Have individuals tell what kind of writing they will do, what activity they will write about, and with whom they will share it.

For more about the Writing Process, refer students to Handbook pages 382–389.

PREWRITE

Say: *Prewrite means to make a plan before you write.* Explain that to plan their summary, students will first draw pictures and then make an experience chart.

▌ Use the Prewriting Support in the **Multi-Level Strategies** to tailor this stage to proficiency levels.

Have partners answer the questions in Think About Your Writing.

Writing That Informs and Explains, continued

Write on Your Own

WRITING PROMPT

Now explain your part in the group activity. Write a summary for your family or friends to read.

Learn to write by doing it.
— P. D. James

PREWRITE

❶ **Show What You Did** Draw pictures of how you did your job.

I went to the beach.	I looked at the trash.	I wrote down the kinds of trash.

❷ **Get Organized** Make an experience chart about your topic.

Experience Chart

> **What I did** recorded the kinds of trash
> **Why I did it** I was the team recorder.
> **Where I did it** Seaside Park
> **When I did it** Friday afternoon
> **How I did it** wrote the name of each item
> **How I felt about it** like to write, important job

Think About Your Writing

- Did you fill in all the details on your chart?
- Are there more you want to add?

Transparency 35 / Master 35

EXPERIENCE CHART

Directions: Write about your part in the class activity.

What I did _____

Why I did it _____

When I did it _____

Where I did it _____

How I did it _____

How I felt about it _____

Transparency 35 Level A, Unit 2 | Cooperation   © Hampton-Brown

▌ **Multi-Level Strategies**

PREWRITING SUPPORT

BEGINNING Display **Transparency 35** and point out that it has the same items on the class experience chart, but with *I* as the subject. Distribute copies of **Master 35** and have students fill in their own charts as you model on the transparency. For each item, recall the entry from the class chart and show how an individual would complete an entry to show his or her own part in the activity. Assist students as needed in writing phrases and including relevant details in their drawings.

INTERMEDIATE / **ADVANCED** Distribute copies of **Master 35** and display **Transparency 33**. (See page T115.) Ask a volunteer to point out the difference. (different subjects: *we, I*) Ask another volunteer to suggest a specific entry for the first item on **Master 35**. Encourage students to discuss the items with a partner as they complete their own charts.

DRAFT

1 **Write Your Summary** Use your chart to write your summary.

2 **Choose the Best Details** Use words that are specific.

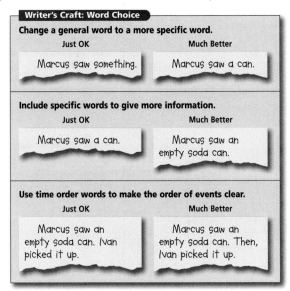

Writer's Craft: Word Choice

Change a general word to a more specific word.

Just OK	Much Better
Marcus saw something.	Marcus saw a can.

Include specific words to give more information.

Just OK	Much Better
Marcus saw a can.	Marcus saw an empty soda can.

Use time order words to make the order of events clear.

Just OK	Much Better
Marcus saw an empty soda can. Ivan picked it up.	Marcus saw an empty soda can. Then, Ivan picked it up.

Collect specific words in categories you are writing about. Use them to add details.

Talent Show	Litter	Lunch Room Decorations
juggle	paper plates	student artwork
play the violin	old newspapers	curtains
dance	candy wrappers	table centerpieces
sing	fast food containers	anti-litter posters

Time Order Words

first
next
then
last
finally
before
after
while
when

Think About Your Writing

• Read your draft. Do you like the way it sounds?

• Are there more specific words to explain what you did?

OBJECTIVES

DRAFT

Function: ❶ Give Information; Write

Learning Strategies and Critical Thinking: Generate Ideas; Self-Assess

Writers Craft: ❶ Word Choice

Writing: ❶ Writing Process

DRAFT

Remind students: *When you draft, you write quickly to get your ideas on paper.*

Study the Writer's Craft to help students use specific and time order words in their writing. Read the examples and talk about why the second sentences are "Much Better."

Go over the word lists. Act out the "Talent Show" entries. Show or draw items on the "Litter" and "Lunch Room Decorations" lists. Use the Time Order words in sample sentences about the lists.

■ Use the Drafting Support in the **Multi-Level Strategies** to tailor this stage to proficiency levels.

For more about the Writer's Craft, refer students to Handbook pages 390–401.

CLOSE AND ASSESS

Have small groups discuss the questions in Think About Your Writing while you work with those who may need more support in assessing their drafts.

Multi-Level Strategies

DRAFTING SUPPORT

BEGINNING Help students turn the information on their experience chart into a summary. As students work, suggest specific words they can use, such as those on the lists on page 117. Use prompts as necessary to assist students in including time order words: *What was the first thing you did? What was the last thing you did?* If necessary, write out sentences that students dictate.

INTERMEDIATE / **ADVANCED** Students can work with a partner to apply the Writer's Craft skill as they create the "Much Better" examples on **Master 36**. Encourage them to brainstorm specific and time order words to record in the Word File for use in their writing.

Transparency 36 / Master 36

WRITING: WORD CHOICE

Directions: Read each writing tip and the example that is "Just Okay." Change the example to make it "Much Better."

Writing Tips	Just Okay	Much Better
Change a general word to a more specific word.	Vi picked up some trash.	Vi picked up some candy wrappers.
Include specific words to give more information.	Vi picked up some candy wrappers.	Vi picked up four large candy wrappers and six small ones.
Use time words to make the order of events clear.	Vi picked up trash. She put it in a pile.	First, Vi picked up trash. Later, she put it in a pile.

Word File Directions: List specific words and time order words you can use in your writing.

Specific Words	Time Order Words

Transparency 36 Level A, Unit 2 | Cooperation   © Hampton-Brown

OBJECTIVES

REVISE

Function: Write; Engage in Discussion

Learning Strategies and Critical Thinking: Generate Ideas; Review; Clarify; Interact with Peers; Self-Assess

Listening and Speaking: Peer-Conferencing

Technology and Media: Use Word-Processing Software

Writing: ❶ Writing Process

REVISE

Remind students: *When you revise, you make changes that will improve your draft.* Have students read their summaries and think about possible changes.

Next, model how to participate in a peer conference. Also model how to make revisions. Then conduct peer conferences and have students revise their writing. If students are writing on a computer, demonstrate the cut-and-paste feature mentioned on page 118.

▌ Use the Peer Conference Support in the **Multi-Level Strategies** to model how to evaluate and revise writing.

CLOSE AND ASSESS

Have peers discuss the questions in Think About Your Writing.

Writing That Informs and Explains, continued

REVISE

❶ **Read Your Summary** Does it make sense?

❷ **Share Your Summary** Have a classmate read your summary. Ask:
- What part do you think is the most interesting? What part could be more interesting?
- Did I tell about events in the right order?
- Do I need to add more specific details?

❸ **Make Your Changes** Think about your classmate's answers to your questions. Then make changes to improve your summary. Use the Revising Marks.

Sample of a Revised Summary

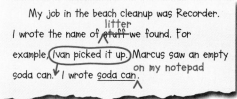

My job in the beach cleanup was Recorder. I wrote the name of ~~stuff~~ litter we found. For example, ⟨Ivan picked it up.⟩ Marcus saw an empty soda can. I wrote soda can. on my notepad

∧   Add.

↶   Move to here.

⋏   Replace with this.

⟋   Take out.

Key In ⟨TO⟩ Technology

You can use the cut-and-paste feature of your word-processing program. It will help you move words or sentences from one place to another.

Think About Your Writing

- What words did you change?
- What details did you add?
- Do you like the way your summary sounds now?

REACHING ALL STUDENTS

Transparency 37 / Master 37

REVISING

Red annotations show changes related to the sample comments. Revisions should vary to reflect comments students make.

Marcus saw an empty soda can. Then, Ivan   *at*   *in a notebook* picked it up. I looked it. I wrote about it. Finally, Ivan put it in the trash bag.

Revising Marks
∧   Add.
↶   Move to here.
⋏   Replace with this.
⟋   Take out.

Help a Writer in a Peer Conference

1. Tell what you like.
- The part I like best is *where she says "an empty soda can." That's very specific. I can picture it.*
- The part I like best is   Students' comments will vary.
- It's really good that you *clearly tell the order of events.*
- It's really good that you   Students' suggestions will vary.

2. Make a suggestion.
- I think you need to say *"I looked at it."*
- I think you need to   Students' comments will vary.
- This would be better if you tell *where you wrote about it. Did you write in a notebook or in a chart?*
- This would be better if   Students' suggestions will vary.

Transparency 37   Level A, Unit 2 | Cooperation   © Hampton-Brown

---

Multi-Level Strategies

PEER CONFERENCE SUPPORT

BEGINNING   Display **Transparency 37**. Read the sample and support comprehension as needed: pantomime or sketch the activity and paraphrase the ideas. Then model how to participate in a peer conference, noting that students should first tell what they like and then make suggestions. Use the sentence starters to develop appropriate language, and have volunteers dictate ways to complete each sentence. Then model how to revise the summary, based on the comments.

INTERMEDIATE / ADVANCED   Distribute copies of **Master 37**. Read the partial summary. Use the sample comments to model how to participate in a peer conference. Have students write more suggestions or comments of each type and share them with the class. Students can then make revisions to the summary, based on the suggestions, and read their revised versions to the group.

GRAMMAR IN CONTEXT

PRONOUNS

A noun is the name of a person, a place, a thing, or an idea. A pronoun takes the place of a noun.

	PRONOUNS	EXAMPLE
I	Use **I** to talk about yourself.	**I** can help in the cleanup.
You	Use **you** to talk to one or more other people.	Carlos, **you** can count the cans.
		Sam and Teresa, **you** can take the cans to the recycle center.
He	Use **he** to talk about a boy or man.	**William** collected the trash.
		He collected the trash.
She	Use **she** to talk about a girl or woman.	**Sara** carried the bag.
		She carried the bag.
It	Use **it** to talk about a place or thing.	**The bag** was heavy.
		It was heavy.
We	Use **we** to talk about other people and yourself.	**María and I** took notes.
		We took notes.
They	Use **they** to talk about other people or things.	**The notes** were helpful.
		They were helpful.

Practice Read each pair of sentences. Write the second sentence and add the correct pronoun.

1. My friends and I had a neighborhood cleanup. __I / We__ collected litter from the streets and sidewalks.
2. Lisa and Tim took the trash to the dump. __He / They__ made three trips.
3. Sylvia got some flower seeds. __He / She__ planted them next to the sidewalk.
4. All the parents admired our work. __They / We__ were proud of us.
5. My mother had a party for us. __She / It__ made cookies and lemonade.

OBJECTIVES
GRAMMAR IN CONTEXT
Grammar: ❶ Pronouns

GRAMMAR IN CONTEXT

1 Teach Pronouns Read the introduction and give examples of the different kinds of nouns, such as *Martin, California, book, peace.* Explain that a pronoun takes the place of the noun, and identify the nouns and pronouns in the examples.

Use student volunteers and classroom objects to illustrate the use of pronouns. Point to the person or item, say the sample sentence with the noun, and then say the sentence again with the pronoun. Then conduct the cooperative learning activity below.

2 Answers to Practice Items

1. We
2. They
3. She
4. They
5. She

CLOSE AND ASSESS

Give each student an oral sentence with a noun or nouns. Ask the student to repeat the sentence using the correct pronoun.

Cooperative Learning

FOR LANGUAGE DEVELOPMENT: Pronouns

Identify Nouns for Pronouns
Review the pronoun chart on page 119 and assign a singular or plural pronoun to each pair of students. In Think Time, individuals think of nouns their pronoun could replace. In Talk Time, give students chart paper and have them brainstorm more nouns their pronoun could replace. Students can include sketches on the chart, as well as words. For Share Time, display the charts and invite students to add nouns to each one.

Debrief the Skill Ask: *Which pronouns can you use to talk about more than one thing? Which pronoun do you use when you are talking about yourself?*

Debrief the Cooperative Process
Have students reflect on how the activity worked out: *Was it hard or easy to think of nouns for the pronouns? What is something you learned from seeing other students' charts?*

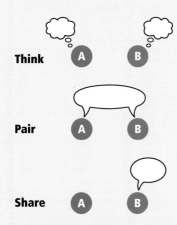

Cooperative Learning Structure: Think, Pair, Share

BUILD WRITING SKILLS

OBJECTIVES

EDIT AND PROOFREAD

Learning Strategies and Critical Thinking: Review; Clarify; Self-Assess

Writing: ❶ Writing Process

PUBLISH

Learning Strategies and Critical Thinking: Interact with Peers; Self-Assess; Make Decisions

Speaking: Read Aloud

Writing: ❶ Writing Process

EDIT AND PROOFREAD

Remind students: *When you edit, you correct errors in spelling, capitalization, punctuation, and grammar. Then you proofread, or check, your final copy.* Use **Transparency 38** to model the process.

PUBLISH

Say: *When you publish your writing, you share a final form with an audience.* Have students choose from the publishing suggestions on page 120.

> Use the Editing and Publishing Support in the **Multi-Level Strategies** to meet the varying needs of students.

CLOSE AND ASSESS

Have groups discuss the questions in Think About Your Writing. Monitor how students complete the checklist.

Writing That Informs and Explains, continued

EDIT AND PROOFREAD

❶ Proofread Your Summary When you find a mistake in spelling, punctuation, or capitalization, correct it. See pages 431–439 in the Handbook for help. Use the Proofreading Marks.

❷ Check Your Pronouns Do the pronouns tell about the right person? Do they tell about the right number of people?

❸ Make a Final Copy If you are working on a computer, print out a final copy of your work. If not, rewrite it and make the corrections you marked.

PUBLISH

Choose a way to share your summary. Here are some ideas.

- Submit your summary to your school newspaper. Add a title. Include your name.

Seaside School News

Park Cleanup
by Christina Villegas

Last Wednesday, our class cleaned up Seaside Park. We divided the class into teams, and each team got a job to do. One team picked up anything that was plastic. Another team collected empty soda cans. Another team gathered pieces of paper. Everything we found filled six garbage bags! At the end we were so tired, but we were proud of our work. Now we can enjoy the park even more.

The park looks so clean now!

- Read your summary to your family, friends, or classmates. Answer any questions they may have.
- Design a scrapbook page. Attach your summary. Add pictures. Then, make a class scrapbook.

Proofreading Marks

∧	Add.
⩔	Add a comma.
⊙	Add a period.
≡	Capitalize.
╱	Make lowercase.
⟋	Take out.
¶	Indent.

Think About Your Writing

- Do you think your summary is interesting?
- ☑ Does it include the important ideas and details?
- ☑ Does it explain what happened in the correct order?
- Do the pronouns tell about the right people?
- What do you like best about your summary?
- Will this summary go in your portfolio? Why or why not?

REACHING ALL STUDENTS

Transparency 38 / Master 38

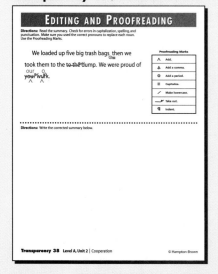

EDITING AND PROOFREADING

Directions: Read the summary. Check for errors in capitalization, spelling, and punctuation. Make sure you used the correct pronouns to replace each noun. Use the Proofreading Marks.

We loaded up five big trash bags, then we took them to the to the dump. We were proud of our your work.

Directions: Write the corrected summary below.

Transparency 38 Level A, Unit 2 | Cooperation   © Hampton-Brown

---

Multi-Level Strategies

EDITING AND PUBLISHING SUPPORT

BEGINNING Model finding and correcting errors in the summary on **Transparency 38**. After marking the edits, have students write out the corrected summary. For publishing, offer students who want to read their summary aloud a chance to tape record it and listen to it with you first.

INTERMEDIATE Guide students in finding and correcting the errors in the summary on **Transparency 38**. Encourage students to bind a copy of their summaries for use in the media center as a reference for class projects.

ADVANCED Distribute copies of **Master 38** and have students work on finding and correcting the errors individually or with partners. Assist students in making a video presentation of their summaries. One student can read his or her summary while another records it.

Debrief **UNITED, WE STAND**

✓ **ASSESSMENT**
The Unit 2 test on page 33 of the Assessment Handbook measures students' progress in reading, language arts, literary study, and writing. Additional forms in the Assessment Handbook allow for:
• Self Assessment on page 32
• Peer Assessment on page 101
• Portfolio Evaluation on page 103

1 Look Back at the Unit

Rank Team Goals This unit showed many kinds of teams.

Teamwork

Together, We Dream

A Dog You Can Count On

A Mountain Rescue

Work with a team of students. Write the title of each selection on an index card. Think about a team from each selection. On the back of each card, list the team's goals, such as *saves lives*, *does a job*, *has fun*. Now decide which team has the most important goal. Rank the teams from 1 to 4.

2 Show What You Know

Sum It All Up Add ideas about cooperation to the mind map. Share what you learned with a partner.

Cooperation		
Looks Like	Sounds Like	Feels Like

Reflect and Evaluate Finish these sentences:
• People cooperate when they _____.
• Cooperation is important because _____.
Put these sentences in your portfolio. Add work that shows what you learned about cooperation.

3 Make Connections

To Your Community Invite a team of community workers to your school. Or, plan a trip to see the team at work. Learn about how they work together.

DEBRIEF UNIT 2

OBJECTIVES

Function: Engage in Discussion; Express Opinions

Learning Strategies and Critical Thinking: Interact with Peers; Generate Ideas; Make Judgments; Summarize; Self-Assess; Evaluate Information; Use Graphic Organizers (mind map)

Literary Analysis: Respond to Literature; Compare and Evaluate Literature

EXPLORE "UNITED, WE STAND"

1 Look Back at the Unit Discuss criteria for ranking the importance of each goal, for example: *Would the outcome have a lasting effect?* Then begin the Cooperative Learning Activity.

2 Show What You Know Encourage students to choose work that illustrates what they consider important about cooperation.

3 Make Connections Prepare students for the visit or trip with a discussion about the contribution the workers make to the community.

CLOSE AND ASSESS

Have students tell you the most important thing they learned in the unit.

Cooperative Learning

FOR CRITICAL THINKING: Make Judgments

Rank Team Goals After agreeing on the ranking criterion, organize groups and number students within the group. Provide individual think time. During talk time, groups discuss the reasoning behind the group's position.

Sharing Ideas Have groups share ideas with a countdown. Call a number and have the students with that number in each group tell the fourth-ranked goal and the reasoning behind the group's choice. Continue with those ranked third, second, and first.

Debrief the Content Ask students what they learned about cooperation from the unit and the presentations. Begin by modeling a response: *I learned that working together helps us accomplish what we cannot do alone.*

Debrief the Cooperative Process Have students evaluate the activity. Ask: *What did the activity help you understand about cooperation? What did you learn about working in a group?*

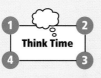
Think Time

Talk Time

Share 2's Time

Cooperative Learning Structure: Numbered Heads

Resources

For Success in Language, Literature, and Content

Student Book pages 122–187

For Skills Practice

Practice Book
pages 62–92

For Planning and Instruction

Teacher's Edition
pages T122a–T187

For Vocabulary and Language Development

Language Tape Sides A and B
Language CD Tracks 5, 6, and 7

For Audio Walk-Throughs and Selection Readings

Selection Tape 3
Selection CD 3

For Technology Support

Inspiration
Visual Learning Software
with Graphic Organizers

For Classroom Activities

Transparencies or Masters 39–58

For Home-School Connections

High Point Newsletters 5 and 6

For Comprehensive Assessment

Language Acquisition Assessment,
Selection Tests, Unit Test, Writing
Assessment, Self-Assessment

In the Theme Library

Mrs. Katz and Tush
by Patricia Polacco

In My Family
by Carmen Lomas Garza

From *The Basics Bookshelf*

▶ *Friends Are Like That*

▶ *Let's Dance!*

▶ *Families*

Theme-related books with
simple text for including
newcomers

Making Connections

AS COMPLEX AS HUMAN RELATIONSHIPS CAN BE, PEOPLE'S LIVES ARE ENRICHED THROUGH THEIR CONNECTIONS WITH OTHERS. THIS UNIT CHALLENGES STUDENTS TO EXPLORE THEIR OWN RELATIONSHIPS AS THEY READ ABOUT THE CONNECTIONS OTHERS HAVE WITH FAMILY AND FRIENDS.

THEME 1 Finding Friendship

Students discover that the qualities that make a true friend are the same around the world and over time.

THEME 2 Across Generations

Students consider how those who came before them have helped to make them who they are.

THEME 1: Finding Friendship

PACING SUGGESTIONS

LESSONS	45–55 MINUTE PERIODS	BLOCK SCHEDULE SESSIONS
1	1 period	4 sessions
2–8	7 periods	
9–10	2 periods	1 session
11–18	6 periods	3 sessions

LESSONS
1

THEME 1 OPENER ▶ pages T124–T125

Function	Learning Strategy	Vocabulary	Critical Thinking
Engage in Discussion	Make a Chart	Words about Careers, Family, and People	Generate Ideas

2–8

The Qualities of Friendship by Aesop   FABLES ▶ pages T128–T136

BUILD LANGUAGE AND VOCABULARY pages T126–T127	Function ⓣ Express Feelings	Learning Strategy Make a Friendship Flow Chart	Vocabulary Friendship Words	Patterns and Structures ⓣ Past Tense Verbs

PREPARE TO READ
page T128

Activate Prior Knowledge
Talk It Over

Vocabulary ⓣ
Use Words in Context

Reading Strategy
ⓣ Identify Sequence

READ THE SELECTION
pages T129–T133

Pre-Reading Strategies
Preview and Predict

  Identify Genre: Fables

  Set Purpose

Strategy Focus
ⓣ Identify Sequence

Vocabulary
Use New Words in Context

Comprehension
Before You Move On: Think and Discuss

📁 **Grammar Minilesson:**
ⓣ Past Tense Verbs

📁 **Literary Analysis Minilesson:**
Dialogue

RESPOND
pages T134–T136

CHECK YOUR UNDERSTANDING

Critical Thinking and Comprehension
Sum It Up:
ⓣ Identify Sequence: Retell the Fables

  Think It Over: Discuss

Function
Express Yourself: Ask for and Give Advice

LANGUAGE ARTS AND LITERATURE

Grammar in Context
ⓣ Use Action Verbs (present and past tense)

Literary Analysis
ⓣ Identify Plot and Character

CONTENT AREA CONNECTIONS

Social Studies
Study Aesop and His World

Technology/Media
Study Aesop's Fables

9–10

We Could Be Friends by Myra Cohn Livingston   POEM ▶ pages T137–T139

PREPARE TO READ
page T137

Activate Prior Knowledge
Idea Exchange

Vocabulary
Relate Words

Reading Strategy
Compare Experiences

READ THE POEM
page T138

Pre-Reading Strategies
Set Purpose

Strategy Focus
Make Comparisons

📁 **Grammar Minilesson:**
ⓣ Present Tense Verbs

RESPOND
page T139

Critical Thinking and Comprehension
Think It Over: Discuss

Function
Express Yourself: Make Comparisons

11–18

My Best Friend by Eloise Greenfield and Lessie Jones Little   AUTOBIOGRAPHY ▶ pages T142–T151

BUILD LANGUAGE AND VOCABULARY pages T140–T141	Function ⓣ Express Likes and Dislikes	Learning Strategy Make a Friendship Chart	Vocabulary Friendship Words	Patterns and Structures ⓣ Verb + Infinitive

PREPARE TO READ
page T142

Activate Prior Knowledge
Quickwrite

Vocabulary ⓣ
Use New Words in Context

Reading Strategy
ⓣ Relate Main Idea and Details

READ THE SELECTION
pages T143–T148

Pre-Reading Strategies
Preview and Predict

  Identify Genre: Autobiography

  Set Purpose

Strategy Focus
ⓣ Relate Main Idea and Details

Vocabulary
Relate Words

Comprehension
Before You Move On: Think and Discuss

📁 **Grammar Minilesson:**
ⓣ Irregular Past Tense Verbs

📁 **Literary Analysis Minilesson:**
Setting—Time and Place

RESPOND
pages T149–T151

CHECK YOUR UNDERSTANDING

Critical Thinking and Comprehension
Sum It Up:
ⓣ Relate Main Idea and Details; Write a Paragraph

  Think It Over: Discuss

Function
Express Yourself: Express Likes and Dislikes

LANGUAGE ARTS AND LITERATURE

Grammar In Context
Use Linking Verbs

Literary Analysis and Writing
Write about a Friendship

CONTENT AREA CONNECTIONS

Social Studies
Compare Generations

THEME 2: Across Generations

PACING SUGGESTIONS		
LESSONS	**45–55 MINUTE PERIODS**	**BLOCK SCHEDULE SESSIONS**
1	1 period	
2–9	7 periods	4 sessions
10–11	2 periods	1 session
12–18	7 periods	4 sessions

LESSONS

1

THEME 2 OPENER ▶ *pages T152–T153*

Function	**Learning Strategy**	**Vocabulary**	**Critical Thinking**
Engage in Discussion	Make a List	Family Words	Generate Ideas

2–9

Honoring Our Ancestors by Stephen Von Mason, Helen Zughaib, and Enrique Chagoya — FAMILY PORTRAITS ▶ *pages T156–T166*

BUILD LANGUAGE AND VOCABULARY pages T154–T155	**Function** ⊤ Give Information	**Learning Strategy** Make a Family Tree	**Vocabulary** Family Words	**Patterns and Structures** ⊤ Past Tense Verbs

PREPARE TO READ page T156

Activate Prior Knowledge
Share Ideas

Vocabulary ⊤
Relate Words

Reading Strategy ⊤
Paraphrase

READ THE SELECTION pages T157–T163

Pre-Reading Strategies
Preview, Predict, and Skim

Set Purpose

Strategy Focus ⊤
Paraphrase

Vocabulary
Relate Words

Comprehension
Before You Move On:
Think and Discuss

🗀 **Grammar Minilessons:**
⊤ Irregular Past Tense Verbs

Linking Verbs

RESPOND pages T164–T166

CHECK YOUR UNDERSTANDING

Critical Thinking and Comprehension
Sum It Up:
Identify Cause and Effect;
⊤ Paraphrase

Think It Over: Discuss

Function
Express Yourself:
Describe Things

LANGUAGE ARTS AND LITERATURE

Vocabulary
⊤ Use Context Clues

Writing/Speaking
Write a Dedication

CONTENT AREA CONNECTIONS

Social Studies and Technology/Media
Research an Ancestor's Country

Fine Arts and Technology/Media
Make a Multimedia Presentation

10–11

Everybody Says by Dorothy Aldis — POEM ▶ *pages T167–T169*

PREPARE TO READ page T167

Activate Prior Knowledge
Share Opinions

Vocabulary
Use New Words in Context

Literary Analysis
Rhyme; Rhythm; Repetition

READ THE POEM page T168

Pre-Reading Strategies
Set Purpose

Strategy Focus
Use Text Features in Poetry (rhyme, rhythm, repetition)

RESPOND page T169

Critical Thinking and Comprehension
Think It Over: Discuss

Writing/Speaking
Write a Poem

12–18

Grandfather's Nose by Dorothy Hinshaw Patent — SCIENCE ARTICLE ▶ *pages T172–T179*

BUILD LANGUAGE AND VOCABULARY pages T170–T171	**Function** ⊤ Define and Explain	**Learning Strategy** Make a Tally Chart of Physical Traits	**Vocabulary** Words About Traits	**Patterns and Structures** Present Tense Verbs; ⊤ Past Tense Verbs

PREPARE TO READ page T172

Activate Prior Knowledge
Share Information

Vocabulary ⊤
Use New Words in Context

Reading Strategy
Use Text Features in Nonfiction; Formulate Questions; Take and Review Notes

READ THE SELECTION pages T173–T176

Pre-Reading Strategies
Preview and Predict

Set Purpose

Strategy Focus
Use Text Features in Nonfiction; Formulate Questions; Take and Review Notes

Comprehension
Before You Move On:
Think and Discuss

🗀 **Grammar Minilesson:**
Demonstrative Pronouns

RESPOND pages T177–T179

CHECK YOUR UNDERSTANDING

Critical Thinking and Comprehension
Sum It Up:
⊤ Relate Main Idea and Details;
Write Sentences

Think It Over: Discuss

Function
Express Yourself:
Define and Explain

LANGUAGE ARTS AND LITERATURE

Grammar in Context
⊤ Use Negative Sentences

Writing
Write Labels

CONTENT AREA CONNECTIONS

Science
Study Genetics

BUILD WRITING SKILLS

WRITING FOR PERSONAL EXPRESSION — EXPRESSIVE: MAIN IDEA PARAGRAPH ▶ *pages T180–T186*

Writing Mode/Form ⊤ Expressive Main Idea Paragraph	**Writing Process** ⊤ Prewrite; Draft; Revise; Edit and Proofread; Publish	**Writer's Craft** ⊤ Elaboration	**Grammar in Context** ⊤ Past Tense Verbs	**Reflect and Evaluate** Self-Assessment

⊤ = Assessed on **Unit 3 Test**   ⊤ = Assessed on **Unit 3 Language Acquisition Assessment**

THEME 1: Finding Friendship

MORE RESOURCES

Mrs. Katz and Tush
by Patricia Polacco
A A special friendship that lasts for years begins when Larnel gives Mrs. Katz a homeless kitten. (Available from Hampton-Brown)

You're Not My Best Friend Anymore
by Charlotte Pomerantz
B Even best friends have arguments. In this story, Molly and Ben learn how to work out a disagreement and stay friends. (Dial)

Robin Hood and Little John
by Barbara Cohen
I Can enemies become friends? That's how a famous friendship begins in this story. It's been told since the Middle Ages! (Putnam & Grosset)

Aesop and Company
by Barbara Bader
B Many of Aesop's best known fables are accompanied here by his biography and several age-appropriate illustrations. (Walter Lorraine)

P.S. Longer Letter Later
by Paula Danziger and Ann Matthews Martin
I A Two popular authors took turns writing this book in the form of letters between two best friends growing up apart. Can friendship overcome the boundary of distance? (Apple)

The Journey of Natty Gann
B I A A charming story of friendship between a young girl searching for her father, a wild dog, and a kind young drifter. Set during the depression. **Film/Video**

THEME 2: Across Generations

MORE RESOURCES

In My Family/En mi familia
by Carmen Lomas Garza
B Paintings and short descriptions present scenes from life in a Mexican American family. (Available from Hampton-Brown)

Honoring Our Ancestors
edited by Harriet Rohmer
I Fourteen artists use words and pictures to honor members of their families. (Children's Book Press)

Yang the Youngest and His Terrible Ear
by Lensey Namioka
A The youngest child of four tries to fit in with his family. It's hard to when everyone else is musical! (Yearling Books)

Regular Guy
by Sarah Weeks
B I Buzz and Bob-o feel like oddballs in their very different families. Could they have been switched at birth? (HarperCollins)

Amazing Schemes Within Your Genes
by Frances R. Balkwill
I A This short nonfiction, part of the Cells and Things series, talks about the science of genetics and the concept of individuality. (First Avenue Editions)

Exploring Genetics and Heredity
I A This interactive CD-ROM uses art and microphotography to explain the concepts of genetics, DNA structure, and more in a clear, engaging manner. (Queue) **Multimedia CD-ROM**

ONGOING, INFORMAL ASSESSMENT

Check for understanding and achieve closure for every lesson with the targeted questions and activities in the **Close and Assess** boxes in your Teacher's Edition.

INDIVIDUAL AND GROUP-ADMINISTERED TESTS

The **Assessment Handbook** includes these comprehensive assessment tools for Unit 3:

▶ **Selection Tests**
Test students' mastery of reading strategies and the vocabulary, comprehension, and language arts skills taught with each main selection of Unit 3.

▶ **Unit Test in Standardized Test Format**
The multiple-choice sections of this test measure students' cumulative understanding of the skills and language developed in Unit 3. A Writing Prompt measures progress in writing skills and fluency. The Read, Think, and Explain section offers open-ended items to measure strategies and comprehension.

▶ **Language Acquisition Assessment**
To verify students' ability to use the vocabulary and grammar structures taught in Unit 3, conduct these performance assessments.

UNIT 3 ASSESSMENT OPPORTUNITIES	
	Assessment Handbook Pages
Unit 3 Language Acquisition Assessment	41–42
Selection Tests	
The Qualities of Friendship	43–44
My Best Friend	45–46
Honoring Our Ancestors	47–48
Grandfather's Nose	49–50
Unit 3 Writing Assessment	51
Unit 3 Self-Assessment Form	52
Unit 3 Test	53–60
Peer-Assessment Form	101
Portfolio Evaluation Form	103

SELF- AND PEER-ASSESSMENT

Students use the Unit 3 Self-Assessment Form in the **Assessment Handbook** to evaluate their own work and develop learning strategies appropriate to their needs. Students offer feedback to their classmates with the Peer-Assessment Form.

WRITING ASSESSMENT / PORTFOLIO OPPORTUNITIES

You can evaluate students' writing using the rubrics and scoring guidelines provided in the **Assessment Handbook**. Then collaborate with students to choose work for their portfolios.

OBJECTIVES

Function: Engage in Discussion

Concepts and Vocabulary: Careers; Family; People

Viewing: Respond to Photographs; Interpret Visual Images

Critical Thinking and Learning Strategies: Classify; Predict; Preview; Build Background; Use Graphic Organizers (mind map)

INTRODUCE UNIT CONCEPT

1 **View the Photographs** Define *relationships:* "connections we have with people in our lives." Ask: *What kinds of relationships does the boy in the photos have?* Then read the activity.

2 **Build Vocabulary About Relationships** Work together as a class to list the relationships in the photos (clockwise from top left: parents, grandfather, godparents, sister and cousins, teacher and classmates, friends). Record the lists on **Transparency 39.** Ask students to complete the chart with professionals not shown in the collage. Then have students build their own lists of important people.

▮ Use the Vocabulary Options in the **Multi-Level Strategies** to work with all proficiency levels.

UNIT 3 Relationships

Fate chooses our relatives; we choose our friends.

—J. DeLille

122

REACHING ALL STUDENTS

Transparency 39 / Master 39

WORDS ABOUT RELATIONSHIPS		
Relatives	Friends	Professionals

Transparency 39 Level A, Unit 3 | Relationships © Hampton-Brown

Multi-Level Strategies
VOCABULARY BUILDING OPTIONS

BEGINNING Use the photographs on page 122 to build vocabulary about relationships. Prompt students to point and give yes/no or one-word answers: *Show me a baby in the photograph. Who is holding the baby?* Repeat each answer as a complete sentence, emphasizing the key word as you write it: *Yes, the* parents *are holding the* baby. *Parents are important people in our lives.*

INTERMEDIATE Use prompts about categories of words to elicit information: *Which family members live at home with you? Who are professional people you see at school every day?* Introduce unfamiliar vocabulary as needed: *Yes, Mrs. Kim is the cashier in the lunchroom.*

ADVANCED Have students share their lists and elaborate about relationships: *Tell me about your sister. How is Mr. Smith important to you?* Then have students introduce one another: *This is Joe. He has a brother named....*

Making Connections

List the important people in your life. Put an *R* next to names of relatives. Put a *P* next to professional people, such as your doctor. Put an *F* next to names of friends. Are the people on your list mostly from one group? Or, do you have people in all groups? Talk with a partner about why each person is important to you.

THEME **1**

Finding Friendship
The qualities that make a true friend are the same around the world and over time.

THEME **2**

Across Generations
Those who come before us help to make us who we are.

123

UNIT 3 Mind Map

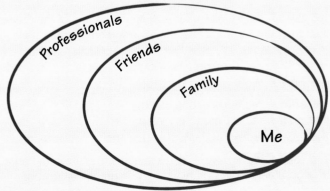

Relationships

Professionals

Friends

Family

Me

Technology Support
See **Inspiration** Visual Learning software for support in creating mind maps.

---

3 Classify and Predict Relationships Discuss answers to these questions:

- Did you place anyone on more than one list?

- Who do you think will still be on your list in five years?

Summarize: *We make connections with friends, family members, and other people who help us in our daily lives. We have relationships with all these important people.*

PREVIEW UNIT THEMES

4 Preview Theme 1: Finding Friendship Read aloud the theme title and the theme statement. Define *qualities* as "traits that make a person special." Then ask: *What kinds of qualities do you think are important in friendships?* (respect, trust)

Invite students to read the saying on page 122, and then look over pages 124–151 to find illustrations or photographs that show friendship.

5 Preview Theme 2: Across Generations Read the theme title and statement. Define *generations* as people born around the same period of time: *You are the young generation, your parents are the adult generation, and your grandparents are the older generation.* "Those who come before us" can include parents, grandparents, aunts and uncles, or more distant relatives. Invite students to look over pages 152–179 to find photographs that portray relationships among family members.

6 Create a Mind Map Model how to add names to the mind map, using yourself as an example. Have students start a map in their notebooks or in the **Practice Book**. Have them add to it as they move through the unit.

▶ **Practice Book** page 62

CLOSE AND ASSESS

Ask students what this unit will be about. (relationships; making connections) Then ask: *Can relationships ever change? How?* (Yes. Families grow. We can meet new friends.)

INTRODUCE THEME 1

OBJECTIVES

Function: Engage in Discussion; Role-Play

Concepts and Vocabulary:
Careers; Family; People

Viewing: Respond to a Photograph;
Interpret a Visual Image

Learning Strategies:
Relate to Personal Experience;
Use Graphic Organizers (chart)

Critical Thinking: Generate Ideas

TAP PRIOR KNOWLEDGE

1 People Hunt Have students write down one thing they like to do with friends. Then, students conduct a People Hunt to find others who wrote down the same thing. Newly formed groups complete this sentence to describe their interest: *Friends can _____.*

VIEW, DISCUSS, AND ROLE-PLAY

2 Imagine Yourself in a Photograph As students look at the photograph, ask: *What are some words you think of when you see good friends together?* Then have students create friendship portraits. Explain to students that in this theme, they will talk and read about how people can be friends.

Use the Activity Options in the **Multi-Level Strategies** to work with all proficiency levels.

3 Dramatize Activities that Friends Share Ask students to act out activities they share with their friends. As students pantomime or role-play, have classmates guess the activity. Record responses on a chart:

Friend 1	Activity	Friend 2
Kim	talks on the phone	with Mike
Rosanna	plays softball	with friends.

Repeat each response as a complete sentence.

124   Unit 3 | Relationships

REACHING ALL STUDENTS

Multi-Level Strategies
ACTIVITY OPTIONS

BEGINNING   Ask students to draw a picture of themselves with a friend, demonstrating in their drawing something they like to do with their friend. As students display their work, ask questions: *What is your friend's name? What are you doing?* Elicit captions and label the drawings.

INTERMEDIATE   Have students draw a picture of a friend and complete these sentence frames to describe the friend and their shared activities. Remind them to use pronouns: *My friend's name is _____. He/She is _____. We _____ together.* Students can share their work with the class.

ADVANCED   Have students imagine they are in the photograph with their best friend. Have them write a paragraph telling about the friendship and the friend's special qualities. Encourage students to illustrate the paragraph and give it the title, *A Photo of _____ and Me.*

Finding Friendship

- What makes a good friend? How can you be a good friend to others?

- What does friendship mean to you? Why is it important?

- How do you make new friends? How do you keep them?

THEME-RELATED BOOKS

You're Not My Best Friend Anymore
by Charlotte Pomerantz

Even best friends have arguments. In this story, Molly and Ben learn how to work out a disagreement and stay friends.

BEGINNING

Robin Hood and Little John
by Barbara Cohen

Can enemies become friends? That's how a famous friendship begins in this story. It's been told since the Middle Ages!

INTERMEDIATE

Mrs. Katz and Tush
by Patricia Polacco

A special friendship that lasts for years begins when Larnel gives Mrs. Katz a homeless kitten.

ADVANCED

125

DISCUSS THE GUIDING QUESTIONS

4 **Set the Theme** Some key points to develop during the discussion are:

- A good friend is thoughtful, honest, respectful, caring, trustworthy, and understanding. These qualities are ones that make us good friends to others as well.

- Friendships can be important for many different reasons. Friends help us feel connected. They provide support, and a sense of belonging. A friend can help us through a difficult time, teach us how to play a game or how to solve a problem. A friend can grow up with us as we change and grow.

- Friends come into our lives in many ways and at different times. We can meet friends in the neighborhood, at school or church, or through other friends. We can keep friendships by caring for and supporting our friends.

Form groups and use the **Multi-Level Strategies** so all students can participate.

CLOSE AND ASSESS

In a round-table activity, ask students to complete the sentence starter *A good friend is _____*. Record student responses and have students join you in reading them aloud.

Multi-Level Strategies
GROUPING GUIDELINES

BEGINNING Work on oral language and listening vocabularies related to friendship. Begin simply, by using sentence frames that each student has a chance to respond to, for example: *I have a friend. (His/her) name is _____. My friend is _____.* Provide guidance as students supply words to describe their friends and as they respond to the guiding questions.

INTERMEDIATE / **ADVANCED** Have Advanced students work with Intermediate students in small groups to discuss the guiding questions. Then have students compile their ideas and make a list of attributes or qualities that characterize a good friendship. Students can use their list of words to create dialogue for a skit that demonstrates some of the aspects of friendship that they identified.

THEME LIBRARY

■ *Mrs. Katz and Tush*
by Patricia Polacco

Invite students to read *Mrs. Katz and Tush*. Ask: *Are Mrs. Katz and Larnel good models for friendship? Why? What can you learn from them about being a friend?* Students can use the questions to continue developing ideas about friendship and how friendships can grow and change. Encourage them to write their ideas in their Reflection Logs, making additions as they read about friendships in other unit selections.

BUILD LANGUAGE AND VOCABULARY

START WITH A COMMON EXPERIENCE

1 Build Background Tell students
that proverbs are short, wise sayings.

2 Discuss the Proverbs Use the art
and the background information to
help develop meaning for the
proverbs. Explain that Slovakia is a
cold, northern land where
strawberries are rare treasures that
come from warmer climates.
Encourage students to restate each
proverb in their own words.

> Use the Discussion Prompts in the
> **Multi-Level Strategies** to invite
> responses from all levels.

3 Listen and Compare
Play the **Language**
Tape/CD or read the script
on page T381. Invite students to tell
which proverb it reminds them of.

Tape 1A
CD 1
Track 5

4 Model How to Express Feelings
Ask what feelings the student on the
recording expressed. *(The student
was upset and worried at first, then felt
good when the problem was solved.)*
Then model the skill:

> **How to Express Feelings**
>
> • Name an event: *I won the game.*
>
> • Name a feeling: *I was so happy
> when I won the game.*
>
> • Tell more: *I held the trophy over
> my head!*

Build Language and Vocabulary
EXPRESS FEELINGS

Read these proverbs. Then listen to a short story about a good
friend. Which friendship proverb does this story remind you of?

FRIENDSHIP

A good friend shields you
from the storm.
—*Chinese proverb*

As for clothes,
the newer the better;
as for friends,
the older the better.
—*Korean proverb*

Real friends will share even
a strawberry.
—*Slovakian proverb*

Who is mighty? One who
makes an enemy into a friend.
—*Jewish proverb*

126   **Unit 3** | Relationships

REACHING ALL STUDENTS

> ### Multi-Level Strategies
> **DISCUSSION PROMPTS**

BEGINNING   Ask questions based on information shown in the art:
*What is the weather like in the picture? How is the person shielding the friend
from the rain?*

INTERMEDIATE   Prompt comment by calling attention to specific details
in the proverbs: *What makes new clothes better than old clothes? What is
important about old friends? Why do you think the proverb states "as for friends,
the older the better"?* Encourage students to express their feelings about
other topics using this formula: *As for socks, the cleaner the better; As for
music, the louder the better.*

ADVANCED   Have students go beyond the literal meanings of the
proverbs. *What meaning could the word* storm *have other than a physical
storm? How can a good friend shield you from problems that arise in life?*

MAKE A FRIENDSHIP FLOW CHART

How do people become friends? Share your ideas with the class. Then, make a chart like this one. Write about the way you made friends with someone you know.

A Friendship Flow Chart

Two people smile at each other.	They sit together in class.	They work on a class project together.	They have fun together after school.

BUILD YOUR VOCABULARY

Friendship Words Good friends do special things for each other. They understand each other's feelings. Work with a group to brainstorm a mind map about how good friends act and feel.

USE LANGUAGE STRUCTURES ▶ PAST TENSE VERBS

Speaking: Tell a Friendship Story Tell the story of how you made friends with someone. Explain how you felt. Use past tense verbs.

Example:
Once I **went** to a new school. I **felt** lonely because I **had** no friends. On my first day, I **saw** a tall girl. She **smiled** at me. That **made** me feel good. Later, we **were** on the same basketball team in gym class. I **passed** her the ball, and she **made** a basket. After that, I **knew** we would be friends.

CONDUCT THE ACTIVITIES

5 Make a Friendship Flow Chart Discuss the question as a group. Have students work on their flow charts individually and then share their charts.

6 Build Your Vocabulary: Friendship Words Remind students to give details for each main idea in the mind map. Invite groups to share and discuss their mind maps.

7 Use Language Structures: Past Tense Verbs Present the skill, using the definition and examples on **Transparency 40**. You may wish to provide additional examples. Then have students complete the sentences in Try It! Remind them to follow the rules for adding -ed.

Speaking: Tell a Friendship Story Conduct the activity at the bottom of page 127. Point out that since students are telling about something that happened in the past, they should use past tense verbs in their stories.

▌ Use the Speaking Activity Options in the **Multi-Level Strategies** to adjust instruction.

▶ **Practice Book** page 63

CLOSE AND ASSESS

Ask students to complete this sentence with a past tense verb: *After school yesterday, I _____.*

Multi-Level Strategies
SPEAKING ACTIVITY OPTIONS

BEGINNING Students might present their stories as a series of drawings. Prompt them to dictate simple captions. Or they may complete sentence frames you provide, using words from a word bank: *I _____ new in my school. I _____ no friends. I felt _____. One day a girl _____ at me. I _____ to her. Then we _____ home together. I felt _____ .* Word bank words: *was, had, sad, smiled, talked, walked, glad.*

INTERMEDIATE / **ADVANCED** Have students prepare for this activity by making a mind map about their feelings and actions when they met their friends. Suggest that students deliver their presentations using appropriate nonverbal cues to convey meaning and express feelings.

Transparency 40 / Master 40

LEARN ABOUT PAST TENSE VERBS

A **past tense verb** tells about an action that already happened. Many past tense verbs end in **-ed**.
Yesterday, we **played** basketball.

Follow these rules.	Verb	Past Tense Verb
For most verbs, add **-ed**.	want	She **wanted** a plum.
For verbs that end in silent **e**, drop the **e** and add **-ed**.	taste	He **tasted** it.
For verbs that end in one vowel and one consonant, double the final consonant and add **-ed**.	chop	They **chopped** it in pieces.
For verbs that end in a consonant and **y**, change the **y** to **i** and add **-ed**.	study	Then they **studied** for the test.

Try It!

Write the past tense form of the verb in parentheses.

1. Enrique _____ schools last year. **(change)**
2. He _____ his old friends. **(miss)**
3. Enrique _____ to make new friends. **(try)**

Transparency 40 Level A, Unit 3 | Relationships   © Hampton-Brown

PREPARE TO READ

OBJECTIVES

THINK ABOUT WHAT YOU KNOW
Reading and Learning Strategies:
Relate to Personal Experience

LEARN KEY VOCABULARY ⊤
Vocabulary Strategy:
Use Words in Context

LEARN TO IDENTIFY SEQUENCE
Reading Strategy: ⊤ Identify Sequence

THINK ABOUT WHAT YOU KNOW

1 Talk It Over List qualities mentioned by students and elicit discussion: *Why is that an important quality? What else do you like about friends?*

LEARN KEY VOCABULARY

2 Use Words in Context Read aloud each vocabulary word and its defining sentence. For the activity, point out context clues: *Which word goes with* song? *Yes, you need music to sing and dance, so* dance *might be right.*

> Use the Vocabulary Options in **Multi-Level Strategies** to tailor instruction to proficiency levels.

▶ **Practice Book** page 64

LEARN TO IDENTIFY SEQUENCE

3 Model How to Identify Sequence Define *sequence.* Use the main events of "A Dog You Can Count On" (pages 95–98) to conduct the activity on **Transparency 41** as a guided practice. Refer to the annotations on this page for ideas.

CLOSE AND ASSESS

Ask: *What do you do when you sequence?* (put events in the order in which they happened, often using words like *first, next, last,* and *finally*)

THE
QUALITIES
of
FRIENDSHIP

fables
by Aesop

Prepare to Read

THINK ABOUT WHAT YOU KNOW

Talk It Over Honesty is one important quality of friendship. Talk about other qualities you look for in a friend.

dance When you **dance**, you move your body to music.

jealous A **jealous** person wants what someone else has.

kindness A **kindness** is something good that you do or say.

show off When you **show off**, you show others how well you can do something. People show off to get attention.

terrified When you are **terrified**, you feel very scared.

trap A **trap** is used to catch animals.

LEARN KEY VOCABULARY

Use Words in Context Study the new words. Then write each sentence. Add the best word to complete each sentence.

1. My friend and I decided to sing and ____dance____ in a contest.

2. She was not scared, but I was __terrified__ .

3. I felt like an animal caught in a ___trap___ !

4. She began to __show off__ her dance steps for the judges.

5. I felt __jealous__ when she won first prize.

6. The judges showed __kindness__ and gave me a prize for my singing.

LEARN TO IDENTIFY SEQUENCE

In stories, events happen in an order called **sequence**. Knowing the sequence of events helps you understand the story.

> **READING STRATEGY**
> **How to Identify Sequence**
> 1. Read the story.
> 2. Ask yourself: What happened first? What happened next?
> 3. Put the events in order. Use order words like: *first, next, then, finally.*

Read "The Qualities of Friendship." Think about the sequence of events.

128 **Unit 3** | Relationships

REACHING ALL STUDENTS

Multi-Level Strategies
VOCABULARY OPTIONS

BEGINNING / **INTERMEDIATE**
Invite volunteers to role-play each word: *Who can pretend to be a person who shows off on a bike?* etc. Then, work as a group to choose the correct word to complete each sentence. Have students role-play the sentences.

ADVANCED Ask partners to write questions using the new words after they have completed the sentences. Each partner chooses three words and uses each in a question. Partners then trade questions and write their answers.

Transparency 41 / Master 41

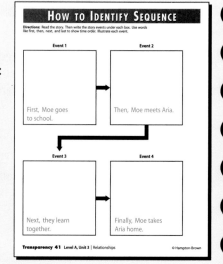

HOW TO IDENTIFY SEQUENCE

Directions: Read the story. Then write the story events under each box. Use words like first, then, next, and last to show time order. Illustrate each event.

Event 1
First, Moe goes to school.

Event 2
Then, Moe meets Aria.

Event 3
Next, they learn together.

Event 4
Finally, Moe takes Aria home.

Transparency 41 Level A, Unit 3 | Relationships   © Hampton-Brown

THE QUALITIES of FRIENDSHIP

BY AESOP

Fables are stories that teach a lesson, or *moral*. These fables about friendship were first told in ancient Greece by Aesop, a famous storyteller. Do you think these lessons are still important, more than a thousand years later?

129

OBJECTIVES

Listening: Listen to a Preview
Reading Strategies: Preview; Predict
Literary Analysis: Fable

INTRODUCE THE SELECTION

4 Preview and Predict Read the title, author, and introduction. Next, have students page through the fables. Ask them to watch for clues about lessons that may be learned by the characters. Ask: *Who do you think will learn a lesson in this fable? Do you think a lion can learn a lesson from a mouse? Why or why not?*

5 Identify Genre: Fables Tell students that characters in fables are often talking animals. Explain that fables usually end with a moral that states the lesson.

6 Audio Walk-Through Play the Audio Walk-Through for "The Qualities of Friendship" on the **Selection Tape/CD** to give students the overall idea of the selection.

Tape 3A
CD 3
Track 1

The Qualities of Friendship
by Aesop

Theme Connection In both fables, "The Mouse and the Lion," and "The Monkey and the Camel," the author makes important points about friendship.

Selection Summary Both stories were first told by Aesop, a famous storyteller in ancient Greece. In "The Mouse and the Lion," the lion learns the importance of doing kind acts for others. In "The Monkey and the Camel," the camel learns that each of us should be true to ourselves and not try to be something we are not. In both of these selections, the characters learn about the importance of friendship.

THE BASICS BOOKSHELF

■ *Friends Are Like That* by Daphne Liu

A friend is someone with whom you can share, someone you can trust. That is what two friends in this story learn about friendship. The simple text describing their confrontation and reconciliation supports the acquisition of the basic feeling words while the illustrations provide opportunities to talk about familiar teen pastimes and interests.

For Lesson Plans: See the Teacher's Guide for *The Basics Bookshelf*.

OBJECTIVES

Function: Read a Selection

Concepts and Vocabulary: Actions

Listening: Listen to a Selection

Reading and Learning Strategies: Set a
Purpose for Reading; ❶ Identify
Sequence; Use Graphic Organizers
(sequence chain)

Comprehension: Identify Details; Relate
to Personal Experience

Literary Analysis: Dialogue

SET PURPOSE

1 Say: *Listen to discover the lesson that
the characters in the story learn.*

READ AND THINK

Tape 3A
CD 3
Track 2

**2 Strategy Focus: Identify
Sequence** Have students identify the
main events in the story in the order
in which they happen.

Choose Reading Options in the
Multi-Level Strategies to tailor
the reading to proficiency levels.

The recording of "The Qualities of
Friendship" on the **Selection
Tape/CD** offers an oral language
model and the opportunity to build
reading fluency.

The Mouse and the Lion

A lion was sleeping in his cave.
He awoke when he felt something **scurry
by**. The lion was surprised to see a small
mouse. **In a flash**, he trapped the mouse
under his huge paw.

"Oh, great lion," the **terrified** mouse
cried, "if you **free me**, I'll never forget
your **kindness**. Someday, I could
help you."

The lion roared with laughter.
"You tiny mouse," he said, "how could
you help me? You're even too tiny to eat.
I shall let you go." And he did.

Ask: Why did the lion let the mouse go?

----

scurry by run past him very quickly
In a flash Very quickly
free me let me go

130 **Unit 3** | Relationships

REACHING ALL STUDENTS

HOME CONNECTION

Friendship Fables Send home a copy
of *High Point Newsletter 5* in the
Teacher's Resource Book. (See pages
125–131.) In this home activity,
students interview family members
to learn about fables or stories that
illustrate a lesson about friendship.
Students take notes (in their home
language or English) and use these
notes to retell the story to the class.

Multi-Level Strategies

READING OPTIONS FOR LESSONS 4–5

BEGINNING As you read aloud each fable, check comprehension to be
certain students understand what is being read: *What did the lion do when he
saw the mouse?* Use the pictures and the red annotations on the facsimile
pages to clarify meaning. Pause after each key event to reword it on the
Sequence Chain on **Transparency 41**. (See page T128.)

INTERMEDIATE Read the fables to students, or play the recording on the
Selection Tape/CD. Work as a group to record events on **Transparency 41**.
Ask questions using sequence words (*first, next, then, finally*) to elicit
information about key events.

ADVANCED Have partners read the fables. They can take turns reading
the dialogue in "The Mouse and the Lion." Distribute copies of **Master 41** for
students to complete for each fable. Then ask volunteers to retell the stories.

Use visuals: Point to the lion in the hunter's trap and ask students to tell what the mouse is doing.

Then one day, the lion was caught in a hunter's **trap**. **In spite of his strength**, the lion could not **escape**. The mouse heard the lion's roars. He **rushed** to the lion's side. Without saying a word, the mouse began to **gnaw at** the ropes. Soon, the lion was free.

"Thank you, little friend," the **grateful** lion said to the mouse. "I never would have guessed that such a small friend could be such a big help."

Moral:
A friend returns one kindness with another.

Restate: Friends help each other.

BEFORE YOU MOVE ON...

1. **Details** Why did the lion think that the mouse could not help him? Was he right or wrong? Explain.
2. **Vocabulary** Make a list of story words that mean "move quickly." Add other words you know that describe the way things move.
3. **Personal Experience** This fable is about friends helping friends. How has a friend helped you?

....

In spite of his strength Even though he was so strong
escape get away, run away
rushed ran very quickly
gnaw at chew on, bite on
grateful thankful

The Qualities of Friendship **131**

CHECK COMPREHENSION

3 Answers to "Before You Move On"

1. **Details** The lion thought that a creature as small as a mouse could not help someone as big as a lion. He was wrong, because the mouse saved him.
2. **Vocabulary** Some possible words include the following: *scurry, rushed, speedy, swift, quick as lightning.*
3. **Personal Experience** Encourage students to tell how a friend helped them, and to put the ideas in sequential order.

CLOSE AND ASSESS

Ask students to write a sentence restating the moral of this fable.

Vocabulary
CHARACTER TRAITS

Have students write an acrostic about a friend. Model how to write the letters of the name vertically and how to use each letter to describe one quality of the friend. Have pairs swap acrostics and write sentences based upon them.

K ind

U ltra-smart

R esponsible

I nteresting

That's my friend Kuri!

Literary Analysis Minilesson

▶ **DIALOGUE**

TEACH Point out to students the conversation between the mouse and the lion on page 130 that begins: "Oh great lion,... " Write the words, noting the quotation marks as you write them.

Explain to students that quotation marks signal to readers that these are the exact words being said by a character. The words within the quotation marks are called *dialogue.* Invite students to act out a dialogue.

PRACTICE Students can practice the use of dialogue by drawing pictures of the story characters, then using quotation marks to indicate what each character says.

Students can then work together in pairs to act out a dialogue. When they are comfortable with the procedure, have them present their dialogue to classmates.

▶ **Practice Book** page 65

OBJECTIVES

Function: Read a Selection

Vocabulary Strategy:
Use New Words in Context

Grammar: ⊤ Past Tense Verbs

Listening: Listen to a Selection

Reading and Learning Strategies: Set a Purpose for Reading; ⊤ Identify Sequence; Use Graphic Organizers (sequence chain)

Comprehension: Identify Details; Make an Inference; Form Opinions

Literary Analysis: Respond to Literature

SET PURPOSE

1 Say: *Listen to find out the lesson that is learned by a character in this fable.*

READ AND THINK

Tape 3A
CD 3
Track 2

2 **Strategy Focus: Identify Sequence** Involve students in reading pages 132–133.

See the **Multi-Level Strategies** on page T130 to include all students in the reading.

Use visuals: Pause to point out the desert in the picture. Ask students to name familiar animals. (zebra, camel, monkey)

The Monkey and the Camel

One day, the **beasts** of the **desert** had a party. All the animals were pleased when the monkey arrived, for she was a great dancer. "**Dance** for us, Monkey," the animals **begged**.

So Monkey danced for them. She put on a great show. The animals clapped. They **praised** her **lively kicks** and her quick steps. But the camel was jealous. He wanted the animals to clap for him. He wanted them to praise *his* dancing. **Ask:** Why was the camel jealous?

---

beasts wild animals
desert dry, sandy land
begged asked over and over again

put on a great show pleased them with her dancing
praised said how much they liked
lively kicks fast, jumping dance steps

132 **Unit 3** | Relationships

REACHING ALL STUDENTS

Vocabulary
SYNONYMS

Say: *Stand up* quickly. Then say: *Stand up* fast. Point out that both commands have the same meaning. Tell students that words like *quickly* and *fast*, are called synonyms. Start a chart similar to the one below. Ask students to suggest words from the story for the left column and synonyms for the right column.

Story Words	Synonyms
pleased	happy, glad, delighted

Language Development
TELL A STORY

Have students do one of the following activities, depending on their level of language proficiency:

• Retell one of the fables.

• Make up a new ending to one of the fables, with a new moral lesson.

• Create a fable to teach a moral related to an event in their own lives.

Students may work with a partner or in small groups. Arrange a storytelling session so students can share their work.

So, to everyone's surprise, Camel began to dance. His tail went up. His head went down. One leg went one way. One leg went another. He looked so silly, all the animals started to laugh. At last, Camel kicked in too many **directions** at once. His legs got **all tangled up**. He fell flat on his face. The animals pointed and **made fun of** him. "That's what you get for trying to **show off**!" they said, and they **drove him away** with their laughter.

Clarify: The camel was embarrassed, so he left.

—❧—

Moral:
The fastest way to lose friends is to try to be something you are not.

—❧—

Restate: It's best to be yourself.

·····································

directions different ways
all tangled up twisted together
made fun of laughed at
drove him away made him leave

BEFORE YOU MOVE ON...

1. **Details** What did the animals like about the way Monkey danced?
2. **Inference** Camel could not dance well because of his long legs. What other animals could have trouble dancing? Why?
3. **Opinion** Do you think the other animals were fair to Camel? Explain.

ABOUT THE AUTHOR

Aesop lived more than 25 centuries ago. He was born a slave around the year 600 BCE. Aesop became famous for the stories he told. His master, Iadmon, set him free from slavery. Aesop's stories were first written down about 200 years after he died.

Aesop, Diego Velázquez, oil on canvas, c. 1639–1640. Museo del Prado, Madrid, Spain.

The Qualities of Friendship   **133**

---

3 Use New Words in Context Check students' comprehension: *How did the Lion show kindness? Why was Camel jealous?*

CHECK COMPREHENSION

4 Answers to "Before You Move On"

1. **Details** They liked her lively kicks and her quick steps.
2. **Inference** Encourage students to give reasons for their responses. For example, students might say that an elephant would not be a good dancer because its trunk would get in the way.
3. **Opinion** Answers will vary.

ABOUT THE AUTHOR

5 Respond to Literature Read aloud About the Author. Talk about the way fables help us understand right and wrong and how to treat others. Start a wall chart for students to record ways they can apply the fable lessons to their lives.

CLOSE AND ASSESS

Have students answer this question on an exit slip: *What important lesson did Camel learn?*

Grammar Minilesson

▶ PAST TENSE VERBS

TEACH Draw students' attention to this sentence from page 133: *He looked so silly, all the animals started to laugh.*

Identify *looked* and *started* as verbs that show the action happened earlier, or in the past. Explain: *Many verbs that show an action that happened in the past end in –ed.*

Use words from the story to illustrate spelling rules for adding **–ed**.

> dance – e + ed = danced
>
> beg + g + ed = begged
>
> try – y + i + ed = tried

PRACTICE Write this paragraph. Have students change the underlined present tense verbs to past tense verbs.

> Camel <u>starts</u> to dance. He <u>dances</u> around and around. He <u>looks</u> so silly, all the animals <u>laugh</u>. Camel <u>kicks</u> his legs out in different directions. He <u>tangles</u> himself in a knot! Camel <u>drops</u> to the ground. The animals <u>point</u> at him and <u>cheer</u>!

▶ Practice Book page 66

RESPOND

OBJECTIVES

SUM IT UP

Function: Write

Reading and Learning Strategies:
⊙ Identify Sequence; Use Graphic
Organizers (storyboard)

Writing: Summary

THINK IT OVER

Function: Engage in Discussion

Critical Thinking and Comprehension:
Identify Author's Purpose;
Make Judgments; Form Opinions;
Relate to Personal Experience

EXPRESS YOURSELF

Function: Ask For and Give Advice

Speaking and Listening: Role-Play

CHECK YOUR UNDERSTANDING

1 Sum It Up Main events for "The
Monkey and the Camel" are: the
animals have a party and Monkey
dances; Camel feels jealous; Camel
dances; the animals laugh at Camel.
If necessary, have students listen to
the **Audio Walk-Through** or reread
the selection.

▶ **Practice Book** page 67

2 Think It Over Possible answers are:

1. Author's Purpose Answers will
vary. The lessons learned by the
animals are good for the people
listening, too.

2. Judgments Good way: Talk
to friends. Bad way: Make fun
of friends.

3. Opinion Answers will vary.

4. Personal Experience Encourage
thoughtful responses.

3 Express Yourself Model how to use
proper intonation when asking for
and giving advice: *What should I... ?
How can I... ? You can.... Maybe you
should....*

CLOSE AND ASSESS

Have students create a graphic organizer
to show Camel's inner feelings and
outward actions.

Respond to the Fables
Check Your Understanding

SUM IT UP

Show Sequence Make a storyboard for the
first fable. Draw pictures and write words to
describe the order of events. Then make another
storyboard for the second fable.

Storyboard

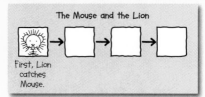

Make a Group Storyboard Make big pictures
from your small drawings. Each person in your
group will draw one picture. Put them in order.
Draw arrows to show sequence. Write a sentence
about each picture.

Retell the Fables Use the storyboards to tell the
fables in your own words. Show each picture and
tell how each character feels about the events.

✓ LANGUAGE ACQUISITION ASSESSMENT
See page 41 of the Assessment Handbook.

THINK IT OVER

Discuss Talk about these questions with
a partner.

1. **Author's Purpose** Why does Aesop write
about animals? Do his fables have good
messages for people, too?

2. **Judgments** The animals made fun of Camel.
Discuss good and bad ways to share your
feelings about a friend.

3. **Opinion** Which fable do you like better?
Why?

4. **Personal Experience** How do you show your
friendship to others?

EXPRESS YOURSELF
▶ ASK FOR AND GIVE ADVICE

Pretend you are Camel. You want to get
attention from the other animals. Ask a partner
for ideas. Then pretend your partner is Camel.
Give advice about how to get attention.

REACHING ALL STUDENTS

Multi-Level Strategies
SUM IT UP OPTIONS

BEGINNING Display the completed Sequence Chain on **Transparency
41** (see page T128) to help partners create their own storyboards. Remind
students to use the words *first, next, then,* and *finally* to show sequence.
Partners can write the text first; then each partner can add illustrations for
one of the fables. Monitor students as they go on to create the group
storyboard.

INTERMEDIATE / ADVANCED Students can use their completed
Sequence Chains from **Master 41** (see page T128) to create their group
storyboards. Then, have them create scripts to add dialogue to each fable.
Students may use their scripts to retell the fables.

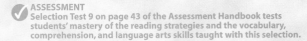

✓ **ASSESSMENT**
Selection Test 9 on page 43 of the Assessment Handbook tests students' mastery of the reading strategies and the vocabulary, comprehension, and language arts skills taught with this selection.

Language Arts and Literature

GRAMMAR IN CONTEXT

USE ACTION VERBS

Learn About Action Verbs An **action verb** tells what the subject does. The **tense** of a verb shows when an action happens.

- Use a **present tense verb** if the action is happening now or if it happens all the time.

- Use a **past tense verb** if the action happened earlier, or in the past.

Present Tense Verbs	Past Tense Verbs
Lion **traps** Mouse.	Lion **trapped** Mouse.
Mouse **helps** Lion.	Mouse **helped** Lion.
Monkey **dances**.	Monkey **danced**.

Use Verbs in Sentences Work with a partner. First your partner does something and uses a present tense verb to describe the action. Then you use a past tense verb to tell what your partner did. Take turns.

Example:
Partner 1: I **clap** my hands.
Partner 2: You **clapped** your hands.

Practice Write the sentences. Change the present tense verbs to past tense verbs.

1. The mouse surprises the lion. *surprised*

2. The lion roars with laughter. *roared*

3. A hunter traps the lion. *trapped*

4. The mouse rushes to the lion. *rushed*

5. The little mouse gnaws the ropes. *gnawed*

LITERARY ANALYSIS

IDENTIFY PLOT AND CHARACTER

Learn About Plot and Character The **plot** tells the events that happen in a story. The events follow a sequence from beginning to end. Stories also have **characters**. Aesop's characters are all animals.

Learn to Map a Story A **story map** shows how the characters and the plot work together in a story. Copy and complete this map for "The Lion and the Mouse."

Story Map

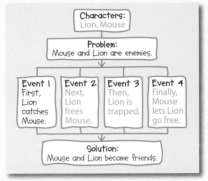

Practice Now make a story map for "The Monkey and the Camel."

Multi-Level Strategies

ACTIVITY OPTIONS FOR PLOT AND CHARACTER

BEGINNING Use questions to ensure that students understand the terms *character, problem,* and *solution: How did Mouse and Lion solve their problem? What was the solution?* etc. Work with students to complete the second story map. After they identify the problem (Camel wants attention), help them see that the solution in this story really is a lesson: Camel learns that showing off is not the way to get attention.

INTERMEDIATE / **ADVANCED** Have small groups with mixed proficiency levels discuss what the problem and solution are in "The Monkey and the Camel." You may need to give them a hint that the solution was the lesson that Camel learned. Then, have groups discuss the key events before having students work independently to complete the story map.

OBJECTIVES

ACTION VERBS

Grammar: ⊕ Present Tense Verbs; ⊕ Past Tense Verbs
Listening and Speaking: Describe Actions

PLOT AND CHARACTER

Function: Write

Concepts and Vocabulary: Words About Story Writing—*plot, characters, solution*

Reading and Learning Strategies: ⊕ Identify Sequence; Use Graphic Organizers (story map)

Literary Analysis: ⊕ Plot (problem and solution); ⊕ Characterization

Representing and Writing: Story Map

LANGUAGE ARTS AND LITERATURE

1 **Use Action Verbs** Pair students with varying proficiency levels to role-play and describe action verbs. Annotations show answers to the practice items.

▶ **Practice Book** page 68

2 **Identify Plot and Character** Students' charts should include: **Characters:** Monkey, Camel; **Problem:** Camel wants attention; **Event 1:** The animals have a party; **Event 2:** When Monkey dances, the animals praise her; **Event 4:** Camel is jealous and begins dancing to get attention; **Event 5:** He falls and the animals laugh at him; **Solution:** Camel learns that showing off is not a good way to get attention.

CLOSE AND ASSESS

Ask students to write a test item for one of the fables. Pool the test items and use them in an oral quiz.

RESPOND

OBJECTIVES

STUDY AESOP AND HIS WORLD

Function: ❶ Give Information

Speaking: Report

Learning Strategies and Research Skills: Gather Information; Take Notes; Use a Map

Representing and Writing: Map; Biography

STUDY AESOP'S FABLES

Function: ❶ Give Information

Learning Strategies, Research Skills, and Technology/Media: Gather Information; Use the Internet

Representing: Illustrated Fable

CONTENT AREA CONNECTIONS

1 Study Aesop and His World Direct students to reference books or to the Internet.

Web Sites and On-line Encyclopedias Web sites undergo frequent modifications, but here are some you may want to suggest to students:

www.pacificnet.net
Click on Aesop to find over 600 fables and narrations, plus a dictionary.

www.umass.edu/aesop
Click on Aesop for traditional and modern illustrations of fables.

www.museum.upenn.edu/greek_world/intro.html
Click on Greek World for information and resources about ancient Greece.

▶ **Practice Book** page 69

2 Study Aesop's Fables Direct students to the Web sites suggested above. Offer guidance in selecting the medium for illustrating the fable.

CLOSE AND ASSESS

Invite students to share their completed projects as a way to demonstrate their understanding of Aesop and his world.

Respond to the Fables, continued

Content Area Connections

▶ SOCIAL STUDIES

STUDY AESOP AND HIS WORLD

Work with a group to research Aesop and ancient Greece. Choose one of these projects:

- **Make a Map** Show where Aesop lived. Use an encyclopedia or an atlas of the ancient world. Label islands, seas, cities, and towns. Show your map to the class.

- **Write a Biography** A **biography** tells about a person's life. Learn more about Aesop. Use library books, encyclopedias, and the Internet to find information. Write a biography to show what you learned.

▶ TECHNOLOGY/MEDIA

STUDY AESOP'S FABLES

Search for more fables by Aesop. Find one to illustrate. Then present your fable to the class.

❶ Find Aesop's Fables Look in books or on the Internet. Find a fable you like and print it. Try these key words and Web sites to begin your search, but remember that new sites appear every day!

INTERNET
INFORMATION ON-LINE

Key Words:
Aesop
fables

Web Sites:
▶ Fables
- www.dusklight.com
- www.pacificnet/~johnr/aesop

❷ Present the Fable Illustrate the fable. Then present the fable and art to the class.

Learn how to use the **Internet**. See Handbook pages 364–365.

REACHING ALL STUDENTS

Research Skills

▶ **USING THE INTERNET**

TEACH Model for students ways to begin their research on Aesop and the world of fables. Explain that information about Aesop is available in books, but they may find more varied resources on the Internet. Help them to narrow their topic. Suggested searches include: + *Aesop* + *fables*, "ancient Greece", "Aesop's fables", *fables*. Work together with small groups to locate search engines and use them to select and gather information.

Search Engines
www.yahooligans.com
www.awesomelibrary.org
ww.ipl.org

PRACTICE Allow small groups to work on the Internet. Remind students to state a research goal: *I want to find out more about the tales that Aesop wrote.* Have students identify at least three sites and tell facts that they learned.

We Could Be Friends

poem
by Myra Cohn Livingston

Prepare to Read Poetry

THINK ABOUT WHAT YOU KNOW

Idea Exchange Who calls you on the telephone? Can telephones help friendships? Share your ideas with the class.

LEARN KEY VOCABULARY

goof around When friends **goof around**, they play together and have fun.

supposed to be The way things are **supposed to be** is how they should be.

Answers to the vocabulary activity will vary.

Relate Words Study the new words. Work with a partner to make a chart. Add your own ideas. Then share your chart with the class.

Friends are supposed to be	Friends goof around when they
honest	ride bikes

LEARN TO MAKE COMPARISONS

Make **comparisons** to see how things are the same and different.

READING STRATEGY
How to Compare Experiences

1. When you read about a person, think about what the person says or does.
2. Ask yourself: Does the person act or think the same way I do? How is the person different from me?
3. Ask yourself: How would I feel or act in the same situation?

As you read "We Could Be Friends," compare your experiences with the narrator's experiences. Do you make friends in the same way?

We Could Be Friends **137**

Multi-Level Strategies
VOCABULARY OPTIONS

BEGINNING Work with the group to complete the chart about friends. Ask leading questions such as *What does your friend love to do? Where does she or he live?*

INTERMEDIATE / ADVANCED
Have partners work together to complete the chart and sentences. Suggest that they proofread each other's work and then revise.

Transparency 42 / Master 42

HOW TO COMPARE EXPERIENCES

Directions: Write the name of a friend in the chart. Write some things you know about your friend's feelings or experiences. Then in the second column, write information about yourself.

Feelings and Experiences

	I
loves to _____	love to _____
lives _____	live _____
helps _____	help _____

Directions: Complete these sentences. Tell how you and your friend are alike and different.

_____ and I are alike because _____
_____
_____

We are different because _____
_____
_____
_____

Transparency 42 Level A, Unit 3 | Relationships   © Hampton-Brown

---

OBJECTIVES

THINK ABOUT WHAT YOU KNOW
Reading and Learning Strategies: Activate Prior Knowledge

LEARN KEY VOCABULARY
Vocabulary Strategy: Relate Words

LEARN TO MAKE COMPARISONS
Reading Strategy: Make Comparisons

THINK ABOUT WHAT YOU KNOW

1 **Idea Exchange** Pantomime hearing the phone ring, picking up the receiver, and greeting the caller. Invite students to do the same. Ask: *Who do you hope is calling you? What would you like to talk to this person about?* Restate student responses in complete sentences. (*Pedro talks to Linda about homework.*)

LEARN KEY VOCABULARY

2 **Relate Words** Read each phrase and its defining sentence aloud. After students understand the meaning of the key vocabulary words, conduct the chart activity.

▌ Use the Vocabulary Options in **Multi-Level Strategies** to help all students participate.

LEARN TO MAKE COMPARISONS

3 **Model How To Compare Experiences** Help students understand the meaning of *make comparisons* or *compare*. Then model the process, using the steps in the box. For guided practice, conduct the activities on **Transparency 42**. Use your feelings and experiences to model completing column two.

CLOSE AND ASSESS

Ask: *What do you do when you compare feelings and experiences?* (look at somebody's feelings and experiences to see if they are the same or different from your own)

Function: Read a Poem
Grammar: ❶ Present Tense Verbs
Listening: Listen to a Poem
Reading and Learning Strategies:
Set a Purpose for Reading;
Make Comparisons

SET PURPOSE

1 Set the purpose for listening to the poem. Say: *As you listen, think about answers to these questions: Why do you think the telephone is important to the two friends? Is the telephone important to you and your friends?*

LISTEN AND READ

Tape 3A
CD 3
Track 3

2 Strategy Focus: Make Comparisons Play "We Could Be Friends" on the **Selection Tape/CD** or read the poem aloud. Then play or read the poem again. Have students think about how the experience of these two friends may be like experiences they have had with their own friends.

> Choose Listening Options in the **Multi-Level Strategies** to tailor the activity to proficiency levels.

WE COULD BE FRIENDS

We could be friends
Like friends are supposed to be.
You, picking up the telephone
Calling me

      to come over and play
      or take a walk,
      finding a place
      to sit and talk,

Or just goof around
Like friends do,
Me, picking up the telephone
Calling you.

—*Myra Cohn Livingston*

138   Unit 3 | Relationships

REACHING ALL STUDENTS

> ### Multi-Level Strategies
> **LISTENING OPTIONS FOR LESSON 10**
>
> **BEGINNING** As you read the poem, use pantomime to act out the actions. Refer to the ideas on the chart on page 137 to support the meaning of *goof around*. As you reread, invite volunteers to act out the events.
>
> **INTERMEDIATE** / **ADVANCED** Have partners with different levels of proficiency work together to create a telephone dialogue between two friends. Encourage them to include the four activities mentioned in the poem in their dialogue (come over and play, walk, talk, goof around). Have partners present their conversations.

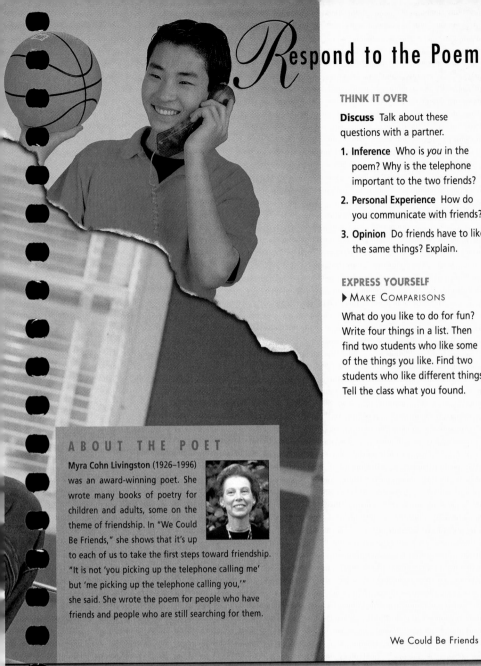

Respond to the Poem

THINK IT OVER

Discuss Talk about these questions with a partner.

1. **Inference** Who is *you* in the poem? Why is the telephone important to the two friends?

2. **Personal Experience** How do you communicate with friends?

3. **Opinion** Do friends have to like the same things? Explain.

EXPRESS YOURSELF

▶ MAKE COMPARISONS

What do you like to do for fun? Write four things in a list. Then find two students who like some of the things you like. Find two students who like different things. Tell the class what you found.

ABOUT THE POET

Myra Cohn Livingston (1926–1996) was an award-winning poet. She wrote many books of poetry for children and adults, some on the theme of friendship. In "We Could Be Friends," she shows that it's up to each of us to take the first steps toward friendship. "It is not 'you picking up the telephone calling me' but 'me picking up the telephone calling you,'" she said. She wrote the poem for people who have friends and people who are still searching for them.

We Could Be Friends **139**

OBJECTIVES

THINK IT OVER
Function: Engage in Discussion
Critical Thinking: Make Inferences; Relate to Personal Experience; Form Opinions

EXPRESS YOURSELF
Function: Make Comparisons

THINK IT OVER

3 Possible answers are:

1. **Inference** "You" is someone the speaker wants to be friends with. The telephone is important as it connects the two friends.

2. **Personal Experience** Possible answers: We talk at school or on the telephone. We write letters, notes, or e-mail.

3. **Opinion** Answers will vary.

EXPRESS YOURSELF

4 **Make Comparisons** Encourage students to compare their likes and dislikes in a chart or on a bar graph.

CLOSE AND ASSESS

Ask: *What would you suggest doing with your friend if you were in the poem?*

COMMUNITY CONNECTION

Materials: telephone books

Scavenger Hunt Introduce the characteristics of a telephone book: white pages contain names, home phone numbers and addresses; yellow pages contain that information for businesses; both sections are in alphabetical order.

Distribute lists of businesses. Have students work in groups to locate listings in the yellow pages.

Grammar Minilesson

▶ **PRESENT TENSE VERBS**

TEACH Ask students to find some action verbs in the poem (*call, play, walk.*) Then say: *Some verbs tell about an action as it is happening. Other verbs tell about an action that happens over and over again.*

Offer examples from daily life:

- I brush my teeth every day.
- I eat breakfast with my father every morning.

Ask for more examples from students.

PRACTICE Have students pretend they are the author of this poem, and that they do all the actions in the poem with a friend every day. Have them write three sentences using present tense verbs to tell about actions that happen over and over again (the habitual present tense). Start them off with this example: *Every day we goof around.*

▶ **Practice Book** page 70

BUILD LANGUAGE AND VOCABULARY

OBJECTIVES

Function: Listen Actively; Recite;
⊕ Express Likes and Dislikes

Concepts and Vocabulary:
Friendship Words

Patterns and Structures:
⊕ Verb + Infinitive

Speaking: Personal Narrative

**Critical Thinking and Learning
Strategies:** Relate to Personal Experience;
Use Graphic Organizers (concept
chart); Classify

START WITH A COMMON EXPERIENCE

1 Introduce Autograph Books
Explain that the book pictured on
page 140 is an autograph book—a
book in which friends sign their
names and write messages.

2 Listen to a Song Play
the **Language Tape/CD**.
Ask students to follow along
in their books as they listen to the
song. Explain that this is the type of
message friends would write in each
other's autograph books during the
last century.

3 Recite a Song Have students sing
the song many times. Then divide
the class into groups, and have them
sing the song as a round.

> Use the Reciting Options in the
> **Multi-Level Strategies** to include
> students at all proficiency levels.

**4 Model How to Express Likes and
Dislikes** Point out that everyone
likes and dislikes things for different
reasons. Then use the following
Think Aloud to help students express
likes and dislikes:

> **How to Express Likes and Dislikes**
>
> • Name something you like: *music*
>
> • Tell what you like about it: *I like
> the way music makes me feel.*
>
> • Name something you dislike:
> *spinach*
>
> • Tell what you do not like about it:
> *I don't like the way it tastes.*

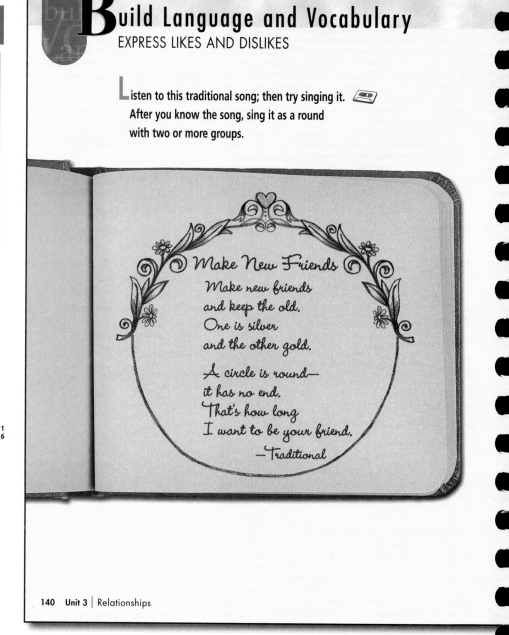

Build Language and Vocabulary
EXPRESS LIKES AND DISLIKES

Listen to this traditional song; then try singing it.
After you know the song, sing it as a round
with two or more groups.

> Make New Friends
>
> Make new friends
> and keep the old.
> One is silver
> and the other gold.
>
> A circle is round—
> it has no end.
> That's how long
> I want to be your friend.
>
> —Traditional

REACHING ALL STUDENTS

Multi-Level Strategies
RECITING OPTIONS

BEGINNING Encourage Beginning students to chime in more each
time the song is repeated. Teach gestures to accompany the song: arms
wide for "Make new friends"; hug self for "keep the old"; hold up right index
finger for "One is silver"; hold up left index finger for "the other gold." Invite
students to lead the group in gesturing to express the feelings of the song.

INTERMEDIATE / ADVANCED Invite students to work in groups to
practice the singing in rounds. Then ask volunteers to lead the class in
singing. Have volunteers take turns choosing ways to act out the second
verse of the song. Those who wish to can write a new verse for the song and
teach it to the class.

MAKE A FRIENDSHIP CHART

There are many kinds of friends—not just old and new ones! Make a chart. Show the kinds of friends you have in the first column and list their names in the second.

Category	Friend's Name	My Friend Is Like
School Friend	Mei	
Family Friend		
Childhood Friend		
Sports or Hobby Friend		
Neighborhood Friend		

BUILD YOUR VOCABULARY

Friendship Words In the third column of your chart, tell about each friend. Use the **Word Bank** to get ideas.

As you work through this unit, you can add different kinds of friends. Also add more words to tell what you like best about each one.

USE LANGUAGE STRUCTURES ▶ VERB + INFINITIVE

Speaking: Express Likes and Dislikes Use the information from your friendship chart to tell about a friend. Tell what you like about your friend and what you don't like. Tell your story to a partner. Then, tell it to the class.

Example:
Jean-Claude was my childhood friend. He was good at sports. I liked to play soccer and ride bikes with him. Sometimes he liked to be bossy. I didn't like that. Since I moved to Miami, we like to write letters to each other.

Word Bank

brave
creative
friendly
funny
good at sports
good dancer
good listener
happy
problem-solver
smart
strong

CONDUCT THE ACTIVITIES

5 **Make a Friendship Chart** Students can use the chart or create categories of their own. Let students share and discuss their completed charts.

6 **Build Your Vocabulary: Friendship Words** Expand the Word Bank by having students brainstorm additional friendship words.

7 **Use Language Structures: Verb + Infinitive** Teach the skill using the definition and examples on **Transparency 43**. Explain that sometimes in speech, the word *to* is dropped; for example: *Lia helped me study.* Then have students complete the sentences in Try It!

Speaking: Express Likes and Dislikes Conduct the activity at the bottom of page 141. Let beginners discuss their ideas with more fluent partners before sharing the information with the class.

▌ Use the Speaking Activity Options in **Multi-Level Strategies** to adjust instruction.

▶ **Practice Book** page 71

CLOSE AND ASSESS

Have students use an infinitive to complete this sentence: *I like _____ .* Then have them use an infinitive to complete a sentence about a friend: *He/She likes _____ .*

Multi-Level Strategies
SPEAKING ACTIVITY OPTIONS

BEGINNING Have students create word cards during the discussion with a partner. They can then use the cards as aids when they share their information with the class.

INTERMEDIATE Suggest that students work with a partner to create an interview in which one student asks questions about the partner's friend. Students then present their interview to the class.

ADVANCED Encourage students to create persuasive speeches telling about their friend. Their purpose is to convince listeners of their friend's good qualities.

Transparency 43 / Master 43

LEARN ABOUT INFINITIVES

An **infinitive** is a verb form that begins with the word *to.* Here are some infinitives:

to move	to like	to play

1. You can use an infinitive to tell about something you have to do.
   We <u>have</u> **to study**.

2. Here are some ways to tell about something you want or need.
   We <u>want</u> **to learn** about sports.
   We <u>need</u> **to know** how to play hockey.

3. You can use an infinitive to tell what you like to do.
   We <u>like</u> **to play** team sports.

Try It!

Choose an infinitive to finish each sentence.

to win	to join	to play	to kick

1. Ana likes _____ soccer.
3. Ana tries _____ goals.

2. Now she wants _____ the school team.
4. She has _____!

Transparency 43 Level A, Unit 3 | Relationships   © Hampton-Brown

OBJECTIVES

THINK ABOUT WHAT YOU KNOW
Reading and Learning Strategy:
Relate to Personal Experience

LEARN KEY VOCABULARY ●
Vocabulary Strategy:
Use New Words in Context

LEARN ABOUT MAIN IDEAS AND DETAILS
Reading Strategy: ● Relate Main Idea and Details

THINK ABOUT WHAT YOU KNOW

1 Quickwrite To help students get started, offer sentence frames: *I would go to ＿＿＿ with my friend ＿＿＿. We would ＿＿＿ and ＿＿＿.*

LEARN KEY VOCABULARY

2 Use New Words in Context Read vocabulary words and defining phrases aloud. After students understand the meaning of the key vocabulary, conduct the dialogue activity.

❚ Use the Vocabulary Options in **Multi-Level Strategies** to involve all proficiency levels.

▶ **Practice Book** page 72

LEARN ABOUT MAIN IDEAS AND DETAILS

3 Model How to Relate Main Ideas and Details Define *main idea* and *details*. Then model the process with the steps in the box. For guided practice, conduct the activity on **Transparency 44**.

CLOSE AND ASSESS

Ask students to agree on the main idea in the dialogue. (When you're best friends, nothing can stop your friendship.) Then ask what ideas led them to this conclusion. (Even though the friends didn't live near each other, they went out of their way to stay in touch; they visited and talked on the phone.)

My Best Friend
autobiography
by Eloise Greenfield and
Lessie Jones Little

Prepare to Read

THINK ABOUT WHAT YOU KNOW

Quickwrite Imagine a day with a friend. What would you do? Where would you go? Write sentences that tell about your day.

best friend A best friend is the friend you like the most.

crazy about When you are **crazy about** something, you really love it.

every chance we got When we did something **every chance we got**, we did it whenever we could.

go out of my way When I choose to take a longer way, I **go out of my way**.

go over You **go over** to a place when you visit.

had our lives all planned out We knew what we wanted to do in the future; we **had our lives all planned out**.

stop to worry When you **stop to worry** about something, you take time to think about it.

talk and talk When people **talk and talk**, they talk for a long time.

that was all there was to it When you were sure of how something would be, you could say, "**that was all there was to it.**"

LEARN KEY VOCABULARY

Use New Words in Context Study the new words. Then take turns reading this dialogue with a partner.

> **Friend 1:** Do you have a **best friend**?
>
> **Friend 2:** Lei was my friend in China. We were **crazy about** the same things. I used to **go out of my way** to **go over** to his house.
>
> **Friend 1:** Have you talked to Lei since you moved here?
>
> **Friend 2:** We called each other **every chance we got**. We would **talk and talk** about the future. We **had our lives all planned out**.
>
> **Friend 1:** Did you **stop to worry** about your friendship when you moved to the United States?
>
> **Friend 2:** No. We were best friends and **that was all there was to it**.

LEARN ABOUT MAIN IDEAS AND DETAILS

The **main idea** of a story is the most important idea. **Details** give examples and information to help you understand the main idea.

> **READING STRATEGY**
> **How to Relate Main Ideas and Details**
> 1. Read the selection.
> 2. Look for the most important idea.
> 3. Look for details that tell about the main idea.

Now read "My Best Friend." Look for the main ideas and details.

REACHING ALL STUDENTS

❚ **Multi-Level Strategies**
VOCABULARY OPTIONS

BEGINNING / **INTERMEDIATE**
Invite volunteers to present the dialogue. Then, pose questions using the phrases to provide additional contextualized practice with new vocabulary: *What were you crazy about when you were in the 5th grade? Do you go over to anyone's house for the weekend?* etc.

ADVANCED Work with students to use the phrases in sentences of their own before they read the dialogue.

Transparency 44 / Master 44

IDENTIFY MAIN IDEA AND DETAILS

Directions: Read the paragraph. Find the most important idea and write it on the Main Idea line. Find examples or more information about the main idea. Write the information on the Details lines.

Jennie Lambert was my best friend. We walked to school together every day. When school was over, we'd stand in front of Jennie's house and talk and talk until Jennie's mother called her to come in. Sometimes we would write each other notes. I'd go over and leave mine in Jennie's mailbox. Then she would write one back. Every chance we got we called each other on the phone. We were best friends, and that was all there was to it!

Main Idea	Details
	We walked to school together every day.
Jennie Lambert was my best friend.	We'd talk and talk.
	We would write each other notes.
	Every chance we got we called each other on the phone.

Transparency 44 Level A, Unit 3 | Relationships   © Hampton-Brown

My Best Friend

from *Childtimes*
by Eloise Greenfield and
Lessie Jones Little

Lessie Jones Little was born in Parmele, North Carolina, in 1906. In many ways, growing up at the beginning of the century was different from growing up today. Women did not have full voting rights. Black people did not have all the same rights as white people. Yet, best friends back then did a lot of the same things they do today. They spent time together and shared their dreams.

143

READ THE SELECTION

OBJECTIVES

Listening: Listen to a Preview
Reading Strategies: Preview; Predict
Literary Analysis: Autobiography

INTRODUCE THE SELECTION

4 Preview and Predict Read the title, authors, and introduction. Encourage discussion about the photographs. Then have students look through the story and discuss the headings, photographs, and captions. Ask: *What do you think this story will be about?*

5 Identify Genre: Autobiography Point out that the seated girl in the photograph is the author Lessie Jones Little. Tell students she uses the words *I, me,* and *my* in her story because it is about herself. Say: *If you write a story about your own life, it is called an autobiography.*

6 Audio Walk-Through Play the Audio Walk-Through for "My Best Friend" on the **Selection Tape/CD** to give students the overall idea of the story.

Tape 3A
CD 3
Track 4

My Best Friend
by Eloise Greenfield
and Lessie Jones Little

Theme Connection This autobiography tells how the author feels about her relationship with her lifelong best friend.

Selection Summary The introduction on page 143 of the student book offers some background and a summary.

Author Awards Eloise Greenfield has written over 30 books of fiction, poetry, and biography for children. She has received dozens of awards, including the Coretta Scott King Award, the Children's Literature and Social Responsibility Award, and citations from the American Library Association and the NCTE. Greenfield's first collaboration with her mother (*I Can Do It By Myself*) was named a Notable Children's Trade Book in Social Studies.

THE BASICS BOOKSHELF

■ *Friends Are Like That* by Daphne Liu

Two best friends share everything until one thinks the other is sharing her boyfriend as well. The simple text describing their confrontation and reconciliation supports the acquisition of basic feeling words, while the realistic illustrations provide opportunities to talk about familiar teen interests and pastimes.

For Lesson Plans: See the Teacher's Guide for **The Basics Bookshelf**.

OBJECTIVES

Function: Read a Selection
Grammar: ❶ Irregular Past Tense Verbs
Listening: Listen to a Selection
Reading and Learning Strategies:
Set a Purpose for Reading;
Use Graphic Organizers (tree diagram);
❶ Relate Main Idea and Details
Comprehension: Make Comparisons

SET PURPOSE

1 Say: *Listen to find out about the kinds of experiences these two friends share. Think about how their friendship is similar to or different from the one you share with your friends.*

READ AND THINK

Tape 3A
CD 3
Track 5

2 Strategy Focus: Relate Main Idea and Details Have students organize ideas in a main idea and details tree diagram for each section during the reading process.

▊ Choose Reading Options in the **Multi-Level Strategies** to tailor the reading to proficiency levels.

The recording of "My Best Friend" on the **Selection Tape/CD** offers an oral language model and the opportunity to build reading fluency.

Red annotations offer opportunities to clarify meaning and check for understanding.

1

LILLIE AND LESSIE

For best friends Lillie and Lessie, even simple things were fun.
That's because they did them together.

⎯⎯⎯⎯

Lillie Belle Draper was my **best friend**. We played together **every chance we got**. When Mama would send me to the store or to the post office, I'd **go out of my way** to go past Lillie's house, and I'd stand at her gate and call, "Hey Lil-lie!" And she'd answer, "Hey Les-sie!" She'd come out to the gate and we'd **talk and talk** until I knew **I had better get going**. **Ask:** Who is telling this story? Is it Lillie or Lessie?

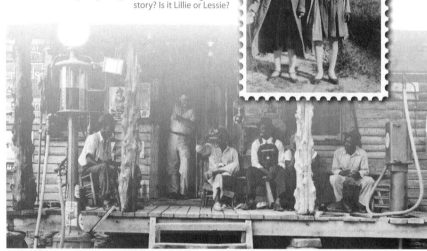

Pattie Ridley Jones, Lessie's mother (above right), with Lessie's sister Lillie Mae (1928).

....

I had better get going it was time to go

REACHING ALL STUDENTS

Transparency 45 / Master 45

TREE DIAGRAM

Directions: Read each part of the autobiography. Find the most important idea and write it on the Main Idea line. Find sentences that support the main idea and write them on the Details lines of the tree diagram.

My Best Friend

Pages 144–146	Lillie and Lessie were best friends.	
Page 147	Lessie thought Lillie was special.	
Page 148	They had plans for the future.	

Transparency 45 Level A, Unit 3 | Relationships   © Hampton-Brown

▊ Multi-Level Strategies
READING OPTIONS FOR LESSONS 13–15

BEGINNING Read aloud the autobiography, one paragraph at a time. Use the photographs and the red annotations on the facsimile pages to clarify meaning. After reading page 144, guide students in identifying the main idea (Lillie and Lessie were best friends who liked to spend time together). Elicit examples of details from students, and model how to record the information on **Transparency 45**. Help students notice that page 145 continues to provide details for the same main idea, and that the last three pages each have different main ideas.

INTERMEDIATE / **ADVANCED** Have students listen to the **Selection Tape/CD** for "My Best Friend," one section at a time. Have them work in groups to discuss these questions: *What is the most important idea? What details help you to understand the main idea?* Together, students can record the main idea and supporting details on **Master 45**.

Lessie and Lillie had fun making frog houses with dirt.

Lillie's married sister, Isabel, lived next door to me, and when Lillie would come in the summer to spend the day with her, I'd **go over**, and we'd sit on the bottom step of **Isabel's front porch** with our **bare feet** on the ground. We'd draw pictures in the dirt while we talked and rub them out with our hands. Or we'd **rake** the cool, **damp** dirt on top of our feet and pack it down tight, then slide our feet out, leaving a little **cave** we called a frog house. And all the time, we'd be just talking.

Encourage elaboration: Why do you think Lillie and Lessie called the caves frog houses?

Ask: Who is Isabel?

BEFORE YOU MOVE ON...

1. **Comparisons** What are some things you do with your friends that are similar to things that Lessie and Lillie did?
2. **Details** Describe how to make a "frog house."

Isabel's front porch the part of the house outside Isabel's front door
bare feet feet with no shoes or socks
rake pull together, gather

damp not very wet, moist
cave open area under the ground

My Best Friend **145**

READ PAGES 146–147

OBJECTIVES

Function: Read a Selection
Vocabulary Strategy: Relate Words
Listening: Listen to a Selection
Reading and Learning Strategies:
Set a Purpose for Reading; Use Graphic
Organizers (tree diagram); ❶ Relate Main
Idea and Details
Comprehension: Identify Details;
Analyze Information; Draw Conclusions
Literary Analysis: Setting

SET PURPOSE

1 Say: *Look for details to find out what Lillie and Lessie were always talking about.*

READ AND THINK

Tape 3A
CD 3
Track 5

2 Strategy Focus: Relate Main Idea and Details Involve students in reading pages 146–147.

See the **Multi-Level Strategies** on page T144 to tailor the reading experience to all proficiency levels.

2
HAPPY TIMES

The girls took lots of long walks. They talked about
books and boys and music.

Build background: Before electricity, people cooked on stoves that used coal or wood to heat them.

Sometimes we'd go walking down the **railroad track**. I'd take my **bucket** with me so I could fill it with the nuggets of **coal** that had fallen from passing trains, and take them home to use in the stove. Lillie would help me, but the bucket didn't always get filled because we stopped so much to talk.

Encourage elaboration: Ask students to name other kinds of musical instruments.

We'd sit on the **silky gray rails** and stretch our legs out toward the **weeds** and tall grass and talk about things like books or boys. And we talked about music a lot. Both of us were **crazy about** the piano. We wished we could play like some of the people we'd seen.

Jelly Roll Morton (above) was a famous jazz pianist in the early 1900s. Many people were crazy about his music. **Explain:** Jazz is a kind of music. Other kinds of music are pop, rock, classical, rap, blues, and country.

railroad track iron track, path for a train
bucket metal or plastic container with a handle, used to carry water or other things

coal a black mineral formed in the earth and used for fuel
silky gray rails train tracks
weeds wild plants that grow in many places

146 **Unit 3** | Relationships

REACHING ALL STUDENTS

Mathematics Connection
TIME CALCULATIONS

Explain that the span of time between a person's birth and the birth of that person's children is called a *generation.* Have students think about the people in their family, and describe the relationships. Have students calculate how many years there are between generations in their family, and how many generations there might be in one century. Or, invite students to base their calculations on this information about the authors: Lessie Jones Little was born in 1906, and her daughter Eloise was born in 1929. Eloise is now a grandmother.

COMMUNITY CONNECTION

Oral History Have students brainstorm questions to ask older people about their childhood friendships. Encourage students to audiotape or videotape interviews with parents, aunts, uncles, grandparents, or neighborhood friends. Using word-processing technology, students can transcribe parts of the interviews to create stories similar to the one about Lessie and Lillie.

Role-Play: Have students act out the way Lillie walked.

I thought everything Lillie did was pretty. The way she walked, **swinging along**, **throwing one foot out** a little more than the other, as if she were **walking to a bouncy kind of music**. The poems she wrote, poems about trees and other growing things, and birds. The way she sang, **leaning** her head back with a **faraway look** in her eyes, as if she were in love with the words and the music, and making the sounds come out so easily.

Ask: How are poems and songs alike and different?

BEFORE YOU MOVE ON...

1. **Details** Where did Lessie's family get some of the coal to use in their stove?

2. **Evidence and Conclusion** Lessie said that "everything Lillie did was pretty." What were some of the "pretty things" that Lessie liked about Lillie?

....

swinging along moving her arms and legs back and forth
throwing one foot out stepping with one foot out
walking to a bouncy kind of music hearing happy music as she walked
leaning tilting, holding at an angle
faraway look dreamy expression

My Best Friend   **147**

REVIEW KEY VOCABULARY

3 Relate Words Make a T-chart with key vocabulary in the first column. Lead students in brainstorming words or phrases that mean the opposite and record them in the second column.

Key Vocabulary	Opposite
best friend	worst friend
every chance we got	never
had our lives all planned out	lived one day at a time
go out of my way	head straight for
go over	stay away

CHECK COMPREHENSION

4 Answers to "Before You Move On"

1. **Details** The coal was from the railroad tracks, dropped by trains.

2. **Evidence and Conclusion** Pretty things were the way she walked, her poetry, and how she sang.

CLOSE AND ASSESS

Ask: *What would you tell a friend about the main ideas and details on pages 146–147?*

Literary Analysis Minilesson

Vocabulary
IDIOMS

Point out idioms in this story, such as *get going* on page 144 or *crazy about* on page 146. Have students work in heterogeneous collaborative groups to define idioms, drawing or writing the idioms and their definitions on large sheets of paper. Post sheets in the class and encourage students to *be on the lookout* (point out that this is also an idiom) for idioms they hear at school, on television or radio, or in their community to add to these collections.

▶ SETTING—TIME AND PLACE

TEACH Use the student book to show places, for example, a forest (page 190), a city (pages 26, 231), or a desert (page 297). Use the word *setting* as students describe what they see. Help students to conclude that a setting is *the location where an event or a story takes place.*

Explain that setting may include the time a story took place—morning or night, fifty years ago, far in the future. Identifying the setting of a story helps the reader understand it.

PRACTICE Ask: *What is the setting of "My Best Friend"? Where and when does the story take place?* Have students locate North Carolina on a map and look for words and photographs that give clues about people's lives during this time period.

Have students work in pairs to list all the clues they find and describe the setting of the story in a brief paragraph. Compare students' work to see what clues they found.

▶ **Practice Book** page 74

SET PURPOSE

1 Say: *Listen to find out how the girls planned for the future.*

READ AND THINK

Tape 3A
CD 3
Track 5

2 **Strategy Focus: Relate Main Idea and Details** Involve students in reading page 148.

> See the **Multi-Level Strategies** on page T144 to tailor the reading experience to all proficiency levels.

CHECK COMPREHENSION

3 **Answers to "Before You Move On"**

1. Setting Some clues are clothing, transportation, use of coal.

2. Prediction Answers will vary.

CLOSE AND ASSESS

Say: *Lillie and Lessie were best friends.* Have each student give a detail that supports this main idea.

3

GROWING UP TOGETHER

Lessie and Lillie shared a goal of going to college together.

Lillie and I **had our lives all planned out**. We were going to be schoolteachers. I was going to be just like Miss Estee Riddick, **stick** a pencil in my hair and walk up and down the **classroom aisles** calling out spelling words to my students. I would pronounce each syllable of every word just the way Miss Estee did. But first we were going to college. We were going to Hampton **Institute** and **be roommates**, and we would make ninety-five to a hundred in all of our **subjects**.

I was a few years older than Lillie was, but we didn't **stop to worry** about how we would manage to go to college at the same time. We were going to be roommates at Hampton Institute, and **that was all there was to it**. After all, we were best friends.

....
stick put
classroom aisles rows between the desks in our class
Institute School, College
be roommates live together
subjects classes

148 Unit 3 | Relationships

BEFORE YOU MOVE ON...

1. **Setting** What can you find in the words or pictures to tell you that the story happened long ago?

2. **Prediction** The story ends here. What do you think will happen to the two friends in the future?

Ask: Who do you think Miss Estee Riddick was?

Restate: Lessie and Lillie dreamed about going to college together and getting good grades in all their classes.

ABOUT THE AUTHORS

After graduating from high school, **Lessie Jones Little** and her best friend Lillie did not go to the Hampton Institute as they had planned. However, Lessie did work as a teacher. She also married Lillie's cousin, Weston. They had five children, including a daughter, Eloise.

Eloise Greenfield grew up to become a well-known author of children's books. Many of her books have won awards. *Childtimes*, which Eloise wrote with her mother, won the Coretta Scott King Honor Award.

REACHING ALL STUDENTS

SOCIAL STUDIES CONNECTION

Have students locate Parmele on a map of North Carolina (northeast of Greenville). Then have pairs use the Internet to find the route they would take to get there from their location. Have students tally miles and estimate travel times. Ask students to map routes to Parmele from other places. Compare students' routes. Where do all the routes merge?

Web Sites

Web sites undergo frequent modification, but here are some sites you may want to suggest to students:

www.mapquest.com   www.maps.yahoo.com
www.mapblast.com   www.city.net/maps

Learning Styles

STRATEGIES FOR CONSTRUCTING MEANING

• **Visual Learners** Students collect photos, illustrations, or art from the early 1900s and create collages.

• **Auditory Learners** Students create auditory collages with music from the early 1900s and dialogue.

• **Kinesthetic Learners** Students create and model early 1900s costumes.

Respond to the Autobiography
Check Your Understanding

SUM IT UP

Relate Main Ideas and Details Study the tree diagram for pages 144–145 of "My Best Friend." Then make diagrams for Parts 2 and 3.

Tree Diagram for Part 1

Main Idea	Details
Lillie and Lessie were best friends	They liked to play together.
	They visited each other.
	They made frog houses together.
	They liked to talk and talk.

Write a Paragraph Use the tree diagram for Part 1 to write your paragraph. Follow these steps:

- Write a **topic sentence** to tell the main idea.
- Write details to support the main idea.
- Write a **concluding sentence** to sum up your paragraph.

> Lessie and Lillie were best friends. They liked to play together. They visited each other every chance they got. They made frog houses together. They liked to talk and talk. **They had fun being best friends.**

Now write paragraphs for Parts 2 and 3. Use your tree diagrams for ideas.

THINK IT OVER

Discuss Talk about these questions with a partner.

1. **Opinion** Would Lessie be a good friend? Why or why not?

2. **Author's Purpose** Why do you think Lessie wrote her autobiography?

3. **Comparisons** How would Lillie and Lessie's story be different if they grew up today? How would it be the same?

4. **Personal Experience** Do you have your life all planned out, like Lessie and Lillie did? Explain.

EXPRESS YOURSELF
▶ EXPRESS LIKES AND DISLIKES

Think about the qualities you like and dislike in a best friend. Share your ideas with the class. Then make a large class T-chart. Write the qualities that most people said.

✓ **LANGUAGE ACQUISITION ASSESSMENT**
See page 41 of the Assessment Handbook.

My Best Friend **149**

Multi-Level Strategies
SUM IT UP OPTIONS

BEGINNING Help students compare the details in the tree diagram in the student book with **Transparency 45**, completed with the group while reading the story. Ask them to decide if they have anything to add or change. Then work as a group to develop the written summary for each part of the story.

INTERMEDIATE / **ADVANCED** Have students work together in small groups to evaluate the tree diagrams they have been developing throughout the story. Allow time for them to update the diagrams. Then have students work in pairs to develop the written summaries. Invite volunteers to share their summaries with the class. Ask listening classmates to identify their topic sentence, the details, and their concluding sentence.

OBJECTIVES

SUM IT UP
Function: Write
Reading and Learning Strategies:
🅣 Relate Main Idea and Details;
Use Graphic Organizers (tree diagram)
Writing: Paragraph

THINK IT OVER
Function: Engage in Discussion
Critical Thinking and Comprehension: Form Opinions; Identify Author's Purpose; Make Comparisons; Relate to Personal Experience

EXPRESS YOURSELF
Function: 🅣 Express Likes and Dislikes
Critical Thinking: Make Comparisons

CHECK YOUR UNDERSTANDING

1 Sum It Up Main ideas for other parts: Lillie and Lessie talked a lot; Lessie thought Lillie was pretty; They had plans for the future.

▶ **Practice Book** page 75

2 Think It Over Possible answers are:

1. **Opinion** Students should support opinions with story details: *I would like to have a friend like Lessie because I like to talk. We would have a lot to talk about.*

2. **Author's Purpose** Sample answer: She has good memories of her childhood.

3. **Comparisons** Lessie and Lillie would still be good friends, but some of their activities would change. They would still talk, but they would not pick up coal by the train tracks.

4. **Personal Experience** Answers will vary.

3 Express Yourself Encourage students to elaborate orally on their chart information.

CLOSE AND ASSESS

Ask students to tell something Lessie enjoyed with Lillie that they also enjoy with a friend.

RESPOND

OBJECTIVES

LINKING VERBS

Grammar: Linking Verbs; ⏺ Present Tense Verbs; ⏺ Past Tense Verbs

WRITE ABOUT A FRIENDSHIP

Function: Write

Critical Thinking and Learning Strategies: Generate Ideas; Use Graphic Organizers (word web)

Literary Analysis: Point of View

Writing: Description

LANGUAGE ARTS AND LITERATURE

1 **Use Linking Verbs** See annotations for answers to Practice items.

▶ **Practice Book** page 76

2 **Write About a Friendship** Provide some examples of how students might develop their descriptions of a friend in both first- and third-person point of view.

Begin with sentence frames: *I have a friend. My friend's name is _____. My friend looks like _____. My friend talks about _____ and acts like _____. I like it when we _____. My friend likes it when we _____.*

Ask another student to tell what the first student said. Help all to see that this second description is in the third-person point of view. (*His friend _____.*)

CLOSE AND ASSESS

Have students read their descriptions to a partner. Ask the partner to identify the linking verbs they hear.

ASSESSMENT
Selection Test 10 on page 45 of the Assessment Handbook tests students' mastery of the reading strategies and the vocabulary, comprehension, and language arts skills taught with this selection.

Respond to the Autobiography, continued

Language Arts and Literature

GRAMMAR IN CONTEXT

USE LINKING VERBS

Learn About Linking Verbs A linking verb connects the subject of a sentence to a word in the predicate. The **predicate** tells what the subject is, has, or does.

The word in the predicate can describe the subject.

Lessie **was** happy.

Or, the word in the predicate can be another way to name the subject.

Lessie **was** a good friend.

All the forms of the verb **be** are linking verbs.

Present Tense	Past Tense
I **am** happy.	I **was** sad.
He **is** funny.	She **was** mad.
We **are** friends.	They **were** sisters.

Use Linking Verbs With a partner, make up sentences about today and the past. Use *am, is, are, was,* and *were* in your sentences.

Example:

Today I **am** a good student. Last year, I **was** lazy.

Practice Copy these sentences. Add *am, is, are, was,* or *were* to finish each sentence.

1. In the past, Lessie _____was_____ a teacher.

2. Today, Lessie _____is_____ a writer.

3. Years ago, the girls _____were_____ neighbors.

150 **Unit 3** | Relationships

LITERARY ANALYSIS
WRITING

WRITE ABOUT A FRIENDSHIP

Learn About Point of View Every story has a **narrator**, who tells the story. In "My Best Friend," Lessie is the narrator. She is part of the story and uses words like *I, me, my,* and *we*. This is called **first-person point of view**.

Example:

Lillie Belle Draper was **my** best friend.

In "The Qualities of Friendship," Aesop is the narrator. He is not part of the story and uses words like *he, she, it,* and *they*. This is **third-person point of view**.

Example:

A lion was sleeping in **his** cave.

Organize Your Ideas Think about a friend and the things you do together. Use a graphic organizer to record your ideas.

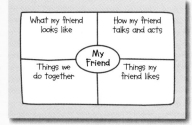

Write About Your Friendship Choose a point of view. Then use it to describe your friendship.

REACHING ALL STUDENTS

Multi-Level Strategies

OPTIONS FOR WRITING ABOUT A FRIENDSHIP

BEGINNING Work with students in a group to generate words to record on the graphic organizer. Then prompt them to use the words in sentences about friends. Record student responses, vocalizing as you write. Help students to use the words and sentences that they generated as they write about their friendship.

INTERMEDIATE After students complete their individual graphic organizers, encourage them to formulate a topic sentence with a main idea and to elaborate using details from the organizer.

ADVANCED Students can participate in written peer conferencing groups. After reading their descriptions of their friends, each peer writes one positive thing and asks one question or offers one suggestion for improvement. The writer then chooses suggestions to include in a revision.

Content Area Connections

SOCIAL STUDIES

COMPARE GENERATIONS

"My Best Friend" shows what life was like in 1906. How has the world changed? Interview an older person about life in the past. Interview a friend about life today. Then compare the information.

1 Prepare Your Questions Write questions about topics like:

music	fashion	famous people
jobs	school	entertainment

Examples:
What kinds of music did you like as a child?
What clothes did people wear?

2 Conduct the Interviews Ask your questions politely. Write the answers. Be sure to say "thank you" when you are finished.

3 Organize Your Information Make a chart. Compare what life was like in the past with how life is now.

Topic	Then (19__)	Now (20__)
music	classical, folk	country, rap, hip hop,
fashion		

4 Share What You Learned Tell your class about your interviews. Listen to your classmates. What discoveries did they make?

Learn how to **listen** and **discuss**. See Handbook pages 373–376.

Talk with an adult about life in the past.

Research Skills

▶ USE A CHART

TEACH Use the sample on page 151 to describe how charts work. Point out the column heads and show how the information in each column corresponds with the head. Explain that while researching a topic, you can add as many rows as necessary to include all the information you find. Point out that charts allow you to present a great deal of information in a small space and make it easy to compare different pieces of information.

PRACTICE Have students make a chart in class. You may wish to have students use this opportunity to create the chart for the "Compare Generations" activity. Or, create a chart about personal information. Draw a grid and help students choose headings. Invite students to take turns filling in information on the chart.

▶ **Practice Book** page 77

OBJECTIVES

COMPARE GENERATIONS

Function: ❶ Ask For and Give Information

Listening and Speaking: Conduct an Interview

Learning Strategies and Research Skills: Gather, Organize, and Synthesize Information; Take Notes; Make Comparisons; Use a Chart

Representing: Comparison Chart

CONTENT AREA CONNECTIONS

1 Compare Generations Help students select topics to focus on, and to prepare questions. Then work with students to brainstorm ideas about interview subjects. (relatives, neighbors, members of congregations, etc.)

Conduct the lesson on presenting information on a chart before students reach that step of the activity.

▶ **Practice Book** page 78

CLOSE AND ASSESS

Invite students to write what they have learned in a dialogue journal. Respond to students' comments.

INTRODUCE THEME 2

> ### OBJECTIVES
>
> **Function:** Engage in Discussion
> **Concepts and Vocabulary:**
> Family—*ancestors, grandmother, grandfather, mother*
> **Viewing:** Interpret a Visual Image
> **Learning Strategies:**
> Relate to Personal Experience
> **Critical Thinking:** Generate Ideas

TAP PRIOR KNOWLEDGE

1 Songs Across Generations Ask students to think of a song their family sings at celebrations or other occasions. Invite volunteers to recite or sing the lyrics, or tell about the song in English if it is in another language. Encourage students to explain the significance of the song and its origins. Discuss how songs and celebrations are passed on across generations in many families.

VIEW AND DISCUSS

2 View *The Family* Point out the title of the painting (*The Family—La Familia*) and ask students to name the family members shown. Record the words, which may include: *baby, parents, grandparents, aunt, uncle.* Then:

- Use this list to clarify the meaning of the word *generations*, using *baby, parent* and *grandparent* as examples.

- Note that one part of the family is looking forward, and the other part is looking back. Point out that those looking back can see what earlier generations left for them.

3 Share Family Legacies Have students do a quickdraw or a quickwrite that represents something that an earlier generation of their family left behind for them. Ask students to share their work.

> Use the Activity Options in the **Multi-Level Strategies** to help all students participate.

The Family (La familia), José Clemente Orozco, mural. Copyright © 2000.

REACHING ALL STUDENTS

Multi-Level Strategies
ACTIVITY OPTIONS

BEGINNING Ask each student to draw a picture of something that was left to them by a previous generation. Help students label their drawings. As students describe the importance of what they have received, paraphrase each sentence for them.

INTERMEDIATE Invite students to write about something they have received from a previous generation. Provide sentence frames: *My _____ left me something very important. I love this _____ because _____. It makes me feel _____. Someday I hope that _____ will have this _____.*

ADVANCED Have students work independently to write about what they have received and why it is important to them. Invite students to exchange papers with a partner and give each other suggestions for changes and corrections.

THEME 2

Across Generations

- What are your special talents? Who else in your family has talents like yours?

- What are your physical features? Who else in your family has features like yours?

- How have earlier generations changed your world? How can you change the world for the generations that will follow you?

THEME-RELATED BOOKS

In My Family/En mi familia
by Carmen Lomas Garza

Paintings and short descriptions present scenes from life in a Mexican American family.

Honoring Our Ancestors
edited by Harriet Rohmer

Fourteen artists use words and pictures to honor members of their families.

NOVEL

Yang the Youngest and His Terrible Ear
by Lensey Namioka

The youngest child of four tries to fit in with his family. It's hard to when everyone else is musical!

153

DISCUSS THE GUIDING QUESTIONS

4 **Set the Theme** Some key points to develop during the discussion are:

- Encourage students to talk about what they and family members like to do. Note that sometimes special talents are passed on from one generation to another.

- Invite students to describe themselves and family members. Point out that sometimes physical features are special and are passed across generations.

- Previous generations often make life easier for us because of their hard work, for example, by starting a family business. They also teach us important lessons and traditions. We can change the world for generations to come by developing and sharing our talents to make the world a better place to live.

▌ Form groups and use the **Multi-Level Strategies** so all students can participate.

CLOSE AND ASSESS

Have students list one thing they have learned from past generations and one thing they hope to teach future generations.

Multi-Level Strategies

GROUPING GUIDELINES

BEGINNING Work on vocabulary development with students as a group. Suggest that they use family members listed in **Master 39** (see page T122) to talk about talents and physical features that have been passed across generations. Model sentences to help students place describing words in context: *My _____ has _____ hair. So do I.*

INTERMEDIATE Have students discuss the guiding questions in small groups. Appoint one student as note-taker in each group. Then have groups share their answers with the class. Encourage additional discussion.

ADVANCED Have students quickwrite answers to the guiding questions and share their answers in groups. Then have groups compile a list of ideas about how generations before them have changed the world, and share them during class discussion.

THEME LIBRARY

▪ **In My Family**
by Carmen Lomas Garza

Invite students to read *In My Family*. Encourage them to draw a picture of something their family—including grandparents, aunts, uncles, cousins—does together and write a paragraph that tells about the picture and the activity. Ask volunteers to share their pictures to begin a discussion of how everyday activities with our families can help us understand who we are and what we can do. Display the pictures or combine them in a class book, *In Our Families*.

BUILD LANGUAGE AND VOCABULARY

OBJECTIVES

Function: Listen Actively; Recite;
T Give Information
Concepts and Vocabulary:
Family Words
Patterns and Structures:
T Past Tense Verbs
Speaking: Personal Narrative
Learning Strategy: Use Graphic
Organizers (tree diagram)
Critical Thinking: Relate to Personal
Experience; Classify

START WITH A COMMON EXPERIENCE

1 Listen to a Song Play
Track 7 on the **Language**
Tape/CD. Tell students that
after they listen to the song, they
will sing it together.

> Use the Reciting Options in the
> **Multi-Level Strategies** to help all
> students participate.

2 Recite a Song Have students sing
the song several times. Explain that
where they see the word *Chorus* on
page 154, they should sing the lines
in the box at the right.

3 Model How to Give Information
Use the following Think Aloud
to help students learn how to
give information:

> **How to Give Information**
>
> • Name a family member:
>   *Grandpa Roberto*
>
> • Tell where the person was born:
>   *He was born in Mexico.*
>
> • Tell more about the person:
>   *Grandpa Roberto lived
>   in Texas.*

Build Language and Vocabulary
GIVE INFORMATION

Listen to this song; then sing along.

Family Tree

Before the days of Jell-O
lived a prehistoric fellow
who loved a maid and courted her
beneath the banyan tree.
And they had lots of children,
and their children all had children,
and they kept on having children
until one of them had me.
    Chorus
My grandpa came from Russia,
my grandma came from Prussia,
they met in Nova Scotia,
had my dad in Tennessee.
Then they moved to Yokohama
where Daddy met my mama.
Her dad's from Alabama
and her mom's part Cherokee.
    Chorus

            —Tom Chapin

> **Chorus**
> We're a family and we're a tree.
> Our roots go deep down in history.
> From my great-great-granddaddy
> reaching up to me,
> we're a green and growing family tree.

154 Unit 3 | Relationships

REACHING ALL STUDENTS

Multi-Level Strategies
RECITING OPTIONS

BEGINNING Read aloud the song, one stanza at a time, restating and
explaining as necessary. For example, you may want to explain that the kind
of gelatin mentioned is a fairly recent invention, and *prehistoric* refers to a
time long, long ago. Clarify all the family-related words. Then play the audio
recording and encourage students to join in, especially on the repetitive
verses in the chorus.

INTERMEDIATE / **ADVANCED** Read the song aloud with students,
inviting questions to clarify meaning. Then play the recording and have
students sing along. Students may wish to look up place names on a world
map or a globe. Partners may then innovate on the song using words that
reflect their own backgrounds.

MAKE A FAMILY TREE

Read the second verse of "Family Tree." Use the information to complete a family tree like this one:

Family Tree

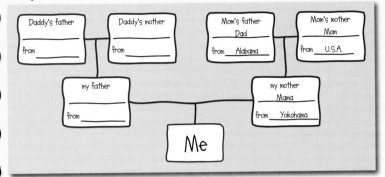

BUILD YOUR VOCABULARY

Family Words Now, make a tree of your family or the people you live with. Show as many people as you can. Use words from the **Word Bank** to label your family tree. As you work through this unit, continue adding the names of other family members.

USE LANGUAGE STRUCTURES ▶ PAST TENSE VERBS: *was/were*

Speaking: Tell About Your Family Use the information from your family tree to tell the class about your family history.

Example:

> My grandpa was from Cuba, and my grandma was from the Dominican Republic. They were in Puerto Rico when they met. My dad was born in San Juan.

Word Bank

aunt
cousin
dad
daddy
father
grandfather
grandma
grandmother
mama
mom
mother
nana
papa
pop
uncle

Build Language and Vocabulary **155**

4 Make a Family Tree Point out that each line of boxes in the family tree represents all the people in one generation. The person in the present generation is on the bottom, that person's parents are just above, and so on.

5 Build Your Vocabulary: Family Words Students may use their own names for family members. Show students how to add other family members, such as aunts, uncles, and cousins, to the family tree.

6 Use Language Structures: Past Tense Verbs *was/were* Use **Transparency 46** to teach the verbs. Then have students complete the sentences in Try It!

Speaking: Tell About Your Family Conduct the activity at the bottom of page 155. Have students use their family trees for ideas.

▌ Use the Speaking Activity Options in the **Multi-Level Strategies** to adjust instruction.

▶ **Practice Book** page 79

CLOSE AND ASSESS

Ask students to agree on a list of five words they could use as signals in a sentence with the verbs *was* and *were*. (*yesterday, last week, etc.*) Then have them write two sentences, one for each verb.

Multi-Level Strategies
SPEAKING ACTIVITY OPTIONS

BEGINNING Suggest that students create two simple sentences that tell about their family members. Remind them to try to use *was* and *were* in their sentences.

INTERMEDIATE Encourage students to use their family trees as a graphic aid during their presentations. Students should point to the appropriate entry on the tree as they give information about a family member.

ADVANCED Have students expand their family histories beyond their places of origin. Students might include such information as occupations and hobbies.

Transparency 46 / Master 46

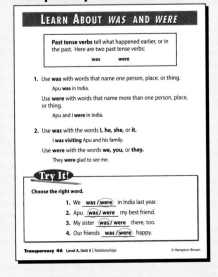

Build Language and Vocabulary **T155**

OBJECTIVES

THINK ABOUT WHAT YOU KNOW

Concepts and Vocabulary: Feelings—
honor, respect, admire

Reading Strategy:
Activate Prior Knowledge

LEARN KEY VOCABULARY ⊙

Vocabulary Strategy: Relate Words

LEARN TO PARAPHRASE

Reading Strategy: ⊙ Paraphrase

THINK ABOUT WHAT YOU KNOW

1 Share Ideas Explain that when you honor someone, you show respect and admiration for that person. Ask partners to discuss a family member they honor. Invite students to take turns sharing their thoughts with the class.

LEARN KEY VOCABULARY

2 Relate Words Read the vocabulary words and defining sentences aloud. Explain that in the example, *education* is a magnet word that attracts other related words to help explain the concept. After students understand the meaning of the key vocabulary words, conduct the activity.

> Use the Vocabulary Options in the **Multi-Level Strategies** to involve all proficiency levels.

▶ **Practice Book** page 80

LEARN TO PARAPHRASE

3 Model How to Paraphrase Define *paraphrase*. Model how to paraphrase following the steps in the box. For guided practice, conduct the activity on **Transparency 47**.

CLOSE AND ASSESS

Ask students to vote on whether the following is true or false: *When you paraphrase, you read a passage and then tell what it means in your own words.*

HONORING
Our
Ancestors

family portraits
by Stephen Von Mason,
Helen Zughaib,
and Enrique Chagoya

Prepare to Read

THINK ABOUT WHAT YOU KNOW

Share Ideas What does it mean to honor someone? Talk about the people you honor and how you honor them.

advise You **advise** someone when you tell what you think he or she should do.

ancestor An **ancestor** is a family member who lived before you.

dedicate When you **dedicate** your work to someone, you make it for that person.

education You get an **education** when you learn.

leader The **leader** of a group tells the others what to do.

pioneer The first person to go some place new or do something new is a **pioneer**.

source of The **source of** something is where it comes from.

support Strength and encouragement are examples of **support**.

LEARN KEY VOCABULARY

Relate Words Study the new words. Then draw eight boxes with a new word in the center of each box. Write words that go with the new word in the corners of each box.

how to paint   read

education

school   learn to cook

LEARN TO PARAPHRASE

When you **paraphrase**, you use your own words to say the same thing as the author. Paraphrasing can help you understand what you read.

> **READING STRATEGY**
> **How to Paraphrase**
> 1. Read a sentence.
> 2. Ask yourself: What does the sentence mean?
> 3. Say it in your own words.

Now read "Honoring Our Ancestors." Stop to paraphrase each difficult sentence.

156   Unit 3 | Relationships

REACHING ALL STUDENTS

Multi-Level Strategies
VOCABULARY OPTIONS

BEGINNING Work with students to complete the boxes. Encourage them to think of words from their home language that are similar to or are cognates of the key words.

INTERMEDIATE / ADVANCED Students could work in pairs. After completing the boxes, pairs write sentences to relate each key word magnet with one other word or phrase it attracted. For example, *We get an education in school.*

Transparency 47 / Master 47

HOW TO PARAPHRASE

Directions: Read the paragraph. Then paraphrase the "Author's Text" in column 2 of the chart.

Our ancestors are a great source of information about our families and traditions. They educate us with lessons and stories. When we honor our ancestors, we show our respect for them. We can dedicate our stories and pictures to our ancestors as a way to honor them.

Author's Text	Paraphrase
1. Our ancestors are a great source of information about our families and traditions.	1. We can learn a lot from our ancestors.
2. They educate us with lessons and stories.	2. They teach us with lessons and stories.
3. When we honor our ancestors, we show our respect for them.	3. We show how much we appreciate our ancestors when we honor them.
4. We can dedicate our stories and pictures to our ancestors as a way to honor them.	4. We show respect for our ancestors when we make stories and pictures about or for them.

Transparency 47 Level A, Unit 3 | Relationships   © Hampton-Brown

HONORING
Our Ancestors

George Crespo, oil paint on burlap; frame is cedar wood and twine. Copyright © 1999.

Three artists describe the paintings they created to honor members of their families.

by Stephen Von Mason
Helen Zughaib
Enrique Chagoya

157

OBJECTIVES

Listening: Listen to a Preview
Reading Strategies: Preview; Predict; Skim

INTRODUCE THE SELECTION

4 **Preview, Predict, Skim** Read aloud the name of the selection and artists as well as the introductory text. Ask: *What does this painting show about generations?* (It shows that young people can learn from older people.) As students skim through the selection and look at the illustrations, read the titles aloud. Ask: *What do you think you will find out about the artists' ancestors?* (who they were, where they lived, what they did)

5 **Audio Walk-Through** Play the Audio Walk-Through for "Honoring Our Ancestors" on the **Selection Tape/CD** to give students the overall idea of the selection.

Tape 3B
CD 3
Track 6

Honoring Our Ancestors
by Stephen Von Mason, Helen Zughaib, and Enrique Chagoya

Theme Connection This selection illustrates in words and pictures how three artists value their relationship with their ancestors, and how the connections have enriched their lives.

Selection Summary Three artists explain how they honor their parents, grandparents, and ancestors in their work. They discuss their ancestors' talents and the special lessons and skills their ancestors taught them.

THE BASICS ➤ BOOKSHELF

■ *Let's Dance* by George Ancona

Dance, like music, is at the heart of cultural tradition passed down from generation to generation. The colorful photos in this book combined with simple text, support the acquisition of basic action words and give beginning English learners opportunities to talk about clothing, culture, and celebrations.

For Lesson Plans: See the Teacher's Guide for *The Basics Bookshelf*.

OBJECTIVES

Function: Read a Selection
Grammar: ❶ Irregular Past Tense Verbs
Listening: Listen to a Selection
Viewing: Describe a Visual Image
Reading and Learning Strategies: Set a Purpose for Reading; Use Graphic Organizers (reflection log); ❶ Paraphrase
Comprehension: Identify Details

SET PURPOSE

1 Say: *Look for details that describe the artist's ancestors.*

READ AND THINK

Tape 3B
CD 3
Track 7

2 **Strategy Focus: Paraphrase**
Prompt students to choose statements to record on the Reflection Log on **Master 48**, paraphrase them, and include their reflections.

▌ Choose Reading Options in the **Multi-Level Strategies** to tailor the reading to proficiency levels.

The recording of "Honoring Our Ancestors" on the **Selection Tape/CD** offers an oral language model and the opportunity to build reading fluency.

Red annotations offer opportunities to clarify meaning and check for understanding.

I HONOR
My Ancestors
by Stephen Von Mason

 Pharoah Jackson Chesney

Cornelius Grant Mason, Jr.

Jordan Douglass Chavis, Jr.

Use visuals: Pause to draw a simple family tree from the author to his great-great-great-grandfather.

This painting is for my **ancestors**. On the left is my great-great-great-grandfather, Pharoah Jackson Chesney. He was a **pioneer**—one of the first **settlers** of Knoxville, Tennessee. He lived to be 120 years old.

On the right is my uncle, Jordan Douglass Chavis, Jr. He was a **famous musician**, the **leader** of a big band called "The Tennessee Collegians" from Tennessee State University. He was a musical pioneer. He started Tennessee State's music **department**.

In the center is my father, Cornelius Grant Mason, Jr., in the clothes he wore when he was a **student pilot** in the late 1940s. He, too, was a pioneer—part of the first group of Black pilots in America.

THE ARTIST
Stephen Von Mason is a painter, printmaker, and fine art framer. He lives in Oakland, California.

---

settlers people who build and live in a new town
famous musician person known for making music
department section (of a school)
student pilot person who is learning how to fly an airplane

Explain: The late 1940s means sometime between 1945 and 1949.
Ask: How many years (or decades) ago was 1940?

Pause for students to view the illustration.

158 Unit 3 | Relationships

REACHING ALL STUDENTS

Transparency 48 / Master 48

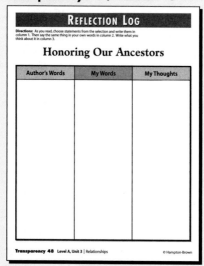

REFLECTION LOG

Directions: As you read, choose statements from the selection and write them in column 1. Then say the same thing in your own words in column 2. Write what you think about it in column 3.

Honoring Our Ancestors

Author's Words	My Words	My Thoughts

Transparency 48 Level A, Unit 3 | Relationships   © Hampton-Brown

▌ **Multi-Level Strategies**
READING OPTIONS FOR LESSONS 4–6

BEGINNING Read aloud each section, using the pictures and the red annotations on the facsimile pages to clarify meaning. Work with the group to identify key ideas from each paragraph for column 1 of the Reflection Log. Guide students in paraphrasing ideas, vocalizing as you record them in column 2. Encourage additional comments and record them in column 3.

INTERMEDIATE Students can listen to the selection on the **Selection Tape/CD**. Then have small groups read aloud and choose statements to record in column 1 of the Reflection Log. Groups should discuss how to paraphrase the author's statements. Have students complete column 3 independently.

ADVANCED Partners read the selection together and identify text for column 1 on the Reflection Log. Have students complete columns 2 and 3 independently and check their work with a partner.

Jordan Douglass "Chick" Chavis Jr.

Cornelius Grant Mason Jr.

A Standard Pilot

Played Carnegie Hall alongside... Billie Holiday and Lester Young...

PARENTS
Cornelius Grant Mason Jr.
m. Josephine Beechum-Mason ... deceased.
m. Loistean Mason Ed.D.

AUNTS and UNCLES
Jordan Douglass Chavis Jr.   Ervin Edward Mason
Katherine M. Mason-Chavis   Angie Snodgrass-Mason

GREAT GRANDPARENTS
Tip Chesney and Uretha B. McFeeter-Chesney

GREAT GREAT GREAT Grandparents
Isaac Burke and Amanda Sharp-Burke
...was a Blacksmith from Algiers, Algeria-N. Africa
Pharoah Jackson and Oria Chesney

Stephen Von Mason, oil on rag paper. Copyright © 1999.

BEFORE YOU MOVE ON...

1. **Details** What did Stephen's three ancestors do?
2. **Viewing and Describing** Look carefully at the painting. Tell your partner what you see.

---

3 Answers to "Before You Move On"

1. **Details** Stephen's great-great-great-grandfather was a pioneer, his uncle was a famous musician, and his father was one of the first African American pilots in America.

2. **Viewing and Describing** Words students might mention are: *airplane, pilot, goggles, sun, moon, great-great-great grandfather, uncle, marriages, history.*

CLOSE AND ASSESS

Ask students to paraphrase a sentence in this section.

Math Connection
STORY PROBLEMS

Tell students that the Ruiz family must count its members to plan a family reunion. Pose these problems to solve:

- Mrs. Ruiz has four children. Each of them has three children. How many grandchildren does Mrs. Ruiz have?

- Each grandchild has two children. How many great-grandchildren does Mrs. Ruiz have?

- Mrs. Ruiz's brother has two sons and three daughters. How many nephews and nieces does Mrs. Ruiz have?

Grammar Minilesson

▶ IRREGULAR PAST TENSE VERBS

TEACH Discuss Stephen Von Mason's ancestors with students. Say, for example: *The three men were very special. Von Mason's father was a pilot, and his uncle was a musician.*

Remind students that most verbs that tell about the past end in **–ed**. Explain that irregular verbs do not add **–ed** to show past tense; they have different forms. Say: Was *and* were *are the past tense forms of the verb* be. *We use* was *with one person or thing and* were *with more than one.*

PRACTICE Write these sentences. Have students rewrite each sentence, choosing *was* or *were* to complete each sentence.

1. Pharoah Jackson Chesney (was, were) a settler in Tennessee.

2. Jordan Douglass Chavis, Jr. (was, were) a famous musician.

3. Cornelius Grant Mason, Jr. (was, were) one of the first African American pilots.

4. All three men (was, were) pioneers.

▶ **Practice Book** page 81

OBJECTIVES

Function: Read a Selection
Vocabulary Strategy: Relate Words
Grammar: Linking Verbs
Listening: Listen to a Selection
Reading and Learning Strategies:
Set a Purpose for Reading; Use Graphic
Organizers (reflection log); ⓣ Paraphrase
Comprehension: Identify Details;
Make an Inference

SET PURPOSE

1 Say: *Look for details that describe what the artist's grandmother did.*

READ AND THINK

Tape 3B
CD 3
Track 7

2 **Strategy Focus: Paraphrase**
Prompt students to choose statements to record on **Transparency 48/Master 48**, paraphrase them, and include their reflections.

> See the **Multi-Level Strategies** on page T158 to adjust instruction to proficiency levels.

I HONOR
My Grandmother
by Helen Zughaib

Miriam Sultani Zughaib

Ask: What other words do you know that mean *grandmother*?

This is Teta, my Lebanese grandmother. (Teta means "grandmother" in Arabic.) She grew up in Syria and Lebanon and came to America after World War II. The man in the picture frame is Teta's husband, my grandfather. When I was a child, I loved going to Teta's house—it was so warm and always **smelled delicious**. Teta would **pinch my cheek** and say, "I love you, I love you, I love you!"

Scraps of cloth, thread and yarn were everywhere. Teta was a wonderful **seamstress**. The clothes she made were beautiful and so unusual that you never knew what she would put together. I learned about colors and patterns from Teta.

She would sit with me for hours, teaching me how to **knit and crochet**. While we were knitting, she would share stories about her childhood. She was an educated woman, which was very **unusual** in those days. She often **advised** me to "put **education** in your heart, not boys!" Well, thanks to you, Teta, I put art in my heart, too.

Ask: What do you have in your heart?

> Define *patterns:* Patterns are designs made of repeated colors, lines, and shapes. Ask students to point out patterns on page 161.

THE ARTIST
Helen Zughaib is a painter. She lives in Washington, D.C., with her two cats, Noodle and Chunky Beef.

Pause for students to view the illustration.

....

smelled delicious had a smell of good things to eat
pinch my cheek squeeze my cheek between her fingers
Scraps of cloth Little pieces of fabric
seamstress woman who makes clothes, woman who sews
knit and crochet make clothes using special needles and yarn
unusual different, special

160 Unit 3 │ Relationships

REACHING ALL STUDENTS

Social Studies Connection
INTER-GENERATIONAL GIFTS

In column 1 of a chart like the one below, have students write a list of the gifts that Teta passed along to Helen. Then ask students to write in column 2 any gifts they have received from ancestors and note gifts they hope to give their descendants in column 3.

Helen's gifts	My gifts	Gifts I will give

INTERNET
SOCIAL STUDIES CONNECTION

Remind students that our ancestors came from different countries. Some family names were changed when people immigrated to the United States. Encourage students to research origins of family names on the Internet and report their findings to the class. Use the key word search to get them started.

Key Words
genealogy
"family names"
"name origins"

Web Site
www.infokey.com

Vocabulary
FAMILY WORDS

Ask partners to list all the family words they can think of in one minute, for example, *mother, father, grandmother, aunt, uncle, cousin.* Encourage students to list family words in their own language as well, for example, *teta* (Arabic for *grandmother*), or *abuela* (Spanish for *grandmother*). Then the class can compile one master list of family words. Invite students to illustrate the list with photographs, original drawings, or pictures cut from magazines.

Helen Zughaib, gouache and ink on board. Copyright © 1999.

BEFORE YOU MOVE ON...

1. Details What did Teta do well?

2. Inference What did Helen learn from Teta?

Honoring Our Ancestors **161**

REVIEW KEY VOCABULARY

3 Relate Words Extend the magnet word activity on page 156. This time, have students copy a sentence from one of the stories in this selection under each box. The sentence should show a connection between the word in the box and the ancestor in the story. For example, for the word *education*, a student might choose this quotation from "I Honor My Grandmother" by Helen Zughaib: *She would sit with me for hours, teaching me how to knit and crochet.*

CHECK COMPREHENSION

4 Answers to "Before You Move On"

1. Details Teta was a seamstress; she made clothes. She also knew how to knit and crochet, and she shared stories with Helen.

2. Inference Helen learned about colors and patterns and how to knit and crochet. She also learned to value education and art.

CLOSE AND ASSESS

Ask students to tell you what they consider the most important thing Helen learned from Teta, and why.

HOME CONNECTION

Ancestor Time Line Send home a copy of *High Point Newsletter 6* in the **Teacher's Resource Book**. (See pages 132–138.) In this home activity, students ask a family member to tell a story about the life of one of their ancestors. With the family member, students make a time line about the ancestor and illustrate it with photographs or drawings. Encourage students to share their time line stories with the class. You may want to invite a family member to visit the class and tell a special story.

Grammar Minilesson

▶ **LINKING VERBS**

TEACH Tell students: *Helen Zughaib uses action verbs like* knit *that tell what the subject of a sentence does. She also uses the verbs* is, was, *and* were. *These are called linking verbs because they connect, or link, one part of a sentence with another part.*

Demonstrate the way linking verbs link the subject with a word in the predicate.

1. To name the subject again:

Teta **was** a seamstress.

2. To describe the subject:

The room **is** colorful.

PRACTICE Write these sentence starters: *The woman... , The man... , The colors... , The cat...* Ask students to finish each sentence with words that describe the portrait, using linking verbs from the list below.

as	are	is
was	were	appear
feel	look	seem

Invite volunteers to share their sentences.

▶ **Practice Book** page 82

Honoring Our Ancestors **T161**

OBJECTIVES

Function: Read a Selection

Concepts and Vocabulary: Art—*colors, patterns, drawing, painting, color theory, landscapes, shape*

Grammar: ❶ Irregular Past Tense Verbs

Listening: Listen to a Selection

Reading and Learning Strategies: Set a Purpose for Reading; Use Graphic Organizers (reflection log); ❶ Paraphrase; Relate to Personal Experience

SET PURPOSE

1 Say: *Look for details that describe the artist's parents.*

READ AND THINK

Tape 3B

CD 3
Track 7

2 Strategy Focus: Paraphrase Involve students in reading pages 162–163.

> See the **Multi-Level Strategies** on page T158 to adjust instruction to proficiency levels.

I HONOR
My Father and Mother
by Enrique Chagoya

I **dedicate** this drawing to my parents because they were my most important **source of** love and **support** when I was growing up.

My father gave me my first drawing and painting lessons and taught me **color theory** when I was seven years old. I remember when I first saw him drawing **landscapes** and animals. I thought his hand was magical. Ever since then, I've always wanted to do the same thing.

> **Restate:** The author loved to watch his father draw. He wanted to learn how to draw, too.

A wedding photo of Enrique's parents— Enrique Chagoya Galicia and Ofelia Flores de Chagoya

My mother **had a big heart**, not only for our family, but for many people who knew her. She **went out of her way** to help people in need and never expected anything back.

I drew the shape of my mother's body using the words "nunca me digas adiós." That's Spanish for "never tell me good-bye." She never wanted to say good-bye to me when I left Mexico. Instead, she said, "See you later." When she died four years ago, we told each other, "See you later."

> **Pause for students to view the illustration.**

THE ARTIST

Enrique Chagoya teaches painting, drawing, and printmaking at Stanford University. He was born in Mexico City and now lives in San Francisco, California.

---

color theory how to mix and use colors

landscapes pictures of trees, mountains, and rivers; scenes that show what the land looks like

had a big heart had a lot of love, was very kind

went out of her way did whatever she could

162 **Unit 3** | Relationships

REACHING ALL STUDENTS

Cooperative Learning

FOR LANGUAGE DEVELOPMENT:
Ask and Answer Questions

Study Painting Details Tell students to look at one of the paintings in the selection. Ask: *What details do you see?* (pyramid, airplane, paintbrushes)

Partner Questions Have students stand in two circles facing each other. Partners ask each other yes/no questions about something in the painting: *Do you see a boy? Does the man have a paintbrush in his hand?* After one question/answer, tell students to move one position to

find a new partner for the next question/answer.

Debrief the Content Instruct students to share what they learned about the paintings that they didn't notice before.

Debrief the Cooperative Process Tell students to think about their participation in the activity. Ask: *Did you find new details to ask your partner about? Did you answer the questions correctly?*

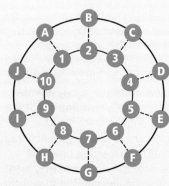

Cooperative Learning Structure: Inside-Outside Circle

Enrique Chagoya, pencil and acrylics on paper. Copyright © 1999.

BEFORE YOU MOVE ON...

1. **Vocabulary** With a partner, list words from the article that tell about art. Can you add more?
2. **Personal Experience** What words would you use to draw the shape of your mother or father?

CHECK COMPREHENSION

3 Answers to "Before You Move On"

1. **Vocabulary** Words from the selection: *colors, patterns, drawing, painting, color theory, landscapes, shape.* Other art-related words: *palette, light, shadow, brushstroke, watercolor, oil.*

2. **Personal Experience** Answers will vary. Encourage students to explain their choices.

CLOSE AND ASSESS

Students write a statement from the selection on an index card. Pairs exchange cards and paraphrase each other's statements.

CULTURAL PERSPECTIVES

World Cultures: Ancestor Album
Explain that many families keep a record of ancestors' stories. Tell students they will make a class album of their ancestors' stories, lessons, and pictures. You may want to group students by home country. Encourage them to bring in photographs or draw pictures to illustrate their ancestors' stories. Students can write or tape record stories and lessons. Students can also include information about their home countries.

Grammar Minilesson

▶ **IRREGULAR PAST TENSE VERBS**

TEACH Draw students' attention to this sentence from page 162: *My father gave me my first drawing and painting lessons and taught me color theory when I was seven years old.*

Guide students to recognize that *gave* and *taught* are verbs that tell about actions that happened in the past.

Remind students that verbs that do not add **-ed** to show past tense are called *irregular verbs.* Help students find more irregular verbs in the lists on Handbook pages 424–425.

PRACTICE Work with students to identify irregular past tense verbs in the selection. Encourage students to make a word file of irregular verbs and use them to write sentences about the selection. Verbs they might use are:

Verb	Earlier— in the Past	Verb	Earlier— in the Past
be give	was, were gave	think draw	thought drew

▶ **Practice Book** page 83

RESPOND

SUM IT UP

Function: Write

Reading and Learning Strategies:
Identify Cause and Effect; Use
Graphic Organizers (cause-and-effect
chart); ⊕ Paraphrase

Writing: Summary

THINK IT OVER

Function: Engage in Discussion

Critical Thinking and Comprehension:
Make Comparisons; Form Opinions; Make
Judgments; Relate to Personal Experience

EXPRESS YOURSELF

Function: Describe

Speaking and Listening:
Oral Description

CHECK YOUR UNDERSTANDING

1 Sum It Up Explain how *because* and
so signal cause and effect. Guide
students in reviewing the selection
before completing the paragraph.

▶ **Practice Book** page 84

2 Think It Over Possible answers are:

1. Comparison Alike: all include
images and descriptions of family
members. Different: two include
text; one shows the artist in the
picture; each focuses on different
generations.

2. Opinion Encourage students to
explain their choices.

3. Judgment People
can be honored with awards,
monuments, and dedications in
books, music, and art.

4. Personal Experience Answers
will vary.

3 Express Yourself Have students use
location words in their descriptions:
on the left, on the right, in the center.

CLOSE AND ASSESS

Students write a statement describing
something in a portrait, then tell why the
artist included that element.

Respond to the Family Portraits
Check Your Understanding

SUM IT UP

Identify Cause and Effect An **effect** is
something that happens. A **cause** is the reason
it happens. Use the word *because* before a
cause. Use the word *so* before an effect.

<u>I went home</u> **because** <u>I missed my family</u>.
   effect   cause

<u>I missed my family</u>, **so** <u>I went home</u>.
   cause   effect

Complete this summary. Write the missing cause
or effect.

    Three artists painted family portraits.
Stephen Von Mason honored his ancestors
because they were pioneers. Helen Zughaib's
grandmother taught her about
art, so she _____. Enrique Chagoya
painted his parents because _____.

Paraphrase the Summary Copy and complete
the paraphrase. Add facts about Helen Zughaib
and Enrique Chagoya.

> Three artists made pictures of their relatives.
> Stephen Von Mason's ancestors were pioneers,
> so he drew them in his painting.

THINK IT OVER

Discuss Talk about these questions with a
partner.

1. **Comparisons** How are the three pictures
alike? How are they different?

2. **Opinion** Which artist's story did you like
most? Why?

3. **Judgment** What is the best way to honor
someone?

4. **Personal Experience** What is something you
have learned from your ancestors?

EXPRESS YOURSELF ▶ DESCRIBE THINGS

Work with a partner to study one of the
portraits. Write notes that describe the portrait.
List things you see. List colors and shapes. Write
about where things are placed. Then use your
notes to describe the painting.

REACHING ALL STUDENTS

Multi-Level Strategies
SUM IT UP OPTIONS

BEGINNING Work with students as a group to complete the summary.
Ask questions to prompt paraphrasing: *What did Helen Zughaib's grandmother
teach her? What did Enrique Chagoya's parents give him?* Write students'
answers and read them aloud.

INTERMEDIATE / ADVANCED Ask students to look for information
in the text of the selection and to paraphrase it to complete the cloze
paragraph. Have them identify the information they provide as either a
cause or an effect.

Language Arts and Literature

VOCABULARY

USE CONTEXT CLUES

Learn About Context Clues Sometimes you can figure out the meaning of a new word by studying context clues. A **context clue** is a hint that you get from the words around the new word.

Find Context Clues Tell the meaning of *seamstress*. What words gave you context clues?

> Scraps of cloth, thread and yarn were everywhere. Teta was a wonderful **seamstress**. The clothes she made were beautiful. . .

Context clues: *The clothes she made, Scraps of cloth, thread and yarn*

Meaning: a woman who sews

Practice Write the meaning and context clues for the underlined words.

1. A underline(portrait) of my mother is on the wall. It looks just like her.

2. My mother is very underline(talented). She writes poetry, plays the piano, and draws.

3. On her birthday, we will honor her with a party. It will be a fun underline(celebration).

4. I am happy to have such a underline(remarkable) mother. She is wonderful and special.

WRITING/SPEAKING

WRITE A DEDICATION

A **dedication** is a way to honor someone special. Dedicate a portrait to someone in your family.

1 **Make a Portrait** You can:
- draw or paint a picture
- take a photograph
- use old photographs to make a collage.

2 **Write a Dedication** Tell why you want to honor this person.

> I dedicate this _____ to _____
> because _____
> _____

3 **Share Your Work** Present your portrait to the class. Read your dedication aloud. Tell about the person you want to honor.

 Learn how to give an **oral presentation**. See Handbook pages 374–376.

Honoring our Ancestors **165**

OBJECTIVES

USE CONTEXT CLUES
Vocabulary Strategy: ⊤ Context Clues

WRITE A DEDICATION
Function: ⊤ Express Feelings; Write
Speaking and Listening: Dedication
Writing: Dedication

LANGUAGE ARTS AND LITERATURE

1 **Use Context Clues** Answers to the Practice items:

1. **New word:** *portrait;* **Context clues:** *on the wall, looks just like her;* **Meaning:** *a picture of a person*

2. **New word:** *talented;* **Context clues:** *writes poetry, plays the piano, draws;* **Meaning:** *has special abilities*

3. **New word:** *celebration;* **Context clues:** *birthday, honor, party, fun;* **Meaning:** *happy event for an important occasion*

4. **New word:** *remarkable;* **Context clues:** *wonderful, special way;* **Meaning:** *unique*

▶ **Practice Book** page 85

2 **Write a Dedication** To help students get started, you may want to share one dedication:

I dedicate this collage to my mother because she taught me how to see the beauty in our world.

CLOSE AND ASSESS

Ask students to write the following sentence and circle the words that provide context clues about the meaning of *dedication: An author can include a dedication in a book to honor or remember a special person.*

Multi-Level Strategies
PRACTICE OPTIONS FOR CONTEXT CLUES

BEGINNING Process each Practice item with the group. Rephrase all the context clues in sentence form and then ask a question. For example: *It is something that hangs on the wall. It is something that looks just like my mother. What hangs on the wall and looks just like my mother?* Confirm and repeat all acceptable answers.

INTERMEDIATE / ADVANCED Have students complete the activity with partners. Then have the groups share their answers. Encourage Advanced students to copy other sentences with difficult words from this unit or a previous unit. Have them underline the target word and challenge a partner to locate the context clues and write the meaning of the underlined word.

RESPOND

OBJECTIVES

RESEARCH AN ANCESTOR'S COUNTRY

Function: ⊤ Give information

Learning Strategies, Critical Thinking, Research Skills, and Technology/Media: Gather Information; Take Notes; Organize and Synthesize Information; Make Comparisons; Use the Internet; Use Search Engines

Representing: Venn Diagram

MAKE A MULTIMEDIA PRESENTATION

Function: ⊤ Give Information

Representing and Technology/Media: Evaluate and Select Appropriate Media for Presentations; Multimedia Presentations

CONTENT AREA CONNECTIONS

1 Research an Ancestor's Country
Direct students to use reference books or the Internet to find out about their ancestor's country.

For Multi-Level Strategies: Guide Beginning students to choose one or two areas to explore, such as *traditions* or *climate.* Group them with higher proficiency students to place facts in the appropriate sections of the Venn diagram.

Encourage Intermediate and Advanced students to use at least three sources (interview, book, Internet).

▶ **Practice Book** page 86

2 Make a Multimedia Presentation
Provide tools for creating the projects, such as poster board, construction paper, paints, colored pencils, tapes and tape recorders, magazines and newspapers.

CLOSE AND ASSESS

Ask: *What did you learn in this lesson?*

Respond to the Family Portraits, continued

Content Area Connections

✔ **LANGUAGE ACQUISITION ASSESSMENT**
See page 42 of the Assessment Handbook.

▶ SOCIAL STUDIES
▶ TECHNOLOGY/MEDIA

RESEARCH AN ANCESTOR'S COUNTRY

Compare an ancestor's life in a different country with your life in the United States.

Gather Information Use your own experience or interview a relative. Find an article or search the Internet. Try the Web sites below, but remember that new sites appear every day! Use the country's name as a key word.

INTERNET

INFORMATION ON-LINE

Web Sites:
➤ Geography
  • www.geographia.com
  • www.emulateme.com

Make Comparisons Make a Venn diagram to compare the countries.

 Learn how to make **diagrams**.
See Handbook pages 343–344.

▶ FINE ARTS
▶ TECHNOLOGY/MEDIA

MAKE A MULTIMEDIA PRESENTATION

Celebrate your class's families in a creative way.

❶ Make a Poster Use a large piece of paper. In the center, put a portrait and dedication that honors your ancestors. Add art that describes your family.

❷ Add Music What music does your family like? Choose a favorite song to play.

❸ Add Photographs Use a camera or a video camera. Record activities like:
  • your family singing a song
  • interviews with family members
  • your family having fun.

❹ Have a Celebration Invite your families to your class. Show off your work.

 Learn how to make a **multimedia presentation**.
See Handbook pages 362–363.

REACHING ALL STUDENTS

Research Skills

▶ **USING THE INTERNET**

TEACH Suggest that students begin researching their ancestors' countries on the Internet. Remind students that the challenge will be narrowing their topic and selecting a useful site. Ask a volunteer to state a research goal: *I want to find out about the country where my grandfather lived.* You may want to model how to search for a country name at www.yahooligans.com.

PRACTICE Provide an opportunity for students to work on the Internet. Have groups studying the same country work together. They should:

1. Narrow the topic.
2. Make a list of possible Web sites.
3. Bookmark useful Web sites.
4. Copy text for diagrams into a word-processing document.

Everybody Says

poem
by Dorothy Aldis

Prepare to Read Poetry

THINK ABOUT WHAT YOU KNOW

Share Opinions Do people say you look "just like" someone? How does it make you feel? Do you want to look like someone else? Share your thoughts with your classmates.

LEARN KEY VOCABULARY

everybody Everyone or every person is **everybody**.

image If you are the **image** of someone, you look a lot like him or her.

look just like When you **look just like** a person, you look the same as the person.

Answers to the vocabulary activity will vary.

Answers on the red lines:
2. image
3. look just like
Answers on black lines will vary.

Use New Words in Context Study the new words. Then write each sentence. Write a new word on the red line. Write the name of a relative or other person on the black line.

1. _Everybody_ says I look like my _father_.

2. My mother says I am the ___image___ of _____.

3. Some day I want to _look just like_ _____.

LEARN ABOUT POETRY

Poems have special **characteristics**, or qualities. They help to give poetry a unique sound. Understanding these characteristics can help you enjoy poetry more.

READING STRATEGY
Characteristics of Poetry
1. When words have the same ending sounds, they **rhyme**.
2. When the number of syllables in the words of a poem has a regular pattern, the poem has **rhythm**.
3. Saying a word again and again is called **repetition**.

Now read "Everybody Says" aloud. As you read, listen for rhyming words, rhythm, and repetition.

Everybody Says **167**

Multi-Level Strategies
VOCABULARY OPTIONS

BEGINNING Work with students as a group to complete the sentences; use yourself as a model. Then ask each student to complete a sentence orally.

INTERMEDIATE / **ADVANCED**
After students complete the sentences independently, have them trade with a partner and rewrite the sentences: *Everybody says you look like your father.*

Transparency 49 / Master 49

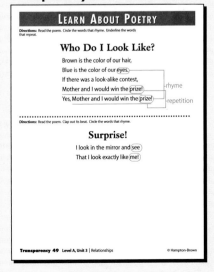

LEARN ABOUT POETRY
Directions: Read the poem. Circle the words that rhyme. Underline the words that repeat.

Who Do I Look Like?
Brown is the color of our hair,
Blue is the color of our eyes.
If there was a look-alike contest,
Mother and I would win the prize! — rhyme
Yes, Mother and I would win the prize! — repetition

Directions: Read the poem. Clap out its beat. Circle the words that rhyme.

Surprise!
I look in the mirror and see
That I look exactly like me!

Transparency 49 Level A, Unit 3 | Relationships   © Hampton-Brown

PREPARE TO READ

OBJECTIVES

THINK ABOUT WHAT YOU KNOW
Reading Strategy:
Relate to Personal Experience

LEARN KEY VOCABULARY ⊕
Vocabulary Strategy:
Use New Words in Context

LEARN ABOUT POETRY
Reading Strategy:
Use Text Features in Poetry

THINK ABOUT WHAT YOU KNOW

1 Share Opinions Use a Think Aloud to model how to express an opinion about your family resemblances. You may want to show a photo of family members who resemble you. Say: *I love it when people say I look like my Aunt Betty, because she is pretty. I don't like it when they say I look like my cousin Paul, because he has big teeth.*

LEARN KEY VOCABULARY

2 Use New Words in Context Read each vocabulary word and the defining sentences. After students understand the meaning of the key vocabulary words, conduct the activity. Model the first sentence for the group, emphasizing the vocabulary word.

> Use the Vocabulary Options in **Multi-Level Strategies** to support proficiency levels.

LEARN ABOUT POETRY

3 Teach Characteristics of Poetry Use **Transparency 49** to teach and illustrate the uses of rhyme, rhythm, and repetition in poetry. Model how to count syllables and keep rhythm in the second poem.

CLOSE AND ASSESS

Ask students to identify three characteristics of a poem.

Everybody Says

Everybody says
I look just like my mother.
Everybody says
I'm the image of Aunt Bee.
Everybody says
My nose is like my father's
But I want to look like ME!

—Dorothy Aldis

168   Unit 3 | Relationships

OBJECTIVES

Function: Read a Poem
Listening: Listen to a Poem
Reading Strategy:
Use Text Features in Poetry
Literary Analysis:
Rhyme; Rhythm; Repetition

SET PURPOSE

1 Read aloud the title and set the purpose for listening to the poem. Say: *As you listen to the poem, think about the rhythm, rhyme, and repetition of the verse.* Ask: *How does the girl feel about what everybody says?*

LISTEN AND READ

Tape 3B
CD 3
Track 8

2 **Strategy Focus: Use Text Features in Poetry** Play "Everybody Says" on the **Selection Tape/CD** or read the entire poem aloud for all students to hear. Then play or read the poem again, pausing to note elements of rhyme, rhythm, and repetition.

▐ Choose Reading Options in the **Multi-Level Strategies** to tailor the reading to all proficiency levels.

REACHING ALL STUDENTS

Learning Styles
STRATEGIES FOR CONSTRUCTING MEANING

• **Visual Learners** Ask students to mark the syllables, accent points, and rhyming words on the board or on a copy of the poem.

• **Auditory Learners** Invite students to clap syllables as you read the poem aloud.

• **Kinesthetic Learners** Encourage students to nod their heads, tap, move feet, or make motions with hands as the poem is read aloud.

Multi-Level Strategies
READING OPTIONS FOR LESSON 11

BEGINNING Begin with an exercise on rhyming, calling out pairs of words and asking students to say whether or not they rhyme. Then read the poem, or play its recording on the **Selection Tape/CD**. Read it aloud again, pausing for students to note rhyme. On later readings, encourage students to chime in on the rhyming or repeating words.

INTERMEDIATE Invite students to read the poem aloud with you. Then invite small groups of students to read it aloud on their own, emphasizing the rhyme and repetition.

ADVANCED Invite partners to memorize the poem and recite it with expression for the class.

Respond to the Poem

THINK IT OVER

Discuss Talk about these questions with a partner.

1. **Character's Motive** What does the speaker in the poem want?

2. **Personal Experience** The speaker says: "I want to look like ME!" Do you feel the same? How do you show the world who you are?

▶ WRITING/SPEAKING

WRITE A POEM

Use "Everybody Says" as a model poem about yourself.

Model Poem

> Everybody says
> I look just like _____.
> Everybody says
> I'm the image of _____.
> Everybody says
> My _____ is like _____.
> But I want to look like _____!

Try to make your poem rhyme. Try to give your poem rhythm. Then recite your poem for the class.

ABOUT THE POET

Dorothy Aldis (1896–1966) may have gotten her love of writing from her father. He was a newspaper man. During her lifetime, Ms. Aldis wrote many novels and books of poetry for young readers. She received the Children's Reading Round Table award for her outstanding work in children's literature. Her work is still read and loved by many.

Everybody Says **169**

OBJECTIVES

THINK IT OVER
Function: Engage in Discussion
Critical Thinking and Comprehension: Identify Character's Motive; Relate to Personal Experience
WRITE A POEM
Function: Write; Recite
Literary Analysis: Rhyme; Rhythm; Repetition
Writing: Poem
ABOUT THE POET
Literary Analysis: Evaluate Impact of Literary Devices on Meaning

THINK IT OVER

3 Possible answers are:

1. **Character's Motive** She wants to look like herself.

2. **Personal Experience** Students might say that they show the world who they are through attitude and actions, hobbies, etc.

WRITE A POEM

4 **Write an Innovation** Tell students that their new poem will probably not rhyme if they use the names of actual family members.

ABOUT THE POET

5 **Evaluate Literature: Literary Devices** Read the About the Poet feature to students. Tell students Dorothy Aldis was an award-winning poet who knew how to use all kinds of literary devices in her poems. Have students evaluate how the repetition of *Everybody Says* affects the meaning of the poem. (It strengthens the contrast between the girl's viewpoint and that of others.)

CLOSE AND ASSESS

Ask: *How are you the image of a family member? What makes you an individual?*

Language Development
NON-VERBAL COMMUNICATION

Model reading the couplets of the poem using different facial expressions and intonations: angry, surprised, happy, and disgusted. Ask students to share their responses to the various intonations. Invite students to select an emotion to express, and then to read couplets with appropriate facial expressions and intonations with partners. Partners can guess the emotions expressed and share their responses to the intonations.

BUILD LANGUAGE AND VOCABULARY

OBJECTIVES

Function: ❶ Define and Explain

Concepts and Vocabulary:
Words About Traits

Patterns and Structures:
Present Tense Verbs; ❶ Past Tense Verbs

Speaking: Oral Report

Viewing: Interpret Visual Information

Learning Strategy: Interact with Peers;
Use Graphic Organizers (observation and
data chart)

Critical Thinking: Make
Comparisons; Summarize

START WITH A COMMON EXPERIENCE

1 **View and Compare** View the
photographs of ears, encouraging
students to describe the
characteristics of each ear. If
necessary, point out that one has an
attached earlobe and the other, a
free earlobe. Let students use a
mirror so that they can compare their
earlobes with the pictures, or have
them work with partners.

2 **Discuss Inherited Traits** Invite
students to speculate about other
traits that are inherited, such as hair
and eye color, hair texture, and so on.
Be sensitive to the possibility that
some students may not know their
biological parents.

> Use the Questioning Techniques
> in the **Multi-Level Strategies** so
> that all students can participate.

3 **Model How to Define and Explain**
Use the following Think Aloud to
help students learn to define
and explain:

> **How to Define and Explain**
>
> • Name a term: *trait*
>
> • Tell what it means: *A trait is a
> feature that sets one individual
> apart from others.*
>
> • Give examples: *Traits include eye
> color, skin color, and height.*

Build Language and Vocabulary
DEFINE AND EXPLAIN

Some physical traits, or features, are inherited from your parents.
The shape of your earlobe is an inherited trait. What shape is your earlobe?
One of your parents probably has the same trait!

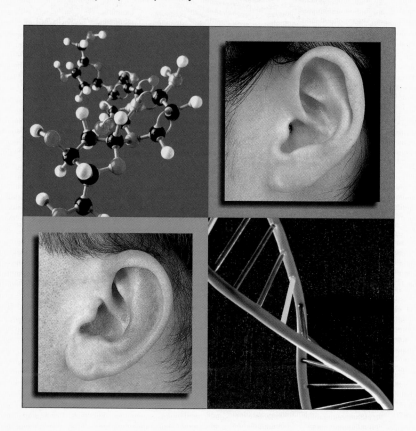

REACHING ALL STUDENTS

Multi-Level Strategies
QUESTIONING TECHNIQUES

BEGINNING Concentrate on questions with yes-no or one-word
answers: *What color are your eyes? Does your father have the same color eyes?
How many family members have eyes that color?*

INTERMEDIATE Ask questions about inherited traits that will expand
language: *Where do you think your eye color came from? What other physical
traits have you inherited from your father/mother?*

ADVANCED Ask these students to make observations about inherited
traits that go beyond the information presented: *Do we inherit only physical
traits? What other characteristics might people inherit from their ancestors?*

MAKE A TALLY CHART OF PHYSICAL TRAITS

Learn about inherited traits. Take a survey of the people in your class. Find out how many:
- can curl their tongue into a long tube shape
- can roll their tongue sideways
- have attached earlobes
- have free earlobes.

Record your findings on a tally chart like this one. Ask your family the same question. Share the information in class.

Can curl tongue	HHt HHt HHt
Can roll tongue	HHt II
Have attached earlobes like this:	IIII
Have free earlobes like this:	HHt HHt HHt

BUILD YOUR VOCABULARY

Words About Traits Read the definition of the word *inherit*.

> **inherit** *verb* When you **inherit** something, you receive it from your parents or ancestors.

Now work with the class to brainstorm a list of features or traits you have inherited from your parents or other family members. As you work through this unit, add to your list.

USE LANGUAGE STRUCTURES ▶ PRESENT AND PAST TENSE VERBS

Writing and Speaking: Define and Explain Work with a partner. Define *physical traits* and *character traits*. Give examples of each type of trait. Share your definitions and examples with the class.

Example:
Your physical traits are the way you look.
You inherit physical traits from your parents.
Sarita inherited green eyes from her grandmother.

Build Language and Vocabulary **171**

CONDUCT THE ACTIVITIES

4 **Make a Tally Chart of Physical Traits** Have students work with a partner to conduct the class survey. After students survey family members, invite discussion of what traits family members share.

5 **Build Your Vocabulary: Words About Traits** Students may want to categorize words into color, shape, and so on.

6 **Use Language Structure: Present and Past Tense Verbs** Review the verb tenses using the definitions and examples on **Transparency 50**. Have students look at Handbook pages 422 and 424–425 to review rules for adding **-ed** and to see irregular past tense forms. Then have them complete the sentences in Try It!

Writing and Speaking: Define and Explain Conduct the activity at the bottom of page 171. Suggest that students review "Discovery" in Unit 1 to review character traits.

▌ Use the Speaking Activity Options in the **Multi-Level Strategies** to adjust instruction.

▶ **Practice Book** page 87

Multi-Level Strategies
SPEAKING ACTIVITY OPTIONS

BEGINNING As a group, list examples of physical traits and character traits that students have already mentioned. Invite them to draw pictures of themselves and a person from whom they have inherited traits. Have them dictate or write captions or labels to show the traits they have in common.

INTERMEDIATE Suggest that students use a T-chart to record physical traits and character traits. Ask them to record examples of character traits from "Discovery," then brainstorm others with a partner. Then have partners brainstorm examples of physical traits. They can present their chart before giving their definitions.

ADVANCED Encourage students to present their definitions and examples in paragraph form.

Transparency 50 / Master 50

PRESENT AND PAST TENSE VERBS

1. The **tense** of a verb shows when an action happens. A **present tense verb** tells what is happening now.

   You **carry** traits from your parents.

2. A **past tense verb** tells what already happened. Past tense verbs end in **-ed**.

   Tim **inherited** red hair from his dad.

3. Other verbs have special forms to show the past tense.

Verb	Past Tense	Example
get	got	I **got** curly hair from my mom.
give	gave	She **gave** me my blue eyes, too.
see	saw	Mom **saw** the family resemblance when I was born.

Try It!

Complete each sentence. Use the past tense form of the underlined verb.

1. Our traits <u>come</u> from our parents. My parents' traits _____ from my grandparents.

2. Tonia <u>looks</u> just like her mother. Tonia's grandmother also _____ like her mother!

3. I hope I <u>grow</u> tall like my father. He _____ taller than his parents.

Transparency 50 Level A, Unit 3 | Relationships   © Hampton-Brown

Build Language and Vocabulary **T171**

PREPARE TO READ

OBJECTIVES

THINK ABOUT WHAT YOU KNOW

Reading Strategy:
Activate Prior Knowledge

LEARN KEY VOCABULARY ⊕

Vocabulary Strategy:
Use New Words in Context

LEARN TO READ NONFICTION

Reading Strategy:
Use Text Features in Nonfiction;
Preview; Formulate Questions;
Take and Review Notes

THINK ABOUT WHAT YOU KNOW

1 Share Information Give students a moment to reflect on the questions. Restate student responses in order to model how to turn questions into answers: *Rita and her sisters all have blue eyes. Jaime's family laughs the same way.* List responses.

LEARN KEY VOCABULARY

2 Use New Words in Context Read the new vocabulary words and the defining sentences aloud.

▌ Use the Vocabulary Options in **Multi-Level Strategies** to clarify meaning for all proficiency levels.

After students understand the meaning of the key vocabulary words, conduct the true/false activity as a group.

▶ **Practice Book** page 88

LEARN TO READ NONFICTION

3 Model How to Read Nonfiction Define *nonfiction*. Demonstrate the four steps of the reading strategy using **Transparency 51**.

CLOSE AND ASSESS

Ask students to tell you what they should do before they are about to read a nonfiction article. (look at the title and headings; formulate questions)

Grandfather's
nose  **P**repare to Read

science article
by Dorothy Hinshaw Patent

THINK ABOUT WHAT YOU KNOW

Share Information How are you like others in your family? Talk about how you look and act like your family.

combination A combination is a mix or a blend.

family resemblance People in some families look like each other. They have a family resemblance.

gene A gene is a part of a cell that tells your body how to form and grow.

genetics The science of genetics studies genes and how they are passed from parent to child.

identical twins Two babies born at the same time are called twins. Identical twins have the same genetic information.

inherit When you inherit something, you get it from your parents or ancestors.

relative A relative is a person in your family.

trait A trait is a person's way of looking or being.

LEARN KEY VOCABULARY

Use New Words in Context Study the new words. Then write these sentences. Write **T** for true. Write **F** for false.

  _T_ **1.** You can **inherit** a **trait** from a **relative**.

  _F_ **2.** You can share a **family resemblance** with a friend.

  _T_ **3.** **Identical twins** have the same **combination** of genes.

  _T_ **4.** Scientists who study **genetics** learn about parts of a **gene**.

LEARN TO READ NONFICTION

Many articles are nonfiction. **Nonfiction** gives facts and information. Reading nonfiction is a good way to learn.

> **READING STRATEGY**
> **How to Read Nonfiction**
> 1. Look at the article before you read. Read the title and headings. Look at the pictures and captions.
> 2. Write your questions about the topic.
> 3. Read and take notes.
> 4. Read your notes and think about what you learned.

Now read "Grandfather's Nose" and follow the steps for reading nonfiction.

REACHING ALL STUDENTS

▌ Multi-Level Strategies
VOCABULARY OPTIONS

BEGINNING Use the family photos on pages 173 and 174 to introduce the words *relatives, traits,* and *family resemblance*. Restate the true/false statements in the activity to clarify, using words from the defining sentences.

INTERMEDIATE / **ADVANCED**
Use a science book or picture dictionary as well as the illustration on page 175 to clarify *genes, genetics, inherit,* and *identical twins*. Ask pairs of students to turn the false statement in the activity into a true statement.

Transparency 51 / Master 51

HOW TO READ NONFICTION

Directions: Read the title and the heading for each paragraph. What questions do you have? Write them in column 1. Now, read each paragraph. Write your notes in column 2. Write what you learned in column 3.

How Traits are Inherited

Physical Traits. A **physical trait** is the special way a person looks. Height, eye color, and hair color are all examples of physical traits. Traits like these are **inherited**—or passed—from parents to children.

Genetic Combinations. Traits come from **genes**, the parts of cells that tell your body how to grow. Each parent gives a child one gene for each trait. The combination of these two genes decides what trait the child will have. For example, a child with two tall parents may be tall, too.

My Questions	Notes from Reading	What I Learned
Students' answers will vary.		

Transparency 51 Level A, Unit 3 | Relationships   © Hampton-Brown

Grandfather's NOSE

by Dorothy Hinshaw Patent

Has anyone ever told you that you have your father's eyes or your mother's hair? In this article, science writer Dorothy Hinshaw Patent explains how we get some of these "special gifts" from our parents.

173

INTRODUCE THE SELECTION

4 Preview and Predict Read the title, author, and introduction to the article on page 173 with students. Talk about the photos they see on the page and what the introduction says about the article. Then have students page through the article and look at the pictures of the families. Ask them to think of questions they might want to ask about genetics.

5 Audio Walk-Through Play the Audio Walk-Through for "Grandfather's Nose" on the **Selection Tape/CD** to give students the overall idea of the story.

Tape 3B
CD 3
Track 9

Grandfather's Nose
by Dorothy Hinshaw Patent

Theme Connection This science article explains what causes us to look like previous generations in our families.

Selection Summary In this article, Dorothy Hinshaw Patent writes about the science of genetics, explaining how we inherit family traits or characteristics from our parents and grandparents.

Author Awards Author Dorothy Hinshaw Patent has won author awards for ALA Best Books for Young Adults in 1986, School Library Journal Best Books of the Year in 1992 and 1986, and Library of Congress Children's Book of the Year in 1985.

THE BASICS BOOKSHELF

■ *Families* by Ann Morris

Inherited characteristics are not the only things that define a family. While the colorful photos in this book support the fact that members of most families look alike in some way, they also expand the concept of family to include how members support, share, and care for one another. The simple text focuses on family activities; i.e., *cook, learn, work, play*, providing beginning English learners an opportunity to learn basic vocabulary about the family.

For Lesson Plans: See the Teacher's Guide for *The Basics Bookshelf*.

Function: Read a Selection
Grammar: Demonstrative Pronouns
Listening: Listen to a Selection
Reading and Learning Strategies: Set a
Purpose for Reading; Use Text Features in
Nonfiction; Formulate Questions; Take
and Review Notes; Relate to Personal
Experience; ⊕ Paraphrase
Comprehension:
Identify Details; Cause and Effect

SET PURPOSE

1 Read aloud the title and the photo
captions. Say: *As you read, look for
the sentence that tells the definition
of* genetics.

READ AND THINK

Tape 3B

CD 3
Track 10

**2 Strategy Focus: Use
Text Features in Nonfiction** Before
students read, ask them to look at the
title, headings, pictures, and captions.
Have them use **Master 52** to write
their questions.

> Choose Reading Options in the
> **Multi-Level Strategies** to tailor
> the reading to proficiency levels.

The recording of "Grandfather's
Nose" on the **Selection Tape/CD**
offers an oral language model
and the opportunity to build
reading fluency.

Red annotations offer opportunities to
clarify meaning and check for understanding.

What Is Genetics?

Do you look like your mother or
father? Do people mix you up with your
brother or sister? People usually do look
like their **relatives** in some ways. They
have a "**family resemblance.**"

How is a grandfather's nose or a
mother's red hair **passed along** to a
daughter or grandson? That is, how are
these features inherited? When you
inherit something, you receive it from
your parents.

Scientists try to understand how we
inherit family **traits,** or characteristics.
They call their work *genetics*
(jen-NET-icks). Genetics is the science
that studies how traits are inherited.
Give examples: Some family traits or characteristics
are eye color, hair color, and height.

passed along given

What kind of family resemblance do you see in
this family?

Clarify: *That is,…* signals that the author will now restate
or explain her idea using other words. What other phrase
could the author have used? *(In other words,…)*

Scientists study
how traits are
inherited.

BEFORE YOU MOVE ON...

1. **Details** What do scientists learn about when
   they study genetics?
2. **Personal Experience** What kind of "family
   resemblances" does your family have?

174 Unit 3 | Relationships

REACHING ALL STUDENTS

Transparency 52 / Master 52

NOTE-TAKING CHART

Directions: Read the title and the heading for each section. What questions do
you have? Write them in column 1. Now, read each section. Write your notes in
column 2 as you read. Write what you learned in column 3.

Grandfather's Nose

| My
Questions | Notes from
Reading | What I
Learned |
|---|---|---|
| | | |
| | | |
| | | |

Transparency 52 Level A, Unit 3 | Relationships   © Hampton-Brown

Multi-Level Strategies

READING OPTIONS FOR LESSONS 14–15

BEGINNING Have students look at the pictures. Ask: *Do you see people
who look alike? What family resemblances can you point to?* Have students
listen to the Audio Walk-Through on the **Selection Tape/CD**, as you point to
the pictures and diagrams. Read headings and captions aloud. Then, help
students formulate questions and record them on **Transparency 52**. Read
each section of the article aloud, using the red annotations to clarify
meaning. Prompt students to complete columns 2 and 3, vocalizing as
you record their ideas.

INTERMEDIATE / **ADVANCED** Have partners with different
proficiencies work together to look at pictures and read headings and
captions before beginning **Master 52**. Encourage them to pause and take
notes as they read the text following each heading. Then, ask partners to
complete column three.

So Many Genes

Genes are the basic **units of inheritance.** Humans have about 50,000 different genes. Even though there are family resemblances, everyone looks different because there are so many ways the genes can be combined. This is one reason why **identical twins** are so **remarkable.** **Ask:** What would your identical twin look like?

Identical twins result when a fertilized egg divides into two separate **cells** that don't stick together. Each of the cells then goes on to **develop into a complete embryo,** a very young baby developing inside its mother. Both twins have exactly the same genes, since they come from the same fertilized egg. That is why they look identical.

Define *fertilized egg*: A fertilized egg has genes from both the mother and the father. A mother's egg is not fertilized until it receives genes from the father. Only a fertilized egg develops into a baby.

The Development of a Single Baby and of Twins

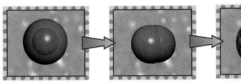

A fertilized egg. The egg divides. An embryo develops. A baby is born.

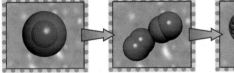

A fertilized egg. The egg divides into two separate cells. Each one divides. Two embryos develop. Two babies are born.

---

units of inheritance pieces of information passed from your parents' cells to yours
remarkable amazing, special
cells tiny parts that make up living things
develop into a complete embryo grow into an unborn baby

BEFORE YOU MOVE ON...

1. **Cause and Effect** Why do most people look different from one another?
2. **Paraphrase/Viewing** Reread paragraph two (above) and look at the flow chart. In your own words, tell how identical twins are formed.

Grandfather's Nose 175

page 174
1. **Details** Scientists learn how we inherit traits and characteristics from family members.
2. **Personal Experience** Answers will vary, but students should discuss physical resemblances such as hair color, eye color, and shape of eyes.

page 175
1. **Cause and Effect** There are many different combinations of genes.
2. **Paraphrase/Viewing** When an egg splits, it becomes two cells that have exactly the same genes.

CLOSE AND ASSESS

Ask students to work with a partner to write a test question about family resemblance and the power of genetics.

Language Development
ASK QUESTIONS

After students have read the selection, give heterogeneous groups vocabulary words (*genetics, family resemblance, genes, embryo, inheritance*). These will serve as "answers." Have each group brainstorm two or three questions for each answer. Students can then reread the selection and revise their questions or come up with new ones: *What is the science that studies how traits are inherited? What tiny part of a cell tells your body how to grow?* Invite groups to pose their questions to the class.

Grammar Minilesson

▶ **DEMONSTRATIVE PRONOUNS**

TEACH Place one book near you and one book farther away. Touching the nearby book, say: *This is on my desk.* (Point to the other book.) *That is on the chalk rail.* Repeat with two groups of objects to introduce *these* and *those* as demonstrative pronouns.

Explain that the pronouns *this, that, these,* and *those* point out people or things. *This* and *these* point to people or things that are near in space or time. *That* and *those* point to people or things that are farther away in space or time.

PRACTICE Write these sentences. Have students write *this, that, these,* or *those* to complete each sentence.

1. _____ are identical twins in that picture.
2. Is _____ your sister standing next to me?
3. _____ are more interesting than those.
4. _____ is a microscope over there.

▶ **Practice Book** page 89

OBJECTIVES

Function: Read a Selection

Listening: Listen to a Selection

Reading and Learning Strategies: Set a Purpose for Reading; Use Text Features in Nonfiction; Take and Review Notes; Relate to Personal Experience

Comprehension: Identify Details

SET PURPOSE

1 Say: *As you read, think about traits that make us unique.*

READ AND THINK

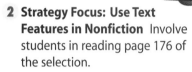

Tape 3B

CD 3
Track 10

2 **Strategy Focus: Use Text Features in Nonfiction** Involve students in reading page 176 of the selection.

> See the **Multi-Level Strategies** on page T174 to tailor the reading experience to all proficiency levels.

CHECK COMPREHENSION

3 **Answers to "Before You Move On"**

 1. Details About six billion.

 2. Personal Experience Answers will vary. Encourage elaboration.

CLOSE AND ASSESS

Have students draw a picture of a cell and write something they have learned about genetics inside it.

So Many Differences

The possible **combinations** of genes are almost **countless**. Even though there are now over six billion people on Earth, no two of them look exactly alike, except for identical twins. Each human being is different from everyone else. People may say you have your grandfather's nose, but no one just like you has ever lived. And no one just like you will ever live again.

Pause to write the numeral 6,000,000,000.

BEFORE YOU MOVE ON...

1. Details About how many people are there on Earth now?

2. Personal Experience What is something about you that is different from everyone else? Is it something you like, or something you'd like to change? Explain.

Each human being is unique.

Define *unique*: different or one-of-a-kind.

countless too many to count

ABOUT THE AUTHOR

In the past 25 years, **Dorothy Hinshaw Patent** has written more than 100 science books for children and young adults. "I have tremendous respect for the minds of children," she says. "They're capable of learning so much. They're like sponges: they just soak stuff up." Dr. Patent dedicated her book, *Grandfather's Nose*, to "the teachers who gave me a love of genetics."

176 **Unit 3** | Relationships

REACHING ALL STUDENTS

Health Connection

LIFESTYLE CHOICES

Sketch a pair of identical adult twins. Label them A and B. Say: *Meet Twins A and B. They were identical as children.* List these lifestyle choices under the sketch of each twin as you present them to the class: *Twin A eats a healthy diet, exercises, and maintains a good weight. Twin B smokes, eats junk food, and never exercises.* Ask: *Do you think they look identical now? What might be different? Can Twin B expect to live as long as Twin A? Why or why not?*

A WORLD OF LANGUAGES

Word Order/Syntax There are many ways to say "no" in English: *No one just like you has ever lived. I do not look like my grandpa.* Compare the ways to show negation in the following languages. Ask bilingual adults in the community who speak the languages of the students to help students discover points of transfer and interference.

Negative Word Before the Verb		Negative Prefix Before the Verb		Negative Word After the Verb	
LANGUAGE	WORD	LANGUAGE	PREFIX	LANGUAGE	WORD
Estonian	*ei*	Cantonese	*m̀h-*	Bengali	*na*
Lao	*baw*	Czech	*ne-*	German	*nicht*
Spanish	*no*				
Tagalog	*Hindî*				

Respond to the Article
Check Your Understanding

SUM IT UP

Relate Main Idea and Details Work with a group. Copy the paragraph. Then use your notes to finish the summary.

Genetics studies <u>how traits are inherited</u>. Parents pass their genes to their <u>children</u>. Genes tell the body to develop certain traits. Humans have about <u>50,000</u> genes. There are many, many possible combinations of genes. That is why each person is <u>special</u>. Only <u>identical twins</u> have the same genes.

Write Sentences Tell what you learned from the article. Tell what you still want to learn.

Example:
Our looks are inherited from our parents.
What other traits are inherited?

THINK IT OVER

Discuss Talk about these questions with a partner.

1. **Inference** The author says: "No one just like you has ever lived." What does she mean?

2. **Judgment** Can identical twins have different personalities? Explain.

3. **Personal Experience** What three traits do you want your children to inherit from you?

4. **Opinion** Some day human parents may be able to choose traits for their children. Is this a good idea? Why or why not?

EXPRESS YOURSELF ▶ DEFINE AND EXPLAIN

Work with a partner to define the term *family resemblance*. Then read your definition to the class. Give an example of a resemblance in your own family.

✓ **LANGUAGE ACQUISITION ASSESSMENT**
See page 42 of the Assessment Handbook.

Grandfather's Nose **177**

Multi-Level Strategies
SUM IT UP OPTIONS

BEGINNING Work as a group to restate the information in the What I Learned column on **Transparency 52**. Then go on to complete the summary paragraph together. Provide sentence frames to help students write their sentences: *I learned _____ from the article. I still want to learn _____.*

INTERMEDIATE / ADVANCED Have students in small, mixed-proficiency groups read aloud their notes from columns 2 and 3 on **Master 52** before completing the summary paragraph. They can refer to column 1 to state what they still want to learn. Have students list resources they could use to find answers. Encourage them to do research and report to the class.

OBJECTIVES

SUM IT UP
Function: Write
Reading and Learning Strategies:
🅣 Relate Main Idea and Details
Writing: Sentences
THINK IT OVER
Function: Engage in Discussion
Critical Thinking: Make Inferences; Form Opinions; Relate to Personal Experience; Make Judgments
EXPRESS YOURSELF
Function: 🅣 Define and Explain
Speaking and Listening: Group Talk

CHECK YOUR UNDERSTANDING

1 **Sum It Up** Group students heterogeneously to discuss their notes and work together to fill in the summary paragraph.

▶ **Practice Book** page 90

2 **Think It Over** Possible answers are:

1. **Inference** The author means that no one has the same genetic material as you.

2. **Judgment** Yes, they can. Answers should show that genetics is only one way that people are different. Experience also shapes personality.

3. **Personal Experience** Answers will vary. Students may answer with physical or character traits.

4. **Opinion** Answers will vary. Some may say genetic choice is good because it will improve people. Students should give reasons for their opinions.

3 **Express Yourself** Prompt the use of describing words and specific examples.

CLOSE AND ASSESS

Ask students to tell something they learned about genes from the article.

RESPOND

OBJECTIVES

NEGATIVE SENTENCES
Grammar: ⊕ Negative Sentences
WRITE LABELS
Function: Write
Writing: Labels

LANGUAGE ARTS AND LITERATURE

1 **Use Negative Sentences** Possible answers to the Practice items are:

1. Anna does not look like her relatives.

2. Not all identical twins are exactly alike.

3. We do not inherit traits from our friends.

▶ **Practice Book** page 91

2 **Write Labels** To provide support, you may want to:

• List possible traits and areas of resemblance students can label: *eye color, height, size of ears, shape of toes.*

• Model making and labeling a drawing: *I have brown eyes like my mother does. I have my father's hands.*

• Offer positive feedback, for example: *I like your ideas. Your drawing and labels really help me imagine how you resemble your family members.*

CLOSE AND ASSESS

Invite students to share their drawings and labels with the class. Ask each student to write a negative sentence telling about a trait not shared with other family members.

 ASSESSMENT
Selection Test 12 on page 49 of the Assessment Handbook tests students' mastery of the reading strategies and the vocabulary, comprehension, and language arts skills taught with this selection.

Respond to the Article, continued
Language Arts and Literature

▶ GRAMMAR IN CONTEXT

USE NEGATIVE SENTENCES

Learn About Negative Sentences Use a **negative word** like one of these to make a sentence mean "no":

no	nothing	never	none
not	nobody	no one	nowhere

Examples:
No one just like you has ever lived.
Not all twins are exactly alike.

Do not use two negative words in the same sentence.

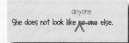

anyone
She does not look like ~~no one~~ else.

Make Up Negative Sentences Ask a friend a question that starts with: *Do you, Can you* or *Have you.* Your friend will answer with a negative sentence. Then change roles.

Example:
You: Do you like milk?
Your partner: I do **not** like milk.

Practice Write these as negative sentences.

1. Anna looks like her relatives.

2. All twins are exactly alike.

3. We inherit traits from our friends.

178   Unit 3 │ Relationships

▶ WRITING

WRITE LABELS

Think of your family or look at the photographs of families in this unit. Find traits that family members share.

1 **Make Your Drawing** Draw a picture of yourself or a child on page 168, 173, or 174.

2 **Find Similarities** Find features that look like the other family members.

Examples:
The boy has dark eyes like both parents.
I have straight hair like my father.

3 **Add Labels** Write family traits next to your drawing. Draw lines to connect the words to the part of the picture they describe.

REACHING ALL STUDENTS

▌Multi-Level Strategies
ACTIVITY OPTIONS FOR WRITING LABELS

BEGINNING Prepare students for the labeling activity by listing possible traits *(big hands; brown hair)* next to a choice of preposition frames *(from my; like my).* Have students practice combining the two to create labels. After they draw and label, ask them to tell about themselves in complete sentences: *I have green eyes like my grandmother.*

INTERMEDIATE / ADVANCED Tell students to create a mind map to organize ideas for the labeling activity. Have them start with the word *Traits* and create six sections, one for traits inherited from each parent and grandparent. After they have completed the drawing and labeling activity, encourage Advanced students to write a paragraph based on their self-portrait. Model the paragraph: *I inherited my brown eyes from my mother and my black hair from both my father and mother. I have my grandmother's small hands.*

Content Area Connections

> SCIENCE

STUDY GENETICS

Parents pass traits to their children. Each parent has two genes for each trait. The parents each pass one gene for each trait to their child.

❶ Learn about Punnet Squares A Punnett square shows all the ways parents' genes can be combined in their children.

Punnett Square 1

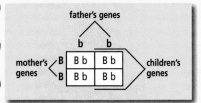

This Punnett square shows how the trait for eye color is passed from parents to children. The father has two genes for blue eyes (**bb**) and the mother has two genes for brown eyes (**BB**). The Punnett square shows that each child will have one **B** gene and one **b** gene.

❷ Learn About Dominant and Recessive Genes Dominant genes block **recessive genes** from being inherited. In Punnett Square 1, each child has one gene for blue eyes (**b**) and one gene for brown eyes (**B**). The gene for brown eyes is dominant. Since all four children have at least one **B** gene, they all will have brown eyes.

❸ Complete a Punnett Square What happens when two parents have mixed genes? Copy and complete Punnett Square 2. How many children will have brown eyes? How many children will have blue eyes?

Punnett Square 2

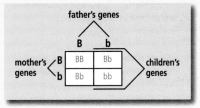

Three children (BB, Bb, Bb) will have brown eyes.
One child (bb) will have blue eyes.

Multi-Level Strategies
PRACTICE OPTIONS FOR STUDYING GENETICS

BEGINNING Model how to fill in the Punnett squares. Ask direct questions to help students understand how to approach the activity: *What color eyes does your mother have? What color eyes does your father have?* Assist students in creating the eye color chart.

INTERMEDIATE Show students how to fill out a Punnett square to figure out how their parents passed along eye color genes. To guide students, ask: *How can you figure out which genes are dominant and recessive?* Encourage pairs to work together and talk over the procedure.

ADVANCED Have students fill out the Punnett squares independently. Ask students to fill out an eye color Punnett square for themselves and write and present a summary explanation for their own eye color: *My mother has brown eyes. This is labeled BB in the Punnett square. . .*

RESPOND

OBJECTIVES

STUDY GENETICS

Function: ❶ Give information

Concepts and Vocabulary: Genetics—*genes, heredity, dominant, recessive*

Learning Strategies and Critical Thinking: Connect New Information to Known; Analyze and Synthesize Information; Visualize

Representing: Punnett Square

CONTENT AREA CONNECTIONS

1 Study Genetics Model how to use the Punnett square to show how traits pass from parents to children. Prepare students by reviewing and previewing content area vocabulary.

- *genetics, genes*: Write the root *gen* and explain that it comes from a Greek word that means *kind* or *type*. Remind students that *genetics* and *genes* have a lot to do with the kind of person we become—at least physically.

- *dominant, recessive*: Describe *dominant* and *recessive* as types of genes. Explain that dominant is "strong" and recessive is "hidden." Help students use what they know about inheriting genes to figure out which genes are dominant and recessive in their families.

▶ **Practice Book** page 92

CLOSE AND ASSESS

Have students agree on a summary statement about dominant and recessive genes. Post it in the classroom.

INTRODUCE WRITING THAT EXPRESSES FEELINGS

1 Discuss Expressive Writing Read the introduction. Ask: *How can writers tell us their thoughts and feelings?*

2 Study the Models After reading the excerpts, ask: *How do you think the author feels about Lillie (Teta)? What tells you the authors' thoughts and feelings?* Make a chart of words and the feelings or thoughts they convey.

Words Used	Thoughts/Feelings
"everything Lillie did was pretty"	admired her, wanted to be like her

Use the Options for Studying Writing in the **Multi-Level Strategies** to adjust instruction.

CLOSE AND ASSESS

Ask students to agree on a summary sentence that defines expressive writing.

Writing for Personal Expression

Writers tell us their thoughts and feelings in expressive writing.

WRITING MODELS

Read these sentences from "My Best Friend." How does the writer feel about Lillie? How do you know?

from "My Best Friend"

> I thought everything Lillie did was pretty. The way she walked, swinging along, throwing one foot out a little more than the other, as if she were walking to a bouncy kind of music.

Here Helen Zughaib describes a visit to her grandmother. What helps you understand how Helen feels?

from "Honoring Our Ancestors"

> When I was a child, I loved going to Teta's house—it was so warm and always smelled delicious. Teta would pinch my cheek and say, "I love you, I love you, I love you!"

REACHING ALL STUDENTS

Multi-Level Strategies
OPTIONS FOR STUDYING EXPRESSIVE WRITING

BEGINNING Have volunteers role-play Lillie walking as described in "My Best Friend," and Helen visiting Teta in "Honoring Our Ancestors." Ask: *How would you feel watching Lillie walk that way? How would you feel at Teta's house?* Ask students to find words in the two models that describe the author's thoughts and feelings, and list them on the chart.

INTERMEDIATE Express some thoughts and feelings and the reasons for them. For example: *I think this flower is pretty because of its deep color; when my dog wags his tail at me, I feel happy.* Invite volunteers to role-play the writers in the models and to restate their thoughts and feelings the same way.

ADVANCED Encourage students to express their own thoughts and feelings about the subjects of the two writing models, and to give reasons for their responses. Add students' ideas to the chart.

Write Together

WRITING PROMPT
Work with your class to write a paragraph. Write about someone you like. Be sure to express your feelings about that person. Then share your work with another class.

1 Brainstorm Ideas Make a list of people to write about. Choose one person to be your topic.

2 Get Ready to Write Before you write, always think about:
- What you are writing, or the **form**
- Who will read your work, or the **audience**
- What you are writing about, or the **topic**
- Why you are writing, or the **purpose**

Fill out an **FATP** chart to get ready to write.

3 Plan and Write the Paragraph A paragraph has one main idea. All the details in the paragraph go with the main idea. Make a chart like the one below. Then use your chart to write the paragraph.

FATP Chart

HOW TO UNLOCK A PROMPT
Form: _paragraph_
Audience: _students in room 24_
Topic: _Lola_
Purpose: _to express how we feel about her_

STUDENT WRITING MODEL

Main Idea
Lola moved away, but we are still good friends.

Detail
We can send e-mails.

Detail
We can send pictures.

Detail
We can call her every week.

A Good Friend

Lola moved away, but we can still be friends. We can send e-mails to each other. It's always great fun to read what Lola has to say. We can send pictures of our class. We can call her every week. I hope that we will stay friends forever!

Writing for Personal Expression   **181**

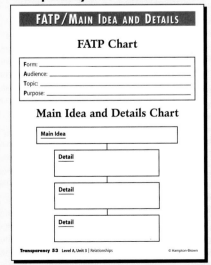

Transparency 53 / Master 53

FATP/MAIN IDEA AND DETAILS

FATP Chart

Form: _____
Audience: _____
Topic: _____
Purpose: _____

Main Idea and Details Chart

Main Idea

Detail

Detail

Detail

Transparency 53   Level A, Unit 3 | Relationships   © Hampton-Brown

Transparency 54 / Master 54

FEATURES OF EXPRESSIVE WRITING

Directions: Read the Student Writing Model. Compare it to the features of an expressive paragraph. Check the box if the model has the feature. Write the words from the model.

An Expressive Paragraph... _My Best Friend_

states the **main idea** clearly	☑ Lola moved away, but we can still be friends.
includes **details** to support the main idea	☑ send e-mails send pictures call her every week
tells the writer's **thoughts** or **feelings** about the subject	☑ great fun to read what Lola has to say we hope to stay best friends forever

Transparency 54   Level A, Unit 3 | Relationships   © Hampton-Brown

---

OBJECTIVES
Function: Write
Learning Strategies and Critical Thinking: Plan; Generate Ideas; Interact with Peers; Analyze and Evaluate Information
Writing: Main Idea Paragraph

WRITE TOGETHER

Discuss the Writing Prompt Remind students that the writing prompt tells what kind of writing to do, what to write about, and who to write for. Read the prompt and ask volunteers to restate it, or paraphrase it yourself, if necessary.

Introduce the FATP Chart Point out the entries in the sample chart to help explain the meaning of *form, audience, topic,* and *purpose.* Tell students that the FATP chart helps you keep these things in mind as you write.

Plan the Paragraph Work with students to choose whom you will write about, and to complete the FATP chart on **Transparency 53**. Then guide students in identifying the main idea and details for the class paragraph on the chart at the bottom of **Transparency 53**.

Analyze and Evaluate a Paragraph Display **Transparency 54**. Guide students in analyzing and evaluating the model against the features.

Write the Paragraph Lead students through adapting the entries on your main idea and details chart into the sentences of your paragraph.

CLOSE AND ASSESS

Distribute copies of **Master 54** and have students work with partners or in small groups to analyze and evaluate your class paragraph against the features.

PREWRITE

Function: Write

Learning Strategies and Critical Thinking: Plan; Generate Ideas; Interact with Peers; Organize Ideas; Self-Assess

Representing: Charts

Writing: ❶ Writing Process

WRITE ON YOUR OWN

Have volunteers tell what form their writing will take, what their paragraph should tell about, and who will read it.

For more about the Writing Process, refer students to pages 382–389 in the Handbook.

PREWRITE

Remind students that the Prewriting stage is for planning their writing. Explain that they will first think of people and experiences they might write about. They will choose one topic, fill out an FATP chart, and organize their ideas on a main idea and details chart.

❚ Use the Prewriting Support in the **Multi-Level Strategies** to tailor this stage to proficiency levels.

CLOSE AND ASSESS

Have partners answer the questions in Think About Your Writing.

Writing for Personal Expression, continued

Write on Your Own

WRITING PROMPT

Now write your own paragraph. It can tell about a person or an experience. Express your feelings about the topic. Then, share your writing with classmates.

PREWRITE

❶ **Choose a Topic** Think about people and experiences that have been special to you. Choose one as your topic. Then fill out an **FATP** chart to help guide your writing.

❷ **Get Organized** Make a main idea chart. Add details about your thoughts and feelings.

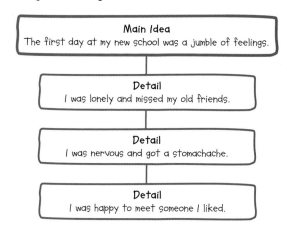

Main Idea
The first day at my new school was a jumble of feelings.

Detail
I was lonely and missed my old friends.

Detail
I was nervous and got a stomachache.

Detail
I was happy to meet someone I liked.

FATP Chart

HOW TO UNLOCK A PROMPT

Form: paragraph

Audience: classmates

Topic: my first day at a new school

Purpose: to share the feelings I had that day

Think About Your Writing

• Are you happy with your topic?

• Do you want to share your feelings about it?

• Will your topic be interesting to your audience?

• Do you have enough details to write about?

REACHING ALL STUDENTS

Transparency 55 / Master 55

TOPIC CHART		
Person or Experience	Thoughts	Feelings
went to get my first library card	wondered what the public library would look like	excited, nervous surprised how big it was

Transparency 55 Level A, Unit 3 | Relationships   © Hampton-Brown

Multi-Level Strategies

GROUPING GUIDELINES

BEGINNING Display **Transparency 55**, explaining that the chart will help students record ideas for topics. Model filling out the chart with a topic of your own. Then distribute copies of **Master 55** and have students record their own ideas, expressed in words and art. Next, have students highlight the topic they choose to write about. Then guide them in filling out FATP and Main Idea and Details charts on copies of **Master 53**. (See page T181.)

INTERMEDIATE / ADVANCED Distribute copies of **Master 55** for students to use in recording topic ideas. Encourage them to complete the chart and then discuss their ideas with a partner before choosing one topic to write about. As students work on the charts, assist with identifying words to express their thoughts and feelings. After they choose a topic, have them fill out FATP and Main Idea and Details charts on **Master 53**. (See page T181.)

DRAFT

1 **Write Your Paragraph** Use your main idea chart to help you write an expressive paragraph.

2 **Use Examples and Details** Study the sentences below.

> I write to clear my own mind, to find out what I think and feel.
>
> — V.S. Pritchett

Writer's Craft: Elaboration

Add details to help explain your thoughts and feelings.

Just OK	Much Better
I was lonely.	I was lonely. I felt as if everyone had a friend—and I had no one.

Add examples to help your readers understand how you feel.

Just OK	Much Better
I did everything alone that day.	I did everything alone that day. I sat alone, I ate alone, and I walked home alone.

Read these lists. Each names a feeling and gives three examples of when you might feel that way. Think of more examples that go with your topic.

Happy
got good grades
had fun at sports
met a new friend

Sad
left a place I like
summer was over
just heard bad news

Nervous
took a test
gave an oral report
met new people

Excited
got chosen for a team
my artwork got displayed
scored my first goal in soccer

Think About Your Writing

- Read your draft. Do you like what you wrote?
- Did you include examples to explain how you felt?

OBJECTIVES

DRAFT

Function: ⊤ Express Feelings; Write
Learning Strategies and Critical Thinking: Generate Ideas; Self-Assess
Writer's Craft: ⊤ Elaboration
Writing: ⊤ Writing Process

DRAFT

Remind students that when they draft their paragraphs, they should quickly write down their ideas. They can make changes and corrections later.

Study the Writer's Craft to help students elaborate when expressing thoughts and feelings. Read the examples and talk about why the second ones are "Much Better."

Go over the word lists together. Dramatize the actions and discuss the feelings. Invite students to suggest other situations for each list.

■ Use the Drafting Support in the **Multi-Level Strategies** to tailor this stage to proficiency levels.

For more about the Writer's Craft, refer students to pages 390–401 in the Handbook.

CLOSE AND ASSESS

Have small groups discuss the questions in Think About Your Writing while you work with those who may need more support in assessing their drafts.

Multi-Level Strategies

DRAFTING SUPPORT

BEGINNING Encourage students to role-play an experience as you describe their actions. Then use prompts to help them relate the experiences and their feelings: *Did you feel happy or sad? Were you nervous? How did you act?* Help students turn the art and writing on their Main Ideas Chart into a paragraph. Encourage them to use words from the lists on page 183, or supply other words, to help them express their feelings.

INTERMEDIATE / ADVANCED Students can work independently to apply the Writer's Craft skill and create "Much Better" examples on **Master 56**. Have them review their work in small groups or go over volunteers' entries with the whole group. Encourage small groups to brainstorm words and phrases that express different thoughts and feelings and record them in the Word File for use in their drafts.

Transparency 56 / Master 56

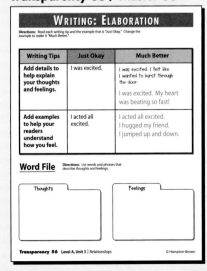

REVISE

Function: Write; Engage in Discussion

Learning Strategies and Critical Thinking: Generate Ideas; Review; Clarify; Interact with Peers; Self-Assess

Listening and Speaking: Peer-Conferencing

Technology and Media: Use Word-Processing Software

Writing: ⊕ Writing Process

REVISE

Explain that when students revise their paragraphs, one type of change they might make is to tell more about their thoughts and feelings. Have students read their paragraphs and think about possible changes.

Next, model how to participate in a peer conference, and how to decide on and make revisions. Then conduct peer conferences and have students revise their writing. If necessary, demonstrate the revising steps on page 184.

▌ Use the Peer Conference Support in the **Multi-Level Strategies** to model how to evaluate and revise writing.

CLOSE AND ASSESS

Have peers discuss the questions in Think About Your Writing.

Writing for Personal Expression, continued

REVISE

1 Read Your Paragraph Does it express your thoughts and feelings?

2 Share Your Paragraph Have your teacher or a friend read your paragraph. Ask:
- Is the topic of my paragraph clear?
- Do you understand how I felt?
- Have I left out any important details?
- Are there interesting details I could add?

3 Make Your Changes Think about the answers to your questions. Then make changes to your paragraph. Use the Revising Marks.

Sample of a Revised Sentence

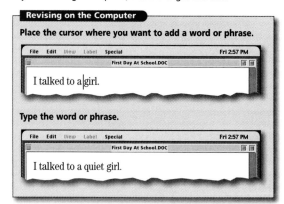

If you are using a computer, make changes like this.

Revising Marks

∧	Add.
↶	Move to here.
⋏	Replace with this.
⤷	Take out.

Think About Your Writing
- What details and examples did you add?
- Did they make your paragraph more interesting?

Transparency 57 / Master 57

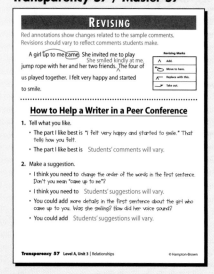

Multi-Level Strategies
PEER CONFERENCE SUPPORT

BEGINNING Display **Transparency 57.** Read the paragraph and support comprehension by leading a group in role-playing the incident. Then model how to participate in a peer conference, noting that students should tell what they like about the writing and make suggestions. Use the sentence starters on the transparency and on page 184 to develop appropriate language, and have volunteers make more suggestions. Then model making revisions based on the comments.

INTERMEDIATE / ADVANCED Distribute copies of **Master 57.** Read the paragraph and model how to offer feedback with the sentence starters there and on page 184. Have students suggest more comments. They can then make revisions to the paragraph and compare changes. Remind students that the writer chooses whether to make the revisions others suggest.

GRAMMAR IN CONTEXT

PAST TENSE VERBS

The tense of a verb shows when an action happens. Use a past tense verb if the action happened earlier, or in the past.

Examples: My family **moved** to Texas last week.
I **walked** to school yesterday.

The past tense form of a regular verb ends in **-ed**.

Follow these rules to add **-ed**:

Spelling Rules

For most verbs, just add **-ed**.	start	I **started** at a new school last week.
	stay	I **stayed** in the hall at first.
For verbs that end in silent **e**, drop the **e** and add **-ed**.	like	I **liked** my teacher right away.
If the verb ends in one vowel and one consonant, double the final consonant and add **-ed**.	tap	I **tapped** my foot because I was so nervous.
For verbs that end in a consonant and **y**, change the **y** to **i** and add **-ed**.	study	We **studied** math before lunch that day.

Irregular verbs do not end with **-ed** to show past tense. They have special forms like the examples at the right. See Handbook pages 424–425 for more examples.

Some Irregular Verb Forms

Present	Past
do	did
feel	felt
fly	flew
get	got
go	went
know	knew
make	made
run	ran
see	saw
take	took
tell	told

Practice Write each sentence. Put the verb in the past tense.

1. I ___(go)___ to my new school.
2. Everything ___(seem)___ to go wrong.
3. I ___(drop)___ all my books in the hall.
4. I ___(study)___ different subjects in my old school, so I couldn't do the science.
5. Finally, at lunch, some kids ___(ask)___ me to sit with them.
6. I really ___(like)___ them. I ___(know)___ everything would be okay.

Writing for Personal Expression **185**

GRAMMAR IN CONTEXT

1 Teach Past Tense Verbs Read the introduction and review what a verb is: the verb tells the action in the sentence. Also review time order words that signal past tense, such as: *yesterday, before, last year, earlier.*

Read aloud the spelling rules and demonstrate adding *-ed* to various verb stems. Give sample sentences for the irregular verbs: *I do my homework every day. Yesterday I did my homework in the evening.* Then conduct the cooperative learning activity below.

2 Answers to Practice Items

1. went
2. seemed
3. dropped
4. studied
5. asked
6. liked, knew

CLOSE AND ASSESS

Assign students different present tense verbs. Ask them to write one sentence using the present tense and another sentence using the past tense of the verb. Then ask them to tell the spelling rule they used to form the past tense.

Cooperative Learning

FOR LANGUAGE DEVELOPMENT:
Past Tense Verbs

Spell Past Tense Verbs Assign a present tense verb to each of the students in the inner circle. Those students use the verb in a sentence and spell the verb aloud. Students in the outer circle change the sentence to the past tense and spell the verb. Allow students to write down their verbs. After everyone shares the sentences and verb spellings, assign present tense verbs to the outer circle. Circles should exchange tasks and repeat the exercise.

Debrief the Skill Ask: *What kinds of spelling changes did we make? What verbs don't change when you add -ed? What happens to irregular verbs?*

Debrief the Cooperative Process Have students reflect on how the activity worked out: *Were you and your partner able to use the verbs in sentences and spell them? What did you do when you didn't know how to spell the verb?*

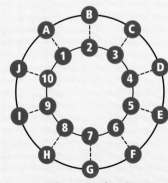

Cooperative Learning Structure:
Inside-Outside Circle

Build Writing Skills **T185**

WRITING ASSESSMENT
Use the Writing Rubric on page 51 of the Assessment
Handbook to evaluate this writing assignment.

BUILD WRITING SKILLS

OBJECTIVES

EDIT AND PROOFREAD

Learning Strategies and Critical Thinking: Review; Clarify; Self-Assess
Writing: ❶ Writing Process

PUBLISH

Learning Strategies and Critical Thinking: Interact with Peers; Self-Assess; Make Decisions
Speaking: Read Aloud
Technology and Media: Use Word-Processing Software
Writing: ❶ Writing Process

EDIT AND PROOFREAD

Explain that when students edit, they should mark corrections. Then they proofread the final copy. Use **Transparency 58** to model the process.

PUBLISH

Tell students that to publish their writing, they need to get it ready to share with an audience. Have them choose a publishing idea from the suggestions on page 186.

Use the Editing and Publishing Support in the **Multi-Level Strategies** to meet the varying needs of students.

CLOSE AND ASSESS

Have groups discuss the questions in Think About Your Writing.

Writing for Personal Expression, continued

EDIT AND PROOFREAD

❶ **Proofread Your Paragraph** When you find a mistake in capitalization, punctuation, or spelling, correct it. See pages 431–439 in the Handbook for help. Use the Proofreading Marks.

❷ **Check Your Verbs** Have you used past tense verbs to describe things that happened in the past? Did you follow the spelling rules for past tense verbs?

❸ **Make a Final Copy** If you are working on a computer, print out a final copy of your work. If not, rewrite it and make the corrections you marked.

PUBLISH

Here are some ways to share your writing.

• Write your paragraph on a large index card. Place it on a bulletin board for others to read.

> I miss my family back home in Mexico. Here in the USA I have only one aunt and a baby cousin nearby. In Mexico, all my family and friends lived near me. I had lots of cousins who were also thirteen. We had so much fun together!
>
> by Magdiel Ramírez

• Read your paragraph aloud to some friends. Ask whether they learned something new about you.

• Type your paragraph on the computer and view it in different kinds of type. Print it in the one you like best.

Proofreading Marks

∧	Add.
⩍	Add a comma.
⊙	Add a period.
≡	Capitalize.
/	Make lowercase.
⌐	Take out.
¶	Indent.

Think About Your Writing

• Are you pleased with your paragraph?
  ☑ Does it express your thoughts or feelings?
  ☑ Do you state the main idea clearly and include details to support it?
  ☑ Did you include enough examples?
  ☑ Did you use past tense verbs and spell them correctly?
• What do you like best about your paragraph?
• Will this paragraph go in your portfolio? Why or why not?

REACHING ALL STUDENTS

Transparency 58 / Master 58

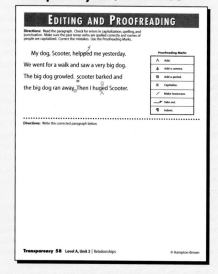

EDITING AND PROOFREADING

Directions: Read the paragraph. Check for errors in capitalization, spelling, and punctuation. Make sure the past tense verbs are spelled correctly and names of people are capitalized. Correct the mistakes. Use the Proofreading Marks.

My dog, Scooter, helped me yesterday.
We went for a walk and saw a very big dog.
The big dog growled. scooter barked and
the big dog ran away. Then I huged Scooter.

Directions: Write the corrected paragraph below.

Transparency 58 Level A, Unit 3 | Relationships   © Hampton-Brown

Multi-Level Strategies
EDITING AND PUBLISHING SUPPORT

BEGINNING Model finding and correcting errors in the paragraph on **Transparency 58**. After marking the edits, have students write out the corrected paragraph. For publishing, encourage students to turn their paragraphs into simple picture books to share with younger siblings or other children.

INTERMEDIATE Guide students in finding and correcting the errors in the paragraph on **Transparency 58**. For publishing, offer students who want to read their poem aloud a chance to tape record it and play the tape for the class.

ADVANCED Distribute copies of **Master 58** and have students work on finding and correcting the errors individually or with partners. Encourage them to send their writing to their audience via e-mail, if appropriate.

Making Connections

✓ **ASSESSMENT**
The Unit 3 test on page 53 of the Assessment Handbook measures students' progress in reading, language arts, literary study, and writing. Additional forms in the Assessment Handbook allow for:
• Self Assessment on page 52
• Peer Assessment on page 101
• Portfolio Evaluation on page 103

▶ Look Back at the Unit

Rate Selections In this unit, you read about friendship and family.

| The Qualities of Friendship | My Best Friend | Honoring Our Ancestors | Grandfather's Nose |

Work with a partner. Write the title of each selection on an index card. Rate each selection with stars. If you liked the story, draw 5 stars. If you didn't like it, draw fewer stars. Now write on the back of the card. Tell one thing you liked about the selection. Then describe a relationship in it.

▶ Show What You Know

Sum It All Up Add new ideas to your mind map about relationships. Talk with a partner. Tell why people have close relationships. Explain how relationships can change.

Reflect and Evaluate Write a sentence. Describe something you learned about relationships. Add this statement to your portfolio. Add work from the unit that shows what you learned.

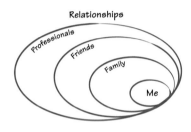

Relationships — Professionals — Friends — Family — Me

▶ Make Connections

To Your Community Build a new relationship by finding a pen pal. Write letters or send e-mail to someone in your school, in your community, or around the world.

OBJECTIVES

Function: Engage in Discussion; Express Opinions

Learning Strategies and Critical Thinking: Interact with Peers; Generate Ideas; Make Judgments; Summarize; Self-Assess; Form Opinions; Use Graphic Organizers (mind map)

Literary Analysis: Respond to Literature; Compare and Evaluate Literature

EXPLORE "MAKING CONNECTIONS"

1 Look Back at the Unit Help students form questions to use when rating the selections, such as: *Was the story exciting?* Then begin the Cooperative Learning Activity.

2 Show What You Know Suggest that students include in their portfolios work that reflects the value of friendship in their lives.

3 Make Connections Help interested students find an e-pal. Try: *www.ks-connection.org/penpal/ penpal.html*

CLOSE AND ASSESS

Have students tell you the most important thing they learned in the unit.

Cooperative Learning

FOR CRITICAL THINKING: Form Opinions

Rate Selections Provide students time to individually think about each selection and what relationship it illustrated. Then have them discuss their ideas with a partner and complete a rating card for each selection.

Sharing Ideas Hold a group discussion about the selections. Partners take turns sharing their ideas. The class may want to tally the results to determine overall ratings.

Debrief the Content Ask students what they learned about relationships from the unit, for example: *I learned that all of my relationships are important to who I am, in different ways.*

Debrief the Cooperative Process Have students evaluate how working with a partner helped them form opinions. Ask: *What ideas did your partner provide that changed your own thinking?*

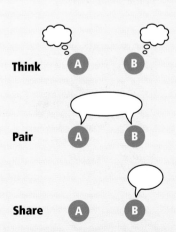

Think A B

Pair A B

Share A B

Cooperative Learning Structure: Think, Pair, Share

Resources

For Success in Language, Literature, and Content

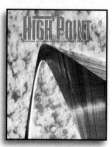

Student Book pages 188–261

For Skills Practice

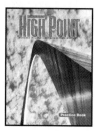

Practice Book
pages 93–132

For Planning and Instruction

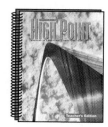

Teacher's Edition
pages T188a–T261

For Vocabulary and Language Development

Language Tape Side B
Language CD Track 8

For Audio Walk-Throughs and Selection Readings

Selection Tape 4
Selection CD 4

For Technology Support

Inspiration
Visual Learning Software
with Graphic Organizers

For Classroom Activities

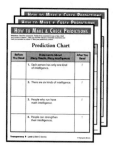

Transparencies or Masters 59–75

For Home-School Connections

High Point Newsletters 7 and 8

For Comprehensive Assessment

Language Acquisition Assessment,
Selection Tests, Unit Test, Writing
Assessment, Self-Assessment

In the Theme Library

Nature's Green Umbrella
by Gail Gibbons

Hurricane!
by Jonathan London

From *The Basics Bookshelf*

▶ *Rachel Carson*

▶ *Power Out!*

Theme-related books with
simple text for including
newcomers

Communities Count

COMMUNITY, FROM THE
LATIN FOR FELLOWSHIP,
GOES BEYOND GEOGRAPHIC
BOUNDARIES. IT IS, AT
HEART, SHAPED AND
MOLDED BY THE
COOPERATION OF ITS
CITIZENS. THIS UNIT
INVITES STUDENTS, AS
COMMUNITY MEMBERS
THEMSELVES, TO EXPLORE
HOW SURVIVAL DEPENDS ON
COMMON FELLOWSHIP.

Seeing the World Through Pictures, Robert Silvers, photomosaic. Copyright © 1997.

THEME **1** **Thinking Ahead**

Students examine why communities must work together to keep
our planet healthy.

THEME **2** **Dealing With Disasters**

Students discover how communities pull together when a natural
disaster strikes.

THEME 1: Thinking Ahead

LESSONS

1

THEME 1 OPENER ▶ pages T190–T191

Function Engage in Discussion	**Learning Strategy** Make a T-Chart	**Vocabulary** Words About Communities and Natural Resources	**Critical Thinking** Formulate Solutions

2–9

Common Ground by Molly Bang PERSUASIVE ESSAY ▶ pages T194–T205

BUILD LANGUAGE AND VOCABULARY pages T192–T193	**Function** Ⓣ Make Comparisons	**Learning Strategy** Make a Comparison Chart	**Vocabulary** Nature Words	**Patterns and Structures** Ⓣ Future Tense Verbs

PREPARE TO READ
page T194

Activate Prior Knowledge
Share Ideas

Vocabulary Ⓣ
Relate Words

Reading Strategy
Make a K-W-L Chart to Connect New Information to Known

READ THE SELECTION
pages T195–T202

Pre-Reading Strategies
Preview and Predict

Identify Genre:
Persuasive Essay

Set Purpose

Strategy Focus
Connect New Information to Known

Vocabulary
Use New Words in Context

Self-Monitoring and Comprehension
Use Visuals to Confirm Meaning

Before You Move On:
Think and Discuss

📁 **Grammar Minilessons:**
Ⓣ Statements with *there is/are, was/were*

Ⓣ Future Tense Verbs

📁 **Literary Analysis Minilesson:**
Theme

RESPOND
pages T203–T205

CHECK YOUR UNDERSTANDING

Critical Thinking and Comprehension
Sum It Up:
Connect New Information to Known;
Ⓣ Evaluate the Essay

Think It Over: Discuss

Function
Express Yourself:
Define and Explain

LANGUAGE ARTS AND LITERATURE

Grammar in Context
Ⓣ Use Adjectives that Compare

Writing
Write an Opinion Paragraph

CONTENT AREA CONNECTIONS

Science
Study Environmental Problems

Science
Explore Recycling

Fine Arts
Picture the Environment

10–19

Protecting Our Planet by Raffi SONGS ▶ pages T208–T221

BUILD LANGUAGE AND VOCABULARY pages T206–T207	**Function** Ⓣ Express Opinions and Persuade	**Learning Strategy** Make a Mind Map	**Vocabulary** Words about the Environment	**Patterns and Structures** Ⓣ Verbs: *should, must, can*

PREPARE TO READ
page T208

Activate Prior Knowledge
Brainstorm Ideas

Vocabulary Ⓣ
Relate Words

Reading Strategy
Ⓣ Preview and Make Predictions

READ THE SELECTION
pages T209–T216

Pre-Reading Strategies
Preview and Predict

Set Purpose

Strategy Focus
Ⓣ Confirm and Revise Predictions

Vocabulary
Use New Words in Context

Self-Monitoring and Comprehension
Visualize

Before You Move On:
Think and Discuss

📁 **Grammar Minilessons:**
Ⓣ Modals

Plural Nouns

Prepositions

RESPOND
pages T217–T221

CHECK YOUR UNDERSTANDING

Critical Thinking and Comprehension
Sum It Up:
Ⓣ Check Predictions;
Analyze Persuasive Techniques;
Ⓣ Evaluate Literature (songs)

Think It Over:
Discuss

Function
Express Yourself:
Recite

LANGUAGE ARTS AND LITERATURE

Grammar in Context
Ⓣ Use Indefinite Pronouns

Literary Analysis and Writing/Representing
Write a Haiku Poem

Literary Analysis
Study Repetition and Author's Style

Writing
Write a Friendly Letter to Raffi

Literary Analysis and Representing/ Speaking
Learn about Propaganda

CONTENT AREA CONNECTIONS

Science and Technology/Media
Research Endangered Species

THEME 2: Dealing With Disasters

PACING SUGGESTIONS

LESSONS	45–55 MINUTE PERIODS	BLOCK SCHEDULE SESSIONS
1	1 period	
2–9	8 periods	5 sessions
10–17	8 periods	4 sessions

LESSONS

1

THEME 2 OPENER ▶ pages T222–T223

Function Engage in Discussion	**Learning Strategy** Make a Venn Diagram	**Vocabulary** Community and Disaster Words	**Critical Thinking** Make Comparisons

2–9

Earthquake at Dawn by Kristiana Gregory PLAY ▶ pages T226–T239

BUILD LANGUAGE AND VOCABULARY pages T224–T225	**Function** 🅣 Give and Carry Out Commands	**Learning Strategy** Brainstorm Ideas	**Vocabulary** Words About Earthquakes	**Patterns and Structures** 🅣 Commands

PREPARE TO READ
pages T226–T227

Activate Prior Knowledge
Idea Exchange

Vocabulary 🅣
Relate Words

Reading Strategy
Use Text Structures and Features in Plays

READ THE SELECTION
pages T228–T236

Pre-Reading Strategies
Preview and Predict

Identify Genre: Stage Play

Set Purpose

Strategy Focus
Use Text Structures and Features in Plays

Vocabulary
Use New Words in Context

Comprehension
Before You Move On: Think and Discuss

📁 **Grammar Minilessons:**
Indefinite Adjectives and Ordinals

Contractions

📁 **Literary Analysis Minilesson:**
Evaluate the Impact of Medium on Meaning

RESPOND
pages T237–T239

CHECK YOUR UNDERSTANDING

Critical Thinking and Comprehension
Sum It Up: Analyze Characters and Setting; Rewrite the Play; 🅣 Evaluate Literature

Think It Over: Discuss

Function
Express Yourself: Give and Carry Out Commands

LANGUAGE ARTS AND LITERATURE

Grammar in Context
🅣 Use Helping Verbs

Literary Analysis and Writing
🅣 Evaluate Literature: Literary Critique

CONTENT AREA CONNECTIONS

Social Studies
Make a Time Line

Science and Technology/Media
Create an Earthquake Data Chart

10–18

When Disaster Strikes by Richie Chevat NEWS ARTICLES ▶ pages T242–T253

BUILD LANGUAGE AND VOCABULARY pages T240–T241	**Function** 🅣 Elaborate	**Learning Strategy** Record Details	**Vocabulary** Words and Phrases	**Patterns and Structures** 🅣 Adjectives, Adverbs and Prepositions

PREPARE TO READ
page T242

Activate Prior Knowledge
Make a Word Web

Vocabulary 🅣
Use New Words in Context

Reading Strategy
🅣 Use Text Features in Nonfiction

READ THE SELECTION
pages T243–T249

Pre-Reading Strategies
Activate Prior Knowledge

Identify Genre: News Article

Set Purpose

Strategy Focus
🅣 Use Text Features in Nonfiction

Vocabulary
Use New Words in Context

Comprehension
Before You Move On: Think and Discuss

📁 **Grammar Minilessons:**
Adverbs that Compare

Count and Noncount Nouns

Adverbs with -ly

RESPOND
pages T250–T253

CHECK YOUR UNDERSTANDING

Critical Thinking and Comprehension
Sum It Up: 🅣 Use Text Features

🅣 Make Comparisons

Think It Over: Discuss

Function
Express Yourself: Ask and Answer Questions; Elaborate

LANGUAGE ARTS AND LITERATURE

Grammar in Context
🅣 Use Helping Verbs

Literary Analysis and Writing
Learn About News Stories

Vocabulary
Classify Science Words

🅣 Use Prefixes and Suffixes

CONTENT AREA CONNECTIONS

Social Studies and Technology/Media
Explore Geography (map)

Social Studies
Create a Public Service Poster

BUILD WRITING SKILLS

WRITING THAT PERSUADES PERSUASIVE: OPINION ESSAY ▶ pages T254–T260

Writing Mode/Form
🅣 Persuasive

Opinion Essay

Writing Process 🅣
Prewrite
Draft
Revise
Edit and Proofread
Publish

Writer's Craft
🅣 Introductory Sentence
🅣 Concluding Sentence

Grammar in Context
🅣 Verb Tense

Reflect and Evaluate
Self-Assessment

THEME 1: Thinking Ahead

MORE RESOURCES

Nature's Green Umbrella
by Gail Gibbons
I This book looks at plant and animal life in tropical rain forests, and describes the importance of this ecosystem. (Available from Hampton-Brown)

The Giving Tree
by Shel Silverstein
B A simple story of a tree that gives all it can to make a person happy. (HarperCollins)

50 Simple Things Kids Can Do to Save the Earth
by The EarthWorks Group
A If you want to protect our planet, this book is full of lots of easy things you can do to help! (Andrews McNeel Publishing)

Song for the Ancient Forest
by Nancy Luenn
B In this picture book, Raven is chosen to carry the message of saving the Earth from destruction. (Macmillan)

She's Wearing a Dead Bird on Her Head!
by Kathryn Lasky
I A An award-winning book about how two well-bred ladies formed a club to protect birds, thereby creating the Massachusetts Audubon Society. (Econo-Clad Books)

The World of Nature
by Allen Say
B I Ecosystems, the environment, and a wealth of information on plants, animals, and insects are featured in this highly illustrated CD-ROM. (Queue) **Multimedia CD-ROM**

THEME 2: Dealing With Disasters

MORE RESOURCES

Hurricane!
by Jonathan London
B The sky grows dark and the wind begins to blow. A family in Puerto Rico hurries to a shelter until an unexpected hurricane is over. (Lothrop, Lee & Shepard)

Flood
by Mary Calhoun
I A family, facing the threat of flood, is determined to save their home. Then the levee breaks and they must flee to save their lives. (Morrow Junior Books)

If You Lived at the Time of the Great San Francisco Earthquake
by Ellen Levine
A How did the 1906 earthquake sound? How did it feel? This book answers these and other questions. (Scholastic)

I Didn't Know That Quakes Split the Ground Open
by Clare Oliver
B I Colorful graphics accompany scientific facts about earthquakes and their aftermath. (Copper Beech Books)

Miloli's Orchids
by Alisandra Jezek
I A When the volcano on Miloli's island home of Kamolo erupts, Miloli risks her life to save the orchids of Makapa. (Raintree/Steck-Vaughn)

SimCity
Students build and manage the growth of their own city, including planning for natural and environmental disasters. (Edmark) **CD-ROM**

ONGOING, INFORMAL ASSESSMENT

Check for understanding and achieve closure for every lesson with the targeted questions and activities in the **Close and Assess** boxes in your Teacher's Edition.

INDIVIDUAL AND GROUP-ADMINISTERED TESTS

The **Assessment Handbook** includes these comprehensive assessment tools for Unit 4:

▶ **Selection Tests**
Test students' mastery of reading strategies and the vocabulary, comprehension, and language arts skills taught with each main selection of Unit 4.

▶ **Unit Test in Standardized Test Format**
The multiple-choice sections of this test measure students' cumulative understanding of the skills and language developed in Unit 4. A Writing Prompt measures progress in writing skills and fluency. The Read, Think, and Explain section offers open-ended items to measure strategies and comprehension.

▶ **Language Acquisition Assessment**
To verify students' ability to use the vocabulary and grammar structures taught in Unit 4, conduct these performance assessments.

UNIT 4 ASSESSMENT OPPORTUNITIES	Assessment Handbook Pages
Unit 4 Language Acquisition Assessment	61–62
Selection Tests	
Common Ground	63–64
Protecting Our Planet	65–66
Earthquake at Dawn	67–68
When Disaster Strikes	69–70
Unit 4 Writing Assessment	71
Unit 4 Self-Assessment Form	72
Unit 4 Test	73–80
Peer-Assessment Form	101
Portfolio Evaluation Form	103

SELF- AND PEER-ASSESSMENT

Students use the Unit 4 Self-Assessment Form in the **Assessment Handbook** to evaluate their own work and develop learning strategies appropriate to their needs. Students offer feedback to their classmates with the Peer-Assessment Form.

WRITING ASSESSMENT / PORTFOLIO OPPORTUNITIES

You can evaluate students' writing using the rubrics and scoring guidelines provided in the **Assessment Handbook**. Then collaborate with students to choose work for their portfolios.

Function: Engage in Discussion

Concepts and Vocabulary:
Communities; Natural Resources

Viewing: Interpret a Visual Image

**Critical Thinking and Learning
Strategies:** Classify; Preview;
Build Background;
Use Graphic Organizers (mind map)

INTRODUCE UNIT CONCEPT

1 Interpret the Title Ask: *What does
the word* count *mean in the title
"Communities Count"?* (have value)
Then ask students to explain the title.
(Communities are important.)

2 Explore the Picture Individually
Distribute a copy of **Master 59** to
each student. Give students time to
list items from the small photos in
the correct categories on Chart 1.

3 Explore the Picture in Groups
Assign students to groups and have
them conduct a timed search,
recording responses on Chart 2 of
Master 59. Invite groups to discuss
the differences between working
alone and with a group.

▌ Use Activity Options in the
Multi-Level Strategies to engage
all proficiency levels.

UNIT
4 Community

Seeing the World Through Pictures, Robert Silvers, photomosaic. Copyright © 1997.

188

REACHING ALL STUDENTS

Transparency 59 / Master 59

CATEGORIZING PICTURES

Chart 1: I Discovered By Myself

Earth	Sea	Sky

Chart 2: We Discovered as a Group

Earth	Sea	Sky

▌**Multi-Level Strategies**
ACTIVITY OPTIONS

BEGINNING For the individual activity, ask students to draw sketches
on the chart of any items whose names they don't know, or to record items
in their home language. They can add labels in English during the group
sharing time. For the group activity, these students can focus on naming or
pointing to pictures for one of the categories.

INTERMEDIATE After the timed searches are conducted, these students
can talk to members of their group to find out which items were recorded by
the most people on Chart 1. Invite them to share their findings with
the class.

ADVANCED After the timed searches are done, ask students to write
one sentence for each column to describe what they discovered.

Communities Count

Write these headings: Earth, Sea, and Sky. Now take one minute to study the picture of planet Earth. List as many of the things in the tiny photos as you can for each category. Next, do this activity with a group of classmates. What did you learn about working together? How does working together make a difference?

THEME 1
Thinking Ahead
If we want to keep our planet healthy, communities must work together to care for the Earth.

THEME 2
Dealing With Disasters
Communities pull together when a natural disaster strikes.

189

UNIT 4 Mind Map

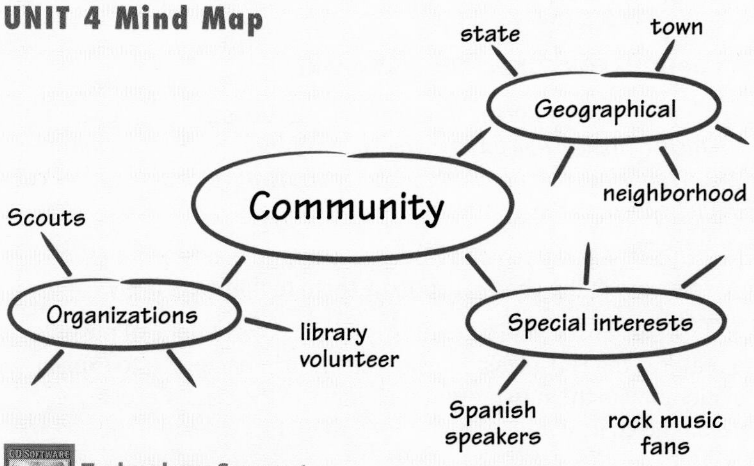

Technology Support
See **Inspiration** Visual Learning software for support in creating mind maps.

4 Preview Theme 1: Thinking Ahead Read aloud the theme title and the theme statement. Explain what *keep our planet healthy* means: *It involves keeping the air and water clean, saving natural resources, and not having more people on the planet than it can support.*

Ask students to name groups they think of as communities. Prompt them to name larger and larger groups who form communities, leading them to the idea that the entire population of the Earth is one large community.

Invite students to leaf through pages 190–221 and tell you some of the environmental problems communities are trying to solve.

5 Preview Theme 2: Dealing With Disasters Read the theme title and statement. Define *pull together* as "to cooperate and think of others' needs as well as your own."

Invite students to leaf through pages 222–253 and describe some of the disasters communities must deal with by pulling together.

6 Create a Mind Map Begin a class mind map on Communities, and have students start a personal map in their notebooks or in the **Practice Book**. Point out that there are many kinds of communities. Help students brainstorm a list of their own communities. They might suggest groups such as Yankee fans, Chinese immigrants, or sports cards collectors. Have students add to the map as they move through the unit.

▶ **Practice Book** page 93

CLOSE AND ASSESS

Ask students what this unit will be about. (how communities bring about change) Then ask: *Why are communities stronger than individuals?* (A group has more resources than individuals working separately.)

INTRODUCE THEME 1

> ### OBJECTIVES
>
> **Function:** Engage in Discussion
>
> **Concepts and Vocabulary:**
> Communities—*responsible, take care of, pull together, common ground;*
> Natural Resources
>
> **Viewing:** Interpret a Visual Image
>
> **Learning Strategies:** Relate to Personal Experience; Use Graphic Organizers (T-chart)
>
> **Critical Thinking:** Solve Problems; Generate Ideas

TAP PRIOR KNOWLEDGE

1 Discuss Responsibility Ask: *What does the word "responsible" mean to you? What kind of responsibilities do you have at school? At home?* Guide students to understand that when you are responsible for something, you are the person in control of it. True responsibility is a feeling that comes from within yourself, not a duty someone else assigns to you.

VIEW AND DISCUSS

2 Solve Problems Ask students to identify what they see in the picture and where it is. (rain forest; South America or Asia) Ask what the weather is like. (hot; humid) Then make a chart to list rain forest problems and solutions.

Problems	Solutions
Cutting trees takes away animals' homes.	Set aside forest preserves.
Industry pollutes the rivers.	Set up government controls.
Unique plants with medical uses may disappear forever.	Grow these plants in forest preserves.

■ Use the Activity Options in the **Multi-Level Strategies** to involve all students.

REACHING ALL STUDENTS

Multi-Level Strategies
ACTIVITY OPTIONS FOR COMPLETING THE CHART

BEGINNING Ask yes/no or short answer questions about tropical rain forests: *Is there a tropical rain forest in this country?* (no) *Are the trees tall or short?* (tall) *What kinds of animals live there?* (parrots, frogs) *If the trees are cut down, what happens to the animals?* (they may die), etc. . . .

INTERMEDIATE Ask students to work in a group to brainstorm a list of solutions to record in the chart. Encourage them to think creatively.

ADVANCED Encourage students to work in pairs to think of possible ways to preserve the Earth's rain forests. Pairs write a paragraph to explain their solution. Invite them to present their ideas to the class. Record solutions on the chart.

Thinking Ahead

- Who is responsible for taking care of our planet?

- What are some of the problems facing our planet? What are some solutions?

- How can we work together in our communities to keep our planet healthy?

THEME-RELATED BOOKS

The Giving Tree
by Shel Silverstein

A simple story of a tree who gives all it can to make a person happy.

BEGINNING

Nature's Green Umbrella
Tropical Rain Forests
by Gail Gibbons

This book looks at plant and animal life in tropical rain forests, and describes the importance of this ecosystem.

INTERMEDIATE

50 Simple Things Kids Can Do to Save the Earth
by The EarthWorks Group

If you want to protect our planet, this book is full of lots of easy things you can do to help!

ADVANCED

191

DISCUSS THE GUIDING QUESTIONS

3 Set the Theme Some key points to develop during the discussion are:

- Governments around the world, large organizations, community groups, families, and individuals must all take responsibility for taking care of our planet.

- Our planet is running out of some natural resources because of population growth. The air, water, and land are becoming polluted. Too many fish are being caught; too many trees are being cut down. Individuals and groups can help by conserving, recycling, and choosing different ways of living.

- We can work with our communities to keep our planet healthy. For example, if a local park is full of trash, we can organize a clean-up day. We can collect bottles and cans for recycling and clean up the streets at the same time. There are many things we can do to keep our planet healthy if we work together.

  ■ Form groups and use the **Multi-Level Strategies** so all students can participate.

CLOSE AND ASSESS

Ask: *What is the most important thing you learned in this lesson? What can you do to help keep our planet healthy?*

▌Multi-Level Strategies
GROUPING GUIDLINES

BEGINNING Group these students so you can define words and pose choices for responses. As you introduce each question, paraphrase it or ask students to restate it in their own words.

INTERMEDIATE Suggest that students work with partners to answer each question. Set a time limit. At the end of that time, have each pair share their answers with another pair and discuss any differences they may have found.

ADVANCED Ask students to do a quickwrite in response to each question. Read the responses to the class and invite other students to comment on them and add any information they wish.

THEME 📖 LIBRARY

■ *Nature's Green Umbrella*
by Gail Gibbons

Ask students to discuss how the theme "Thinking Ahead" is presented in this book, and to compare it to the way it is presented in the selections in Theme 1 of Unit 4. Partners can make charts with columns for author, title, genre, and description to help organize ideas for making comparisons. Invite them to share their opinions on the approach they prefer.

BUILD LANGUAGE AND VOCABULARY

OBJECTIVES

Function: ⊤ Make Comparisons

Concepts and Vocabulary:
Nature Words

Patterns and Structures:
⊤ Future Tense Verbs

Speaking: Predictions

Viewing: Respond to a Photograph

**Critical Thinking and Learning
Strategies:** Make Comparisons;
Formulate Predictions; Use Graphic
Organizers (T-chart)

Writing: Predictions

START WITH A COMMON EXPERIENCE

1 View and Describe View the
photograph and have students
describe the scene.

> Use the Questioning Techniques
> in the **Multi-Level Strategies** to
> invite responses.

2 Discuss the Quotation Invite
students to offer examples of how
things that happened long ago
might affect people living today. Ask:
*What can we do today that will affect
future generations?* Explain that "the
next seven generations" refers to
future children, the children's
children, and so on.

3 Model How to Make Comparisons
Explain that when we talk about the
ways in which the past and present
are the same or different, we are
comparing them. Model how to
make an effective comparison:

> **How to Make Comparisons**
>
> • Name something in nature: *a tree*
>
> • Name something that shares some
>   of the same characteristics: *a bush*
>
> • Tell ways the two things are alike:
>   *A tree and a bush both grow out of
>   the ground; both have leaves.*
>
> • Tell ways they are different: *A tree
>   can grow tall; a bush is short.*

Build Language and Vocabulary
MAKE COMPARISONS

View this photograph and read the quote. What effect could
clearing the forest have on the next seven generations?

> *We must consider the impact of our
> decisions on the next seven generations.*
>
> —*from the Great Law of the Iroquois Confederacy,*
> *16th Century*

REACHING ALL STUDENTS

Multi-Level Strategies
QUESTIONING TECHNIQUES

BEGINNING   Ask yes/no questions or questions that will result in short
answers, and then expand language. *Have most of the trees in this forest been
cut down? What do you think the man will do to the rest of the trees?*

INTERMEDIATE   Encourage students to speculate about the changes in the
forest. *How do you think the forest looked before the man started cutting down
the trees? What do you think happened to the animals that lived there?*

ADVANCED   Have students speculate beyond the specifics of the
photograph. *What effect does cutting down a forest have on the animals that
lived there? On the soil? On people? It takes many years for a tree to grow.
What do you think this place will look like in ten years? In twenty years?*

MAKE A COMPARISON CHART

Compare the pictures on pages 190 and 192. Then brainstorm words to describe each one. Record them in a chart. Discuss how tree-cutting can affect the next seven generations.

Before	After
green forest	burned trees
homes for birds	smoke
beautiful	ugly

BUILD YOUR VOCABULARY

Nature Words Trees are an important part of our Earth. Read this definition to learn what trees and other special parts of our planet are called.

> **nat·u·ral re·sourc·es** *noun*
> **Natural resources** are the minerals, air, plants, animals, and water that are part of our planet. Natural resources come from the earth.

Now, think of as many natural resources as you can and list them. Add to your list as you go through this unit.

USE LANGUAGE STRUCTURES ▶ FUTURE TENSE VERBS

Speaking: Compare Possibilities for the Future Choose a natural resource from your list. Think about what the resource will mean for the next seven generations. Write a sentence to tell what will happen if we do not take care of that resource. Write another sentence to tell what will happen if we do take care of that resource. Share your sentences with the group. Compare the possibilities.

Example:
If we cut down all the trees, the soil will wash away.
If we take care of the trees, we will have clean air and beautiful forests.

Build Language and Vocabulary **193**

CONDUCT THE ACTIVITIES

4 Make a Comparison Chart Work with the class to develop a chart comparing the two scenes. Ask: *What word would you use to describe the forest on page 190? What about the forest on page 192?*

5 Build Your Vocabulary: Nature Words Have students work in small groups to brainstorm a list of natural resources. Students should list words under the five categories mentioned.

6 Use Language Structures: Future Tense Verbs Present the skill, using the definition and examples on **Transparency 60**. For item 3, stress that a sentence of this type expresses a possibility—something that *may* happen. Then have students complete the sentences in Try It!

Speaking: Compare Possibilities for the Future Conduct the activity at the bottom of page 193. Have students work with a partner or in a small group to develop ideas.

▌ Use the Speaking Activity Options in the **Multi-Level Strategies** to adjust instruction.

▶ **Practice Book** page 94

CLOSE AND ASSESS

Have students tell what a future tense verb shows. Then ask them to complete this sentence: *If we protect our planet, future generations _____ .*

REACHING ALL STUDENTS

Multi-Level Strategies
SPEAKING ACTIVITY OPTIONS

BEGINNING Draw a simple time line. Mark the middle, and label the halves Now and In the Future. Write this sentence under the first half of the time line: *We cut down all of the trees.* Under the second half write: *The soil will wash away.* Model how to combine the sentences in an *If… then* format. As a group, do the same with the second example on page 193.

INTERMEDIATE Tell students to create a time line to organize their thoughts. They can work in pairs to discuss ideas before composing the sentences.

ADVANCED Encourage students to conduct research to discover the potential effects of misusing or wasting various natural resources. Have them take notes on what can be done to protect these resources. They can then write a series of detailed sentences to share with the group.

Transparency 60 / Master 60

LEARN ABOUT FUTURE TENSE VERBS

A **future tense verb** tells about an action that will happen later, or in the future.

Tomorrow, the man **will plant** a tree.

1. To show the future tense, use the helping verb **will** along with a main verb.

   We **will protect** our forests from now on.
   helping verb/main verb

2. In a question, the subject comes between the helping verb and the main verb.

   Will we **protect** our forests from now on?
   subject

3. You can use a future tense verb to tell about something that may happen.

   If we protect our forests, animals **will have** a place to live.

Try It!

Use future tense verbs to complete each sentence.

1. If we waste water, _____
2. If we pollute the air, _____
3. If we keep the air clean, _____

Transparency 60 Level A, Unit 4 | Community   © Hampton-Brown

Build Language and Vocabulary **T193**

THINK ABOUT WHAT YOU KNOW

Reading Strategy: Relate to Personal Experience

LEARN KEY VOCABULARY ⓣ

Vocabulary Strategy: Relate Words

LEARN TO MAKE A K-W-L CHART

Reading Strategy: Connect New Information to Known; Use Graphic Organizers (K-W-L chart)

THINK ABOUT WHAT YOU KNOW

1 Share Ideas List shared items. Then ask students to tell how their families share each one. Record various methods and discuss which work best.

LEARN KEY VOCABULARY

2 Relate Words Read the words and definitions aloud. Give sample sentences, such as *The athletic field is common ground at our school.*

> Use Vocabulary Options in the **Multi-Level Strategies** to create more sample sentences.

Then conduct the sorting activity.

▶ **Practice Book** page 95

LEARN TO MAKE A K-W-L CHART

3 Model How to Make a K-W-L Chart Use **Transparency 61** to model the process following the steps in the box.

- Together, page through the essay and sum up the topic: *This essay is about Earth's resources. One thing I know is that our planet is mostly water.* Record that idea under "K."

- Then model forming a question about what you want to know: *Why should we conserve water?* Write the question under "W."

Students will complete their own K-W-L charts in the next lesson.

| CLOSE AND ASSESS |

Ask which part of the K-W-L chart always contains information found in the reading. (the "L" column)

Common Ground
persuasive essay
by Molly Bang

Prepare to Read

THINK ABOUT WHAT YOU KNOW

Share Ideas You share things like rooms, food, telephones, and the television with your family. How do you decide how to share these things?

benefit When you **benefit** from something, you are helped by it.

common If something is **common**, it may be shared.

common ground Land shared by everyone is **common ground**.

commons A **commons** is a piece of land that is shared by the whole town.

forest A **forest** is a large area with many trees.

fossil fuel A **fossil fuel** is a source of energy found in the earth. Coal, oil, and natural gas are **fossil fuels**.

natural resource A **resource** is something people use. A **natural resource** comes from the earth.

sustain When you **sustain** something, you keep it going.

village A **village** is a small community.

villager A **villager** is a person who lives in a village.

Answers to the vocabulary activity will vary.

LEARN KEY VOCABULARY

Relate Words Study the new words. Sort them into groups. Draw a circle and label each group. Think of more words to add.

Places to Live
(village forest)
city, farm

Words That Look Alike
(village villager)
common, common ground

Natural Resources
(forest water)
commons, coal, oil, fossil fuel

LEARN TO MAKE A K-W-L CHART

A **K-W-L chart** helps you connect new information to what you already know. It also helps you think about what you want to learn before you read.

K | W | L

READING STRATEGY

How to Make a K-W-L Chart

1. Look at the essay. Think about the topic.
2. Write what you **know** about the topic under **K**.
3. Write what you **want to learn** under **W**.
4. Read the essay. Write what you **learned** under **L**.

Make a K-W-L chart. Follow the steps in the Reading Strategy as you read "Common Ground."

194 Unit 4 | Community

REACHING ALL STUDENTS

Multi-Level Strategies
VOCABULARY OPTIONS

BEGINNING Work with students to write a sample sentence for each vocabulary word. Discuss the differences among the words that look alike: *common, common ground, commons; village, villager.*

INTERMEDIATE / **ADVANCED** Invite students to write sentence frames on index cards, leaving out key vocabulary words. Have them exchange cards and complete each other's sentences.

Transparency 61 / Master 61

HOW TO MAKE A K-W-L CHART

Directions: Look at the essay and think about the topic. Write what you already know about the topic in Column 1. Write what you want to learn in Column 2. Read the essay. Then, write what you learned in Column 3.

Common Ground

K What I Know	W What I Want to Learn	L What I Learned
The earth is mostly water.	Why should we worry about water?	We need to keep our water clean and free of polution.

Transparency 61 Level A, Unit 4 | Community   © Hampton-Brown

Common Ground
The Water, Earth, and Air We Share
by Molly Bang

*O*ur Earth has many wonderful natural resources. In this essay, Molly Bang describes how these resources can be destroyed and presents a persuasive argument for working together to take care of them. If communities don't care for our resources, there will be nothing left for future generations.

195

OBJECTIVES

Listening: Listen to a Preview
Reading Strategies: Preview; Predict
Literary Analysis: Essay

INTRODUCE THE SELECTION

4 **Preview and Predict** Read aloud the title, subtitle, and author. Ask: *What do you think you will learn about in this selection?* Then read the introduction and have students confirm or revise their prediction.

5 **Identify Genre: Persuasive Essay** Explain that the author cares about Earth's natural resources and that she wrote this selection to convince other people that they should care, too. Say: *A text written to persuade people to agree with the author is a persuasive essay.*

6 **Audio Walk-Through** Play the Audio Walk-Through for "Common Ground" on the **Selection Tape/CD** to give students an overall idea of the story.

Tape 4A
CD 4
Track 1

Common Ground: The Water, Earth, and Air We Share
by Molly Bang

Theme Connection This selection cites some very good reasons for thinking ahead to help protect Earth's environment.

Selection Summary and Awards The introduction on page 195 of the student book offers a summary of this selection.

Common Ground won the 1998 Giverny Award for Best Children's Science Picture Book. It was inspired by a classic biology article, "The Tragedy of the Commons," published in *Science* in 1968 by Garrett Hardin. Molly Bang has also received two Caldecott Awards and the School Library Journal Best Book of the Year award.

THE BASICS BOOKSHELF

■ *Rachel Carson: A Woman Who Loved Nature*
adapted from *Rachel Carson* by William Accorsi

Rachel Carson was one of the first environmentalists to recognize that everyone is responsible for protecting the air we breathe. In this biography, simple text introduces basic vocabulary for land and sea plants and animals. Labeled wildlife sketches and photographs of Rachel Carson increase access for beginning English learners.

For Lesson Plans: See the Teacher's Guide for *The Basics Bookshelf*.

READ PAGES 196–197

OBJECTIVES

Function: Read a Selection

Grammar: Statements with *there is/are, was/were*

Listening: Listen to a Selection

Reading and Learning Strategies: Set a Purpose for Reading; Connect New Information to Known; Use Graphic Organizers (K-W-L chart)

Comprehension: Identify Cause and Effect; Make an Inference; Form Opinions

---

SET PURPOSE

1 Read aloud the introduction to pages 196–197. Say: *Find out what plan people make in order to be fair to everyone.*

READ AND THINK

Tape 4A
CD 4
Track 2

2 Strategy Focus: Connect New Information to Known Have students record what they know and want to learn in columns 1 and 2 of **Master 61**. As students read, have them use the third column to record what they have learned.

▌ Choose Reading Options in the **Multi-Level Strategies** to tailor the reading to proficiency levels.

The recording of "Common Ground" on the **Selection Tape/CD** offers an oral language model and the opportunity to build reading fluency.

Red annotations offer opportunities to clarify meaning and check for understanding.

1

THE VILLAGE COMMONS

Hundreds of years ago, people made a plan to share land for their animals in a way that was fair for everyone.

———

*L*ong ago, a **village** was built around a **commons**. The commons was **"common ground"** which belonged to everyone in the village. All the **villagers** could bring their sheep to the commons to **graze**. But there was a problem.

A villager who owned many sheep used more of the commons than a villager who owned a few sheep, or one, or none at all. And because the **common** grass was free, people put as many sheep to graze there as they could. Soon there were too many sheep.

There was not enough grass for all of them. This was not good for the commons, or for the sheep, or for the villagers. So the people did one of two things.

Some people stayed in the village, but they made a plan together. They **agreed** to keep the commons **lush and green**, and to do a better job of sharing it. Each person could only put one sheep on the commons.

Everyone had to follow this rule. Other people chose to move away. There was always someplace else to go.

Ask: What might have happened if the villagers had not made a plan to share the commons?

BEFORE YOU MOVE ON...

1. **Cause and Effect** What problem was caused by having too many sheep on the commons?

2. **Opinion** Do you think the villagers' plan for using the commons was fair? Why or why not?

3. **Inference** Why did some of the villagers move away?

---

graze eat grass
agreed decided together
lush and green healthy and beautiful

196 **Unit 4** | Community

REACHING ALL STUDENTS

▌ **Multi-Level Strategies**
READING OPTIONS FOR LESSONS 4–6

BEGINNING Elicit information to complete columns 1 and 2 of **Transparency 61**. Then, read the selection aloud. After reading each page, review **Transparency 61** and record answers in column 3.

INTERMEDIATE Students can work in a group to brainstorm information to record in column 1 of **Master 61**. Students work independently to complete column 2. Then have students listen to the recording on the **Selection Tape/CD**. Pause so students can add notes to column 3 of **Master 61**.

ADVANCED Have students work independently to complete columns 1 and 2 of **Master 61**. Then have partners take turns reading the selection to each other. Ask them to pause after each section to record answers to their questions in column 3.

The commons was "common ground."

There was not enough grass for all the sheep.

They agreed to do a better job of sharing it.

3 Answers to "Before You Move On"

1. **Cause and Effect** Soon all the grass was gone, leaving the commons ugly and the sheep hungry.

2. **Opinion** Some students may feel it's fair because the same rules apply to everyone. Others may feel it's unfair because large families need more food and wool than small ones.

3. **Inference** Possible answers: Some people may have been unhappy with the new rules. Large families may have needed to keep more than one sheep in order to survive.

CLOSE AND ASSESS

Ask students to share the new information they have recorded on their K-W-L charts.

Grammar Minilesson

▶ **STATEMENTS WITH *THERE IS/ARE, WAS/WERE***

TEACH Call attention to this sentence on page 196: *But there was a problem.* Explain that in sentences that begin with *There is* or *There are,* the subject comes after the verb. If the subject is singular, the verb must be singular. In this sentence, *problem* is singular, so the singular verb *was* is used.

	One	More Than One
In the Present	is	are
In the Past	was	were

PRACTICE Write these sentences. Have students choose *is, are, was,* or *were* to complete each sentence.

1. There (was, were) a problem.

2. There (was, were) too many animals.

3. There (was, were) not enough grass.

4. There (is, are) many ways to solve the problem.

▶ **Practice Book** page 96

READ PAGES 198–199

OBJECTIVES

Function: Read a Selection
Vocabulary Strategies: Relate Words;
Use New Words in Context
Reading and Learning Strategies:
Set a Purpose for Reading;
Connect New Information to Known; Use
Graphic Organizers (K-W-L chart)
Comprehension:
Identify Details, Cause and Effect
Literary Analysis: Theme

SET PURPOSE

1 Read aloud the introduction to
pages 198–199. Ask: *What are some
common resources that are being used
up in today's world?*

READ AND THINK

Tape 4A
CD 4
Track 2

2 **Strategy Focus: Connect
New Information to Known** Involve
students in reading pages 198–199 of
the selection. Have them record new
information on their K-W-L charts as
they read.

See the **Multi-Level Strategies**
on page T196 to tailor the reading
experience to proficiency levels.

THE WORLD TODAY

Today, our common resources are being used up.

*T*oday the world is much like that
village. Now our commons are our parks,
reserves, and **natural resources**, and
the waters and air of the whole world.
Today we have almost the same problem
that the villagers had.

Today each fisherman tries to catch
as many fish as he can from the common
sea. This way, the fisherman has more
fish to sell—**in the short run**. But soon
there are fewer and fewer fish. This is
not good for the fish, the sea, or for
the people. **Ask:** How is this not good for the fish,
the sea, or the people?

Today each **lumber company** wants
to cut down as many trees as it can, to
sell for wood, paper, and **fuel**. The more
trees the lumber company cuts down, the
more money it makes—in the short run.
But after cutting down so many trees,
there are fewer and fewer **forests**.
This is not good for the trees, or for the
forest creatures, or the forest **soil**.

Encourage elaboration: Tell how cutting down
trees affects the forest creatures and soil.

BEFORE YOU MOVE ON...

1. **Vocabulary** In the short run means "now."
What do you think in the long run means?
2. **Details** The villagers almost used up all the
grass on the commons. List two resources
that we are in danger of using up today.
3. **Cause and Effect** What would happen if
we used all the fish and trees now?

reserves land that is saved for a special reason
in the short run now, at the present time
lumber company company that cuts down trees
for use in making products
fuel something used to give heat and power
forest creatures animals that live in the woods
soil dirt, ground, earth

198 Unit 4 | Community

REACHING ALL STUDENTS

Vocabulary
RELATE WORDS

Help students keep track of vocabulary
related to natural resources with a mind
map. Brainstorm several natural
resources and model how to set up the
the map. Ask students to copy it in their
notebooks and add new words as they
continue to read the selection.

HOME CONNECTION

How We Use Resources Send home a
copy of *High Point Newsletter 7* in the
Teacher's Resource Book. (See
pages 139–145.) In this home activity,
students will interview family
members about what they are doing
to conserve resources and protect the
environment. Then, they develop a
plan to improve conservation practices
at home.

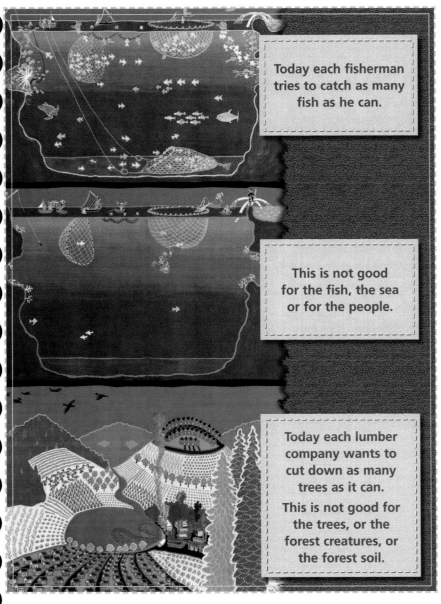

Today each fisherman tries to catch as many fish as he can.

This is not good for the fish, the sea or for the people.

Today each lumber company wants to cut down as many trees as it can.

This is not good for the trees, or the forest creatures, or the forest soil.

3 **Use New Words in Context** Assign different key vocabulary words to pairs of students and ask them to write a sentence using their word. Ask partners to read their sentence aloud, omitting the key vocabulary word. Classmates write the missing vocabulary words, then review the answers together.

CHECK COMPREHENSION

4 **Answers to "Before You Move On"**

1. **Vocabulary** Students may say that "in the long run" means "over a long period of time," "later," or "after many years."

2. **Details** Some resources that we are in danger of using up include coal, oil, fish, forests, and clean water.

3. **Cause and Effect** Answers will vary, but should include the idea that there would be no fish or trees for future generations.

CLOSE AND ASSESS

Ask students to share with the class the most important idea they have put on their K-W-L charts so far.

Literary Analysis Minilesson

▶ **THEME**

TEACH Define *theme* as "a universal idea found in the literature of many cultures." Ask for examples of fairytales, fables and other stories that illustrate a theme such as right wins over might. Then read aloud the description of Theme 1 on page 189. Ask students how "Common Ground" fits the theme, "Thinking Ahead." (It shows how people in a community long ago cooperated to save a common resource, and how people today must do the same to save Earth's natural resources for future generations.)

PRACTICE Ask students to suggest other fables, stories, poems, and songs that also fit this theme. Make a chart.

Fables	The Grasshopper and the Ant
Books	Leo Lionni's "Frederick"
Poems	
Songs	

▶ **Practice Book** page 97

SET PURPOSE

1 Read aloud the introduction to pages 200–201. Say: *As you read, think about what will probably happen if we don't plan ways to conserve natural resources now.*

READ AND THINK

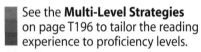

Tape 4A

CD 4
Track 2

2 Strategy Focus: Connect New Information to Known Involve students in reading pages 200–201 of the selection. Have them add information to their K-W-L charts as they read.

> See the **Multi-Level Strategies** on page T196 to tailor the reading experience to proficiency levels.

3

PLANNING FOR THE FUTURE

If we want to preserve our natural resources for
future generations, we must plan together *now*.

W̲e use our common **oil**, **gas**, and **coal** to heat our houses and run our cars. Companies use them to make plastics and other chemicals. In this way, we can stay warm, travel long distances, and visit stores full of amazing things to buy—in the short run. But some day, these **fossil fuels** will be used up.

We all need water for drinking, cooking, and washing. Farms need water for crops and livestock.

And businesses need water to cool equipment and clean up **wastes**.

So we pump as much of our common water as we can. This works pretty well—in the short run.

But over time, the wells **run dry**, and the wastes **pollute the water**. There is not enough clean water for all the people, the farms, and the businesses.

Fresh water, fossil fuels, forests, fish—one by one, we are destroying the natural resources that **sustain** our lives.

So then here is our common question:

If our country, our companies, and each one of us **benefit** more in the short run from using as many natural resources as we can, then what will stop us from destroying our whole world— our common ground?

We need to answer this question TOGETHER, because today we are different from those long-ago villagers in one very important way . . .

Give examples: Some crops are corn, wheat, and potatoes. Some examples of livestock are chickens, pigs, cattle, and sheep.

Define *pump*: When you pump, you bring water up from deep in the ground.

oil liquid found in Earth that can be used for fuel
gas vapor—like air or steam—found in Earth that can be used for fuel
coal black mineral that is burned to make heat or energy

wastes garbage and other unwanted materials
run dry have no more water
pollute the water make the water dirty

200 **Unit 4** | Community

REACHING ALL STUDENTS

Cooperative Learning

FOR CRITICAL THINKING:
Generate Ideas and Solve Problems

Describe the Problem Four settlers arrive on the moon: a farmer who needs 4 gallons of water a day to grow food, a cook who needs 2 gallons a day to prepare dehydrated food, and two scientists who each need a gallon a day for experiments. Healthy settlers need to drink one gallon of water daily, but one scientist must drink 2 gallons daily. They have 250 gallons of water to last until the next supply ship arrives in 30 days. How should they share the water?

Set up the Learning Situation Have students work in groups of four, with each student representing one of the settlers. Each group develops a plan for sharing the water, then describes their plan to the class.

Debrief the Content Ask: *Which plan is the fairest?* Invite students to share any new insights they gained.

Debrief the Cooperative Process Ask students how they and the other students in their group reached compromises and agreements.

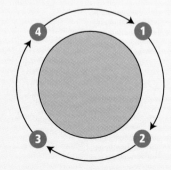

Cooperative Learning Structure:
Roundtable

We use our common oil, gas, and coal to heat our houses and run our cars. But someday, these fossil fuels will be used up.

We pump as much of our common water as we can. But over time, the wells run dry.

MONITOR YOUR READING

3 Use Visuals to Confirm Meaning

- Refer students to the pictures on pages 196–197 and point out how well they illustrate the meaning of key ideas on page 196. (The open green space with houses around it shows what a "village commons" is. The animals in the middle of page 197 illustrate the overcrowding they were experiencing. The circle of people at the bottom of the page shows the villagers meeting to discuss the problem.)

- Ask students to look through the illustrations that accompany the other parts of the story they have read so far. Have partners take turns describing to each other how the illustrations confirm the meaning of the words on the page.

Grammar Minilesson

▶ FUTURE TENSE VERBS

TEACH Draw attention to this sentence on page 201: *But someday, these fossil fuels will be used up.* Ask whether this sentence tells about the past, the present, or the future.

Remind students that the tense of a verb shows when an action happens. Explain: *One way to show that an action will happen later, or in the future, is to use the helping verb* will *along with a main verb.*

PRACTICE Ask: *What does the author of this selection say will happen to our planet in the future?* Have pairs of students work together to write two or three sentences that tell what she says will happen. (There will be no fish. There will be fewer forests; that will cause problems for forest creatures. Wells will run dry and water will be polluted.)

Call on volunteers to write their sentences for the class. Ask students to circle the helping verb that shows the future tense.

▶ **Practice Book** page 98

Now we don't have any place else to go.

BEFORE YOU MOVE ON...

1. **Details** How do we use natural resources like water and fossil fuels today?
2. **Inference** What does the author mean when she says that we don't have any place else to go?
3. **Author's Purpose** Why do you think Molly Bang wrote this story?

ABOUT THE AUTHOR

Molly Bang has written and illustrated more than 20 books for young readers. She enjoys learning stories from around the world, and has lived in Mali, Japan, and India. Molly Bang was inspired to write *Common Ground* after talking with a group of geologists—scientists who study the earth. She was so concerned by what she learned from them that she wrote *Common Ground* that very evening! She believes that people must plan ways to take care of the Earth's resources now—before it's too late.

OBJECTIVES

Function: Read a Selection
Listening: Listen to a Selection
Reading Strategy: Connect New Information to Known;
Use Graphic Organizers (K-W-L chart)
Comprehension: Identify Details;
① Identify Author's Purpose; Make an Inference
Literary Analysis: ① Evaluate Literary Quality

CHECK COMPREHENSION

4 Answers to "Before You Move On"

1. **Details** Water: to drink, cook, wash, grow crops, run machines, clean up waste. Fossil fuels: to heat houses, run cars.

2. **Inference** We have already used most of Earth's resources.

3. **Author's Purpose** She wants us to conserve natural resources.

ABOUT THE AUTHOR

5 Evaluate Literary Quality Read aloud About the Author. Ask students to comment on the effectiveness of Molly Bang's persuasive argument.

CLOSE AND ASSESS

Ask students to explain whether they agree with the author's beliefs, and why.

REACHING ALL STUDENTS

COMMUNITY CONNECTION

Neighborhood Tour Conduct a tour of the neighborhood with students and collect information about the use and misuse of resources. Ask students to record examples on charts. Suggest that they take note of how water, air, heating fuel, gasoline, paper, and food are used and misused. Help students plan a public meeting to present their findings and try to persuade community members and leaders to improve the situation.

Resource	Use/ Misuse	Notes
Water	M	When they water the park, a lot of water runs into the street.
Water	U	When there's a fire, they use water to put it out.

INTERNET

SCIENCE CONNECTION

Have groups each research a different business whose operations could have a negative impact on the environment, such as the lumber, fishing, and petroleum industries. Groups complete a chart showing problems caused by the industry they researched and how the industry is trying to minimize the problem.

Key Word Search
"oil spill prevention"
"dolphin-safe"
reforestation

Respond to the Essay
Check Your Understanding

SUM IT UP

Connect New Information to What You Know Follow these steps to complete your K-W-L chart:

- Read the **K** column. Correct any mistakes.
- Read the questions under **W**. Write any answers you learned under **L**.
- Write new things you learned under **L**.
- What questions do you still have? Think of ways to find answers.

Evaluate the Essay Look at your K-W-L chart and think about the essay. Then copy and complete these sentences. *Answers will vary.*

The author, wants us to *save natural resources*.
The essay is good because *it explains a problem*.
The essay would be better if *it told us how to save resources*.

THINK IT OVER

Discuss Talk about these questions with a partner.

1. **Inference** The author suggests that we must plan together to save our world. Who does she mean by "we"?

2. **Personal Experience** What natural resources are important where you live? How can you help save these resources?

3. **Opinion** What will the world be like in 100 years?

EXPRESS YOURSELF
▶ DEFINE AND EXPLAIN

Work in a group. Discuss a problem that can happen when people use natural resources. Brainstorm ways to solve the problem. Then share your group's ideas with the class.

Problems:

- We need lumber to build houses, but our forest has lost too many trees.
- We need energy for cars and heat, but we are using up our fossil fuels.

Common Ground **203**

Multi-Level Strategies
SUM IT UP OPTIONS

BEGINNING Invite students to brainstorm together possible completions for each part of the writing frame. Write out the responses. Rephrase, or ask a student to rephrase each one. Then invite students to complete the writing activity by choosing from these responses.

INTERMEDIATE Have each student complete the sentences in the writing frame. Then invite students to discuss their responses in a group and work together to come up with a summary of the group's views. This summary can be presented orally to the class.

ADVANCED Ask students to use the writing frame as a starting point for a paragraph about the essay. Encourage them to elaborate on their views by referring back to their K-W-L charts.

RESPOND

OBJECTIVES

SUM IT UP
Function: Write
Reading and Learning Strategies: Connect New Information to Known; Use Graphic Organizers (K-W-L chart)
Critical Thinking: ❶ Evaluate Literature; ❶ Identify Author's Purpose
Writing: Literary Critique

THINK IT OVER
Function: Engage in Discussion
Critical Thinking and Comprehension: Relate to Personal Experience; Make Inferences, Judgments; Form Opinions

EXPRESS YOURSELF
Function: Define and Explain
Speaking and Listening: Discussion

CHECK YOUR UNDERSTANDING

1 **Sum It Up** Possible responses: The author wants us to *care about saving our planet*. The essay is good because *she shows that people need to work together*. The essay would be better if *she gave some ideas for how people could start planning together*.

▶ **Practice Book** page 99

2 **Think It Over** Possible answers are:

1. **Inference** "We" can mean everyone on Earth including individuals, families, governments, businesses, and communities.

2. **Personal Experience** Students may mention open land, timber, water, air, plants, animals, beaches, rivers, minerals, and petroleum. Answers on preserving resources will vary.

3. **Opinion** Encourage positive responses.

3 **Express Yourself** Invite students to create posters to illustrate their ideas.

CLOSE AND ASSESS

Ask students to sum up in one sentence what they learned in this lesson.

RESPOND

OBJECTIVES

ADJECTIVES THAT COMPARE

Grammar: ➊ Adjectives that Compare
Critical Thinking: Make Comparisons

OPINION PARAGRAPH

Function: ➊ Express Opinions; Write
Research Skills: Gather Information
Learning Strategies:
Use Graphic Organizers (chart)
Writing: Paragraph
Writer's Craft: Topic Sentence;
Supporting Details

LANGUAGE ARTS AND LITERATURE

1 Use Adjectives That Compare As
students make comparisons:

- Point out that the word *than* is
  always used when comparing two
  things: *Hilmi is happier than Esin.*

- Point out that the words *the* and *of*
  are often used when comparing
  three or more things: *Ali is happiest.
  Ali is the happiest. Ali is the happiest
  of all.*

▶ **Practice Book** page 100

2 Write an Opinion Paragraph As
students complete the activity:

- Encourage them to include on
  their charts all the non-food items
  they find.

- Provide a list of natural resources
  and materials made from them,
  such as plastics which are made
  with petroleum products, and
  cardboard and paper which are
  made from trees.

- Review how to use the index
  volume of an encyclopedia as a
  starting point for research.

CLOSE AND ASSESS

Ask each student to create a test item that
requires the correct use of a comparative
adjective. Form groups and have students
test other members of the group.

ASSESSMENT
Selection Test 13 on page 63 of the Assessment Handbook tests students' mastery of the reading
strategies and the vocabulary, comprehension, and language arts skills taught with this selection.

Respond to the Essay, continued
Language Arts and Literature

GRAMMAR IN CONTEXT

USE ADJECTIVES THAT COMPARE

Learn About Adjectives That Compare
Adjectives can help you make comparisons. To
compare two things, add **-er** to the adjective. To
compare three or more things, add **-est**.

> The pine tree is **tall**.
>
> The oak tree is **taller** than the pine.
>
> The redwood is the **tallest** of the three.

For long adjectives, use **more** and **the most** to
make comparisons.

- To compare two things, use **more**:

  The oak is **more beautiful** than the pine.

- To compare three or more things, use
  the most:

  The redwood is **the most beautiful** tree of all.

Make Comparisons Act out a feeling with two
friends. For example, one of you can act happy.
The next can act happier, and the third, the
happiest of all. Ask classmates to make
comparisons to describe your actions.

Practice Write the sentences. Choose the
correct adjective to complete each sentence.

1. Brazil has the (big) rain forests in the world.
   biggest
2. Rain forests are (wet) than regular forests.
   wetter
3. Rain forest animals are the (interesting)
   animals in the world. most interesting

WRITING

WRITE AN OPINION PARAGRAPH

What resources are used in your lunch? Save
your non-food trash from lunch. Make a chart to
show what you found.

Do Research Paper, plastic, and metal are
made from natural resources. Use an electronic
or print encyclopedia to learn which resources
are used to make them. Make a chart like this:

I found:	It is made of:	Natural resources:	Can it be recycled?
a napkin	paper	wood	yes
a straw	plastic	petroleum	yes

Write a Paragraph Give your opinion about
the use of natural resources in your lunch. Then
explain your ideas.

Learn how to improve your writing
in the **writer's craft**.
See Handbook pages 390–401.

REACHING ALL STUDENTS

Multi-Level Strategies
PRACTICE OPTIONS FOR ADJECTIVES THAT COMPARE

BEGINNING Before completing the practice items with students, make
comparisons using people and things in the classroom. Provide sentence
frames with blanks for students to add adjectives that compare:

   (tall)   Anna is _____ than Jasmine.

   (old)   Ricardo is the _____ student of all.

   (interesting) English is the _____ class.

INTERMEDIATE / **ADVANCED** Ask students to write four original
sentences that compare the height and age of people in the class. Then ask
them to write two sentences using *most*. Have them share answers with a
partner and make revisions.

Content Area Connections

✓ **LANGUAGE ACQUISITION ASSESSMENT**
See page 61 of the Assessment Handbook.

▶ SCIENCE

STUDY ENVIRONMENTAL PROBLEMS

How can we save natural resources? Work with a group. Study a problem that threatens a natural resource like:

acid rain	air pollution
water pollution	loss of forests

1 Gather Information Research your topic in the library or on the Internet. Take notes as you read.

2 Find Solutions How can people help? Brainstorm ideas with your group.

3 Organize Information Make a chart to show what you learned.

Environmental Problems and Solutions

Problems	Causes	Effects	Solutions
air pollution	smoke from fires and cars makes the air dirty	people get sick	don't burn trash, carpool

Learn how to do **research**.
See Handbook pages 366–370.

▶ SCIENCE

EXPLORE RECYCLING

We can **recycle** used natural resources to make new things. For example, we can recycle paper so that new trees do not need to be cut down. Most products made of glass, aluminum, paper, and plastic can be recycled.

Look for recyclable materials in your school and at home. List the things your class found. Discuss how your class can help recycle natural resources.

▶ FINE ARTS

PICTURE THE ENVIRONMENT

Study the environmental collage on page 188. How do you see the world? Make a collage. Use pictures of the environment. You can:

- use magazine and newspaper pictures
- download pictures from the Internet
- create your own pictures.

Put the pictures together in a creative way. Then share your work with your classmates.

Common Ground **205**

Research Skills

▶ **USING AN ENCYCLOPEDIA**

TEACH Introduce students to encyclopedias in print and electronic formats. Explain that an encyclopedia has information on many topics and is organized in alphabetical order. Guide students to choose a research topic related to this selection.

PRACTICE Have students survey an encyclopedia, noting organizational features such as the index. Tell students that they should look quickly through an entry, or scan it, to help locate key information. Model how text features like headings, subheadings, and sidebars lead to specific information. Ask students how various features helped them locate specific information. Have students use the copyright and title pages to record information about sources and evaluate timeliness of information.

▶ **Practice Book** page 101

RESPOND

OBJECTIVES

STUDY ENVIRONMENTAL PROBLEMS
Function: Give Information;
🅣 Make Comparisons
Learning Strategies, Critical Thinking, and Research Skills: Choose a Topic; Use an Encyclopedia; Gather Information; Take Notes; Solve Problems
Representing: Chart

EXPLORE RECYCLING
Function: Engage in Discussion
Learning Strategy and Critical Thinking: Plan; Generate Ideas; Solve Problems

PICTURE THE ENVIRONMENT
Representing: Collage

CONTENT AREA CONNECTIONS

1 Study Environmental Problems

- Guide groups in choosing research topics to ensure variety.

- Ask the groups to divide up the research tasks before they begin.

- Invite groups to share their charts. Encourage students to make comments and ask questions.

▶ **Practice Book** page 102

2 Explore Recycling

- Discuss materials that can be recycled in your community. Suggest that students try to find an example of each type.

- When debriefing the activity in class, use a two-column chart. In the left column list the various materials, and in the right column list ideas on how the class can help recycle this type of material.

3 Picture the Environment Invite students to rehearse their presentations with a partner before talking with the class.

CLOSE AND ASSESS

Ask students to vote on what they consider the most serious environmental problem facing the world today.

BUILD LANGUAGE AND VOCABULARY

OBJECTIVES

Function: ❶ Express Opinions; ❶ Persuade

Concepts and Vocabulary: Words About the Environment

Patterns and Structures: ❶ Modals: *should, must, can*

Viewing: Interpret Visual Information

Learning Strategy: Use Graphic Organizers (concept map)

Critical Thinking: Form Opinions; Make Judgments

Representing and Writing: Poster, Caption

START WITH A COMMON EXPERIENCE

1 View and Interpret Ask two students to take the roles of the two characters and read the knock-knock joke aloud. Explain, if necessary, that knock-knock jokes involve plays on words. The joke comes from words that sound alike, in this case, *garden* and *guarding.* Have students identify the message.

2 Persuade Others to Agree with an Opinion Point out that the message of the knock-knock joke—the importance of guarding, or protecting, the environment—is an opinion, someone's belief or judgment. Then model how to persuade people to accept an opinion:

How to Persuade

- State something you believe is important: *We should not pollute water.*

- Tell why: *All life on Earth depends on water.*

- Give reasons to support your opinion: *Polluted water is not safe to drink. Fish can't live in polluted water.*

Have students try their hands at expressing opinions and save their ideas for the writing activity on page T207.

Use the Options in the **Multi-Level Strategies** to allow all students to participate.

Build Language and Vocabulary

EXPRESS OPINIONS • PERSUADE

View this cartoon and read the joke. What is the real message in this joke?

Knock, knock.

Who's there?

Garden.

Garden who?

Garden the environment is important.

REACHING ALL STUDENTS

Multi-Level Strategies

OPTIONS FOR EXPRESSING OPINIONS

BEGINNING Have students draw pictures to illustrate an opinion and its supporting reasons. Pair Beginning students with more fluent partners to create sentence strips to label the pictures and summarize their ideas. Read the sentence strips aloud and have students repeat.

INTERMEDIATE Have students work with partners to create a main idea sentence stating their opinion and detail sentences that add to or support the opinion. After getting feedback from partners, students can present their opinions to the class.

ADVANCED Invite students to express opinions and reasons on the importance of a specific natural resource. Students should present their opinion and reasons to the class. Invite classmates to vote on how persuasive their reasons are. Encourage revisions to make the argument stronger.

MAKE A MIND MAP

Do you agree that "guarding the environment" is important? What are some of the natural resources that we should protect? Use the pictures in this unit for ideas. Then record your ideas on a mind map. Share your ideas about why each resource is important.

BUILD YOUR VOCABULARY

Words About the Environment Read this definition to learn a word about caring for our natural resources.

> **con·ser·va·tion** *noun*
> **Conservation** is careful planning to stop natural resources from being destroyed or ruined.

What are some ways that conservation can help us take care of our natural resources? Add your ideas to your mind map.

USE LANGUAGE STRUCTURES ▶ VERBS: *should, must, can*

Writing: Express Your Opinion Think of a way to conserve natural resources. Use it to make a poster. Use *should*, *must*, or *can* to write a caption to persuade people to take care of that resource.

Examples:
We **can** pick up trash to help keep our beaches clean.
We **must** recycle paper to help save trees.

CONDUCT THE ACTIVITIES

3 Make a Mind Map Have students work individually and then share their mind maps.

4 Build Your Vocabulary: Words About the Environment Demonstrate how to add spokes and ideas to the mind map. Remind students to link new ideas to the category that makes the most sense.

5 Use Language Structures: Verbs: *should, must, can* Present the helping verbs, using the definition and examples on **Transparency 62**. Explain that these words signal possibilities, not facts or definite actions. Then have students complete the sentences in Try It!

Writing: Express Your Opinion Conduct the activity at the bottom of page 207. Tell students that a poster should be lively in order to capture the viewer's attention and interest. They should choose persuasive words for their captions.

■ Use the Writing Activity Options in the **Multi-Level Strategies** to adjust instruction.

▶ **Practice Book** page 103

CLOSE AND ASSESS

Have students tell the purpose of *should, must,* and *can*. Then ask them to use each verb in an oral or written sentence.

Multi-Level Strategies
WRITING ACTIVITY OPTIONS

BEGINNING Students' posters may depend heavily on visual imagery. Offer a sentence frame for their caption, such as:

> We should take care of _____ because _____.

INTERMEDIATE Students can work in pairs to select and expand ideas from their mind maps. Remind students to use the words *should, must,* and *can* in the sentences on their posters.

ADVANCED Encourage students to provide as many facts as possible to support the opinions they express on their posters. Have them label the poster with these additional facts as well as writing the caption.

Transparency 62 / Master 62

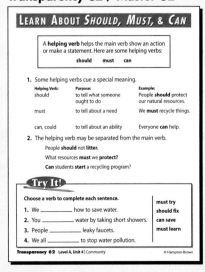

OBJECTIVES

THINK ABOUT WHAT YOU KNOW
Reading Strategy:
Activate Prior Knowledge

LEARN KEY VOCABULARY ⓣ

Vocabulary Strategy: Relate Words

LEARN TO PREVIEW AND PREDICT

Reading Strategy: Preview;
ⓣ Make Predictions

THINK ABOUT WHAT YOU KNOW

1 Brainstorm Ideas Suggest that students visualize themselves walking around inside and outside the school. Have them write down any ideas about cleaning up the school that they "see" during their virtual tour.

LEARN KEY VOCABULARY

2 Relate Words Read each vocabulary word and its defining sentence aloud. Then conduct the activity.

> Use the Vocabulary Options in the **Multi-Level Strategies** to work with all proficiency levels.

▶ **Practice Book** page 104

LEARN TO PREVIEW AND MAKE PREDICTIONS

3 Model How to Preview and Predict Define *preview*. Then preview the songs on pages 210–216 with students.

Read aloud About the Songwriter on page 216. Ask students to predict the author's purpose. Record students' predictions on a chart.

CLOSE AND ASSESS

Ask students to define *preview* and *predict* in their own words.

PROTECTING
our planet

songs
by Raffi

Prepare to Read Songs

THINK ABOUT WHAT YOU KNOW

Brainstorm Ideas Make a class list of ideas for cleaning up your school. What can students do alone? How must adults help?

LEARN KEY VOCABULARY

crystal clean When something is **crystal clean**, it is clear and pure.

earth/Earth The ground or dirt is **earth**. The planet we live on is called **Earth**.

life Something that has **life** is alive. **Life** can also mean living things.

nation People who live in one country form a **nation**.

planet A **planet** is any one of the large objects in space that travel around the sun.

rain forest A **rain forest** is an area covered by trees that gets at least 100 inches of rain each year.

source of power A **source of power** is where energy comes from.

stream A **stream** is a small river of moving water.

up to me When something is **up to me**, I am the one who should do something.

valley A **valley** is the land between hills or mountains.

Relate Words Study the new words. Then look at the table of contents. Tell a partner what each chapter title means in your own words.

LEARN TO PREVIEW AND MAKE PREDICTIONS

When you **preview**, you look at a selection before you read. You figure out what it is about. **Previewing** helps you to **predict** what you may read.

READING STRATEGY
How to Preview and Predict

1. Look at the titles and illustrations. Ask yourself: What do they tell me about the subject?

2. Think about the author. Ask yourself: What do I know about this author? How does the author feel about this subject?

3. Write predictions about what you will read.

Before you read "Protecting Our Planet," predict why Raffi wrote these songs. Then read to see if your predictions are correct.

REACHING ALL STUDENTS

Multi-Level Strategies
VOCABULARY OPTIONS

BEGINNING Use pictures to illustrate the meanings of these vocabulary words. (*Earth, planet:* page 188; *nation:* map, page 26; *rain forest:* page 190; *source of power:* page 201; *stream, valley:* page 199) Pose questions to ensure comprehension of other vocabulary words: *Is it a good idea to drink crystal clean water?*

INTERMEDIATE Give each student an index card with a key vocabulary word or phrase on one side. On the back, have each student write an original sentence using the word. Students exchange cards with partners and check each other's work.

ADVANCED Ask students to write paragraphs using as many of the key vocabulary words as possible. Have students share their work with partners and suggest ways for their partners to include additional vocabulary words.

PROTECTING
our planet

by Raffi Cavoukian

In this collection of songs, popular singer Raffi describes our beautiful planet, as well as some of the threats facing our world today. His songs call on us to work in our communities to protect the wonders of our natural world.

209

OBJECTIVES

Reading Strategies: Preview;
❶ Make Predictions

INTRODUCE THE SONGS

4 Preview and Make Predictions
Read the title, author, and introduction to the collection of songs. Invite students to read the titles of the three sections of the selection. Ask: *What topics do you think Raffi will be singing about?* Have students add predictions about the topics to the prediction chart.

Protecting Our Planet
by Raffi Cavoukian

Theme Connection Raffi's songs ask people everywhere to think of themselves as one big community that can work together and think ahead to save the environment.

Selection Summary and Awards The introduction on page 209 of the student book provides a summary of the songs.

Songwriter Awards Raffi won an Earth Achievement Award in 1992 for his songs encouraging people to protect the environment. He has also been honored by the International Reading Association and the Children's Book Council, and has received the Children's Choice Award and the Child Study Association Book of the Year Award.

Red annotations offer
opportunities to clarify
meaning and check for
understanding.

OBJECTIVES

Function: Read Songs
Grammar: ❶ Modals
Listening: Listen to Songs
Reading and Learning Strategies: Set a Purpose for Reading; ❶ Make, Confirm, and Revise Predictions
Comprehension: ❶ Make Comparisons
Literary Analysis: Author's Style; Theme; Evaluate Impact of Literary Devices and Genre on Meaning

SET PURPOSE

1 Say: *As you listen to each song, ask yourself what natural beauty and resources the song is about.*

LISTEN AND READ

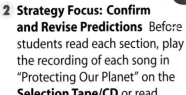

Tape 4A
CD 4
Track 3

2 **Strategy Focus: Confirm and Revise Predictions** Before students read each section, play the recording of each song in "Protecting Our Planet" on the **Selection Tape/CD** or read it aloud.

▌ See the **Multi-Level Strategies** for Listening and Reading Options to adjust instruction.

Review the prediction chart (see page T208), and revise or add predictions as needed.

1

O U R   W O N D E R F U L   W O R L D

The world we live in is full of natural beauty
and resources for all of us.

One Light, One Sun

One light, one sun.
One sun lighting everyone.
One world turning.
One world turning everyone.

One world, one home.
One world home for everyone.
One dream, one song.
One song heard by everyone.

One love, one heart.
One heart warming everyone.
One hope, one joy.
One love filling everyone.
Restate: One love felt by everyone.

One light, one sun.
One sun lighting everyone.
One light warming everyone.

One sun lighting everyone. The sun gives light to everyone who lives on Earth.
One world turning everyone. As the Earth turns, everyone on the planet turns, too.
joy strong feeling of happiness

210 Unit 4 | Community

REACHING ALL STUDENTS

Vocabulary
NUMBER WORDS

Materials: Old magazines and newspapers

Ask students to make a two-part collage to compare and contrast the healthy natural world and the polluted world. One panel of the collage will show natural items such as trees, animals, and flowers, while the other panel will show things that cause pollution, such as cars, garbage, and factories. Students label the items on the collage, including number words as in "One Light, One Sun." Labels might include: *one factory, three trees, four bottles.*

Multi-Level Strategies
LISTENING AND READING OPTIONS FOR LESSONS 12–14

BEGINNING After students listen to the song, reread it in sections, pausing after each stanza to paraphrase its meaning in a sentence or two. Invite students to add their comments and ask about anything they don't understand.

INTERMEDIATE After students listen to the song, ask them to work in small groups. Each person in the group selects a stanza and practices singing or reading it aloud. Students then sing or recite the song for each other and discuss what it means to them.

ADVANCED After the initial listening, ask students to close their books and listen to each song again. Encourage them to listen to the overall message, not individual words and phrases. Then invite them to write a sentence or two about each song in a Reflection Log.

Big Beautiful Planet

Chorus:

There's a big, beautiful planet in the sky.
It's my home, it's where I live.
You and many others live here, too.
The Earth is our home; it's where we live.

We can feel the power of the noonday sun—
A blazing ball of fire up above—
Shining light and warmth enough for everyone:
A gift to every nation from a star.

Clarify: The sun is a star. Earth is a planet.

Chorus

We can feel the spirit of a blowing wind—
A mighty source of power in our lives—
Offering another way to fill our needs:
Nature's gift to help us carry on.

Chorus

Ask: What two elements of nature are described in this song?

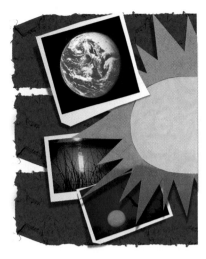

BEFORE YOU MOVE ON...

1. **Author's Style** Why does Raffi repeat the word *one* in his song "One Light, One Sun"?
2. **Theme** What is Raffi's message to community members with these two songs?
3. **Comparisons** What is the message in these songs? What is different?

---

noonday sun sun at noon, when it reaches its highest point in the sky
blazing brightly burning, shining
spirit of a blowing wind strength of moving air

mighty great, strong
Offering Giving
fill our needs give us what we need to live
carry on go on, keep living

---

3 Answers to "Before You Move On"

1. **Author's Style** The writer wants to emphasize that everyone on Earth shares the same light from the same sun.

2. **Theme** He is saying that we are all members of a single community. He is also saying that if we are careful, Earth can provide us with enough resources to take care of everyone.

3. **Comparisons** They are both optimistic and they both praise the beauty and richness of the natural world. However, "One Light, One Sun" emphasizes the unity of humanity while "Big Beautiful Planet" suggests that we need to look at ways to conserve resources— "another way to fill our needs."

CLOSE AND ASSESS

Have students choose one of the songs and illustrate the message.

Grammar Minilesson

▶ MODALS

TEACH Draw attention to these lines of the song: *We can feel the power of the noonday sun. . . . We can feel the spirit of a blowing wind.* Explain that verbs like *can* tell about things that are possible, not facts or things that are definite.

Provide several examples of sentences with modals to help students understand the concept. For example: *It might rain tomorrow. We could go on a field trip next week. You should all do well on tomorrow's test.*

PRACTICE Write a list of modals for students to refer to:

can	could	may	might
must	should	will	would

Ask pairs of students to choose at least two words from the list and write a sentence for each word that tells about something that is possible. Invite volunteers to share their sentences.

▶ **Practice Book** page 105

READ PAGES 212–213

OBJECTIVES

Function: Read Songs
Listening: Listen to a Song
Grammar: Plural Nouns
Reading and Learning Strategies:
Set a Purpose for Reading; ❶ Make, Confirm, and Revise Predictions
Comprehension: Make an Inference; ❶ Identify Author's Point of View
Literary Analysis: Tone

SET PURPOSE

1 Read and discuss the introduction to pages 212–213. Say: *What kind of pollution does Raffi sing about in this song? Which natural resource does it affect?*

LISTEN AND READ

Tape 4A
CD 4 Track 3

2 **Strategy Focus: Confirm and Revise Predictions** Play the song on the **Selection Tape/CD**. Then involve students in reading pages 212–213.

See the **Multi-Level Strategies** on page T210 to adjust instruction.

THE THREAT OF POLLUTION

Pollution threatens to destroy our natural resources and our health.

Clean Rain

Clean rain, crystal clean rain.

Clean rain. **Clarify:** Crystal is fine quality, clear glass with no imperfections. When something is crystal clean, it is as clean and pure as possible.

I remember the days when the rain fell clean
Into the valleys and into the streams,
Clean through the air and clean to the Earth.
They say that the rain fell clean.

Rain on the land and rain in the water,
Clean fell the rain from the skies above.
The rain brought life, life in every drop,
The rain that we used to know.

Clean rain, crystal clean rain.

Clean rain. **Encourage elaboration:** Explain how rain brings life to the land and water on Earth.

---

the rain fell clean the water in the rain was clean when it came down

life in every drop each drop of rain helped living things grow

212 Unit 4 | Community

REACHING ALL STUDENTS

Cooperative Learning

FOR LANGUAGE DEVELOPMENT
Ask and Answer Questions

Pose the Questions Students will share information about their reactions to Raffi's songs. First ask them to think about these two questions:

• Which song do you like the best? Why?

• Which song includes a topic that you would like to learn more about? How could you do that?

Students Interview Each Other and Report Have partners take turns interviewing each other and taking notes about what they learn. Each pair of

students joins another pair to form a group of four. Each person reports what he or she learned in the interview.

Debrief the Content Ask students to share insights they gained about how to learn more about topics of interest. Have them evaluate whether people in their group have similar or different preferences.

Debrief the Process Students can say if they prefer interviewing or being interviewed, and tell how it felt to hear someone else present their ideas.

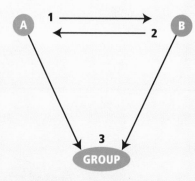

Cooperative Learning Structure:
Three-Step Interview

I remember the days when the rain fell clean
Into the valleys and into the streams,
Clean through the air and clean to the Earth.
They say that the rain fell clean.

There's life in the woods and life in our waters,
Moving in the beauty of this Earth that we love,
And praying for the day when the rain falls clean
Like the rain we used to know.

Clean rain, crystal clean rain.   **Ask:** Why is the rain
not clean anymore?
Clean rain.

BEFORE YOU MOVE ON...

1. **Author's Point of View** Raffi writes about the clean rain that fell in the past. What do you think Raffi thinks about the rain that falls today?
2. **Inference** What happens when the rain that falls is not clean?
3. **Tone** How do you think Raffi felt when he was writing this song? Explain.

CHECK COMPREHENSION

3 Answers to "Before You Move On"

1. **Author's Point of View** He thinks the rain that falls today is not clean or clear.
2. **Inference** When the rain is not clean, our water sources are polluted. Fish and other animals may die out.
3. **Tone** He probably felt sad. He mentions several times how clean the rain was in the past, but he doesn't say that it will be clean again in the future.

CLOSE AND ASSESS

Ask students to name a way that rain affects life on Earth.

Health Connection
WATER AND HEALTH

Ask students why so many people have started drinking bottled water. Lead into a discussion of water pollution and the possible health risks it poses. Divide the class into two groups. One group uses the Internet to research sources of water pollution. The other group collects ads for pure water sources such as bottled water and filter systems. Have the two groups report their findings to each other. Evaluate the claims made by companies promoting safe water.

Grammar Minilesson

▶ PLURAL NOUNS

TEACH Ask students to identify words in "Clean Rain" that name one and more than one. Write the nouns in two columns. Use the words *valleys* and *skies* to review the rules for forming plurals of words ending in **y**. Introduce changing **f** to **v** and adding **–es** using related nature words, such as *leaf leaves.*

Point out the word *children* in the song on page 216. Say: *Some nouns form their plurals in special ways.* Children *is the plural of* child. Refer students to Handbook pages 410–411 for more examples of plural nouns.

PRACTICE Write these sentences. Ask students to rewrite each sentence, changing the singular noun in parentheses into a plural noun.

1. Our (life) depend on having clean water.
2. Once, clean rain fell from the (sky).
3. People tell (story) about the clean water of long ago.
4. The rain is not clean these (day).

▶ **Practice Book** page 106

OBJECTIVES

Function: Read a Song

Vocabulary Strategy:
Use New Words in Context

Grammar: Prepositions

Listening: Listen to a Song

Reading and Learning Strategies: Set a Purpose for Reading; ❶ Make, Confirm, and Revise Predictions; Visualize

SET PURPOSE

1 Say: *As you listen to the song, think about what the words* evergreen *and* everblue *refer to.*

LISTEN AND READ

Tape 4A
CD 4
Track 3

2 Strategy Focus: Confirm and Revise Predictions Encourage students to predict the meaning of *evergreen* and *everblue* before playing the song on the **Selection Tape/CD**. Then involve students in reading pages 214–215.

See the **Multi-Level Strategies** on page T210 to adjust instruction.

Communities must join together to protect the plants and animals of our planet from destruction.

Evergreen, Everblue

Evergreen, everblue,
As it was in the beginning,
We've got to see it through.
Evergreen, everblue.
At this point in time
It's up to me, it's up to you.

Restate: You and I must help.

Amazon is calling, "Help this planet Earth,"

With voices from the jungle,
   "Help this planet Earth."

Hear the tree that's falling:
   "Help this planet Earth."

Rainforests are crying,
   "Help this planet Earth to stay

Evergreen, everblue,
As it was in the beginning,
We've got to see it through."
Evergreen, everblue.
At this point in time
It's up to me, it's up to you.

Clarify: The Amazon is a rain forest in South America. The Amazon river flows through it.

----

see it through do everything we can to get the result we want

At this point in time Right now, At this moment

214 Unit 4 | Community

REACHING ALL STUDENTS

Science Connection
WATER CYCLE

Materials: hotplate, 2 pots (1 larger than the other), 1 pie tin, a potholder, ice

Give a simple demonstration of how the water cycle works. Fill the smaller pot with ice, and the larger one with water. Heat the water until it boils. Then hold the ice-filled pot an inch above the boiling water. When it is well covered with condensation, slide the pie tin under it. Ask students to look closely as water drops fall on the pie tin. Have students describe what they see. Explain that the water cycle in nature follows the same principles. The small drops that have condensed on the outside of the ice pot represent a cloud. The drops mix together and when they become larger they begin to fall as rain. Discuss how falling rain might pick up pollutants from the air.

Vocabulary
COINED WORDS

Ask students to describe what an *evergreen* is. (a tree, like a pine or a fir that is green all year round) Point out how Raffi used the idea behind *evergreen* to create the word *everblue* to describe waters that he hoped would always be clear and blue, not dirty and brown. Give other examples of coined words in English, such as a *cheeseburger* to describe a hamburger with cheese on it. Invite students to make up new coined words.

Ocean's wave is rumbling, "Help this planet Earth,"
With voices from the seaway, "Help this planet Earth."

Water's for the drinking: "Help this planet Earth."
Beluga whales are singing, "Help this planet Earth to stay

Evergreen, everblue,
As it was in the beginning,
We've got to see it through."
Evergreen, everblue.

At this point in time
It's up to me, it's up to you.

Right now is when we're needed.
We can all do something.
The young, the old together.
The more we get together,
The more we help this planet Earth.

Ask: How can we help the planet Earth?

continued next page

Clarify: Belugas are white whales that live near Canada. Their numbers have dropped because of hunters.

....

seaway oceans

Protecting Our Planet **215**

Grammar Minilesson

▶ PREPOSITIONS

TEACH Referring to "Clean Rain," ask: *Where did the rain fall?* (into the ____ valleys/streams, through the air, to the Earth, on the land, in the water) Referring to "Evergreen, Everblue," ask: *Where did the voices come from?* (from the jungle/seaway)

Identify the underlined words as prepositions. Explain that prepositions begin a prepositional phrase and that prepositional phrases provide details.

Create a chart, organizing prepositions under the headings: **Location** (on, in), **Time** (in), **Direction** (to, into, through, from), **Other** (at, for).

Work with students to add other prepositions to the chart. See Handbook page 429.

PRACTICE Write these cloze sentences. Have students add a preposition from the chart to finish each sentence.

1. Raffi writes songs ____ everyone.
2. Once, clean rain fell ____ the skies.
3. What will happen ____ the future?

▶ **Practice Book** page 107

REVIEW KEY VOCABULARY

3 **Use New Words in Context** Ask students to use the key vocabulary words as they create magazine advertisements to persuade people to help take care of the environment. Each ad should feature a picture with a caption that uses one or more of the words on the list. For the term *source of power,* for example, a student might show a hydroelectric dam and the caption, "Hydroelectric Dams—a Safe Source of Power."

MONITOR YOUR READING

4 **Visualize** Ask students to listen to the song once with their eyes closed, focusing on the images that they see in their "mind's eye." Then have them read the words of the song again and notice how the pictures they "saw" may have helped to deepen their understanding of the song. Encourage volunteers to share what they experienced.

READ PAGE 216

OBJECTIVES

Function: Read a Song
Listening: Listen to a Song
Comprehension: Identify Details;
❶ Identify Author's Purpose
Literary Analysis: Figurative Language;
Evaluate Impact of Author's Beliefs
on Literature

CHECK COMPREHENSION

5 Answers to "Before You Move On"

1. Classify Things that should
stay "evergreen" are trees and
rainforests. Things that should
stay "everblue" are the oceans and
the seaway.

2. Figurative Language Raffi is
describing "mother Earth."

3. Author's Purpose He wants
people to help save the planet.

ABOUT THE AUTHOR

**6 Evaluate Literature: Author's
Beliefs** Read aloud About the
Songwriter. Say: *How do Raffi's
songs reflect his beliefs about
helping our planet?*

CLOSE AND ASSESS

Ask students to describe how they
corrected or revised predictions made at
the beginning of the selection.

So come all united nations, help this planet Earth.   **Restate:** Let everyone agree to
come help this planet Earth.
Children of one mother, help this planet Earth.

With love for one another, help this planet Earth.

For our sons' and daughters' future, help this planet Earth to stay

Evergreen, everblue,

As it was in the beginning,

We've got to see it through.

Evergreen, everblue.

At this point in time

It's up to me, it's up to you.

BEFORE YOU MOVE ON...

1. Classify List things from the song that
should stay "evergreen" and "everblue."

2. Figurative Language How are humans
"children of one mother?" What "mother" is
Raffi describing?

3. Author's Purpose Why do you think Raffi
wrote this song?

ABOUT THE SONGWRITER

Raffi Cavoukian was born in Egypt in 1948. His first language
was Armenian, his family language. Raffi learned English at
the age of 10, when his family moved to Canada.

Today, Raffi is a popular entertainer. He uses his songs to
express his love of nature and his wish to preserve it.

"I believe that we can rescue our beleaguered planet only through a change of
heart and mind," says Raffi. "My new music celebrates our power to act together
to preserve the beauty and bounty of the Earth for our children's future."

---

united nations countries that agree to work together

REACHING ALL STUDENTS

Vocabulary
CONSERVATION WORDS

A popular environmental motto is
"Reduce, Reuse, and Recycle." Ask
students to look up these words and
examine the differences among the
actions they represent. Have them
make a chart to compare the three
terms, giving examples of each. Have
students explain whether or not this
is a good motto to promote a healthy
environment.

Reduce	use less	Use less gas by carpooling.
Reuse	use again	Clean plastic containers and use them to store food.
Recycle	make into something new	Make used soda cans into new cans.

COMMUNITY CONNECTION

Environmental Action Discuss the
chart students made in the Vocabulary
activity. Encourage them to write
letters or e-mail to local businesses
to find out what they are doing to
reduce, reuse, and recycle materials.
Brainstorm a list of places students
can contact, such as fast-food
restaurants, grocery stores, utility
companies, and newsstands.

Respond to the Songs
Check Your Understanding

SUM IT UP

Check Predictions Review your predictions. Why did you think Raffi wrote these songs? Were your predictions correct?

Raffi wants to **persuade**, or encourage, people to take care of the Earth. Think about what Raffi wants people to do in each song.

Analyze Persuasive Techniques Raffi uses different ways, or **techniques**, to persuade his readers to take care of the Earth. Think of words and phrases to add to the chart.

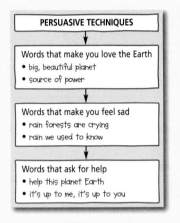

PERSUASIVE TECHNIQUES

Words that make you love the Earth
• big, beautiful planet
• source of power

Words that make you feel sad
• rain forests are crying
• rain we used to know

Words that ask for help
• help this planet Earth
• it's up to me, it's up to you

Evaluate the Songs Did Raffi's techniques persuade you to take care of the Earth? Tell why or why not.

THINK IT OVER

Discuss Talk about these questions with a partner.

1. **Summarize** What part of the environment is each song about? How are the songs alike?

2. **Inference** How can you tell that Raffi cares about the Earth?

3. **Opinion** Can these songs change peoples' ideas about our environment?

4. **Personal Experience** What questions would you like to ask Raffi?

EXPRESS YOURSELF ▶ RECITE

Work with a group. Choose a song to **recite**, or say out loud. Decide who will read each part of the song. Decide which parts the whole group will read together. Practice reading. Then recite your song for the class. Use your voice to make the words persuade.

Multi-Level Strategies
SUM IT UP OPTIONS

BEGINNING After reviewing the prediction chart, work with the group to find examples of persuasive language in the songs. Ask students: *Does it make you feel sad or happy when you hear* "Rainforests are crying"? Ask students to say which song they think will persuade the most people.

INTERMEDIATE Form three groups and ask each group to focus on one section of the persuasive techniques chart. Have them check all the songs for words and phrases that fit that section. Invite the groups to share their findings. Then have students write their opinions individually.

ADVANCED Ask students to complete the persuasive techniques chart individually. When they finish, ask them to write paragraphs telling which of Raffi's persuasive techniques worked for them and which did not. Prompt them to cite specific lines or stanzas and to give reasons for their answers.

OBJECTIVES

SUM IT UP
Function: Write; ❶ Express Opinions
Reading and Learning Strategies:
❶ Make, Confirm, and Revise Predictions; Classify; Analyze Information; Use Graphic Organizers (category chart)
Critical Thinking: ❶ Evaluate Literature
Writer's Craft: Word Choice

THINK IT OVER
Function: Engage in Discussion
Critical Thinking and Comprehension: Summarize; Make Inferences; Form Opinions; Relate to Personal Experience

EXPRESS YOURSELF
Function: Recite
Speaking and Listening: Choral Reading

CHECK YOUR UNDERSTANDING

1 Sum It Up Possible answers are:

- Words that make you love the Earth—*home, light and warmth*

- Words that make you feel sad—*threat, pollution*

- Words that ask for help—*we've got to see it through*

▶ **Practice Book** page 108

2 Think It Over Possible answers are:

1. **Summarize** "One Light, One Sun"—the sun. "Big Beautiful Planet"—Earth. "Clean Rain"—rain and water. "Evergreen, Everblue"—rain forests and oceans. All the songs are about the environment.

2. **Inference** He tries to persuade others to help care for the Earth.

3. **Opinion** They can make us think about protecting the environment.

4. **Personal Experience** Answers will vary.

3 Express Yourself Record each group.

CLOSE AND ASSESS

Ask: *Which song is your favorite? Why?*

RESPOND

OBJECTIVES

INDEFINITE PRONOUNS
Grammar: ❶ Indefinite Pronouns
HAIKU POEM
Function: Express Feelings; Write
Concepts and Vocabulary: Nature Words
Literary Analysis: Poem
Writing: Poem

LANGUAGE ARTS AND LITERATURE

1 **Use Indefinite Pronouns** See annotations for possible answers to the Practice items.

▶ **Practice Book** page 109

2 **Write a Haiku Poem** Read aloud the haiku poem or ask a student to read it. Prompt students to name the elements of nature in the poem (raindrops, valleys, streams).

Ask students to count the syllables to themselves as you read the poem again, emphasizing each syllable.

You may want to introduce the activity by writing a class haiku:

• Start by brainstorming various aspects of nature and choosing one to write about.

• Then brainstorm a list of words and phrases related to that topic.

• Encourage students to suggest five- and seven-syllable lines for the poem.

• Shape students' suggestions into a haiku poem.

CLOSE AND ASSESS

Ask students to state one thing they learned in this lesson.

Respond to the Songs, continued
Language Arts and Literature

> GRAMMAR IN CONTEXT

USE INDEFINITE PRONOUNS

Learn About Indefinite Pronouns When you don't know the name of a specific person, place, or thing, use an **indefinite pronoun**.

Some Indefinite Pronouns

person	anyone	someone	everyone
place	anywhere	somewhere	everywhere
thing	anything	something	everything

Examples:
Everyone can help save the planet Earth.
We should help **anywhere** we can.
Is there **something** you can do?

Use Indefinite Pronouns How can you and your classmates help this planet Earth? Finish these sentences:

• Something I can do is . . .
• Everyone should . . .
• Anyone can . . .

Practice Write the sentences. Use an indefinite pronoun to complete each sentence. Answers will vary.

1. __Anyone__ can help save the planet.
2. What is __something__ you can do to help?
3. __Everyone__ can help by saving water.
4. Try to recycle __everywhere__ you go.
5. Do __everything__ you can to keep Earth "evergreen, everblue."

218 Unit 4 | Community

> LITERARY ANALYSIS
> WRITING/REPRESENTING

WRITE A HAIKU POEM

A **haiku poem** tells one idea about nature. Write your own feelings about nature.

❶ **Learn the Haiku Pattern** Each haiku has seventeen syllables in three lines.

Line 1
5 syllables   Crys tal clear rain drops
Line 2
7 syllables   Gone from the val leys
             and streams

Line 3
5 syllables   A tear falls for you

❷ **Write Your Draft** Create a poem about nature. Use the haiku pattern.

❸ **Edit Your Poem** Trade poems with a partner. See if you understand the poem. Check to see that the poem matches the haiku pattern. Give your partner ideas about how to make the poem better.

❹ **Make a Final Draft** Make a new copy of your haiku poem. Write neatly or use a word-processing program on a computer. Add pictures of nature.

Learn how to use a **word-processing program**.
See Handbook pages 354–361.

REACHING ALL STUDENTS

Multi-Level Strategies
WRITING OPTIONS FOR HAIKU POEMS

BEGINNING Suggest that students look for five- and seven-syllable phrases in Raffi's songs. Have them use one or two of these phrases as a starting point for their haikus. (From "Clean Rain": *Into the valleys—Crystal clean rain is falling—Sun peeks through the clouds.*)

INTERMEDIATE Invite students to work in pairs. Together they can brainstorm ideas, write a draft, and edit the poem. For the final draft, have each student copy and illustrate the poem individually.

ADVANCED Give students photographs of natural settings and ask them to write haiku poems inspired by the picture they receive. Have them exchange poems, but not pictures. Then display the pictures and poems and invite the group to match each poem with the appropriate picture.

OBJECTIVES

REPETITION AND AUTHOR'S STYLE
Function: Write
Learning Strategies: Review
Literary Analysis: Repetition; Style

FRIENDLY LETTER TO RAFFI
Function: Give Information; Write
Concepts and Vocabulary: Environment
Critical Thinking: Generate Ideas
Writing: Friendly Letter

LANGUAGE ARTS AND LITERATURE

1 Study Repetition and Author's Style Other examples of repetition:

- the words *one* and *everyone* in "One Light, One Sun"
- the verb *live* in "Big Beautiful Planet"
- the word *clean* in "Clean Rain."

Ask students to suggest a variety of possible repetitive phrases to add to the verse. Write them all, and have students try them out.

2 Write a Friendly Letter to Raffi Read the sample letter aloud. Call attention to the heading, greeting, body, and closing.

Ask students to point out the parts of the letter they will leave the same and the parts they will have to change when they write their own letters:

- The address will have to change.
- The greeting can stay the same.
- The body will change.
- The word "Sincerely" can stay but the names in the closing will change.

Suggest that students reread the songs in order to remember details they will need to write their letters.

CLOSE AND ASSESS

Have students write you a friendly letter about what they learned in this lesson.

LITERARY ANALYSIS

STUDY REPETITION AND AUTHOR'S STYLE

Learn About Repetition When writers use **repetition**, they say words or phrases more than once. Repetition shows the author's important ideas.

In "Evergreen, Everblue," Raffi wants people to protect our planet. He repeats the phrase "Help this planet Earth" to make his point.

Find Repetition Look back at the songs in "Protecting Our Planet." What words are repeated? How does repetition help you remember Raffi's main points?

Practice Copy the poem. Add a repetitive phrase.   Answers will vary.

> Drivers are driving everywhere,
> Their smog pollutes the nice, fresh air.
> Try to find a different way to go —
> Try a bike or the bus.
> A different way to go—
> Come on! It's up to us.

WRITING

WRITE A FRIENDLY LETTER TO RAFFI

Work with a partner. Tell Raffi what you learned from his songs. Be sure to tell:

- which song you like the most
- your ideas about the environment
- how you will help the Earth.

Write a Letter Use this model:

Heading	Cabrillo Middle School
	1423 Veteran Avenue
	Los Angeles, CA 90010
	March 19, 2004
Greeting	Dear Raffi,
Body	Our class read four of your songs. Our favorite is "Big Beautiful Planet" because it talks about how much we need the sun and the wind. We care about our environment, too. We are going to pick up trash at our school. Thank you for writing your songs.
Closing and signature	Sincerely, Binh and Tony

Send Your Letter Use this address:

c/o Troubadour Records
1078 Cambie Street
Vancouver, BC
Canada V6B 5L7

Multi-Level Strategies
WRITING OPTIONS FOR A FRIENDLY LETTER

BEGINNING Work with students to brainstorm two lists: one about threats to our environment and another listing ways students can help the Earth. Help students turn these ideas into sentences and record them, vocalizing as you write. Use some of these sentences to write a group letter.

INTERMEDIATE Ask students to review the instructions and take notes before they begin writing. Have them look back at the songs to choose their favorite one. Suggest that students review each other's letters and offer suggestions for improvement.

ADVANCED Ask students to do a Quickwrite. Suggest that they reread the instructions and then write their letters all the way through without stopping. Then have them review what they have written, make additions and revisions, and write out a final copy.

RESPOND

OBJECTIVES

PROPAGANDA

Function: Give Information

Concepts and Vocabulary:
Propaganda—*glittering generalities, bandwagon, name calling*

Speaking: Oral Report

Research Skills: Gather Information

Comprehension and Critical Thinking:
Identify Propaganda (glittering generalities, bandwagon, name-calling); Analyze Information; Evaluate Information

Literary Analysis: Advertisements

Representing: Chart

LANGUAGE ARTS AND LITERATURE

1 Learn About Propaganda As you introduce the list of propaganda techniques, include these ideas:

- The word *glittering* refers to something that sparkles and shines. A *glittering generality* may distract the reader from seeing the truth.

- The *bandwagon* was the vehicle that carried musicians at a circus. It was fun to join them for a ride.

- *Name calling* makes a competitor's product seem less desirable than the advertised product.

Ask students to illustrate the three propaganda techniques in the sample ad:

- Glittering generalities: "New," "Great"

- Bandwagon technique: "All the coolest kids are buying it."

- Name calling: "Other shampoos use chemicals that hurt the environment. We don't."

▶ **Practice Book** pages 110–111

CLOSE AND ASSESS

Ask: *What is the purpose of propaganda techniques?* (to make you feel or think a certain way)

ASSESSMENT
Selection Test 14 on page 65 of the Assessment Handbook tests students' mastery of the reading strategies and the vocabulary, comprehension, and language arts skills taught with this selection.

Respond to the Songs, continued
Language Arts and Literature

LITERARY ANALYSIS
REPRESENTING/SPEAKING

LEARN ABOUT PROPAGANDA

Propaganda techniques try to make you feel or think a certain way. Advertisements use propaganda techniques because they want you to buy what they are selling.

- A **glittering generality** says that the product is special. Some ads may say: *New!* and *Improved!*

- The **bandwagon technique** says that everyone buys the company's product. They may say: *Everyone should have this!*

- Companies use **name calling** to show that they are better than others. For example: *Other brands are more expensive.*

① Identify Propaganda Techniques Work with a partner. Find propaganda techniques in the ad.

② Study Modern Propaganda Techniques Find examples of propaganda techniques in magazines, newspapers, or television commercials. Make a T-chart to list the techniques that you find. Give examples of each technique.

③ Give an Oral Presentation Show the advertisement to the class. Talk about the propaganda techniques you found. Tell if the advertisement made you want to buy the product.

 Learn how to make a **chart**.
See Handbook page 341.
Learn how to give an **oral presentation** on pages 374–376.

REACHING ALL STUDENTS

Multi-Level Strategies
OPTIONS FOR LEARNING ABOUT PROPAGANDA

BEGINNING / **INTERMEDIATE** Post a chart showing the three propaganda techniques. Partners with different ability levels review print ads from magazines and newspapers and categorize the techniques they find. Partners can share their findings with the class.

ADVANCED Ask students to review radio and television ads for propaganda techniques. They can tape the ads and play them for the class, pausing to comment on techniques; or they can work with partners to act out the ads, encouraging the class to identify the techniques.

Content Area Connections

LANGUAGE ACQUISITION ASSESSMENT
See page 61 of the Assessment Handbook.

▶ SCIENCE

▶ TECHNOLOGY/MEDIA

RESEARCH ENDANGERED SPECIES

Endangered species are animals that are disappearing from our planet. Work with a group to study animals that are in danger today.

❶ **Find Information** Use science books, magazines, encyclopedias, or the Internet. Take notes. Try these Web sites, but remember that new sites appear every day!

INTERNET

INFORMATION ON-LINE

Web Sites:
➤ **Endangered Species**
  • www.sprint.com/epatrol
  • www.epa.gov/kids
  • www.amnh.org/exhibitions/endangered

❷ **Organize Your Information** Make a chart.

Endangered Species	Where They Live	Why They Are Endangered	How People Can Help
Bengal Tigers	India, China, Siberia,	hunting, fewer forests	save forests

❸ **Prepare Your Presentation** Tell your class about the endangered species you studied. Use drawings and maps to show information. Then listen to the other groups in your class. Add their information to your chart.

❹ **Write a Persuasive Statement** Study your chart. Then write about how people can help animals that are in danger.

Learn how to do **research**.
See Handbook pages 366–370.
Learn to use the **Internet** on pages 364–365.

Protecting Our Planet **221**

Research Skills

▶ **USE AUDIO-VISUAL RESOURCES**

TEACH Show students how audio-visual materials can enhance a presentation such as their endangered species presentations. Show a photo or video of Bengal tigers; find a map of India, China, or Siberia; play a CD or audio file recording of tiger sounds. Ask students how these materials helped them understand more about Bengal tigers.

Tell students that they can find audio and visual resources on the Internet, such as the live footage of the pandas on the San Diego Zoo link:

www.sandiegozoo.org/special/pandacam/index.html

PRACTICE Encourage students to find and include audio-visuals that complement their presentations.

▶ **Practice Book** pages 112–113

RESPOND

OBJECTIVES

ENDANGERED SPECIES

Function: Give Information; ❶ Persuade

Concepts and Vocabulary: Endangered Species—*ecology, ecosystem, endangered species, extinction*

Learning Strategies and Research Skills: Gather Information; Organize and Synthesize Information; Take Notes; Use the Library; Use an Encyclopedia; Use Audio-Visual Resources

Technology/ Media: Use the Internet

Representing: Chart

CONTENT AREA CONNECTIONS

❶ **Research Endangered Species** Ask students to help gather magazine and newspaper articles about endangered species. Arrange a library trip to allow students to use print or on-line encyclopedias and the Internet.

To Build Content Area Vocabulary Prepare students by introducing the following terms:

• *ecology, ecosystem*: Explain that *eco* is a Greek prefix meaning "house." Elicit that *ology* means "the study of." Have students put the meanings together to define *ecology* as "the study of where we live." Then define *ecosystem* as "the relationship between a community of animals, plants, and microscopic living things and the area in which they live." Give examples such as forests, deserts, jungles.

• *endangered species*: Explain that under the Endangered Species Act, the U.S. Fish and Wildlife Service lists animals or plants that need protection to prevent them from dying out. Once a species is listed, plans are put in place to help the species recover.

• *extinction*: define extinction as "the dying out of a species or animal."

CLOSE AND ASSESS

Ask each student to summarize the status of one of the endangered species the class studied.

INTRODUCE THEME 2

OBJECTIVES

Function: Engage in Discussion

Concepts and Vocabulary:
Community—*people, contributions, individual;* Disasters—*strike, recover*

Viewing: Interpret a Visual Image

Learning Strategies: Relate to Personal Experience; Use Graphic Organizers (Venn diagram)

Critical Thinking: Generate Ideas;
🟡 Make Comparisons

TAP PRIOR KNOWLEDGE

1 **Discuss Disasters** Ask: *What is a disaster?* Give examples of natural disasters, such as tornadoes and hurricanes. Ask: *What other kinds of natural disasters can you think of?* (floods, earthquakes, droughts)

Point out that disasters affect everyone in a community. Ask: *Has a disaster ever happened to your community? What happened? What did you do? What did people in your community do?*

VIEW AND DISCUSS

2 **Make Comparisons** Focus students' attention on the picture on page 222. Ask: *What do you think has happened here? What are these people doing?*

Make Venn diagrams comparing earthquakes to other events in which people in a community help each other. Prompt discussion with possible events such as a lost pet, a broken water main, or a fire.

After an Earthquake — After a Pet Loss

People:
need shelter
need food
need clothing

People help each other

People:
look for pet
post signs
make phone calls

Use the Discussion Prompts in the **Multi-Level Strategies** to allow all students to participate.

222 Unit 4 | Community

REACHING ALL STUDENTS

Multi-Level Strategies
DISCUSSION PROMPTS

BEGINNING Use the pictures on pages 240 and 248 or other images of people helping each other during community disasters or times of need. Ask students to point to the pictures that are similar to events they have experienced. Prompt discussion with yes/no and choice questions.

INTERMEDIATE Have students form small groups and discuss both personal and community times of need. Prompt discussion with multiple-choice questions and open-ended scenarios. Ask students to choose one comparison for their group's diagram.

ADVANCED Students may brainstorm several different community events and their needs with a partner and then create Venn diagrams.

Dealing With Disasters

- How do people in communities help each other every day?

- When disaster strikes, how do the contributions of each individual help the whole community recover?

- When is it important to help out in your community—every day, or when disaster strikes? Why?

THEME-RELATED BOOKS

Hurricane!
by Jonathan London

The sky grows dark and the wind begins to blow. A family in Puerto Rico hurries to a shelter until an unexpected hurricane is over.

BEGINNING

Flood
by Mary Calhoun

A family, facing the threat of flood, is determined to save their home. Then the levy breaks and they must flee to save their lives.

INTERMEDIATE

...If You Lived at the Time of the Great San Francisco Earthquake
by Ellen Levine

How did the 1906 earthquake sound? How did it feel? This book answers these and other questions.

ADVANCED

223

DISCUSS THE GUIDING QUESTIONS

3 Set the Theme Some key points to develop during the discussion are:

- People in communities help each other every day. The people who deliver mail, people who work at stores, and people who keep your community clean are helping you and everyone else in your community.

- When disaster strikes, it takes the efforts of every individual to help the community recover. Working together, tasks that may have seemed impossible to achieve are accomplished with greater ease.

- It is important to remember to help people in your community every day, not just when disaster strikes.

Form groups and use the **Multi-Level Strategies** to allow all students to participate.

CLOSE AND ASSESS

Ask small groups of students to summarize what they have learned in the lesson in one sentence. Have them report their sentences to the class.

Multi-Level Strategies

GROUPING GUIDELINES

BEGINNING Work with students as a group. Rephrase the questions for yes/no responses. Ask several yes/no questions for each concept to ensure students' comprehension. After each response, record the questions as statements on a chart, vocalizing as you write. Share these ideas with the class.

INTERMEDIATE Have students discuss the questions in small groups. Ask groups to share their responses with the class.

ADVANCED Invite students to discuss the questions with partners. Pairs can compare and discuss answers. Suggest that each group write their conclusions on a chart to share with the class.

THEME LIBRARY

■ *Hurricane!* by Jonathon London

Invite students to read *Hurricane!* Then help them evaluate the story by asking: *How well did the words and pictures convey the intensity of a hurricane? Think about what you learned about the 1998 hurricane in the Caribbean from "When Disaster Strikes." What does that help you understand about this story?* Encourage students to articulate the author's purpose in writing each hurricane selection, and the impact of genre on conveying the message.

OBJECTIVES

Function: Listen Actively; Recite;
⊕ Give and Carry Out Commands

Concepts and Vocabulary:
Words About Earthquakes

Patterns and Structures: ⊕ Commands

Speaking and Listening: Role-Play

Learning Strategy: Use Graphic
Organizers (category chart)

Critical Thinking: Generate Ideas

START WITH A COMMON EXPERIENCE

1 **Listen to a Poem** Play
the **Language Tape/CD**
or read aloud the poem
"When the Ground Shakes." Use the
photos and diagrams to develop
meaning for the description of an
earthquake. Have students point to
visual examples of *slipping, cracking,
earth layers shifting, shock waves.*

Tape 1B
CD 1
Track 8

2 **Recite a Poem** Have students recite
the poem several times.

> Use the Reciting Options in the
> **Multi-Level Strategies** to include
> students at all proficiency levels.

3 **Model How to Give Commands** Tell
students that in a disaster, such as an
earthquake, emergency personnel
need to give commands to help
people survive. Use the following
Think Aloud to help students learn to
give commands:

> **How to Give Commands**
>
> • Name something to do in an
>   earthquake: *People should get in
>   doorways. They should not be near
>   a window.*
>
> • Tell someone else what to do:
>   *Get in that doorway. Stay away
>   from the windows.*

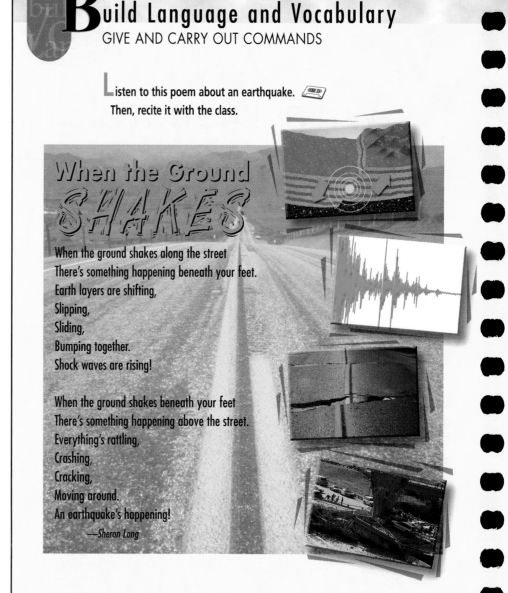

Build Language and Vocabulary
GIVE AND CARRY OUT COMMANDS

Listen to this poem about an earthquake.
Then, recite it with the class.

When the Ground SHAKES

When the ground shakes along the street
There's something happening beneath your feet.
Earth layers are shifting,
Slipping,
Sliding,
Bumping together.
Shock waves are rising!

When the ground shakes beneath your feet
There's something happening above the street.
Everything's rattling,
Crashing,
Cracking,
Moving around.
An earthquake's happening!

—*Sheron Long*

224 Unit 4 | Community

REACHING ALL STUDENTS

Multi-Level Strategies
RECITING OPTIONS

BEGINNING Read aloud the poem one stanza at a time, using gestures
and illustrations to clarify meaning. Then play the audio recording from the
Language Tape/CD. Prompt students to chime in as they can, particularly
on the one-word middle section of each stanza.

INTERMEDIATE Read aloud the poem or play the audio recording, as
students read along in the book. Assign some students to be shock waves
rising and others to be earth layers shifting. Ask them to role-play the actions
described in the poem as they recite.

ADVANCED Have students participate in the read-aloud/role-play.
Invite a group of volunteers to memorize the poem and present it as a
rhythmic chant with additional role-play ideas as well as sound effects.

BRAINSTORM IDEAS

What should you do when an earthquake happens? Record your ideas in a list and discuss each of them.

> **What To Do During an Earthquake**
> - get under a table
> - go outside in the open
> - stay away from windows and other glass

BUILD YOUR VOCABULARY

Words About Earthquakes You never know when an earthquake will happen, but it is a good idea to be prepared. Add a column to the chart with ideas about how to prepare for an earthquake. Then, add another column with ideas about ways to help after an earthquake. Use words from the **Word Bank**.

Word Bank

batteries
clothing
food
mess
plan
shelter
supplies
water

How To Prepare for an Earthquake	What To Do During an Earthquake	How To Help After an Earthquake
• make a plan to meet family members • keep candles, flashlights, and batteries in the house	• stand in a doorway • get under a table • go outside in the open • stay away from windows and other glass	• give extra clothing to shelters • serve food at a shelter • help clean up the mess

---

USE LANGUAGE STRUCTURES ▶ COMMANDS

Speaking and Listening: Role-Play Disaster Responses Work with a group. Choose one person to be an earthquake expert. The expert will give the group commands about what to do before, during, or after an earthquake. Use ideas from the chart. The other group members will act out each command.

Examples:
Make a plan to meet family members before an earthquake.
Stand in a doorway during an earthquake.
Give extra clothing to shelters after an earthquake.

Build Language and Vocabulary **225**

---

4 Brainstorm Ideas Remind students to give every group member a chance to share ideas during the brainstorm. Stress the importance of consensus about what to include in the list.

5 Build Your Vocabulary: Words About Earthquakes You may want to provide action verbs and/or sentence frames for students to use in building sentences.

6 Use Language Structures: Commands Teach commands, using the definition and examples on **Transparency 63**. Then have students complete the Try It! activity.

Speaking and Listening: Role-Play Disaster Responses Conduct the activity at the bottom of page 225. Suggest that students rotate the role of earthquake expert to give everyone a chance to practice giving commands.

▌ Use the **Multi-Level Strategies** for Speaking and Listening Options to adjust instruction.

▶ **Practice Book** page 114

CLOSE AND ASSESS

Have students form a circle. Provide the group with an eraser, and have them take turns giving and following commands about the eraser. For example: *Toss the eraser to Juan. Put the eraser on a desk.*

Multi-Level Strategies
SPEAKING AND LISTENING OPTIONS

BEGINNING / **INTERMEDIATE** Beginning students may want to role-play the commands given by Intermediate students. Encourage the student acting as an earthquake expert to use gestures to clarify meaning for the students acting out the commands. Assign an assistant earthquake expert to repeat each command, in order to provide practice to as many students as possible.

ADVANCED Encourage students to expand upon the chart ideas when issuing commands. For example: *Stand in a doorway with your arms protecting your head. Get under a table and put your head on your knees.*

Transparency 63 / Master 63

Build Language and Vocabulary **T225**

PREPARE TO READ

OBJECTIVES

THINK ABOUT WHAT YOU KNOW

Reading Strategies: Build Background; Activate Prior Knowledge

Critical Thinking:
Relate Causes and Effects

LEARN KEY VOCABULARY Ⓣ

Vocabulary Strategy: Relate Words

LEARN ABOUT PLAYS

Reading Strategy: Use Text Structures and Features in Plays

THINK ABOUT WHAT YOU KNOW

1 Idea Exchange Group students with different English proficiency levels. Use the suggestions on page T227 to guide the Idea Exchange. As students discuss earthquakes, be sensitive to and acknowledge their fears.

LEARN KEY VOCABULARY

2 Relate Words Read each vocabulary word and its defining text aloud. Then conduct the activity.

▌ Use the Vocabulary Options in the **Multi-Level Strategies** to adjust instruction.

▶ **Practice Book** page 115

LEARN ABOUT PLAYS

3 Model How to Read a Script Define *play* and *script*. Demonstrate the steps in the box with **Transparency 64**:

- Use the red annotations on the transparency to introduce the *scene, setting,* and *stage directions.*

- Discuss stage directions and dialogue. Invite volunteers to take the parts of Edith, Daisy, and Mrs. Somers and act out the scene.

CLOSE AND ASSESS

Ask: *What could you teach a friend about how to read a script?*

EARTHQUAKE AT DAWN

play
by Kristiana Gregory

Prepare to Read

THINK ABOUT WHAT YOU KNOW

Idea Exchange Work with a group to study the diagrams on the next page. Discuss how earthquakes happen with your group.

epidemic An **epidemic** is a sickness or disease that spreads quickly.

restore power When you **restore power**, you get the electricity to work again.

rise When things begin to **rise**, they start to get up.

ruins Fallen buildings, damaged roads, or bridges that cannot be fixed are called **ruins**.

separate When something is **separate**, it is by itself.

sewer A **sewer** is an underground tunnel that carries wastes from houses and buildings.

supplies Materials that people need are called **supplies**.

take good care of When you **take good care** of someone, you give that person special attention.

tent city A **tent** is a shelter made of cloth. A **tent city** is a large area with many tents.

threatened If you are **threatened**, you are warned that something bad may happen.

Answers to the vocabulary activity will vary. See sample responses on word web.

LEARN KEY VOCABULARY

Relate Words Study the new words. Then copy the web below. Work with a group to sort the new words into the web.

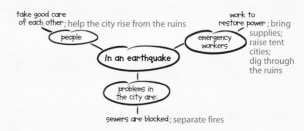

LEARN ABOUT PLAYS

A **play** is a story that is acted out. The written form of a play is the **script**. The script tells the actors what to say and do.

> **READING STRATEGY**
> **How to Read a Script**
> 1. **Acts** and **scenes** show the time and setting of the action.
> 2. **Stage directions** tell the players what to do.
> 3. **Speaker words** tell who is speaking.
> 4. **Dialogue** is words the characters say.

Now read "Earthquake at Dawn." Picture the stage. Imagine the players speaking. Imagine them acting out the stage directions.

226 Unit 4 | Community

REACHING ALL STUDENTS

▌ **Multi-Level Strategies**
VOCABULARY OPTIONS

BEGINNING Draw simple pictures (*sewers, tent city*) Use realia (*supplies*), pictures from the selections (*ruins*), and pantomime to demonstrate meaning. Create a group word web.

INTERMEDIATE / **ADVANCED** Students work in small groups to create word webs using the new vocabulary. Display and discuss their work as a class. Advanced students can also use the completed web to write a paragraph.

Transparency 64 / Master 64

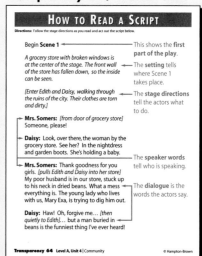

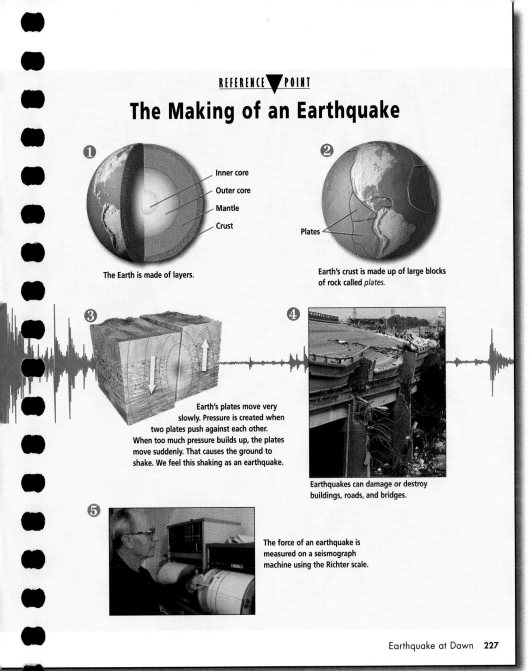

The Making of an Earthquake

1

Inner core
Outer core
Mantle
Crust

The Earth is made of layers.

2

Plates

Earth's crust is made up of large blocks
of rock called *plates*.

3

Earth's plates move very
slowly. Pressure is created when
two plates push against each other.
When too much pressure builds up, the plates
move suddenly. That causes the ground to
shake. We feel this shaking as an earthquake.

4

Earthquakes can damage or destroy
buildings, roads, and bridges.

5

The force of an earthquake is
measured on a seismograph
machine using the Richter scale.

Earthquake at Dawn **227**

CONDUCT THE IDEA EXCHANGE

Learn About Earthquakes Read aloud the captions and labels. Have students create a cause/effect graphic organizer to summarize key information. Point out that an effect can also be the cause of another effect.

Cause #1 Earth's plates move slowly.

↓

Effect #1
Cause #2 Plates press together.

↓

Effect #2
Cause #3 This makes pressure.

↓

Effect #3
Cause #4 Pressure builds up.

↓

Effect #4
Cause #5 The plates move suddenly.

↓

Effect #5 The ground shakes.

Use the images on pages 222, 224, 227, and 244 to prompt further discussion about earthquakes and their aftermath.

Science Connection

PLATE TECTONICS

Materials: clay slabs, sliced bread (fresh, stale, and toasted), graham crackers, or other materials to represent various types of earth; toothpicks; tape

Define *plate tectonics* as "the movement in the Earth's crust that creates changes to the surface of the Earth." Students conduct an experiment to demonstrate how plate tectonics can cause the ground to move and cause damage. Partners place materials representing Earth's plates side-by-side and touching, on a flat surface. They stand toothpicks in the "plates" to represent trees, buildings, and people, and lay tape across the "plates" to represent roads. Have students slowly push the edges of the "plates" against each other until something gives.

Before students begin, model how to complete the Scientific Method Chart on **Transparency 65** by reviewing the steps taken to set up the experiment and recording several hypotheses suggested by students. Then, distribute copies of **Master 65** to partners and have them perform the experiment, record the results they observe, and draw conclusions.

Transparency 65 / Master 65

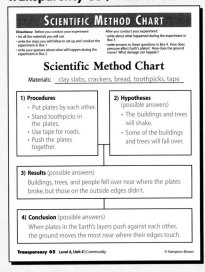

SCIENTIFIC METHOD CHART

Directions: Before you conduct your experiment:
• list all the materials you will use
• write the steps you will follow to set up and conduct the experiment in Box 1
• write your guesses about what will happen during the experiment in Box 2

After you conduct your experiment:
• write about what happened during the experiment in Box 3
• write answers to these questions in Box 4. How does pressure affect Earth's plates? How does the ground move? What damage can happen?

Scientific Method Chart

Materials: clay slabs, crackers, bread, toothpicks, tape

1) Procedures
• Put plates by each other.
• Stand toothpicks in the plates.
• Use tape for roads.
• Push the plates together.

2) Hypotheses (possible answers)
• The buildings and trees will shake.
• Some of the buildings and trees will fall over.

3) Results (possible answers)
Buildings, trees, and people fell over near where the plates broke, but those on the outside edges didn't.

4) Conclusion (possible answers)
When plates in the Earth's layers push against each other, the ground moves the most near where their edges touch.

Transparency 65 Level A, Unit 4 | Community   © Hampton-Brown

Earthquake at Dawn **T227**

READ THE SELECTION

OBJECTIVES

Listening: Listen to a Preview
Reading Strategies: Preview; Predict
Literary Analysis: Stage Play

INTRODUCE THE SELECTION

1. **Preview and Predict** Read aloud the title, author, and text on the page. Ask: *What year and in what city does this play take place? What has happened? Who are the characters? What do you think will happen to them?*
2. **Identify Genre: Stage Play** Ask students if they have ever seen a play. Have them turn back to the pictures of student performances on pages 37–38. Then, explain that this selection is a script for a stage play. Review the text features of a script: acts, scenes, stage directions, dialogue.
3. **Audio Walk-Through** Tape 4B CD 4 Track 4 Play the Audio Walk-Through for "Earthquake at Dawn" on the **Selection Tape/CD** to give students an overall idea of the play.

EARTHQUAKE AT DAWN

A PLAY IN ONE ACT
by
Kristiana Gregory

Twenty-two year old photographer Edith Irvine, her father, and her traveling companion, Daisy Valentine, travel from their home in Stockton, California, to San Francisco. There, the young women plan to board a ship to Australia to exhibit Edith's work. They arrive in San Francisco on April 18, 1906, just in time to experience a powerful earthquake. As they wander the streets of the city, they are separated from Edith's father and soon become involved in helping victims of the disaster.

SETTING

TIME:
MORNING OF APRIL 18, 1906

PLACE:
CITY OF SAN FRANCISCO, CALIFORNIA,
AFTER AN ENORMOUS EARTHQUAKE

CHARACTERS

EDITH IRVINE:
A 22-YEAR-OLD PHOTOGRAPHER PREPARING FOR A TRIP TO AUSTRALIA

DAISY VALENTINE:
EDITH'S 15-YEAR-OLD TRAVELING COMPANION

CITIZENS OF SAN FRANCISCO:
MR. AND MRS. SOMERS, STORE OWNERS
MARY EXA, FRIEND OF THE SOMERS
MR. AND MRS. WESTLAKE, AN ELDERLY COUPLE

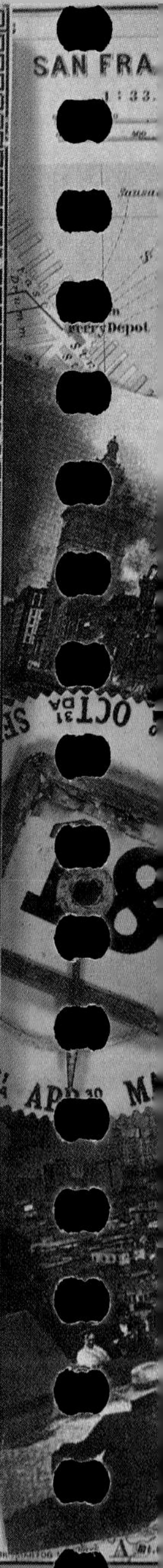

Earthquake at Dawn
by Kristiana Gregory

Theme Connection "Earthquake at Dawn" tells the story of how people in the community of San Francisco helped each other after the earthquake disaster of 1906.

Selection Summary and Background The play's main character, Edith Irvine, is based on a young photographer by the same name who photographed post-quake San Francisco and later wrote about her experiences.

Author Awards Kristiana Gregory's historical novel, *Earthquake at Dawn*, was the 1992 NCSS-CBC Outstanding Trade Book in the field of Social Studies. Her first book, *Jenny of the Tetons*, was also an NCSS-CBC award winner in addition to receiving the Golden Kite Award.

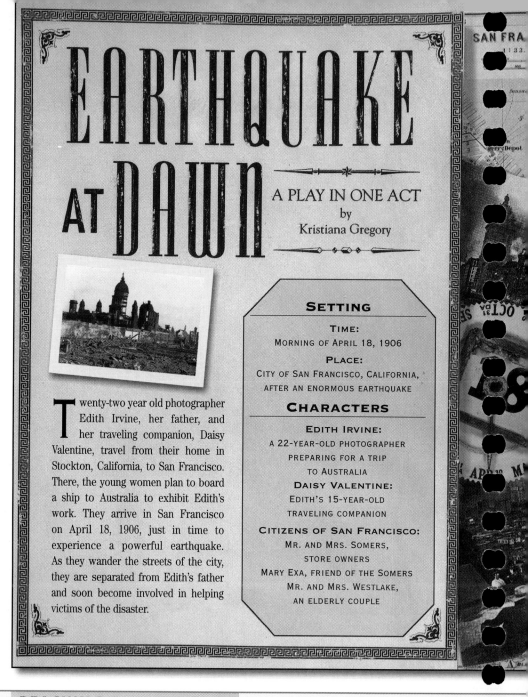

REACHING ALL STUDENTS

THE BASICS BOOKSHELF

■ ***Power Out!*** by Sherilin Chanek

It doesn't take an earthquake to throw a city into turmoil—a simple power-outage will do it. This minute-by-minute account of how a city copes with a potential disaster combines simple text and bold illustrations to introduce basic vocabulary related to community, community services, and telling time.

For Lesson Plans: See the Teacher's Guide for ***The Basics Bookshelf***.

1

HELPING HANDS

Edith and Daisy meet some earthquake victims and help with a rescue.

Begin Scene 1

A grocery store with broken windows is at the center of the stage. The front wall of the store has fallen down, so the inside can be seen.

*[Enter Edith and Daisy, walking though the **ruins** of the city. Their clothes are torn and dirty.]*

Mrs. Somers: *[from door of grocery store]*

Someone, please!

Daisy: Look, over there, the woman by

Use text features: Point to the setting and stage direction. Say: This is the setting of Scene 1. This is a stage direction that tells the actors what to do.

the grocery store. See her? In the **nightdress** and garden boots. She's holding a baby.

Mrs. Somers: Thank goodness for you girls. *[pulls Edith and Daisy into her store]* My poor husband is in our store, **stuck** up to his neck in dried beans. **What a mess** everything is. The young lady who lives with us, Mary Exa, is trying to dig him out.

Daisy: Haw! Oh, forgive me . . . *[then quietly to Edith]* . . . but a man buried in beans is the funniest thing I've ever heard!

Edith: Hush up now, Daisy. Let's help the poor **fellow**. He may be hurt, you know. Clarify: *Hush up means "be quiet".*

Mrs. Somers: It was that last **shock** that did it. **Eight-fourteen sharp**, and everything that didn't fall the first time fell then. Mercy!

---

nightdress clothing for sleeping, women's pajamas
stuck trapped, unable to move
What a mess How dirty, How untidy

fellow man
shock small earthquake
Eight-fourteen sharp At exactly fourteen minutes after eight o'clock

Earthquake at Dawn   **229**

READ PAGE 229

OBJECTIVES

Function: Read a Selection
Listening: Listen to a Selection
Reading and Learning Strategies: Set a Purpose for Reading; Use Text Structures and Features in Plays

SET PURPOSE

4 Read aloud the introduction to pages 229 to 231. Say: *As you read the stage directions and dialogue in the script, try to imagine the play on stage.*

READ AND THINK

Tape 4B
CD 4
Track 5

5 Strategy Focus: Use Text Structures and Features in Plays
Involve students in reading pages 229 to 231 of the selection, completing **Transparency 66** as they read. Encourage them to include details they might use to create a set and costumes for a production.

Invite volunteers to point out examples of speaker words, dialogue, and stage directions.

Choose Reading Options in the **Multi-Level Strategies** to include students at all proficiency levels.

The recording of "Earthquake at Dawn" on the **Selection Tape/CD** offers an oral language model and the opportunity to build reading fluency.

Multi-Level Strategies
READING OPTIONS FOR LESSONS 4–6

BEGINNING Read aloud the script, changing your inflection for each character and following the stage directions, or play the recording of the play on the **Selection Tape/CD**. Pause frequently to restate and clarify meaning. Refer to the pictures and the red annotations on the facsimile pages. Record clues to the setting on **Transparency 66** as a group.

INTERMEDIATE / **ADVANCED** Ask students to read the script independently, using a dictionary to learn the meaning of unfamiliar words. Distribute **Master 66** and have students complete the chart on their own as they read. Students can work in groups of seven to compare their charts, and then choose parts to read the play aloud.

Transparency 66 / Master 66

NOTE-TAKING CHART

Directions: "Earthquake at Dawn" takes place in 1906. As you read the script, look for clues in the text and pictures that tell you how people dress and talk and how the city looks. Write clues about the setting in the chart below.

Earthquake at Dawn

1. How people dress	women wear petticoats men and women wear hats women wear long skirts
2. How people talk	"Mercy!" "Ladies, I thank you." "Please take no offense"
3. How the city looks	stores keep food in barrels ruins everywhere buildings don't look modern

Transparency 66 Level A, Unit 4 | Community   © Hampton-Brown

Earthquake at Dawn **T229**

OBJECTIVES

Vocabulary Strategy:
Use New Words in Context

Grammar: Indefinite Adjectives;
Ordinal Numbers

Reading Strategies: Use Text Structures
and Features in Plays

Comprehension: Make an Inference;
Identify Details, Cause and Effect

REVIEW KEY VOCABULARY

6 Use New Words in Context Have
students reread the vocabulary
words and definitions on page 226.
Write each word or phrase and its
definition on a sheet of paper.
Distribute one of these sheets to
partners or triads and ask them to
write a sentence on it using the new
word or phrase.

After a few minutes, each group
passes its paper to another group.
Groups will then write a sentence for
their new word.

Continue the process, with groups
passing the words and sentences
around until they receive the
sheet they started with and its
accompanying sentences. Have each
group choose one or two sentences
to read aloud.

Use visuals: Pause to show students a map of northern California. Point out San Francisco and Stockton.

*[Edith and Daisy join Mary Exa. They
begin digging into the beans with their
hands to free Mr. Somers.]*

Edith: Hoist!   **Role-Play:** Students can act out hoist-
ing Mr. Somers out of the dry beans.

Mary Exa: Here he comes! Uh!

Mr. Somers: *[brushing himself off]*
Ladies, I thank you. I seem to be fine.
Are you all right, dear?

Mrs. Somers: Yes, baby Timothy and
I are fine, but I have never seen such
a mess in my life!

Edith: Allow me to **introduce myself**.
I'm Edith Irvine and this is **my
traveling companion**, Daisy

Valentine. We were **to set sail** for
Australia this afternoon. The **docks**
are such a mess, I doubt that any
ships will sail. Now, I guess we'll
be going back home to Stockton.

Mrs. Somers: *[looking at the girls
kindly]* How dreadful for you. But
mercy, where are my manners? You
must be hungry. Let's see what we
can offer you. Edith and Daisy, will
you take baby Timothy while we look
through this mess for something we
can eat? Mary, see what you can find.

Hoist Lift
introduce myself tell you who I am, tell you my name
my traveling companion the friend I am traveling with

to set sail going to travel on a boat
docks place where the ships load and unload goods
and people

REACHING ALL STUDENTS

Vocabulary
DRAMA WORDS

Brainstorm a list of stage directions with
students: *enter, exit, center stage, left,
right, loudly, quietly, slowly, quickly.* Ask
volunteers to demonstrate these
directions. Write each stage direction on
an index card or slip of paper. Have
students form two teams and play
charades with the cards.

Social Studies Connection
COMMUNITY SERVICES

Make a class chart showing
organizations and how they serve the
community on a daily basis. Then, create
a third column that shows the services
these organizations might perform in a
disaster situation, such as an earthquake.

Organization	Everyday Services	Disaster Services
fire dept.	fire safety inspections, put out fires, rescue people and animals	control and put out fires, rescue people and animals
police dept.	patrol streets, direct traffic	protect people from violence and theft
EMT/ambulance	take hurt or sick people to hospital	give medical service to hurt people

Ask: Why does Edith think that the baby's diaper needs changing?

Edith: *[holding the baby up and at arm's length]* Daisy, I think the baby **needs changing**. But I'm smelling something else. I smell smoke.

Mr. Somers: Look, over there, toward the **harbor**! Can you see all those **plumes** of smoke? . . . nine . . . ten . . . eleven . . . Eleven **separate** fires . . . Chief Sullivan's going to be busy this morning!

Mary Exa: *[proudly]* Chief Sullivan has an **outstanding fire department**. San Francisco will **be safe in his hands**.

Mr. Somers: Oh yes, dear, no worries. *[pulling two wooden chairs out to the sidewalk and motioning for his wife and Edith to sit]*

Daisy: Oh, look. There's a sign on that pole down the street. Edith, let's go see what it says.

[Edith hands the baby to Mrs. Somers. She and Daisy exit the stage.]

Ask: Who is left on stage?

End Scene 1

BEFORE YOU MOVE ON...

1. **Inference** When Edith and Daisy meet Mrs. Somers, she is wearing a nightdress. What do you think she was doing when the earthquake happened?
2. **Details** Why can't Edith and Daisy sail to Australia as they had planned?
3. **Cause and Effect** What might cause a fire to start after an earthquake?

---

needs changing needs to have his diaper changed, has a dirty diaper

harbor place where ships stay when they are not sailing

plumes long, vertical clouds

outstanding fire department excellent team that puts out fires

be safe in his hands not be in danger because he is in charge

Earthquake at Dawn **231**

CHECK COMPREHENSION

7 Answers to "Before You Move On"

1. **Inference** Answers may vary. Mrs. Somers was probably sleeping or had just gotten up when the earthquake happened.

2. **Details** Edith and Daisy can't sail to Australia as planned because the ships' docks were damaged by the earthquake.

3. **Cause and Effect** Students' answers may include such events as gas explosions and candles falling over.

CLOSE AND ASSESS

Ask: *What have you learned about reading a script? What do stage directions tell? What is dialogue?*

Vocabulary
MULTIPLE-MEANING WORDS

Explain that some words can mean different things depending on how they're used in a sentence. As an example, define the word *poor* as "to have no money." Then read aloud Mrs. Somers' line on page 229: *My poor husband is in our store, stuck up to his neck in dried beans.* Have students discuss the differing meanings of *poor.* Help students find other examples of multiple meaning words in the selection.

Grammar Minilesson

▶ **INDEFINITE ADJECTIVES AND ORDINALS**

TEACH Ask: *What was the first thing that happened in the play? The last thing?* After students answer, say: *Words like* first *and* last *tell the order of things.*

Line up objects, such as pencils, and give students directions using ordinals: *Pick up the second pencil.* As students carry out the direction, have them say: *This is the second pencil.*

Use a similar procedure for quantity words: *many, some, few,* and so on. Introduce them by saying: *Mr. Somers was buried in some beans.*

PRACTICE Have small groups work together to create illustrated charts of ordinals and quantity words. The chart of ordinals, or order words, should show a row of objects, with each object labeled: *first, second, third,* and so on. The quantity words chart should show groups of objects representing indefinite numbers. Provide a word bank of quantity words for students.

some	a few	all
several	many	

▶ **Practice Book** page 116

Earthquake at Dawn **T231**

OBJECTIVES

Function: Read a Selection
Grammar: Contractions
Listening: Listen to a Selection
Reading and Learning Strategies: Set a Purpose for Reading; Use Text Structures and Features in Plays
Comprehension: Identify Details; Identify Character's Motive; Make an Inference

SET PURPOSE

1 Read aloud the introduction to page 232. Say: *Read to understand how the mayor tries to keep the city under control.*

READ AND THINK

Tape 4B
CD 4
Track 5

2 Strategy Focus: Use Text Structures and Features in Plays
Involve students in reading page 232 of the selection.

See the **Multi-Level Strategies** on page T229 to involve all students in the reading experience.

---

② SIGNS OF TROUBLE

The mayor tries to keep the city under control.
His message scares Edith and Daisy.

Ask students to point to the setting and stage direction for Scene 2.

Begin Scene 2

A street corner with a telephone pole.

[Enter two men carrying hammers and signs. Edith and Daisy then enter as the men begin to nail the signs to the telephone pole.]

Daisy: *[grabs Edith's arm]* What do those signs say? The ones those men are nailing on the telephone pole.

Edith: *[reads aloud]* **SEWERS** BLOCKED. DON'T USE TOILETS. **EPIDEMIC THREATENED. OBEY ORDERS** OR GET SHOT.

[men exit stage]

Daisy: Do you think they're serious?

Edith: *[laughing]:* Of course not. There's not a man alive who would shoot a lady for doing what she needs to do.

Daisy: What does this one say, Edith?

Edith: It's from the mayor of San Francisco. **Basically** it says, oh dear, oh dear . . . !

Daisy: Edith! What?

Edith: It says that soldiers and police are **authorized** to KILL any and all persons caught **looting** or **committing** any other crime . . . and the gas and lighting companies won't **restore power** until the mayor says to. Dear me. Isn't this **illegal**?

[sound of gunshot]

Clarify: *Alarmed* means "surprised" or "frightened." Daisy is alarmed by what the signs say.

Daisy: *[alarmed]:* Oh!

Edith: There's trouble somewhere. Let's get back to Mrs. Somers' house!

[Edith and Daisy rush off stage.]

End Scene 2

BEFORE YOU MOVE ON...

1. Details What warnings were posted after the earthquake?
2. Character's Motive At first Edith laughs about the warning signs. Why does she change her mind?
3. Inference Why do you think the mayor threatens to shoot people who don't follow the rules?

OBEY ORDERS Do what you are told, Follow instructions
Basically The main thing
authorized given permission

looting stealing
committing carrying out, doing
illegal against the law, not allowed

232 Unit 4 | Community

REACHING ALL STUDENTS

INTERNET

HEALTH CONNECTION

Tell students that people who live in earthquake-prone areas should take precautions. Have students use the Internet to research earthquake safety precautions and then create public service posters.

Web Sites
Web sites undergo frequent modifications, but here are some you may want to suggest to students:

quake.wr.usgs.gov
wwwneic.cr.usgs.gov

Language Development
GIVE INFORMATION

Assign each of the three scenes from the play to a different team. Although radio broadcasting was not widespread until 1916, ask students to imagine that they are radio news reporters in San Francisco at the time of the 1906 earthquake. Ask students to create news reports of the events from their scene. Each team can perform their reports in order of the scenes as "late-breaking news." Students might play the role of eye-witnesses and conduct interviews as part of their reports.

San Francisco, California. April 18, 1906. Soldiers walk past burning buildings and ruins.

Earthquake at Dawn **233**

1. **Details** Warnings were posted not to use toilets because sewers were blocked and an epidemic was threatened. Police were authorized to shoot anyone looting or committing other crimes. Gas and lighting companies would not restore power until the mayor gave his permission.

2. **Character's Motive** Edith stops laughing about the warning signs when she hears a gunshot and realizes that the warnings are real.

3. **Inference** Answers may vary. The mayor threatens to shoot people who don't follow the rules because he wants everyone to know this is a serious situation and people should obey the rules.

CLOSE AND ASSESS

Give partners an index card. Ask students to illustrate or write a description of the setting in Scene 2. Each student signs the card and partners present it as they exit the class. Check cards to assess students' comprehension.

Science Connection
TECHNOLOGY

Tell students that telephones existed in 1906, but many other communication technologies available today did not exist at that time. Invite students to think about how messages such as those nailed to the telephone poles would be posted today. Then ask: *What technologies do we have today that would help us survive an earthquake?* (seismology equipment, radio, Internet, cellular phones, etc.) Make a chart showing how these technologies could help in a disaster.

Grammar Minilesson

▶ **CONTRACTIONS**

TEACH Point to Daisy's second line on page 232: *Do you think they're serious?* Then say: *The word* they're *is a contraction—a short way of writing two words. The apostrophe shows where letters were left out when the two words were joined.*

Write *they are;* then erase the letter *a* and replace it with an apostrophe to illustrate how the contraction was formed.

PRACTICE Divide students into small groups. Assign two pages of the play to each group. Ask students to find and list all of the contractions on their assigned pages of the play. Have students use Handbook page 437 to determine which words make up each contraction. Students should then rewrite the sentences containing contractions, replacing each contraction with the two words that form it.

▶ **Practice Book** page 117

READ PAGES 234–235

OBJECTIVES

Function: Read a Selection
Listening: Listen to a Selection
Reading and Learning Strategies: Set a Purpose for Reading; Use Text Structures and Features in Plays; Visualize
Literary Analysis: Evaluate the Impact of Medium on Meaning

SET PURPOSE

1 Read aloud the introduction to pages 234 to 236. Set the purpose for reading: *Read to see how people cope with the continuing aftershocks. Continue to look for clues to the setting.*

READ AND THINK

Tape 4B
CD 4
Track 5

2 **Strategy Focus: Use Text Structures and Features in Plays** Involve students in reading pages 234–236 of the selection.

▮ Use the **Multi-Level Strategies** on page T229 to tailor the reading experience to proficiency levels.

3

MOVING ON

Aftershocks continue. Edith, Daisy, and their new friends decide to join the people in the park.

Begin Scene 3

Inside the upstairs apartment above the Somers' grocery store.

[Mr. and Mrs. Somers and Mary Exa are pulling blankets and mattresses off beds.]

Ask: What is the setting for Scene 3? What do the actors do first in this scene?

Edith: *[offstage]* Hello, where is everybody?

Mrs. Somers: We're here, upstairs. We're just getting some things. Mr. Somers, please carry that **mattress** and those blankets out to the yard.

[Mr. Somers exits with mattress and blankets. Edith and Daisy enter.]

Mrs. Somers: Ladies, please **take no offense** if I offer you a fresh change of clothes. *[hands clothes to Edith and Daisy]* There is a clean blouse for each of you, and two clean **petticoats**. **Unfortunately**, there is only one **spare** hat.

[Another powerful jolt strikes. Everybody falls to the ground, hands over head.] **Restate:** Another strong earthquake occurs.

Mrs. Somers: Oh, my! More glass is breaking . . . watch out!

Edith: *[hugs Daisy]* Are you all right? Hurry. Let's **change into** these clothes while we can. Here you go, Daisy. You take this lovely hat. You look so good in blue. It seems silly to worry about our clothing at a time like this, but I do feel better somehow.

---

mattress pad to sleep on—usually on a bed
take no offense do not be angry with me
petticoats skirts to wear under dresses

Unfortunately Sadly
spare extra
change into put on, get dressed in

234 **Unit 4** │ Community

REACHING ALL STUDENTS

COMMUNITY CONNECTION

Disaster Relief Invite community workers from the fire department, Red Cross, or neighborhood emergency response to talk to the class about dealing with disasters. Prepare students by brainstorming questions about how they can help their community in times of disaster. Have students write their questions on a chart. At the conclusion of the talk, complete the chart and have students make individual lists of things they can do to help during a disaster.

HOME CONNECTION

Are We Prepared? Send home a copy of *High Point Newsletter 8* in the **Teacher's Resource Book**. (See pages 146–152.) In this home activity, students enlist the help of family members to list supplies they have at home that would be useful after a natural disaster. Then, they determine what supplies they might gather to be better prepared, and list these as well. Have students bring their lists to class and compare them.

[*Edith and Daisy go behind a screen, change clothes, and return.*]

Mary Exa: I don't think it's safe to go down into the store right now . . . things keep shaking so . . . but Mr. Somers did bring up some fruit. We have no water to drink, but these oranges will help our **thirst**. Here . . .

[*Mary hands out oranges.*]

[*Enter an elderly couple.*]

Mrs. Somers [*greeting the couple*]: Hello! Daisy and Edith, these are our neighbors, Mr. and Mrs. Westlake!

Mrs. Westlake: We've had **a terrible time**. Our **canaries flew off** when their **cages** fell over. We barely saved the cat before the chimney crashed onto our bed. I **hollered** to the Davenports, but they didn't answer. Not a word. Oh dear . . . I'm afraid something **horrible** has happened to them. **Pose choices:** Do you think the Davenports are neighbors or canaries?

[*Enter Mr. Somers.*]

Mr. Somers: We have to get out of here. The city is burning. Every **jolt brings down** more buildings. I don't think the store is safe anymore.

Mr. Westlake: We saw people **heading for** Golden Gate Park. They are using whatever they have to **set up** a **tent city**. **Clarify:** Golden Gate Park is a large, open area in the city of San Francisco. It was a safe place after the earthquake.

---

thirst need to drink something
a terrible time bad experiences
canaries flew off pet birds flew away
cages wire houses for birds
hollered called out, yelled

horrible very bad, awful
jolt brings down aftershock knocks down
heading for going to, moving towards
set up put up, build

MORE TO EXPLORE

Act Out the Play Invite students to stage a performance of the play. Work with students to assign roles, collect props and costumes, and rehearse lines. Suggest that students invite friends and family to their performance. Several students can work together to make posters and invitations. Include all students in the preparations and performance.

For Multi-Level Strategies: To include all proficiency levels in acting out the play, assign Beginning students to make posters, and collect props. Create non-speaking roles for these students if necessary. Intermediate students can make invitations and work with Beginning students to design posters and props. Advanced students can be "directors" and help other students in their roles.

Literary Analysis Minilesson

▶ **EVALUATE THE IMPACT OF MEDIUM ON MEANING**

TEACH Have students read pages 229–231 again. Present different types of reports about the 1906 San Francisco earthquake: newspaper reports from the time, photographs, eyewitness accounts, textbook and history book descriptions of the event. (Gregory's novel *Earthquake at Dawn* includes an excellent bibliography of resources.)

Ask students which format for telling this story made the most powerful impression on them and why.

PRACTICE Ask students to collect various media reports of a recent disaster—newspaper reports, television coverage, Internet postings, and personal accounts. Ask students to identify the strengths and weaknesses of each media report. Ask: *What did you learn from each report? Which format did you prefer, and why?*

▶ **Practice Book** page 118

CHECK COMPREHENSION

3 Answers to "Before You Move On"

1. **Details** The Somers family helped the girls find safety; the girls helped the Somers family carry supplies to the tent city in Golden Gate Park.

2. **Comparisons** The store building could collapse. In the open space of the park, there were no buildings that could fall on them.

3. **Figurative Language** Answers may vary, but should focus on rebuilding the city after the fire.

ABOUT THE AUTHOR

4 Evaluate Literary Quality Read aloud or have students read About the Author. Ask students how the author's experience as a reporter may have helped her research the subject. Invite them to find examples of historical information incorporated in the play. Ask: *How does using historical details make the play better?*

CLOSE AND ASSESS
Ask small groups of students to write a sentence that summarizes what they learned in this lesson.

Ask: Why do you think Golden Gate Park was the safest place?

Mrs. Somers: Yes. That's the safest place to be. Maybe we'll find water there.

Edith: Daisy and I will go, too. We'll help you carry whatever we can.

Mr. Somers *[taking charge]*: It's **settled**, then. We'll go to Golden Gate Park!

[All exit except Daisy.]

Daisy *[to audience]*: Edith and I did finally return to our home in Stockton. Her father got home safely, too. The people of San Francisco **took good care** of each other until more help arrived. **Communities from all over the nation** sent food and **supplies**.

....

settled decided, agreed on
Communities from all over the nation People in towns and cities all across the country

Nearly all of the city burned to the ground, but not for long! Within weeks, a new San Francisco began to **rise** out of the ashes. **Clarify:** Ashes are what's left after a fire burns out.

[Exit Daisy.]

The End

BEFORE YOU MOVE ON...
1. **Details** How did the Somers family and the girls help each other?
2. **Comparisons** Why was it safer to stay in the park than in the store?
3. **Figurative Language** What do you think Daisy meant when she said that a new San Francisco began to rise out of the ashes?

ABOUT THE AUTHOR

Kristiana Gregory has been a reporter, editor, and children's book reviewer. Her books, *Earthquake at Dawn* and *Jenny of the Tetons*, were chosen as Notable Children's Trade Books for Social Studies. Kristiana lives in California and has experienced dozens of earthquakes. She hopes that by learning about the past, her readers will be able to help their communities prepare for the future.

236 Unit 4 | Community

REACHING ALL STUDENTS

Non-Verbal Language In any language, we communicate verbally and nonverbally. Misunderstanding may result if people are not aware of the traditions of other cultures. Discuss the correct type of greeting to use with persons from the following cultures.

CULTURE	GREETING
American	Sometimes hug if the person is a friend. Shake hands if the person is not a close friend.
Asian	Nod the head and give a verbal greeting.
Latino	Hug and kiss on the cheek.
Middle Eastern	Avoid body contact with persons of the opposite sex.

Respond to the Play
Check Your Understanding

SUM IT UP

Analyze Characters and Setting "Earthquake at Dawn" takes place in 1906. What clues from the script and the illustrations show this? Make a chart like the one below.

How Do You Know It Was 1906?	
How people dress	women wear petticoats people wear hats women wear long skirts
How people talk	"Mercy!" "Ladies, I thank you." "Please take no offense."
How the city looks	stores keep food in barrels

Rewrite the Play Imagine that the story happened today. Choose a scene from the play to rewrite. Where would it take place? How would people talk? What commands would they give? How could they help each other? Remember to include stage directions and other parts of a script.

Evaluate Literature Talk with a partner about how the time and place cause the plays to be different. Write a sentence or two to summarize your ideas.

THINK IT OVER

Discuss Talk about these questions with a partner.

1. **Literary Analysis** Imagine what the play would be like as a short story. Which would you like better?

2. **Generalization** Read this saying: "Disaster brings out the best in some people, the worst in others." What does this mean? Use details from the play to explain.

3. **Cause and Effect** What problems do earthquakes cause?

4. **Personal Experience** Have you ever been in a disaster? Describe your experience.

EXPRESS YOURSELF

▶ GIVE AND CARRY OUT COMMANDS

Form groups. A volunteer pretends to be a character in the play in a Hot Seat!

- The rest of the group acts as the director and tells the character what to do.

- The character carries out the commands.

 **LANGUAGE ACQUISITION ASSESSMENT** See page 62 of the Assessment Handbook.

Earthquake at Dawn **237**

Multi-Level Strategies
SUM IT UP OPTIONS

BEGINNING Review **Transparency 66**, completed with the group during reading. Then, have students choose the part of the play they want to update. Create a third column for the graphic organizer and record students' ideas about how people in the contemporary version dress and talk, and how the modern city looks. Use these ideas to create new dialogue and stage directions for the updated scene. Encourage students to include references to modern technology as well, e.g., Mrs. Somers: *Excuse me. Do you girls have a cell phone to call 911?*

INTERMEDIATE / ADVANCED Have students review **Master 66**, then create a third column to record ideas about contemporary clothing, language and cities. Ask partners or small groups to work together to choose an episode to rewrite and to brainstorm dialogue and stage directions for their script. Have groups rehearse and present their scenes to the class.

OBJECTIVES

SUM IT UP
Function: Write
Reading and Learning Strategies: Use Text Structures and Features In Plays
Critical Thinking and Literary Analysis: Analyze Information; ⊕ Evaluate Literature

THINK IT OVER
Function: Engage in Discussion
Critical Thinking and Comprehension: Form Generalizations; Identify Cause and Effect; Relate to Personal Experience
Literary Analysis: Play; Short Story

EXPRESS YOURSELF
Function: ⊕ Give and Carry Out Commands
Speaking and Listening: Role-Play

CHECK YOUR UNDERSTANDING

1 **Sum It Up** Refer students to the chart they started earlier in the lesson.

▶ **Practice Book** page 119

2 **Think It Over** Possible answers are:

1. **Literary Analysis** Students' preferences may vary.

2. **Generalization** During crises, some people do heroic things while others react selfishly. Edith and Daisy and the Somers family act heroically as they help each other to safety.

3. **Cause and Effect** Problems might include contaminated drinking water, explosions, car accidents, and homelessness.

4. **Personal Experience** Answers will vary.

3 **Express Yourself** Review the descriptions of the players on page 228.

CLOSE AND ASSESS

Ask: *What could you tell a friend about the San Francisco earthquake of 1906?*

Earthquake at Dawn **T237**

OBJECTIVES

HELPING VERBS
Grammar: ❶ Helping Verbs

LITERARY CRITIQUE
Function: ❶ Express Opinions; Write
Critical Thinking: Form Opinions;
Make Judgments; ❶ Evaluate Literature
Literary Analysis: Characterization
Technology/Media and Writing: Literary
Critique; Use Word-Processing Software

LANGUAGE ARTS AND LITERATURE

1 Use Helping Verbs Possible answers
to the Practice items are:

1. could

2. should

3. Will

4. must

5. will

▶ **Practice Book** page 120

2 Write a Literary Critique To
support students through each step
of the activity, you may want to:

• Brainstorm character traits.

• Prompt critical thinking with
questions about each character.

• Encourage students to use a word-
processing program to write their
paragraphs.

CLOSE AND ASSESS

Ask students to work in small groups to
describe one of the characters from the
play, using sentences that include at least
one helping verb.

✓ **ASSESSMENT**
Selection Test 15 on page 67 of the Assessment Handbook tests students' mastery of the reading
strategies and the vocabulary, comprehension, and language arts skills taught with this selection.

Respond to the Play, continued
Language Arts and Literature

> **GRAMMAR IN CONTEXT**

USE HELPING VERBS

Learn About Helping Verbs Some verbs are
made up of more than one word. The last word
is called the main verb. It shows the action. The
verb that comes before the main verb is the
helping verb. Here are some helping verbs.

can	could	may	might
must	should	will	would

Examples:

An earthquake **can** cause great damage.
People **must** cooperate in an emergency.

In a negative sentence, the word *not* comes
between the helping verb and the main verb.

The ships **may** not sail today.

Use Helping Verbs Write the helping verbs
listed above on cards. Put the cards in a pile.
With a group, take turns choosing a card. Use
the word in a sentence to tell or ask something
about an earthquake.

Practice Copy these sentences. Add a helping
verb to complete each sentence.

1. Damaged buildings _____ fall down.

2. Everyone _____ go to a safe place.

3. _____ the people find water to drink?

4. Other cities _____ come to help.

5. The city _____ rise from the ashes.

238　**Unit 4** | Community

> **LITERARY ANALYSIS**
> **WRITING**

WRITE A LITERARY CRITIQUE

When you **critique** a character, you tell what is
good and bad about the character. Critique the
characters in the play.

❶ **Set the Standards** What traits are
important to have in a disaster? Write the
traits in your chart.

❷ **Critique the Characters** Give each
character a grade for each trait.
Answers will vary.

Literary Report Card

name	courage	generosity
Edith Daisy Mrs. S.	A+	

❸ **Write a Paragraph** Critique one character.
Explain what you liked and didn't like about
the character. Give examples from the story.

REACHING ALL STUDENTS

▍ Multi-Level Strategies
ACTIVITY OPTIONS FOR USING HELPING VERBS

BEGINNING Work with students as a group to create sentences using
helping verbs on cards. To complete Practice items, ask volunteers to identify
the main verb in each sentence and to choose a helping verb.

INTERMEDIATE / ADVANCED Students work with partners to
complete the Practice sentences. Encourage them to identify all the helping
verbs that can complete each Practice item.

Content Area Connections

▶ **SOCIAL STUDIES**

MAKE A TIME LINE

In **historical fiction**, some people and events were real. Other parts could have happened. Find examples of these.

① Find Information Look for facts about the San Francisco earthquake that happened on April 18, 1906. Use history books, encyclopedias, and the Internet.

You can try these sites for information:
• www.sfmuseum.org
• quake.wr.usgs.gov/more/1906
• www.exploratorium.edu/covis/earthquake

② Organize Your Information Take notes about what happened during and after the earthquake. Put your facts in the order they happened.

③ Make a Time Line Write the historical events in one color. Add the events of the play in a different color. What parts of the play were real and what were imaginary?

Time Line

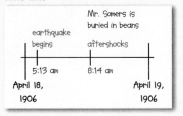

▶ **SCIENCE**
▶ **TECHNOLOGY/MEDIA**

CREATE AN EARTHQUAKE DATA CHART

Learn about recent earthquakes.

Gather Information Use newspapers or the Internet. Take notes about three earthquakes. Try these Web sites to begin your search, but remember that new sites appear every day!

INTERNET
INFORMATION ON-LINE

Web Sites:
▶ **Current Earthquakes**
• www.discovery.com
• www.planetdiary.com

Make a Chart Compare the earthquakes. List the location, date, size, and damage for each earthquake. Share your chart with the class.

  Learn how to make **charts**. See Handbook pages 340–341.

Research Skills

▶ USE PARTS OF A BOOK

TEACH Show students a reference book on earthquakes. Demonstrate how to find a subject, such as *earthquakes in San Francisco*, in the book's **table of contents**.

Then, turn to the book's **index** and demonstrate how to find a more specific topic in the index, such as the 1906 earthquake. Explain that entries in an index are organized alphabetically.

Demonstrate **skimming** through each referenced page to determine if the information is useful to you. Note new information on a notecard or in a notebook along with the page number, title, and author of the book.

PRACTICE Ask students to use reference books to find out the real events of the 1906 earthquake and record them on their time lines.

▶ **Practice Book** pages 121–122

OBJECTIVES

TIME LINE

Function: Confirm Information

Learning Strategies, Critical Thinking, and Research Skills: Gather Information; Use Parts of a Book; Skim; Take Notes; ⊕ Make Comparisons; Draw Conclusions

Representing: Time line

EARTHQUAKE DATA CHART

Function: ⊕ Make Comparisons

Concepts and Vocabulary: Scientific Instruments—*seismogram, seismograph, seismometer, seismoscope*

Learning Strategies, Critical Thinking, and Research Skills: Gather Information; Take Notes; ⊕ Make Comparisons; Summarize

Technology/Media: Use the Internet

Representing: Comparison Chart

CONTENT AREA CONNECTIONS

1 Make a Time Line Some facts of note about the 1906 earthquake are:

• The earthquake struck at 5:13 a.m. on April 18, 1906.

• A major aftershock struck at 8:14 a.m.

• The fire burned for four days.

The Museum of the City of San Francisco's web site (www.sfmuseum.org) offers a comprehensive time line of the 1906 earthquake.

2 Create an Earthquake Data Chart To prepare students, introduce the following content area vocabulary:

• *seismograph, seismometer, seismoscope:*
These scientific tools use mathematical calculations to detect, record, measure, and predict earthquakes. A **seismogram** is a read-out. Write the root *seismo-* and ask students to guess what it means. (earthquake)

▶ **Practice Book** page 123

CLOSE AND ASSESS

Ask students to write a sentence that tells the sequence of events in an earthquake.

OBJECTIVES

Function: ❶ Elaborate

Concepts and Vocabulary:
Words and Phrases

Patterns and Structures:
❶ Adjectives, Adverbs, and Prepositions

Viewing: Respond to a Photograph;
Interpret Visual Information

Learning Strategy: Use Visuals

Critical Thinking: Make Comparisons

Writing: Paragraph

START WITH A COMMON EXPERIENCE

1 View and Describe View the
photograph, inviting students to
describe what they see. Encourage
them to use exact words in their
descriptions.

> Use the Questioning Techniques
> in the **Multi-Level Strategies** to
> meet all levels.

2 Model How to Elaborate Use the
following Think Aloud to help
students learn to elaborate.

> **How to Elaborate**
>
> • Tell something that is happening
>   in the picture: *People are
>   passing sandbags.*
>
> • Tell what kind of people: *Men and
>   women are passing sandbags.*
>
> • Tell what kind of sandbags:
>   *Men and women are passing
>   heavy sandbags.*
>
> • Tell where: *Men and women are
>   passing heavy sandbags in front
>   of the restaurant.*
>
> • Tell why: *Men and women are
>   passing heavy sandbags in front
>   of the restaurant to help stop
>   the flood.*

Build Language and Vocabulary
ELABORATE

View this picture. How do these people help during a disaster
in their community?

REACHING ALL STUDENTS

Multi-Level Strategies
QUESTIONING TECHNIQUES

BEGINNING Show students a variety of photographs of flood
situations—water pouring over flood banks, people escaping in boats,
people building sandbag walls. Ask: *What is happening here? What are the
people doing?* Then discuss the photograph on page 240: *What are these
people doing?* (building a sandbag wall)

INTERMEDIATE Call attention to specific details in the scene to prompt
comments from students: *People are lined up to pass the sandbags along.
What benefits are there to this system?* Elicit that when people work together,
the work goes faster and everyone feels a sense of community.

ADVANCED Ask students to speculate and make observations that go
beyond the scene shown. *What do you think caused this flood? How well do
you think the sandbags will work to hold the water back? etc.*

RECORD DETAILS

Look at the picture on page 240 with a small group. Each person plays an important part in building the wall of sandbags. Write a sentence to describe what is happening in the picture.

> People work to stack the sandbags.

Compare sentences. Look at the details in each person's sentence. Notice the differences.

BUILD YOUR VOCABULARY

Words and Phrases Look again at one sentence your group wrote. Add details to tell more about the picture.

- Add an **adjective** to tell what something is like.

> People work to stack the **heavy** sandbags.

- Add an **adverb** to tell how, when, or where something is done.

> People work **quickly** to stack the heavy sandbags.

This adverb tells **how**.

- Add a **prepositional phrase** to give more information. Some phrases, like this one, tell where someone is.

> People **near the water** work quickly to stack the heavy sandbags.

USE LANGUAGE STRUCTURES ▶ ADJECTIVES, ADVERBS, PREPOSITIONS

Writing: Elaborate Copy this paragraph. Add adjectives, adverbs, and prepositional phrases to tell more about the picture. Use the **Word Bank** to help you get ideas.

People form a line. Some people fill bags with sand. Some people pass the sandbags. Some people stack the sandbags. A wall of sandbags is forming. The wall helps to stop the water. The volunteers work to build a taller wall.

Word Bank

Adjectives
heavy
muddy

Adverbs
carefully
quickly

Prepositions
by
on top of

Build Language and Vocabulary **241**

CONDUCT THE ACTIVITIES

3 **Record Details** Have students work individually to write their sentences and then compare them with those of other group members.

4 **Build Your Vocabulary: Words and Phrases** Teach adjectives, adverbs, and prepositions, using the definitions and examples on **Transparency 67**. Point out that most adverbs that tell *how* end in *-ly*. Then have students complete the sentences in Try It!

5 **Use Language Structures: Adjectives, Adverbs, Prepositions** Tell students that they will be using what they have learned about adjectives, adverbs, and prepositions in the next activity.

Writing: Elaborate Conduct the activity at the bottom of page 241. Suggest that students refer to the definitions on **Transparency 67** as well as the Word Bank for ideas.

▮ Use the Writing Activity Options in the **Multi-Level Strategies** to adjust instruction.

▶ **Practice Book** page 124

CLOSE AND ASSESS

Write this sentence and have students identify an example of an adjective, an adverb, and a preposition: *The muddy water swirls dangerously near the top of the wall.*

Multi-Level Strategies
WRITING ACTIVITY OPTIONS

BEGINNING Suggest that students add one type of word at a time. For example, they might just add adjectives the first time, adverbs on a second go-round, and prepositional phrases the last time.

INTERMEDIATE Encourage students to conduct a peer conference with a partner to discuss the additions they have made to the paragraph. Following feedback, students can revise their paragraphs.

ADVANCED Invite students to use a thesaurus or a dictionary to choose exact and vivid adjectives and adverbs to add to the paragraph. Students might extend the activity and replace weak verbs with stronger ones.

Transparency 67 / Master 67

ADJECTIVES, ADVERBS, PREPOSITIONS

1. An **adjective** is a word that describes, or tells about, a person, place, or thing.

Colors: purple brown	**Sizes:** wide tall
Shapes: square round	**Feelings:** worried proud
Traits: gentle friendly	**Other Adjectives:** swift rough

2. An **adverb** is a word that tells **how, where,** or **when.**

How: rapidly slowly	**Where:** everywhere outside
When: tomorrow later	

3. A **preposition** can show location, direction, time, and many other things. A **prepositional phrase** starts with a preposition and ends with a noun or pronoun.

Location: above beside	**Direction:** around down
Time: during after	**Other Prepositions:** from with

   Try It!

   Choose adjectives, adverbs, and prepositions from the charts to complete the sentences.

   1. The _____ river rose _____ over the banks.

   2. _____ workers stacked sandbags _____ the river.

Transparency 67 Level A, Unit 4 | Community   © Hampton-Brown

Build Language and Vocabulary **T241**

THINK ABOUT WHAT YOU KNOW

Reading Strategies:
Activate Prior Knowledge;
Use Graphic Organizers (word web)

LEARN KEY VOCABULARY ⓣ

Vocabulary Strategy:
Use New Words in Context.

LEARN TO READ FOR INFORMATION

Reading Strategies:
ⓣ Use Text Features in Nonfiction

THINK ABOUT WHAT YOU KNOW

1 Make a Word Web Ask: *Why are some events called natural disasters?* Brainstorm types of natural disasters. Ask: *What makes a natural disaster different from other kinds of disasters?*

LEARN KEY VOCABULARY

2 Use New Words in Context Read aloud the new vocabulary and definitions. Clarify meanings. Then conduct the activity.

> Use the Vocabulary Options in the **Multi-Level Strategies** to tailor the activity to proficiency levels.

▶ **Practice Book** page 125

LEARN TO READ FOR INFORMATION

3 Model How to Find Information Demonstrate with **Transparency 68**:

- Read the photo caption aloud and summarize the information.

- Point to the map as you identify and define the compass rose, legend, and scale of miles.

- Read aloud the caption and labels on the diagram. Have students restate the information.

CLOSE AND ASSESS

Have students work in pairs or small groups to create a test question about how to read for information.

WHEN DISASTER STRIKES

news articles
by Richie Chevat

Prepare to Read

THINK ABOUT WHAT YOU KNOW

Make a Word Web Work with your class to complete the word web about disasters.

aid Money, food, and supplies for people who need help is called **aid**.

damage Harm and destruction are kinds of **damage**.

evacuee A person who must move away from a disaster is called an **evacuee**.

recovery When something gets back to normal after a problem, it is called **recovery**.

relief worker A **relief worker** is someone who helps people after a disaster.

rescue worker A **rescue worker** tries to save people in emergencies.

shelter People can stay in a **shelter** when they have no home.

struggle When you **struggle**, you try hard to do something.

survivor Someone who is still alive after a disaster is called a **survivor**.

wreckage What is left after things are destroyed or ruined is called **wreckage**.

LEARN KEY VOCABULARY

Use New Words in Context Study the new words. Use these ideas to write a paragraph about a disaster and how people struggle to rebuild.

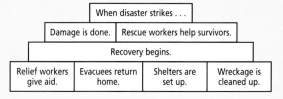

Example:
When disaster strikes, damage is done. Rescue workers help survivors.

LEARN TO READ FOR INFORMATION

When you read nonfiction, you can use photos, maps, and diagrams to find information. These pictures help you understand information.

> **READING STRATEGY**
> **Where to Find Information**
> - A **photo** is a picture of someone or something real.
> - A **caption** describes what is in a photo or picture.
> - A **map** shows where events happen.
> - A **diagram** is a drawing that explains information.

Now read "When Disaster Strikes." Use the information in photos, captions, maps, and diagrams to help you understand the articles.

REACHING ALL STUDENTS

Multi-Level Strategies
VOCABULARY OPTIONS

BEGINNING Work with students to write a paragraph as a group.

INTERMEDIATE In small groups, students restate definitions in their own words, then write paragraphs. Encourage students to trade paragraphs with a partner and offer suggestions for improvement.

ADVANCED Have students include information about several types of disasters in their paragraphs.

Transparency 68 / Master 68

HOW TO READ FOR INFORMATION

Directions: Use these strategies when you look at photos, maps, and diagrams.

Much of San Francisco was in ruins after the 1906 earthquake.

Photos and Captions
1. Look at the photo. Ask yourself: What does it show?
2. Read the caption. Think about how it explains the photo.

California's San Andreas Fault

Maps
1. Use the compass rose to see which direction is north, south, east, and west on the map.
2. Use the legend to find out what symbols on the map mean.
3. Use the scale of miles to estimate distance.
4. Read titles or captions, to help you understand what the map shows.

When plates move against each other, pressure is created.

Diagrams
1. Look at the picture.
2. Read the labels, captions, and other text.
3. Describe what you see. Explain what the picture shows in your own words.

Transparency 68 Level A, Unit 4 | Community   © Hampton-Brown

WHEN DISASTER STRIKES

By RICHIE CHEVAT

Natural disasters can occur at any time, in any place around the world. When natural disasters strike, communities pull together to help each other and to rebuild. Sometimes, people of the world act together as a global community when disaster strikes. These events, taken from newspaper articles, tell about three real-life disasters.

243

READ THE SELECTION

OBJECTIVES

Listening: Listen to a Preview
Reading Strategies:
Activate Prior Knowledge
Literary Analysis: News Article

INTRODUCE THE SELECTION

4 Activate Prior Knowledge
Read aloud the title, author, and introduction. Ask: *Can you think of any natural disasters that have happened in other places in the world? What can we do to help when natural disasters occur?*

5 Identify Genre: News Article
Explain that news articles tell us about events around the world. Read some current headlines in the newspaper. Then ask students to page through "When Disaster Strikes" and read the headlines.

6 Audio Walk-Through
Play the Audio Walk-Through for "When Disaster Strikes" on the **Selection Tape/CD** to give students the overall idea of the selection.

Tape 4B
CD 4
Track 6

When Disaster Strikes
by Richie Chevat

Theme Connection This selection includes news accounts of three recent natural disasters. The articles illustrate the efforts of rescue workers who risk their own lives to help others as they deal with the disaster.

Selection Summary The introduction on page 243 of the student book offers a summary of the selection.

Background Disaster relief organizations provide shelter, food, clothing, medicine, and other services to victims of disasters. These services are free of charge and rely on volunteer efforts.

OBJECTIVES

Function: Read a Selection

Concepts and Vocabulary: Quantity Words

Grammar: Adverbs that Compare

Listening: Listen to a Selection

Reading and Learning Strategies:
Set a Purpose for Reading;
🌀 Use Text Features in Nonfiction;
Use Graphic Organizers
(note-taking chart)

Comprehension: Identify Cause and
Effect, Details

SET PURPOSE

1 Read aloud the headline and article titles on pages 244–245. Say: *As you read, note details about the earthquake in Taiwan and find out what rescue workers did to help.*

READ AND THINK

Tape 4B
CD 4
Track 7

2 **Strategy Focus: Use Text Features in Nonfiction** Have students record information on **Master 69** during the reading process. Encourage them to refer to text and graphic elements for information.

Choose Reading Options in the **Multi-Level Strategies** to include students at all proficiency levels.

The recording of "When Disaster Strikes," on the **Selection Tape/CD**, offers the opportunity to build reading fluency.

Red annotations offer opportunities to clarify meaning and check for understanding.

Earthquake in Taiwan, 1999

2:00 A.M.

Massive Quake Rocks Taiwan— Hundreds Feared Dead
Restate: Hundreds of people may have died.

A huge earthquake **rocked** the island of Taiwan just before 2 a.m. It sent twelve-
Clarify: 2 a.m. is 2 o'clock in the morning.
story buildings crashing to the ground. Hundreds are **feared dead** and hundreds more are trapped in the **rubble**.

The quake measured 7.6 on the Richter scale and may be the strongest quake ever to hit this area. **Power is out** in many places. Government officials **call for calm** and **warn of continuing aftershocks**.

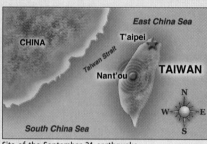
East China Sea
CHINA
T'aipei
Taiwan Strait
Nant'ou
TAIWAN
N
W E
S
South China Sea
Site of the September 21 earthquake

6:00 A.M.

Taiwan Quake Kills More Than 1,400

The **death toll** from today's early morning earthquake stands at 1,450. **Rescue workers** fear it will go even higher. Hundreds of people are still trapped in wrecked buildings. Dozens of aftershocks, several as strong as a major earthquake, make rescue work dangerous. Everywhere, rescuers are working to dig out **survivors** Cranes and bulldozers are
Clarify: Cranes and bulldozers are
being used. machines that can move heavy rubble and earth.

Often, friends and neighbors are using their bare hands to remove the rubble.

A 12-story building lies on its side after an earthquake jolted Taiwan.

---

rocked shook, moved

feared dead thought to be dead

rubble ruins of destroyed buildings

Power is out There is no electricity, Electric power is not working

call for calm ask people to be calm

warn of continuing aftershocks let people know there may be more earthquakes

death toll number of people who died

REACHING ALL STUDENTS

Transparency 69 / Master 69

NOTE-TAKING CHART

Directions: Fill in the chart with information from the articles. Use the photos, captions, maps, and diagrams to help you.

When Disaster Strikes

	Earthquake	Hurricane	Flood
Date	September 21, 1999	September 21–27, 1998	April 11–22, 1997
Location	Taiwan	Puerto Rico, Haiti, and Dominican Republic	Grand Forks, North Dakota
Damage	fallen buildings	ruined houses, no electricity, mudslides	flooded homes, fire, no water or electricity
Rescue Work	search for and dig out survivors	bring food, water, shelter, and medicine	fight fires, set up shelters
What Survivors Do	stay away from homes, help rescue	go to shelters, get water from river	flee their homes, rebuild

Transparency 69 Level A, Unit 4 | Community   © Hampton-Brown

---

Multi-Level Strategies

READING OPTIONS FOR LESSONS 12–14

BEGINNING Read aloud the articles about each disaster in the selection, or play the recording of "When Disaster Strikes" on the **Selection Tape/CD**. Pause frequently to restate and clarify meaning. Refer to the red annotations on the facsimile pages. As a group, fill in each column on **Transparency 69**.

INTERMEDIATE / **ADVANCED** Ask students to read the articles independently. Remind them to read the captions, maps, and diagrams. Direct them to complete the chart on **Master 69** as they read about each disaster. Encourage students to compare and discuss their work with a partner.

11:00 A.M.

Rescue Effort Grows

As many as 3,000 people were trapped in fallen buildings after a pre-dawn earthquake. Rescue teams **comb through** the **wreckage** to find those still trapped. Trained dogs are searching the rubble. Survivors are still being pulled from under the **concrete.**

"My wife was buried under **debris** for nine hours. Luckily, she was pulled out alive," says a 59-year-old grocer from the town of Puli. **Define** *grocer:* A grocer is someone who sells groceries or food.

Tens of thousands of people are on the streets, afraid to return to their homes. **Soup kitchens** are being set up in parks. Countries around the world— including the United States, Germany, and Japan—offer to send **aid**. A team from Turkey is **rushing to the scene**. Aftershocks keep coming. The terrible search for survivors continues, but it seems that the worst is over.

---

comb through search carefully in
concrete strong, hard building material, made from cement and minerals
debris rocks and rubble created by the earthquake

Soup kitchens places where food is served for free to people who need it
rushing to the scene coming to the disaster site as quickly as possible

---

> **POINT-BY-POINT**
>
> **HOW COMMUNITIES RESPOND TO DISASTERS**
>
> **After an Earthquake:**
> - The government calls for calm.
> - Community members and rescuers search for survivors.
> - The international community sends aid.

Ask: Do you think rescue teams used combs to find people? **Clarify:** No, to comb through wreckage is an expression that means to search everywhere.

B E F O R E   Y O U   M O V E   O N . . .

1. **Vocabulary** The article reports that hundreds of people were killed. List other words from the article that tell numbers of things.
2. **Cause and Effect** Why does the death toll rise as the days go by?
3. **Details** Why was it difficult for rescue workers to help the people who were trapped?

CHECK COMPREHENSION

3 Answers to "Before You Move On"

1. **Vocabulary** Words include: *dozens of aftershocks; tens of thousands of people*

2. **Cause and Effect** More and more victims are found each day as the rescue efforts continue.

3. **Details** Dozens of aftershocks made rescue work dangerous.

> **CLOSE AND ASSESS**
>
> Ask students to share their charts. Did they fill in each row under Earthquake on their charts? Have students write a sentence summarizing what they learned about this earthquake.

Grammar Minilesson

▶ **ADVERBS THAT COMPARE**

TEACH Using adverbs that compare, discuss the reports about the Taiwan earthquake. Ask, for example: *Why might rescue workers think the death toll would go higher? Do you think the aftershocks were stronger than the earthquake?*

List adverbs that you use and explain that they compare two or more actions:

stronger	highest
calmer	greatest

Teach three rules:

- Add **–er** to compare two actions.
- Add **–est** to compare three or more.
- If the adverb ends in **–ly**, use **more, most, less,** or **least.**

PRACTICE Write these sentences. Have students choose the correct word.

1. The first quake lasted (longer, longest) than the aftershocks.
2. The government calls (more, less) urgently for calm.

▶ **Practice Book** page 126

Science Connection
RICHTER SCALE

Explain that the size of an earthquake is measured on a Richter Scale, a system named after its inventor, Charles F. Richter. Present related vocabulary, such as *seismologist* (scientist who studies earthquakes), *seismograph* (instrument that records ground movement) and *magnitude* (size and strength). Have students research Richter and the Richter Scale. Suggest that they study degrees of damage caused by earthquakes of different magnitude and compare earthquake statistics around the world.

OBJECTIVES

Function: Read a Selection
Grammar: Count and Noncount Nouns
Listening: Listen to a Selection
Reading and Learning Strategies:
Set a Purpose for Reading;
❶ Use Text Features in Nonfiction;
Use Graphic Organizers
(note-taking chart)
Comprehension: Identify Cause and
Effect, Details

SET PURPOSE

1 Read aloud the headline and article titles on pages 246–247. Say: *As you read, note details about the hurricane in the Caribbean and find out what rescue workers did to help the victims.*

READ AND THINK

Tape 4B
CD 4
Track 7

2 Strategy Focus: Use Text Features in Nonfiction Involve students in reading pages 246–247 of the selection.

| See the **Multi-Level Strategies** on page T244 to involve all students in the reading experience.

Build background: Hurricanes are named in alphabetical order.
Ask: How many hurricanes happened in 1998 before Hurricane Georges?

Hurricane in the Caribbean, 1998

The path of Hurricane Georges

MONDAY, SEPTEMBER 21, 1998

Hurricane Georges Hits Puerto Rico

Hurricane Georges slammed into the island of Puerto Rico at around 6 p.m. today. Winds **reached** over 115 miles per hour. Airplanes flipped over like toys. Trees were **uprooted** and flew through the air like missiles. Over 80 percent of the island is without electricity. Seventy percent of all homes are without water.

Use visuals: Pause to draw a simple pie chart to demonstrate eighty and seventy percent.

Inside a Hurricane

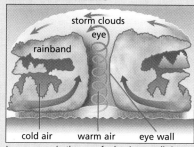

storm clouds
eye
rainband
cold air   warm air   eye wall

Low pressure in the eye of a hurricane pulls in cooler air, creating a powerful storm with winds over 74 miles per hour.

TUESDAY, SEPTEMBER 22, 1998

Georges Blasts Dominican Republic— Rescue Efforts Begin

Hurricane Georges spreads its destruction to the Dominican Republic. **Mudslides** and **flooding** kill over 200 people. More than 100,000 people are left **homeless**.

Meanwhile, rescue workers bring aid to Puerto Rico. More than 20,000 people **crowd into shelters** in San Juan and other cities.

FRIDAY, SEPTEMBER 25, 1998

Hurricane Relief Underway

Rescue workers in the Dominican Republic and Haiti **struggle** to bring food, water, and shelter to people. House

---

reached got as fast as
uprooted pulled from the ground
Mudslides Rushing rivers of mud and rain

flooding water overflowing the banks of rivers
homeless without homes, with nowhere to live
crowd into are pushed together in

246 Unit 4 | Community

REACHING ALL STUDENTS

Vocabulary
COMPOUND WORDS

Define *compound words* as words that are made of two words. Point out that *earthquake* combines the words *earth* and *quake*. Define these words. Then, ask students to define *earthquake*. Invite students to find and define more compound words in the selection, such as *mudslide, aftershock,* and *firefighters*. Remind students that compound words can always be split into two smaller words. Ask: *How do the smaller words help you understand the meaning of the compound word?*

Language Development
GIVE AND CARRY OUT COMMANDS

Brainstorm a Do/Don't list of actions to take during an earthquake, hurricane, or flood. Present the commands for these actions, such as *Don't stand in front of a window. Stand in a doorway.* Have students work in pairs to illustrate one command. Each group then presents their illustration to the class. One student reads the command while the other student acts it out.

after house **lies in ruins** or without a roof.

"There's no water. There's no power. There is nothing," says Domingo Osvaldo Fortuna as he fills a plastic jug with water from the garbage-filled Ozama River in Santo Domingo. **Ask:** Do you think the water in the river is safe to drink?

Aid from the United States begins to arrive. A French cargo plane brings **relief workers**, food, and medicine. Sixty-three firefighters from New York help to search for survivors.

SUNDAY, SEPTEMBER 27, 1998

Hurricane Continues— Tons of Food On the Way

Tons of food and supplies begin to arrive in the Dominican Republic and Haiti. Volunteers fly in with tons of bottled water and enough **plastic sheeting** to repair 15,000 houses. Members of the U.S. military carry aid to towns **cut off by** flooding and mudslides.

Although it will take weeks or even years for the islands to **repair** the **damage**, **recovery** has slowly begun.

---

lies in ruins sits on the ground in pieces
Tons Several thousands of pounds
plastic sheeting waterproof covering

cut off by unable to have contact with the outside world because of
repair fix, correct

HOW COMMUNITIES RESPOND TO DISASTERS

After a Hurricane:

- Emergency shelters are set up for people who are left homeless.
- Rescue workers bring food, water, and medicine to disaster victims.
- Rescue workers search for survivors.
- The international community sends aid to help victims recover and rebuild.

Restate: A large plane from France brings relief workers, food, and medicine.

BEFORE YOU MOVE ON...

1. **Vocabulary** What words or phrases describe the strength of the hurricane?
2. **Cause and Effect** What problems did the hurricane cause?
3. **Details** How did other countries help the people on the islands?

CHECK COMPREHENSION

3 Answers to "Before You Move On"

1. **Vocabulary** *Hurricane Georges slammed into the island; Winds reached over 115 miles per hour; Airplanes flipped over like toys; Trees were uprooted and flew through the air like missiles.*

2. **Cause and Effect** Problems included loss of water and electricity; mudslides and flooding; homelessness.

3. **Details** French cargo planes brought relief workers, food, and medicines. Firefighters from the United States helped search for survivors. Volunteers flew in with bottled water and plastic sheeting. U.S. military carried aid to towns cut off by flooding and mudslides.

CLOSE AND ASSESS

Ask: *What could you tell a friend about this hurricane?* Have partners write exit slip summary statements. Check students' comprehension.

Language Development
EXPRESS PROBABILITY

Ask: *What kind of warnings prepare people for a hurricane?* Brainstorm ways that the media and government prepare people for disasters, such as storm warnings and public service announcements about emergency preparedness. Ask students to prepare a P.S.A. or a hurricane warning. Provide sentence frames: *This is a special report. A storm _____ is in effect until _____ P.M. tonight. The storm may strike _____ at _____ P.M. It is expected to _____. People in the area should _____.*

Grammar Minilesson

▶ COUNT AND NONCOUNT NOUNS

TEACH Draw students' attention to this sentence on page 246: *Trees were uprooted and flew through the air like missiles.* Identify *trees* and *missiles* as nouns that can be counted and *air* as a noun that cannot be counted. Remind students that nouns that cannot be counted have only one form for "one" and "more than one."

Use Handbook page 411 to introduce types of noncount nouns, such as weather words (*flooding*) and materials (*water, electricity*).

PRACTICE Begin a chart of noncount nouns, using these categories: *Ideas and Feelings, Activities and Sports, Category Nouns, Food, Weather Words,* and *Materials.* Have small groups of students look through the selection to find examples of noncount nouns. Work with students to place the words in the correct categories.

Suggest that students copy the chart and add new noncount nouns that they come across in their reading.

▶ **Practice Book** page 127

Function: Read a Selection
Vocabulary Strategy:
Use New Words in Context
Grammar: Adverbs
Listening: Listen to a Selection
Reading and Learning Strategies:
Set a Purpose for Reading;
🅣 Use Text Features In Nonfiction;
Use Graphic Organizers
(note-taking chart)
Comprehension:
Identify Cause and Effect, Details
Literary Analysis: Evaluate Impact of
Medium on Quality

SET PURPOSE

1 Read aloud the headline and article
titles on pages 248–249. Say: *As you
read, note details about the flood in
the American Midwest and find
out how rescue workers
helped the victims.*

READ AND THINK

Tape 4B
CD 4
Track 7

2 **Strategy Focus: Use Text
Features in Nonfiction** Involve
students in reading pages 248–249 of
the selection.

> See the **Multi-Level Strategies** on
> page T244 to involve all students
> in the reading experience.

Flood in the American Midwest, 1997

FRIDAY, APRIL 11, 1997

Red River Keeps Rising
While Volunteers Build Levees

   Swollen by melting snow and spring
rains, the Red River continued to rise today.
It has already reached 39 feet in Fargo,
North Dakota, about 80 miles downstream
from Grand Forks.

   In Grand Forks, thousands of volunteers
worked round-the-clock, **piling** sandbags
on **dikes and levees**. The National
Weather Service predicts the river will
crest here at 49 feet sometime in the next
few days. **Clarify:** When people work round-the-
clock, they do not stop to sleep at night.

Volunteers help to pile sandbags in Grand Forks.

Grand Forks, North Dakota, was the site
of severe flood damage. **Clarify the depth of 52
feet. Ask:** How many 8-f
deep swimming pools st
on top of each other would
you need to reach 52 feet?

SUNDAY, APRIL 20, 1997

Grand Forks Flooded and On Fire,
Levees Fail, River Keeps Rising

   Grand Forks was in the middle of a **vast**
lake today, surrounded by the waters of the
Red River. The river **surged** to over 52 feet,
washing away dikes and levees and
flooding over 60 percent of the town. Tens
of thousands of people were forced to flee
their homes.

   Meanwhile, firefighters struggled to
stop a blaze in the downtown area.
The fire has destroyed at least seven
buildings. "With two to three feet of water

Swollen Made larger
piling putting stacks of
dikes and levees walls, often of dirt, built to keep
water from overflowing a river or stream

crest reach its highest point
vast wide and open
surged rose quickly

Learning Styles
**STRATEGIES FOR CONSTRUCTING
MEANING**

- **Visual Learners** Ask students to draw
  or paint a picture that represents how a
  disaster victim might feel.

- **Auditory Learners** Ask students to
  imagine the sounds of the disaster.
  Invite them to use pencils, hands,
  voices, and simple percussion
  instruments to create these sounds.

- **Kinesthetic Learners** Ask students to
  imagine they are victims of the disaster
  and to use facial expressions, gestures,
  and body language to show reactions.

INTERNET

SOCIAL STUDIES CONNECTION

Working in small groups, students
research a flood, earthquake, or
hurricane and complete a chart with
details about their disaster. Have
students present findings, highlighting
the role of the global community.

Disaster	Location/ Time	Details/ Disaster	Relief Services

Web Sites
Web sites undergo frequent
modifications, but here are some you
may want to suggest to students:

www.disasterrelief.org
www.redcross.org
www.disasterium.com
www.usgs.gov

in the area, it's very difficult," said Captain Wade Davis of the National Guard. Helicopters dropped 2,000-gallon buckets of muddy water on the fires.

Ask: Why did firefighters have to drop buckets of water from helicopters on the fires?

TUESDAY, APRIL 22, 1997

President Visits Grand Forks

The President of the United States visited the flooded town of Grand Forks today, taking a helicopter tour of the area and speaking to **evacuees** at a nearby Air Force base. The President offered **words of sympathy** and also promises of federal aid to flooded areas.

"It may be hard to believe now," he told his audience, "but you can rebuild stronger and better than ever."

Grand Forks is nearly **deserted**. The water supply, gas, and electricity have been cut off to most of the city. Almost all of the people have fled.

"You can't believe the emotion that goes through your mind and your heart," said one resident. "Please help these people."

Clarify: *Emotion* is another word for *feeling.*

words of sympathy words to show that he understood and was sad about their problem
deserted empty of people

> ## POINT-BY-POINT
>
> **HOW COMMUNITIES RESPOND TO DISASTERS**
>
> **Before a Flood:**
> - Volunteers pile sandbags to hold back water.
> - People are evacuated from the flood zone.
>
> **After a Flood:**
> - The government sets up shelters for people left homeless.
> - The government provides aid to help people rebuild and recover.

Define *federal aid*: money and help provided by the government

BEFORE YOU MOVE ON...

1. **Cause and Effect** What caused the Red River to rise?
2. **Details** How did people try to stop the flood damage?

ABOUT THE AUTHOR

Richie Chevat lives with his wife and two daughters in New Jersey. Earthquakes and hurricanes are very rare in New Jersey. Richie is glad that he has never been the victim of a flood or any other natural disaster. He hopes that these articles will get people thinking about how they can help when disaster strikes.

When Disaster Strikes **249**

REVIEW KEY VOCABULARY

3 **Use New Words in Context** Ask students to write sentences about each kind of disaster using the key vocabulary words.

CHECK COMPREHENSION

4 **Answers to "Before You Move On"**

1. **Cause and Effect** Melting snow and spring rains caused the Red River to rise.

2. **Details** People piled sandbags on dikes and levees to try to stop the flood.

ABOUT THE AUTHOR

5 **Evaluate Literature: Medium** Have students read About the Author. *What is the advantage of using newspaper articles to get information?* (The information is current; reporters must check the accuracy of their facts before publishing the article; photographs allow readers to feel the emotions of the victims).

> **CLOSE AND ASSESS**
>
> Have students share their note-taking charts. Check that each column is complete.

Vocabulary
SHORTENED WORDS

Present some shortened words from the selection: *plane* (page 247) for *airplane* (page 246), *quake* for *earthquake* (both on page 244). Read aloud sentences from the selection containing these words. Explain that the shortened words are another way to say the longer version of the words. Begin a chart of these words. Then, brainstorm more examples, such as *photo* for *photograph, auto* for *automobile, burger* for *hamburger.* Post the chart and invite students to collect other examples to add.

Grammar Minilesson

▶ ADVERBS WITH *-LY*

TEACH Point out this sentence on page 249: *Grand Forks is nearly deserted.* Identify *nearly* as an adverb that tells *how;* it tells about the verb *deserted.* Explain that adverbs that tell *how* usually end in **-ly**.

Work with **-ly** adverbs using concrete examples. Have students walk across the room in different ways—quickly, slowly, carefully. Describe what is happening: *Nico is walking slowly.*

PRACTICE Have students add an adverb to finish each sentence. They can make adverbs from the list below, by adding **-ly**.

fearful	careful	swift
quick	slow	kind

1. The Red River rose _____ .
2. Volunteers worked _____ to prevent flooding.
3. Thousands of people fled _____ from the city.
4. The President spoke _____ to the people.

▶ **Practice Book** page 128

When Disaster Strikes **T249**

RESPOND

OBJECTIVES

SUM IT UP

Function: Write

Reading and Learning Strategies:
➊ Use Text Features in Nonfiction; Use Graphic Organizers (note-taking chart)

Critical Thinking: ➊ Make Comparisons

Writing: Paragraph

THINK IT OVER

Function: Engage in Discussion

Critical Thinking and Comprehension:
Relate to Personal Experience;
Make an Inference; Form Opinions;
Draw Conclusions

EXPRESS YOURSELF

Function: Ask and Answer Questions;
➊ Elaborate

Speaking and Listening: Question Game

CHECK YOUR UNDERSTANDING

1 Sum It Up Invite students to share the information they recorded on their note-taking charts. Annotations for the chart appear on the facsimile of **Transparency 69** on page T244.

▶ **Practice Book** page 129

2 Think It Over Possible answers are:

1. **Personal Experience** Answers will vary by region.

2. **Inference** These articles show us that disaster victims count on people working together to help them during and after emergencies.

3. **Opinion** Answers will vary. Be sensitive to students' fears or traumatic experiences.

4. **Conclusions** Communities can develop disaster plans that designate places for shelters and sources of aid and food.

3 Express Yourself Remind students to use the new vocabulary in their questions and answers.

CLOSE AND ASSESS

Ask students to write a sentence expressing something specific they learned from a photo caption or map.

Respond to the Articles
Check Your Understanding

SUM IT UP

Read for Information Fill in the chart with information from the articles. Use the photos, captions, maps, and diagram to help you.

Details	Earthquake	Hurricane	Flood
Date			
Location			
Damage			
Rescuer Work			
What Survivors Do			

Make Comparisons Write a paragraph. Tell how two disasters are the same and different.

• Write a **topic sentence** to tell the main idea.

• Add **details** to support the main idea.

• Use **comparison words** like these:

same	different
both	unlike
alike	but

Example:
  A hurricane and an earthquake are the **same** in some ways, but **different** in others. They **both** cause a lot of damage and wreckage. A hurricane brings rain, **but** an earthquake does not.

THINK IT OVER

Discuss Talk about these questions with a partner.

1. **Personal Experience** What natural disasters happen where you live? What do people do when they happen?

2. **Inference** What lessons can we learn about helping others from these articles?

3. **Opinion** Which disaster would frighten you the most? Why?

4. **Conclusions** How can communities prepare for natural disasters?

EXPRESS YOURSELF

▶ ASK AND ANSWER QUESTIONS, ELABORATE

Play a quiz game about natural disasters.

1. Join one of these groups: *A*, *B*, or *C*.

   • *A* will study the Taiwan earthquake.

   • *B* will study the Caribbean hurricane.

   • *C* will study the Grand Forks flood.

2. Write questions about the disaster your group is studying. Write the answers.

3. Take turns asking the other groups questions about your disaster. Ask them to elaborate on their ideas.

4. The team with the most correct answers wins.

LANGUAGE ACQUISITION ASSESSMENT
See page 62 of the Assessment Handbook.

REACHING ALL STUDENTS

Multi-Level Strategies
SUM IT UP OPTIONS

BEGINNING Clarify the meaning of comparison words. Then, refer to your group chart on **Transparency 69** and prompt students to participate in writing a paragraph. Ask yes/no questions: *Are earthquakes, hurricanes, and floods all natural disasters? Do they all cause damage? Do people know when disaster is about to strike?* Work with students to write a paragraph.

INTERMEDIATE Read aloud or have students read the sample paragraph. Point out the topic sentence. Then, ask: *How are earthquakes, hurricanes, and floods the same? How are they different? Use examples from your chart to write a paragraph.*

ADVANCED Students write paragraphs independently. Ask partners to proofread each other's paragraphs. Students can then revise their work as necessary. Invite volunteers to read their paragraphs aloud.

Language Arts and Literature

GRAMMAR IN CONTEXT

USE HELPING VERBS

Learn About Helping Verbs The words **is** and **are** are **helping verbs**. Use them with verbs that end in **–ing** to show that an action is still happening.

- Use **is** when the subject is one person or thing.

    An earthquake **is** rocking the island.

- Use **are** when the subject is more than one person or thing.

    Buildings **are** crashing to the ground.

Find Verbs Make a list of the helping verbs and main verbs in this paragraph. Then use them in a new sentence:

> Everywhere, rescuers are working. Cranes and bulldozers are digging. A neighbor is removing the rubble. The workers are looking for survivors.

Practice Copy the paragraph. Add the helping verb *is* or *are* to complete each sentence.

Hurricane Georges ___is___ hitting Puerto Rico. Trees ___are___ flying through the air. Airplanes ___are___ flipping over like toys. Mud ___is___ pouring down the hillsides. Homes ___are___ washing away in the storm.

LITERARY ANALYSIS
WRITING

LEARN ABOUT NEWS STORIES

A **news story** gives facts about an event. News stories have these parts:

- The **headline** is the title of the article.

- The **lead paragraph** gives a summary of the article. In the article called "President Visits Grand Forks," the lead paragraph tells:

    Who: President of the U.S.

    What: visited the flooded town

    When: April 22, 1997

    Where: Grand Forks

    Why: to offer words of sympathy

- The **body** gives more details and facts about the event.

Write a News Story Tell about news in your school or community. Put the news stories together to make a class newspaper.

 Learn how to improve your writing in the **writer's craft**. See Handbook pages 390–401.

When Disaster Strikes **251**

Multi-Level Strategies
PRACTICE OPTIONS FOR HELPING VERBS

BEGINNING Read each sentence of the Practice paragraph aloud. Ask: *What is the sentence about? Is it about one or more than one?* Ask a volunteer to point to the helping verb that fits in the sentence. Read the sentence aloud with the correct helping verb.

INTERMEDIATE Have students work with a partner to complete Practice items. Review exercises with students and guide them in making necessary revisions.

ADVANCED Students can complete Practice items independently, then add two new sentences to the paragraph. One sentence should use *is* as a helping verb, and the other should use *are*. Review students' paragraphs with them and guide them in making revisions.

RESPOND

OBJECTIVES

HELPING VERBS

Grammar: ❶ Helping Verbs

NEWS STORIES

Function: Give Information; Write
Critical Thinking: Analyze Information
Literary Analysis and Writing: News Article

LANGUAGE ARTS AND LITERATURE

1 **Use Helping Verbs** Possible answers to the Practice items are:

1. is

2. are

3. are

4. is

5. are

▶ **Practice Book** page 130

2 **Learn About News Stories**
Encourage students to write stories about their class. Students might write about field trips or upcoming school events, or they may choose to write a profile of a classmate.

Encourage students to use word-processing software to write their articles and compile them into a class newspaper.

CLOSE AND ASSESS

Have students explain what they have learned in this lesson.

RESPOND

OBJECTIVES

CLASSIFY WORDS

Vocabulary Strategy: Relate Words; Use Context Clues to Meaning

Critical Thinking: Classify

PREFIXES AND SUFFIXES

Vocabulary Strategy:
🄣 Structural Clues (prefixes and suffixes)

LANGUAGE ARTS AND CONTENT AREA CONNECTIONS

1 Classify Science Words Annotations on the chart show possible ways to classify words.

2 Use Prefixes and Suffixes See annotations for answers to Practice items.

▶ **Practice Book** page 131

CLOSE AND ASSESS

Ask students to write a sentence about each disaster that includes a word with a prefix or suffix.

✓ **ASSESSMENT**
Selection Test 16 on page 69 of the Assessment Handbook tests students' mastery of the reading strategies and the vocabulary, comprehension, and language arts skills taught with this selection.

Respond to the Articles, continued

Language Arts and Content Area Connections

▶ VOCABULARY

CLASSIFY SCIENCE WORDS

Learn to Classify Words When you **classify** words, you put them into groups. The words in the group all have something in common.

These words all tell about weather:

wind   rain   snow   sunshine

Classify Disaster Words Put these words where they belong on a chart like the one below.

aftershocks, blasts, crest, mudslides, Richter scale, rocked, sandbags, swollen, winds

Earthquake	Hurricane	Flood
aftershocks Richter scale rocked	blasts sandbags winds	crests mudslides swollen

Use Your New Vocabulary Copy the paragraph. Use words from the chart to fill in the missing words.

Rescue workers are very important during natural disasters. They pile _____ (1) on dikes to prevent floods. They look for survivors in the rubble caused by an earthquake and its _____ (2). Some workers help evacuees get out of the way of winds and fast-moving _____ (3) caused by hurricanes.

1. sandbags
2. aftershocks
3. mudslides

▶ VOCABULARY

USE PREFIXES AND SUFFIXES

Learn About Prefixes and Suffixes A prefix is a word part that comes at the beginning of a word.

The prefix **re-** means "again."

People had to **rebuild** their homes.
People had to **build** their home **again**.

A **suffix** is a word part that comes at the end of the word.

The suffix **-less** means "without."

100,000 people are **homeless**.
100,000 people are **without homes**.

The suffix **-ous** means "full of."

The work is **dangerous**.
The work is **full of danger**.

Adding prefixes and suffixes changes the meaning of the word.

Practice Copy the sentences. Add the prefix **re-** or the suffix **-ous** or **-less** to make new words. Use a dictionary to check your work.

1. I was speech___-less___ when I saw the damage from the earthquake.

2. The woman gave a joy___-ous___ shout when she saw that her cat was safe.

3. It will take years to ___re-___construct the area.

REACHING ALL STUDENTS

▌ Multi-Level Strategies

PRACTICE OPTIONS FOR CLASSIFYING SCIENCE WORDS

BEGINNING Classify the disaster words and complete the cloze activity as a group. Clarify meaning as necessary.

INTERMEDIATE Assign each pair of students a disaster word. Ask them to find the disaster word in the news articles and then invite them to write it in the correct category on the class chart. Encourage peer teaching and discussion.

ADVANCED Ask students to classify the words *food, rebuild, water, shelter, repair,* and *recover* under two or more headings in their charts. Have them write a second paragraph using these words. Share students' work with the class.

SOCIAL STUDIES
TECHNOLOGY/MEDIA

EXPLORE GEOGRAPHY

Make a Disaster Map Show where major earthquakes, hurricanes, and floods happened in the past. Use almanacs or try the Web sites below, but remember that new sites appear every day! Use the disasters as key words to begin your search.

INTERNET

INFORMATION ON-LINE

➤ **On-line Almanacs**
- kids.infoplease.com/world.html
- www.yahooligans.com/content/ka/index.html

Study the Data Look for patterns about where disasters happen. Share your ideas and map with your class.

Learn how to use the **Internet**.
See Handbook pages 364–365.

SOCIAL STUDIES

CREATE A PUBLIC SERVICE POSTER

Public service posters help people prepare for disasters. Work with a group to make a poster about earthquakes, hurricanes, or floods.

Research a Disaster Find information from the library, public services like the fire department or the American Red Cross, or on the Internet.

Make the Poster Include these things:
- what people should have ready
- what people should and shouldn't do
- emergency phone numbers.

Display the Poster Maybe your poster will help someone prepare for a disaster!

HURRICANES!

HAVE	DON'T
a flashlight	Go outside during a hurricane
a radio	Touch fallen wires
batteries	
cans of food	
bottles of water	

EMERGENCY PHONE NUMBERS
✳ Police and Fire Departments 911

When Disaster Strikes **253**

Research Skills

▶ **HOW TO USE AN ALMANAC**

TEACH Display an almanac and tell students to consult it when they need facts and figures about a topic. Explain that almanacs are rewritten every year, so the information is current.

Then state a research goal: *I want to find where major natural disasters happened.* Model how to look up the key word *earthquakes* in the index to find entries. Model how to skim each entry, looking at photos, captions, maps, and diagrams

to determine if it fits the research goal.

PRACTICE Have pairs of students locate several entries in a print or on-line almanac, skim them, and select entries of interest for the geography activity. They should then:

1. List the titles of the entries.

2. Describe the main ideas.

3. Tell which entry was the most helpful and why.

LANGUAGE ARTS AND CONTENT AREA CONNECTIONS

3 Explore Geography To help prepare students, introduce the following content area vocabulary:

- ***boundaries, borders:*** Define *boundaries* and *borders* as the lines where regions and countries meet. Display a map of North America and point out the boundaries of states and the borders between countries.

- ***topographic, oceanographic:*** Explain that maps often show land and water features. Say: *Topographic maps show details of land features. Oceanographic maps show details about oceans.* Point out that the root—*graphic* is from the Greek for "to show or illustrate."

▶ **Practice Book** page 132

4 Create a Public Service Poster If students created public service posters for earthquake preparedness in Lesson 5 of this Theme, steer them towards another kind of disaster for this activity.

CLOSE AND ASSESS

Have students work together to present a public service announcement for one of the disasters they researched, using a map as they present the announcement.

OBJECTIVES

Function: Engage in Discussion
Critical Thinking: Infer; Interpret Opinions
Writing: ❶ Persuasive (essay)

INTRODUCE WRITING THAT PERSUADES

1 **Discuss Persuasive Writing** Read the introduction. Ask students when they might use persuasive language.

2 **Study the Models** Make a chart of what Molly Bang and Raffi describe.

Author	Molly Bang	Raffi
Problem	using up fossil fuels	The Earth needs help.
Opinion	They will be used up.	We are needed now.
Action	Protect the planet.	Work together.

▌ Use the Options for Studying Writing in the **Multi-Level Strategies** to adjust instruction.

CLOSE AND ASSESS

Ask students to agree on a summary sentence that defines persuasive writing.

Writing That Persuades

Persuasive writing presents an opinion and tries to get the reader to agree with the opinion. Some persuasive writing describes a problem and persuades people to help solve it.

WRITING MODELS

Read the following sentences from the essay "Common Ground," by Molly Bang. What problem does she see? What is her opinion? What action does she want you to take? Why?

from "Common Ground"

> Today each lumber company wants to cut down as many trees as it can, to sell for wood, paper, and fuel. The more trees the lumber company cuts down, the more money it makes— in the short run. But after cutting down so many trees, there are fewer and fewer forests. This is not good for the trees, or for the forest creatures, or the forest soil.

In "Evergreen, Everblue," Raffi tries to persuade us. What action does he want us to take?

from "Evergreen, Everblue"

> Right now is when we're needed.
> We can all do something.
> The young, the old together.
> The more we get together,
> The more we help this planet Earth.

REACHING ALL STUDENTS

▌ Multi-Level Strategies

OPTIONS FOR STUDYING PERSUASIVE WRITING

BEGINNING Have students find magazine pictures that illustrate the problem described in "Common Ground" and the actions Molly Bang and Raffi want their audiences to take. Encourage students to paraphrase the authors' opinions and state their own opinions.

INTERMEDIATE Give an example of a problem, an opinion, and a solution. For example, play loud music for a few seconds; then say: *This music is too loud. It hurts my ears.* Then turn the volume down to demonstrate the solution to the problem. Encourage students to act out the problem and solution in "Common Ground" and help them restate the author's opinion.

ADVANCED Engage students in a discussion of the problem described in "Common Ground," the opinion of the author, and what they could do to take action. Take notes and ask students to write summary statements.

Write Together

OBJECTIVES

Function: Write
Learning Strategies and Critical Thinking: Plan; Generate Ideas; Interact with Peers; Analyze and Evaluate Information
Writing: Persuasive Essay

WRITING PROMPT

First write a class essay about a problem in your community. Persuade your readers to do something about it.

1 Brainstorm Topics What problem does your class want to solve? What is your opinion about it? Brainstorm a list and choose a topic for the class essay.

2 Plan the Essay Your essay will have three paragraphs. Make an outline to plan it:

I. State the problem and tell your opinion about it.

II. Tell why there is a problem.

III. Summarize your opinion and tell your readers what you want them to do.

3 Write the Essay Follow your outline to write the class essay.

Sample Outline

I. Kids are getting hurt on school buses. We need to make the buses safer.

II. Buses are dangerous because they are too crowded.

III. We need to get more buses.

STUDENT WRITING MODEL

School Bus Problem

Riding the bus can be a disaster. A lot of kids are getting hurt. We need to make the buses safer to ride.

The buses are just too crowded. There are not enough seats. Kids have to stand. Then they start fighting and won't listen to the driver.

We must all help solve the bus problem. The school should get enough buses for all the students to have seats. Students need to follow the rules and show respect.

Use **persuasive words** to persuade your readers to take action.

Writing That Persuades **255**

WRITE TOGETHER

Discuss the Writing Prompt Read the prompt aloud and ask volunteers to tell

- what kind of writing you will do together (an essay)
- what the essay will be about (a problem in the community)
- what the essay should do (describe the problem and persuade readers to do something about it)

Plan the Persuasive Essay Work with students to brainstorm a list of problems and choose one to write about. Go over the explanation of what each paragraph should tell and study the sample outline. Then complete the outline on **Transparency 70** for your class essay.

Analyze and Evaluate a Persuasive Essay Display **Transparency 71**. Guide students in analyzing and evaluating the Student Model against the features.

If students have difficulty finding a feature, have them look at the sample outline again. The organization there may help them discover the feature.

Write the Class Essay Help students turn their outline into an essay. Guide them in clearly stating their opinion, backing up their opinion with facts, and using persuasive words.

CLOSE AND ASSESS

Distribute copies of **Master 71** and have students work with partners or in small groups to analyze and evaluate your class essay against the features.

Transparency 70 / Master 70

OUTLINE

I. The problem is _____

_____

Our/My opinion about the problem is _____

_____

II. There is a problem because _____

_____

III. In summary, _____

_____

We/I want readers to _____

_____

Transparency 70 **Level A, Unit 4** | Community   © Hampton-Brown

Transparency 71 / Master 71

FEATURES OF PERSUASIVE WRITING

Directions: Read the Student Writing Model. Compare it to the features of a persuasive essay. Check the box if the model has the feature. Write the details.

A Persuasive Essay... School Bus Problem

describes a **problem** and tells the writer's **opinion**.	☑ problem: Kids are getting hurt on school buses. ☑ opinion: The buses should be safer.
tells **why** there is a problem.	☑ buses are too crowded; there aren't enough seats; kids have to stand up; kids fight; kids don't listen to the driver
summarizes the writer's opinion in the last paragraph and **tells the action readers should take.**	☑ opinion: We should all help solve the bus problem. ☑ action: get more buses; follow the rules and show more respect
includes **persuasive words.**	☑ must, should, need to

Transparency 71 **Level A, Unit 4** | Community   © Hampton-Brown

PREWRITE

Function: Write

Learning Strategies and Critical Thinking: Plan; Generate Ideas; Interact with Peers; Organize Ideas; Self-Assess

Representing: Chart; Outline

Writing: ❶ Writing Process

WRITE ON YOUR OWN

Read the prompt together. Have volunteers tell what kind of writing they will do, what it will be about, and what they will include in their essay.

For more about the Writing Process, refer students to Handbook pages 382–389.

PREWRITE

Explain to students that they will fill out an FATP chart to help them think about the form, their audience, topic, and purpose. Then they will complete an outline to show the problem, their opinion, and ways to solve the problem.

▮ Use the Prewriting Support in the **Multi-Level Strategies** to tailor this stage to proficiency levels.

CLOSE AND ASSESS

Have partners discuss the questions in Think About Your Writing.

Writing That Persuades, continued

Write on Your Own

WRITING PROMPT

Now write your own opinion essay about a problem in your school. Persuade your classmates to agree with your opinion.

PREWRITE

❶ **Choose a Problem to Write About** Think about problems in your school. Choose a problem that you think can be solved. This is your **topic**. Fill out an **FATP** chart to guide your writing.

❷ **Get Organized** Complete an outline. Name the topic in your title.

> **Title:** Stop School Damage
>
> I. Kids should not damage school property.
>
> II. Students cause damage in two ways.
>   A. They write graffiti on the walls.
>   B. They destroy books.
>
> III. Students need to take care of school property.
>   A. Make them clean off the walls.
>   B. Have them pay for the books.

FATP Chart

HOW TO UNLOCK A PROMPT
Form: opinion essay
Audience: students who don't take care of school property
Topic: damage to school property
Purpose: to persuade students to take care of school property

Think About Your Writing

• Do you care a lot about your topic? If not, choose one you do care about.

• Do you have enough good ideas for solutions?

Transparency 72 / Master 72

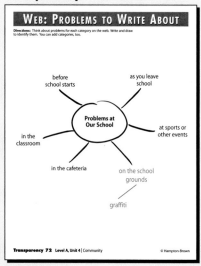

WEB: PROBLEMS TO WRITE ABOUT

Directions: Think about problems for each category on the web. Write and draw to identify them. You can add categories, too.

before school starts

as you leave school

Problems at Our School

at sports or other events

in the classroom

in the cafeteria

on the school grounds

graffiti

Transparency 72 Level A, Unit 4 | Community   © Hampton-Brown

Multi-Level Strategies
PREWRITING SUPPORT

BEGINNING Use **Transparency 72** to help students brainstorm writing topics. Go over the web and model adding to it, using the example. Then distribute copies of **Master 72** and have students write phrases or draw pictures to represent problems. Afterward, guide students in stating their opinions about the problems: *Is this dangerous? Why do you think this is a bad thing? What happens when people do this?* Next, have students highlight the information for their essay, and guide them in filling out FATPs. You may want to help them organize their ideas in a simple outline.

INTERMEDIATE / ADVANCED Partners can use **Master 72** to brainstorm problems to write about. Encourage them to discuss opinions and solutions. After students fill out FATP charts, they can use the outline format on page 256 or on **Master 70** (see page T255) to plan essays.

DRAFT

1 **Write Your Essay** Follow your outline to write your essay.

2 **Consider Your Audience** Think about who will read your essay. Start out with a statement of your opinion. Try different ways to get your reader's attention.

Writing is a way of cutting away at the surface of things, of exploring, of understanding.

— Robert Duncan

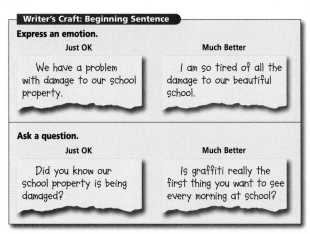

Writer's Craft: Beginning Sentence

Express an emotion.

Just OK	Much Better
We have a problem with damage to our school property.	I am so tired of all the damage to our beautiful school.

Ask a question.

Just OK	Much Better
Did you know our school property is being damaged?	Is graffiti really the first thing you want to see every morning at school?

End your essay with a strong sentence. It should encourage your reader to take action.

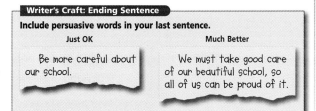

Writer's Craft: Ending Sentence

Include persuasive words in your last sentence.

Just OK	Much Better
Be more careful about our school.	We must take good care of our beautiful school, so all of us can be proud of it.

Think About Your Writing

- Read your draft. Have you stated your opinion clearly?
- Does your draft have good beginning and ending sentences?
- Does your draft include enough persuasive words?
- Will it persuade your readers?

Writing That Persuades **257**

DRAFT

Remind students to write their drafts quickly, without worrying about making mistakes. They can fix errors later.

Study the Writer's Craft to help students write strong beginning and ending sentences for their essays. Read the examples and ask volunteers to point out the changes. Talk about why the second examples are better.

Go over the Words to Persuade Others. Use the phrases in sentences, restating as necessary to clarify meaning.

■ Use the Drafting Support in the **Multi-Level Strategies** to tailor this stage to proficiency levels.

For more about the Writer's Craft, refer students to Handbook pages 390–401.

CLOSE AND ASSESS

Have small groups discuss the questions in Think About Your Writing while you work with those who may need more support in assessing their drafts.

Multi-Level Strategies
DRAFTING SUPPORT

BEGINNING To draft their opinion essays, students may need for you to write the sentences they dictate. If so, read each sentence aloud after you write it. Help students turn the information on their outline into the three paragraphs of the essay. Help students make a list of persuasive words to include in their writing.

INTERMEDIATE / ADVANCED Students can work with a partner to apply the Writer's Craft skill as they create the "Much Better" examples on **Master 73**. They can read persuasive essays or listen to persuasive speeches for additional words to use in their writing. Have them record emotions, questions, and persuasive words they will use in their writing in the Word File.

Transparency 73 / Master 73

BEGINNING/ENDING SENTENCES

Directions: Read each writing tip and the example that is "Just Okay." Change the example to make it "Much Better."

Writing Tips	Just Okay	Much Better
Begin by expressing an emotion.	It is too bad that teenage drivers have accidents.	It frightens me that so many teenage drivers have accidents.
Begin by asking a question.	Do teenage drivers have accidents?	Do teenage drivers have an unusual number of accidents?
End with persuasive words.	Go to driving school.	We must go to driving school to learn to drive safely.

Word File Directions: List emotions, questions, and persuasive words for your essay.

Emotions/Questions	Persuasive Words

OBJECTIVES

REVISE

Function: Write; Engage in Discussion

Learning Strategies and Critical Thinking: Generate Ideas; Review; Clarify; Interact with Peers; Self-Assess

Listening and Speaking: Peer-Conferencing

Writing: ❶ Writing Process

REVISE

Explain that in revising their opinion essays, students will decide on changes to make that will explain the problem more clearly and persuade their readers to do what they suggest. Have students reread their essays and think about possible changes.

Next, model how to participate in a peer conference. Also model how to make revisions. Then conduct peer conferences and have students revise their writing.

▌ Use the Peer Conference Support in the **Multi-Level Strategies** to model how to evaluate and revise writing.

CLOSE AND ASSESS

Have peers discuss the questions in Think About Your Writing.

Writing That Persuades, continued

REVISE

1 Read Your Essay Does your essay persuade your reader to take action? Do you have strong beginning and ending sentences?

2 Share Your Essay Work in a group of four students. Read each essay. First tell what you like about it. Then ask questions and make suggestions:

- To tell what you like, start with:
  I really like the part where . . .
  It's great how you . . .
  The best thing about your essay is . . .

- To suggest changes, start with:
  You could add . . .
  This would be clearer if . . .
  What do you mean when you say . . .?

3 Make Your Changes Think about your group's comments and questions. Then make changes to improve your essay. Use the marks for revising your writing.

I am so tired of all the damage to our beautiful
   mean things about people
school. Students write on the walls. They ought to
   how this makes ∧ feel
think about other students.

They should also think about how damage makes
our school look ~~sometimes.~~ I think you will agree
that we want to be proud of our building (always).

Revising Marks

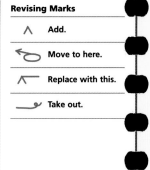

∧	Add.
↶	Move to here.
⋏	Replace with this.
⤸	Take out.

Think About Your Writing

- Do you like your first and last sentence?
- Did you persuade your readers to help with the problem?
- Do you like the way your essay sounds now?

REACHING ALL STUDENTS

Transparency 74 / Master 74

REVISING

Red annotations show changes related to the sample comments. Revisions should vary to reflect comments students make.

We must all help solve the bus problem.
   for all the students to have seats
The school should get enough buses.
   need to
Students can follow the rules and show respect.

Revising Marks

∧	Add.
↶	Move to here.
⋏	Replace with this.
⤸	Take out.

Help a Writer in a Peer Conference

1. Tell what you like.
   - The best thing about your essay is where you clearly summarize your opinion.
   - It's great how you Students' comments will vary.

2. Suggest changes.
   - You could add that there should be enough buses for everyone to get a seat.
   - This would be clearer if Students' comments will vary.
   - The best thing about your essay is Students' comments will vary.
   - You could add Students' suggestions will vary.

Transparency 74 Level A, Unit 4 | Community   © Hampton-Brown

---

Multi-Level Strategies

PEER CONFERENCE SUPPORT

BEGINNING   Display **Transparency 74**. Read the essay and support comprehension by paraphrasing it. Then model how to participate in a peer conference. Use the examples on the transparency and have volunteers dictate comments, using the sentence starters there or from page 258. Model how to revise the essay, based on the comments. Point out how revising the last sentence can make it more persuasive.

INTERMEDIATE / ADVANCED   Distribute **Master 74**. Read the essay and model commenting in a peer conference. Have students suggest more comments. They can then make revisions to the essay, based on the comments. You may want to suggest adding more persuasive language at the end. Remind students that, in revising, they can choose which changes to make from their own ideas and others' suggestions.

GRAMMAR IN CONTEXT

VERB TENSE

The tense of a verb shows when an action happens.

Earlier	Now	Later
Past Tense	Present Tense	Future Tense

The **present tense** of a verb tells about an action that is happening now.

> **Example:** Leon **cleans** the wall.

A present tense verb can also tell about something that happens all the time.

> **Example:** Leon **goes** to our middle school.

The **past tense** of a verb tells about an action that happened earlier, or in the past.

> **Examples:** Some kids **painted** pictures on the wall.
> They **wrote** on it, too.

The **future tense** of a verb tells about an action that will happen later, or in the future.

> **Examples:** We **will help** Leon.
> All of us **are going to clean** the wall.

The word **won't** also shows future tense. **Won't** is a contraction of the words **will** and **not.**

> **Example:** We **won't** finish today.

Practice Write each sentence. Choose the correct verb.

1. Ms. Vega ___works / worked___ in the school library every day.
2. Last week she ___will see / saw___ many damaged books.
3. Tomorrow, she ___will speak / spoke___ to us about the books.
4. She ___asked / is going to ask___ us to help.
5. Bill ___will tape / taped___ the torn pages.
6. I ___am going to fix / fix___ the backs of the books.
7. Last year, I also ___will help / helped___ in the school library.
8. It ___felt / won't feel___ good to do something for my school.

GRAMMAR IN CONTEXT

1 **Teach Verb Tense** Read the introduction and examples. Use a wall calendar to illustrate the tenses:

- Point to the current date and say: *This is now. We talk about things happening now in the present tense.*

- Point to the previous day and month and say: *Things that happened earlier are in the past. Yesterday, we talked about...* (Name a topic from the previous day.)

- Point to the next day and month and say: *Things that will happen are in the future. Soon, we will...* (Name an upcoming event.)

2 **Answers to Practice Items**

1. works	5. will tape
2. saw	6. am going to fix
3. will speak	7. helped
4. is going to ask	8. felt

CLOSE AND ASSESS

Give each student an index card with a verb in one tense. Mark sections of the room: *Present, Past, Future.* Students go to the correct section and read their verbs aloud.

Cooperative Learning

FOR LANGUAGE DEVELOPMENT:
Verb Tenses

Brainstorm Verbs Have teams divide chart paper into four columns and label them *Past, Present, Future,* and *Future—Won't.* Display a list of verbs.

talk	play
start	sew
bake	paint
live	walk

Team members should take turns filling in the chart with sentences using different verbs correctly in each tense. Encourage team members to assist one another so that all team members contribute.

Debrief the Skill Ask: *Which tense tells about an action that is happening now? What are the ways to show future tense?*

Debrief the Cooperative Process Have students reflect on the activity: *Did your group always agree on how to write the verb tense? If not, how did you decide what to write?*

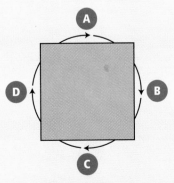

Cooperative Learning Structure:
Team Word Webbing

Build Writing Skills **T259**

✔ **WRITING ASSESSMENT**
Use the Writing Rubric on page 71 of the Assessment
Handbook to evaluate this writing assignment.

BUILD WRITING SKILLS

OBJECTIVES

EDIT AND PROOFREAD
Learning Strategies and Critical Thinking: Review; Clarify; Self-Assess
Writing: ❶ Writing Process

PUBLISH
Learning Strategies and Critical Thinking: Interact with Peers; Self-Assess; Make Decisions
Speaking: Read Aloud
Technology and Media: Use Word-Processing Software; Use Video
Writing: ❶ Writing Process

EDIT AND PROOFREAD

Remind students that to edit their essays, they will look for and mark errors. Use **Transparency 75** to model the process.

PUBLISH

Tell students that it is time to publish, or share, their essays. Have them choose from the publishing suggestions on page 260 or display the essays on a bulletin board titled "In My Opinion."

▌ Use the Editing and Publishing Support in the **Multi-Level Strategies** to meet the varying needs of students.

CLOSE AND ASSESS

Have groups discuss the questions in Think About Your Writing.

Writing That Persuades, continued

EDIT AND PROOFREAD

❶ **Proofread Your Essay** When you find a mistake in capitalization, punctuation, or spelling, correct it. See pages 431–439 of the Handbook for help. Use the Proofreading Marks.

❷ **Check Verb Tenses** Did you use present, past, and future tenses correctly?

❸ **Make a Final Copy** If you are working on a computer, print out a final copy of your work. If not, rewrite it and make the corrections you marked.

PUBLISH

Choose one of these ideas for sharing your essay.

• Tape your essay to a poster. Draw pictures around it.

• Make a video presentation. Videotape students cleaning up graffiti, for example. Edit the tape. Read your essay like a news reporter and show your video.

Proofreading Marks

∧	Add.
⩘	Add a comma.
⊙	Add a period.
≡	Capitalize.
/	Make lowercase.
℘	Take out.
¶	Indent.

Think About Your Writing

• Do you think your essay is effective?
  ☑ Did you state the problem and your opinion about it?
  ☑ Did you tell why there is a problem?
  ☑ Did you tell what action your readers should take?
  ☑ Did you use persuasive words?

• Will this essay go in your portfolio? Why or why not?

REACHING ALL STUDENTS

Transparency 75 / Master 75

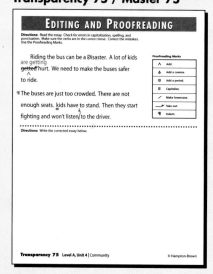

Multi-Level Strategies
EDITING AND PUBLISHING SUPPORT

BEGINNING Model finding and correcting errors in the essay on **Transparency 75**. After marking the edits, have students write out the corrected essay. For publishing, assist students who make a poster with finding photos or illustrations to go with their essays.

INTERMEDIATE Guide students in finding and correcting the errors in the essay on **Transparency 75**. For publishing, encourage students to read their essays aloud several times to a partner or small group before beginning to record their videos. Listeners should give feedback about voice expression and tone.

ADVANCED Distribute copies of **Master 75** and have students work on finding and correcting the errors individually or with partners. Students can create an introduction to the video, telling about their concerns. They can also write a conclusion summarizing the issues presented on the video.

✓ **ASSESSMENT**
The Unit 4 Test on page 73 of the Assessment Handbook measures students' progress in reading, language arts, literary study, and writing.
Additional forms in the Assessment Handbook allow for:
• Self Assessment on page 72
• Peer Assessment on page 101
• Portfolio Evaluation on page 103

❶ Look Back at the Unit

Rank Communities In this unit, you read about many communities.

Common Ground

Protecting Our Planet

Earthquake at Dawn

When Disaster Strikes

care a lot

not so much

Work with a partner. Draw a large thermometer. Mark a place for each selection. If the selection made you think or care more about your own community, mark it near the top. If the selection did not make you think about your community, put it near the bottom.

❷ Show What You Know

Sum It All Up Add new ideas to your mind map about community. Tell a partner about the community that is the most important to you.

Geographical

Community

Organizations

Special interests

Reflect and Evaluate Finish this sentence:
• The most important community is _____.
Add the sentence to your portfolio. Choose work from the unit that shows what you learned.

❸ Make Connections

To Your Community Host a science assembly at your school. Invite scientists to talk about natural disasters or the environment. Give reports and make displays. Invite other classes and people in your community to attend.

Unit Debrief **261**

EXPLORE "COMMUNITIES COUNT"

1 Look Back at the Unit After students draw their thermometers and place the selections, tally results to determine the selection that made students care the most about their community. Then begin the Cooperative Learning Activity.

2 Show What You Know Suggest that students include in their portfolios work that reflects the notion that communities do count.

3 Make Connections Help students center the assembly on an environmental issue that affects the community right now.

CLOSE AND ASSESS

Have students tell you the most important thing they learned in the unit.

Cooperative Learning

FOR CRITICAL THINKING:
Make Comparisons

Interview and Report Have partners compare their thermometers and interview each other about each placement. Students should justify their decisions, sharing information that informed their rankings. Then pairs compare and contrast how they ranked selections as they report to the group.

Debrief the Content Ask students what they learned about how much they care about their own communities by doing this exercise.

Debrief the Cooperative Process Have students evaluate their interview techniques. Ask: *What questions helped you understand your partner's ideas? What will you do differently the next time you interview someone?*

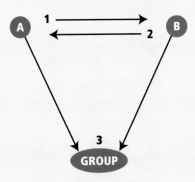

Cooperative Learning Structure: Three-Step Interview

Resources

For Success in Language, Literature, and Content

Student Book pages 262–333

For Skills Practice

Practice Book
pages 133–172

For Planning and Instruction

Teacher's Edition
pages T262a–T333

For Vocabulary and Language Development

Language Tape Side B
Language CD Tracks 9–12

For Audio Walk-Throughs and Selection Readings

Selection Tape 5
Selection CD 5

For Technology Support

Inspiration
Visual Learning Software
with Graphic Organizers

For Classroom Activities

Transparencies or Masters 76–93

For Home-School Connections

High Point Newsletters 9 and 10

For Comprehensive Assessment

Language Acquisition Assessment,
Selection Tests, Unit Test, Writing
Assessment, Self-Assessment

In the Theme Library

Coyote: A Trickster Tale from the American Southwest
by Gerald McDermott

Gilgamesh the King
by Ludmila Zeman

From *The Basics Bookshelf*

▶ *Gift of Fire*

▶ *All Across America*

▶ *Sunny and Moonshine: A Love Story*

Theme-related books with
simple text for including
newcomers

STORIES TO TELL

Ulysses and the Sirens. 4th century CE, mosaic tile.

WHETHER TOLD TO ENTERTAIN OR TO EXPLAIN, A STORY NOTES SOMETHING ABOUT WHO WE ARE AND WHAT WE ARE MADE OF. THROUGH A FOCUS ON THE STORYTELLING TRADITION, THIS UNIT INVITES STUDENTS, WHO ARE LIVING EVER-CHANGING STORIES OF THEIR OWN, TO EXPLORE THE POWER AND THE MYSTERY OF BEING HUMAN.

THEME 1 In the Beginning

Students look back at the stories told by earlier cultures to explain the way things were.

THEME 2 Telling the Tale

Students discover that storytellers around the world have many stories and many ways to share their tales.

THEME 1: In the Beginning

PACING SUGGESTIONS

LESSONS	45–55 MINUTE PERIODS	BLOCK SCHEDULE SESSIONS
1	1 period ⎤	
2–8	8 periods ⎥→	4 sessions
9–17	8 periods	4 sessions

LESSONS

1

THEME 1 OPENER ▶ pages T264–T265

Function	Learning Strategy	Vocabulary	Critical Thinking
Engage in Discussion	Make a Chart	Storytelling Words	Formulate Questions

2–8

Echo & Narcissus by Antonia Barber *Ancient Greece*   GREEK MYTH AND ARTICLE ▶ pages T268–T277

BUILD LANGUAGE AND VOCABULARY pages T266–T267	Function ⊤ Describe	Learning Strategy Make a Character Chart	Vocabulary Describing Words	Patterns and Structures ⊤ Complete Sentences

PREPARE TO READ
page T268

Activate Prior Knowledge
Quickwrite

Vocabulary ⊤
Relate Words

Reading Strategy
⊤ Monitor Your Reading

READ THE SELECTION
pages T269–T275

Pre-Reading Strategies
Preview and Predict

Identify Genre:
Greek Myth

Set Purpose

Strategy Focus
⊤ Monitor Your Reading

Self-Monitoring and Comprehension
⊤ Use Text Features in Fiction and Nonfiction

Before You Move On:
Think and Discuss

📁 **Grammar Minilesson:**
Phrases

📁 **Literary Analysis Minilessons:**
Character Traits and Motives

⊤ Goal and Outcome

RESPOND
pages T276–T277

CHECK YOUR UNDERSTANDING

Critical Thinking and Comprehension
Sum It Up:
Analyze Information;
Make Judgments

Think It Over:
Discuss

Function
Express Yourself:
Express Opinions;
Describe

LANGUAGE ARTS AND CONTENT AREA CONNECTIONS

Grammar in Context
⊤ Use Complete Sentences

Writing/Speaking
Write a New Ending for a Myth

Social Studies
Compare Governments

9–17

How the Ox Star Fell from Heaven by Lily Toy Hong *Ancient China*   CHINESE MYTH AND ARTICLE ▶ pages T280–T291

BUILD LANGUAGE AND VOCABULARY pages T278–T279	Function ⊤ Make Comparisons	Learning Strategy Make a Comparison Chart	Vocabulary Antonyms	Patterns and Structures ⊤ Compound Sentences

PREPARE TO READ
page T280

Activate Prior Knowledge
Brainstorm

Vocabulary ⊤
Locate and Use Definitions

Reading Strategy
⊤ Recognize Fiction and Nonfiction

READ THE SELECTION
pages T281–T287

Pre-Reading Strategies
Preview and Predict

Set Purpose

Strategy Focus
⊤ Use Text Features in Fiction and Nonfiction

Self-Monitoring and Comprehension
Use Visuals

Before You Move On:
Think and Discuss

📁 **Grammar Minilesson:**
⊤ Compound Sentences

📁 **Literary Analysis Minilessons:**
Description

Fantasy and Reality

RESPOND
pages T288–T291

CHECK YOUR UNDERSTANDING

Critical Thinking and Comprehension
Sum It Up:
⊤ Relate Events in a Sequence;
⊤ Compare Literature

Think It Over: Discuss

Function
Express Yourself:
Negotiate

LANGUAGE ARTS AND LITERATURE

Grammar in Context
⊤ Use Complete Sentences

⊤ Use Compound Sentences

Literary Analysis and Writing
⊤ Compare Myths in an Essay

⊤ Compare Fiction and Nonfiction

CONTENT AREA CONNECTIONS

Social Studies and Technology/Media
Study Modern China

THEME 2: Telling the Tale

1

	45–55 MINUTE	BLOCK SCHEDULE
LESSONS	PERIODS	SESSIONS
1	1 period	
2–9	7 periods	4 sessions
10–18	8 periods	4 sessions
19–22	3 periods	2 sessions

PACING SUGGESTIONS

THEME 2 OPENER
▶ *pages T292–T293*

Function	Learning Strategy	Vocabulary	Critical Thinking
Engage in Discussion	Make Observations	Storytelling Words	Generate Ideas

2–9

The Art of the Tall Tale by Chuck Larkin
ARTICLE AND TALL TALE ▶ *pages T296–T305*

BUILD LANGUAGE AND VOCABULARY pages T294–T295	Function ⓣ Retell a Story	Learning Strategy Complete a Story Map	Vocabulary Time and Cause Words	Patterns and Structures ⓣ Complex Sentences

PREPARE TO READ
page T296

Activate Prior Knowledge
Play a Game

Vocabulary ⓣ
Relate Words

Reading Strategy
ⓣ Use Graphic Organizers (time line)

READ THE SELECTION pages T297–T302

Pre-Reading Strategies
Preview and Predict

Set Purpose

Strategy Focus
ⓣ Use Graphic Organizers (time line)

Comprehension
Use Text Features (sidebar)

Before You Move On: Think and Discuss

Grammar Minilesson:
ⓣ Complex Sentences

Literary Analysis Minilesson:
Setting

RESPOND pages T303–T305

CHECK YOUR UNDERSTANDING

Critical Thinking and Comprehension
Sum It Up:
ⓣ Relate Events in a Sequence; Retell a Story; Synthesize Information

Think It Over: Discuss

Function
Express Yourself: Elaborate

LANGUAGE ARTS AND LITERATURE

Grammar in Context
ⓣ Use Complex Sentences

Writing/Speaking
Write a New Episode

CONTENT AREA CONNECTIONS

Social Studies
Explore Geography (map)

Science and Technology/Media
Study Wild Animals

10–18

Unwinding the Magic Thread by Diane Wolkstein
ARTICLE AND HAITIAN FOLK TALE ▶ *pages T308–T320*

BUILD LANGUAGE AND VOCABULARY pages T306–T307	Function Tell an Original Story	Learning Strategy Interact with Peers	Vocabulary Story Words	Patterns and Structures ⓣ Present Perfect Tense

PREPARE TO READ
page T308

Activate Prior Knowledge
Make a Storytelling Web

Vocabulary ⓣ
Relate Words

Reading Strategy
ⓣ Relate Goals and Outcomes

READ THE SELECTION pages T309–T317

Pre-Reading Strategies
Preview and Predict

Set Purpose

Strategy Focus
ⓣ Relate Goals and Outcomes

Comprehension
Before You Move On: Think and Discuss

Grammar Minilessons:
ⓣ Complex Sentences
ⓣ Present Perfect Tense

Past Progressive Forms of Verbs

Helping Verbs

RESPOND pages T318–T320

CHECK YOUR UNDERSTANDING

Critical Thinking and Comprehension
Sum It Up:
ⓣ Relate Goals and Outcomes

Think It Over: Discuss

Function
Express Yourself: Tell an Original Story

LANGUAGE ARTS AND LITERATURE

Grammar in Context
ⓣ Use Present Perfect Tense

Literary Analysis and Writing
Write a Character Study

Writing
Write a Friendly Letter

CONTENT AREA CONNECTIONS

Social Studies and Technology/Media
Make a Travel Guide

19–22

When I Taste Salt by Carmen Agra Deedy
NEVER-ENDING POEM ▶ *pages T321–T325*

PREPARE TO READ
page T321

Activate Prior Knowledge
Share Memories

Vocabulary
Use Context Clues

Reading Strategy
ⓣ Interpret Figurative Language

READ THE POEM
pages T322–T323

Pre-Reading Strategies
Set Purpose

Strategy Focus
ⓣ Interpret Figurative Language

RESPOND pages T324–T325

CHECK YOUR UNDERSTANDING

Critical Thinking and Comprehension
Sum It Up: Paraphrase;
ⓣ Draw Conclusions

Think It Over: Discuss

Function
Express Yourself: Clarify

LANGUAGE ARTS AND LITERATURE

Literary Analysis
Learn About Alliteration

Vocabulary and Writing
ⓣ Use Sensory Words

BUILD WRITING SKILLS

WRITING THAT TELLS A STORY
NARRATIVE: STORY ▶ *pages T326–T332*

Writing Mode/Form ⓣ Narrative Story	Writing Process ⓣ Prewrite; Draft; Revise; Edit and Proofread; Publish	Writer's Craft ⓣ Show, Don't Tell	Grammar in Context ⓣ Complete Sentences	Reflect and Evaluate Self-Assessment

ⓣ = Assessed on **Unit 5 Test**   ⓣ = Assessed on **Unit 5 Language Acquisition Assessment**

THEME 1: In the Beginning

MORE RESOURCES

Coyote: A Trickster Tale from the American Southwest
by Gerald McDermott
B An amusing tale that tells why Coyote is the color of dust and has a burnt tip on his tail. (Available from Hampton-Brown)

Why Rat Comes First
by Clara Yen
I The story of how Rat wins a contest and becomes the first of 12 animals in the Chinese Calendar. (Children's Book Press)

Creation: Read-Aloud Stories from Many Lands
retold by Ann Pilling
A Stories from around the world explain the wonders of Earth and its creatures. (Candlewick Press)

Dateline: Troy
by Paul Fleischman
I The famous author parallels events of the Trojan war with real news clippings from around the world. (Candlewick Press)

Favorite Greek Myths
by Mary Pope Osborne
A Classic stories of ancient Greece are beautifully told and illustrated in this edition by a famous author. (Scholastic)

The Greek and Roman World
B I A The history and culture of ancient Greece and Rome come to life for students in this fascinating program. (Clearvue/SVE) **CD-ROM**

THEME 2: Telling the Tale

MORE RESOURCES

Gilgamesh the King
by Ludmila Zeman
I In one of the world's oldest stories, Enkidu teaches the evil Gilgamesh how to become a good king. (Available from Hampton-Brown)

John Henry and His Mighty Hammer
by Patsy Jensen
B The story of an American folk hero who splits rock faster than a machine. (Dragonfly-Knopf)

The Singing Man
by Angela Shelf Medearis
A Long ago in West Africa, a young man leaves home to become a musician. He returns years later as the king's singing storyteller. (Holiday House)

Listen to the Storyteller
by Kristen Balouch
B I A collection of three vibrantly illustrated stories from around the world. A separate CD/cassette offers narrations with original soundtracks by famous musicians. (Viking)

Paul Bunyan
by Steven Kellogg
I The legendary escapades of Paul Bunyan are cleverly told and illustrated in this version of his story. (Econo-Clad Books)

Pecos Bill
from Shelley Duvall's "Tall Tales and Legends" series
B I The hilarious adventures of an American folk hero are reenacted in this entertaining video. **Video**

ONGOING, INFORMAL ASSESSMENT

Check for understanding and achieve closure for every lesson with the targeted questions and activities in the **Close and Assess** boxes in your Teacher's Edition.

INDIVIDUAL AND GROUP-ADMINISTERED TESTS

The **Assessment Handbook** includes these comprehensive assessment tools for Unit 5:

▶ **Selection Tests**
Test students' mastery of reading strategies and the vocabulary, comprehension, and language arts skills taught with each main selection of Unit 5.

▶ **Unit Test in Standardized Test Format**
The multiple-choice sections of this test measure students' cumulative understanding of the skills and language developed in Unit 5. A Writing Prompt measures progress in writing skills and fluency. The Read, Think, and Explain section offers open-ended items to measure strategies and comprehension.

▶ **Language Acquisition Assessment**
To verify students' ability to use the vocabulary and grammar structures taught in Unit 5, conduct these performance assessments.

UNIT 5 ASSESSMENT OPPORTUNITIES	
	Assessment Handbook Pages
Unit 5 Language Acquisition Assessment	81–82
Selection Tests	
Echo and Narcissus	83–84
How the Ox Star Fell from Heaven	85–86
The Art of the Tall Tale	87–88
Unwinding the Magic Thread	89–90
Unit 5 Writing Assessment	91
Unit 5 Self-Assessment Form	92
Unit 5 Test	93–100
Peer-Assessment Form	101
Portfolio Evaluation Form	103

SELF- AND PEER-ASSESSMENT

Students use the Unit 5 Self-Assessment Form in the **Assessment Handbook** to evaluate their own work and develop learning strategies appropriate to their needs. Students offer feedback to their classmates with the Peer-Assessment Form.

WRITING ASSESSMENT / PORTFOLIO OPPORTUNITIES

You can evaluate students' writing using the rubrics and scoring guidelines provided in the **Assessment Handbook**. Then collaborate with students to choose work for their portfolios.

INTRODUCE UNIT 5

OBJECTIVES

Function: Engage in Discussion

Concepts and Vocabulary:
Storytelling—*culture, tradition, tales, storytellers*; Ancient Greece

Viewing: Interpret a Visual Image

Critical Thinking and Learning Strategies: Preview; Build Background; Use Graphic Organizers (mind map); Make Comparisons

Writing: Story

INTRODUCE UNIT CONCEPT

1 Interpret the Unit Title Ask: *What is a story? Who tells stories? Can pictures tell stories?*

2 View *Ulysses and the Sirens* Say: *In ancient Greece, people believed that sirens were magical women who lived on islands in the sea. When sailors heard their beautiful singing, they would go to the island and stay forever.*

3 Tell a Story and Build Vocabulary Use **Transparency/Master 76** for partners or small groups to tell a story about the mosaic.

> Use the Vocabulary Options in the **Multi-Level Strategies** to work with all proficiency levels.

After the activity, tell students that in this scene from *The Odyssey*, Ulysses is tied to the ship so he won't follow the sirens.

Ulysses and the Sirens, 4th century CE, mosaic tile.

262

REACHING ALL STUDENTS

Transparency 76 / Master 76

TELLING STORIES THROUGH ART

Directions: List as many details as you can about what you see in the picture on page 262.

People	Place/Time	Things	Actions

Directions: Tell a story that goes with the picture of *Ulysses and the Sirens*. Use words from your list.

Tell the Story:

_____

_____

_____

_____

Transparency 76 Level A, Unit 5 | Traditions   © Hampton-Brown

Multi-Level Strategies
VOCABULARY BUILDING OPTIONS

BEGINNING Use simple questions to reinforce new vocabulary and build story concepts: *Can you see sirens on an island here? Where do you think they are? Are shields used for fighting? Do you think the men fight in the boat or on land?* Work as a group to complete **Transparency 76**. Prompt students to use information from the chart to create story text. Students can create and tell about individual pictures to accompany the group story.

INTERMEDIATE / ADVANCED Have heterogeneous pairs work together to complete the chart on **Master 76**; then review it with the group. Make sure to include these words: (for *people*) *sailor, leader*; (for *things*) *oars, sails, mast, ship*; (for *actions*) *row, fight, sail, stand, sit*, etc. Brainstorm story ideas, and then have partners write and tell stories.

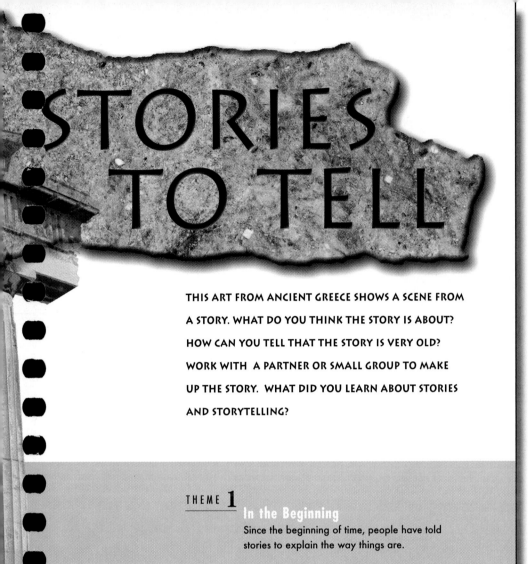

STORIES TO TELL

THIS ART FROM ANCIENT GREECE SHOWS A SCENE FROM
A STORY. WHAT DO YOU THINK THE STORY IS ABOUT?
HOW CAN YOU TELL THAT THE STORY IS VERY OLD?
WORK WITH A PARTNER OR SMALL GROUP TO MAKE
UP THE STORY. WHAT DID YOU LEARN ABOUT STORIES
AND STORYTELLING?

THEME **1**
In the Beginning
Since the beginning of time, people have told
stories to explain the way things are.

THEME **2**
Telling the Tale
Storytellers from around the world have many
stories and many ways to share their tales.

263

UNIT 5 Mind Map

People who
tell stories

How people
tell stories

Storytelling

What people
tell stories about

Why people
tell stories

Technology Support
See **Inspiration** Visual Learning
software for support in creating mind maps.

---

4 **Compare Stories and Discuss
Storytelling** Ask: *How can you tell
that the story in the picture is very old?
What does this tell you about stories
and storytelling?*

Summarize: *We can tell that the story
is old from the style of the clothing and
the boat. Stories can be told through
art, writing, and oral traditions. We are
all storytellers.*

PREVIEW UNIT THEMES

5 **Preview Theme 1: In the Beginning**
Read aloud the theme title and the
theme statement. Define *beginning* as
"the start" or "first." Tell students that
today, science and knowledge from
our ancestors help us understand
many things about our world. Long
ago, before people understood as
much, they made up stories to explain
things about the world.

Invite students to look over
pages 264–291 to see some of these
stories from long ago.

6 **Preview Theme 2: Telling the Tale**
Read the theme title and statement.
Help students understand that
people from around the world and
from the beginning of time have
been telling stories or tales. Invite
them to look over pages 292–325
and find pictures, captions, and
headings about telling tales.

7 **Create a Mind Map** Begin a class
mind map on storytelling and have
students start a personal map in their
notebooks or in the **Practice Book**.
As you work through the unit,
encourage students to add to the
mind map.

▶ **Practice Book** page 133

CLOSE AND ASSESS

Ask:
- *What will this unit be about?* (traditional
  stories; telling stories)
- *Who tells stories? What do people tell
  stories about?* (People from all times and
  all cultures tell stories to inform, share
  ideas, pass down traditions, entertain.)

INTRODUCE THEME 1

OBJECTIVES

Function: Engage in Discussion
Concepts and Vocabulary:
Storytelling—*ancient, culture, tradition, beliefs*
Viewing: Respond to a Visual Image
Learning Strategies:
Relate to Personal Experience;
Use Graphic Organizers (planning chart)
Critical Thinking: Generate Ideas;
Formulate Questions

TAP PRIOR KNOWLEDGE

1 **Imagine Beginnings** Ask: *What do we know about a book when we open to its first page? What about when we begin a new day?* Help students conclude that sometimes we don't have all the information we need to understand things in the beginning. Explain that, in this theme, they will read stories that were first told long ago, when people tried to understand the world around them.

VIEW, DISCUSS, AND TELL A STORY

2 **Generate Ideas and Formulate Questions** After students view the painting, explain that people have told stories about the sun since the beginning of time. Ask: *What other elements of nature do you think people wanted to understand long ago?* Record student responses on a chart.

Element of Nature	Questions
The sun	Where did it come from?
The stars	Why do stars shine?
Rain	How does it get in the sky?

3 **Tell How It Came To Be** Have mixed proficiency groups choose one of the natural forces from the chart and tell a traditional or original story about how it came to be.

> Use the Storytelling Options in the **Multi-Level Strategies** to work with all students.

Ad Marginem, Paul Klee, oil on canvas, 1930.

264 **Unit 5** | Traditions

REACHING ALL STUDENTS

Multi-Level Strategies
STORYTELLING OPTIONS

BEGINNING After mixed groups brainstorm story ideas, have students create an illustration to go with their group's story. Ask questions about the drawings: *Pia, why is the star red? Jalil, is the sun coming up or going down?* Provide sentence frames for students to use as captions: *The sun is _____. The rain comes from the _____.*

INTERMEDIATE / ADVANCED After groups brainstorm story ideas, Intermediate students can tell the story while an Advanced partner writes it. When students present stories to the class, ask Advanced students to give a short introduction to the story before Intermediate students present the telling.

In the Beginning

- Why did ancient peoples use stories to explain how things happen?

- What makes the stories of one culture different from the stories of another culture?

- What do stories tell you about the traditions and beliefs of a culture?

THEME-RELATED BOOKS

Coyote: a Trickster Tale from the American Southwest
by Gerald McDermott

An amusing tale that tells why Coyote is the color of dust and has a burnt tip on his tail.

BEGINNING

Why Rat Comes First
by Clara Yen

The story of how Rat wins a contest and becomes the first of 12 animals in the Chinese calendar.

INTERMEDIATE

ANTHOLOGY

Creation: Read-Aloud Stories from Many Lands
retold by Ann Pilling

Stories from around the world explain the wonders of Earth and its creatures.

ADVANCED

265

THEME 1

DISCUSS THE GUIDING QUESTIONS

4 Set the Theme Some key points to develop during the discussion are:

- Ancient peoples, just like all peoples, wanted to understand their world. Stories can help people accept and understand their world. Stories can help give shape and meaning to the world around us.

- Different cultures have different ways of life that reflect different geographic settings, languages, traditions, religions, and values, as well as different ways to access food, shelter, and clothing.

- Stories tell how people of varying cultures relate to the world around them and to other people. A story can tell us how societies are structured or organized, for example, with kings or queens or other leaders. It can tell how people relate to nature, Earth, and their environment.

Form groups and use the **Multi-Level Strategies** so all students can participate.

CLOSE AND ASSESS

Have students draw the outline of an open book. Invite each student to draw a picture or write a brief description of what stories can tell us about a culture.

Multi-Level Strategies
GROUPING GUIDELINES

BEGINNING Guide students in talking about formulaic story words (e.g. *Once upon a time, lived happily ever after*). Encourage students to share and explain examples in their home language, and to discuss characters from traditional stories they know. Remind them of Aesop's animal characters.

INTERMEDIATE In small groups, encourage students to share stories from their own cultures or family traditions. Ask: *Do you know a story about why the sun rises and sets? Why the seasons change? Why disasters occur?* Have students list stories and track how many versions they know.

ADVANCED Let students work in culturally heterogeneous groups. Have them discuss a story common to more than one culture and identify the elements of tradition and belief that influenced the way the tale is told in each culture.

THEME LIBRARY

■ *Coyote* by Gerald McDermott
After students read *Coyote,* ask them to talk about how this book fits the theme of "In the Beginning." Ask: *Does this book tell the story of how something came to be? What does it explain?* Encourage students to point out how the culture that produced this story is reflected in story details, and to note specific cultural influences in the other selections in this theme.

Theme Opener **T265**

BUILD LANGUAGE AND VOCABULARY

Function: Listen Actively; ❶ Describe

Concepts and Vocabulary:
Describing Words

Patterns and Structures:
❶ Complete Sentences

Listening and Speaking: Poem

Critical Thinking and Learning Strategy:
Generate Ideas; Use Graphic Organizers
(character chart)

Writing: Description

START WITH A COMMON EXPERIENCE

1 Listen to a Rap Play
the recording of "The
Mount Olympus Rap" on
the **Language Tape/CD,** or read the
rap aloud. Then play the tape again
and ask students to point to the
picture of each god or goddess as
he or she is named.

Tape 1B
CD 1
Track 9

2 Conduct a Choral Reading Invite
students to chime in or take parts in
a group reading of the rap.

> Use the Choral Reading Options
> in the **Multi-Level Strategies**
> to include all students.

3 Model How to Describe Use the
following Think Aloud to help
students learn to describe characters.

> **How to Describe**
>
> • Name a character: *Athena*
>
> • Tell what she looked like: *She looked powerful and warlike.*
>
> • Tell what she did: *She protected Greek cities.*
>
> • Tell what she was like inside: *She was wise and charming.*

Build Language and Vocabulary
DESCRIBE

Listen to this rap about the gods and goddesses of ancient Greece.

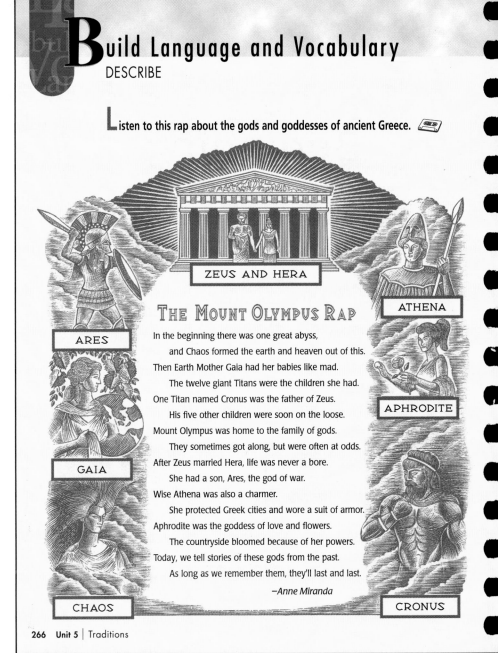

ZEUS AND HERA

ARES

ATHENA

GAIA

APHRODITE

CHAOS

CRONUS

THE MOUNT OLYMPUS RAP

In the beginning there was one great abyss,
    and Chaos formed the earth and heaven out of this.
Then Earth Mother Gaia had her babies like mad.
    The twelve giant Titans were the children she had.
One Titan named Cronus was the father of Zeus.
    His five other children were soon on the loose.
Mount Olympus was home to the family of gods.
    They sometimes got along, but were often at odds.
After Zeus married Hera, life was never a bore.
    She had a son, Ares, the god of war.
Wise Athena was also a charmer.
    She protected Greek cities and wore a suit of armor.
Aphrodite was the goddess of love and flowers.
    The countryside bloomed because of her powers.
Today, we tell stories of these gods from the past.
    As long as we remember them, they'll last and last.

        —Anne Miranda

REACHING ALL STUDENTS

Multi-Level Strategies
CHORAL READING OPTIONS

BEGINNING Read aloud the poem several times, restating as necessary
to clarify meaning (e.g., *bottomless space* for *abyss, arguing* for *at odds*). Play
the recording from the **Language Tape/CD**, and ask students to listen and
try to chime in on the rhyming word at the end of each two-line verse.

INTERMEDIATE Read the poem aloud or play the recording from the
Language Tape/CD as students follow along. Then assign groups of
students to represent one god or goddess. On a rereading, have them stand
and read aloud when they hear the verses mentioning their character.

ADVANCED Have students read the poem as they listen to the recording.
Assign each verse to a pair of students, then have the group recite the whole
poem with each pair speaking their verse in turn. Advanced students can read
the whole poem through as Intermediates and Beginners chime in.

MAKE A CHARACTER CHART

Work with the group to list all the characters in the poem on a chart. Also record what each character did. Follow this model:

Name	What Character Did
Chaos	formed earth and heaven
Gaia	had the 12 Titans

BUILD YOUR VOCABULARY

Describing Words Look at the pictures of the gods and goddesses on page 266. Think of a word to describe each one, or choose one from the **Word Bank**. Add a third column to your chart. In it, write a word to describe each character:

Name	What Character Did	What Character Was Like
Chaos	formed earth and heaven	powerful
Gaia	had the 12 Titans	strong

Word Bank

beautiful
big
dark
fierce
powerful
strong
tall
ugly

USE LANGUAGE STRUCTURES ▶ COMPLETE SENTENCES

Writing: Describe Greek Gods Choose a Greek god or goddess. Use the information from the character chart to write two complete sentences. Tell what the god or goddess did, and what he or she was like. Be sure each sentence includes a subject and a predicate.

Example:
Athena protected Greek cities. She was powerful.

CONDUCT THE ACTIVITIES

4 **Make a Character Chart** Have students work in small groups to create their charts.

5 **Build Your Vocabulary: Describing Words** Point out that students can choose describing words that tell what the character was like inside as well as what the character looked like.

6 **Use Language Structures: Complete Sentences** Present the skill using the definition and examples on **Transparency 77**. You may want to explain and identify the simple subject and simple predicate for students. Then have them complete the sentences in Try It!

Writing: Describe Greek Gods
Conduct the activity at the bottom of page 267. Some students may want to illustrate their sentences.

Use the Writing Activity Options in the **Multi-Level Strategies** to adjust instruction.

▶ **Practice Book** page 134

CLOSE AND ASSESS

Ask students to name the two parts of a complete sentence. Then ask them to add a subject or a predicate to complete these sentences: _____ *is a Greek god/goddess. He/She _____.*

Multi-Level Strategies
WRITING ACTIVITY OPTIONS

BEGINNING Model how each sentence must contain a subject that tells whom the sentence is about and a predicate—beginning with a verb—that tells what the subject does, is, or has. Write the sentences as a group.

INTERMEDIATE Remind students of the lesson on elaborating in Unit 4. Suggest that students expand their descriptions with adjectives, adverbs, and prepositional phrases to make their writing more interesting and vivid.

ADVANCED After writing their sentences, Advanced learners may be interested in conducting research into the attributes of other Greek gods and goddesses. They should then write sentences about one of these new characters and share the information with the class.

Transparency 77 / Master 77

LEARN ABOUT COMPLETE SENTENCES

A complete sentence has a **subject** and a **predicate**.
The ancient Greeks   had many gods.
   subject   predicate

1. The **subject** tells what the sentence is about. The subject can have one word or more than one word.
   Myths tell stories about the gods.
   All the gods lived on Mount Olympus.

2. The **predicate** tells what the subject is, does, or has. The predicate can have one word or more than one word.
   Ares **was the god of war.**
   This powerful god **fought many enemies.**
   He **had a suit of armor.**

Try It!

Add a subject or a predicate to complete each sentence.

1. Wise Athena _____
2. _____ made the flowers bloom.
3. _____ often fought among themselves.
4. Many stories _____

Transparency 77 Level A, Unit 5 | Traditions   © Hampton-Brown

OBJECTIVES

THINK ABOUT WHAT YOU KNOW

Concepts and Vocabulary: Nature Words

Reading and Learning Strategies:
Activate Prior Knowledge

LEARN KEY VOCABULARY ⓣ

Vocabulary Strategy: Relate Words

LEARN TO MONITOR YOUR READING

Reading Strategy: ⓣ Monitor Your
Reading (preview, visualize,
clarify, paraphrase)

THINK ABOUT WHAT YOU KNOW

1 Quickwrite Brainstorm nature topics. Ask: *Have you ever wondered what causes lightning or why leaves change color in autumn? Do you know why roses have thorns?* Give students time to write and then share ideas.

LEARN KEY VOCABULARY

2 Relate Words Read each vocabulary word and its defining sentence aloud.

After students understand the meaning of key vocabulary words conduct the word-pairing activity.

▌ Use the Vocabulary Options in **Multi-Level Strategies** to tailor instruction to proficiency levels.

▶ **Practice Book** page 135

LEARN TO MONITOR YOUR READING

3 Model How to Monitor Your Reading Define *monitor* as "to watch or keep track of." Help students see the purpose of monitoring: to make sure we understand the meaning of what we read. Conduct the activity on **Transparency 78** with the group. Record students' ideas on the Transparency after each monitoring pause; students can use paper to draw what they visualize.

CLOSE AND ASSESS

Ask students to agree on three questions to monitor their reading. (*What is the selection about? Do the events make sense? What words go together?*)

Echo & Narcissus

Greek myth retold
by Antonia Barber

Prepare to Read

THINK ABOUT WHAT YOU KNOW

Quickwrite Choose something in nature, such as thunder, fire, or the ocean. Write why or how you think it came to be. Give a real or imaginary explanation. Share your ideas with the class.

adorable Something is **adorable** when it is pretty and delightful.

attendant An **attendant** is someone who serves another person.

disrespectful You are **disrespectful** when you are rude or impolite.

echo You hear an **echo** when you hear the same sound repeated many times in a row.

pine When you **pine** for something, you feel sad and sick because you want it.

repeat When you **repeat** something, you say it again.

took pity If you **took pity** on someone, you felt sorry for that person.

wept When you **weep**, you cry. **Wept** is the past tense of *weep*.

wood nymph In Greek myths, a **wood nymph** is a spirit that lives in the forest and looks like a beautiful young woman.

Answers to the vocabulary activity will vary.

LEARN KEY VOCABULARY

Relate Words Study the new words. Then work with a partner to connect pairs of words in the list. Explain why they go together.

Example:

__Echo__ and __repeat__ go together

because __an echo repeats a sound__.

LEARN TO MONITOR YOUR READING

When you **monitor your reading**, you make sure that you understand the selection as you read.

> **READING STRATEGY**
> **How to Monitor Your Reading**
> 1. **Preview** the selection. Ask yourself: What will the selection be about?
> 2. **Visualize** the events as you read. Ask yourself: What pictures does the story make me see?
> 3. **Clarify** the meaning of words. Ask yourself: What words go together? How are the words used in a sentence?
> 4. **Paraphrase** the selection. Ask yourself: How can I retell the selection in my own words?

Monitor your reading as you read "Echo and Narcissus" and the article on ancient Greece.

REACHING ALL STUDENTS

▌ **Multi-Level Strategies**
VOCABULARY OPTIONS

BEGINNING Use expressions and gestures to illustrate *disrespectful, pine,* and *wept*. Use your voice for *echo* and *repeat*. Invite students to suggest something that is *adorable*.

INTERMEDIATE Work with students to paraphrase the definitions. Then ask pairs to create their own definition sentences.

ADVANCED Have students write original sentences using two vocabulary words in each one.

Transparency 78 / Master 78

HOW TO MONITOR YOUR READING

Directions: Read the title to preview the story. As you read, complete the activities in the boxes.

Pandora's Box

Long ago, Earth was a beautiful place. The green fields were full of flowers. Animals and people lived in harmony. Pandora was the first woman on Earth. Like everyone else, she was happy.

One day, Pandora was called by Zeus, the king of the gods. He gave her a beautiful box with a golden clasp.

"Pandora," he said, "I am giving you this box. It must never be opened. I can trust you."

Pandora hid the box, but she thought about it all the time. At last, she took a quick peek. When she opened the lid, evil, grief, and misery escaped from the box.

Visualize: What picture of the world forms in your mind as you read?

Students may draw a picture or describe it in words.

Clarify: What is the meaning of *clasp*?

A device for holding things together, a fastener

Paraphrase: "Pandora hid the box, but she thought about it all the time."

Pandora put the box away, out of sight, but she couldn't stop thinking about it.

Transparency 78 Level A, Unit 5 | Traditions   © Hampton-Brown

Echo & Narcissus

a Greek myth retold by Antonia Barber

L ong ago people made up stories to explain things they did not understand. This story tells how the narcissus flower came to be—and why we hear echoes.

269

READ THE SELECTION

OBJECTIVES

Listening: Listen to a Preview
Reading Strategies: Preview; Predict
Literary Analysis: Myth

INTRODUCE THE SELECTION

4 **Preview and Predict** Read the title, author, and introduction. Ask: *What do you think you will learn about how the narcissus flower and echoes came to be?*

5 **Identify Genre: Greek Myth** Define *myth* as a traditional story that often explains how a practice, belief, or something in nature came to be. Tell students that many famous myths originated in ancient Greece, and these are called Greek myths.

6 **Audio Walk-Through** Play the Audio Walk-Through for "Echo and Narcissus" on the **Selection Tape/CD** to give students the overall idea of the story. Before reading the nonfiction article on pages 274–275, play the Audio Walk-Through for "Life in Ancient Greece."

Tape 5A
CD 5
Track 1

Echo and Narcissus
retold by Antonia Barber

Theme Connection This selection is a retelling of a classic Greek myth that explains how two elements of nature came to be "in the beginning."

Selection Summary and Background The introduction on page 269 of the student book offers a summary of the selection. This myth is one of many that tell how Hera, the queen of the Greek gods, used her powers to punish others for inappropriate behavior.

Author Award Author Antonia Barber has been a Carnegie Award nominee.

READ PAGES 270–271

OBJECTIVES

Function: Read a Selection
Concepts and Vocabulary: Feelings
Listening: Listen to a Selection
Reading and Learning Strategies:
❶ Monitor Your Reading (visualize, clarify, paraphrase); Set a Purpose for Reading
Comprehension: Summarize
Literary Analysis:
Character Traits and Motives

SET PURPOSE

1 Say: *Listen to find out what Hera, the queen of the gods, does to Echo for talking too much.*

READ AND THINK

Tape 5A
CD 5
Track 2

2 Strategy Focus: Monitor Your Reading As students read the myth, remind them to pause to monitor their reading by visualizing, clarifying, and paraphrasing. Have students use their journals to record ideas. Use a similar process with the article on pages 274–275.

Choose Reading Options in the **Multi-Level Strategies** to tailor the reading to proficiency levels.

The **Selection Tape /CD** offers an oral language model and the opportunity to build reading fluency.

Red annotations offer opportunities to clarify meaning and check for understanding.

1

ECHO IS PUNISHED

The queen of the gods gets angry with Echo for talking too much. To punish her, the queen allows Echo to only repeat other people's words.

ℋera was the queen of the gods. Among her many **attendants** was a **lovely wood nymph** named **Echo**. Hera **was very fond of her**. But the little nymph talked too much, and Hera grew tired of the sound of her voice. What was worse, Echo always tried to **have the last word**. That was **disrespectful** to the queen of the gods. It was also very **irritating**.

One day, Hera **could bear it no longer**. "You shall have the last word," she told Echo angrily. "But you shall have no other. And the last word you have shall not be your own." From that moment, Echo was unable to speak unless she **repeated** words already spoken.

The poor nymph **pined** until she became a thin shadow. She left her companions and **roamed** the lonely valleys, where her **faint** voice could sometimes be heard repeating the calls of happier mortals.

Define *mortals:* Mortals are ordinary people like you and me, not gods and goddesses.

---

lovely beautiful, pretty
was very fond of her liked her a lot
have the last word be the person who said the last thing in a conversation, have a clever answer
irritating annoying, bothersome

could bear it no longer was very upset, lost her patience
roamed walked around
faint weak, quiet

REACHING ALL STUDENTS

Art Connection
CAMPAIGN POSTERS

Provide an opportunity for students to research deities from Greek mythology. Then have them imagine that they live in early Greece and that they are young activists who are running a campaign to raise funds to build a new temple to their favorite deity. Ask students to promote support of their chosen deity by publicizing the deity's powers, human qualities, deeds, and ways the deity can help humans.

Multi-Level Strategies
READING OPTIONS FOR LESSONS 4–6

BEGINNING / **INTERMEDIATE** Read aloud the selection, using the pictures and the red annotations on the facsimile pages to clarify meaning. As you read, pause from time to time to engage students in the monitoring strategies: *What picture do you see in your mind of Echo when she becomes a thin shadow? What other words in this part of the story help us understand what mortals are? Tell me in your own words what this paragraph is about.* Prompt students to articulate generalizations about how the strategies help with comprehension and record ideas in their reflection journals.

ADVANCED Have students read the selection, using monitoring strategies to help them as they read. Encourage students to write in their reflection journals as they read each section, giving examples of when and how they used each strategy and whether the strategy was helpful to them.

One day, as she **wandered**, Echo came upon Narcissus. He was a young boy **on the brink of** manhood. Narcissus was so beautiful that all women loved him, and Echo **was no exception**. She **longed** to speak her love but could not; she could only wait for his words.

Hearing her footstep, Narcissus called out, "Who is here?"

"Here! . . . here!" answered Echo, stepping forward and reaching out her arms to him.

Narcissus drew back. "No! Do not touch me!" he said.

"Touch me! . . . touch me!" **pleaded** Echo, and she grasped his hand.

Restate: She held his hand.

Narcissus frowned and pulled his hand away. "Never can I love you!" he told her coldly.

"I love you! . . . I love you!" cried Echo **desperately**, but Narcissus would not **heed** her.

Ask: Why does Echo love Narcissus?

⋯⋯⋯⋯⋯⋯⋯⋯⋯⋯⋯⋯⋯⋯⋯⋯⋯⋯⋯

wandered walked from place to place
on the brink of about to reach
was no exception was no different, was the same, also loved him
longed wanted very much
pleaded asked again and again, begged
desperately anxiously, in despair, without hope
heed pay attention to, listen to

> **BEFORE YOU MOVE ON...**
>
> 1. **Vocabulary** Write words from the story that tell how Hera felt about Echo.
> 2. **Summary** In your own words, describe how and why Hera punished Echo.
> 3. **Prediction** Do you think that Echo and Narcissus will fall in love? Why or why not?

Echo and Narcissus **271**

CHECK COMPREHENSION

3 Answers to "Before You Move On"

1. **Vocabulary** Student responses will vary but might include such words as *fond of, irritating, disrespectful*.

2. **Summary** Hera felt that Echo was disrespectful because she never stopped talking and always had to have the last word. Hera punished Echo by allowing her to speak only other peoples' words.

3. **Prediction** Student responses will vary. Some might say they will *not* fall in love because Echo can no longer speak her own words. Others may say they *will* fall in love because Narcissus will come to see that Echo cares for him.

CLOSE AND ASSESS

Ask students to summarize the story so far by paraphrasing story events.

HOME CONNECTION

Learn a Family Story Send home a copy of *High Point Newsletter 9* in the **Teacher's Resource Book**. (See pages 153–159.) In this home activity, students ask family members to share some of their favorite stories that have been passed down through the years. Then students retell the story or stories family members have shared on a tape recorder, either at home or at school. Provide an opportunity for students to share their recordings with others.

Literary Analysis Minilesson

▶ **CHARACTER TRAITS AND MOTIVES**

TEACH Before reading the first paragraph of the story, say: *Listen to the way the author describes Echo. What do you think Echo is like?* When students suggest that Echo talks all the time, explain that "talkative" is a **trait** that describes this character. Then ask: *Why does Hera punish Echo?* Explain that Hera is a queen and likes to have things her way. Her reason, or **motive**, for punishing Echo is to show her power. Point out that recognizing character traits and motives can help us understand story events.

PRACTICE Have students identify the words the author uses to describe each character and then complete a chart of character traits and motives.

Name of Character	Traits	Motives
Hera		
Echo		
Narcissus		

▶ **Practice Book** page 136

Echo and Narcissus **T271**

OBJECTIVES

Function: Read a Selection

Listening: Listen to a Selection

Reading and Learning Strategies:
Set a Purpose for Reading; ❶ Monitor Your Reading (visualize, clarify, paraphrase)

Comprehension and Critical Thinking:
Identify Main Idea, Details; Make Comparisons

Literary Analysis: Characterization; Evaluate Impact of Culture on Meaning; Plot (goal and outcome)

SET PURPOSE

1 Read aloud the introduction to pages 272–273. Say: *Now, let's read to find out what Hera, the queen of the gods, does to Narcissus for being cruel to Echo.*

READ AND THINK

Tape 5A
CD 5
Track 2

2 **Strategy Focus: Monitor Your Reading** Involve students in reading pages 272–273.

See the **Multi-Level Strategies** on page T270 to tailor reading to all proficiency levels.

2

NARCISSUS IS PUNISHED

Echo wants Narcissus to feel the pain of love, too. She hopes he loves someone who does not return his love.

*E*cho thought him **cruel and heartless**. She prayed to Hera that he too might love **without return**. And the goddess heard her.

As Narcissus turned away from Echo, he **caught sight of** a most beautiful face in a pool nearby. **Enchanted**, he leaned over the pool, tracing each line of the **adorable** features, and, for the first time, he fell in love. But the face he saw was his own, and when he reached to **embrace** it, his fingers met only the coldness of water. Narcissus **wept**, but his falling tears only **blurred the image**.

Then the unhappy youth began to pine, as Echo had pined for him. **Unable to tear himself away** from the **vision** of his own face, he **grew thin and faded**. "Alas!" he murmured, "I shall die of my love."

Ask: Who did Narcissus fall in love with?

Ask: What did Echo want to happen? Was her prayer answered?

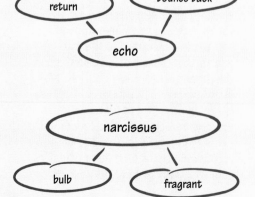

cruel and heartless mean, uncaring	**embrace** hug, hold
without return without being loved by the person he loves	**blurred the image** made the picture less clear
caught sight of saw	**Unable to tear himself away** Not able to leave
Enchanted Interested and attracted	**vision** picture
	grew thin and faded lost weight and became pale

272   Unit 5 | Traditions

REACHING ALL STUDENTS

Vocabulary
CONTENT AREA WORDS

Have some students use science books or articles on acoustics to research the scientific explanation of echoes and why certain geographic configurations are particularly conducive to this phenomenon. Have other students research the narcissus flower, its parts, and life cycle. Students can make word webs about their topic and share findings with the class.

return
bounce back
echo

narcissus
bulb
fragrant

Learning Styles
STRATEGIES FOR CONSTRUCTING MEANING

Have students make up a new god or goddess, different from any they have read about or studied, but embodying special powers and human qualities. Students can work in triads, each focusing on a different modality.

- **Visual Learners** Draw the deity.
- **Auditory Learners** Find or create music and sound effects for the deity.
- **Kinesthetic Learners** Develop gestures and means of locomotion for the deity.

BEFORE YOU MOVE ON...

1. **Main Idea and Details** This story explains how two things came to be. What are these two things?
2. **Character** Echo thought Narcissus was cruel and heartless. How would you describe him? Explain your answer.
3. **Comparisons** How is the goddess Hera different from the wood nymph Echo? Explain your answer.

Use visuals: Point out the narcissus in the illustration.

And poor Echo replied, "My love! . . . my love!"

Narcissus died beside the pool, but Aphrodite, goddess of love and of flowers, **took pity** on the lovely boy. Where he **had lain**, a new flower sprang up, a flower with white and golden petals, which to this day we call the narcissus.

Ask: Why did Aphrodite make a new flower when Narcissus died?

had lain had put his body on the ground

ABOUT THE AUTHOR

Antonia Barber is the author of more than 25 books for readers of all ages. *Apollo and Daphne* is her sixteenth book. She believes that young people need to know about myths because they are part of our cultural heritage. People who are not aware of these stories will not understand many things in art and literature. Myths are the author's favorite stories. For her, the characters are not separate from ordinary life because their stories are about things that we all experience. Antonia Barber lives in Kent, England.

Echo and Narcissus **273**

CHECK COMPREHENSION

3 Answers to "Before You Move On"

1. **Main Idea and Details** The story explains how echoes and the narcissus flower came to be.

2. **Character** Answers may vary, but may indicate that Narcissus was not nice to Echo; he was self-centered and in love with himself.

3. **Comparisons** Hera has supernatural powers; Echo does not have power. Hera can make things happen and change people; Echo cannot.

ABOUT THE AUTHOR

4 Evaluate Literature: Impact of Culture Point out to students how the illustrations and the language of this myth can help them understand more about the culture of ancient Greece. For instance, belief in a certain power structure of gods and goddesses are evident in Hera's actions, as well as the belief that gods and goddesses hold power over mortals. Ask: *What else have you learned or observed about ancient Greek culture from reading this myth?*

CLOSE AND ASSESS

Have students write several sentences that paraphrase what happened to Narcissus.

Vocabulary
SUFFIXES

Write words from the story that have suffixes: *desperately, angrily, disrespectful, beautiful, heartless, adorable,* and *coldness.* Underline the **-ly** suffix in the first two words, and explain that this ending means "in this way." Provide other examples of words with that suffix: *beautifully, deeply.* Continue with other words on the list, noting that **-ful** means *full of,* **-less** means *without,* **-able** means *can be,* and **-ness** describes the quality of something. Encourage students to look for suffixes to help them figure out the meaning of words.

Literary Analysis Minilesson

▶ **PLOT: GOAL AND OUTCOME**

TEACH Direct students to read the first paragraph on page 272. Restate what has happened: *Hera heard Echo praying and decided to act.* Remind students that Hera's motive is to show her power. She also has a goal—to teach Narcissus a lesson. Tell students:

* The goals of characters provide a reason for actions and events in stories.
* These goals have outcomes.
* The outcomes are not always what the character intended.

PRACTICE Assign partners to look for the outcomes of Hera's action in this part of the story.

Intended	Unintended
Narcissus loved without return.	Aphrodite created a flower, called Narcissus.
Echo may never speak her own words.	Echo falls in love and cannot express herself.

▶ **Practice Book** page 137

Echo and Narcissus **T273**

READ PAGES 274–275

OBJECTIVES

Function: Read a Selection

Grammar: Phrases

Listening: Listen to a Selection

Reading and Learning Strategies: Set a Purpose for Reading; ❶ Monitor Your Reading (visualize, clarify, paraphrase); ❶ Use Text Features in Fiction and Nonfiction

Critical Thinking and Comprehension: Form Generalizations; Make Comparisons; Make Inferences

Literary Analysis: Evaluate Impact of Genre on Meaning

SET PURPOSE

1 Read aloud the title and give students some time to look at the images from ancient Greece. Say: *Do you think life in ancient Greece was similar to or different from the way we live today?*

READ AND THINK

2 **Strategy Focus: Monitor Your Reading** Involve students in reading pages 274–275.

▌ See the **Multi-Level Strategies** on page T270 to tailor reading to all proficiency levels.

Clarify: Events and dates in ancient history use the abbreviation BCE. BCE means Before the Common Era.

Greece about 500 BCE

Use visuals: Point out that parts of buildings from ancient Greece still remain in Athens today.

LIFE IN ANCIENT GREECE

an article by Shirleyann Costigan

THE GREEK CITY-STATES

Ancient Greece was not a country. It was a group of many **territories** separated by sea and mountains. These territories were called city-states. The people in each city-state **formed** their own government. They lived off their own land. They sometimes fought with other city-states. Even so, all the people of these city-states were Greeks. They **shared** the same language. They believed in many of the same gods. They held a deep love for beauty. Most of all, they firmly believed in **personal liberty** and **public laws**.

territories areas of land, each with its own government

formed created, made

shared all used

personal liberty each person's rights and freedoms

public laws the laws that people in the land must follow

In the 5th Century BCE, one Greek city-state rose above the others. It was Athens (far left), a beautiful city named for Athena, the Goddess of Wisdom (left).

274 Unit 5 │ Traditions

REACHING ALL STUDENTS

Language Development
DESCRIBE

Have students work in pairs, taking turns to describe people, objects, and events from the myth and the article. They might choose to describe Echo's personality, the physical appearance of Narcissus, the Acropolis, the statue of Athena, etc. Have partners use prompts to elicit more detailed descriptions: *Where? How much? What color? What's another word for that?*

A WORLD OF LANGUAGES

Common Word Structures Students' knowledge of word structure in their native language can transfer and help them learn English. Native speakers of Vietnamese, Mandarin, Thai, and Indonesian may have more difficulty, since these languages do not use endings to form adverbs. Following are some common endings that transfer.

ENGLISH	SPANISH	FRENCH
-ly: rapidly	*-mente*: rápidamente	*-ment*: rapidement
-able: adorable	*-able*: adorable	*-able*: adorable
-tion: exception	*-ción*: excepción	*-tion*: exception

THE GREEK SYSTEM OF JUSTICE

The Greeks believed that gods and goddesses lived **atop** Mount Olympus in Northern Greece. In Greek myths, these powerful gods controlled the lives of people. Sometimes, the gods even punished humans, as Hera punished Narcissus. The punishment of the gods was often **harsh and unpredictable**.

In reality, the ancient Greeks believed in order and fairness. They had laws for all people to follow. They had courts to punish people who broke the laws. They even created a system that allowed people to choose their leaders by voting. This system of government was called *demokratia*, meaning "the rule of the people." The first democratic system of government began in Athens around 500 BCE. The United States' democratic system of government is **based on** ancient Greek democracy.

....

atop on top of
harsh and unpredictable hard and always changing
In reality In everyday life
based on created from
property belongings

GREEK LAW

- was based on what the people decided
- could be changed only by the people's vote
- protected the life and **property** of all citizens.

"Our constitution is called a democracy because power is in the hands of the whole people...everyone is equal before the law."

—*Pericles, statesman, 5th Century, BCE*

Bust of Pericles

BEFORE YOU MOVE ON...

1. **Generalization** What were the gods and goddesses of ancient Greece like?
2. **Comparisons** How are the governments of Greece and the United States alike?
3. **Inference** What does *democracy* mean?

INTERNET

ART CONNECTION

Have students research the art of ancient Greece through the Internet. You might want to point out the statue of Athena on page 274. Students can visit web sites for the Louvre, www.smartweb.fr/louvre/, the J. Paul Getty Museum, www.getty.edu, and the British Museum, at www.british-museum.ac.uk. Ask students to choose one piece of art and tell about it: the date of the work, the artist, and what the piece tells about the culture from which it came.

Grammar Minilesson

▶ **PHRASES**

TEACH Draw students' attention to this sentence on page 274: *The people in each city-state formed their own government.* Write *in each city-state,* and point out that this group of words helps describe the subject of the sentence, *The people.*

Say: *This group of words is called a phrase. A phrase is a group of words that does not have a subject or a verb.* Explain that in the example sentence, the phrase *in each city-state* acts like an adjective—it tells more about the noun *people.* Tell students that many phrases begin with a preposition—a word such as *in, from, by, with,* or *about.*

PRACTICE Write these sentences. Have students identify the prepositional phrase and the word it describes.

1. The Greeks lived off their own land.
2. Greek city-states sometimes fought with each other.
3. All the people of these city-states were Greeks.

▶ **Practice Book** page 138

OBJECTIVES

SUM IT UP
Function: Write
Learning Strategy:
Use Graphic Organizers (chart)
Critical Thinking and Comprehension:
Analyze Information (important and unimportant); Make Judgments

THINK IT OVER
Function: Engage in Discussion
Critical Thinking and Comprehension:
Make Comparisons; Make Inferences; Synthesize Information

EXPRESS YOURSELF
Function: Express Opinions; ⊤ Describe
Speaking and Listening: Speech

CHECK YOUR UNDERSTANDING

1 Sum It Up Have students refer to their reflection journals to share the strategies they used to monitor their reading.

▶ **Practice Book** page 139

2 Think It Over Possible answers are:

1. Comparisons Echo loves Narcissus because he is beautiful; he loves himself for the same reason. Both Echo and Narcissus love someone who will never love them back.

2. Opinion Answers will vary.

3. Inference Pericles meant that everyone should have the same rights, responsibilities, and punishments.

3 Express Yourself Suggest how students might express their opinions. Ask: *Was Hera fair? What other options did Hera have?*

CLOSE AND ASSESS

Have students write a summary statement on an exit slip about what they learned from this selection.

Respond to the Myth and Article
Check Your Understanding

SUM IT UP

Identify Important Information What are the main events of the myth? What did you learn about ancient Greece? Make and complete a chart like this:

Visualize	The selections made me see pictures of:
Clarify	I learned these important words:
Paraphrase	The selections were mostly about:

Make Judgments Write statements from the selections. Then write whether you agree or disagree and why.

Example:
"Echo always tried to have the last word. That was disrespectful to the queen of the gods."

I don't think Echo was disrespectful. She just liked to talk too much.

THINK IT OVER

Discuss Talk about these questions with a partner.

1. **Comparisons** How is Echo's love for Narcissus like Narcissus' love for himself?

2. **Opinion** Which character do you like the most in the story? Explain your answer.

3. **Inference** Pericles said, "Everyone is equal before the law." What did he mean?

EXPRESS YOURSELF

▶ EXPRESS OPINIONS; DESCRIBE

Pretend that you are talking to Hera. Do you agree with how she treated Echo and Narcissus? Describe her actions in your own words. Then tell Hera how you feel about her actions. Tell her how you think she should behave in the future. Present your speech to the group.

✓ **LANGUAGE ACQUISITION ASSESSMENT**
See page 81 of the Assessment Handbook.

REACHING ALL STUDENTS

Multi-Level Strategies
SUM IT UP OPTIONS

BEGINNING After reviewing monitoring strategies with the reflection journals, work with students to identify important infomation. Ask questions and have students vote on whether the answer is important: *Who is Hera?* (important) *Where did Echo roam?* (not important)

INTERMEDIATE / **ADVANCED** Have students label information recorded in their reflection journals as important and unimportant information. Have them add any other important information that they did not include. After students write their opinions about statements from the selections, have pairs who disagree debate. Invite the class to vote on who presents the most convincing reasons in support of a position.

Language Arts and Content Area Connections

▶ **GRAMMAR IN CONTEXT**

USE COMPLETE SENTENCES

Learn About Subjects and Predicates Every complete sentence has two main parts, the subject and the predicate.

The **subject** tells whom or what the sentence is about. The complete subject includes all the words that tell about the subject.

The Ancient Greeks lived in city-states.

The **predicate** tells what the subject is, has, or does. The complete predicate includes all the words in the predicate.

Citizens voted for their rulers.

Create Complete Sentences Make up a sentence. Write the complete subject on one card and the complete predicate on another card. Trade your predicate card with a partner. Write a subject to go with it. Then compare your sentence with your partner's original sentence.

Practice Write each sentence. Add a subject or a predicate to make a complete sentence.
Answers will vary.
1. Each city-state _____.

2. _____ believed in order and fairness.

3. The Greeks _____.

4. _____ is based on *demokratia*.

▶ **WRITING/SPEAKING**

WRITE A NEW ENDING FOR A MYTH

Write a different ending for "Echo and Narcissus." Will Hera change her mind? Will Echo and Narcissus ever fall in love? Share your story with the class.

▶ **SOCIAL STUDIES**

COMPARE GOVERNMENTS

Copy and complete the chart. Use the article to find information about ancient Greece. Do research in the library or on the Internet to find information about the United States.

Democracy in Ancient Greece and in the U.S.A.

Questions	Ancient Greece	United States
When did democracy begin?	Democracy began around 500 BCE.	Democracy began in 1776.
Where do the people live?		
How do they choose leaders?		
How are people punished?		

Learn how to do **research**.
See Handbook pages 366–370.

Multi-Level Strategies
WRITING OPTIONS FOR A NEW ENDING FOR A MYTH

BEGINNING As you work with students to brainstorm new endings, first discuss at what point in the story the new endings will be inserted (e.g., when Narcissus looks in the water, after he becomes a flower). Have students draw each one of the new endings to the myth. Then use student drawings to generate language to narrate the new endings.

INTERMEDIATE / ADVANCED After participating in a group brainstorm of new endings, have students work independently to choose one of the endings and develop it in writing. Encourage them to think about characters' goals, actions, and the outcomes of their actions as they plan their writing. Invite students to read their new endings to the class.

RESPOND

OBJECTIVES

COMPLETE SENTENCES

Grammar: ❶ Complete Sentences; Subjects and Predicates

WRITE A NEW ENDING FOR A MYTH

Function: Write

Writing: Ending for a Myth

COMPARE GOVERNMENTS

Function: Write

Concepts and Vocabulary: Government

Critical Thinking and Research Skills: Gather and Organize Information; Classify; Make Comparisons

Representing/Writing: Chart

LANGUAGE ARTS AND CONTENT AREA CONNECTIONS

1 **Use Complete Sentences** See annotations for answers to Practice items.

▶ **Practice Book** page 140

2 **Write a New Ending for a Myth** Brainstorm other endings as a class. Record them on a web. Have students trade endings and verify that each sentence is complete.

3 **Compare Governments** Prepare students by previewing the following content area vocabulary:

• *territories, city-states, states, leaders, president, law*: Use maps of ancient Greece and the United States to help explain the concepts and vocabulary related to territories, city-states, and states. Help students to use vocabulary related to leaders—what leaders do, how they become leaders, and how they implement the laws.

▶ **Practice Book** page 141

CLOSE AND ASSESS

Ask: *What did you learn in this lesson?*

BUILD LANGUAGE AND VOCABULARY

OBJECTIVES

Function: ❶ Make Comparisons; Listen Actively

Concepts and Vocabulary: Antonyms

Patterns and Structures:
❶ Compound Sentences

Viewing: Respond to a Photograph; Interpret a Visual Image

Critical Thinking and Learning Strategy: Make Comparisons; Use Graphic Organizers (comparison chart)

Writing: Comparison

START WITH A COMMON EXPERIENCE

1 View and Compare Encourage students to point out differences between the two people. Explain that the photograph shows a Chinese peasant, or farmer, and the inset art shows the emperor, or ruler of the country. Then model how to make a comparison:

How to Make a Comparison

- Name something common to both people: *clothing*

- Tell what the peasant's clothing looks like: *The peasant's clothing is simple, plain, and has no decoration.*

- Tell how the emperor's clothing is different: *The emperor's clothing is fancy, colorful, and beautiful.*

2 Read and Discuss a Traditional Song Tell students that peasants in ancient China sang this song as they worked. Invite students to speculate on its meaning. *(The work the peasant does and his everyday life are all that matter to him, not how the emperor lives.)* Develop the idea that getting to know the traditions of another culture is important to understanding the people in that culture.

Tape 1B / CD 1 Track 10

▌ Use the Questioning Techniques in the **Multi-Level Strategies** to invite responses.

Build Language and Vocabulary
MAKE COMPARISONS

Listen to this traditional song. How does the Chinese peasant feel?

Peasant's Song

At sunup to work,

Sundown to rest,

Eating off the fields I plow—

The Emperor and his might—what are they to me?

—traditional Chinese peasant's song

REACHING ALL STUDENTS

Multi-Level Strategies
QUESTIONING TECHNIQUES

BEGINNING Ask students questions with yes/no or one-word answers and questions that include alternatives from which to choose: *Does the emperor look as though he works hard? Do you think the peasant's work is hard? Does the peasant work all day or just part of the day?*

INTERMEDIATE Ask students questions that require longer answers or that are more open-ended. *What work is the peasant in the photograph doing?* (He is planting rice.) *What kinds of work might the emperor do?* (make laws, rule his people)

ADVANCED Invite students to speculate on the lives of the peasant and the emperor. *What do you think the peasant does after a day in the fields? Why does this song seem to say that the peasants are not interested in the emperor? How do you think the emperor feels toward the peasants?*

MAKE A COMPARISON CHART

In traditional China, peasants had a hard life working the land. The Emperor had a much easier life in the palace. Brainstorm differences between the life of the peasants and the Emperor. Record them on a chart like this:

Peasants	Emperor
grew food	in charge of government
did hard work	had servants to do work
had simple clothing	had fancy clothing

BUILD YOUR VOCABULARY

Antonyms Words that have opposite meanings are called *antonyms*. Work with a partner to find pairs of antonyms in the **Word Bank**. Add the words to the comparison chart.

Word Bank

educated
fat
hungry
poor
rich
thin
uneducated
well-fed

USE LANGUAGE STRUCTURES ▶ COMPOUND SENTENCES

Writing: Compare the Peasants and the Emperor Use the information on the comparison chart to make comparisons. Write compound sentences and join your ideas with one of these words: *or, and,* or *but.*

Example:
The peasants were thin, **but** the Emperor was fat.
The peasants grew the food, **and** the Emperor ate it.
The peasants worked for the Emperor, **or** the Emperor punished them.

CONDUCT THE ACTIVITIES

3 Make a Comparison Chart Let students work in small groups to brainstorm ideas. Have groups share and discuss their charts.

4 Build Your Vocabulary: Antonyms Explain that knowing words that are antonyms can help students make clearer comparisons.

5 Use Language Structures: Compound Sentences Present the skill using the definition and examples on **Transparency 79**. You may want to tell students that the words *and, but,* and *or* are called *coordinating conjunctions.* Then have students combine the sentences in Try It! to form compound sentences.

Writing: Compare the Peasants and the Emperor Conduct the activity at the bottom of page 279. Remind students of the differences in meaning and use of *and, but,* and *or.*

■ Use the Writing Activity Options in the **Multi-Level Strategies** to adjust instruction.

▶ **Practice Book** page 142

CLOSE AND ASSESS

Have students tell what a compound sentence is. Then ask them to combine these two sentences to form a compound sentence: *The emperor sat on his throne. His subjects bowed to him.*

Multi-Level Strategies
WRITING ACTIVITY OPTIONS

BEGINNING Write two individual sentences: *The peasants were thin. The emperor was fat.* As a group, students add a coordinating conjunction to form and write the compound sentence: *The peasants were thin, but the emperor was fat.*

INTERMEDIATE Suggest that students work in pairs to ask each other questions about the descriptions on their charts. Encourage students to write their answers as compound sentences: *Who grew the food? Who ate the food? The peasants grew the food, and the emperor ate it.*

ADVANCED Encourage Advanced students to go beyond the information on their charts. Students can look through the next selections for ideas to include in their sentences. For example: *Peasants lived in small huts, but their lords lived in large manor houses.*

Transparency 79 / Master 79

LEARN ABOUT COMPOUND SENTENCES

You can put two sentences together to make a **compound sentence**. Join the two sentences with a comma and one of these words: **and, but, or**

1. Use **and** to join two ideas that are alike.

   An ox pulled the plow.
   The peasant walked behind it. → An ox pulled the plow, **and** the peasant walked behind it.

2. Use **but** to show a difference between two ideas.

   The emperor had an easy life.
   The peasants' lives were hard. → The emperor had an easy life, **but** the peasants' lives were hard.

3. Use **or** to show a choice between two ideas.

   The peasants could grow food.
   They could starve. → The peasants could grow food, **or** they could starve.

Try It!

Join each pair of sentences to make a compound sentence.

1. The rice was ripe. The peasants harvested it.
2. The peasants grew the food. The emperor got most of the crop.
3. The emperor could read a poem. He could listen to music.

Transparency 79 Level A, Unit 5 | Traditions   © Hampton-Brown

THINK ABOUT WHAT YOU KNOW
Concepts and Vocabulary: Agriculture
Reading and Learning Strategies:
Activate Prior Knowledge; Use Graphic
Organizers (word web, diagram)
LEARN KEY VOCABULARY Ⓣ
Vocabulary Strategy: Locate and
Use Definitions
LEARN ABOUT FICTION AND NONFICTION
Reading Strategy: Ⓣ Use Text Features
in Fiction and Nonfiction

THINK ABOUT WHAT YOU KNOW

1 Brainstorm Brainstorm ideas with
the class. Write *farmer* at the center
of the web. Write *what a farmer does*
and *what a farmer needs* as spokes.

LEARN KEY VOCABULARY

2 Locate and Use Definitions Model
how to look up words in the Glossary.
After students understand the
meaning of key vocabulary words,
conduct the writing activity.

> Use the Vocabulary Options in
> **Multi-Level Strategies** to tailor
> instruction to proficiency levels.

▶ **Practice Book** page 143

LEARN TO RECOGNIZE FICTION AND NONFICTION

**3 Model How to Recognize Fiction
and Nonfiction** Define *fiction*
and *nonfiction*. Guide students in
reviewing the steps on the diagram
on **Transparency 80**:

- Read aloud the section titles and
summaries on pages 282–284. Ask:
*Is the Emperor real or imaginary?
How do you know?*

- As students preview "A Peasant's
Life in Ancient China," ask: *Is this
article about real or imaginary places
or people? How do you know?*

CLOSE AND ASSESS

Ask students to name two features of
fiction (imaginary characters, entertains)
and of nonfiction (gives facts, informs).

Ox Star Prepare to Read

Chinese myth retold
by Lily Toy Hong

THINK ABOUT WHAT YOU KNOW

Brainstorm Imagine that you are a farmer. How do you work your
fields? How do you harvest your crops? Show your ideas on a mind map.

blessing A **blessing** is
something good that brings happiness.
crop A **crop** is a field of
plants that farmers grow.
harvest time At **harvest time**
farmers pick and gather their crops.
labor You **labor** when you
work hard.
peasant A **peasant** is a very poor
person who works on the land.
plow A **plow** is a large tool that opens
the earth for planting.
sundown Evening begins at **sundown,**
when the sun goes down.
sunup Morning begins at
sunup, when the sun comes up.
thick When something is
thick, it is big and solid.

Answers to the vocabulary
activity will vary.

LEARN KEY VOCABULARY

Locate and Use Definitions Find the definition for each word in the
Glossary. Then use the web to write a paragraph about the ox.

must labor from
sunup to sundown
helps the peasant
plant a crop
The Ox
is a blessing
pulls a plow
has a thick neck
works during
harvest time

LEARN ABOUT FICTION AND NONFICTION

Fiction and nonfiction are kinds of literature. In **fiction**, the events are
from the author's imagination. In **nonfiction**, the events are from real life.

READING STRATEGY
How to Recognize Fiction and Nonfiction

1. To identify fiction, look for imaginary characters and
events. There is a sequence from beginning to end.

2. To identify nonfiction, look for facts about real people
or events.

3. Preview the selection to see if it is fiction or nonfiction.
Fiction is for entertainment. You can read it quickly.
Nonfiction is for information. You should read it slowly
and carefully.

Read "How the Ox Star Fell from Heaven" and the article. Look for clues
to help you recognize if the selections are fiction or nonfiction.

REACHING ALL STUDENTS

Multi-Level Strategies
VOCABULARY OPTIONS

BEGINNING Use story illustrations
to clarify *crop, harvest, labor, peasant,
plow.* Guide students in writing their
ideas in a paragraph.

INTERMEDIATE Have partners look
through the selection to find pictures
illustrating the vocabulary words.

ADVANCED Suggest that
students write sentence fragments from
the web on separate slips of paper.
Students then arrange fragments in
order to plan their paragraphs.

Transparency 80 / Master 80

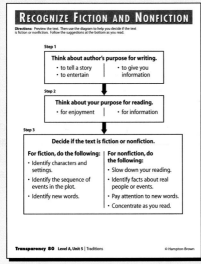

RECOGNIZE FICTION AND NONFICTION

Directions: Preview the text. Then use the diagram to help you decide if the text
is fiction or nonfiction. Follow the suggestions at the bottom as you read.

Step 1
Think about author's purpose for writing.
- to tell a story
- to entertain
- to give you
  information

Step 2
Think about your purpose for reading.
- for enjoyment
- for information

Step 3
Decide if the text is fiction or nonfiction.

For fiction, do the following:	For nonfiction, do the following:
• Identify characters and settings.	• Slow down your reading.
• Identify the sequence of events in the plot.	• Identify facts about real people or events.
• Identify new words.	• Pay attention to new words.
	• Concentrate as you read.

Transparency 80 Level A, Unit 5 | Traditions   © Hampton-Brown

HOW THE Ox Star FELL FROM Heaven

by Lily Toy Hong

This ancient Chinese story tells about a message that gets mixed up. It also explains why people use oxen to help grow crops for food.

281

THE BASICS BOOKSHELF

■ **The Eagle and the Moon Gold, A Fable from the Hmong People** adapted by Yeemay Chan

With Eagle's help, Yaoh, a peasant orphan, takes just enough moon gold to make life easier, but his friend, Gwa, wants too much. Yaoh is happy with just enough. Gwa is greedy. The simple text for this delightful tale introduces words with opposite meanings, while the beautiful illustrations provide picture support for beginning English learners.

For Lesson Plans: See the Teacher's Guide for **The Basics Bookshelf**.

Listening: Listen to a Preview
Reading Strategies: Preview; Predict

INTRODUCE THE SELECTION

4 Preview and Predict Read the title, author, and introduction to the Chinese myth. Have students talk about the illustrations they see on the page. Then have them look through the story and note the headings and illustrations. Ask: *Based on what you learned about the Greek gods and goddesses, what do you think might happen to cause the ox to fall from heaven?* (The gods may have punished the ox.)

5 Audio Walk-Through Play the Audio Walk-Through for "How the Ox Star Fell from Heaven" on the **Selection Tape/CD** to give students the overall idea of the story. Pause to allow students to preview pages 286–287 before playing the Audio Walk-Through for "A Peasant's Life in Ancient China."

Tape 5A
CD 5 Track 3

How the Ox Star Fell from Heaven

retold by Lily Toy Hong

Theme Connection This Chinese myth is part of a tradition of tales that explain how something came to be.

Selection Summary and Awards "How the Ox Star Fell from Heaven," retold by Lily Toy Hong, is a Chinese myth about how the ox came to Earth to help the people of China with their laborious farm tasks. In 1991, it was named "One of the Year's Ten Best Books" by *Parenting* magazine and received a picture book honor seal from *Parents' Choice*.

OBJECTIVES

Function: Read a Selection
Grammar: ❶ Compound Sentences
Listening: Listen to a Selection
Reading and Learning Strategies: Set a Purpose for Reading; ❶ Use Text Features in Fiction and Nonfiction; Relate Reading Rate to Purpose; Use Graphic Organizers (diagram); Make Predictions
Comprehension and Critical Thinking: Identify Details, Cause and Effect; Make Comparisons; Make Judgments
Literary Analysis: Myth

SET PURPOSE

1 Say: *Read to find out why the Emperor sends the Ox Star to Earth.*

READ AND THINK

Tape 5A
CD 5
Track 4

2 Strategy Focus: Use Text Features in Fiction and Nonfiction Remind students that they identified this selection as fiction. Have them use Step 3 of **Master 80** to guide their reading.

▌ Choose Reading Options in the **Multi-Level Strategies** to tailor the reading to proficiency levels.

The recording of "How the Ox Star Fell from Heaven" on the **Selection Tape/CD** offers an oral language model. Wait until students preview pages 286–287 to play the recording of "A Peasant's Life in Ancient China."

1

LIFE ABOVE AND BELOW

Long ago, the Emperor had an easy life up in the heavens. Down on Earth, the life of the peasants was hard.

1

In the beginning, oxen did not live on Earth. They could only be found in **the heavens**, among the stars. They lived with the Emperor of All the Heavens in his Imperial Palace.

Clothed in robes of the finest **silk**, they **reclined** on **billowy** clouds. They never had to work, and their lives were easy.

Life on Earth was hard, especially hard since oxen did not live here. Farmers had no **beast of burden** to help with the planting of vegetables and rice in the spring, or with the gathering of **crops** at **harvest time**.

People were always tired and hungry. They **labored** from **sunup** to **sundown**, yet they could never finish all their work.

Because there was so little food, they sometimes went three, four, even five days without **one single meal**.

Ask: Why were oxen's lives easy in the beginning?

---

the heavens the sky
silk soft, shiny cloth
reclined leaned back, rested
billowy soft and fluffy
beast of burden animal used for heavy work
one single meal one meal to eat, anything to eat

BEFORE YOU MOVE ON...

1. **Details** What made life on Earth difficult for the farmers?
2. **Comparisons** How were the lives of the oxen and the humans different?
3. **Prediction** This story describes what life was like "in the beginning." How do you think the story may change by the end?

REACHING ALL STUDENTS

Vocabulary
SIGNAL WORDS

Explain to students that in a story, certain words can signal when, why, or how events happen. Point out the phrase *In the beginning* in the first sentence on page 282. Ask: *What question does that answer?* (when) *What about the word* Because, *at the bottom of page 282?* (why) Categorize signal words as time and cause words. Assign categories of signal words to small groups. Give them two minutes to find and list all the signal words in that category that they can find on pages 282–283. Have them explain their word choices.

Multi-Level Strategies
READING OPTIONS FOR LESSONS 11–13

BEGINNING Read aloud the text or play the **Selection Tape/CD**. Use the red annotations on the facsimile pages to clarify meaning. Point out the suggestions for reading each genre on **Master 80**. (See page T280.) Take class notes about the setting, characters, and sequence of events in "How the Ox Star Fell from Heaven" and about facts in the nonfiction piece. Work with students to define new words. Save these notes for use in the Sum It Up activity on page 288.

INTERMEDIATE / ADVANCED Have students read the selections in small groups, charting details from both the myth and the article as they read. Invite them to refer to Step 3 of **Master 80** (see page T280) for suggestions of what to record. After reading, have them explain in their response journals how they were able to recognize fiction and nonfiction.

The Emperor decides to make life a little easier for the peasants, but his messenger, Ox Star, mixes up an important message.

The Emperor of All the Heavens had not forgotten the Earth, however. He knew that the poor **peasants** worked long and hard, and he believed that they should be able to eat every third day. With this in mind, he **issued a decree**: "The people of Earth shall eat at least once every three days!" Ask: Would you like to eat only once every three days?

He called upon his most **trusted** messenger, the Ox Star, to **deliver the message**. Dressed in a magnificent silk robe and a golden crown, the Ox Star
Define *magnificent*: very beautiful and special

issued a decree announced a new law
trusted honest and dependable
deliver the message tell them about the law, take the message to the peasants
set off on began
twisted mixed up
declared said, announced

set off on the long and lonely journey down to Earth.

When he arrived, all the peasants hurried out to meet him. "I come with a message from the Emperor of All the Heavens," he bellowed. But the Ox Star, while strong, was not very smart. He **twisted** the Emperor's words: "The Emperor has **declared** that you shall eat three times a day, every day!" The peasants cheered and cheered.

Restate *bellowed*: He said loudly.

BEFORE YOU MOVE ON...

1. **Details** What was the Ox Star's job in the heavens?
2. **Judgment** Do you think the Emperor's new law was a good law? Why or why not?
3. **Cause and Effect** How did the Ox Star change the Emperor's message? What did this change mean for the peasants?

How the Ox Star Fell from Heaven **283**

CHECK COMPREHENSION

3 Answers to "Before You Move On"

page 282

1. **Details** The farmers had no beasts of burden to help with planting and harvesting.
2. **Comparisons** Oxen lived in heaven, were clothed in silk, and reclined on billowy clouds; the humans worked hard on Earth.
3. **Prediction** Answers will vary but students might say that the Ox Star will come to Earth to help.

page 283

1. **Details** trusted messenger
2. **Judgment** Answers may vary. Students may say it was not a good law because people need to eat more often.
3. **Cause and Effect** The Ox Star mixed up the order of the words in the message: he told them they could eat three times a day instead of once every three days.

CLOSE AND ASSESS

Have students classify characters as to whether they live in heaven or on Earth. *(heaven: Emperor, oxen, Ox Star; Earth: farmers/peasants)*

Grammar Minilesson

▶ **COMPOUND SENTENCES**

TEACH Point out the sentence on page 282: *They never had to work, and their lives were easy.* Identify this as a compound sentence. Explain: *You can join two sentences to make a compound sentence by using a comma and the word* and, but, *or* or.

Present these rules, giving examples:

• Use *and* when you join two ideas that are alike.

• Use *but* when you want to show a difference between two ideas.

• Use *or* when you want to show a choice between two ideas.

PRACTICE Write these pairs of sentences. Have students rewrite them as compound sentences.

1. The Emperor had an easy life. The life of the peasants was hard. (but)
2. The people labored all day. They could never finish all their work. (but)
3. The peasants had to work hard. They would have no food. (or)

▶ **Practice Book** page 144

| OBJECTIVES |

Function: Read a Selection
Listening: Listen to a Selection
Reading and Learning Strategies: Set a Purpose for Reading; **T** Use Text Features in Fiction and Nonfiction; Relate Reading Rate to Purpose; Use Graphic Organizers (diagram); Use Visuals
Comprehension and Critical Thinking: Make Comparisons; Identify Cause and Effect; Summarize
Literary Analysis: Myth; Evaluate Impact of Author's Background on Meaning; Description

SET PURPOSE

1 Say: *Ox Star confused the message. What do you think the Emperor of All the Heavens will do? Read to find out.*

READ AND THINK

Tape 5A
CD 5
Track 4

2 **Strategy Focus: Use Text Features in Fiction and Nonfiction** Involve students in using the suggestions in Step 3 of **Master 80** as they read pages 284–285.

> See the **Multi-Level Strategies** on page T282 to tailor the reading to proficiency levels.

3

A HELPFUL MISTAKE

The Emperor punishes Ox Star for his mistake. The Ox's life becomes harder, but the life of the peasants becomes a little easier.

The Emperor of All the Heavens heard his messenger's **mistake** and was angry. When the Ox Star arrived back at the Imperial Palace, he found the gates were locked. His princely robe and royal crown **vanished**. "Since you have

betrayed my trust," the Emperor **roared**, "you shall never again be allowed in the heavens." The sky filled with lightning and thunder, and the Ox Star wept. **Ask:** What mistake did the Ox Star make?

Suddenly everything turned dark. In a **whirlwind**, the Ox Star was hurried through the stormy sky. Down, down, down to Earth he fell.

From that day, the Ox Star became a beast of burden, helping farmers. Around his **thick** neck he wore a heavy yoke, and through his nose he wore a ring.

The other oxen were sent to Earth, too. They labored day after day in the fields, pulling **plows** through the ground at planting time and helping to gather the crops at harvest time. **Restate:** They worked day after day.

---

mistake error, (something that is wrong or incorrect)
vanished went away, disappeared
betrayed my trust shown me that I cannot count on you

roared yelled
whirlwind strong wind, a spinning wind

284 **Unit 5** | Traditions

REACHING ALL STUDENTS

| Language Development
RETELL A STORY

Teach the ordinals *first* through *sixth*. Then have students use the ordinals to retell the story events in sequence. Provide sentence frames: *First, the Ox Star _____. Second, the Emperor _____.* Have students stand and take turns retelling the story one sentence at a time. Help students realize how identifying the sequence of story events in fiction can help them understand and remember what they have read.

| Vocabulary
DESCRIBING WORDS

Have students collect describing words from the selection, for example, *finest, billowy, easy, hard, tired, hungry.* Create a web for each word to show items the words might describe, for example, *finest* might describe a *dress* or a *restaurant.*

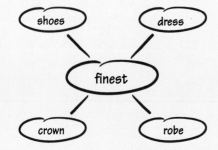

Today, because of the Ox Star's **ill fortune** and his **careless mistake**, a bit of heaven **remains** on Earth. For those who have an ox, good soil, and enough rain, life is not as hard as it once was. Best of all, they can eat warm rice, **tender** vegetables, and Chinese sweet cakes three times a day, every day!

Now when you look up at the night sky, so beautiful and bright, think of the Ox Star, who fell from the heavens, and of his **blunder**, which became a **blessing**.

Ask: How do oxen help farmers?

BEFORE YOU MOVE ON...

1. **Comparisons** What were the Ox Star's clothes like when he lived in the heavens? How did they change when he fell to Earth?

2. **Cause and Effect** In your own words, explain what caused the Ox Star to fall from the heavens to Earth.

3. **Summary** How did the Ox Star's blunder become a blessing for the peasants?

---

ill fortune bad luck
careless mistake error caused by not being careful
remains stays
tender soft, not tough or hard
blunder mistake

ABOUT THE AUTHOR

Lily Toy Hong grew up as one of nine children. From the time she was a child, she wanted to write books for young people. Here is her message to her readers: "I was delighted when I found the myth about how oxen came to Earth. It was a joy for me to turn it into a book for young readers. My parents are from China, but I was born in America. This story helps me to better understand my family roots. It also explains why I love to eat rice three times a day!"

How the Ox Star Fell from Heaven **285**

MONITOR YOUR READING

3 **Use Visuals** Tell students they can gain more understanding of the story and the Chinese culture from the illustrations. Ask: *What details of dress do you observe? What are the peasants eating on page 285?* Have students record their observations.

CHECK COMPREHENSION

4 **Answers to "Before You Move On"**

1. **Comparisons** In the heavens, the Ox Star wore a silk robe and a royal crown; on Earth, he wore a heavy yoke and a nose ring.

2. **Cause and Effect** His mistake angered the Emperor, who forced Ox Star to live on Earth.

3. **Summary** The peasants got the help they needed.

ABOUT THE AUTHOR

5 **Evaluate Literature: Author's Background** Read About the Author to students. Ask: *Do you think the author would have been so happy about finding this myth if the myth had been from ancient Greece? Why?* Discuss how an author's background influences his or her writing.

CLOSE AND ASSESS

Have students return to the unit mind map on page 263 and add new ideas.

Vocabulary
TWO-WORD VERBS

Teach the concept of two-word verbs by going back to page 283 and pointing out the phrases *called upon* (chose) and *set off* (began). Write these sentences using other two-word verbs containing *called* and *set* and have students use the context to determine their meaning:

1. Jenna *called up* her friend.
2. Rob *called out* loudly to get help.
3. Ms. Green *set up* the chairs at the front of the classroom.
4. Let's gather up our books and *get set* to go home.

Literary Analysis Minilesson

▶ **DESCRIPTION**

TEACH Have students close their eyes and visualize a scene from the story, such as the description of the Ox Star on page 283. Ask students to make a word web and record words that help the reader visualize.

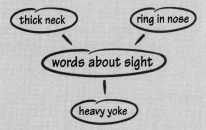

thick neck → words about sight ← ring in nose
words about sight → heavy yoke

PRACTICE Tell students that other words can be used to describe things experienced with other senses. Have students work with partners to rewrite a section of the story, using words which emphasize a sensory perception other than sight. For touch, use the second paragraph on page 282; for hearing, use the first paragraph on page 284; for taste, use the first paragraph on page 285. Add words from these re-writings to the web.

▶ **Practice Book** page 145

OBJECTIVES

Function: Read a Selection

Listening: Listen to a Selection

Reading and Learning Strategies: Set a Purpose for Reading; ❶ Use Text Features in Fiction and Nonfiction; Relate Reading Rate to Purpose; Use Graphic Organizers (diagram);

Comprehension and Critical Thinking: Draw Conclusions; Make Comparisons; Identify Details

Literary Analysis: Fantasy and Reality

SET PURPOSE

1 Read aloud the title, and have students identify images related to ancient China. Say: *As you read the article, see if the life of the farmer is described the way it was in the Ox Star story.*

READ AND THINK

Tape 5A
CD 5
Track 4

2 Strategy Focus: Use Text Features in Fiction and Nonfiction Remind students that they identified this selection as nonfiction (see page T280) and have them use the suggestions in Step 3 of **Master 80** to guide their reading.

> See the **Multi-Level Strategies** on page T282 to tailor the reading to proficiency levels.

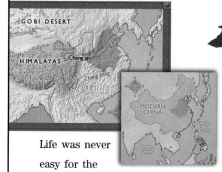

Ancient China during the Zhou Dynasty, 1050 BCE–256 CE

GOBI DESERT

HIMALAYAS Chang'an

Chang Jiang

MODERN CHINA

A Peasant's Life in ANCIENT CHINA

an article by Shirleyann Costigan

Life was never easy for the peasant farmers of ancient China. They worked the earth, planted, and **harvested** the crops by hand. It was slow, **backbreaking** work. Around 700 BCE, many farmers began to use oxen or water buffalo to pull the plows and seed the fields. **Food production increased**. Everyone ate better. Life got a little easier, but not by much.

Most peasants lived in small villages near the **manor houses** of their **lords**. Their small huts were made of **packed earth** with dirt floors. Peasants rented the land they lived and worked on. They gave a large part of every crop to **their landlord**. They paid taxes to the Emperor. For the most part, they lived simply, died quietly, and in time were forgotten.

Restate: Peasants did not own the land they lived and worked on.

In ancient China, the lords and scholars lived in big houses and dressed in silks. They depended on the peasant farmers for all their needs, but they did not do much to make the peasants' lives easier.

Clarify: The Emperor ruled ancient China. Taxes are money that is paid to a country's government.

---

harvested collected, gathered
backbreaking physically hard
Food production increased. They grew more crops.
manor houses large houses for the rich, mansions

lords rulers
packed earth dirt that is pressed together to make solid walls
their landlord the person who owned the land

286 Unit 5 | Traditions

REACHING ALL STUDENTS

Language Development
ASK FOR AND GIVE INFORMATION

Play a question-and-answer game. Assign small groups to focus on one aspect of ancient China covered in the myth and article, such as Peasants, Ox Star, Emperor, Farming, Social Groups. Each group writes five questions about their topic. Students write each question on a separate index card and stack the cards. Groups take turns selecting cards from another group's stack and answering the questions.

Sample Topics and Questions:

Group 1: Peasants How did peasants plow before oxen? How often did they eat? Where did peasants fit into the social order?

Group 2: Ox Star How did Ox Star help the peasants? What were some of Ox Star's traits? What was Ox Star's job in heaven? on Earth?

Group 3: Emperor In the beginning, where did the Emperor live? How did he make new laws? What was another name for the Emperor?

Group 4: Farming Did crops grow all year 'round? What crops did peasants grow? What animals were beasts of burden in farming? How were crops harvested before oxen?

Group 5: Social Groups Who were protectors of the land? Who made laws? Who were rulers of the land? How many social classes were there in ancient China? Which class was at the bottom?

Emperor
the Son of Heaven

Lords & Scholars
rulers of the land

Knights
protectors of the land

Peasants
workers of the land

CLASSES OF SOCIETY IN ANCIENT CHINA, 700 BCE

There were three classes of people under the Emperor of ancient China. The people of each class had a place to fill in the Chinese order of life. The order rarely changed.

Peasant farmers worked from sunup to sundown all year long. They also had to work on roads and canals that ran through the countryside.

Peasants grew their own food, as well as food for the ruling classes. Rice, soybeans, and millet were all common crops.

Rice

Soybeans

Millet

Ask: What were the four classes of people in ancient China?

BEFORE YOU MOVE ON...

1. **Evidence and Conclusion** How did the oxen help the farmers produce more crops?
2. **Comparisons** How were the lives of the peasants and the lords different?
3. **Details** The peasants ate what they grew. What are some examples of this?

CHECK COMPREHENSION

3 Answers to "Before You Move On"

1. **Evidence and Conclusion** It was easier to plow, plant, and harvest more land when oxen helped humans.

2. **Comparisons** The lords ruled the lands—they were the scholars and rulers. The peasants were the laborers who paid rent to the landlord and taxes to the Emperor.

3. **Details** The peasants grew and ate rice, soybeans, and millet, among other things.

CLOSE AND ASSESS

Ask students to write a test item about life in ancient China. Collect test items and use in an oral quiz.

INTERNET

ART CONNECTION

Explain that ancient China has been the setting for many great works of art. Have students search the Internet for photos and download samples of Chinese art.

Web Sites

Web sites undergo frequent modifications, but here are some you may want to suggest to students:

www.asianart.com
www.artic.edu
www.chinapage.com

Literary Analysis Minilesson

▶ **FANTASY AND REALITY**

TEACH Direct students to the first paragraph of "A Peasant's Life in Ancient China," which states "Around 700 BCE, many farmers began to use oxen or water buffalo to pull the plows and seed the fields." Point out that this is a fact. It is an example of *reality*. Yet, this fact is used as the basis for the myth about the Ox Star. Explain that the events of the myth (ox wearing silk and living in heaven) are things that cannot happen in real life. They are examples of *fantasy*.

PRACTICE Ask students to point to other elements of reality and fantasy in "How the Ox Star Fell from Heaven" and record their ideas on a chart.

Character or Events	Fantasy Elements	Reality Elements
Ox comes to live on Earth.	Ox fell from heaven as punishment.	Oxen live on Earth and help farmers.

▶ **Practice Book** page 146

How the Ox Star Fell from Heaven **T287**

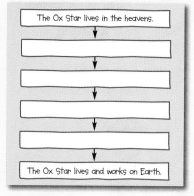

Respond to the Myth and Article
Check Your Understanding

OBJECTIVES

SUM IT UP

Function: Write

Critical Thinking, Reading and Learning Strategies: ❶ Relate Events in a Sequence; Use Graphic Organizers (sequence chart)

Literary Analysis: ❶ Compare Literature

THINK IT OVER

Function: Engage in Discussion

Comprehension and Critical Thinking: Identify Character's Motive; Make Comparisons; Form Opinions; Relate to Personal Experience

EXPRESS YOURSELF

Function: Negotiate

Speaking and Listening: Role-Play

CHECK YOUR UNDERSTANDING

1 Sum It Up Sample answers for the sequence chart are:

- The Emperor issues a decree that peasants on Earth should eat once every three days.
- The Emperor sends Ox Star to Earth to deliver the message.
- Ox Star tells the peasants to eat three times a day, every day.
- The Emperor gets angry at Ox Star and banishes him from heaven.

▶ **Practice Book** page 147

2 Think It Over Possible answers are:

1. **Character's Motive** The Emperor could not trust the Ox Star to get the message right.

2. **Comparisons** Both are powerful, get angry, and are quick to punish.

3. **Opinion** Answers will vary.

4. **Personal Experience** Answers will vary. Encourage elaboration.

3 Express Yourself Help students brainstorm better solutions.

CLOSE AND ASSESS

Ask: *What would you tell a friend about reading fiction and nonfiction?*

SUM IT UP

Identify a Sequence of Events Make a sequence chart for the myth.

Sequence Chart

```
┌─────────────────────────────────────┐
│  The Ox Star lives in the heavens.   │
└─────────────────────────────────────┘
                  ↓
┌─────────────────────────────────────┐
│                                     │
└─────────────────────────────────────┘
                  ↓
┌─────────────────────────────────────┐
│                                     │
└─────────────────────────────────────┘
                  ↓
┌─────────────────────────────────────┐
│                                     │
└─────────────────────────────────────┘
                  ↓
┌─────────────────────────────────────┐
│                                     │
└─────────────────────────────────────┘
                  ↓
┌─────────────────────────────────────┐
│ The Ox Star lives and works on Earth.│
└─────────────────────────────────────┘
```

Compare Literature The myth about the Ox Star is fiction, but some parts of the story are based on facts. Make a list of events in the story that agree with facts from the article.

Oxen still help farmers in Asia work their fields.

THINK IT OVER

Discuss Talk about these questions with a partner.

1. **Character's Motive** Why didn't the Emperor send the Ox Star back with the correct message?

2. **Comparisons** How is the Emperor like Hera in "Echo and Narcissus"?

3. **Opinion** Would you want to live in ancient China? Explain why or why not.

4. **Personal Experience** Think about a time that you made a mistake. Were the results good or bad?

EXPRESS YOURSELF ▶ NEGOTIATE

Work with a partner. Role-play a conversation between the Ox Star and the Emperor. The Ox Star can:

- try to show the Emperor another way to fix his mistake
- suggest a better punishment or solution
- explain how he feels about living on Earth.

288 Unit 5 | Traditions

REACHING ALL STUDENTS

Multi-Level Strategies
SUM IT UP OPTIONS

BEGINNING Work with students to complete the sequence chart. Then, help students identify similar characters, events, and details in the myth and article and tell how they are alike and different. (Both texts have an emperor: in the myth he lives in heaven while in the article he lives on Earth; real and mythical peasants use oxen to farm, and so on.)

INTERMEDIATE / ADVANCED Students may complete their sequence charts independently, then use their charts to retell the myth to a partner. As they compare the myth and article, have them evaluate the suggestions for reading in Step 3 of **Master 80**. Ask: *How helpful were the suggestions in guiding your reading? Did they help you sequence the events? Will using these strategies help you read other selections?* Students may write their evaluations in a response journal.

Language Arts and Literature

USE COMPLETE SENTENCES

Learn About Subjects and Predicates Every complete sentence has two main parts, the subject and the predicate.

The simple subject is the most important word in the complete subject. It tells whom or what the sentence is about.

The poor peasants labored all day.

The simple predicate is the most important word in the complete predicate. It is the verb.

The rulers lived in big houses.

Identify Simple Subjects and Predicates Write a sentence about ancient China. Trade your work with a partner. Circle the simple subject. Underline the verb. Compare your sentences.

Practice Write each sentence. Add a simple subject on each green line. Add a verb on each blue line.

1. Most __peasants__ slept in small huts.
2. They __worked__ hard in the fields.
3. Farmers __paid__ taxes to the Emperor.
4. The __peasants__ in ancient China lived quietly.

LANGUAGE ACQUISITION ASSESSMENT
See page 81 of the Assessment Handbook.

LITERARY ANALYSIS
WRITING

COMPARE MYTHS IN AN ESSAY

Write an essay to compare the two myths in this unit. Follow these steps.

1 **Prewrite** Make a T-chart like this:

Similarities	Differences
Both myths tell how something in nature came to be.	"Echo" happens in ancient Greece, but "Ox Star" happens in ancient China.

2 **Write a Draft** Include these paragraphs:

- Write an **introduction** to tell what your essay is about.
- Write a paragraph to show how the two myths are alike.
- Write a paragraph to show how the two myths are different.
- Write a **conclusion** to sum up your essay.

3 **Revise Your Work** Think of ways to improve your essay. Ask a classmate or a teacher for ideas. Then write a better, final draft.

 Learn how to improve your writing in the **writer's craft**. See Handbook pages 390–401.

OBJECTIVES

COMPLETE SENTENCES
Grammar: ❶ Complete Sentences; Subjects and Predicates

COMPARE MYTHS IN AN ESSAY
Function: ❶ Make Comparisons; Write
Critical Thinking and Learning Strategies: Use Graphic Organizers (T-chart)
Literary Analysis: Myth; ❶ Compare Literature
Writing: Essay

LANGUAGE ARTS AND LITERATURE

1 **Use Complete Sentences** See annotations for answers to Practice items.

▶ **Practice Book** page 148

2 **Compare Myths in an Essay** You might want to use a story map as a way for students to recall and record events from the myths. Have them use what they have identified to complete a T-chart.

CLOSE AND ASSESS

Have students circle the simple subjects and underline the verbs in their essays.

TEACHING ALL STUDENTS

Multi-Level Strategies
WRITING OPTIONS FOR COMPARING MYTHS

BEGINNING Work with students to complete the prewriting chart together. Then lead them in writing an introductory paragraph as a group. Solicit volunteers to read the paragraph aloud and to suggest ideas for continuing the group essay. Restate their ideas to write the rest of the paragraphs.

INTERMEDIATE Have students complete the prewriting activity independently. Work as a group to write an introductory paragraph. As a group, model the editing process. Then, have the students complete the essay on their own. Conduct "read back feedback" peer editing where partners exchange papers and read each other's paper aloud. The writer listens and makes notes about changes he or she would like to make.

ADVANCED Have students complete their essays and then participate in peer conferencing groups: each peer writes one positive thing and asks one question or offers one suggestion for improvement to a classmate.

RESPOND

OBJECTIVES

COMPOUND SENTENCES

Grammar: ❶ Compound Sentences

COMPARE FICTION AND NONFICTION

Function: Write

Critical Thinking, Reading and Learning Strategies: ❶ Use Text Features in Fiction and Nonfiction; Analyze Information (fantasy and reality); Use Graphic Organizers (comparison chart)

Literary Analysis: ❶ Compare Literature

Writing: Comparison Chart

LANGUAGE ARTS AND LITERATURE

1 Use Compound Sentences

Possible answers to Practice items:

1. The Ox Star was happy, and he enjoyed an easy life in the heavens.

2. He had a message, but he twisted the Emperor's words.

3. The Ox Star worked, and he wore a heavy yoke.

▶ **Practice Book** page 149

2 Compare Fiction and Nonfiction

Encourage students to ask questions to help them identify fiction and nonfiction. For example, students might ask: *Could this happen in real life? Does this selection give facts about a topic?* Annotations in the chart show possible answers.

CLOSE AND ASSESS

Have students identify pairs of books from the classroom or school library as fiction or nonfiction.

Respond to the Myth and Article, continued

Language Arts and Literature, continued

> **GRAMMAR IN CONTEXT**

USE COMPOUND SENTENCES

Learn About Clauses A **clause** is a group of words with a subject and a verb. An **independent clause** tells a complete thought. It can stand alone as a sentence.

Independent Clauses:
The Emperor lived in the Heavens
The peasants lived on Earth

Learn About Compound Sentences
A **compound sentence** is made up of two independent clauses. To join the clauses, use a comma and the word **and**, **but**, or **or**.

Compound Sentence:
The Emperor lived in the Heavens, **and** the peasants lived on Earth.

Make up Compound Sentences Work with a partner. Join each pair of independent clauses to make a compound sentence.

• I am a farmer. I push a plow.

• I worked alone. Now I have an ox.

Practice Write compound sentences. Put **and**, **but**, or **or** on the red line. Finish the sentence by adding an independent clause on the black line.

1. The Ox Star was happy, _____ _____ .

2. He had a message, _____ _____ .

3. The Ox Star worked, _____ _____ .

> **LITERARY ANALYSIS**

COMPARE FICTION AND NONFICTION

Work with a group to copy and complete a comparison chart. Use "Echo and Narcissus" and "How the Ox Star Fell From Heaven" to fill in the fiction section. Use information from the articles on ancient Greece and ancient China to fill in the nonfiction section.

Story Elements	In Fiction	In Nonfiction
Characters	imaginary people, gods, and animals	real people; Pericles; emperor
Setting	Heaven	real place in the real world
Events	did not really happen	really happened
Sequence	events in time order	events are not in sequence
Author's Purpose	to entertain	to inform

REACHING ALL STUDENTS

▌ **Multi-Level Strategies**

PRACTICE OPTIONS FOR COMPOUND SENTENCES

BEGINNING Brainstorm clauses that might be added to the Practice items with students. Work together to select an appropriate clause for each item. Then have students choose the correct coordinating conjunction for each compound sentence.

INTERMEDIATE Have students work with partners of differing proficiency levels to complete the Practice items. Then have pairs compose an original compound sentence.

ADVANCED Students can complete the Practice items independently. Then, have students write three original compound sentences. Students exchange sentences with a partner to check for compound sentences.

Content Area Connections

SOCIAL STUDIES
TECHNOLOGY/MEDIA

STUDY MODERN CHINA

What is life like in China today? Work in a group. Choose a topic like:

farming   culture   languages
geography   holidays people

❶ Gather Information Use encyclopedias, maps, and almanacs. Talk to someone who has lived in China. Take notes. Here are some key words and Web sites that may help you get started, but remember that new sites appear every day.

INTERNET

INFORMATION ON-LINE

Key Words:
China
"People's Republic of China"

Web Sites:
➤ China
  • www.geographia.com
  • kids.infoplease.com

❷ Prepare a Multimedia Presentation Work with a team. Think of ways to share what you learned. Think of pictures you found in your research. Think of diagrams, charts, or maps you could show. You may want to download photos for a poster.

Modern and traditional styles are used in the buildings around Hong Kong harbor.

❸ Have a Chinese Celebration Plan a special day with your class. Decorate the room with Chinese art. Bring food to share. Then watch each group's presentation.

 Learn how to make a **multimedia presentation**. See Handbook pages 362–363.

How the Ox Star Fell from Heaven **291**

Research Skills

▶ **REPRESENTING INFORMATION**

TEACH Direct students' attention to graphic organizers in selections throughout the student book. Point out the ways that charts and diagrams can help them to access information by organizing it in a clear, visual manner. Display a map, a pie graph, a T-chart, a word cluster, a sequence chart, and a comparison chart. Discuss with students the best uses for each one.

PRACTICE Ask students to look through content area textbooks and Internet Web sites and find examples of charts and diagrams that clarify meaning. Then have them work with partners as they prepare their research reports on modern China to develop at least three kinds of charts and graphs that will help them present and explain the infomation they have found.

▶ **Practice Book** pages 150–151

RESPOND

OBJECTIVES

STUDY MODERN CHINA
Function: Give Information
Critical Thinking and Research Skills: Gather and Organize Information; Take Notes; Use Charts, Diagrams, and Maps
Technology/Media: Use the Internet
Representing: Research Report

CONTENT AREA CONNECTIONS

1 Study Modern China Prepare students by previewing information about modern China:

- **Geography** Display a map of Asia, pointing out the location of China in relation to other countries. Show students the huge range of climate zones, time zones, and terrain encompassed by China.

- **Language and Culture** Point out that modern China includes a population with a myriad of ethnic backgrounds, cultural heritages, and languages. Explain that some of these differences are related to the geographical features of the country. Lead a discussion about why this might be so (people separated by mountains and rivers develop independently) before having students choose their topics and do their research.

▶ **Practice Book** page 152

CLOSE AND ASSESS

Ask students to list one fact they learned from each presentation.

INTRODUCE THEME 2

OBJECTIVES

Function: Engage in Discussion

Concepts and Vocabulary:
Storytelling—*techniques, exaggeration, tall tale*

Viewing: Interpret a Visual Image

Learning Strategies: Relate to Personal Experience; Use Graphic Organizers (observation chart)

Critical Thinking: Generate Ideas

TAP PRIOR KNOWLEDGE

1 **Think, Pair, Share on Storytelling Techniques** Define *technique* as "a way of doing something," and suggest that there are many different storytelling techniques. Tell students that one popular technique is *exaggeration*, or "stretching the truth." Add that a story that uses exaggeration is a *tall tale*.

Invite students to think about storytellers they have heard. Ask: *What techniques does a good storyteller use? What makes a good story?* Have students think about these questions, discuss with a partner, and then share what they have learned. List the responses.

VIEW AND DISCUSS

2 **Observe Details of a Visual Image** After students view the artwork, have them make a chart to record observations. Help students see that the storyteller in the statue has captured the attention of many children. Ask: *What story do you think she is telling the children? Who is the storyteller?* (grandmother, friend, aunt)

Observation Chart
Who?
What?
Where?

Use the Observation Options in the **Multi-Level Strategies** to include all proficiency levels.

Storyteller statue from Jemez Pueblo, New Mexico, © 1997 Helen Sands.

292 **Unit 5** | Traditions

REACHING ALL STUDENTS

Multi-Level Strategies
OBSERVATION OPTIONS

BEGINNING Read the caption of the visual image, *Storyteller statue*. Model how to make observations of the image, using the following frame: *I see a lady and she is singing/talking in the garden . I see children and they are singing/talking , too.* Fill out the observation chart with students, and compare observations within the group.

INTERMEDIATE Encourage students to work with a partner to discuss and write observations in the observation chart. Have them summarize their ideas and then compare observations with another pair, noting ideas that are different and those that are alike.

ADVANCED Ask students to make their observations on their own, then compare their ideas with a partner. Encourage them to write a story about what they think is happening in the image.

THEME 2

Telling the Tale

- How has storytelling changed over time? How has it remained the same?

- How do storytellers pass along the history of a culture?

- What techniques can storytellers use to make their tales come alive?

THEME-RELATED BOOKS

John Henry and His Mighty Hammer
by Patsy Jensen

The story of an American folk hero who splits rock faster than a machine.

BEGINNING

Gilgamesh the King
by Ludmila Zeman

In one of the world's oldest stories, Enkidu teaches the evil Gilgamesh how to become a good king.

INTERMEDIATE

The Singing Man
by Angela Shelf Medearis

Long ago in West Africa, a young man leaves home to become a musician. He returns years later as the king's singing storyteller.

ADVANCED

293

DISCUSS THE GUIDING QUESTIONS

3 Set the Theme Some key points to develop during the discussion are:

- Storytelling has changed in terms of where and how a story is told. In the old days, people often sat around a fire telling stories; now they may sit around their kitchen table or in their living rooms. The purpose of storytelling has remained the same. It is a tradition for many cultures to share stories from one generation to the next, usually at family gatherings or ceremonies.

- Storytellers pass along the history of a culture through stories, images, and dramatizations. Oral traditions are part of many cultures and a way for generations to appreciate and honor their ancestors.

- Storytellers can use vivid descriptions, dramatic images, humor, exaggerations, and examples from personal experiences.

  Form groups and use the **Multi-Level Strategies** so all students can participate.

CLOSE AND ASSESS

Ask students to define storytelling techniques and give examples.

Multi-Level Strategies
GROUPING GUIDELINES

BEGINNING Use modeling and sentence frames to support students. Model complete sentences: *Storytelling is different today than in the past. Today, _____. A long time ago, people _____. A technique that storytellers use is _____.* Provide guidance as students supply words to compare storytelling over time.

INTERMEDIATE / ADVANCED Have Advanced students work with Intermediate students in small groups to discuss the guiding questions. Then have students agree on a list of qualities of a good storyteller and techniques to use to tell a good story. Students present their lists to the class.

THEME LIBRARY

■ Gilgamesh the King
by Ludmila Zeman

Invite students to read *Gilgamesh the King* and compare its style with the styles of the stories in Unit 5, including the Theme Library book *Coyote*. Ask: *What is the difference between reading an illustrated story and hearing a story told?* Encourage volunteers to choose one of the stories to retell to the class. Remind them that storytellers use their own words and add their own ideas to the stories they retell.

BUILD LANGUAGE AND VOCABULARY

OBJECTIVES

Functions: Listen Actively; ⓣ Retell a Story

Concepts and Vocabulary: Time and Cause Words

Patterns and Structures: ⓣ Complex Sentences

Speaking and Listening: Storytelling

Critical Thinking and Learning Strategy: Use Graphic Organizers (story map)

START WITH A COMMON EXPERIENCE

1 Listen to a Story Play the recording on the **Language Tape/CD** or read aloud the script on page T382. Ask students to listen for enjoyment but also to think about how they might retell the story themselves.

Tape 1B
CD 1
Track 11

> Use the Options for Listening in the **Multi-Level Strategies** to include all proficiency levels.

2 Model How to Retell a Story Explain that a storyteller like Sarah Ross takes the elements of a traditional story and retells it in her own words. Model retelling a fragment of the story for students:

> **How to Retell a Story**
>
> • Select part of the story: *King Solomon was known for his great wisdom and people came from near and far to have him solve their problems.*
>
> • Rephrase the ideas: *Word of King Solomon's wisdom spread far and wide. People from all across the land came to him with their problems, knowing the great king would solve them.*
>
> • Act out parts of the story: *The woman was so poor that all she could afford to do was smell the delicious bread.* (Breathe in deeply.)

Build Language and Vocabulary
RETELL A STORY

Listen to this story from the Jewish tradition. It has been told for hundreds of years. Here a student, Sarah Ross, tells the story as she learned it from her mother, a professional storyteller.

Sarah Ross tells "King Solomon and the Smell of Bread."

294 Unit 5 | Traditions

REACHING ALL STUDENTS

Multi-Level Strategies
OPTIONS FOR LISTENING

BEGINNING First, have students listen to the whole story. Then, on another listening, use gestures, pause frequently to clarify meaning, and restate as necessary to ensure comprehension. Ask questions: *What was the name of the king? Who came to see the king? What is the problem?*

INTERMEDIATE Encourage students to listen with a purpose or goal in mind, such as to determine the sequence of events in the story. Tell students to listen for words that signal the order of events—such as *one day* and *when*—and reasons for actions—such as *so* and *as*.

ADVANCED Have students concentrate on the storyteller's pacing, tone, and expression to learn how to retell a story effectively. Encourage students to think about how they will use their voices to get across meaning and feelings when it is their turn to retell the story.

COMPLETE A STORY MAP

Work with the group to complete a story map like this one for "King Solomon and the Smell of Bread." Listen to the story again if you need to.

Story Map

Title:	King Solomon and the Smell of Bread
Setting:	Ancient Jerusalem
Characters:	Baker, poor woman, King Solomon
Problem:	Poor woman smells baker's bread. Baker wants to be paid.
Event 1	_____
Event 2	_____
Event 3	_____
Event 4	_____
Solution:	_____

BUILD YOUR VOCABULARY

Time Order and Cause Words A signal gives you a clue about something. Some words signal special information in a sentence.

Time order words, such as *after* or *while*, signal when something happens.

Cause words, such as *because* or *since*, signal the reason for something. When you speak or write, you can use words like these to show how ideas go together.

Example:
The poor woman smelled the bread **because** she could not buy it.
King Solomon made a decision **after** he talked to the baker and the woman.

In these complex sentences, the words *because* and *after* are **conjunctions**.

USE LANGUAGE STRUCTURES ▶ COMPLEX SENTENCES

Speaking: Retell a Story Practice telling "King Solomon and the Smell of Bread" with a partner. Use ideas from the story map. Tell your story to the group.

Example:
The baker was upset **when** the woman smelled the bread.
The baker took her to court **because** he wanted to get paid.

Word Bank

Time Order Words
after
before
when
while

Cause Words
because
since

Build Language and Vocabulary **295**

---

3 Complete a Story Map Suggest that groups listen to the story as often as necessary to complete the story map.

4 Build Your Vocabulary: Time Order and Cause Words Explain that the sentences in the examples are called *complex sentences*. Present the skill, using the definitions and examples on **Transparency 81**. For item 3, point out that some of these words are time order words, and some are cause words. Give examples to clarify the meaning of each conjunction. Then have students form the complex sentences in Try It!

5 Use Language Structures: Complex Sentences Teach the skill using **Transparency 81**.

Speaking: Retell a Story Conduct the activity at the bottom of page 295. Remind students that their story maps show the order in which events in the story took place.

▋ Use the Speaking Activity Options in the **Multi-Level Strategies** to adjust instruction.

▶ **Practice Book** page 153

CLOSE AND ASSESS

Have students tell what a complex sentence is. Then ask them to create a clause that completes this sentence: *King Solomon was wise, _____ .*

Multi-Level Strategies
SPEAKING ACTIVITY OPTIONS

BEGINNING Encourage Beginning students to retell the story as well as they can, giving the main events in the order in which they happened. Suggest that students use gestures, pantomime, and facial expressions to help get meaning across to their listeners.

INTERMEDIATE Suggest that students tape-record their retellings and play them back so that they can judge how effective the retelling is. After students revise their presentations, they can tell the story to the group.

ADVANCED Encourage students to use appropriate volume, stress, pacing, and tone as they retell the story. Remind them to make eye contact with their listeners and to use gestures and facial expressions to help get meaning across.

Transparency 81 / Master 81

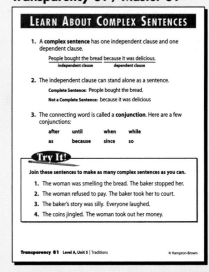

LEARN ABOUT COMPLEX SENTENCES

1. A **complex sentence** has one independent clause and one dependent clause.

   People bought the bread because it was delicious.
   <u>independent clause</u>   <u>dependent clause</u>

2. The independent clause can stand alone as a sentence.

   Complete Sentence: People bought the bread.
   Not a Complete Sentence: because it was delicious

3. The connecting word is called a **conjunction**. Here are a few conjunctions.

after	until	when	while
as	because	since	so

   Try It!

   Join these sentences to make as many complex sentences as you can.

   1. The woman was smelling the bread. The baker stopped her.
   2. The woman refused to pay. The baker took her to court.
   3. The baker's story was silly. Everyone laughed.
   4. The coins jingled. The woman took out her money.

   Transparency 81 Level A, Unit 5 | Traditions   © Hampton-Brown

Build Language and Vocabulary **T295**

PREPARE TO READ

OBJECTIVES

THINK ABOUT WHAT YOU KNOW

Reading Strategy: Relate to Personal Experience

LEARN KEY VOCABULARY ⊤

Vocabulary Strategy: Relate Words

LEARN TO USE GRAPHIC ORGANIZERS

Reading Strategy:
Use Graphic Organizers (time line)

THINK ABOUT WHAT YOU KNOW

1 **Play "Stretch the Truth"** Discuss the meaning of *stretch* and model stretching the truth.

Truth: *It rained a lot.*
Stretching the Truth: *It rained so hard there were puddles as big as a lake.*

LEARN KEY VOCABULARY

2 **Relate Words** Read each vocabulary word and its defining sentence aloud; then conduct the matching activity.

▌ Use the Vocabulary Options in **Multi-Level Strategies** to tailor instruction to proficiency levels.

▶ **Practice Book** page 154

LEARN TO USE GRAPHIC ORGANIZERS

3 **Model How to Make a Time Line** Read the story on **Transparency 82** and record events. Then follow the steps in the strategy box on page 296 to make a vertical time line of the events like the one on page 303 of the student book.

CLOSE AND ASSESS

Ask students: *What have you learned?* Compile student responses on a graphic organizer, such as a cluster web, to model how it can help to organize information.

The Tall Tale

article and tall tale retold
by Chuck Larkin

Prepare to Read

THINK ABOUT WHAT YOU KNOW

Play "Stretch the Truth" Work with a group to make exaggerated sentences. *The baby was bigger than a bear. No, it was bigger than _____. No, it was bigger than _____.* Play as long as you can.

LEARN KEY VOCABULARY

Relate Words Study the new words. Then write sentences by combining a beginning from column 1 with an ending from column 2.

Beginning	Ending
1. A **exaggerated** event is C	A. and that it is the **absolute truth**.
2. You **insist** that you are not lying A	B. the storyteller's **humor**.
3. A rainstorm was the **cause** and E	C. funny, but not **believable**.
4. The **audience** laughed at B	D. has its own funny **logic**.
5. An **outlandish** tale D	E. a flood was the **effect**.

absolute truth When something is completely true, it is the **absolute truth**.

audience An **audience** is a group of people who watch and listen to a performance.

believable A **believable** event could really happen.

cause A **cause** is something that makes something else happen.

effect An **effect** is something that happens because of something that happened earlier.

exaggerated Something is **exaggerated** when it is bigger and wilder than the truth.

humor When something makes you laugh, it has **humor**.

insist When you **insist** on something, you will not change your mind.

logic When something has **logic**, it makes sense.

outlandish Something is **outlandish** if it is very strange or odd.

LEARN TO USE GRAPHIC ORGANIZERS

A **graphic organizer** helps you "see" information quickly. Word webs, mind maps, time lines, and charts are graphic organizers.

READING STRATEGY
How to Make a Time Line
1. Think of the main events in a story.
2. Write the events in order. Use words like *first*, *after*, and *finally* to help you.
3. Draw a line and divide it into parts to show time.
4. Write the events in order along the time line.

As you read "Pecos Bill," write the important events. After reading, you can put the events in order to make a time line.

REACHING ALL STUDENTS

▌ **Multi-Level Strategies**
VOCABULARY OPTIONS

BEGINNING Work with students to understand vocabulary words. Then have them watch the pantomimes (see below) and guess the words.

INTERMEDIATE / **ADVANCED**
Have students work in groups to pantomime the meaning of vocabulary words. Students perform the pantomimes for the class to reinforce meaning.

Transparency 82 / Master 82

HOW TO IDENTIFY SEQUENCE

Directions: Read the story. Record the events on the chart. Then, on your own paper, make a time line to show the order of the events. Include dates on your time line.

The Giant Peach

I found a giant peach. I decided to take my peach to a festival. I pulled it along the road with 16 mules. When I got to the festival, I stuck a faucet into the side of the peach, turned it on, and sold 1,300 gallons of peach juice! That's a fact. I was there.

First	Then	Finally
Sample entries are shown. I found a giant peach.	I had 16 mules pull it to a festival.	At the festival, I stuck in a faucet and sold 1,300 gallons of peach juice.

Transparency 82 Level A, Unit 5 | Traditions   © Hampton-Brown

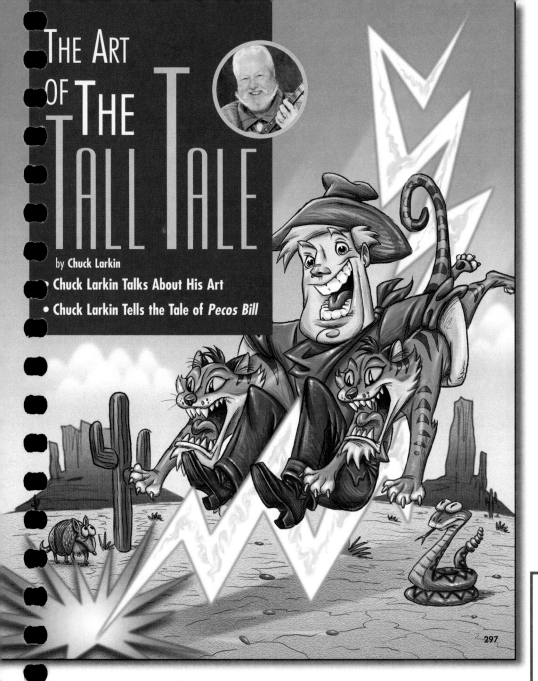

THE ART OF THE TALL TALE

by **Chuck Larkin**

- **Chuck Larkin Talks About His Art**
- Chuck Larkin Tells the Tale of *Pecos Bill*

297

OBJECTIVES
Listening: Listen to a Preview
Reading Strategies: Preview; Predict

INTRODUCE THE SELECTION

4 Preview and Predict Read the title, author, and the headings for the two parts of the selection on page 297 with students. Define a tall tale as a funny story made up of exaggerated characters and events. It uses realistic details to describe impossible events. Talk about the story characters they see on the page. Ask: *What do you think this tall tale will be about?*

Next, have students page through the tall tale and look at the pictures of Pecos Bill in the story. Ask them to predict exaggerated truths that this tall tale might include.

5 Audio Walk-Through Play the Audio Walk-Through for "The Art of the Tall Tale" on the **Selection Tape/CD** to give students the overall idea of the selection.

Tape 5B
CD 5
Track 5

The Art of The Tall Tale
by Chuck Larkin

Theme Connection As the storyteller talks about his art, and then spins a yarn about the West, the reader becomes acquainted with one of many storytelling styles.

Selection Summary Both parts of this selection help students understand the art of the tall tale and its unique characteristics. This Pecos Bill story tells how Pecos Bill becomes a cowboy. The author stretches the truth to make the story humorous and entertaining.

THE BASICS 📚 BOOKSHELF

■ ***All Across America*** by Daphne Liu

In many ways, America is the greatest tall tale of all. The rhyming text of this lively song introduces vocabulary for people who formed the United States, such as *explorers, pioneers, inventors,* and *dreamers.* Colorful illustrations and labeled maps give increased access to beginning English learners.

For Lesson Plans: See the Teacher's Guide for *The Basics Bookshelf*.

Red annotations offer
opportunities to clarify meaning
and check for understanding.

OBJECTIVES

Function: Read a Selection

Grammar: **T** Complex Sentences

Listening: Listen to a Selection

Reading and Learning Strategies:
Set a Purpose for Reading; Use Text
Features (sidebar)

Comprehension: Identify Author's
Purpose; Summarize; Relate to Personal
Experience

Literary Analysis: Respond to Literature

SET PURPOSE

1 Say: *Listen for details that tell
about the storyteller and how
he creates tall tales.*

LISTEN AND READ

Tape 5B
CD 5
Track 6

2 Learn About Tall Tales
Play the recording of pages 298–299,
or read them aloud, pausing
frequently to check comprehension
of humor: *Flames from a fire are hot,
but are they hot like pepper?* etc.

CHUCK LARKIN TALKS ABOUT HIS ART

ABOUT THE AUTHOR

Chuck Larkin loves to tell tall tales. Here's what he
has to say about himself: "I was raised in the small
town of Pocomoke. Pocomoke is so small that its
zip code is a **fraction.** In Pocomoke, the winters
were so cold that the **flames** in the fireplace
would freeze up **solid**! Momma would **grind
up** that frozen fire and we'd **sprinkle** it on our
food for red pepper. That's a fact. I was there."
Chuck Larkin makes up his own tall tales
and also retells classics like "Pecos Bill."

Pose choices: Is this a believable
event or an exaggerated event?

298 Unit 5 | Traditions

Tall tales are funny stories. They are
made up of **exaggerated** events. The
events describe a **cause** and an **effect**.
The cause is a **believable** event—
something that could be true in real life:
Pocomoke was a small town. But it's
followed by an **outlandish** effect: *The
zip code is a fraction.* You know that
it can't be true, but there is a strange
logic to it that makes you laugh. Of
course, the storyteller **insists** that the
story is the **absolute truth**. That just
adds to the **humor**.

I always tell about **my personal
experiences**. As I always say to my
audience: "I was there, and I'd walk
on my lips before I would tell a lie."

Clarify: Can a person walk on their lips?
They could try, but they'd look funny
doing it, and it would probably hurt!

....

fraction number that is less than 1 ($\frac{1}{2}, \frac{1}{4}$, etc.)
flames the burning part of a fire
solid strong and hard
grind up crush, break into small pieces
sprinkle drop a small amount of
my personal experiences things that have happened
to me

REACHING ALL STUDENTS

Vocabulary
FIGURATIVE LANGUAGE: HYPERBOLE

Define *hyperbole* as "exaggeration," and
use examples from the giant peach
story to clarify. Remind students about
the Stretching the Truth game. Have
students work with a partner to make
a T-chart listing as many examples of
hyperbole as they can find in the story
in a given time period.

What It Says	What It Means

Vocabulary
CONTRACTIONS

Have students play "Contraction
Concentration." Point out that
contractions are used in this very
informal style of writing. (*I'm, I've,
name's, That's, 'til*) Challenge students
to find as many contractions as they
can as they read the selection, and to
think of others they have heard. Have
students write each contraction and
its uncontracted form on index cards.
Students place cards face down to
play "Concentration" and turn them
over to match contracted and
uncontracted forms.

CULTURAL PERSPECTIVES

Home and U.S. Cultures: Heroes
Invite students to share some of the
larger-than-life heroes they know
about. Give examples from cultures
outside the United States. (Mohandas
Gandhi, Nelson Mandela, Mother
Teresa) Then share with students a list
of several U.S. heroes (John Glenn,
Martin Luther King Jr., Rosa Parks, Helen
Keller, Elizabeth Cady Stanton) and
explain why they are famous.

I have one tale about a giant peach. Storytellers around the country have used it. You can use it, too, to make your own tall tale. **Clarify:** This tale is an example. It will show you how to make an event into a tall tale.

Imagine you had a giant peach. What would you do with it? I decided to take my peach to a festival. I pulled it along the road with 16 mules. When I got to the festival, I stuck a faucet into the side of the peach, turned it on, and sold 1,300 gallons of peach juice!

That's a fact. I was there. **Ask:** Why is the story about a giant peach a tall tale?

Now, read the tall tale of . . .

Pecos Bill

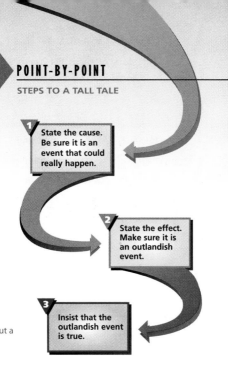

POINT-BY-POINT
STEPS TO A TALL TALE

1. State the cause. Be sure it is an event that could really happen.

2. State the effect. Make sure it is an outlandish event.

3. Insist that the outlandish event is true.

BEFORE YOU MOVE ON...

1. **Author's Purpose** Why does Chuck Larkin say: "Pocomoke is so small that its zip code is a fraction."?

2. **Summary** Describe how to create a tall tale.

3. **Personal Experience** Think of a true event that you could turn into a tall tale. Share your idea with a partner.

CHECK COMPREHENSION

3 **Use Text Features: Sidebar** Summarize the key points in the text with the Point-by-Point feature. Ask students to give an example of each point.

4 **Answers to "Before You Move On"**

1. **Author's Purpose** A zip code is made of 5 numbers. By saying that his zip code is only a fraction of one number, he is emphasizing how small his town was.

2. **Summary** Refer to the Point-by-Point Steps to a Tall Tale.

3. **Personal Experience** Answers will vary. Encourage students to think of a funny event, an adventure, a mishap, or a fall that can be turned into a tall tale.

ABOUT THE AUTHOR

5 **Respond to Literature** Ask students how they feel about this kind of storytelling: *Does it make you laugh? Does it make you want to hear more tall tales? Does it make you want to become a storyteller?*

CLOSE AND ASSESS

Ask students: *What did you learn about telling tall tales?*

Mathematics Connection
CALCULATING DISTANCE

Tell students, in the selection they are about to read, Pecos Bill's family traveled from New England to Pecos, Texas. Using U.S. maps or an Internet map site (mapquest.com) with roads and distances indicated, ask students to trace the modern version of the route. As they read each page of the story, students can trace the route and record the miles or kilometers the family traveled. At the end of the selection, have students determine the total distance.

Grammar Minilesson

▶ **COMPLEX SENTENCES**

TEACH Write this sentence: *If you write a tall tale, then you must exaggerate things.* Point out that this sentence has two parts, each of which has a subject and a verb. Say: *A group of words within a sentence that has a subject and a verb is called a* clause.

Help students identify the two clauses. Point out that the first clause cannot stand alone as a sentence, so it is a dependent clause. The second clause can stand alone, so it is a main, or independent, clause.

Say: *A sentence that contains a dependent clause and an independent clause is called a* complex sentence.

PRACTICE Write these cloze sentences. Have students complete the clauses.

1. If I had a giant peach, then _____.
2. If _____, then I would spend ten years counting all my money.
3. If I grew as tall as a tree, then _____.
4. If _____, then I would hitch a ride to the moon.

▶ **Practice Book** page 155

OBJECTIVES

Function: Read a Selection

Listening: Listen to a Selection

Reading and Learning Strategies:
Set a Purpose for Reading; Use Graphic
Organizers (note-taking chart)

Comprehension: Make Comparisons;
Identify Details, Characters' Traits

Literary Analysis: Setting; Style

SET PURPOSE

1 Read the introduction on page 300
and briefly discuss the pictures. Say:
*As you read, notice the outlandish
events and the exaggerations.*

READ AND THINK

Tape 5B
CD 5
Track 6

**2 Strategy Focus: Use
Graphic Organizers** Involve
students in reading pages 300–301
and taking notes about the events
in Bill's early life and when he
grows up.

> Choose Reading Options in the
> **Multi-Level Strategies** to tailor
> the reading to proficiency levels.

The recording of "The Art of the Tall
Tale" on the **Selection Tape/CD**
offers an oral language model
and the opportunity to build
reading fluency.

1

THE EARLY LIFE OF PECOS BILL

The story of Pecos Bill begins when he is born in New England during a
wild tornado. His family soon moves West, near the Pecos River in Texas.

I'm Pecos Bill. I'm part man and
part **coyote**. I've slid down lightning
bolts holding wildcats under both arms
and never been scratched. I was raised
in Texas along the Pecos River, but my
life began in New England. I was born
while my Ma was **taming a tornado**.
Pa had caught the tornado **tearing up**
our farm. **Ask:** Do you think this is true?
Why or why not?

After the tornado, we needed a new
farm. **My folks** decided to move West.
They **hitched up** their wagon to Tillie—
that's what Pa named that tornado.
Finally, we got to the Pecos River and
settled down. I was five years old.

My, how I loved that Pecos River!
One day I **rigged up** a fishing line and
hooked a baby fish that measured about
six feet from eye to eye. I held that
fishing pole and stepped into the water.
That little fish pulled me barefoot down

the river! That's how water skiing got
started. I **wound up** so far away from
home that I decided to just keep on
going. **Clarify:** Water skiing is a sport. People
stand on a ski on top of the water as a
boat pulls them across the water.

BEFORE YOU MOVE ON...

1. **Cause and Effect** Why did Bill's family
   decide to move West?
2. **Character** What were Bill's parents like?
3. **Details** Describe some of the events of
   Bill's childhood.

---

coyote wild animal, like a dog or wolf
taming a tornado making a wild storm calm and peaceful
tearing up destroying, ruining
my folks my parents

hitched up tied
settled down made our home there
rigged up made, set up
wound up ended up

300 **Unit 5** | Traditions

REACHING ALL STUDENTS

Transparency 83 / Master 83

NOTE-TAKING CHART

Directions: Record the key events from the story.

The Art of the Tall Tale

Section	Important Events
The Early Life of Pecos Bill	
Pecos Bill Grows Up	
Pecos Bill Becomes a Cowboy	

Transparency 83 Level A, Unit 5 | Traditions   © Hampton-Brown

Multi-Level Strategies

READING OPTIONS FOR LESSONS 5–6

BEGINNING Read the selection aloud or play its recording on the
Selection Tape/CD. Use red annotations on the facsimile pages to clarify
meaning. Then read the text together and record events on **Transparency
83**. Add sketches to clarify meaning and say the text as you write it.

INTERMEDIATE / ADVANCED Have students read the selection
independently, taking notes on **Master 83**. As students complete each
section, have them compare notes with a partner and make sure they have
recorded the key events.

PECOS BILL GROWS UP

Pecos Bill grows up in the wild with a family of coyotes. One day, he meets Cactus Joe and learns to get honey from bees.

For a while I **lived off the land**, eating rattlesnakes and horned toads. Then I joined a **clan** of coyotes. They **raised me**. Pretty soon, I thought I *was* a coyote. **Pose choices:** Was Pecos Bill a coyote or a person?

One day, it was so hot that the shade and I moved under a bush to keep cool. A beekeeper came walking by. He said, "Howdy there. My name's Cactus Joe. What are you doing in the bushes? Where are your clothes?"

I said, "I've been living with the coyotes for years. I outgrew all my clothing." Cactus Joe laughed **mighty** hard at that, and he gave me a blanket to wear 'til I could get some clothes.

After that, I worked with Cactus Joe as a beekeeper. We **herded** honey bees out of their **hives**. We sang beekeeper songs as the bees gathered **nectar**.

Clarify: A beekeeper is someone who keeps honey bees and gathers honey from their hives.

BEFORE YOU MOVE ON...

1. **Setting/Vocabulary** Study the text and pictures. Then list things Bill could find to eat in the desert.
2. **Comparisons** How did Bill's life change after he met Cactus Joe?
3. **Author's Style** How does the author use exaggeration to describe a hot day?

lived off the land found all my food around the land nearby

clan family with many members and generations

raised me took care of me and helped me grow up

mighty very

herded led, gathered

hives homes made by or for bees

nectar the sweet liquid produced by plants and used by bees to make honey

---

CHECK COMPREHENSION

3 Answers to "Before You Move On"

page 300
1. **Cause and Effect** Bill's family decided to move West after a tornado tore up the farm.
2. **Character** Bill's mother was a strong woman and his father was adventurous.
3. **Details** He was born during a tornado; he rode from New England to Pecos, Texas, with his family in the covered wagon; he liked to fish.

page 301
1. **Setting/Vocabulary** Things Bill could find to eat in the desert were: rattlesnakes, horned toads, rabbits, honey.
2. **Comparisons** Cactus Joe invited Pecos Bill to work with him as a beekeeper.
3. **Author's Style** He uses exaggeration to explain that it was so hot that the shade wanted to hide under a bush to keep cool.

CLOSE AND ASSESS

Ask students to write down their favorite exaggeration from Pecos Bill's life.

Vocabulary
COLLOQUIALISMS

Define colloquialisms as "words used in informal conversation." Point out the large number of colloquialisms in the Pecos Bill tale. (*Howdy, mighty, barefoot, outgrew, get ourselves*) Help students discover the meaning of these terms through context, or by using a dictionary/glossary. Then have them practice using the colloquialisms in dialogues with a partner. For example: *Howdy. How are you? I'm mighty tired. Are you going to the party barefoot? No. We're having a mighty hard time getting ourselves ready to go.*

Literary Analysis Minilesson

▶ **SETTING**

TEACH Define *setting* as "the time and place of a story." Point out that the setting makes a difference in the reader's expectations. For example, a tall tale about coyotes and snakes would not make as much sense outside of a desert setting.

Explain that the setting in a story can change, as it does in "Pecos Bill," from New England to Texas, and from Bill's early years to his later years.

PRACTICE Have students chart the changes in setting over the course of the tall tale "Pecos Bill." Then have them do the same for the tale "How the Ox Star Fell from Heaven." Guide students to conclude that the setting has an important impact on the characters and events in any fictional selection.

▶ **Practice Book** page 156

READ PAGE 302

OBJECTIVES

Function: Read a Selection

Listening: Listen to a Selection

Reading and Learning Strategies:
Set a Purpose for Reading;
Use Graphic Organizers
(note-taking chart)

Comprehension: Identify Cause and
Effect, Character; Make Comparisons

SET PURPOSE

1 Say: *Look for details about how Pecos Bill
is different from other cowboys.*

READ AND THINK

Tape 5B
CD 5
Track 6

2 **Strategy Focus: Use
Graphic Organizers** Involve
students in reading page 302 and
taking notes.

> See the **Multi-Level Strategies**
> on page T300 to tailor reading to
> all proficiency levels.

CHECK COMPREHENSION

3 **Answers to "Before You Move On"**

1. **Cause and Effect** He thought it
   would be like herding bees.

2. **Comparisons** He rode a cougar.

3. **Character** wild, crazy, funny

CLOSE AND ASSESS

Have buzz groups retell this adventure.

Cactus Joe and Pecos Bill become cowboys. They herd cows instead of
bees, and begin the first cattle drives in the West.

Use visuals: Look at the Texas
longhorn cows in the picture.
Point to their horns.

One day, Cactus Joe found out
that **folks** in Kansas wanted their own
big Texas cows.

I said, "Let's get ourselves a couple
of **cougars** to ride. We can **round up** a
bunch of cows and herd them north to
Kansas. It can't be much different from
herding bees." **Ask:** What do you think?
Is this true or exaggerated?

So that's what we did. Let me tell
you, the horns on those Texas longhorn
cows are good for **picking your teeth**!
Just make sure you don't use a horn
that's **attached to** a cow. Those Texas
longhorns have a mighty kick!

After that first cattle drive, other
Texas boys decided to herd cattle, too,
but they had to ride horses. Horses
were easier to **come by** than cougars.
Together, we chased those cows from
Texas to Kansas and back. And that's
how the great **cattle drives** began.

BEFORE YOU MOVE ON...

1. **Cause and Effect** Why did Bill think that
   herding cows would be easy?

2. **Comparisons** What was one difference
   between Bill and the other cowboys who
   herded cows?

3. **Character** What are some words you could
   use to describe Bill?

folks people
cougars mountain lions
round up gather
picking your teeth cleaning food from between your
teeth

attached to connected to, part of
come by get
cattle drives travels over land with cowboys taking cows
from one place to another

302 Unit 5 | Traditions

REACHING ALL STUDENTS

Language Development
TELL AN ORIGINAL STORY

Have students work together to write
and tell a group tall tale. Each group
should make a chart with three rows
labeled "Event" (cause), "Outlandish
Event" (effect), and "Insist it's true."

Have groups construct the tall tales
through the following rotation (about
thirty minutes):

• Round 1: Each group brainstorms an
"Event" (cause), records it in row 1 of
the chart, then passes the chart to
the next group.

• Round 2: Each group brainstorms,
fills in the "Outlandish Event" (effect)
row, and passes the chart on.

• Round 3: Groups brainstorm and fill
in the "Insist it's true" space, writing
an expression that attests to their
truthfulness. (*I'd die before I'd lie.*)
They keep this card.

Groups then practice the tall tale on
their card and tell it to the class.

Respond to the Tall Tale
Check Your Understanding

SUM IT UP

Identify Sequence Copy and complete this time line to show the events in Pecos Bill's life.

Time Line

> Early Life
> First Bill was born in New England.
> Then his family moved to the Pecos River.

Retell a Story and Synthesize Information
Tell Pecos Bill's story to a partner. Also tell it to your family. Ask them what they thought about the story. Then write sentences that **synthesize**— or put together— your family's ideas.

Example:
My family liked the humor in Pecos Bill's story.

Possible events for the time line are:
Early Life: born in New England; moved to Pecos River; invented water skiing.
Bill Grows Up: joined coyote clan; met Cactus Joe; got clothing; herded bees.
Becoming a Cowboy: Joe and Bill get cougars; first cattle drive to Kansas; cattle drives with Texas boys.

✓ **LANGUAGE ACQUISITION ASSESSMENT**
See page 82 of the Assessment Handbook.

THINK IT OVER

Discuss Talk about these questions with a partner.

1. **Author's Style** What does Chuck Larkin say at the end of his tales? Why does he say that?

2. **Figurative Language** Bill says that the baby fish was "about six feet from eye to eye." What does he mean? How else could you describe a huge fish?

3. **Comparisons** How is a tall tale different from other kinds of stories?

4. **Judgments** Do you like the tall tale style? Explain.

EXPRESS YOURSELF ▶ ELABORATE

When you **elaborate**, you add new ideas and details. With a group, change an event in "Pecos Bill" to make it even more unbelievable! Then share your stories with other groups. Think of an outlandish prize for the best story.

The Art of the Tall Tale **303**

Multi-Level Strategies
SUM IT UP OPTIONS

BEGINNING Review with students the notes on **Transparency 83**. (See page T300.) Have students create individual time lines, writing complete sentences to describe each event and using *first, then, after, next, finally*. Make sure students add labels to the new time line to indicate periods of Pecos Bill's life. Have students practice retelling the tale to partners before they retell it to their families.

INTERMEDIATE / **ADVANCED** Have students review the notes they took on **Transparency 83**. Have them set up a vertical time line and record the events in order. They should add headings to the time line to show the stages of Paul's life. Students then use their time lines to retell the story to a partner. Advanced students can also write a summary of "Pecos Bill".

OBJECTIVES

SUM IT UP
Function: ❶ Retell a Story; Write
Reading and Learning Strategies: Summarize; Use Graphic Organizers (time line); ❶ Identify Sequence
Representing and Writing: Time line; Sentences

THINK IT OVER
Function: Engage in Discussion
Critical Thinking: Make Judgments
Literary Analysis: ❶ Compare Literature; Evaluate Author's Style; ❶ Figurative Language (hyperbole)

EXPRESS YOURSELF
Function: Elaborate
Speaking and Listening: Storytelling

CHECK YOUR UNDERSTANDING

1 Sum It Up See annotations on the student page for sample events for the time line.

▶ **Practice Book** page 157

2 Think It Over Possible answers are:

1. **Author's Style** He says, "That's a fact. I was there." This adds to the humor because you know it can't possibly be true.

2. **Figurative Language** He means that fish was *really* big. Answers will vary on how to describe a huge fish.

3. **Comparisons** A tall tale is a funny story about exaggerated events that describe a cause and an effect. The cause is believable.

4. **Judgments** Answers will vary.

3 Express Yourself Prompt the use of unbelievable events and exaggerated language.

CLOSE AND ASSESS

Ask students to complete the following sentence on an exit slip: *We can use a time line to _____.*

RESPOND

OBJECTIVES

COMPLEX SENTENCES
Grammar: ❶ Complex Sentences

WRITE A NEW EPISODE
Function: Write
Speaking and Listening: Storytelling
Learning Strategies: Use Graphic Organizers (cause-and-effect story chart)
Writing: Tall Tale

LANGUAGE ARTS AND LITERATURE

1 Use Complex Sentences Possible answers to Practice items:

1. Bill left his family when he caught a big fish.

2. Bill ate toads since they live in the desert.

3. Bill got a cougar because he wanted to ride it.

▶ **Practice Book** page 158

2 Write a New Episode Brainstorm outlandish events as a class. Work with students to fill in the chart. Encourage students to use complex sentences. Invite volunteers to share their stories with the class.

CLOSE AND ASSESS

Have students underline or circle complex sentences in their stories.

✔ **ASSESSMENT**
Selection Test 19 on page 87 of the Assessment Handbook tests students' mastery of the reading strategies and the vocabulary, comprehension, and language arts skills taught with this selection.

Respond to the Tall Tale, continued
Language Arts and Literature

GRAMMAR IN CONTEXT

USE COMPLEX SENTENCES

Learn About Clauses A **clause** is a group of words that has a subject and a verb.

An **independent clause** is a complete sentence.

> Chuck Larkin uses exaggerated events

A **dependent clause** is not a complete sentence.

> when he tells tall tales

Learn About Complex Sentences To make a **complex sentence**, join an independent clause and a dependent clause. Words like **when**, **because**, and **since** signal the dependent clause.

Chuck exaggerates **because** it adds humor.
<u>independent clause</u>   <u>dependent clause</u>

Make Up Complex Sentences Choose one independent clause and one dependent clause to make a complex sentence.

Independent Clauses	Dependent Clauses
Cattle drives began	because he lived alone
Bill was wild	when Bill went to Kansas

Practice Write complex sentences. Put **when**, **because**, or **since** on the red line, then finish the sentence.

1. Bill left his family _____ _____ .

2. Bill ate toads _____ _____ .

3. Bill got a cougar _____ _____ .

WRITING/SPEAKING

WRITE A NEW EPISODE

Add to the tall tale about Pecos Bill.

❶ **Make a Story Chart** Copy and complete the chart with your ideas.

Cause (a realistic event)	Effect (an outlandish event)	Insist that the story is true
Pecos Bill caught a big fish.	The fish pulled him many miles down the river.	That's a fact. I saw it with my own eyes.
Pecos Bill saw an eagle fly by.		
	Pecos Bill made a lasso out of a rattlesnake.	

❷ **Write Your Episode** Include exaggeration, or **hyperbole**, in your writing.

Examples:
The eagle was as big as an airplane.
The rattlesnake was a block long.

❸ **Share Your Episode** Tell the tale with expression. Use a different voice for each character.

REACHING ALL STUDENTS

▌Multi-Level Strategies
WRITING OPTIONS FOR A NEW EPISODE

BEGINNING   Work with students on a skit representing segments of the Pecos Bill story. Then have them modify the skit, changing the events for the development of a new episode. As students act out the episode, attach English words to their actions. Use what they have done to develop a shared writing of a new episode.

INTERMEDIATE   Have students work with partners or small groups as they develop their ideas using the Cause/Effect/Insist It's True model. Ask them if they need any help with vocabulary to develop their ideas. Suggest that they use a thesaurus to find outlandish synonyms. Ask students to act out their episodes, while a partner narrates.

ADVANCED   Have students write, illustrate, and put their tall tales together in a book. Invite them to read their new episodes to classmates.

Content Area Connections

EXPLORE GEOGRAPHY

Make a Tall Tale Map Start with a map of the United States. Mark the places described in the story. Then label the events that happened to Bill in each place. Look for other tall tales in books at the library or on the Internet.

Find characters like:

- Paul Bunyan
- Annie Christmas
- John Henry
- Mike Fink

On your map, find and label the places where these new stories happen.

SCIENCE
TECHNOLOGY/MEDIA

STUDY WILD ANIMALS

Research an animal of the Wild West:

| rattlesnake | coyote | cougar |
| mustang | buffalo | horned toad |

Find Information Use books or the Internet. Use the animal's name as a key word for your search. Try these Web sites, but remember that new sites appear every day!

INTERNET

INFORMATION ON-LINE

Web Sites:
➤ Animals
- www.AllAboutNature.com/coloring
- www.desertusa.com

Take notes about where the animal lives, what it eats, and other interesting facts.

Write a Report Describe your animal. Add photos, illustrations, and other art.

 Learn how to write a **research report**. See Handbook pages 366–372.

Research Skills

▶ USING AN ATLAS

TEACH Display an atlas and demonstrate how to look up a map of the United States. Page through the book and identify other kinds of information available in an atlas, such as geographical maps, distances, climate, topographical information, and population in cities, states, and countries. Also point out that an atlas identifies mountain ranges, rivers, and oceans. Demonstrate how the index in the back of the atlas can be helpful.

PRACTICE List these places on self-stick notes and ask students to locate them in an atlas:

- Texas
- Massachusetts
- Wyoming
- California

Then have them take turns looking up locations they have been or places where friends or relatives live.

▶ **Practice Book** page 159

RESPOND

OBJECTIVES

EXPLORE GEOGRAPHY

Function: Give Information

Concepts and Vocabulary: Geography—*country, states, mountain ranges, rivers, oceans*

Learning Strategies, Critical Thinking, and Research Skills: Gather Information; Take Notes; Use an Atlas

Representing and Writing: Map; Labels

STUDY WILD ANIMALS

Function: Write; Give Information

Concepts and Vocabulary: Animals

Technology/Media: Use the Internet

Writing: Report

CONTENT AREA CONNECTIONS

1 Explore Geography Prepare students by previewing the following vocabulary, using an atlas or geography text: *country, states, mountain ranges, rivers, oceans*.

▶ **Practice Book** pages 160–161

2 Study Wild Animals Prepare students by previewing the following content area vocabulary:

- **habitat:** Write *habitat, habitation,* and *inhabit.* Tell students that these words come from a Latin root (*habitare*), meaning "to live." Define each word, explaining *habitat* as "a region where a plant or animal naturally lives."

- **desert:** Model pronouncing *desert* with the stress on the first syllable. Define it as "a dry, barren, sandy region." Tell students that a desert is an example of a habitat.

- **poisonous:** Define *poisonous* as "capable of injuring or killing by poison or venom." Ask: *Are all snakes poisonous?* (no)

CLOSE AND ASSESS

Have students mark on their maps where in the U.S. the animals they researched are most likely to be found.

BUILD LANGUAGE AND VOCABULARY

OBJECTIVES

Function: Listen Actively;
T Tell an Original Story

Concepts and Vocabulary:
T Story Words

Patterns and Structures:
T Present Perfect Tense

Speaking: Storytelling

Viewing: Interpret Visual Information

Critical Thinking and Learning Strategy:
Interact with Peers; Summarize;
Use Text Structures (goal and outcome);
Use Graphic Organizers
(goal-and-outcome chart)

START WITH A COMMON EXPERIENCE

1 View Illustrations and Listen to a Story Beginning Play the recording of the beginning of "The Boy Who Looked for the Wind" on the **Language Tape/CD** or read aloud the audio script on page T382. Refer to the illustrations on page 306.

Tape 1B
CD 1
Track 12

2 Summarize Story Events Work with students to summarize the story events and record them on a story map.

> Use the Summarizing Options in the **Multi-Level Strategies** to invite responses.

3 Model How to Tell an Original Story Explain that when telling an original story, you have to invent the characters and story events. Use the following Think Aloud:

> **How to Tell an Original Story**
> • Name a place and time: *a faraway land, long ago*
> • Name a character: *a young girl*
> • Tell what the character wants to do: *find the rainbow's end*
> • Tell what the character does to reach the goal: *Long ago, in a faraway land, a young girl set out to find the rainbow's end. As she walked, the rainbow seemed to get farther away. She decided to ask the animals for help.*

Build Language and Vocabulary

TELL AN ORIGINAL STORY

View the pictures and listen to the beginning of a story.

Multi-Level Strategies

SUMMARIZING OPTIONS

BEGINNING Suggest that students draw pictures to go with the story events they hear in the audio recording. Students can then sequence their pictures and label them or dictate labels. They can use this storyboard technique to tell more of the story later in the lesson.

INTERMEDIATE / ADVANCED Have students work with partners to complete story maps as they listen to the story beginning. As a group, work to develop a good summary of the story. Students should then write individual summaries to use later in the lesson.

DISCUSS STORY EPISODES

Who else did the boy talk to? What else did he get? Look at the pictures on page 306 and share your ideas with a partner.

BUILD YOUR VOCABULARY

Story Words Every story happens in a time and a place. That is called the **setting**. The people or animals in a story are called the **characters**. The **goal** is what the character is trying to get or do. The **outcome** is what happens at the end of the story. It tells you if the goal was met. Fill in information about "The Boy Who Looked for the Wind" on a chart like this. Add your own ideas for the outcome of this story.

Setting	Characters	Goal	Outcome

USE LANGUAGE STRUCTURES ▶ PRESENT PERFECT TENSE

Speaking: Tell a Story Use the information on your chart to tell your version of "The Boy Who Looked for the Wind." Practice with a partner, then tell your story to the group.

Example:
Once upon a time, a boy who lived in the country went looking for the wind. "Have you seen the wind?" he asked everyone he met.

Build Language and Vocabulary **307**

CONDUCT THE ACTIVITIES

4 **Discuss Story Episodes** Students should recognize that the boy has talked to a tree, which has given him some leaves.

5 **Build Your Vocabulary: Story Words** Tell students that the main, or most important, character in a story is the person who is trying to achieve the goal.

6 **Use Language Structures: Present Perfect Tense** Use the definition and examples on **Transparency 84** to teach this tense. Have students identify examples of the present perfect tense in the story beginning. Then have students complete the sentences in Try It!

Speaking: Tell a Story Conduct the activity at the bottom of page 307.

▌ Use the Speaking Activity Options in the **Multi-Level Strategies** to adjust instruction.

▶ **Practice Book** page 162

CLOSE AND ASSESS

Ask students to use present perfect tense verbs to complete these sentences: *The boy _____ the wind. No animal _____ the wind.*

Multi-Level Strategies
SPEAKING ACTIVITY OPTIONS

BEGINNING Invite Beginning students to expand their storyboards to create their story ending. Encourage students to use gestures, pantomime, and facial expressions to help get meaning across to their listeners. You may wish to narrate their actions to help them tell their stories.

INTERMEDIATE Have partners conference with each other and confirm that they have included ideas for each category of the chart. Suggest that students then make a story map to show the order of events. After students practice their presentations, they can tell the story.

ADVANCED Remind students that when they tell a story, they should use appropriate volume and tone of voice. Tell them to make eye contact with their listeners, and encourage them to use gestures and facial expressions to help communicate meaning and feelings.

Transparency 84 / Master 84

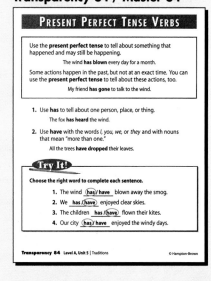

PRESENT PERFECT TENSE VERBS

Use the **present perfect tense** to tell about something that happened and may still be happening.

The wind **has blown** every day for a month.

Some actions happen in the past, but not at an exact time. You can use the **present perfect tense** to tell about these actions, too.

My friend **has gone** to talk to the wind.

1. Use **has** to tell about one person, place, or thing.
   The fox **has heard** the wind.

2. Use **have** with the words *I, you, we,* or *they* and with nouns that mean "more than one."
   All the trees **have dropped** their leaves.

Try It!

Choose the right word to complete each sentence.
1. The wind (has/ have) blown away the smog.
2. We (has /have) enjoyed clear skies.
3. The children (has /have) flown their kites.
4. Our city (has/ have) enjoyed the windy days.

Transparency 84 Level A, Unit 5 | Traditions   © Hampton-Brown

Build Language and Vocabulary **T307**

PREPARE TO READ

OBJECTIVES

THINK ABOUT WHAT YOU KNOW

Concepts and Vocabulary:
Storytelling —*techniques, elaboration, sequence, hyperbole*

Reading and Learning Strategies:
Activate Prior Knowledge; Use Graphic Organizers (word web)

LEARN KEY VOCABULARY ●T

Vocabulary Strategy: Relate Words

LEARN TO RELATE GOALS AND OUTCOMES

Reading Strategy:
●T Relate Goal and Outcome

THINK ABOUT WHAT YOU KNOW

1 **Make a Storytelling Web** Begin a word web with *storytelling techniques* at the center, then brainstorm with students techniques storytellers use.

LEARN KEY VOCABULARY

2 **Relate Words** Read each vocabulary word and its defining sentence aloud. After students understand the key vocabulary words, have partners complete the sentences.

> Use the Vocabulary Options in **Multi-Level Strategies** to tailor instruction to proficiency levels.

▶ **Practice Book** page 163

LEARN TO RELATE GOALS AND OUTCOMES

3 **Model How to Relate Goals and Outcomes** Define *goal* and *outcome*.

Use **Transparency 85** to model the steps in the box and record answers.

• Read aloud the beginning of "The Fox and the Crow." Ask: *What do Fox and Crow want to do? What does each character need to do to reach the goal?*

• Ask: *What do the characters do? What is the outcome of their actions?*

CLOSE AND ASSESS

Ask small groups: *How do you identify goal and outcome?*

MAGIC **T**HREAD

article and Haitian folk tale retold by Diane Wolkstein

Prepare to Read

THINK ABOUT WHAT YOU KNOW

Make a Storytelling Web Storytellers use techniques like elaboration, sequence, and hyperbole. Write more storytelling techniques on a word web.

LEARN KEY VOCABULARY

Relate Words Study the new words. With a group, use vocabulary words to complete this sentence: *Talented storytellers can . . .* Make a new sentence for each vocabulary word.

Example:
Talented storytellers can show **inventiveness**.

expression Your **expression** is the way you make your face look. Smiling is an **expression** that shows happiness.

familiar Things you know well are **familiar**.

full attention You give your **full attention** when you watch and listen carefully.

gesture A **gesture** is a movement you make with your hands and arms.

inventiveness The ability to think up new things is called **inventiveness**.

present **Present** means at this time.

respond When you answer back, you **respond**.

talent When you have a **talent** for something, you do it well.

Answers to the vocabulary activity will vary.

LEARN TO RELATE GOALS AND OUTCOMES

In many stories, the character's **goal** is to have or do something. The **outcome** tells if the goal is reached. When you relate the goals and outcomes in a story, you will know the most important ideas.

> **READING STRATEGY**
>
> **How to Relate Goals and Outcomes**
> 1. Read the beginning of the story.
> 2. Think about what the character wants to do or have.
> 3. Ask yourself: What does the character need to do to reach the goal?
> 4. Read the rest of the story to find the outcome.

As you read "Owl," find goals and outcomes for the characters.

REACHING ALL STUDENTS

Multi-Level Strategies
VOCABULARY OPTIONS

BEGINNING Use pantomime to help students understand *decide, expression, full attention, gesture, respond.* Help students write sentences with key vocabulary.

INTERMEDIATE Have partners complete sentences together, using more than one vocabulary word in a sentence, if possible.

ADVANCED Have students write sentences independently. In groups, ask students to write a paragraph about storytellers.

Transparency 85 / Master 85

IDENTIFY GOAL AND OUTCOME

Directions: Read the fable. Look for the characters' goals. Ask yourself: *What does each character want to do?* Write the characters' goals and actions on the chart. Does each character reach his or her goal? Fill in the last two columns.

The Fox and the Crow

Crow found a piece of cheese. She flew into a tree to eat it. A hungry fox saw her and sat down under the tree. "Hello, Crow," he called out. "Your shiny feathers are so beautiful."

Crow was pleased, but said nothing. She did not want the cheese to fall out of her mouth.

Then Fox said, "I have heard that your voice is also beautiful. I would love to hear you sing!"

Crow was even more pleased. She opened her mouth to sing. The cheese fell to the ground, where Fox swiftly gobbled it up.

"Next time," said Fox as he ran off, "don't believe all the good things you hear about yourself."

Character	Goal	Actions	Outcome	Goal Reached
Crow	Wants to eat the cheese.	Opens mouth to sing for Fox.	Drops the cheese.	No.
Fox	Wants to eat the cheese.	Calls Crow beautiful; asks to hear her voice.	Eats the cheese.	Yes.

Transparency 85 Level A, Unit 5 | Traditions   © Hampton-Brown

UNWINDING the MAGIC THREAD

STORYTELLING IN HAITI
by Diane Wolkstein

- Diane Wolkstein Talks About Haitian Storytelling
- Diane Wolkstein Tells the Tale of *Owl*

INTRODUCE THE SELECTION

4 Preview and Predict Read the title, author, and the headings for the two parts of the selection on page 309. Discuss the pictures on this page and point out that there are two features included in this selection. Ask: *Do you think the first feature will be fiction or nonfiction? Where do you think the story of "Owl" is from?*

Next, have students page through the selection, look at the pictures of Owl in the story, and think about Owl's goal and the outcome.

5 Audio Walk-Through Play the Audio Walk-Through for "Unwinding the Magic Thread" on the **Selection Tape/CD** to give students the overall idea of the selection. (You might pause after the nonfiction walk-through, and read the article before playing the walk-through for "Owl."

Tape 5B
CD 5
Track 7

Unwinding the Magic Thread
by Diane Wolkstein

Theme Connection Through this selection, we learn about storytelling traditions in Haiti.

Selection Summary and Awards Both parts of this selection familiarize students with the techniques used by storytellers in Haiti. The story of "Owl" is a favorite Haitian tale that is shared with family, friends, and neighbors. Each storyteller adds something new and different to the story each time it is told. "Unwinding the Magic Thread" won an ALA Notable Book award in 1979, and its author, Diane Wolkstein, has won a Parent's Choice Award.

THE BASICS BOOKSHELF

■ *Sunny and Moonshine: A Love Story*
by Shirleyann Costigan

Moonshine is in love with Sunny, but she has never met him face to face. This modern pourquoi tale explains how the Sun and Moon at last come face to face during a full eclipse of the Sun. Simple text introduces the names of the planets and other celestial bodies. Illustrations about the solar system and a solar eclipse give beginning English learners access to the facts behind the fiction.

For Lesson Plans: See the Teacher's Guide for *The Basics Bookshelf*.

SET PURPOSE

1 Say: *Listen for the ways the storyteller
and the audience work together to
enjoy a good story in Haiti.*

LISTEN AND READ

Tape 5B
CD 5
Track 8

**2 Learn About Haitian
Folktales** Play the recording of
pages 310–311 or read them aloud,
pausing frequently to check
comprehension. Ask: *How do
Haitian storytellers "unwind the
magic thread"?*

DIANE WOLKSTEIN TELLS ABOUT
THE MAGIC THREAD

Red annotations offer opportunities to clarify
meaning and check for understanding.

"*Cric?*" the Haitian storyteller calls
out. "*Crac!*" the audience answers if they
want the storyteller to begin. If they do
not **respond** with *crac*, the storyteller
cannot begin.

Ask: What does it mean when
people say *crac* in Haiti?

"*Cric?*" another storyteller calls out,
hoping for the **welcoming** "*crac!*" If the
listeners cry *crac!*, they **are expected
to** give their **full attention** to the
storyteller. They will listen to hear that
the story is told correctly. They will
comment on the events and characters
of the stories. They will comment on the
storyteller's **talents**. As soon as a song
within a story begins, the listeners will
join in. I have heard groups **joyously** sing
the **chorus** of a song ten or twenty times.

Storytelling in Haiti takes place in the
plains, mountains, and countryside.
When the adults are not too tired, and
especially when the moon is full, families
gather on their steps to talk and **gossip**.
Soon someone may think of a story. *Cric?*

In moments, others may join the
family: friends, neighbors, teenagers,
children, and toddlers. Many are ready
to tell a story, so the storytellers must

Use visuals: Pause to show students
Haiti on a world map.

---

welcoming encouraging, friendly
are expected to must, are supposed to
comment on talk about
joyously happily

chorus repeating part
gossip tell about what's happening in
the lives of other people

REACHING ALL STUDENTS

CULTURAL PERSPECTIVES

Home and U.S. Cultures: Traditions
Provide examples of phrases that start
and end stories in the English-speaking
tradition, for example, *Once upon a time*
or *happily ever after*. Discuss the
purpose of such elements (a formula for
beginning or ending a story, a signal
that tells listeners what to expect, etc.).
Then, ask students to think about
storytelling traditions they know.
Collect phrases that start and end
stories in the students' cultures.

HOME CONNECTION

Make Up a New Story Ending Send
home a copy of *High Point Newsletter 10*
in the **Teacher's Resource Book**. (See
pages 160–166.) In this home activity,
students retell a story from the theme—
either "Pecos Bill" or "Owl"—and invite
family members to help them create a
new ending. Students share their new
story endings with the class.

compete for a chance. A storyteller
will call out *cric?* But perhaps someone
else has already called out *cric?* Then
the audience must decide who will be
the next one to **unwind the magic
thread of the story**.

Most of the stories are well-known.
Each story has its own **familiar** set
of **gestures** and **expressions**.
What is most exciting to see is the
inventiveness of the storyteller.
Everyone may know the tale, but they
are **eager** to see what the storyteller
will give to it this time.

It is my hope that you, my reader,
will turn the page and **bite into the
strange fruit of the Haitian night;**
that your **present** world will **dissolve;**
that you will **be possessed by** the
mysterious world of the story.

Let's begin the story of

Owl

Cric?

Crac! Encourage students to participate by repeating "Crac!"

Restate: Everybody knows most of the stories.

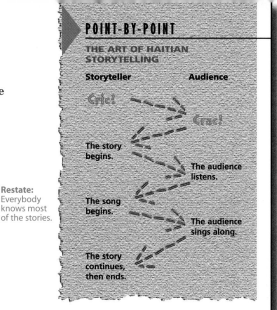

POINT-BY-POINT

THE ART OF HAITIAN STORYTELLING

Storyteller   Audience

Cric!

Crac!

The story begins.

The audience listens.

The song begins.

The audience sings along.

The story continues, then ends.

BEFORE YOU MOVE ON...

1. **Steps in a Process** In your own words, describe the steps for telling a story in Haiti.
2. **Comparisons** How is Haitian storytelling different from reading a book aloud?
3. **Evidence and Conclusion** In Haiti, the audience is as important as the storyteller. What are some ways that the audience becomes a part of the storytelling?

---

compete for try to win
unwind the magic thread of the story tell a story
eager wanting very much

bite into the strange fruit of the Haitian night
enjoy an unusual story told at night in Haiti
dissolve melt away, disappear
be possessed by become a part of

Unwinding the Magic Thread **311**

CHECK COMPREHENSION

3 **Use Text Features: Sidebar** Go over the call-and-response storytelling process represented in the Point-by-Point feature. Explain that this process is very similar to storytelling in Africa. Tell students that many Haitians have ancestors in Africa, and that this form of storytelling is part of a long tradition.

4 **Answers to "Before You Move On"**

1. **Steps in a Process** Answers should include the elements in the Point-by-Point sidebar.

2. **Comparisons** In Haitian storytelling, the story changes in each telling and the audience is invited to participate.

3. **Evidence and Conclusion** The audience encourages the storyteller and can also join in singing songs and making comments during the story.

CLOSE AND ASSESS

Ask students to describe the art of Haitian storytelling in a round-robin style. Invite each student to contribute an example or step in the storytelling event.

Grammar Minilesson

▶ **COMPLEX SENTENCES**

TEACH Draw attention to this sentence on page 310: *If they do not respond with* crac, *the storyteller cannot begin.* Identify this as a complex sentence. Ask students to identify the independent clause and the dependent clause. Point out the word *If,* and explain that it shows how the two ideas are related. Provide examples of complex sentences with other subordinating conjunctions, such as *since, until,* or *because.*

PRACTICE Have students add a clause to finish each sentence. They can use a conjunction from the list.

since	after	when
because	until	before
if	as long as	

1. The storyteller begins _____.
2. Listeners sing the chorus of a song _____.
3. _____, the storytellers must compete for a chance.

▶ **Practice Book** page 164

Unwinding the Magic Thread **T311**

OBJECTIVES

Function: Read a Selection
Grammar: ❶ Present Perfect Tense Verbs
Listening: Listen to a Selection
Reading and Learning Strategies:
Set a Purpose for Reading;
❶ Relate Goal and Outcome;
Make Predictions
Comprehension: Identify Character's
Motive; Make an Inference

SET PURPOSE

1 Say: *Look for details that tell what Owl wants to do.*

READ AND THINK

Tape 5B
CD 5
Track 8

2 **Strategy Focus: Relate Goals and Outcomes** Involve students in reading pages 312–313. Tell them to begin looking for details about the goals and actions of the characters.

> ▌Choose Reading Options in the **Multi-Level Strategies** to tailor the reading to proficiency levels.

The recording of "Unwinding the Magic Thread" on the **Selection Tape/CD** offers an oral language model and the opportunity to build reading fluency.

1

OWL FALLS IN LOVE

Owl and a young woman fall in love. Owl is afraid to visit during the day. He believes the woman will think he's ugly if she sees his face in the daylight.

Owl thought he was **very ugly**. One evening he met a girl and talked with her and she liked him. "If it had been day," Owl thought, "and she had seen my face, she never would have liked me." Still, she had liked him.

Ask: Why did Owl think the girl wouldn't like him if it was day?

very ugly not very good-looking
arrive at come to
politely nicely, in a respectful or courteous way
your fiancé the man you are engaged to marry
change put on clean clothing

312 Unit 5 | Traditions

So Owl went to her house the next night. And the next. And the night after that. Every evening he would **arrive at** the girl's house at seven, and they would sit outside on the porch steps, talking together **politely**. **Clarify:** Evening is the time of day after the sun has set.

Then one evening after Owl had left, the girl's mother said to her, "Why doesn't **your fiancé** come and visit you during the day?"

"But Mama, he's explained that to me. He works during the day. Then he must go home and **change** and he cannot get here before seven." **Ask:** What reason did Owl give for not coming to see the girl during the day?

"Still, I would like to see his face before the marriage," the mother said. "Let's invite him to our house for a dance this Sunday afternoon. Surely he doesn't work on Sunday."

REACHING ALL STUDENTS

Transparency 86 / Master 86

GOAL-AND-OUTCOME CHART

Directions: Write the goal of each character in "Owl." Write the character's actions and the outcome of those actions. Was the goal reached?

Unwinding the Magic Thread

Character	Goal	Actions	Outcome	Goal Reached
Owl				
Rooster				
Girl				
Mother				

Transparency 86 Level A, Unit 5 | Traditions   © Hampton-Brown

▌ ## Multi-Level Strategies

READING OPTIONS FOR LESSONS 12–15

BEGINNING Read the selection with students, using the red annotations on the facsimile pages to help clarify meaning as needed. Pause for students to identify each new character. Prompt them to state goals and actions for you to record on **Transparency 86**. At the end of the story, elicit the outcome of each character's actions, and whether the goal was met. Vocalize as you record information on the transparency.

INTERMEDIATE Have partners read the selection or listen to its recording on the **Selection Tape/CD**. As they read the story of Owl, have partners record information on **Master 86**.

ADVANCED Students can read the selection independently. Remind them to record information on **Master 86**. Ask partners to prepare a summary of the story that includes goals and outcomes.

Owl was very pleased with the invitation: a dance **in his honor**. He was also very **frightened**. He told his cousin, Rooster, about the girl and asked him to **accompany** him to the dance. That Sunday afternoon, as Owl and Rooster were riding on their horses to the dance, Owl **glanced** over at Rooster. Rooster **held himself with such assurance**, he was so elegantly and fashionably dressed, that Owl imagined the girl seeing the two of them and **was filled with shame**.

"I can't go on," he choked. "You go and tell them I've had an accident and will be there later."

Rooster rode to the dance. "Tsk tsk, poor Owl," he explained. "He has had an accident, and he has asked me to let you know that he will be here later."

Restate: Owl imagined that the girl would prefer Rooster after she saw how handsome Rooster was in his fancy clothes.

Clarify: Owl made up an excuse, or a reason, that he couldn't go to the dance until later. **Ask:** Why do you think he wanted to go later?

in his honor especially for him
frightened afraid, scared
accompany go with
glanced looked quickly
held himself with such assurance felt so comfortable about himself
was filled with shame became embarrassed, felt badly about himself

BEFORE YOU MOVE ON...

1. **Character's Motive** Why didn't Owl want to visit the girl during the day?
2. **Prediction** What do you think the girl will do if she sees what Owl looks like? Why?
3. **Inference** How did Owl feel about going to the dance? Why?

Unwinding the Magic Thread **313**

Science Connection
ZOOLOGY

Invite students to research the habitats and habits of roosters and owls. Encourage them to find out the birds' scientific names and determine how they are classified. Ask: *What characteristics do they share? How are they different?* Suggest that students present their information in a Venn diagram to highlight similarities and differences.

Grammar Minilesson

▶ **PRESENT PERFECT TENSE VERBS**

TEACH Direct attention to what Rooster told the girl's family on page 313: *"He has had an accident, and he has asked me to let you know that he will be here later."*

Point out that Rooster is telling about something that happened at an indefinite time before the present. Say: *When you speak of a time before the present that is not definite, use the helping verb* has *or* have *with the past participle of the main verb.*

PRACTICE Write these sentences. Have students choose the correct helping verb to complete each sentence.

1. Owl (has, have) fallen in love.
2. The girl's parents (has, have) become curious about Owl.
3. They (has, have) invited Owl to a dance.
4. Rooster (has, have) told the people that Owl had an accident.

▶ **Practice Book** page 165

Unwinding the Magic Thread **T313**

SET PURPOSE

1 Read aloud the introduction to pages 314–315. Say: *Look for details about Owl's goal at the dance.*

READ AND THINK

Tape 5B
CD 5
Track 8

2 Strategy Focus: Relate Goals and Outcomes Involve students in reading pages 314–315. Have them continue looking for details about the characters' goals and actions.

See the **Multi-Level Strategies** on page T312 to tailor the reading to proficiency levels.

OWL GOES TO THE PARTY

Owl arrives at the party, hiding his head under a hat. Owl's fiancée is pleased to see how well he dances, but Owl is worried that people will see his face.

When it was quite dark, Owl tied his horse **a good distance** from the dance and **stumbled** up to the porch steps. "Pssst," he whispered to a young man sitting on the steps. "Is Rooster here?"

"Well now, I don't know."

"Go and look. Tell him a friend is waiting for him by **the mapou tree**."

Rooster came out. "OWL!"

"Shhhhhh—"

"Owl!"

"Shhh—"

"Owl, what are you wearing over your head—I mean your face?"

"It's a hat. Haven't you ever seen a hat before? Look, tell them anything. Tell them I **scratched** my eyes on a branch as I was riding here and the light—even the light from a lamp—hurts them. And you must be certain to watch for the day for me, and to **crow** as soon as you see the light, so we can leave."

"Yes, yes," Rooster said. "Come in and I shall **introduce you to** the girl's relatives." **Define *relatives*:** Relatives are family members.

Ask: Is Owl telling the truth about his eyes?

---

a good distance far away
stumbled walked while tripping or dragging his feet
the mapou tree a type of tree that grows in Haiti

scratched hurt, cut
crow make the sound of a rooster
introduce you to take you to meet

314 Unit 5 | Traditions

REACHING ALL STUDENTS

Vocabulary
SYNONYMS

Explain to students that Owl thinks he is ugly. Ask: *What are some other, kinder, terms he could use to describe himself?* (unattractive, plain, homely) Invite students to use a thesaurus to find variations for other words commonly used to describe how people look. They can chart these in their individual or class dictionaries as follows:

Synonyms

ugly	unattractive	plain	homely
fat	chubby	heavy	plump
funny	hilarious	silly	goofy
nice	generous	kind	caring

Rooster introduced Owl to everyone, explaining Owl's **predicament**. Owl went around shaking hands, his hat hung down almost completely covering his face. Owl then tried to **retreat into** a corner, but the girl came over.

"Come into the yard and let's dance," she said.

Dong ga da, Dong ga da, Dong ga da, Dong. Dong ga da, Dong. Eh-ee-oh.

Owl danced. And Owl could dance well. The girl was proud of Owl. Even if he wore his hat strangely and had **sensitive** eyes, he could dance.

Dong ga da, Dong ga da, Dong ga da, Dong. Dong ga da, Dong. Eh-ee-oh.

Rooster was dancing, too. When Owl noticed that Rooster was dancing, instead of watching for the day, Owl was afraid that Rooster would forget to warn him, and he **excused himself** to the girl. He ran out of the yard, past the houses to a **clearing** where he could see the **horizon**. No, it was still night. Owl came back.

Dong ga da, Dong ga da, Dong ga da, Dong. Dong ga da, Dong. Eh-ee-oh.

Restate: Owl tried to get Rooster's attention, but Rooster was busy dancing and didn't see him.

Owl motioned to Rooster, but Rooster was lost in the dance. Owl excused himself again to the girl, ran to the clearing; no, it was still night. Owl returned.

Dong ga da, Dong ga da, Dong ga da, Dong. Dong ga da, Dong. Eh-ee-oh.

Owl tried to excuse himself again, but the girl held on to him. "Yes, stay with me," she said. And so they danced and danced and danced.

Dong ga da, Dong ga da, Dong ga da, Dong. Dong ga da, Dong. Eh-ee-oh.

Ask: What do you think will happen?

BEFORE YOU MOVE ON...

1. **Details** How did Owl try to hide his face?
2. **Cause and Effect** Why did Owl want Rooster to crow when the new day began?
3. **Character's Motive** Why did Owl keep leaving the party?

---

predicament problem
retreat into get away to, hide in
sensitive easily hurt

excused himself said he had to leave for a moment
clearing place with no trees, open place
horizon place where the sun comes up

CHECK COMPREHENSION

3 Answers to "Before You Move On"

1. **Details** Owl tried to hide his face by pulling his hat way down.

2. **Cause and Effect** Owl wanted to know when daylight was near so he could run away and no one would see his face.

3. **Character's Motive** Owl kept leaving the party to check whether or not it was daylight because he was afraid Rooster would forget to warn him.

CLOSE AND ASSESS

Ask students to predict what the outcome will be on a signed and dated slip of paper. Return the slips after students complete the story so they may confirm their predictions.

Grammar Minilesson

▶ **PAST PROGRESSIVE FORMS OF VERBS**

TEACH Call attention to this sentence on page 315: *Rooster was dancing, too.*

Point out that this action was going on while Owl watched. Say: *When you are talking about something that is still happening, use the –ing form of the main verb. To show that the action is happening in the past, use the helping verb was or were.*

PRACTICE Write these sentences. Have students add the *–ing* form of a verb to finish each sentence. You may wish to provide a word bank of verbs.

worry	hide	hope
have	enjoy	cover

1. The girl's relatives were _____ to meet Owl.
2. Owl was _____ his face with a hat.
3. The people were _____ a good time at the dance.
4. Owl was _____ about the daylight.

▶ **Practice Book** page 166

SET PURPOSE

1 Say: *Read to find out what the outcome of the characters' actions is.*

READ AND THINK

Tape 5B
CD 5
Track 8

2 **Strategy Focus: Relate Goals and Outcomes** Involve students in reading pages 316–317. Have them look for details about the outcome of the characters' actions.

▪ See the **Multi-Level Strategies** on page T312 to tailor the reading to proficiency levels.

OWL RUNS AWAY

When Owl's fiancée sees his face, he becomes embarrassed
and runs away forever.

The sun moved up in the sky, higher and higher, until it filled the house and the yard with light.

"Now—let us see your fiancé's face!" the mother said.

"Kokioko!" Rooster crowed.

And before Owl could hide, she reached out and pulled the hat from his face.

"MY EYES!" Owl cried, and covering his face with his hands, he ran for his horse.

"Wait, Owl!" the girl called.

"Kokioko!" Rooster crowed.

"Wait, Owl, wait." **Ask:** Why is Rooster crowing?

And as Owl put his hands down to **untie** his horse, the girl saw his face.

Ask: When did the girl see Owl's face?

....

untie take the knot out of the rope that held

REACHING ALL STUDENTS

│ Vocabulary
ONOMATOPOEIA

Define *onomatopoeia* as the use of words that imitate sounds. Illustrate the concept, using examples from "Owl": *tsk tsk* (page 313), *pssst, shhhhhh* (page 314), *Kokioko* (page 316). To help students understand the concept, have them say the words out loud. Have students make a chart in their individual or class dictionaries to record these examples and others they have heard.

A WORLD OF LANGUAGES

Borrowed Words Borrowed words are words from other languages that are used in their original form, or a slightly altered form, in English. See how many of these words students recognize and point out that the origins of these words are French, one of the official languages of Haiti.

WORD	MEANING
fiancé	a man to whom a woman is engaged to be married
fiancée	a woman to whom a man is engaged to be married
marriage	from *mariage*, "the ceremony of becoming husband and wife"
dance	from *danser*, "to move in time with music"

It was **striking** and **fierce**, and the girl thought it was the most **handsome** face she had ever seen.

"Owl—"

But Owl was already on his horse, riding away, farther and farther away.

Owl never came back.

The girl waited. Then she married Rooster. She was happy, except sometimes in the morning when Rooster would crow "kokioko-o-o." Then she would think about Owl and wonder where he was.

Ask: Is this a sad or a happy ending? Why?

....

striking unusual and good-looking
fierce strong and wild
handsome good-looking, attractive

BEFORE YOU MOVE ON...

1. **Vocabulary** The author uses the words *striking*, *fierce*, and *handsome* to describe Owl's face. What words would you use to describe Owl's personality?
2. **Opinion** Did the story have a happy ending for everyone? Explain.
3. **Theme** What do you think is the moral, or lesson, of this story?

ABOUT THE AUTHOR

Diane Wolkstein is a storyteller who has visited Haiti many times. She began writing down Haitian folk tales after she saw a talented storyteller sing and dance the story of "Owl." "I will write the stories, write about the storytellers, and write about the storytelling experience that creates community," she decided. She put 27 of her stories into a collection called *The Magic Orange Tree and Other Haitian Folktales*. Today, more than 20 years later, the stories are still being told around the world. "Now when I tell these stories," she says, "I am exploring, like the Haitians. Both the audience and I know the beginning and the ending, but we don't know until we come to the heart of the story what we will discover."

Unwinding the Magic Thread   **317**

CHECK COMPREHENSION

3 Answers to "Before You Move On"

1. **Vocabulary** Students may use words such as *shy, insecure, nervous,* or *anxious* to describe Owl's personality. Encourage them to support their answers.

2. **Opinion** Answers will vary, but remind students to support their opinions based upon the actions and events in the story.

3. **Theme** Answers will vary and may include: *You shouldn't assume that you know what others think of you.*

ABOUT THE AUTHOR

4 Evaluate Literature: Culture Read aloud or have students read About the Author. Explain that the author is not Haitian but has visited Haiti and understands its storytelling culture. Ask: *Do you think it's important to help understand and preserve parts of other cultures? Why?*

CLOSE AND ASSESS

Have students work with a partner to summarize the outcome of the story in one or two sentences. Return their prediction cards from Lesson 14 and have students compare them with the story outcome. Then ask students to write what they learned about goals and outcomes on an index card, sign the card, and turn it in before leaving class.

Language Development
ROLE-PLAY

Assign roles to students: Owl, Rooster, girl, mother. Have them brainstorm the characteristics of each, and make simple masks to wear. Encourage students to first present themselves to the class: *I am Owl. I feel worried about how ugly I am. But I love to dance.* Have players act out various scenes from the story, using appropriate gestures and facial expressions.

Grammar Minilesson

▶ **HELPING VERBS**

TEACH Ask students questions about the story that can be answered with *do* or *does*. For example: *Do Owl and Rooster make up a silly story?* (They do.)

Identify *do* and *does* as forms of the helping verb *do*. Present rules for using *do* and *does*:

- Use **do** with *I, you, we, they,* and plural nouns.
- Use **does** with *he, she, it,* and singular nouns.

PRACTICE Write the sentences. Have students make two columns labeled *Helping Verb* and *Main Verb*. Ask them to find the parts of the verb in each sentence and write them in the proper columns.

1. Owl does not visit the girl during the day.
2. Do the girl's parents like Owl?
3. Why does Owl hide his face?
4. Rooster and Owl do act strangely.

▶ **Practice Book** page 167

Respond to the Folk Tale
Check Your Understanding

CHECK YOUR UNDERSTANDING

1 Sum It Up As students discuss
actions that would have led to other
outcomes, share these ideas:

- The girl could have run after Owl
  and told him he was handsome.

- Owl could have gone back to tell
  the girl he loved her.

- Rooster could have sent a message
  to Owl to tell him the truth.

▶ **Practice Book** page 168

2 Think It Over Possible answers are:

1. **Opinion** The girl married Rooster
   because Owl never came back.

2. **Prediction** Answers will vary.

3. **Generalization** You should ask
   what people are thinking instead
   of guessing.

4. **Personal Experience** Answers
   will vary.

3 Express Yourself Remind students
that a good listener gives full
attention to the storyteller.

CLOSE AND ASSESS

Ask: *What did you learn from this tale?*
Have students write a note to Owl, advising
him to accept himself for who he is.

SUM IT UP

Make a Goal and Outcome Chart Show the
goals, actions, and outcomes for each character
in "Owl."

Goal and Outcome Chart for the Girl

Goal	Actions	Outcome	Goal Met?
She wanted to marry Owl.	She invited Owl to meet her family.	She married Rooster after Owl ran away.	No

Generate Ideas Work with a group. Think of
actions the characters should have taken to meet
their goals.

THINK IT OVER

Discuss Talk about these questions with
a partner.

1. **Opinion** Why did the girl marry Rooster?
   Do you think she made the right decision?

2. **Prediction** What do you think happened to
   Owl after he ran away?

3. **Generalization** Owl believed his fiancée
   thought he was ugly. Is it a good idea to
   guess what others think without asking?
   Explain.

4. **Personal Experience** Who are you more like,
   Owl or Rooster? Explain.

EXPRESS YOURSELF

▶ TELL AN ORIGINAL STORY;
  LISTEN ACTIVELY

Work with a group to make up your own folk
tale. Tell your story to another group as they
listen carefully. A member of the other group
will retell your story. Then listen to their folk
tale. Choose someone from your group to retell
their story.

✔ LANGUAGE ACQUISITION ASSESSMENT
  See page 82 of the Assessment Handbook.

REACHING ALL STUDENTS

Multi-Level Strategies
SUM IT UP OPTIONS

BEGINNING Use the completed chart on **Transparency 86** (see
page T312) to prompt students to use complete sentences to describe each
character's role in the story: *The girl wants to be with Owl, so she invites him to
a party. She marries Rooster after Owl runs away.* Then, prompt students to
suggest alternate actions and outcomes: *Could she have sent Owl a message
with his cousin Rooster? What might have happened?* Invite volunteers to share
alternative scenarios with the class.

INTERMEDIATE / ADVANCED Have partners work in small groups
to share ideas from the goal-and-outcome charts they have completed. Have
students brainstorm alternate actions and outcomes and formulate new
endings for the story. Encourage groups to use the *Cric? Crac!* technique to
present the new versions to the class.

Language Arts and Literature

GRAMMAR IN CONTEXT

USE PRESENT PERFECT TENSE

Learn About Tense A verb in the **present perfect tense** can tell about an action that began in the past and may still be going on.

Storytellers **have told** tales for many years. Some actions happened in the past, but you don't know when. Use a verb in the present perfect tense to tell about these actions, too.

My friend **has heard** "Owl" three times. To form the present perfect tense, use the helping verb **have** or **has** plus the **past participle** of the main verb.

- Use **have** with *I, you, we,* or *they.*
  I **have told** the tale often.

- Use **has** with *he, she,* or *it.*
  It **has become** famous.

Write in the Present Perfect Tense Write a sentence for each of these verbs. Then read your sentences aloud.

has said	have talked
has danced	have played

Practice Write the sentences. Add *has* or *have* to complete each sentence.

1. Haitians ___have___ told stories for centuries.
2. My father ___has___ told many stories.
3. I ___have___ always loved Papa's stories.
4. My aunt ___has___ started tape-recording them.

LITERARY ANALYSIS

WRITING

WRITE A CHARACTER STUDY

Study the characters in "Owl," then write about how each character's traits affect the story.

Make a Character Chart Copy and complete this chart. Show what each character is like. Tell how the character's traits affect the story.

	Girl	Owl	Rooster
Character Traits	generous kind loving	shy nervous insecure	confident well-dressed stylish
Example from the Story	She loved Owl before she saw his face.	He does not want anyone to see his face.	He is comfortable going to the party alone.
Outcome of the Story	She still cared about Owl after he left.	He runs away and thinks no one can love him.	He marries the girl.

Write Your Ideas Use your chart to write about what each character is like. Then tell how the characters' traits affect the story.

Example:
The girl in the story is generous, kind, and loving.

She loved Owl even before she saw his face. She still cared about Owl after he ran away.

Unwinding the Magic Thread **319**

OBJECTIVES

PRESENT PERFECT TENSE

Grammar: Helping Verbs;
T Present Perfect Tense Verbs

WRITE A CHARACTER STUDY

Function: Write

Learning Strategy:
Use Graphic Organizers (chart)

Literary Analysis: Evaluate Impact of Characterization on Meaning

Writing: Character Study

LANGUAGE ARTS AND LITERATURE

1 **Use Present Perfect Tense** See annotations for answers to Practice items.

▶ **Practice Book** page 169

2 **Write a Character Study** Annotations in the character chart show possible answers. Have students share their character studies and compare any differences.

CLOSE AND ASSESS

Have students revisit the mind map begun on page T263 and add ideas to it based on what they have learned about storytelling in Haiti.

Multi-Level Strategies
WRITING OPTIONS FOR CHARACTER STUDIES

BEGINNING Work with students to brainstorm words to describe each character. Look through the story to find information for the chart. Use sentence frames to write about the characters:

The girl was _____ and she showed it by _____.

At the end of the story, she _____.

INTERMEDIATE Have students work in groups to complete the chart. Assign each group one character to write the character study about. Have groups share their paragraphs.

ADVANCED Encourage students to work independently to write a character study paragraph for each character.

RESPOND

OBJECTIVES

WRITE A FRIENDLY LETTER

Function: Write

Concepts and Vocabulary: Letters—
heading, greeting, body, closing, signature

Critical Thinking: Generate Ideas

Writing: Friendly Letter

MAKE A TRAVEL GUIDE

Function: Give Information

Concepts and Vocabulary: Travel—
location, climate, cultural traditions, sightseeing

Learning Strategies and Critical Thinking: Gather and Organize Information; Connect New Information to Known

Representing and Writing: Travel Guide

LANGUAGE ARTS AND CONTENT AREA CONNECTIONS

1 **Write a Friendly Letter** Have students focus on the labeled elements in the model and discuss what goes in each section, including some options and what they connote. (*My Dearest Owl, Beloved Owl; Sincerely, Rooster*)

2 **Make a Travel Guide** Show sample travel guides. Prepare students by previewing content area vocabulary.

• *location:* Explain that a travel guide gives information about a particular *location,* or place.

• *climate:* Define *climate* as weather patterns.

• *cultural traditions, customs, heritage:* Explain that these words all refer to ways in which people in a certain place or of a certain background act—either typically or on special occasions.

• *sightseeing tips:* Tell students that *sightseeing tips* are suggestions for what to see and how best to enjoy a visit.

▶ **Practice Book** pages 170–171

CLOSE AND ASSESS

Have students list the elements of a friendly letter and/or the elements of a travel guide.

Respond to the Folk Tale, continued

Language Arts and Content Area Connections

▶ WRITING

WRITE A FRIENDLY LETTER

Imagine you are a character in "Owl." Write a letter to tell how you feel. Here are some ideas:

• Owl explains why he left.

• The girl tries to get Owl to come back.

• Rooster explains why he married the girl.

Use this model to write your friendly letter.

Heading—	June 3, 2004
Greeting—	Dear Owl,
Body—	
Closing—	Your friend,
Signature—	Rooster

▶ SOCIAL STUDIES
▶ TECHNOLOGY/MEDIA

MAKE A TRAVEL GUIDE

Travel guides give information about places you can visit. Make a travel guide about a country you want to visit.

1 **Gather Information** Use the Internet, an encyclopedia, or library books to research facts about the country. Take notes.

2 **Organize Your Information** Make a chart.

Haiti

location	
climate	
foods	
places to see	
things to do	

3 **Make a Travel Guide** Write your information in a way that encourages people to visit your country. You can use a word-processing program on a computer to make a travel guide look professional.

4 **Take a World Tour** Display your travel guide. Then look at your classmates' travel guides. Find new places you want to visit.

 Learn how use a **word-processing program**. See Handbook pages 354–361.

REACHING ALL STUDENTS

Multi-Level Strategies

OPTIONS FOR WRITING A FRIENDLY LETTER

BEGINNING / INTERMEDIATE Demonstrate how to write a friendly letter. Create a large format model of the outline on the student page. Explain the purposes of each part of the letter. As a group, fill in each section of the letter using one of the ideas given. Then work on generating a chart with more ideas. Record them for partners with varying proficiency to use in letters they write together.

ADVANCED Encourage students to work individually to write letters that follow the frame. Then, have partners trade letters and write a response to their partner's letter.

When I Taste Salt

never-ending poem
by Carmen Agra Deedy

Prepare to Read Poetry

THINK ABOUT WHAT YOU KNOW

Share Memories Have you ever felt sad and happy at the same time? Talk about a time that you felt this way.

dance 1. *noun* A **dance** is a party where people move to music. **2.** *verb* When you **dance**, you move to a rhythm.

salt 1. *noun* **Salt** is a natural product that adds flavor to food. **2.** *verb* You can **salt** food to add flavor.

skirt 1. *noun* A **skirt** is a piece of women's clothing that hangs from the waist. **2.** *verb* When you **skirt** something, you go along its edge.

taste 1. *noun* A **taste** of something is a small amount of it. **2.** *verb* You **taste** something when you put it in your mouth.

water 1. *noun* Living things need **water**. **2.** *verb* You **water** plants to help them grow.

wave 1. *noun* In the ocean, water comes to the shore in a **wave**. **2.** *verb* You **wave** when you move your hand back and forth.

Answers to the vocabulary activity:

nouns   verbs
water   skirts
waves   dance
salt   taste

LEARN KEY VOCABULARY

Use Context Clues to Meaning Study the new words. They are **multiple-meaning words**, or words that can mean more than one thing. Read the paragraph. Find the correct meaning of each underlined word.

> When I sit on the wall that <u>skirts</u> the ocean, memories <u>dance</u> in my mind. I swam in the <u>water</u> when I was young. I moved back and forth with the <u>waves</u>. My memories are so strong that I can <u>taste</u> the <u>salt</u> of the sea.

LEARN TO INTERPRET FIGURATIVE LANGUAGE

Some writers use **figurative language** when they put words together in creative ways to make comparisons. Understanding figurative language can help you get a clear picture of people, places, and events in a selection.

> **READING STRATEGY**
> **How to Interpret Figurative Language**
> 1. As you read, make a picture in your mind of the people, places, and events.
> 2. Think about comparisons that the poet makes. How are the two people or two things alike?
> 3. Ask yourself: What does the poet really mean? Then explain the meaning in your own words.

As you read "When I Taste Salt," look for examples of figurative language. Try to figure out what the poet means.

Multi-Level Strategies
VOCABULARY BUILDING OPTIONS

BEGINNING Use each vocabulary word in two sentences, as a noun and a verb. Help students identify the part of speech. Work through the paragraph as a group.

INTERMEDIATE Use vocabulary words in sentences as nouns and verbs. Have partners identify the part of speech and then work through the paragraph together.

ADVANCED Students complete the activity on their own, then write additional sentences, identifying vocabulary words as nouns or verbs.

Transparency 87 / Master 87

INTERPRET FIGURATIVE LANGUAGE

Directions: Read the poem. In the first column, write the poet's words. In the second column, write what the poem means in your own words.

from When I Taste Salt
by Carmen Agra Deedy

I watch my sister dance with the sea.
She is a hero
and a goddess
and a mermaid
With laughing coffee-colored eyes.

What the Poem Says	What the Poem Means
dance with the sea	swim, play in the waves, run in and out of the water
She is a hero	She is strong
and a goddess	She is powerful
and a mermaid	She swims well
With laughing coffee-colored eyes	She has bright, brown eyes

Transparency 87 Level A, Unit 5 | Traditions   © Hampton-Brown

---

OBJECTIVES

THINK ABOUT WHAT YOU KNOW
Reading Strategy:
Relate to Personal Experience

LEARN KEY VOCABULARY
Vocabulary Strategy:
Use Context Clues to Meaning

LEARN TO INTERPRET FIGURATIVE LANGUAGE
Literary Analysis:
❶ Figurative Language

THINK ABOUT WHAT YOU KNOW

1 Share Memories Model how to share memories using sentence frames: *I felt sad because... I also felt happy because...*

LEARN KEY VOCABULARY

2 Use Context Clues to Meaning Read each vocabulary word and the defining sentences aloud. Point out that each word has two meanings: one is a thing (noun) and one is an action (verb). After students understand the meanings of the key vocabulary words, conduct the context clue activity.

> Use the Vocabulary Options in **Multi-Level Strategies** to tailor the activity to proficiency levels.

▶ **Practice Book** page 172

LEARN TO INTERPRET FIGURATIVE LANGUAGE

3 Model How to Interpret Figurative Language Define *figurative language* and give examples (*in a flash* for *quickly*). Use the poetry stanza on **Transparency 87** to model the strategy by reading aloud and asking students to visualize. Then record the literal and figurative meanings.

CLOSE AND ASSESS

Ask students to restate a line of the stanza on **Transparency 87**, using a different word or phrase to create a different image.

OBJECTIVES

Function: Read a Poem
Concepts and Vocabulary: Memories
Vocabulary Strategy:
Interpret Figurative Language
Listening: Listen to a Poem
Literary Analysis: ❶ Figurative
Language; Evaluate Impact of Author's
Background on Meaning

SET PURPOSE

1 Read aloud the title and give
students a moment to look at the
photo. Say: *As you listen, try to make
a picture in your mind of what the
poet is describing.*

LISTEN AND READ

Tape 5B

CD 5
Track 9

**2 Strategy Focus: Interpret
Figurative Language** Play
"When I Taste Salt" on the **Selection
Tape/CD** or read the poem aloud for
all students to hear. Then play or
read the poem again, pausing after
each stanza to discuss and record
paraphrases of figurative language.

▮ Choose Reading Options in the
Multi-Level Strategies to tailor
the reading to all proficiency levels.

When I Taste Salt

When I taste salt,
I think of Cuban waters.
I hear my sister shriek
As she tries to outrun the waves
That break over *el Malecón*,
The sea-wall
That skirts Havana harbor.

I watch my sister dance with the sea.
She is a hero
　　　　and a goddess
　　　　　　and a mermaid
With laughing coffee-colored eyes.
She turns wet arms to me.
I shake my dry head
At the invitation.
I am too timid.
I am the little sister.

Our mother returns with melting
Snow cones and fire on her lips.
She scolds and sighs as she wrings the salt
From my sister's hair.

In silence, then, we three
Walk home at dusk.
But our mother is in a mood
For remembering,
And, as the breeze makes my sister shiver,
Mother tells how she, too,
Once raced the waves.

This memory always makes me cry,
And when I cry, I taste salt . . .

　　　　　　　—Carmen Agra Deedy

shriek scream, yell
outrun the waves run faster than the waves
el Malecón the Jetty (in Spanish); the name of the
wall along the oceanfront in Havana, Cuba
mermaid part fish, part girl; an imaginary creature
timid shy, scared
wrings squeezes out

322　Unit 5 | Traditions

REACHING ALL STUDENTS

▮ **Multi-Level Strategies**
READING OPTIONS FOR LESSON 20

BEGINNING Read the poem aloud one stanza at a time. Use elements
in the photo to point out *el Malecón/the sea-wall, sister, waves,* and *outrun.*
Then, use questions to help students identify figurative language: *Does the
mother really have fire on her lips?* Brainstorm attributes of fire to help
students realize that the mother is angry. Continue recording figurative
language and paraphrases on **Transparency 87**. (See page T321.)

INTERMEDIATE In groups, have one student read aloud a stanza while
the others listen. The group identifies figurative language to record on
Master 87 (see page T321), and agrees on a way to paraphrase meaning.

ADVANCED After students finish recording examples of figurative
language on **Master 87** (see page T321), they can compare their work with a
partner, and work together to write what expressions mean.

3 **Evaluate Literature: Author's Background** Explain that since the Cuban Revolution in 1959, many Cubans have come to the United States because they prefer life in a democratic country. Tell students that once Cubans leave Cuba, it is not easy to go back to visit. Invite students to talk about how it might feel to leave a place that you cannot return to, especially if you have happy memories of that place. Ask them to speculate about why this memory makes the author cry.

CLOSE AND ASSESS

Ask: *What is figurative language? Why do writers use figurative language?*

ABOUT THE POET

Carmen Agra Deedy was born in Havana, Cuba. She and her family immigrated to the United States after the Cuban Revolution. They settled in Decatur, Georgia. Her combined Latin American and Southern heritage has had a rich influence on her work. Carmen is a professional storyteller. She has delighted audiences across the nation with her tales. She is also the author of several award-winning books for children.

When I Taste Salt **323**

Vocabulary
OCEAN WORDS

Have students make a mind map that identifies words related to the ocean with subtopics as shown.

Water

Animals — Ocean Words — Objects to Collect

Things to Do

Sounds

Plant Life

RESPOND

OBJECTIVES

SUM IT UP

Function: Write

Learning Strategy and Critical Thinking: Paraphrase; Use Graphic Organizers (chart); ❶ Draw Conclusions

Writing: Sentences

THINK IT OVER

Function: Engage in Discussion

Critical Thinking: Make Inferences; Form Opinions; Relate to Personal Experience

Literary Analysis: Style

EXPRESS YOURSELF

Function: Clarify

Speaking and Listening: Questions and Answers

CHECK YOUR UNDERSTANDING

1 Sum It Up Invite students to read aloud their paraphrases, eliciting several examples for each instance of figurative language.

▶ **Practice Book** page 173

2 Think It Over Possible answers are:

1. Inference The memory makes her cry and taste her salty tears.

2. Author's Style Part of the first line is repeated at the end of the poem, so the poem can start all over again, in a sort of circle.

3. Opinion Answers will vary.

4. Personal Experience Answers will vary. Encourage students to elaborate.

3 Express Yourself Model how to clarify memories to make them clearer. Ask: *Why is this memory special to me? Who else shares this memory? What happened in this memory?*

CLOSE AND ASSESS

Ask students to explain the relationships of the three characters. (The narrator is the little sister; the big sister is the one playing in the water; the mother brings them snow cones.)

Respond to the Poem
Check Your Understanding

SUM IT UP

Paraphrase Make a chart to help you paraphrase "When I Taste Salt."

What the Poem Says	What the Poem Means
I watch my sister dance with the sea.	I see her run in and out of the waves.
She is a hero . . .	she is strong
. . . and a goddess . . .	she is powerful
. . . and a mermaid	she can swim well
Our mother returns with . . . fire on her lips.	our mom yells at us when she comes back

Draw Conclusions When you **draw a conclusion**, you combine what you have read with what you know and make an opinion about it. Draw conclusions about the poet or the poem.

Examples:

The poet thinks her sister is special.

The poet has good memories of her childhood.

THINK IT OVER

Discuss Talk about these questions with a partner.

1. **Inference** Why does the poet "taste salt" when she thinks of this memory?

2. **Author's Style** What does the poet do to make this a never-ending poem?

3. **Opinion** Do you think that this is a happy or sad poem? Explain.

4. **Personal Experience** What older person do you admire? Why?

EXPRESS YOURSELF ▶ CLARIFY

Work with a group. Talk about memories you each have.

Example:

When I ___smell roses___ ,

I think of ___playing in my aunt's garden___ .

When you **clarify** something, you make it clearer. Help to clarify each other's memories. Take turns asking questions like these:

• Where did your memory take place?

• Is there a smell, taste, sound, or color that comes with this memory?

• What does this memory mean to you?

REACHING ALL STUDENTS

Multi-Level Strategies
SUM IT UP OPTIONS

BEGINNING / **INTERMEDIATE** Remind students that to draw conclusions they should use evidence from the text and their own experience. Ask: *If you described an experience this way, what would you be thinking? How would you feel? What do you know about the poet? How do you think the poet feels?* Have partners of different ability levels work together to write conclusion statements.

ADVANCED Students can write conclusions on their own. Then small groups can share their conclusions, supporting their ideas with examples from the poem and making connections with their experience. Challenge students to find other poems that express similar ideas.

Language Arts and Literature

LITERARY ANALYSIS

LEARN ABOUT ALLITERATION

Learn About Alliteration Look at these lines from "When I Taste Salt."

> The sea-wall
> That skirts Havana harbor.

Sea-wall and *skirts* have the same beginning sounds. So do *Havana* and *harbor*. The repetition of beginning sounds is called **alliteration**. Poets often choose to use words with alliteration because they sound good together.

Find Examples of Alliteration Find the words in the sentence that begin with the same sound.

> She scolds and sighs as she wrings the salt
> From my sister's hair.

Practice Use the words in parentheses to rewrite this poem using alliteration.

In the hot summer days	(sunny)
My brother and I used to	(big)
Walk by a river	(Run)
Where we caught fish and	(found)
Gathered pebbles.	(Picked up)
Then we sat on rocks and	(rested)
Listened to the water.	(Watched)

VOCABULARY
WRITING

USE SENSORY WORDS

Learn About Sensory Words Writers use **sensory words** to tell how things look, sound, smell, taste, and feel. Use sensory words to write about a memory.

❶ **Find Sensory Words** Copy the chart below. Then add words from the poem.

See	Hear	Smell	Taste	Touch

❷ **Think About a Memory** Think of a special place or event from your childhood. What sensory words can you use to describe the memory? Add them to the chart.

❸ **Write About Your Memory** Write a story or a poem about your memory. Try to help your reader see, hear, smell, taste, and feel the place or event.

Learn how to improve your writing in the **writer's craft**. See Handbook pages 390–401.

When I Taste Salt **325**

Multi-Level Strategies
WRITING OPTIONS FOR FIGURATIVE LANGUAGE

BEGINNING Have students draw a picture of an experience they've had, perhaps one they have enjoyed with their families. Encourage them to visualize the event, thinking carefully about the sounds, sights, smells, tastes, and feel of the event. Have students share their drawings. Use them to develop language related to the five senses. Have them dictate words or phrases, which you can write for them in the form of a poem. Then read the poem aloud.

INTERMEDIATE / **ADVANCED** Ask students to think about an event from their past. Encourage students to visualize as much detail as they can, focusing on all of their senses. Have them complete the chart to plan their writing. Then have them tell about the event through a poem or a descriptive paragraph. Encourage students to use figurative language.

RESPOND

OBJECTIVES

ALLITERATION

Concepts and Vocabulary: Literary Devices—*alliteration; word choice*

Literary Analysis: Alliteration

Writing: Rewrite a Poem

SENSORY WORDS

Function: Write; Express Feelings

Concepts and Vocabulary: Senses

Reading and Learning Strategy: Use Graphic Organizers (chart)

Literary Analysis:
❶ Figurative Language

Writing: Story or Poem

LANGUAGE ARTS AND LITERATURE

1 Learn About Alliteration To provide support, you may want to give more examples of alliteration:

- We're wishing for a wonderful, wet world this winter.

- Sand, sun, surf, and sails are some sights of summer.

Invite students to make up some of their own alliterative sentences.

▶ **Practice Book** page 174

2 Use Sensory Words Sensory words from the poem include: see—*sister, waves, sea-wall, mother;* hear—*shriek, waves, scolds;* smell—*sea, waves, salt;* taste—*snow cones, salt;* touch—*sea-wall, wet arms, hair;* etc.

CLOSE AND ASSESS

Ask partners to think of alliteration that describes something you could experience at the beach with one of your senses. *(loud laughing, wild waves, soft sand, salty seaweed)*

When I Taste Salt **T325**

OBJECTIVES

Function: Engage in Discussion
Critical Thinking: Identify
Story Elements
Writing: ❶ Narrative (story)

INTRODUCE WRITING THAT TELLS A STORY

1 Discuss Narrative Writing Read the introduction. Ask: *What are some stories you know? Who are the characters in them? Where do the stories take place?*

2 Study the Models Ask: *Who are the characters in the stories? Which words tell where each story takes place?*

Give each student three small self-adhesive notes to label *beginning, middle,* and *end.* Have students work with partners to label the parts of "Owl" on pages 312–317. Then invite students to share where they put the notes and why.

▌ Use the Options for Studying Writing in the **Multi-Level Strategies** to adjust instruction.

CLOSE AND ASSESS

Ask students to agree on a summary sentence that defines narrative writing.

T326 Unit 5 | Traditions

Writing That Tells a Story

Narrative writing tells a story. The plot tells what the story is about. The characters are the people or animals in the story. The setting is where and when the story takes place.

WRITING MODELS

Read these sentences from "Pecos Bill." How does the writer describe the main character? What kind of setting do you see?

from "Pecos Bill"

> I'm Pecos Bill. I'm part man and part coyote. I've slid down lightning bolts holding wildcats under both arms and never been scratched. I was raised in Texas along the Pecos River, but my life began in New England. I was born while my Ma was taming a tornado. Pa had caught the tornado tearing up our farm.

The plot of a story has a beginning, a middle, and an end. Read these paragraphs from the beginning of "Owl." They introduce the characters and tell about a problem. What events happened in the middle of the story? How did they lead up to the end?

from "Owl"

> Owl thought he was very ugly. One evening he met a girl and talked with her and she liked him. "If it had been day," Owl thought, "and she had seen my face, she never would have liked me." Still, she had liked him.
>
> So Owl went to her house. Every evening he would arrive at the girl's house at seven, and they would sit outside on the porch steps, talking together politely.
>
> Then one evening after Owl had left, the girl's mother said to her, "Why doesn't your fiancé come and visit you during the day?"

REACHING ALL STUDENTS

Multi-Level Strategies
OPTIONS FOR STUDYING NARRATIVE WRITING

BEGINNING Make a three-column chart labeled *characters, setting,* and *plot.* Help students identify these elements in the models, and write key words or draw simple illustrations on the chart.

INTERMEDIATE Focus on the excerpt from *Owl.* Ask: *What is Owl's problem? What events happen in this part of the story? Could any of these events be left out? How might the story end if this event is left out?*

ADVANCED Lead students in a discussion of the writing models. Ask: *How do you find out about the problems of each of the main characters? Which setting is described in more detail? Which part of the plot is presented in the excerpt from "Pecos Bill"? Which parts are presented in the excerpt from "Owl"?*

Write Together

WRITING PROMPT

Write a class story for a younger class, for another class, or for your families and friends to read.

1 Plan the Story Your story will need two or more characters. It also will need a setting and a plot. Here is a map to help you plan your story. Study the example.

Characters: Who is the story about?

Setting: Where and when does the story take place?

Plot:

Beginning
What happens first?

Middle
1.
2. What events take place
3. in the middle?
4.

End
What happens last?

Characters: Ant, Grasshopper, Shrimp

Setting: a field, "once upon a time"

Plot:

Beginning
Ant sees Grasshopper eating all the crops.

Middle
1. Ant and Grasshopper fight.
2. Grasshopper bites Ant's waist.
3. Ant pulls out Grasshopper's hair.
4. Shrimp bends over and laughs.

End
The animals all change. Ant has a slim waist, Grasshopper is bald, and Shrimp has a bent back.

2 Write the Story Use the story map to write a class story. Or, make a map for a new story and write it.

Transparency 88 / Master 88

STORY MAP

Characters: _____
Setting: _____
Plot:

Beginning

Middle
1.	3.
2.	4.

End

Transparency 89 / Master 89

FEATURES OF NARRATIVE WRITING

Directions: Compare the "Owl" to the features of a story. Check the box if the story has the feature. Write the details.

A Story. . . _____"Owl"_____

has people or animals as **characters**	☑ Owl, girl, Rooster, girl's mother
tells the **setting**—where and when the story takes place	☑ at night, on a porch, in a yard, at a dance
has a **plot** with	
• **beginning**	☑ **beginning**: Owl thinks he is ugly. He meets a girl one evening, but is afraid she won't like him when she sees his face in the light.
• **middle**	☑ **middle**: Owl and Rooster go to a dance at the girl's house. Owl wears a hat that covers his face. Owl runs away when the girl sees his face, and never returns.
• **end**	☑ **end**: The girl marries Rooster.

OBJECTIVES

Function: Write

Learning Strategies and Critical Thinking: Plan; Generate Ideas; Interact with Peers; Analyze and Evaluate Information

Writing: Class Story

WRITE TOGETHER

Discuss the Writing Prompt Read the prompt aloud and ask volunteers to tell

• what you will write together (a story)

• who will read the story you write (a younger class, another class, or family and friends).

Plan the Story Go over the sample story map, and then ask students to suggest possible characters, settings, and plots for a story. Record their responses on a three-column chart. (You may want to use **Transparency 90** on page T328.) Have students vote on the ideas to use in the class story. Then fill out the Story Map on **Transparency 88**. Guide students in developing the plot.

Analyze and Evaluate a Story Display **Transparency 89**. Guide students in analyzing and evaluating the story "Owl" on pages 312–317 against the features.

Write the Class Story Help students turn the details on the Story Map into a story. Guide students in including details about the characters, setting, and story events to make their writing interesting and entertaining.

CLOSE AND ASSESS

Distribute copies of **Master 89** and have students work with partners or in small groups to analyze and evaluate your class story against the features.

PREWRITE

Function: Write

Learning Strategies and Critical Thinking: Plan; Generate Ideas; Interact with Peers; Organize Ideas; Self-Assess

Representing: Chart

Writing: ❶ Writing Process

WRITE ON YOUR OWN

Read the prompt. Have volunteers tell what kind of writing they will do, who the audience will be, and what the story should do.

For more about the Writing Process, refer students to pages 382–389 in the Handbook.

PREWRITE

Explain to students that to plan their story, they will first make a chart of characters, settings, and plot ideas. Then they will complete an FATP chart and continue their planning on a story map.

> Use the Prewriting Support in the **Multi-Level Strategies** to tailor this stage to proficiency levels.

CLOSE AND ASSESS

Have partners answer the questions in Think About Your Writing.

Writing That Tells a Story, continued

Write on Your Own

WRITING PROMPT

Now write your own story for classmates to read. Tell an adventure story. Make it exciting!

PREWRITE

❶ **Choose a Story Idea** What adventure would you like to write about? Record your ideas in a chart.

Characters	Setting	Plot Idea
space aliens	Earth, 2010	They come here to try to make friends.
two hikers	mountain, today	They get caught in a terrible storm.

Choose one of your story ideas. Fill in an **FATP** chart.

❷ **Get Organized** Make a story map to show your characters, setting, and plot.

Story Map

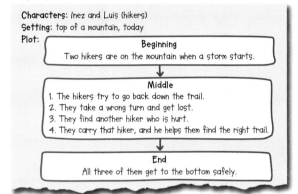

Characters: Inez and Luis (hikers)
Setting: top of a mountain, today
Plot:

Beginning
Two hikers are on the mountain when a storm starts.

Middle
1. The hikers try to go back down the trail.
2. They take a wrong turn and get lost.
3. They find another hiker who is hurt.
4. They carry that hiker, and he helps them find the right trail.

End
All three of them get to the bottom safely.

FATP Chart

HOW TO UNLOCK A PROMPT

Form: _story_

Audience: _classmates_

Topic: _surviving a thunderstorm on a mountaintop_

Purpose: _to tell an exciting story about hikers caught in the storm_

Think About Your Writing

• Are you happy with your story idea?

• Do you have enough details to show what the characters and setting are like?

• Will the events make an interesting plot?

REACHING ALL STUDENTS

Transparency 90 / Master 90

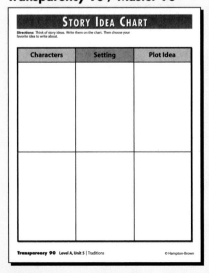

STORY IDEA CHART

Directions: Think of story ideas. Write them on the chart. Then choose your favorite idea to write about.

Characters	Setting	Plot Idea

Transparency 90 Level A, Unit 5 | Traditions   © Hampton-Brown

Multi-Level Strategies
PREWRITING SUPPORT

BEGINNING With **Transparency 90**, help students get started thinking of different parts of a story. For each part, talk through an example, using an idea of your own or one from the chart on page 328. Then distribute copies of **Master 90** and have students fill in their charts with words, phrases, and/or simple illustrations. Next, have students choose the story ideas they will write about, and guide them in filling out FATP charts. Finally, have them expand their plot ideas on copies of **Master 88**. (See page T327.)

INTERMEDIATE / **ADVANCED** Have individuals brainstorm items for each story part on **Master 90**, and discuss their ideas in a small group. Encourage them to explore their plot ideas to see if they'll work well for a story. Then have students choose one story idea, fill out an FATP chart, and continue their planning on the story map on **Master 88**. (See page T327.)

DRAFT

1 **Write Your Story** Use your story map to write your story.

2 **Use Dialogue and Descriptive Details** Study these examples.

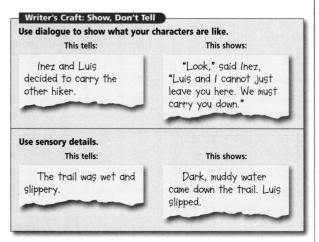

Writer's Craft: Show, Don't Tell

Use dialogue to show what your characters are like.

This tells:

Inez and Luis decided to carry the other hiker.

This shows:

"Look," said Inez, "Luis and I cannot just leave you here. We must carry you down."

Use sensory details.

This tells:

The trail was wet and slippery.

This shows:

Dark, muddy water came down the trail. Luis slipped.

Study these examples of sensory details. What sensory details would go with your topic?

Sight	**Sound**	**Touch**
bare branches	branches snapping	wet clothes
darkening sky	cries of "help!"	frozen fingers
sharp rocks	rumbling thunder	a hot meal

Taste	**Smell**
salty tears	a burning fire
sweet cocoa	sweet pine trees
bitter greens	baking bread

Key In To Technology

Your word-processing software probably has a feature that allows you to check your spelling. Click on Spelling in your Tools window. A screen will then show each misspelled word and how to correct it.

Think About Your Writing

• Read your draft. Do you like what you wrote?

• Will the dialogue help your readers understand the characters?

• Did you include sensory details?

OBJECTIVES

DRAFT

Function: **1** Tell A Story; Write

Learning Strategies and Critical Thinking: Generate Ideas; Self-Assess

Technology: Use Word-Processing Software

Writer's Craft: **1** Show, Don't Tell

Writing: **1** Writing Process

DRAFT

Remind students to write their drafts quickly, without worrying about making mistakes. They can make changes and fix errors later.

Study the Writer's Craft to help students use dialogue and sensory details in their stories. Explain how one example tells and the other shows.

Go over the word lists together. Use pictures and real objects to illustrate and explain the sensory details.

■ Use the Drafting Support in the **Multi-Level Strategies** to tailor this stage to proficiency levels.

For more about the Writer's Craft, refer students to pages 390–401 in the Handbook.

CLOSE AND ASSESS

Have small groups discuss the questions in Think About Your Writing while you work with those who may need more support in assessing their drafts.

Multi-Level Strategies

DRAFTING SUPPORT

BEGINNING To help students use dialogue and descriptive details in their writing, have them dramatize scenes from their story. Take notes on the words and actions, such as: *You yelled, "Watch out! There's a monster behind you!" Then you cheered and clapped your hands to show you were happy.*

INTERMEDIATE / ADVANCED Distribute copies of **Master 91**. Students can work in small groups to create examples that show instead of tell. Point out that the sample story map on page 327 gives details they can use to write their examples. Review the five senses, and then have partners brainstorm sensory words for use in their specific stories. Point out the word file on **Master 91**, where they can record the words. If students are using a word-processing program, show them how to access the thesaurus to find synonyms for sensory words.

Transparency 91 / Master 91

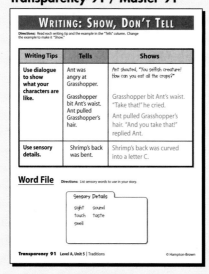

WRITING: SHOW, DON'T TELL

Directions: Read each writing tip and the example in the "Tells" column. Change the example to make it "Show."

Writing Tips	Tells	Shows
Use dialogue to show what your characters are like.	Ant was angry at Grasshopper.	Ant shouted, "You selfish creature! How can you eat all the crops?"
	Grasshopper bit Ant's waist. Ant pulled Grasshopper's hair.	Grasshopper bit Ant's waist. "Take that!" he cried. Ant pulled Grasshopper's hair. "And you take that!" replied Ant.
Use sensory details.	Shrimp's back was bent.	Shrimp's back was curved into a letter C.

Word File Directions: List sensory words to use in your story.

Sensory Details

sight sound
touch taste
smell

Transparency 91 Level A, Unit 5 | Traditions © Hampton-Brown

Build Writing Skills T329

REVISE

Function: Write; Engage in Discussion

Learning Strategies and Critical Thinking: Generate Ideas; Review; Clarify; Interact with Peers; Self-Assess

Listening and Speaking: Peer-Conferencing

Technology and Media: Use Word-Processing Software

Writing: ❶ Writing Process

REVISE

Explain that to revise their stories, students will decide on changes to make their stories clearer and more interesting. Have them reread their stories and think about possible changes.

Next, conduct peer conferences and have students revise their writing. If students are writing on a computer, demonstrate the revising steps illustrated on page 330.

▌ Use the Peer Conference Support in the **Multi-Level Strategies** to model how to evaluate and revise writing.

CLOSE AND ASSESS

Have peers discuss the questions in Think About Your Writing.

Writing That Tells a Story, continued

REVISE

❶ **Read Your Story** Does it have a beginning, a middle, and an end?

❷ **Share Your Story** Have your teacher or a friend read your story. Ask:
- Does the dialogue help you understand the characters?
- Do I have a variety of long and short sentences?
- Do my sentences begin in different ways?

❸ **Make Your Changes** If you are using a computer, make the changes like this:

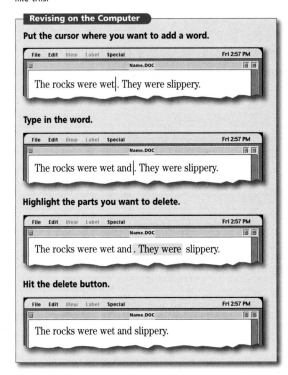

Revising on the Computer

Put the cursor where you want to add a word.

> The rocks were wet|. They were slippery.

Type in the word.

> The rocks were wet and|. They were slippery.

Highlight the parts you want to delete.

> The rocks were wet and. They were slippery.

Hit the delete button.

> The rocks were wet and slippery.

Think About Your Writing

- Does your dialogue sound like real conversation?
- Does your plot have a beginning, a middle, and an end?
- Did you vary your sentences?

Transparency 92 / Master 92

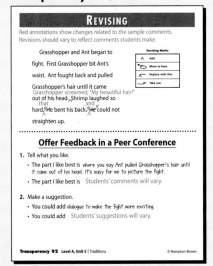

REVISING

Red annotations show changes related to the sample comments. Revisions should vary to reflect comments students make.

Grasshopper and Ant began to fight. First Grasshopper bit Ant's waist. Ant fought back and pulled Grasshopper's hair until it came out of his head. Shrimp laughed so hard. He bent his back. He could not straighten up.

Grasshopper screamed, "My beautiful hair!"

and that

Revising Marks
- ∧ Add.
- Move to here.
- Replace with this.
- Take out.

Offer Feedback in a Peer Conference

1. Tell what you like.
   - The part I like best is *where you say Ant pulled Grasshopper's hair until it came out of his head. It's easy for me to picture the fight.*
   - The part I like best is *Students' comments will vary.*

2. Make a suggestion.
   - You could add *dialogue to make the fight more exciting.*
   - You could add *Students' suggestions will vary.*

Transparency 92 Level A, Unit 5 | Traditions   © Hampton-Brown

Multi-Level Strategies

PEER CONFERENCE SUPPORT

BEGINNING Display **Transparency 92**. Read the paragraph and support comprehension as needed: draw the three characters before and after the fight or invite volunteers to role-play it (safely!) as you lead them through it. Then model how to participate in a peer conference, noting that students should first tell what they like and then make suggestions. Use the sentence starters, and have volunteers dictate additional comments. Then model how to revise the story, based on the comments.

INTERMEDIATE / ADVANCED Distribute copies of **Master 92**. Read the paragraph. Use the sample comments to model how to participate in a peer conference. Have students write more comments of each type and share suggestions with the class. Students can then make revisions to the paragraph, based on the comments, and compare their changes.

GRAMMAR IN CONTEXT

COMPLETE SENTENCES

A complete sentence has two main parts—the subject and the predicate. Together, they tell a complete thought.

- The **subject** tells whom or what the sentence is about. It usually comes at the beginning of the sentence.
- The **predicate** tells what the subject is, does, or has. The most important word in the predicate is the **verb**.

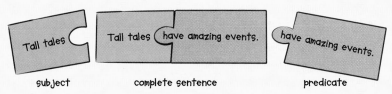

subject   complete sentence   predicate

Study these examples:

Subject	Predicate
We	**love** to read tall tales!
Characters in tall tales	**do** impossible things.
The story of Pecos Bill	**is** a tall tale.
Bill's mother	once **tamed** a tornado.
The family	**moved** west.

Practice Look at the words in the box. Use each as a subject to complete the sentences below.

1. _____ decided to race against each other.
2. _____ came to watch.
3. _____ hopped ahead very quickly.
4. _____ took a nap because he was so far ahead.
5. _____ crawled past the sleeping rabbit and won the race!

Word Box

Turtle
Rabbit
Turtle and Rabbit
All the other animals
He

GRAMMAR IN CONTEXT

1 Teach Complete Sentences Read the introduction and explain the meaning of a "complete thought": *A complete thought tells who is doing the action and what the action is.* Have volunteers read the descriptions of *subject* and *predicate*.

Use the illustration of the interlocking puzzle pieces to show how the subject and predicate go together. Then conduct the cooperative learning activity below.

2 Answers to Practice Items

1. Turtle and Rabbit
2. All the other animals
3. Rabbit
4. He
5. Turtle

CLOSE AND ASSESS

Have partners read a short paragraph from a familiar story. One partner writes the subject and the other writes the predicate for each sentence, each on a separate strip of paper. Then partners reassemble the sentences and read them aloud together.

Cooperative Learning

FOR LANGUAGE DEVELOPMENT:
Complete Sentences

Materials: subjects and predicates written on index cards

Create Complete Sentences Write subjects and predicates on index cards, one subject or predicate per card. Give a card to the first person in the group. That person reads aloud the card and identifies it as a subject or predicate. The other three group members take turns contributing a subject or predicate to form a complete sentence. Play continues until all index cards have been used.

Debrief the Skill Ask: *How did you know if the card contained a subject or a predicate? Why does a sentence need both a subject and a predicate?*

Debrief the Cooperative Process Have students reflect on how the activity worked out: *Was everyone in your group able to think of subjects or predicates? How did you help each other if one of you had difficulty?*

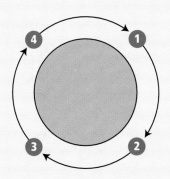

Cooperative Learning Structure:
Roundtable

OBJECTIVES

EDIT AND PROOFREAD

Learning Strategies and Critical Thinking: Review; Clarify; Self-Assess

Writing: ❶ Writing Process

PUBLISH

Learning Strategies and Critical Thinking: Interact with Peers; Self-Assess; Make Decisions

Speaking: Read Aloud

Technology and Media: Use E-Mail; Use Web Pages

Writing: ❶ Writing Process

EDIT AND PROOFREAD

Remind students that to edit their stories, they will mark errors. Use **Transparency 93** to model the process.

PUBLISH

Have students choose from the publishing suggestions on page 332. They can also bind the class stories together to make a book.

■ Use the Editing and Publishing Support in the **Multi-Level Strategies** to adjust instruction.

CLOSE AND ASSESS

Have groups discuss the questions in Think About Your Writing.

Writing That Tells a Story, continued

EDIT AND PROOFREAD

❶ **Proofread Your Story** When you find a mistake in capitalization, punctuation, or spelling, correct it. See pages 431–439 in the Handbook for help. Use the Proofreading Marks.

❷ **Check Your Sentences** Did you use complete sentences? Did you begin your sentences in different ways?

❸ **Make a Final Copy** If you are working on the computer, print out the corrected work. If not, rewrite it. Make the corrections you marked.

PUBLISH

Here are some ways to share your writing.

• Write your story and print it from your computer. Add a picture. Combine all the class stories into a book.

Mountain Adventure
by Anne Narkpraset

"We're almost there, Luis!" Inez shouted happily. "I can see the top of the mountain."

The two friends were excited. They had hiked all morning and now they were almost at the top of the trail.

Suddenly, there was a loud crash. "That was lightning," Luis said.

"It's raining!" Inez cried. Large raindrops fell in every direction. "We have to go back!"

• Read your story aloud to a friend. When you are done, ask your friend to describe the main characters and the setting.

• If your family or school has a Home Page on the Web, include a copy of your story to share with others. Invite readers to e-mail their comments.

Proofreading Marks

∧	Add.
⩘	Add a comma.
⊙	Add a period.
≡	Capitalize.
/	Make lowercase.
⤴	Take out.
¶	Indent.

Think About Your Writing

• Are you pleased with your story?
☑ Does it have a beginning, a middle, and an end?
☑ Does it include dialogue that shows what the characters are like?
• What do you like best about your story?
• Will this story go in your portfolio? Why or why not?

REACHING ALL STUDENTS

Transparency 93 / Master 93

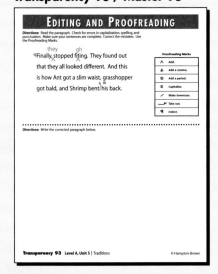

Multi-Level Strategies
EDITING AND PUBLISHING SUPPORT

BEGINNING Model finding and correcting errors in the paragraph on **Transparency 93**. After marking the edits, have students write out the corrected paragraph. For publishing, students can work in small groups to develop a puppet show based on one of their stories.

INTERMEDIATE Guide students in finding and correcting the errors in the paragraph on **Transparency 93**. For publishing, encourage students to practice their speaking skills by tape recording the stories and using different voices for the characters.

ADVANCED Distribute copies of **Master 93** and have students work on finding and correcting the errors individually or with partners. If you make a book of class stories, students might develop a television commercial to advertise the book.

STORIES TO TELL

✔ **ASSESSMENT**
The Unit 5 Test on page 93 of the Assessment Handbook measures students' progress in reading, language arts, literary study, and writing. Additional forms in the Assessment Handbook allow for:
• Self Assessment on page 92
• Peer Assessment on page 101
• Portfolio Evaluation on page 103

1 Look Back at the Unit

Rate Stories In this unit, you read about many stories and storytellers.

Echo and Narcissus

How the Ox Star Fell From Heaven

The Art of the Tall Tale

Unwinding the Magic Thread

Work with a partner. Talk about the four selections. Organize them on one side of a pyramid. Put the selection you liked best at the top. Put others in order below. On the opposite side of the pyramid, tell what you liked best about each story.

2 Show What You Know

Sum It All Up Add new ideas to your mind map about traditions. Tell a partner something you learned about storytelling.

People who tell stories — How people tell stories — **Storytelling** — What people tell stories about — Why people tell stories

Reflect and Evaluate Finish this sentence:
• Good storytellers can _____.
Add the sentence to your portfolio. Choose work from the unit that shows what you learned.

3 Make Connections

To Your School and Community Plan a storytelling day for your class or school. Invite storytellers from your community. Then visit other classes. Share the stories you've heard with younger students.

Unit Debrief **333**

OBJECTIVES

Function: Engage in Discussion; Express Opinions

Learning Strategies and Critical Thinking: Interact with Peers; Generate Ideas; Summarize; Self-Assess; Form Opinions; Justify; Use Graphic Organizers (mind map)

Literary Analysis: Respond to Literature; Compare and Evaluate Literature

EXPLORE "STORIES TO TELL"

1 **Look Back at the Unit** Discuss criteria students might use to rate the stories, such as: *Can I apply the story's message to my own life?* Then begin the Cooperative Learning Activity.

2 **Show What You Know** Urge students to include work that helped them understand the importance of the storytelling tradition.

3 **Make Connections** Ask a librarian to give a workshop on "How to Be an Effective Storyteller." Provide preparation time for students who share stories with younger classes.

CLOSE AND ASSESS

Have students tell you the most important thing they learned in the unit.

Cooperative Learning

FOR CRITICAL THINKING: Evaluate and Justify

Rate Stories After deciding on criteria for rating stories, give partners time to make their rating pyramids. Then have them form teams of 3–5 according to their highest rated selection. Provide each team with a large piece of paper.

Justify Ratings Students make a web with the title in the center. Each student uses a different color marker to add ideas that support the rating. The team then presents their web to the class.

Debrief the Content Ask students what they learned about storytelling traditions from the unit, for example: *I learned how stories from long ago helped explain things that people did not understand.*

Debrief the Cooperative Process Ask students to share insights they gained by working with a partner and a team. Ask: *Did your partner's or other group members' ideas help you understand your own?*

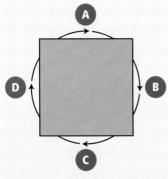

Cooperative Learning Structure: Team Word Webbing

High Point Handbook

This Handbook is especially designed for English learners. Students can use the Handbook independently as a resource for learning as they participate in the language arts and content area activities that follow each literature selection. You may also want to use appropriate sections to teach or reinforce skills and strategies developed in the program.

HIGH POINT
Handbook

Handbook: Language and Learning

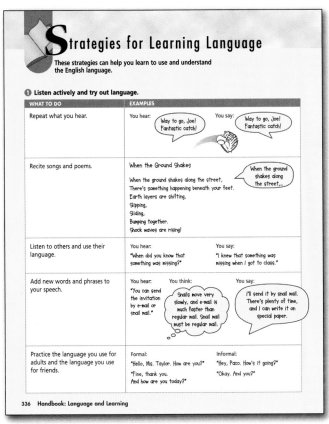

Strategies for Learning Language

These strategies can help you learn to use and understand the English language.

1 Listen actively and try out language.

WHAT TO DO	EXAMPLES
Repeat what you hear.	You hear: Way to go, Joe! Fantastic catch! You say: Way to go, Joe! Fantastic catch!
Recite songs and poems.	**When the Ground Shakes** When the ground shakes along the street, There's something happening beneath your feet. Earth layers are shifting, Slipping, Sliding, Bumping together. Shock waves are rising! *When the ground shakes along the street...*
Listen to others and use their language.	You hear: "When did you know that something was missing?" You say: "I knew that something was missing when I got to class."
Add new words and phrases to your speech.	You hear: "You can send the invitation by e-mail or snail mail." You think: Snails move very slowly, and e-mail is much faster than regular mail. Snail mail must be regular mail. You say: I'll send it by snail mail. There's plenty of time, and I can write it on special paper.
Practice the language you use for adults and the language you use for friends.	Formal: "Hello, Ms. Taylor. How are you?" "Fine, thank you. And how are you today?" Informal: "Hey, Paco. How's it going?" "Okay. And you?"

336 Handbook: Language and Learning

page 336

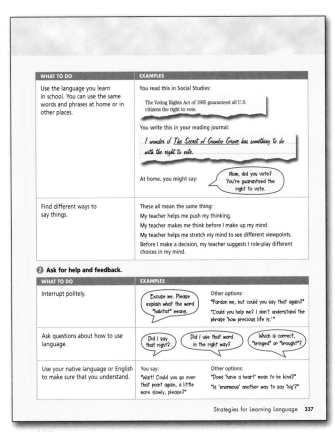

WHAT TO DO	EXAMPLES
Use the language you learn in school. You can use the same words and phrases at home or in other places.	You read this in Social Studies: The Voting Rights Act of 1965 guaranteed all U.S. citizens the right to vote. You write this in your reading journal: I wonder if The Secret of Gumbo Grove has something to do with the right to vote. At home, you might say: Mom, did you vote? You're guaranteed the right to vote.
Find different ways to say things.	These all mean the same thing: My teacher helps me push my thinking. My teacher makes me think before I make up my mind. My teacher helps me stretch my mind to see different viewpoints. Before I make a decision, my teacher suggests I role-play different choices in my mind.

2 Ask for help and feedback.

WHAT TO DO	EXAMPLES
Interrupt politely.	Excuse me. Please explain what the word "habitat" means. Other options: "Pardon me, but could you say that again?" "Could you help me? I don't understand the phrase 'how precious life is.'"
Ask questions about how to use language.	Did I say that right? Did I use that word in the right way? Which is correct, "bringed" or "brought"?
Use your native language or English to make sure that you understand.	You say: "Wait! Could you go over that point again, a little more slowly, please?" Other options: "Does 'have a heart' mean to be kind?" "Is 'enormous' another way to say 'big'?"

Strategies for Learning Language 337

page 337

Strategies for Learning Language, continued

3 Use nonverbal clues.

WHAT TO DO	EXAMPLES
Use gestures and movements to help others understand your idea.	I will hold up five fingers to show that I need five more minutes.
Look for clues from people's movements and expressions. They can help you understand the meaning.	Maria wants me to go to the Subhumans' concert, but I think their music is awful—and insulting. I'm not sure what she said about the Subhumans' music, but I can tell she doesn't like it. Just look at her!
Watch people as they speak. The way they move can help you understand the meaning of their words.	Let's give him a hand. Everyone is clapping. "Give him a hand" must mean to clap for him.

4 Verify how language works.

WHAT TO DO	EXAMPLES
Test your ideas about language.	You try out what you learned: I can add -ation to the verb observe to get the noun observation. So maybe I can make a noun by adding -ation to all verbs that end in -e. Let's see. Prepare and preparation. Yes, that works! Preserve and preservation. That works, too. Compare and comparation. That doesn't sound right. I will see what the dictionary says... Now I see — it's comparison.

338 Handbook: Language and Learning

page 338

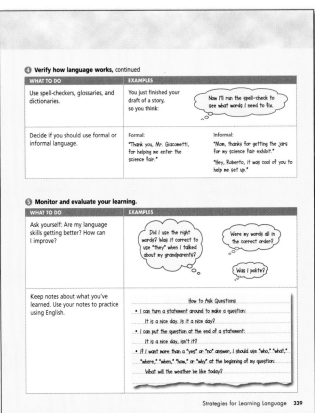

4 Verify how language works, continued

WHAT TO DO	EXAMPLES
Use spell-checkers, glossaries, and dictionaries.	You just finished your draft of a story, so you think: Now I'll run the spell-check to see what words I need to fix.
Decide if you should use formal or informal language.	Formal: "Thank you, Mr. Giacometti, for helping me enter the science fair." Informal: "Mom, thanks for getting the jars for my science fair exhibit." "Hey, Roberto, it was cool of you to help me set up."

5 Monitor and evaluate your learning.

WHAT TO DO	EXAMPLES
Ask yourself: Are my language skills getting better? How can I improve?	Did I use the right words? Was it correct to use "they" when I talked about my grandparents? Were my words all in the correct order? Was I polite?
Keep notes about what you've learned. Use your notes to practice using English.	**How to Ask Questions** • I can turn a statement around to make a question: It is a nice day. Is it a nice day? • I can put the question at the end of a statement: It is a nice day, isn't it? • If I want more than a "yes" or "no" answer, I should use "who," "what," "where," "when," "how," or "why" at the beginning of my question: What will the weather be like today?

Strategies for Learning Language 339

page 339

Handbook: Language and Learning

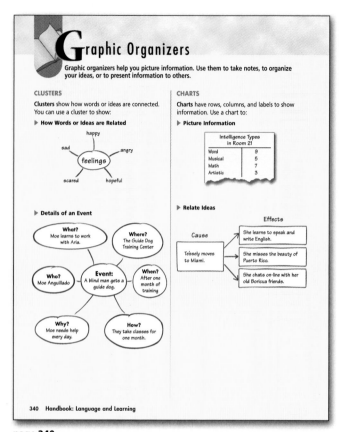

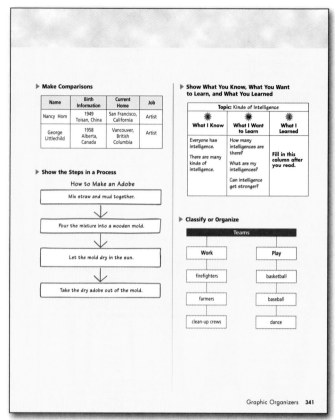

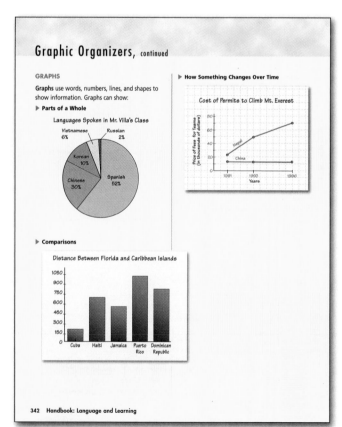

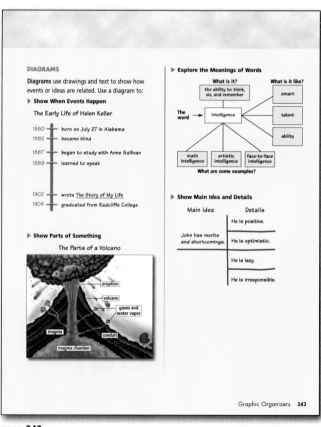

Handbook: Language and Learning

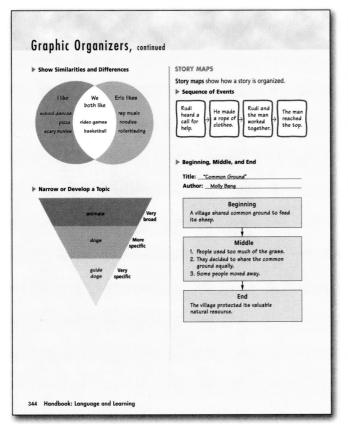

page 344

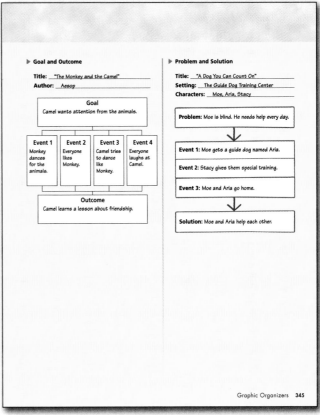

page 345

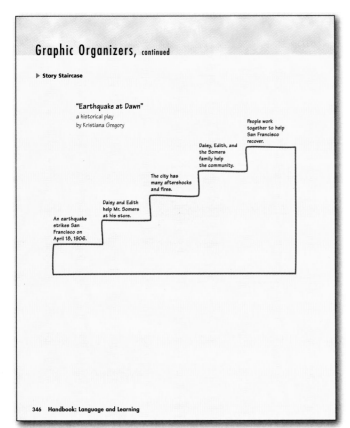

page 346

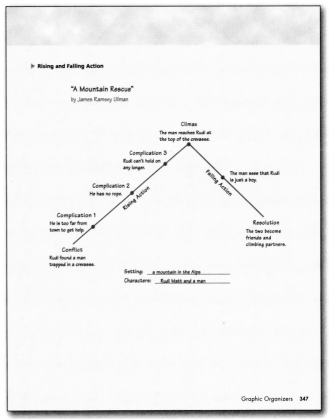

page 347

Handbook: Language and Learning

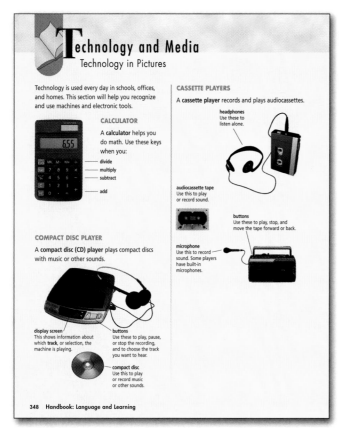

Technology and Media
Technology in Pictures

Technology is used every day in schools, offices, and homes. This section will help you recognize and use machines and electronic tools.

CALCULATOR

A **calculator** helps you do math. Use these keys when you:

- divide
- multiply
- subtract
- add

COMPACT DISC PLAYER

A **compact disc (CD) player** plays compact discs with music or other sounds.

display screen
This shows information about which track, or selection, the machine is playing.

buttons
Use these to play, pause, or stop the recording, and to choose the track you want to hear.

compact disc
Use this to play or record music or other sounds.

CASSETTE PLAYERS

A **cassette player** records and plays audiocassettes.

headphones
Use these to listen alone.

audiocassette tape
Use this to play or record sound.

buttons
Use these to play, stop, and move the tape forward or back.

microphone
Use this to record sound. Some players have built-in microphones.

page 348

CAMCORDER

A **camcorder** is a hand-held video camera. It records pictures and sounds on videotape. You can watch the videotape on a television.

microphone
This records sound.

view finder
Use this to see the picture as you record.

lens
Aim this at the action you want to record.

videotape
Use this or smaller tapes to record or play pictures and sounds.

VIDEOCASSETTE RECORDER

A **videocassette recorder (VCR)** records and plays videotapes through a television. You can record television programs or watch videos that you make, buy, rent, or check out from the library.

television
Use this to watch programs.

remote control
Use this to control the television and other machines from far away.

VCR and videotape
Use these to record and watch programs.

DIGITAL VIDEODISC PLAYER

A **digital videodisc (DVD) player** plays discs that have very clear pictures and sounds. You can watch movies by connecting a DVD player to a television or a computer.

digital videodisc
This holds recordings of programs.

page 349

Technology and Media, continued
Technology in Pictures, continued

FAX MACHINE

A **fax machine** uses phone lines to send or receive a copy of pages with pictures or words.

input tray
Load the paper you want to send here.

keypad
Enter the telephone numbers here. Then press START.

output tray
Receive messages and your original copy here.

WIRELESS TELEPHONE

A **wireless telephone** lets you talk to people wherever you are.

power key
Use this to turn the phone on and off.

talk key
Press TALK or SEND to dial the phone number you set.

number keys
Enter the phone number with these keys.

end key
Press this when your call is finished.

page 350

THE COMPUTER

A **computer** is an electronic tool that helps you create, save, and use information.

Compact Disc Read-Only Memory (CD-ROM) Drive
Use this to read or play CD-ROMs with text, sound, video, photographs, and computer software.

monitor and screen
These show the text and pictures that are in the computer.

digital camera
Use this to take photographs you can use on the computer. You can view, print, or work on your pictures.

scanner
Use this to take a picture of words or pictures that are already on a page. You can view, print, or work on whatever you scan on your computer.

keyboard
This has letter, number, symbol, and function keys. Type here to add information and give commands to the computer.

mouse
Use this to choose and move things on your screen.

printer
Use this to make a paper copy of the information on your computer.

page 351

Handbook: Language and Learning

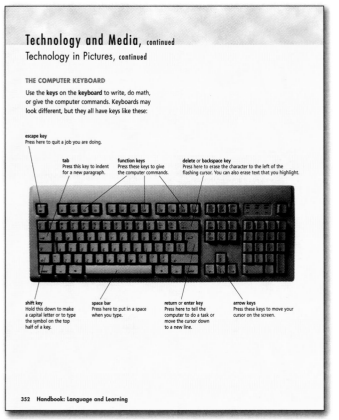

page 352

Technology and Media, continued
Technology in Pictures, continued

THE COMPUTER KEYBOARD

Use the **keys** on the **keyboard** to write, do math, or give the computer commands. Keyboards may look different, but they all have keys like these:

escape key
Press here to quit a job you are doing.

tab
Press this key to indent for a new paragraph.

function keys
Press these keys to give the computer commands.

delete or backspace key
Press here to erase the character to the left of the flashing cursor. You can also erase text that you highlight.

shift key
Hold this down to make a capital letter or to type the symbol on the top half of a key.

space bar
Press here to put in a space when you type.

return or enter key
Press here to tell the computer to do a task or move the cursor down to a new line.

arrow keys
Press these keys to move your cursor on the screen.

352   Handbook: Language and Learning

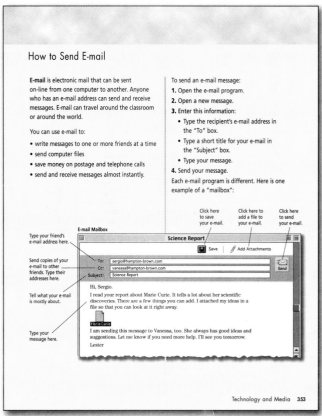

page 353

How to Send E-mail

E-mail is electronic mail that can be sent on-line from one computer to another. Anyone who has an e-mail address can send and receive messages. E-mail can travel around the classroom or around the world.

You can use e-mail to:
- write messages to one or more friends at a time
- send computer files
- save money on postage and telephone calls
- send and receive messages almost instantly.

To send an e-mail message:
1. Open the e-mail program.
2. Open a new message.
3. Enter this information:
   - Type the recipient's e-mail address in the "To" box.
   - Type a short title for your e-mail in the "Subject" box.
   - Type your message.
4. Send your message.

Each e-mail program is different. Here is one example of a "mailbox":

Click here to save your e-mail.

Click here to add a file to your e-mail.

Click here to send your e-mail.

E-mail Mailbox

Type your friend's e-mail address here.

Send copies of your e-mail to other friends. Type their addresses here.

Tell what your e-mail is mostly about.

Type your message here.

Science Report

Save   Add Attachments

To: sergio@hampton-brown.com
Cc: vanessa@hampton-brown.com
Subject: Science Report

Send

Hi, Sergio.
I read your report about Marie Curie. It tells a lot about her scientific discoveries. There are a few things you can add. I attached my ideas in a file so that you can look at it right away.

I am sending this message to Vanessa, too. She always has good ideas and suggestions. Let me know if you need more help. I'll see you tomorrow.
Lester

Technology and Media   353

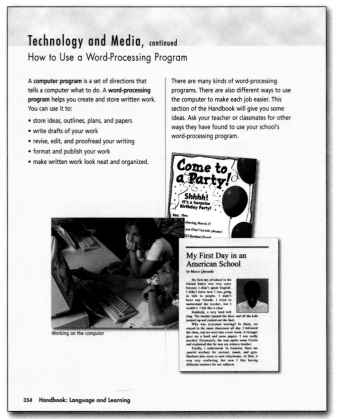

page 354

Technology and Media, continued
How to Use a Word-Processing Program

A **computer program** is a set of directions that tells a computer what to do. A **word-processing program** helps you create and store written work. You can use it to:
- store ideas, outlines, plans, and papers
- write drafts of your work
- revise, edit, and proofread your writing
- format and publish your work
- make written work look neat and organized.

There are many kinds of word-processing programs. There are also different ways to use the computer to make each job easier. This section of the Handbook will give you some ideas. Ask your teacher or classmates for other ways they have found to use your school's word-processing program.

Working on the computer

354   Handbook: Language and Learning

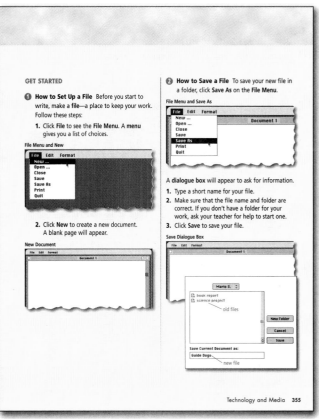

page 355

GET STARTED

1 **How to Set Up a File** Before you start to write, make a **file**—a place to keep your work. Follow these steps:

1. Click **File** to see the **File Menu**. A menu gives you a list of choices.

File Menu and New

2. Click **New** to create a new document. A blank page will appear.

New Document

2 **How to Save a File** To save your new file in a folder, click **Save As** on the **File Menu**.

File Menu and Save As

A **dialogue box** will appear to ask for information.

1. Type a short name for your file.
2. Make sure that the file name and folder are correct. If you don't have a folder for your work, ask your teacher for help to start one.
3. Click **Save** to save your file.

Save Dialogue Box

Technology and Media   355

Handbook: Language and Learning

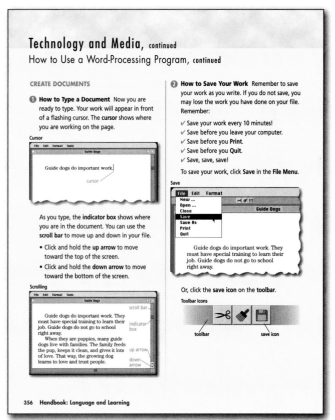

page 356

Technology and Media, continued
How to Use a Word-Processing Program, continued

CREATE DOCUMENTS

❶ **How to Type a Document** Now you are ready to type. Your work will appear in front of a flashing cursor. The **cursor** shows where you are working on the page.

Cursor

> Guide dogs do important work.
> cursor

As you type, the **indicator box** shows where you are in the document. You can use the **scroll bar** to move up and down in your file.

- Click and hold the **up arrow** to move toward the top of the screen.
- Click and hold the **down arrow** to move toward the bottom of the screen.

Scrolling

> Guide dogs do important work. They must have special training to learn their job. Guide dogs do not go to school right away.
> When they are puppies, many guide dogs live with families. The family feeds the pup, keeps it clean, and gives it lots of love. That way, the growing dog learns to love and trust people.

❷ **How to Save Your Work** Remember to save your work as you write. If you do not save, you may lose the work you have done on your file. Remember:

✓ Save your work every 10 minutes!
✓ Save before you leave your computer.
✓ Save before you **Print**.
✓ Save before you **Quit**.
✓ Save, save, save!

To save your work, click **Save** in the **File Menu**.

Save

> New ...
> Open ...
> Close
> Save
> Save As
> Print
> Quit

> Guide dogs do important work. They must have special training to learn their job. Guide dogs do not go to school right away.

Or, click the **save icon** on the **toolbar**.

Toolbar Icons

> toolbar   save icon

356   Handbook: Language and Learning

page 357

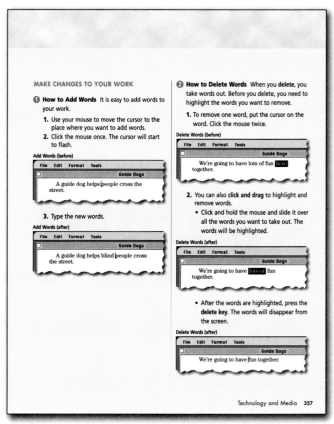

MAKE CHANGES TO YOUR WORK

❶ **How to Add Words** It is easy to add words to your work.

1. Use your mouse to move the cursor to the place where you want to add words.
2. Click the mouse once. The cursor will start to flash.

Add Words (before)

> A guide dog helps people cross the street.

3. Type the new words.

Add Words (after)

> A guide dog helps blind people cross the street.

❷ **How to Delete Words** When you delete, you take words out. Before you delete, you need to highlight the words you want to remove.

1. To remove one word, put the cursor on the word. Click the mouse twice.

Delete Words (before)

> We're going to have lots of fun here together.

2. You can also **click and drag** to highlight and remove words.
   - Click and hold the mouse and slide it over all the words you want to take out. The words will be highlighted.

Delete Words (after)

> We're going to have lots of fun together.

   - After the words are highlighted, press the **delete key**. The words will disappear from the screen.

Delete Words (after)

> We're going to have fun together.

Technology and Media   357

page 358

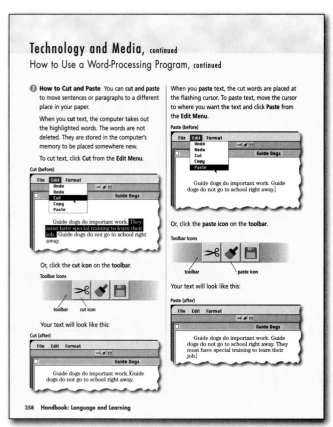

Technology and Media, continued
How to Use a Word-Processing Program, continued

❸ **How to Cut and Paste** You can cut and paste to move sentences or paragraphs to a different place in your paper.

When you **cut** text, the computer takes out the highlighted words. The words are not deleted. They are stored in the computer's memory to be placed somewhere new.

To cut text, click **Cut** from the **Edit Menu**.

Cut (before)

> Undo
> Redo
> Cut
> Copy
> Paste

> Guide dogs do important work. They must have special training to learn their job. Guide dogs do not go to school right away.

Or, click the **cut icon** on the **toolbar**.

Toolbar Icons

> toolbar   cut icon

Your text will look like this:

Cut (after)

> Guide dogs do important work. Guide dogs do not go to school right away.

When you paste text, the cut words are placed at the flashing cursor. To paste text, move the cursor to where you want the text and click **Paste** from the **Edit Menu**.

Paste (before)

> Undo
> Redo
> Cut
> Copy
> Paste

> Guide dogs do important work. Guide dogs do not go to school right away.

Or, click the **paste icon** on the **toolbar**.

Toolbar Icons

> toolbar   paste icon

Your text will look like this:

Paste (after)

> Guide dogs do important work. Guide dogs do not go to school right away. They must have special training to learn their job.

358   Handbook: Language and Learning

page 359

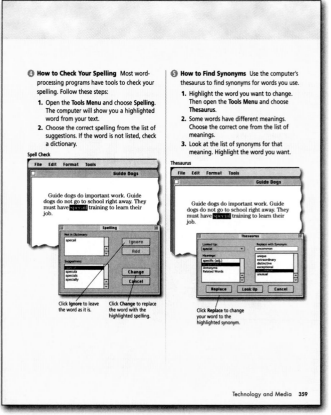

❹ **How to Check Your Spelling** Most word-processing programs have tools to check your spelling. Follow these steps:

1. Open the **Tools Menu** and choose **Spelling**. The computer will show you a highlighted word from your text.
2. Choose the correct spelling from the list of suggestions. If the word is not listed, check a dictionary.

Spell Check

> Guide dogs do important work. Guide dogs do not go to school right away. They must have special training to learn their job.

> Spelling
> Not in Dictionary: special
> Ignore
> Add
> Suggestions:
> specula
> specials
> specially
> Change
> Cancel

Click **Ignore** to leave the word as it is.   Click **Change** to replace the word with the highlighted spelling.

❺ **How to Find Synonyms** Use the computer's thesaurus to find synonyms for words you use.

1. Highlight the word you want to change. Then open the **Tools Menu** and choose **Thesaurus**.
2. Some words have different meanings. Choose the correct one from the list of meanings.
3. Look at the list of synonyms for that meaning. Highlight the word you want.

Thesaurus

> Guide dogs do important work. Guide dogs do not go to school right away. They must have special training to learn their job.

> Thesaurus
> Looked Up: special
> Replace with Synonym: uncommon
> Meanings: specific (adj.)
> unique
> extraordinary
> distinctive
> exceptional
> Antonyms
> Related Words
> unusual
> Replace   Look Up   Cancel

Click **Replace** to change your word to the highlighted synonym.

Technology and Media   359

Handbook: Language and Learning

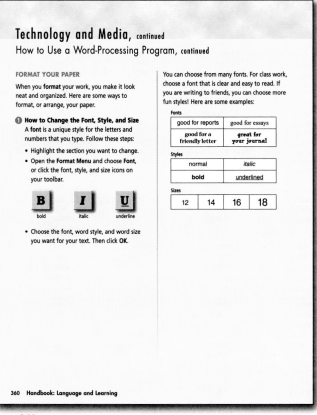

page 360

Technology and Media, continued
How to Use a Word-Processing Program, continued

FORMAT YOUR PAPER

When you **format** your work, you make it look neat and organized. Here are some ways to format, or arrange, your paper.

① How to Change the Font, Style, and Size
A **font** is a unique style for the letters and numbers that you type. Follow these steps:

- Highlight the section you want to change.
- Open the **Format Menu** and choose **Font**, or click the font, style, and size icons on your toolbar.

B	**I**	**U**
bold	italic	underline

- Choose the font, word style, and word size you want for your text. Then click **OK**.

You can choose from many fonts. For class work, choose a font that is clear and easy to read. If you are writing to friends, you can choose more fun styles! Here are some examples:

Fonts

good for reports	good for essays
good for a friendly letter	*great for your journal*

Styles

normal	*italic*
bold	underlined

Sizes

12	14	16	18

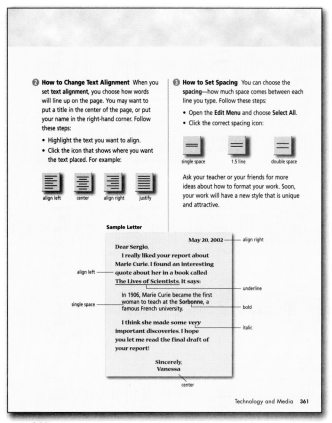

page 361

② How to Change Text Alignment When you set text **alignment**, you choose how words will line up on the page. You may want to put a title in the center of the page, or put your name in the right-hand corner. Follow these steps:

- Highlight the text you want to align.
- Click the icon that shows where you want the text placed. For example:

align left   center   align right   justify

③ How to Set Spacing You can choose the **spacing**—how much space comes between each line you type. Follow these steps:

- Open the **Edit Menu** and choose **Select All**.
- Click the correct spacing icon:

single space   1.5 line   double space

Ask your teacher or your friends for more ideas about how to format your work. Soon, your work will have a new style that is unique and attractive.

Sample Letter

> May 20, 2002 — align right
>
> Dear Sergio,
>   I really liked your report about Marie Curie. I found an interesting
> align left — quote about her in a book called
>   The Lives of Scientists. It says: — underline
>
> single space — In 1906, Marie Curie became the first woman to teach at the **Sorbonne**, a — bold
>   famous French university.
>
>   I think she made some *very* — italic
>   important discoveries. I hope you let me read the final draft of your report!
>
>   Sincerely,
>   Vanessa
>   — center

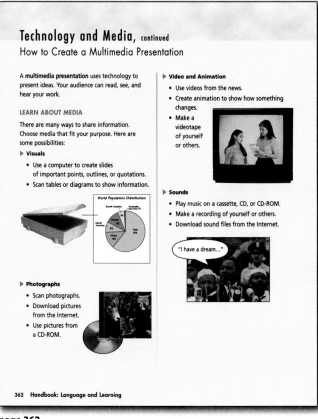

page 362

Technology and Media, continued
How to Create a Multimedia Presentation

A **multimedia presentation** uses technology to present ideas. Your audience can read, see, and hear your work.

LEARN ABOUT MEDIA

There are many ways to share information. Choose media that fit your purpose. Here are some possibilities:

▶ Visuals
- Use a computer to create slides of important points, outlines, or quotations.
- Scan tables or diagrams to show information.

▶ Photographs
- Scan photographs.
- Download pictures from the Internet.
- Use pictures from a CD-ROM.

▶ Video and Animation
- Use videos from the news.
- Create animation to show how something changes.
- Make a videotape of yourself or others.

▶ Sounds
- Play music on a cassette, CD, or CD-ROM.
- Make a recording of yourself or others.
- Download sound files from the Internet.

"I have a dream…"

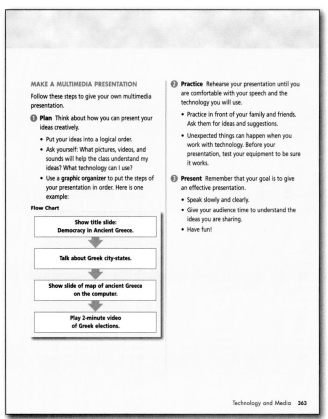

page 363

MAKE A MULTIMEDIA PRESENTATION

Follow these steps to give your own multimedia presentation.

① Plan Think about how you can present your ideas creatively.
- Put your ideas into a logical order.
- Ask yourself: What pictures, videos, and sounds will help the class understand my ideas? What technology can I use?
- Use a **graphic organizer** to put the steps of your presentation in order. Here is one example:

Flow Chart

> Show title slide:
> **Democracy in Ancient Greece.**
>   ↓
> **Talk about Greek city-states.**
>   ↓
> **Show slide of map of ancient Greece on the computer.**
>   ↓
> **Play 2-minute video of Greek elections.**

② Practice Rehearse your presentation until you are comfortable with your speech and the technology you will use.
- Practice in front of your family and friends. Ask them for ideas and suggestions.
- Unexpected things can happen when you work with technology. Before your presentation, test your equipment to be sure it works.

③ Present Remember that your goal is to give an effective presentation.
- Speak slowly and clearly.
- Give your audience time to understand the ideas you are sharing.
- Have fun!

Handbook: Language and Learning

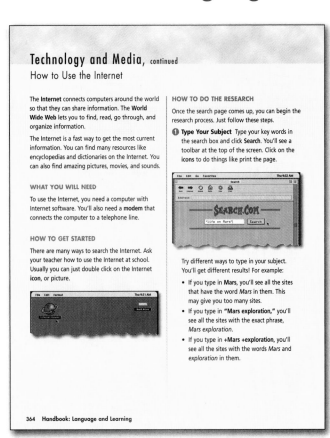

page 364

Technology and Media, continued
How to Use the Internet

The **Internet** connects computers around the world so that they can share information. The **World Wide Web** lets you to find, read, go through, and organize information.

The Internet is a fast way to get the most current information. You can find many resources like encyclopedias and dictionaries on the Internet. You can also find amazing pictures, movies, and sounds.

WHAT YOU WILL NEED

To use the Internet, you need a computer with Internet software. You'll also need a **modem** that connects the computer to a telephone line.

HOW TO GET STARTED

There are many ways to search the Internet. Ask your teacher how to use the Internet at school. Usually you can just double click on the Internet **icon**, or picture.

HOW TO DO THE RESEARCH

Once the search page comes up, you can begin the research process. Just follow these steps.

❶ **Type Your Subject** Type your key words in the search box and click **Search**. You'll see a toolbar at the top of the screen. Click on the **icons** to do things like print the page.

Try different ways to type in your subject. You'll get different results! For example:

- If you type in **Mars**, you'll see all the sites that have the word *Mars* in them. This may give you too many sites.
- If you type in **"Mars exploration,"** you'll see all the sites with the exact phrase, *Mars exploration*.
- If you type in **+Mars +exploration**, you'll see all the sites with the words *Mars* and *exploration* in them.

page 365

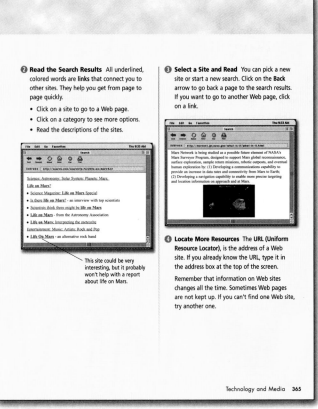

❷ **Read the Search Results** All underlined, colored words are **links** that connect you to other sites. They help you get from page to page quickly.

- Click on a site to go to a Web page.
- Click on a category to see more options.
- Read the descriptions of the sites.

This site could be very interesting, but it probably won't help with a report about life on Mars.

❸ **Select a Site and Read** You can pick a new site or start a new search. Click on the **Back** arrow to go back a page to the search results. If you want to go to another Web page, click on a link.

❹ **Locate More Resources** The URL (Uniform Resource Locator), is the address of a Web site. If you already know the URL, type it in the address box at the top of the screen.

Remember that information on Web sites changes all the time. Sometimes Web pages are not kept up. If you can't find one Web site, try another one.

page 366

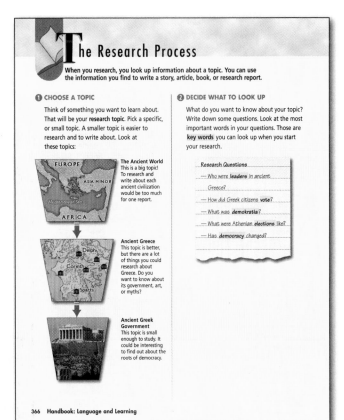

The Research Process

When you research, you look up information about a topic. You can use the information you find to write a story, article, book, or research report.

❶ **CHOOSE A TOPIC**

Think of something you want to learn about. That will be your **research topic**. Pick a specific, or small topic. A smaller topic is easier to research and to write about. Look at these topics:

The Ancient World
This is a big topic! To research and write about each ancient civilization would be too much for one report.

Ancient Greece
This topic is better, but there are a lot of things you could research about Greece. Do you want to know about its government, art, or myths?

Ancient Greek Government
This topic is small enough to study. It could be interesting to find out about the roots of democracy.

❷ **DECIDE WHAT TO LOOK UP**

What do you want to know about your topic? Write down some questions. Look at the most important words in your questions. Those are **key words** you can look up when you start your research.

> *Research Questions*
> — Who were **leaders** in ancient Greece?
> — How did Greek citizens **vote**?
> — What was **demokratia**?
> — What were Athenian **elections** like?
> — Has **democracy** changed?

page 367

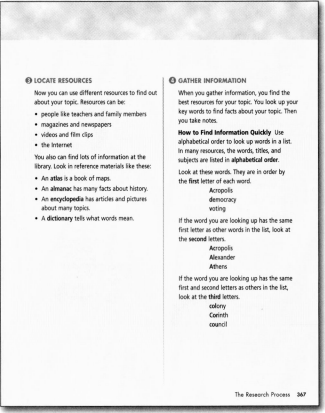

❸ **LOCATE RESOURCES**

Now you can use different resources to find out about your topic. Resources can be:

- people like teachers and family members
- magazines and newspapers
- videos and film clips
- the Internet

You also can find lots of information at the library. Look in reference materials like these:

- An **atlas** is a book of maps.
- An **almanac** has many facts about history.
- An **encyclopedia** has articles and pictures about many topics.
- A **dictionary** tells what words mean.

❹ **GATHER INFORMATION**

When you gather information, you find the best resources for your topic. You look up your key words to find facts about your topic. Then you take notes.

How to Find Information Quickly Use alphabetical order to look up words in a list. In many resources, the words, titles, and subjects are listed in **alphabetical order**.

Look at these words. They are in order by the **first** letter of each word.

> Acropolis
> democracy
> voting

If the word you are looking up has the same first letter as other words in the list, look at the **second** letters.

> Acropolis
> Alexander
> Athens

If the word you are looking up has the same first and second letters as others in the list, look at the **third** letters.

> colony
> Corinth
> council

Handbook: Language and Learning

page 368

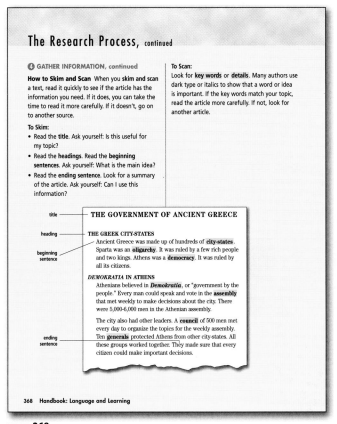

The Research Process, continued

4 GATHER INFORMATION, continued

How to Skim and Scan When you **skim and scan** a text, read it quickly to see if the article has the information you need. If it does, you can take the time to read it more carefully. If it doesn't, go on to another source.

To Skim:
- Read the **title**. Ask yourself: Is this useful for my topic?
- Read the **headings**. Read the **beginning sentences**. Ask yourself: What is the main idea?
- Read the **ending sentence**. Look for a summary of the article. Ask yourself: Can I use this information?

To Scan:
Look for **key words** or **details**. Many authors use dark type or italics to show that a word or idea is important. If the key words match your topic, read the article more carefully. If not, look for another article.

title — **THE GOVERNMENT OF ANCIENT GREECE**

heading — **THE GREEK CITY-STATES**

beginning sentence — Ancient Greece was made up of hundreds of **city-states**. Sparta was an **oligarchy**. It was ruled by a few rich people and two kings. Athens was a **democracy**. It was ruled by all its citizens.

***DEMOKRATIA* IN ATHENS**
Athenians believed in ***Demokratia***, or "government by the people." Every man could speak and vote in the **assembly** that met weekly to make decisions about the city. There were 5,000-6,000 men in the Athenian assembly.

ending sentence — The city also had other leaders. A **council** of 500 men met every day to organize the topics for the weekly assembly. Ten **generals** protected Athens from other city-states. All these groups worked together. They made sure that every citizen could make important decisions.

368　Handbook: Language and Learning

page 369

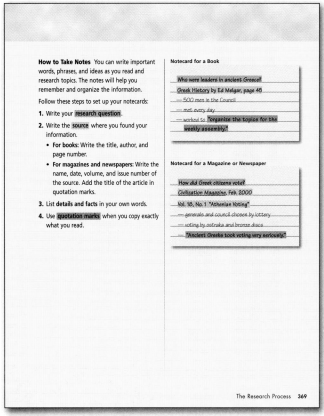

How to Take Notes You can write important words, phrases, and ideas as you read and research topics. The notes will help you remember and organize the information.

Follow these steps to set up your notecards:

1. Write your **research question**.

2. Write the **source** where you found your information.
   - **For books:** Write the title, author, and page number.
   - **For magazines and newspapers:** Write the name, date, volume, and issue number of the source. Add the title of the article in quotation marks.

3. List **details** and facts in your own words.

4. Use **quotation marks** when you copy exactly what you read.

Notecard for a Book

Who were leaders in ancient Greece?
Greek History by Ed Melgar, page 45
— 500 men in the Council
— met every day
— worked to "organize the topics for the weekly assembly."

Notecard for a Magazine or Newspaper

How did Greek citizens vote?
Civilization Magazine, Feb. 2000
Vol. 18, No. 1 "Athenian Voting"
— generals and council chosen by lottery
— voting by ostraka and bronze discs
— "Ancient Greeks took voting very seriously."

The Research Process　369

page 370

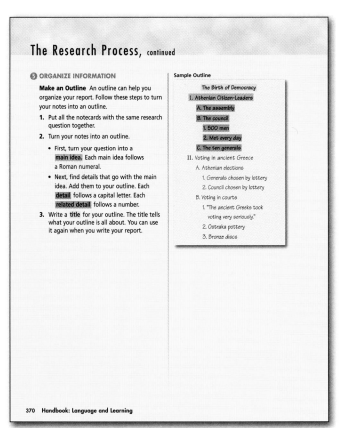

The Research Process, continued

5 ORGANIZE INFORMATION

Make an Outline An outline can help you organize your report. Follow these steps to turn your notes into an outline.

1. Put all the notecards with the same research question together.

2. Turn your notes into an outline.
   - First, turn your question into a **main idea**. Each main idea follows a Roman numeral.
   - Next, find details that go with the main idea. Add them to your outline. Each **detail** follows a capital letter. Each **related detail** follows a number.

3. Write a **title** for your outline. The title tells what your outline is all about. You can use it again when you write your report.

Sample Outline

The Birth of Democracy
I. Athenian Citizen-Leaders
　A. The assembly
　B. The council
　　1. 500 men
　　2. Met every day
　C. The ten generals
II. Voting in ancient Greece
　A. Athenian elections
　　1. Generals chosen by lottery
　　2. Council chosen by lottery
　B. Voting in courts
　　1. "The ancient Greeks took voting very seriously."
　　2. Ostraka pottery
　　3. Bronze discs

370　Handbook: Language and Learning

page 371

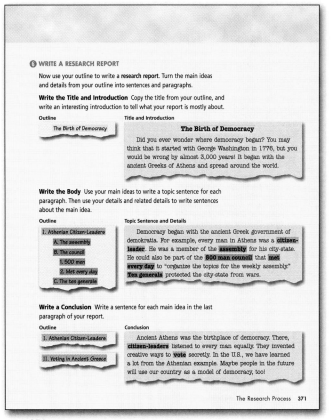

6 WRITE A RESEARCH REPORT

Now use your outline to write a **research report**. Turn the main ideas and details from your outline into sentences and paragraphs.

Write the Title and Introduction Copy the title from your outline, and write an interesting introduction to tell what your report is mostly about.

Outline

The Birth of Democracy

Title and Introduction

The Birth of Democracy
　Did you ever wonder where democracy began? You may think that it started with George Washington in 1776, but you would be wrong by almost 3,000 years! It began with the ancient Greeks of Athens and spread around the world.

Write the Body Use your main ideas to write a topic sentence for each paragraph. Then use your details and related details to write sentences about the main idea.

Outline

I. Athenian Citizen-Leaders
　A. The assembly
　B. The council
　　1. 500 men
　　2. Met every day
　C. The ten generals

Topic Sentence and Details

　Democracy began with the ancient Greek government of demokratia. For example, every man in Athens was a **citizen-leader**. He was a member of the **assembly** for his city-state. He could also be part of the **500 man council** that **met every day** to "organize the topics for the weekly assembly." **Ten generals** protected the city-state from wars.

Write a Conclusion Write a sentence for each main idea in the last paragraph of your report.

Outline

I. Athenian Citizen-Leaders

II. Voting in Ancient Greece

Conclusion

　Ancient Athens was the birthplace of democracy. There, **citizen-leaders** listened to every man equally. They invented creative ways to **vote** secretly. In the U.S., we have learned a lot from the Athenian example. Maybe people in the future will use our country as a model of democracy, too!

The Research Process　371

Handbook: Language and Learning

page 372

The Research Process, continued

The Birth of Democracy

Did you ever wonder where democracy began? You may think that it started with George Washington in 1776, but you would be wrong by almost 3,000 years! It began with the ancient Greeks of Athens and spread around the world.

Democracy began with the ancient Greek government of demokratia. For example, every man in Athens was a citizen-leader. He was a member of the assembly for his city-state. He could also be part of the 500 man council that met every day to "organize the topics for the weekly assembly." Ten generals protected the city-state from wars.

Athenian citizens "took voting very seriously." They knew that elections could be unfair. Council members and generals were chosen by lottery. In courts, ostraka pottery and bronze voting discs made sure that people voted privately.

Ancient Athens was the birthplace of democracy. There, citizen-leaders listened to every man equally. They invented creative ways to vote secretly. In the U.S., we have learned a lot from the Athenian example. Maybe people in the future will use our country as a model of democracy, too!

INTRODUCTION
The **title** and **introduction** tell what your report is about.

BODY
The **body** of the report tells the facts you found. Each paragraph goes with a main idea from your outline.

CONCLUSION
The **conclusion** is a summary of the topic.

page 373

Speaking and Listening

You talk, or speak, to others every day. That's how you express your ideas.
You also listen to others to learn about new ideas.

HOW TO BE A GOOD LISTENER

Good listeners listen carefully to what others say.

How to Be a Good Listener
- Pay attention. Open your eyes and ears. Look at the speaker as you listen.
- Be quiet while the speaker talks.
- Only interrupt when you need the speaker to talk louder.
- Save your questions until the speaker is finished.

HOW TO PARTICIPATE IN A DISCUSSION

Sometimes you will discuss ideas as a class, in a group, or with a partner. You may also have a conference with a teacher or a peer to talk about your writing. Discussions are good ways to find information, check your understanding, and share ideas.

How to Participate in a Discussion
- Use good listening skills.
- Give the speaker a chance to finish before you respond.
- Make positive comments about the ideas of others.
- Respect everyone's ideas and feelings.
- Only talk about one topic at a time.
- Ask questions if you need more information.

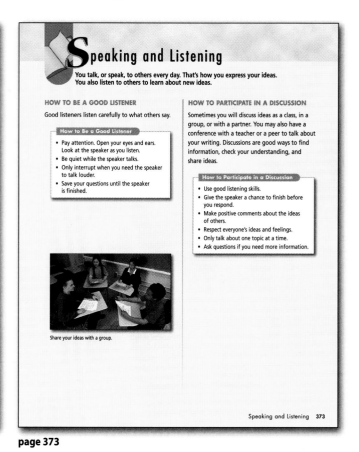

Share your ideas with a group.

page 374

Speaking and Listening, continued

HOW TO LISTEN CAREFULLY

When you listen carefully, you can find out how to do something or learn more about a topic. As you listen:

- Think about what you hear. How does it relate to what you already know?
- Listen for key words and important details. Take notes to help you remember the ideas.

Example:
ecosystem: things in nature and how they work together

- Ask yourself: What is the speaker's purpose? Does the speaker want to inform, entertain, or persuade the audience?
- Pay attention to the speaker's voice, gestures, and expressions. What do they tell you about how the speaker feels about the topic?
- Think about the speaker. Ask yourself: What does the speaker know about the topic?
- Summarize what the speaker says in your own mind. Do you agree or disagree? What new information did you learn?

HOW TO GIVE AN ORAL PRESENTATION

There are many kinds of oral presentations. Decide if you want to make a speech, give a report, recite a poem, or give a performance. Follow these steps to prepare your presentation.

❶ Plan Your Presentation Think about your audience. What ideas do you want to share? What is the best way to share your ideas?

- Organize your information. You can use a graphic organizer to show the details and the order you will use to present ideas.

Outline

I. Ecosystem
  A. Is like a community
  B. Includes all living things in nature
II. Food Chain
  A. Is different in different places
  B. Has a sequence
    1. Microorganisms in soil
    2. Plants grow
    3. Animals eat plants

page 375

- Think of a way to interest the audience and introduce your topic. You may want to use a quotation, make a startling statement, or ask a question.
- Write your main ideas on notecards. You can look at them as you speak to help you remember what to say.

Beginning of food chain
—microorganisms in the soil
create food for plants
—plants grow

- Use visuals and technology to support your ideas. Organize them to match your notes.

Food Chain Poster

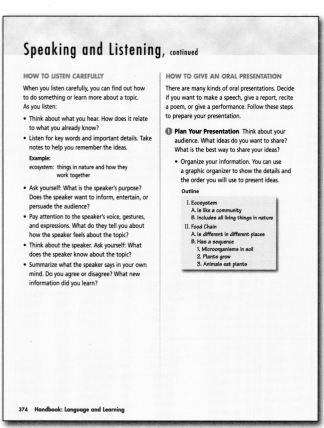

hawk
snake
frog
cricket
plants

- Use your notecards, visuals, and technology to practice your presentation in front of a mirror or your family. You can videotape or tape record your presentation as you practice. This can help you find ideas about how to improve.

Handbook: Language and Learning

page 376

Speaking and Listening, continued

HOW TO GIVE AN ORAL PRESENTATION
continued

❷ Choose the Right Language and Tone Will you speak to your friends, to young kids, or to adults? Think about your topic, audience, and purpose. Then decide the best way to give your presentation.

To give a persuasive speech:
- Use a strong, clear voice. Change your tone to describe important points.
- Use formal language to tell the facts. Use persuasive words to give opinions.

To tell a story:
- Use informal language to make the characters seem real. Change your voice to show when a new character speaks.
- Use expressions, gestures, and other movements to show the characters' feelings and the action.

To give a formal report:
- Use formal language to tell the facts and information.
- Speak slowly and clearly so everyone can understand the information.
- Tell the information in a logical order.
- Use examples and visuals that show your main points.

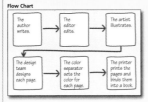
Use formal language to give a report.

❸ Give Your Presentation Now you are ready. As you present your ideas:
- Stand up straight.
- Look at everyone in the audience.
- Speak slowly and clearly. Use a loud voice so everyone can hear you.
- Use expressions and movements that go with the information you are presenting.
- Make sure that the audience can see you and your visuals.
- Stay calm and relaxed.
- Thank the audience when you're done. Ask for questions when you are finished.

page 377

Viewing and Representing

You can get information from the things you see, or view. You can also use visuals to help you show your ideas.

HOW TO EVALUATE WHAT YOU SEE

There are many things to view—photographs, videos, graphs, charts, and Web sites. You can also watch when people use movements to send messages without words. Try this process with the visual below.

❶ View and Look for Details Study the visual. Ask yourself:
- Who or what does the image show? Are there other details that tell when, where, why, or how?
- How does the visual make me feel? Do I like looking at it?
- Do I like the colors? How does the size or shape of the visual affect me?

❷ Think About the Purpose and the Message What you see can change the way you feel about a topic. Ask yourself:
- What message does the visual give?
- Why did the artist create the visual? Does it make me want to do something? Does it give me new information?
- What does the visual tell about the topic?
- How does the artist want me to feel when I look at the visual?

❸ Look for Stereotypes A stereotype is a general opinion that is not always true. It's like saying that because one dog is mean, all dogs are mean. Try to find any stereotypes in the visual.

page 378

Viewing and Representing, continued

HOW TO REPRESENT YOUR IDEAS

There are many resources, or **media**, to help you make your point more clearly. Choose media that match your purpose and your topic.

A beautiful **illustration** can add creativity and make a story come alive.

Illustration

A **flow chart** can show steps in a process.

Flow Chart

A **chart** or a **graph** can show comparisons. You can find more graphic organizers on pages 340–347.

Chart

Number of Endangered Species in the United States	
Classification	Number of Species
Mammals	61
Birds	75
Reptiles	14
Fishes	69
Insects	28

Graph

Number of Endangered Species in the United States

page 379

HOW TO MATCH MEDIA TO YOUR MESSAGE

Choose the best media to give your message and help you get your audience's attention. Look at the different media you can use on pages 362–363. Here are a few examples.

❶ To Entertain Include props, illustrations of the setting, or slides for a backdrop. Create a film strip, animation, or a video.

❷ To Inform Use maps and charts to show information. You can make a time line to show the order of events or use a transparency to show information on an overhead projector.

Most Giant Pandas originated in China.

❸ To Persuade Show images that will change people's opinions. You might use slides or photographs to touch people's emotions.

Fewer than 1,000 pandas live in the wild.

Handbook: Language and Learning

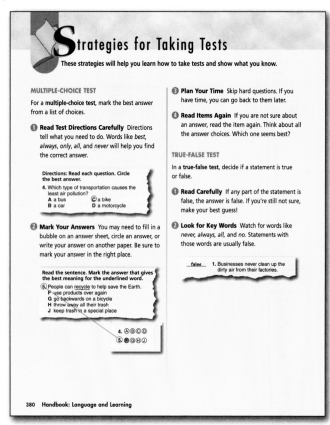

Strategies for Taking Tests

These strategies will help you learn how to take tests and show what you know.

MULTIPLE-CHOICE TEST

For a **multiple-choice test**, mark the best answer from a list of choices.

❶ **Read Test Directions Carefully** Directions tell what you need to do. Words like *best*, *always*, *only*, *all*, and *never* will help you find the correct answer.

> **Directions: Read each question. Circle the best answer.**
>
> 4. Which type of transportation causes the least air pollution?
> A a bus   Ⓒ a bike
> B a car   D a motorcycle

❷ **Mark Your Answers** You may need to fill in a bubble on an answer sheet, circle an answer, or write your answer on another paper. Be sure to mark your answer in the right place.

> **Read the sentence. Mark the answer that gives the best meaning for the underlined word.**
>
> 5. People can <u>recycle</u> to help save the Earth.
> F use products over again
> G go backwards on a bicycle
> H throw away all their trash
> J keep trash in a special place
>
> 4. Ⓐ Ⓑ Ⓒ D
> 5. Ⓔ Ⓕ Ⓖ Ⓗ

❸ **Plan Your Time** Skip hard questions. If you have time, you can go back to them later.

❹ **Read Items Again** If you are not sure about an answer, read the item again. Think about all the answer choices. Which one seems best?

TRUE-FALSE TEST

In a **true-false test**, decide if a statement is true or false.

❶ **Read Carefully** If *any* part of the statement is false, the answer is false. If you're still not sure, make your best guess!

❷ **Look for Key Words** Watch for words like *never, always, all*, and *no*. Statements with those words are usually false.

> ___false___   1. Businesses never clean up the dirty air from their factories.

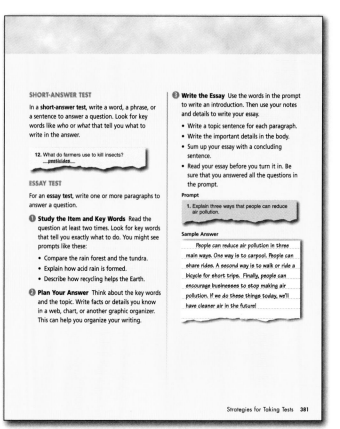

SHORT-ANSWER TEST

In a **short-answer test**, write a word, a phrase, or a sentence to answer a question. Look for key words like *who* or *what* that tell you what to write in the answer.

> 12. What do farmers use to kill insects?
> ___pesticides___

ESSAY TEST

For an **essay test**, write one or more paragraphs to answer a question.

❶ **Study the Item and Key Words** Read the question at least two times. Look for key words that tell you exactly what to do. You might see prompts like these:

- Compare the rain forest and the tundra.
- Explain how acid rain is formed.
- Describe how recycling helps the Earth.

❷ **Plan Your Answer** Think about the key words and the topic. Write facts or details you know in a web, chart, or another graphic organizer. This can help you organize your writing.

❸ **Write the Essay** Use the words in the prompt to write an introduction. Then use your notes and details to write your essay.

- Write a topic sentence for each paragraph.
- Write the important details in the body.
- Sum up your essay with a concluding sentence.
- Read your essay before you turn it in. Be sure that you answered all the questions in the prompt.

Prompt

> 1. Explain three ways that people can reduce air pollution.

Sample Answer

> People can reduce air pollution in three main ways. One way is to carpool. People can share rides. A second way is to walk or ride a bicycle for short trips. Finally, people can encourage businesses to stop making air pollution. If we do these things today, we'll have cleaner air in the future!

page 380   page 381

Handbook: Writing

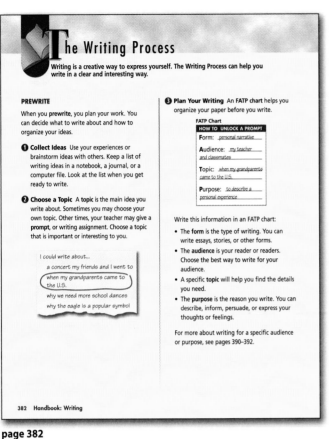

The Writing Process

Writing is a creative way to express yourself. The Writing Process can help you write in a clear and interesting way.

PREWRITE

When you **prewrite**, you plan your work. You can decide what to write about and how to organize your ideas.

❶ Collect Ideas Use your experiences or brainstorm ideas with others. Keep a list of writing ideas in a notebook, a journal, or a computer file. Look at the list when you get ready to write.

❷ Choose a Topic A **topic** is the main idea you write about. Sometimes you may choose your own topic. Other times, your teacher may give a **prompt**, or writing assignment. Choose a topic that is important or interesting to you.

> I could write about...
> a concert my friends and I went to
> when my grandparents came to the U.S.
> why we need more school dances
> why the eagle is a popular symbol

❸ Plan Your Writing An FATP chart helps you organize your paper before you write.

FATP Chart

HOW TO UNLOCK A PROMPT
Form: _personal narrative_
Audience: _my teacher and classmates_
Topic: _when my grandparents came to the U.S._
Purpose: _to describe a personal experience_

Write this information in an FATP chart:

- The **form** is the type of writing. You can write essays, stories, or other forms.
- The **audience** is your reader or readers. Choose the best way to write for your audience.
- A specific **topic** will help you find the details you need.
- The **purpose** is the reason you write. You can describe, inform, persuade, or express your thoughts or feelings.

For more about writing for a specific audience or purpose, see pages 390–392.

page 382

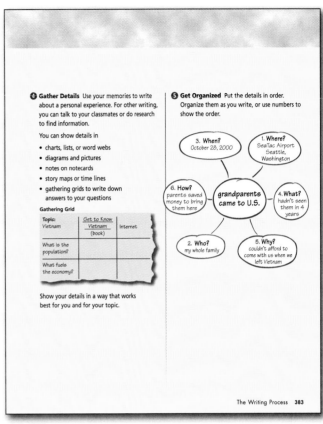

❹ Gather Details Use your memories to write about a personal experience. For other writing, you can talk to your classmates or do research to find information.

You can show details in

- charts, lists, or word webs
- diagrams and pictures
- notes on notecards
- story maps or time lines
- gathering grids to write down answers to your questions

Gathering Grid

Topic: Vietnam	Get to Know Vietnam (book)	Internet
What is the population?		
What fuels the economy?		

Show your details in a way that works best for you and for your topic.

❺ Get Organized Put the details in order. Organize them as you write, or use numbers to show the order.

- 3. When? October 28, 2000
- 1. Where? SeaTac Airport Seattle, Washington
- 6. How? parents saved money to bring them here
- **grandparents came to U.S.**
- 4. What? hadn't seen them in 4 years
- 2. Who? my whole family
- 5. Why? couldn't afford to come with us when we left Vietnam

page 383

The Writing Process, continued

DRAFT

Now you are ready to write. Write a **first draft** that has all your ideas. Don't worry about mistakes! Use your details to write sentences and paragraphs. As you write, you may think of new ideas and details. Add the new ideas as you think of them.

Trang Bui's Draft

> My family stood by the windows and watched the plane land at SeaTac Airport in Seattle on October 28, 2000. We were so excited to see the plane. The people started coming through the door. We lined up so we could see. I had to lift my little brother up so he could see.
>
> Suddenly everyone was hugging and crying. "I see them," my mother cried. My little brother tried to hide. My brother didn't know my grandparents. He was feeling shy.

REVISE

When you **revise**, you make your draft better.

❶ Read Your Draft Make sure that your ideas are clear, complete, and written in the best way. Ask yourself questions from the Revision Checklist:

Revision Checklist

- ☑ Did I follow the plan on my FATP chart?
- ☑ Is my writing interesting?
- ☑ Did I use different kinds of sentences?
- ☑ Does my writing have a beginning, a middle, and an ending?
- ☑ Are my ideas clear?
- ☑ Do I need to add more details?
- ☑ Are my details in the best order?
- ☑ Did I use words that say what I mean?

page 384

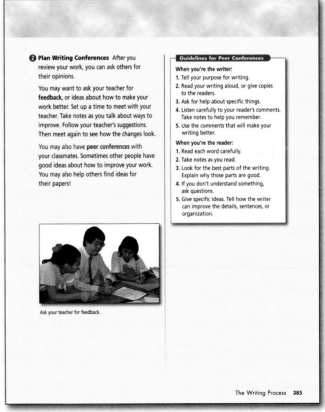

❷ Plan Writing Conferences After you review your work, you can ask others for their opinions.

You may want to ask your teacher for **feedback**, or ideas about how to make your work better. Set up a time to meet with your teacher. Take notes as you talk about ways to improve. Follow your teacher's suggestions. Then meet again to see how the changes look.

You may also have **peer conferences** with your classmates. Sometimes other people have good ideas about how to improve your work. You may also help others find ideas for their papers!

Ask your teacher for feedback.

Guidelines for Peer Conferences

When you're the writer:
1. Tell your purpose for writing.
2. Read your writing aloud, or give copies to the readers.
3. Ask for help about specific things.
4. Listen carefully to your reader's comments. Take notes to help you remember.
5. Use the comments that will make your writing better.

When you're the reader:
1. Read each word carefully.
2. Take notes as you read.
3. Look for the best parts of the writing. Explain why those parts are good.
4. If you don't understand something, ask questions.
5. Give specific ideas. Tell how the writer can improve the details, sentences, or organization.

page 385

Handbook: Writing

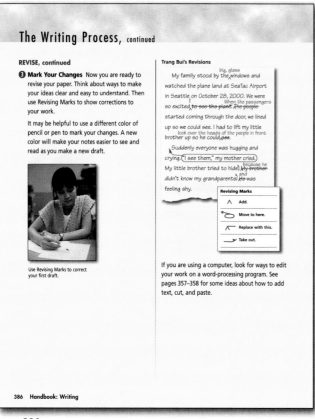

page 386

The Writing Process, continued

REVISE, continued

③ Mark Your Changes Now you are ready to revise your paper. Think about ways to make your ideas clear and easy to understand. Then use Revising Marks to show corrections to your work.

It may be helpful to use a different color of pencil or pen to mark your changes. A new color will make your notes easier to see and read as you make a new draft.

Use Revising Marks to correct your first draft.

Trang Bui's Revisions

> My family stood by the windows and
> *big, glass*
> watched the plane land at SeaTac Airport
> in Seattle on October 28, 2000. We were
> so excited to see the plane. The people
> *When the passengers*
> started coming through the door, we lined
> up so we could see. I had to lift my little
> *look over the heads of the people in front*
> brother up so he could see.
>
> Suddenly everyone was hugging and
> crying. "I see them," my mother cried.
> My little brother tried to hide. My brother
> *because he*
> didn't know my grandparents. He was
> *and*
> feeling shy.

Revising Marks

∧	Add.
↶	Move to here.
⤬	Replace with this.
⤴	Take out.

If you are using a computer, look for ways to edit your work on a word-processing program. See pages 357–358 for some ideas about how to add text, cut, and paste.

386   Handbook: Writing

page 387

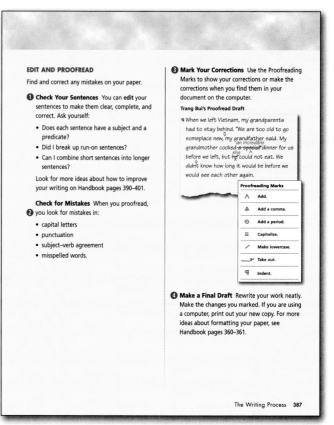

EDIT AND PROOFREAD

Find and correct any mistakes on your paper.

① Check Your Sentences You can **edit** your sentences to make them clear, complete, and correct. Ask yourself:

- Does each sentence have a subject and a predicate?
- Did I break up run-on sentences?
- Can I combine short sentences into longer sentences?

Look for more ideas about how to improve your writing on Handbook pages 390–401.

Check for Mistakes When you proofread, **②** you look for mistakes in:

- capital letters
- punctuation
- subject–verb agreement
- misspelled words.

③ Mark Your Corrections Use the Proofreading Marks to show your corrections or make the corrections when you find them in your document on the computer.

Trang Bui's Proofread Draft

> ¶ When we left Vietnam, my grandparents
> had to stay behind. "We are too old to go
> someplace new," my grandfather said. My
> *an incredible*
> grandmother cooked a special dinner for us
> *she*
> before we left, but he could not eat. We
> didn't know how long it would be before we
> would see each other again.

Proofreading Marks

∧	Add.
⋏	Add a comma.
⊙	Add a period.
≡	Capitalize.
/	Make lowercase.
⤴	Take out.
¶	Indent.

④ Make a Final Draft Rewrite your work neatly. Make the changes you marked. If you are using a computer, print out your new copy. For more ideas about formatting your paper, see Handbook pages 360–361.

The Writing Process   387

page 388

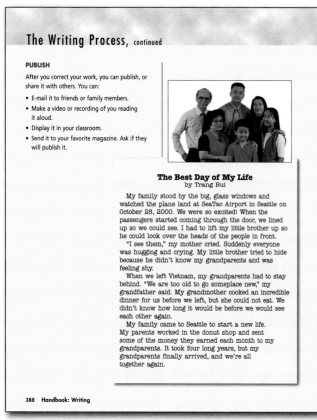

The Writing Process, continued

PUBLISH

After you correct your work, you can publish, or share it with others. You can:

- E-mail it to friends or family members.
- Make a video or recording of you reading it aloud.
- Display it in your classroom.
- Send it to your favorite magazine. Ask if they will publish it.

The Best Day of My Life
by Trang Bui

My family stood by the big, glass windows and watched the plane land at SeaTac Airport in Seattle on October 28, 2000. We were so excited! When the passengers started coming through the door, we lined up so we could see. I had to lift my little brother up so he could look over the heads of the people in front.

"I see them," my mother cried. Suddenly everyone was hugging and crying. My little brother tried to hide because he didn't know my grandparents and was feeling shy.

When we left Vietnam, my grandparents had to stay behind. "We are too old to go someplace new," my grandfather said. My grandmother cooked an incredible dinner for us before we left, but she could not eat. We didn't know how long it would be before we would see each other again.

My family came to Seattle to start a new life. My parents worked in the donut shop and sent some of the money they earned each month to my grandparents. It took four long years, but my grandparents finally arrived, and we're all together again.

388   Handbook: Writing

page 389

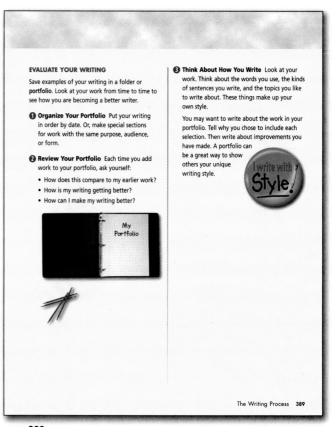

EVALUATE YOUR WRITING

Save examples of your writing in a folder or **portfolio**. Look at your work from time to time to see how you are becoming a better writer.

① Organize Your Portfolio Put your writing in order by date. Or, make special sections for work with the same purpose, audience, or form.

② Review Your Portfolio Each time you add work to your portfolio, ask yourself:

- How does this compare to my earlier work?
- How is my writing getting better?
- How can I make my writing better?

③ Think About How You Write Look at your work. Think about the words you use, the kinds of sentences you write, and the topics you like to write about. These things make up your own style.

You may want to write about the work in your portfolio. Tell why you chose to include each selection. Then write about improvements you have made. A portfolio can be a great way to show others your unique writing style.

I write with Style!

The Writing Process   389

Handbook: Writing

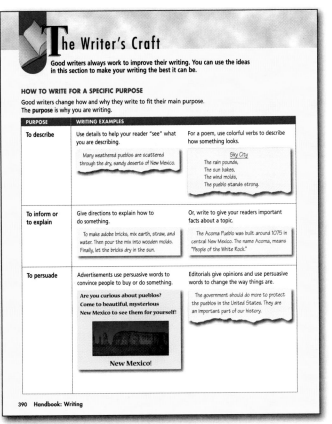

The Writer's Craft

Good writers always work to improve their writing. You can use the ideas in this section to make your writing the best it can be.

HOW TO WRITE FOR A SPECIFIC PURPOSE

Good writers change how and why they write to fit their main purpose. The **purpose** is why you are writing.

PURPOSE	WRITING EXAMPLES	
To describe	Use details to help your reader "see" what you are describing.	For a poem, use colorful verbs to describe how something looks.
	Many weathered pueblos are scattered through the dry, sandy deserts of New Mexico.	Sky City The rain pounds, The sun bakes, The wind molds, The pueblo stands strong.
To inform or to explain	Give directions to explain how to do something.	Or, write to give your readers important facts about a topic.
	To make adobe bricks, mix earth, straw, and water. Then pour the mix into wooden molds. Finally, let the bricks dry in the sun.	The Acoma Pueblo was built around 1075 in central New Mexico. The name Acoma, means "People of the White Rock."
To persuade	Advertisements use persuasive words to convince people to buy or do something.	Editorials give opinions and use persuasive words to change the way things are.
	Are you curious about pueblos? Come to beautiful, mysterious New Mexico to see them for yourself! New Mexico!	The government should do more to protect the pueblos in the United States. They are an important part of our history.

page 390

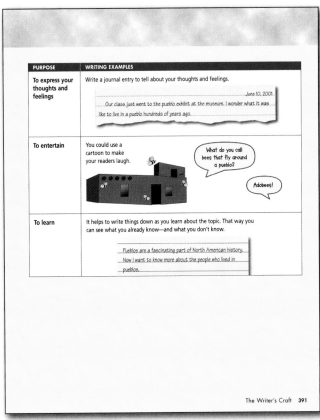

PURPOSE	WRITING EXAMPLES
To express your thoughts and feelings	Write a journal entry to tell about your thoughts and feelings. June 10, 2001. Our class just went to the pueblo exhibit at the museum. I wonder what it was like to live in a pueblo hundreds of years ago.
To entertain	You could use a cartoon to make your readers laugh. What do you call bees that fly around a pueblo? Adobees!
To learn	It helps to write things down as you learn about the topic. That way you can see what you already know—and what you don't know. Pueblos are a fascinating part of North American history. Now I want to know more about the people who lived in pueblos.

page 391

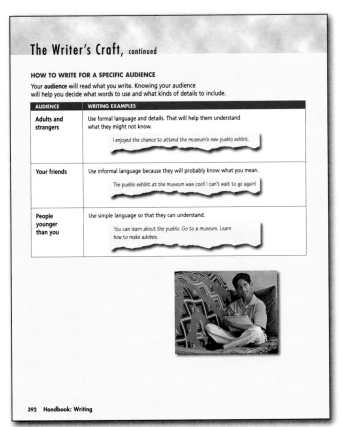

The Writer's Craft, continued

HOW TO WRITE FOR A SPECIFIC AUDIENCE

Your **audience** will read what you write. Knowing your audience will help you decide what words to use and what kinds of details to include.

AUDIENCE	WRITING EXAMPLES
Adults and strangers	Use formal language and details. That will help them understand what they might not know. I enjoyed the chance to attend the museum's new pueblo exhibit.
Your friends	Use informal language because they will probably know what you mean. The pueblo exhibit at the museum was cool! I can't wait to go again!
People younger than you	Use simple language so that they can understand. You can learn about the pueblo. Go to a museum. Learn how to make adobes.

page 392

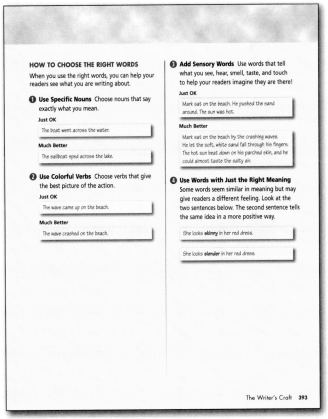

HOW TO CHOOSE THE RIGHT WORDS

When you use the right words, you can help your readers see what you are writing about.

❶ Use Specific Nouns Choose nouns that say exactly what you mean.

Just OK
The boat went across the water.

Much Better
The sailboat sped across the lake.

❷ Use Colorful Verbs Choose verbs that give the best picture of the action.

Just OK
The wave came up on the beach.

Much Better
The wave crashed on the beach.

❸ Add Sensory Words Use words that tell what you see, hear, smell, taste, and touch to help your readers imagine they are there!

Just OK
Mark sat on the beach. He pushed the sand around. The sun was hot.

Much Better
Mark sat on the beach by the crashing waves. He let the soft, white sand fall through his fingers. The hot sun beat down on his parched skin, and he could almost taste the salty air.

❹ Use Words with Just the Right Meaning Some words seem similar in meaning but may give readers a different feeling. Look at the two sentences below. The second sentence tells the same idea in a more positive way.

She looks **skinny** in her red dress.

She looks **slender** in her red dress.

page 393

Handbook: Writing

page 394

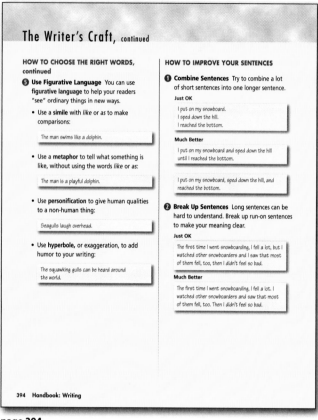

The Writer's Craft, continued

HOW TO CHOOSE THE RIGHT WORDS, continued

5 Use Figurative Language You can use figurative language to help your readers "see" ordinary things in new ways.

- Use a **simile** with *like* or *as* to make comparisons:

  > The man swims like a dolphin.

- Use a **metaphor** to tell what something is like, without using the words *like* or *as*:

  > The man is a playful dolphin.

- Use **personification** to give human qualities to a non-human thing:

  > Seagulls laugh overhead.

- Use **hyperbole**, or exaggeration, to add humor to your writing:

  > The squawking gulls can be heard around the world.

HOW TO IMPROVE YOUR SENTENCES

1 Combine Sentences Try to combine a lot of short sentences into one longer sentence.

Just OK
> I put on my snowboard.
> I sped down the hill.
> I reached the bottom.

Much Better
> I put on my snowboard and sped down the hill until I reached the bottom.

> I put on my snowboard, sped down the hill, and reached the bottom.

2 Break Up Sentences Long sentences can be hard to understand. Break up run-on sentences to make your meaning clear.

Just OK
> The first time I went snowboarding, I fell a lot, but I watched other snowboarders and I saw that most of them fell, too, then I didn't feel so bad.

Much Better
> The first time I went snowboarding, I fell a lot. I watched other snowboarders and saw that most of them fell, too. Then I didn't feel so bad.

page 395

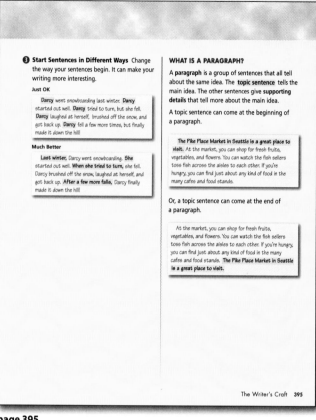

3 Start Sentences in Different Ways Change the way your sentences begin. It can make your writing more interesting.

Just OK
> Darcy went snowboarding last winter. Darcy started out well. Darcy tried to turn, but she fell. Darcy laughed at herself, brushed off the snow, and got back up. Darcy fell a few more times, but finally made it down the hill!

Much Better
> Last winter, Darcy went snowboarding. She started out well. When she tried to turn, she fell. Darcy brushed off the snow, laughed at herself, and got back up. After a few more falls, Darcy finally made it down the hill!

WHAT IS A PARAGRAPH?

A **paragraph** is a group of sentences that all tell about the same idea. The **topic sentence** tells the main idea. The other sentences give **supporting details** that tell more about the main idea.

A topic sentence can come at the beginning of a paragraph.

> **The Pike Place Market in Seattle is a great place to visit.** At the market, you can shop for fresh fruits, vegetables, and flowers. You can watch the fish sellers toss fish across the aisles to each other. If you're hungry, you can find just about any kind of food in the many cafes and food stands.

Or, a topic sentence can come at the end of a paragraph.

> At the market, you can shop for fresh fruits, vegetables, and flowers. You can watch the fish sellers toss fish across the aisles to each other. If you're hungry, you can find just about any kind of food in the many cafes and food stands. **The Pike Place Market in Seattle is a great place to visit.**

page 396

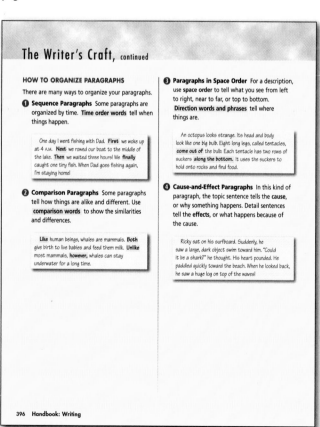

The Writer's Craft, continued

HOW TO ORGANIZE PARAGRAPHS

There are many ways to organize your paragraphs.

1 Sequence Paragraphs Some paragraphs are organized by time. **Time order words** tell when things happen.

> One day I went fishing with Dad. **First** we woke up at 4 A.M. **Next** we rowed our boat to the middle of the lake. **Then** we waited three hours! We **finally** caught one tiny fish. When Dad goes fishing again, I'm staying home!

2 Comparison Paragraphs Some paragraphs tell how things are alike and different. Use **comparison words** to show the similarities and differences.

> **Like** human beings, whales are mammals. **Both** give birth to live babies and feed them milk. **Unlike** most mammals, **however**, whales can stay underwater for a long time.

3 Paragraphs in Space Order For a description, use **space order** to tell what you see from left to right, near to far, or top to bottom. **Direction words and phrases** tell where things are.

> An octopus looks strange. Its head and body look like one big bulb. Eight long legs, called tentacles, **come out of** the bulb. Each tentacle has two rows of suckers **along the bottom**. It uses the suckers to hold onto rocks and find food.

4 Cause-and-Effect Paragraphs In this kind of paragraph, the topic sentence tells the **cause**, or why something happens. Detail sentences tell the **effects**, or what happens because of the cause.

> Ricky sat on his surfboard. Suddenly, he saw a large, dark object swim toward him. "Could it be a shark?" he thought. His heart pounded. He paddled quickly toward the beach. When he looked back, he saw a huge log on top of the waves!

page 397

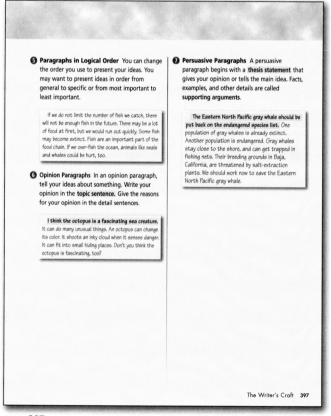

5 Paragraphs in Logical Order You can change the order you use to present your ideas. You may want to present ideas in order from general to specific or from most important to least important.

> If we do not limit the number of fish we catch, there will not be enough fish in the future. There may be a lot of food at first, but we would run out quickly. Some fish may become extinct. Fish are an important part of the food chain. If we over-fish the ocean, animals like seals and whales could be hurt, too.

6 Opinion Paragraphs In an opinion paragraph, tell your ideas about something. Write your opinion in the **topic sentence**. Give the reasons for your opinion in the detail sentences.

> **I think the octopus is a fascinating sea creature.** It can do many unusual things. An octopus can change its color. It shoots an inky cloud when it senses danger. It can fit into small hiding places. Don't you think the octopus is fascinating, too?

7 Persuasive Paragraphs A persuasive paragraph begins with a **thesis statement** that gives your opinion or tells the main idea. Facts, examples, and other details are called **supporting arguments**.

> **The Eastern North Pacific gray whale should be put back on the endangered species list.** One population of gray whales is already extinct. Another population is endangered. Gray whales stay close to the shore, and can get trapped in fishing nets. Their breeding grounds in Baja, California, are threatened by salt-extraction plants. We should work now to save the Eastern North Pacific gray whale.

Handbook: Writing

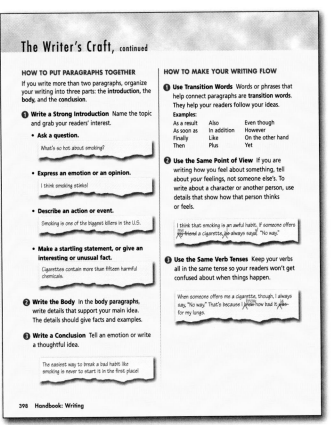

page 398

The Writer's Craft, continued

HOW TO PUT PARAGRAPHS TOGETHER

If you write more than two paragraphs, organize your writing into three parts: the **introduction**, the **body**, and the **conclusion**.

1 Write a Strong Introduction Name the topic and grab your readers' interest.

- **Ask a question.**

  What's so hot about smoking?

- **Express an emotion or an opinion.**

  I think smoking stinks!

- **Describe an action or event.**

  Smoking is one of the biggest killers in the U.S.

- **Make a startling statement, or give an interesting or unusual fact.**

  Cigarettes contain more than fifteen harmful chemicals.

2 Write the Body In the body paragraphs, write details that support your main idea. The details should give facts and examples.

3 Write a Conclusion Tell an emotion or write a thoughtful idea.

  The easiest way to break a bad habit like smoking is never to start it in the first place!

HOW TO MAKE YOUR WRITING FLOW

1 Use Transition Words Words or phrases that help connect paragraphs are transition words. They help your readers follow your ideas.

Examples:

As a result	Also	Even though
As soon as	In addition	However
Finally	Like	On the other hand
Then	Plus	Yet

2 Use the Same Point of View If you are writing how you feel about something, tell about *your* feelings, not someone else's. To write about a character or another person, use details that show how that person thinks or feels.

  I think that smoking is an awful habit. If someone offers
  my friend a cigarette, he always says, "No way."

3 Use the Same Verb Tenses Keep your verbs all in the same tense so your readers won't get confused about when things happen.

  When someone offers me a cigarette, though, I always
  say, "No way." That's because I know how bad it was
  for my lungs.

398 Handbook: Writing

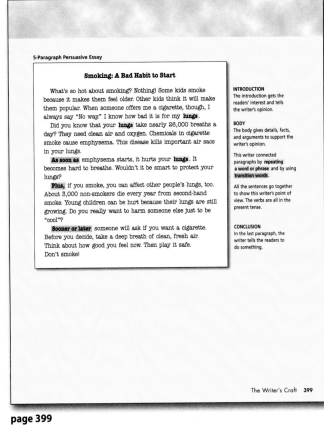

page 399

5-Paragraph Persuasive Essay

Smoking: A Bad Habit to Start

What's so hot about smoking? Nothing! Some kids smoke because it makes them feel older. Other kids think it will make them popular. When someone offers me a cigarette, though, I always say "No way." I know how bad it is for my **lungs**.

Did you know that your **lungs** take nearly 26,000 breaths a day? They need clean air and oxygen. Chemicals in cigarette smoke cause emphysema. This disease kills important air sacs in your lungs.

As soon as emphysema starts, it hurts your **lungs**. It becomes hard to breathe. Wouldn't it be smart to protect your lungs?

Plus, if you smoke, you can affect other people's lungs, too. About 3,000 non-smokers die every year from second-hand smoke. Young children can be hurt because their lungs are still growing. Do you really want to harm someone else just to be "cool"?

Sooner or later someone will ask if you want a cigarette. Before you decide, take a deep breath of clean, fresh air. Think about how good you feel now. Then play it safe. Don't smoke!

INTRODUCTION
The introduction gets the readers' interest and tells the writer's opinion.

BODY
The body gives details, facts, and arguments to support the writer's opinion.

This writer connected paragraphs by **repeating a word or phrase** and by using **transition words**.

All the sentences go together to show this writer's point of view. The verbs are all in the present tense.

CONCLUSION
In the last paragraph, the writer tells the readers to do something.

The Writer's Craft 399

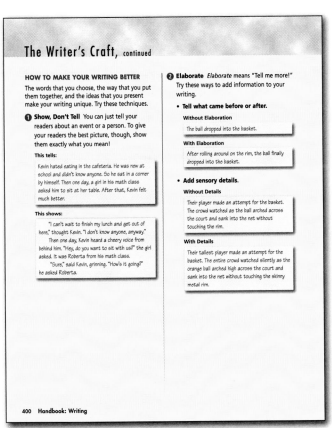

page 400

The Writer's Craft, continued

HOW TO MAKE YOUR WRITING BETTER

The words that you choose, the way that you put them together, and the ideas that you present make your writing unique. Try these techniques.

1 Show, Don't Tell You can just tell your readers about an event or a person. To give your readers the best picture, though, show them exactly what you mean!

This tells:

  Kevin hated eating in the cafeteria. He was new at school and didn't know anyone. So he sat in a corner by himself. Then one day, a girl in his math class asked him to sit at her table. After that, Kevin felt much better.

This shows:

  "I can't wait to finish my lunch and get out of here," thought Kevin. "I don't know anyone, anyway."
  Then one day, Kevin heard a cheery voice from behind him. "Hey, do you want to sit with us?" the girl asked. It was Roberta from his math class.
  "Sure," said Kevin, grinning. "How's it going?" he asked Roberta.

2 Elaborate *Elaborate* means "Tell me more!" Try these ways to add information to your writing.

- **Tell what came before or after.**

  Without Elaboration

  The ball dropped into the basket.

  With Elaboration

  After rolling around on the rim, the ball finally dropped into the basket.

- **Add sensory details.**

  Without Details

  Their player made an attempt for the basket. The crowd watched as the ball arched across the court and sank into the net without touching the rim.

  With Details

  Their tallest player made an attempt for the basket. The entire crowd watched silently as the orange ball arched high across the court and sank into the net without touching the skinny metal rim.

400 Handbook: Writing

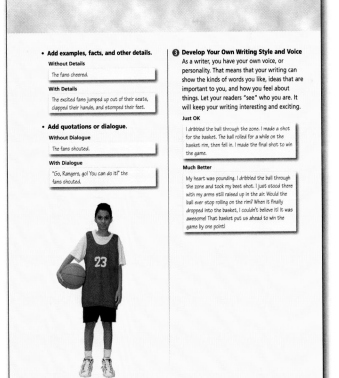

page 401

- **Add examples, facts, and other details.**

  Without Details

  The fans cheered.

  With Details

  The excited fans jumped up out of their seats, clapped their hands, and stomped their feet.

- **Add quotations or dialogue.**

  Without Dialogue

  The fans shouted.

  With Dialogue

  "Go, Rangers, go! You can do it!" the fans shouted.

3 Develop Your Own Writing Style and Voice As a writer, you have your own voice, or personality. That means that your writing can show the kinds of words you like, ideas that are important to you, and how you feel about things. Let your readers "see" who you are. It will keep your writing interesting and exciting.

Just OK

  I dribbled the ball through the zone. I made a shot for the basket. The ball rolled for a while on the basket rim, then fell in. I made the final shot to win the game.

Much Better

  My heart was pounding. I dribbled the ball through the zone and took my best shot. I just stood there with my arms still raised up in the air. Would the ball ever stop rolling on the rim? When it finally dropped into the basket, I couldn't believe it! It was awesome! That basket put us ahead to win the game by one point!

The Writer's Craft 401

Handbook: Grammar, Usage, Mechanics, Spelling

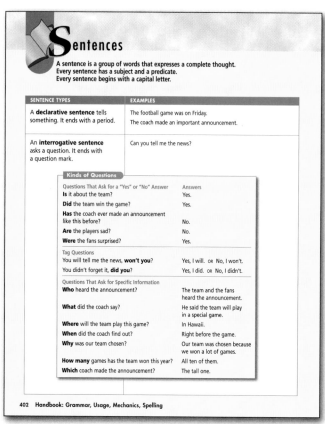

page 402

Sentences

A sentence is a group of words that expresses a complete thought.
Every sentence has a subject and a predicate.
Every sentence begins with a capital letter.

SENTENCE TYPES	EXAMPLES
A **declarative sentence** tells something. It ends with a period.	The football game was on Friday. The coach made an important announcement.
An **interrogative sentence** asks a question. It ends with a question mark.	Can you tell me the news?

Kinds of Questions

Questions That Ask for a "Yes" or "No" Answer	Answers
Is it about the team?	Yes.
Did the team win the game?	Yes.
Has the coach ever made an announcement like this before?	No.
Are the players sad?	No.
Were the fans surprised?	Yes.

Tag Questions	
You will tell me the news, **won't you**?	Yes, I will. OR No, I won't.
You didn't forget it, **did you**?	Yes, I did. OR No, I didn't.

Questions That Ask for Specific Information	
Who heard the announcement?	The team and the fans heard the announcement.
What did the coach say?	He said the team will play in a special game.
Where will the team play this game?	In Hawaii.
When did the coach find out?	Right before the game.
Why was our team chosen?	Our team was chosen because we won a lot of games.
How many games has the team won this year?	All ten of them.
Which coach made the announcement?	The tall one.

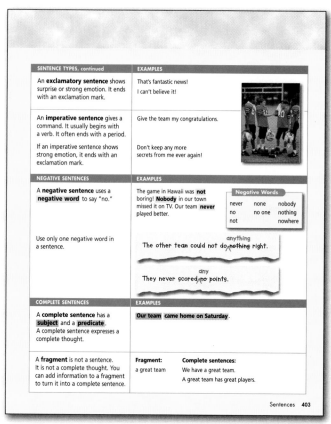

page 403

SENTENCE TYPES, continued	EXAMPLES
An **exclamatory sentence** shows surprise or strong emotion. It ends with an exclamation mark.	That's fantastic news! I can't believe it!
An **imperative sentence** gives a command. It usually begins with a verb. It often ends with a period. If an imperative sentence shows strong emotion, it ends with an exclamation mark.	Give the team my congratulations. Don't keep any more secrets from me ever again!

NEGATIVE SENTENCES	EXAMPLES
A **negative sentence** uses a **negative word** to say "no."	The game in Hawaii was **not** boring! **Nobody** in our town missed it on TV. Our team **never** played better.

Negative Words		
never	none	nobody
no	no one	nothing
not		nowhere

Use only one negative word in a sentence.

The other team could not do ~~nothing~~ anything right.

They never scored ~~no~~ any points.

COMPLETE SENTENCES	EXAMPLES
A **complete sentence** has a **subject** and a **predicate**. A complete sentence expresses a complete thought.	Our team came home on Saturday.
A **fragment** is not a sentence. It is not a complete thought. You can add information to a fragment to turn it into a complete sentence.	**Fragment:** a great team **Complete sentences:** We have a great team. A great team has great players.

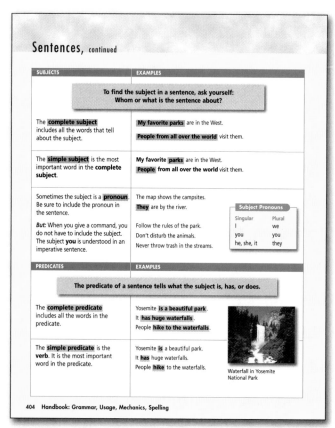

page 404

Sentences, continued

SUBJECTS	EXAMPLES
To find the subject in a sentence, ask yourself: **Whom or what is the sentence about?**	
The **complete subject** includes all the words that tell about the subject.	**My favorite parks** are in the West. **People from all over the world** visit them.
The **simple subject** is the most important word in the **complete subject**.	My favorite **parks** are in the West. **People** from all over the world visit them.
Sometimes the subject is a **pronoun**. Be sure to include the pronoun in the sentence. *But:* When you give a command, you do not have to include the subject. The subject **you** is understood in an imperative sentence.	The map shows the campsites. **They** are by the river. Follow the rules of the park. Don't disturb the animals. Never throw trash in the streams.

Subject Pronouns	
Singular	Plural
I	we
you	you
he, she, it	they

PREDICATES	EXAMPLES
The predicate of a sentence tells what the subject is, has, or does.	
The **complete predicate** includes all the words in the predicate.	Yosemite **is a beautiful park**. It **has huge waterfalls**. People **hike to the waterfalls**.
The **simple predicate** is the **verb**. It is the most important word in the predicate.	Yosemite **is** a beautiful park. It **has** huge waterfalls. People **hike** to the waterfalls.

Waterfall in Yosemite National Park

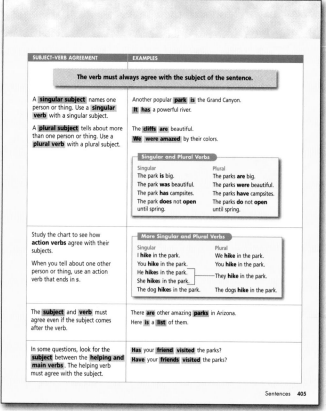

page 405

SUBJECT–VERB AGREEMENT	EXAMPLES
The verb must always agree with the subject of the sentence.	
A **singular subject** names one person or thing. Use a **singular verb** with a singular subject. A **plural subject** tells about more than one person or thing. Use a **plural verb** with a plural subject.	Another popular **park is** the Grand Canyon. **It has** a powerful river. The **cliffs are** beautiful. **We were** amazed by their colors.

Singular and Plural Verbs	
Singular	Plural
The park **is** big.	The parks **are** big.
The park **was** beautiful.	The parks **were** beautiful.
The park **has** campsites.	The parks **have** campsites.
The park **does** not **open** until spring.	The parks **do** not **open** until spring.

Study the chart to see how **action verbs** agree with their subjects. When you tell about one other person or thing, use an action verb that ends in s.	

More Singular and Plural Verbs	
Singular	Plural
I **hike** in the park.	We **hike** in the park.
You **hike** in the park.	You **hike** in the park.
He **hikes** in the park.	
She **hikes** in the park.	They **hike** in the park.
The dog **hikes** in the park.	The dogs **hike** in the park.

The **subject** and **verb** must agree even if the subject comes after the verb.	There **are** other amazing **parks** in Arizona. Here **is** a **list** of them.
In some questions, look for the **subject** between the **helping and main verbs**. The helping verb must agree with the subject.	**Has** your **friend visited** the parks? **Have** your **friends visited** the parks?

Handbook: Grammar, Usage, Mechanics, Spelling

page 406

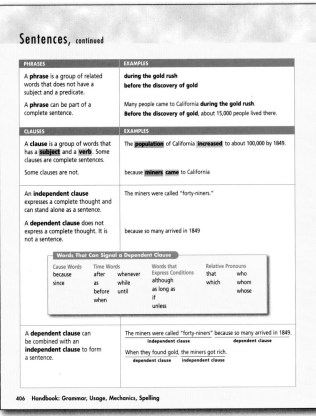

Sentences, continued

PHRASES	EXAMPLES
A **phrase** is a group of related words that does not have a subject and a predicate.	during the gold rush before the discovery of gold
A **phrase** can be part of a complete sentence.	Many people came to California **during the gold rush**. **Before the discovery of gold**, about 15,000 people lived there.

CLAUSES	EXAMPLES
A **clause** is a group of words that has a **subject** and a **verb**. Some clauses are complete sentences. Some clauses are not.	The **population** of California **increased** to about 100,000 by 1849. because **miners** **came** to California
An **independent clause** expresses a complete thought and can stand alone as a sentence.	The miners were called "forty-niners."
A **dependent clause** does not express a complete thought. It is not a sentence.	because so many arrived in 1849

Words That Can Signal a Dependent Clause

Cause Words	Time Words		Words that Express Conditions	Relative Pronouns	
because	after	whenever	although	that	who
since	as	while	as long as	which	whom
	before	until	if		whose
	when		unless		

	EXAMPLES
A **dependent clause** can be combined with an **independent clause** to form a sentence.	The miners were called "forty-niners" because so many arrived in 1849. *independent clause* *dependent clause* When they found gold, the miners got rich. *dependent clause* *independent clause*

406 Handbook: Grammar, Usage, Mechanics, Spelling

page 407

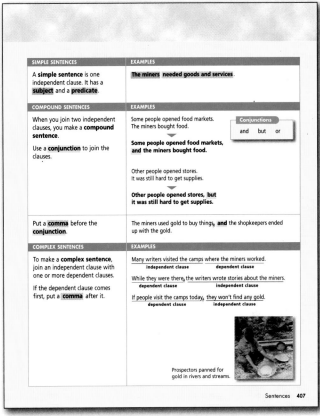

SIMPLE SENTENCES	EXAMPLES
A **simple sentence** is one independent clause. It has a **subject** and a **predicate**.	The miners needed goods and services.

COMPOUND SENTENCES	EXAMPLES
When you join two independent clauses, you make a **compound sentence**. Use a **conjunction** to join the clauses.	Some people opened food markets. The miners bought food. **Conjunctions** and but or **Some people opened food markets, and the miners bought food.** Other people opened stores. It was still hard to get supplies. **Other people opened stores, but it was still hard to get supplies.**
Put a **comma** before the **conjunction**.	The miners used gold to buy things, **and** the shopkeepers ended up with the gold.

COMPLEX SENTENCES	EXAMPLES
To make a **complex sentence**, join an independent clause with one or more dependent clauses. If the dependent clause comes first, put a **comma** after it.	Many writers visited the camps where the miners worked. *independent clause* *dependent clause* While they were there, the writers wrote stories about the miners. *dependent clause* *independent clause* If people visit the camps today, they won't find any gold. *dependent clause* *independent clause*

Prospectors panned for gold in rivers and streams.

Sentences 407

page 408

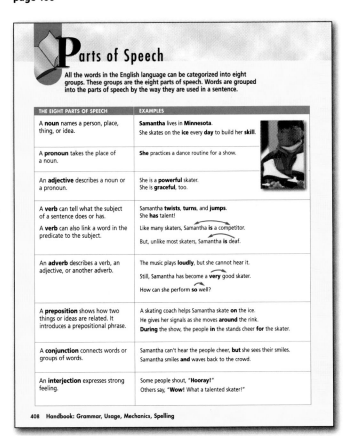

Parts of Speech

All the words in the English language can be categorized into eight groups. These groups are the eight parts of speech. Words are grouped into the parts of speech by the way they are used in a sentence.

THE EIGHT PARTS OF SPEECH	EXAMPLES
A **noun** names a person, place, thing, or idea.	**Samantha** lives in **Minnesota**. She skates on the **ice** every **day** to build her **skill**.
A **pronoun** takes the place of a noun.	**She** practices a dance routine for a show.
An **adjective** describes a noun or a pronoun.	She is a **powerful** skater. She is **graceful**, too.
A **verb** can tell what the subject of a sentence does or has. A **verb** can also link a word in the predicate to the subject.	Samantha **twists**, **turns**, and **jumps**. She **has** talent! Like many skaters, Samantha **is** a competitor. But, unlike most skaters, Samantha **is** deaf.
An **adverb** describes a verb, an adjective, or another adverb.	The music plays **loudly**, but she cannot hear it. Still, Samantha has become a **very** good skater. How can she perform **so** well?
A **preposition** shows how two things or ideas are related. It introduces a prepositional phrase.	A skating coach helps Samantha skate **on** the ice. He gives her signals as she moves **around** the rink. **During** the show, the people **in** the stands cheer **for** the skater.
A **conjunction** connects words or groups of words.	Samantha can't hear the people cheer, **but** she sees their smiles. Samantha smiles **and** waves back to the crowd.
An **interjection** expresses strong feeling.	Some people shout, "**Hooray!**" Others say, "**Wow!** What a talented skater!"

408 Handbook: Grammar, Usage, Mechanics, Spelling

page 409

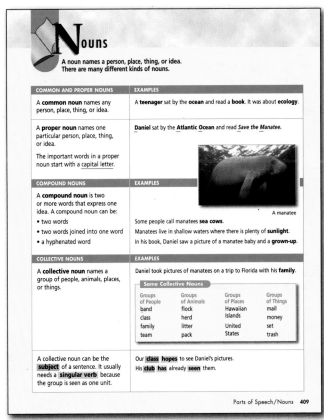

Nouns

A noun names a person, place, thing, or idea. There are many different kinds of nouns.

COMMON AND PROPER NOUNS	EXAMPLES
A **common noun** names any person, place, thing, or idea.	A **teenager** sat by the **ocean** and read a **book**. It was about **ecology**.
A **proper noun** names one particular person, place, thing, or idea. The important words in a proper noun start with a capital letter.	**Daniel** sat by the **Atlantic Ocean** and read *Save the Manatee*.

COMPOUND NOUNS	EXAMPLES
A **compound noun** is two or more words that express one idea. A compound noun can be: • two words • two words joined into one word • a hyphenated word	Some people call manatees **sea cows**. Manatees live in shallow waters where there is plenty of **sunlight**. In his book, Daniel saw a picture of a manatee baby and a **grown-up**.

A manatee

COLLECTIVE NOUNS	EXAMPLES
A **collective noun** names a group of people, animals, places, or things.	Daniel took pictures of manatees on a trip to Florida with his **family**.

Some Collective Nouns

Groups of People	Groups of Animals	Groups of Places	Groups of Things
band	flock	Hawaiian Islands	mail
class	herd		money
family	litter	United States	set
team	pack		trash

	EXAMPLES
A collective noun can be the **subject** of a sentence. It usually needs a **singular verb** because the group is seen as one unit.	Our **class** **hopes** to see Daniel's pictures. His **club** **has** already **seen** them.

Parts of Speech/Nouns 409

Handbook: Grammar, Usage, Mechanics, Spelling

page 410

Nouns, continued

SINGULAR AND PLURAL NOUNS	EXAMPLES

The singular form of a count noun names one thing. The plural form names more than one thing.

Count nouns are nouns that you can count. Follow these rules to make a count noun plural:

- Add **-s** to most count nouns.

desk	book	teacher	apple	line
desks	books	teachers	apples	lines

- If the noun ends in **x, ch, sh, s,** or **z,** add **-es.**

box	lunch	dish	glass	waltz
boxes	lunches	dishes	glasses	waltzes

- For nouns that end in a consonant plus **y,** change the **y** to **i** and add **-es.**

story	sky	city	penny	army
stories	skies	cities	pennies	armies

- For nouns that end in a vowel plus **y,** just add **-s.**

boy	toy	day	monkey	valley
boys	toys	days	monkeys	valleys

- For most nouns that end in **f** or **fe,** change the **f** to **v** and add **-es.** For some nouns that end in **f,** just add **-s.**

leaf	knife	half	roof	chief
leaves	knives	halves	roofs	chiefs

- If the noun ends in a vowel plus **o,** add **-s.** For some nouns that end in a consonant plus **o,** add **-s.** For others, add **-es.**

radio	kangaroo	banjo	potato	tomato
radios	kangaroos	banjos	potatoes	tomatoes

- A few count nouns have irregular plural forms.

child	foot	person	man	woman
children	feet	people	men	women

- For a few count nouns, the singular and plural forms are the same.

deer	fish	salmon	sheep	trout
deer	fish	salmon	sheep	trout

410 Handbook: Grammar, Usage, Mechanics, Spelling

page 411

Nouns, continued

SINGULAR AND PLURAL NOUNS	EXAMPLES
Noncount nouns are nouns that you cannot count. A noncount noun does not have a plural form.	My favorite museum has **furniture** and **art.** Sometimes I wonder how much **money** each item is worth.

Types of Noncount Nouns

Activities and Sports

				Examples
baseball	camping	dancing	fishing	I love to play **soccer.**
golf	singing	soccer	swimming	

Category Nouns

clothing	equipment	furniture	hardware	jewelry	My **equipment** is in the car.
machinery	mail	money	time	weather	

Food

bread	cereal	cheese	corn	flour	I'll drink some **water** on my way
lettuce	meat	milk	rice	salt	to the game.
soup	sugar	tea	water		

You can count some food items by using a measurement word like **cup, slice, glass,** or **head** plus the word **of.** To show the plural form, just make the measurement word plural.

I'll drink **two glasses of water** on my way to the game.

Ideas and Feelings

democracy	enthusiasm	freedom	fun	health	I'll also listen to the radio for
honesty	information	knowledge	luck	work	**information** about the weather.

Materials

air	fuel	gasoline	gold	The radio says the **air** is heavy.
metal	paper	water	wood	What does that mean?

Weather

fog	hail	heat	ice	lightning	Uh-oh! First came the **lightning**
rain	smog	snow	sunshine	thunder	and the **thunder.** I want **sunshine** for my next soccer game!

Some words have more than one meaning. Add **-s** for the plural only if the noun means something you can count.	Throw me those **baseballs.** I want to learn to play **baseball.**

Nouns 411

page 412

Nouns, continued

ARTICLES	EXAMPLES
An **article** is a word that helps identify a noun. An article often comes before a count noun.	After **the** game, we found **a** coat and **an** umbrella on **the** field.
Use **a** or **an** before **nouns** that are not specific. Use **the** before **nouns** that are specific.	**A boy** walked around the field. **The coach's son** walked around the field.
Use **a** before a word that starts with a consonant sound.	a **ball** a **gate** a **player** a **one-way street** (o is pronounced like w) a **cap** a **kick** a **net** a **uniform** (u is pronounced like y)
Use **an** before a word that starts with a vowel sound.	a e i o u silent h an **ant** an **elbow** an **inch** an **olive** an **umbrella** an **hour** an **apron** an **eel** an **idea** an **ocean** an **amount** an **election** an **owl** an **artist** an **orange**
Do not use **a** or **an** before a noncount noun.	The soccer ball was made of ~~a~~ leather.
Do not use **the** before the name of: • a city or state • most countries • a language • a day, a month, or most holidays • a sport or activity • most businesses • a person.	Our next game will be in **Dallas.** Games in **Texas** are always exciting. We will play a team from **Mexico.** People will be cheering in **Spanish** and **English.** The game will take place on **Monday.** Is that in **February**? Yes, on **President's Day.** That will be a good day to play **soccer.** The fans will have hot dogs to eat from **Sal's Market.** You may even see **Sal** himself.

412 Handbook: Grammar, Usage, Mechanics, Spelling

page 413

POSSESSIVE NOUNS	EXAMPLES
A **possessive noun** is the name of an owner. All possessive nouns include an **apostrophe.**	Several bands performed in our **town's** parade. Everyone liked the **musicians'** costumes.
Follow these rules to make a noun possessive: • If there is one owner, add **'s** to the owner's name.	Some kids played the trumpet. One **boy's** trumpet was very loud. **Marsha's** baton went high in the air.
But: If the owner's name ends in **s,** you can add **'s** or just the apostrophe. Either is correct.	**Louis's** hat fell off. **Louis'** hat fell off.
• A noun that names two or more owners is plural and often ends in **s.** If so, just add **'.**	The **girls'** section sang loud songs. I could barely hear my **brothers'** tubas.
But: If the plural noun that names the owners does not end in **s,** add **'s.**	The **men's** cooking club marched with the band. The **children's** band rode on tricycles.

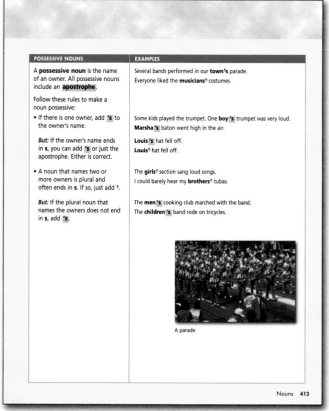

A parade

Nouns 413

Handbook: Grammar, Usage, Mechanics, Spelling

page 414

Pronouns

A pronoun takes the place of a noun or refers to a noun.

PRONOUN AGREEMENT	EXAMPLES
Use a **pronoun** to tell about the right person or thing.	
• For yourself, use **I** and **me**.	**I** want to find out about careers. What career will be good for **me**?
• When you speak to another person, use **you**.	What career are **you** interested in?
• For a boy or man, use **he** or **him**.	Scott likes art. **He** wants to be a photographer. It will be a good career for **him**.
• For a girl or woman, use **she** or **her**.	Janet likes animals. **She** wants to be a veterinarian. That career will give **her** a chance to take care of animals.
• For a thing, use **it**.	What about music? Is **it** a good career?

Use a **pronoun** to tell about the right number of people or things. **Singular pronouns** refer to one person. **Plural pronouns** refer to more than one person. Here are some examples:	**Some Singular and Plural Pronouns** Singular Pronouns: I, me, my, mine; you, your, yours; he, him, his; she, her, hers; it, its — Plural Pronouns: we, us, our, ours; you, your, yours; they, them, their, theirs
• These pronouns tell about one person or thing.	**I** am thinking about lots of careers. Ted says **he** is, too.
• This pronoun is used to speak to one or more than one person.	Are **you** set on a career?
• Use these pronouns to speak about yourself and another person.	Ted and I are doing interviews on careers. **We** talked to **our** friends. They talked to **us**.
• These pronouns are used to speak about other people or things.	**They** told us about careers in the computer industry. We told **them** about careers in health care.

414 Handbook: Grammar, Usage, Mechanics, Spelling

page 415

SUBJECT PRONOUNS	EXAMPLES
Use a **subject pronoun** as the **subject** of a sentence.	Janet likes animals. **She** works at a pet shop. **Subject Pronouns** — Singular: I, you, he, she, it — Plural: we, you, they
The pronoun **it** can be used as a **subject** to refer to a noun.	Janet lives near the **shop**. **It** is on First Street.
But: The pronoun **it** can be the **subject** without referring to a specific noun.	**It** is interesting to work in the shop. **It** is fun to play with the animals. **It** is important to take care of them, too.

REFLEXIVE PRONOUNS	EXAMPLES
Sometimes you talk about a person twice in a sentence. Use a **reflexive pronoun** to refer to the **subject**.	Janet taught **herself** about the life cycle of parrots. The shop **owners themselves** learned some things from Janet. **Subject and Reflexive Pronouns** — Singular: I myself, you yourself, he himself, she herself, it itself — Plural: we ourselves, you yourselves, they themselves

OBJECT PRONOUNS	EXAMPLES
You can use an **object pronoun** after an **action verb**. You can also use an **object pronoun** after a **preposition**.	The parrots get hungry at 5 o'clock. Janet **feeds them** every day. The parrots squawk **at her** to say "thank you." **Object Pronouns** — Singular: me, you, him, her, it — Plural: us, you, them

Pronouns 415

page 416

Pronouns, continued

POSSESSIVE PRONOUNS	EXAMPLES
A **possessive pronoun** tells who or what owns something. A **possessive pronoun** can refer to the name of an owner. It is sometimes called a **possessive adjective**. A **possessive pronoun** can take the place of a **person's name and what the person owns**.	**Janet's** posters are about pet care. **Her** posters show what dogs need. Which one is **Janet's poster**? The big one is **hers**. **Possessive Pronouns** Use these pronouns to refer to the name of an owner. These pronouns always come before a noun and act as adjectives. Singular: my, your, his, her, its — Plural: our, your, their. Use these pronouns to replace a person's name and what the person owns. These pronouns are always used alone. Singular: mine, yours, his, hers, its — Plural: ours, yours, theirs

DEMONSTRATIVE PRONOUNS	EXAMPLES
A **demonstrative pronoun** points out a specific noun without naming it.	Look at the puppies. **That** is a cute puppy. **Those** are sleeping. **Demonstrative Pronouns** — Nearby: this (Singular), these (Plural) — Far Away: that (Singular), those (Plural)

INDEFINITE PRONOUNS	EXAMPLES
When you are not talking about a specific person or thing, use an **indefinite pronoun**.	**Everybody** loves to visit the pet shop. **Something** is happening in the pet shop today. **Several** of the puppies are getting a bath! **Some Indefinite Pronouns** — Singular: each, everybody, everyone, everything, no one, nothing, someone, something — Plural: both, few, many, several

416 Handbook: Grammar, Usage, Mechanics, Spelling

page 417

Adjectives

An adjective describes or modifies a noun or pronoun. It can tell what kind, which one, how many, or how much.

DESCRIPTIVE ADJECTIVES	EXAMPLES
An **adjective** can tell what something is like. It can tell the color, size, or shape. It can describe a feeling.	Where can you find **brown** rabbits and **white** egrets? A swamp has **large** and **small** animals like these. The egret has **round** eyes and a **pointed** beak. I feel **happy** when I spend a day in the swamp.
An adjective can tell how something sounds, feels, looks, tastes, or smells. 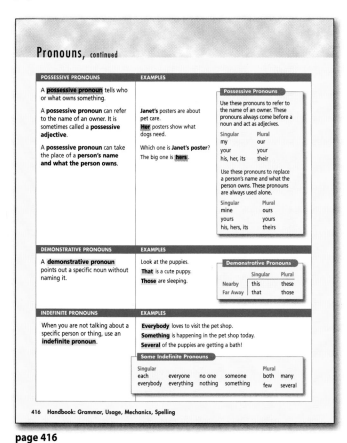 An egret	I like the **noisy** birds. The egrets are **beautiful**.

Adjectives That Appeal to the Senses

Hearing	Touch	Sight	Taste	Smell
crunchy	hard	beautiful	bitter	fishy
noisy	rough	dark	salty	fragrant
quiet	smooth	huge	sour	fresh
soft	wet	shiny	sweet	rotten

Usually, an **adjective** comes before the noun it describes.	An **old alligator** hides in the **dark mud**.
But: A **predicate adjective** appears in the predicate and still describes the noun or pronoun in the **subject**.	The **alligator** is **powerful**. 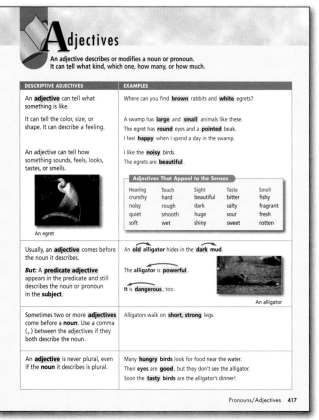 **It** is **dangerous**, too. An alligator
Sometimes two or more **adjectives** come before a **noun**. Use a comma (**,**) between the adjectives if they both describe the noun.	Alligators walk on **short**, **strong** legs.
An **adjective** is never plural, even if the **noun** it describes is plural.	Many **hungry birds** look for food near the water. Their **eyes** are **good**, but they don't see the alligator. Soon the **tasty birds** are the alligator's dinner!

Pronouns/Adjectives 417

Handbook: Grammar, Usage, Mechanics, Spelling

page 418

Adjectives, continued

DEMONSTRATIVE ADJECTIVES	EXAMPLES
A **demonstrative adjective** points out the noun that follows it. It answers the question "Which one?"	**These** otters are by my boat. **That** otter over there belongs to one of them. **Demonstrative Adjectives** 		Singular	Plural	 Nearby	this	these Far Away	that	those

NUMBER WORDS	EXAMPLES
Number words are often used as **adjectives**.	Today in the swamp I saw **one** snake, **two** alligators, and **six** turtles.
Sometimes the number word tells the **order** that things are in.	The **first** day I saw many kinds of birds. The **second** day I saw a lot of alligators. What will I see on the **third** day?

INDEFINITE ADJECTIVES	EXAMPLES
Use an **indefinite adjective** when you are not sure of the exact number.	I didn't see **much** wildlife on the third day. All I saw were a **few** frogs.
Some indefinite adjectives tell **how many** things there are. Use these adjectives before nouns you can count. Some indefinite adjectives tell **how much** there is of something. Use these adjectives before nouns you cannot count.	**Some Indefinite Adjectives** To Tell How Many: **many** insects, **a few** insects, **some** insects, **several** insects, **no** insects To Tell How Much: **much** sunshine, **a little** sunshine, **some** sunshine, **not much** sunshine, **no** sunshine
In a negative sentence, use **any** instead of **some**.	I saw some turtles, too. However, I didn't see ~~some~~ any insects.

PROPER ADJECTIVES	EXAMPLES
A **proper adjective** is formed from a proper noun. It always begins with a **capital letter**.	There are many swamps in America. The **American** alligator is found in the southeastern United States.

418 Handbook: Grammar, Usage, Mechanics, Spelling

page 419

ADJECTIVES THAT COMPARE	EXAMPLES
Adjectives can help you show how things are alike or different.	
Use a **comparative adjective** to show how **two** things are alike or different. Add **-er** to most adjectives. Also use **than**. Use **more. . .than** if the adjective has three or more syllables.	Deserts may be small or large. The Sechura Desert in South America is **smaller than** the Sahara Desert in Africa. *Sahara Desert* Is the Sechura Desert **more interesting than** the Sahara Desert?
You can use either **-er** or **more** to make a comparison with some two-syllable adjectives. **Be sure not to use both.**	Most desert animals are ~~more~~ livelier at night than during the day. Desert flowers are ~~more~~ prettier than swamp grasses.
Use a **superlative adjective** to compare **three or more** things. Add **-est** to most adjectives. Use **the** before the adjective. Use **the most** with the adjective if it has three or more syllables.	The Sahara Desert is **the largest** desert in the world. The Libyan Desert has the world's **highest** record temperature. Both habitats have some of **the most interesting** animals in the world.
Some **adjectives** have **special forms** for comparing things: good bad some little better worse more less best worst most least	Today's weather in the desert is **bad**. Tomorrow's weather will be **worse**. Next week's weather is expected to be **the worst** of the summer.
Use **less** or **the least** to compare things you cannot count. Use **fewer** or **the fewest** to compare things you can count.	Deserts have **less** rainfall than swamps. Deserts have **the least** rainfall of any habitat. Some deserts have **fewer** days of rain than others. Which desert had **the fewest** number of visitors last year?

Adjectives 419

page 420

Verbs

Every sentence is divided into two parts: a subject and a predicate. The verb is the key word in the predicate. A verb tells what a subject does or links words in a sentence.

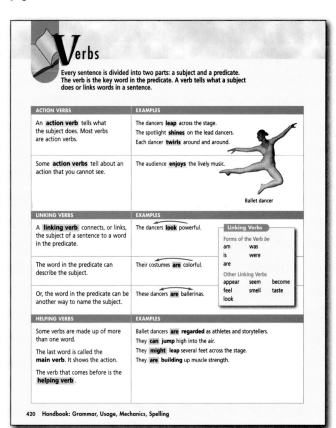

Ballet dancer

ACTION VERBS	EXAMPLES
An **action verb** tells what the subject does. Most verbs are action verbs.	The dancers **leap** across the stage. The spotlight **shines** on the lead dancers. Each dancer **twirls** around and around.
Some **action verbs** tell about an action that you cannot see.	The audience **enjoys** the lively music.

LINKING VERBS	EXAMPLES
A **linking verb** connects, or links, the subject of a sentence to a word in the predicate.	The dancers **look** powerful. **Linking Verbs** Forms of the Verb *be* am was is were are
The word in the predicate can describe the subject.	Their costumes **are** colorful.
Or, the word in the predicate can be another way to name the subject.	These dancers **are** ballerinas. Other Linking Verbs appear seem become feel smell taste look

HELPING VERBS	EXAMPLES
Some verbs are made up of more than one word. The last word is called the **main verb**. It shows the action. The verb that comes before is the **helping verb**.	Ballet dancers **are** regarded as athletes and storytellers. They **can** jump high into the air. They **might** leap several feet across the stage. They **are building** up muscle strength.

420 Handbook: Grammar, Usage, Mechanics, Spelling

page 421

HELPING VERBS, continued	EXAMPLES
The **helping verb** agrees with the subject.	The dancers **have practiced** for hours. The exercise **has made** them strong.
The word not always comes between the **helping verb** and the main verb.	The dancers **do** not **tell** a story in the usual way.
Other adverbs can come between a **helping verb** and the **main verb**, or appear in other places in the sentence.	They **will** never **use** their voices to tell a story. The story **is** always **told** through their graceful movements. Often slow movements **will show** an emotion like sadness. Happiness **is shown** best by quick, springy movements.
In questions, the subject comes between the **helping verb** and the **main verb**.	**Have** you **seen** a performance? **Does** your family **enjoy** ballet?

Helping Verbs

Forms of the Verb *be*		Other Helping Verbs
am	was	To express ability: I **can** dance. I **could** do the jump.
is	were	
are		To express possibility: I **may** dance tonight. I **might** dance tonight. Perhaps I **could** do the dance.
Forms of the Verb *do*		
do	did	To express a need or want: I **must** dance more often. I **would** like to dance more often.
does		
Forms of the Verb *have*		To express an intent: I **will** dance more often.
have	had	To express something you ought to do: I **should** practice more often. I **ought** to practice more often.
has		

Verbs 421

Handbook: Grammar, Usage, Mechanics, Spelling

page 422

Verbs, continued

PRESENT TENSE VERBS	EXAMPLES
The tense of a verb shows when an action happens.	
The **present tense** of a verb tells about an action that is happening now.	My mom **looks** at her charts. She **checks** her computer screen.
The **present tense** of a verb can also tell about an action that happens regularly or all the time.	My mom **works** for the local TV station. She **is** a weather forecaster. She **reports** the weather every night at 5 p.m.
The **present progressive** form of a verb tells about an action as it is happening. It uses the helping verb **am, is,** or **are** and a main verb. The main verb ends in **-ing**.	Right now, she **is getting** ready for the show. "I can't believe it!" she says. "I **am looking** at the biggest storm of the century!" "**Are** those high winds **travelling** toward the coast?" asks her boss.

PAST TENSE VERBS	EXAMPLES
The **past tense** of a verb tells about an action that happened earlier, or in the past.	Yesterday, my mom **warned** everyone about the hurricane. The storm **moved** over the ocean toward land. We **did** not **know** exactly when it would hit.
The past tense form of a **regular verb** ends with **-ed**. See page 439 for spelling rules.	The shop owners in our town **covered** their windows with wood. We **closed** our shutters and **stayed** inside.
Irregular verbs have special forms to show the past tense. See the chart on pages 424–425.	The storm **hit** land. The sky **grew** very dark. It **began** to rain.

Some Irregular Verbs

Present Tense	Past Tense
begin	began
do	did
grow	grew
hit	hit

page 423

Verbs

PAST TENSE VERBS, continued	EXAMPLES
The **past progressive** form of a verb tells about an action that was happening over a period of time in the past. It uses the helping verb **was** or **were** and a main verb. The main verb ends in **-ing**.	The wind **was blowing** at high speeds. Our shutters **were** really **shaking** during the storm. **Were** the trees **falling** down?

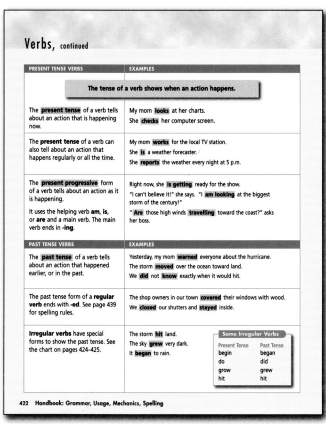

Wind damage from Hurricane Floyd, 1999

FUTURE TENSE VERBS	EXAMPLES
The **future tense** of a verb tells about an action that will happen later, or in the future. To show future tense, use one of the following:	
• the helping verb **will** plus a main verb	After the storm, everyone **will come** out of their houses. They **will inspect** the damage.
• the phrase am going to, is going to, or are going to plus a verb.	I **am going to take** the tree branches out of my yard. The city **is** not **going to clean** every street. We **are** all **going to help** each other.

PRESENT PERFECT TENSE VERBS	EXAMPLES
Use the **present perfect tense** of a verb when you want to tell about:	
• an action that happened in the past, but you are not sure of the exact time.	The people in our neighborhood **have helped** each other during other disasters.
• an action that began in the past and may still be going on.	Our neighborhood **has** even **received** awards for teamwork. The newspaper **has written** stories about our neighborhood for three days now.
To form the present perfect tense, use the helping verbs **has** or **have** and the **past participle** of the main verb.	

page 424

Verbs, continued

FORMS OF IRREGULAR VERBS

Irregular Verb	Past Tense	Past Participle	Irregular Verb	Past Tense	Past Participle
be: am, is	was	been	eat	ate	eaten
are	were	been	fall	fell	fallen
beat	beat	beaten	feed	fed	fed
become	became	become	feel	felt	felt
begin	began	begun	fight	fought	fought
bend	bent	bent	find	found	found
bind	bound	bound	fly	flew	flown
bite	bit	bitten	forget	forgot	forgotten
blow	blew	blown	freeze	froze	frozen
break	broke	broken	get	got	got, gotten
bring	brought	brought			
build	built	built	give	gave	given
burst	burst	burst	go	went	gone
buy	bought	bought	grow	grew	grown
catch	caught	caught	have	had	had
choose	chose	chosen	hear	heard	heard
come	came	come	hide	hid	hidden
cost	cost	cost	hit	hit	hit
creep	crept	crept	hold	held	held
cut	cut	cut	hurt	hurt	hurt
dig	dug	dug	keep	kept	kept
do	did	done	know	knew	known
draw	drew	drawn	lay	laid	laid
dream	dreamed, dreamt	dreamed, dreamt	lead	led	led
			leave	left	left
drink	drank	drunk	lend	lent	lent
drive	drove	driven	let	let	let

page 425

FORMS OF IRREGULAR VERBS, continued

Irregular Verb	Past Tense	Past Participle	Irregular Verb	Past Tense	Past Participle
lie	lay	lain	sink	sank	sunk
light	lit	lit	sit	sat	sat
lose	lost	lost	sleep	slept	slept
make	made	made	slide	slid	slid
mean	meant	meant	speak	spoke	spoken
meet	met	met	spend	spent	spent
pay	paid	paid	stand	stood	stood
prove	proved	proved, proven	steal	stole	stolen
			stick	stuck	stuck
put	put	put	sting	stung	stung
quit	quit	quit	strike	struck	struck
read	read	read	swear	swore	sworn
ride	rode	ridden	swim	swam	swum
ring	rang	rung	swing	swung	swung
rise	rose	risen	take	took	taken
run	ran	run	teach	taught	taught
say	said	said	tear	tore	torn
see	saw	seen	tell	told	told
seek	sought	sought	think	thought	thought
sell	sold	sold	throw	threw	thrown
send	sent	sent	understand	understood	understood
set	set	set	wake	woke, waked	woken, waked
shake	shook	shaken			
show	showed	shown	wear	wore	worn
shrink	shrank	shrunk	weep	wept	wept
shut	shut	shut	win	won	won
sing	sang	sung	write	wrote	written

Handbook: Grammar, Usage, Mechanics, Spelling

page 426

Verbs, continued

TWO-WORD VERBS	EXAMPLES
A **two-word verb** is a verb followed by a preposition. The meaning of the two-word verb is different from the meaning of the verb by itself.	I like to **call** you, but you never answer me. The coach **calls off** the game because of the rain. The workers **call for** higher pay.

Some Two-Word Verbs

Verb	Meaning	Example
break	to split into pieces	I didn't **break** the window with the ball.
break down	to stop working	Did the car **break down** again?
break up	to end	The party will **break up** before midnight.
	to come apart	The ice on the lake will **break up** in spring.
bring	to carry something with you	**Bring** your book to class.
bring up	to suggest	She **brings up** good ideas at every meeting.
	to raise children	**Bring up** your children to be good citizens.
check	to make sure you are right	We can **check** our answers at the back of the book.
check in	to stay in touch with someone	I **check in** with my mom at work.
check up	to see if everything is okay	The nurse **checks up** on the patient every hour.
check off	to mark off a list	Look at your list and **check off** the girls' names.
check out	to look at something carefully	Hey, Marisa, **check out** my new bike!
fill	to put as much as possible into a container or space.	**Fill** the pail with water.
fill in	to color or shade in a space	Please **fill in** the circle.
fill out	to complete	Marcos **fills out** a form to order a book.
get	to go after something	I'll **get** some milk at the store.
	to receive	I often **get** letters from my pen pal.
get ahead	to go beyond what is expected of you	She worked hard to **get ahead** in math class.
get along	to be on good terms with	Do you **get along** with your sister?
get out	to leave	Let's **get out** of the kitchen.
get over	to feel better	I hope you'll **get over** the flu soon.
get through	to finish	I can **get through** this book tonight.

426 Handbook: Grammar, Usage, Mechanics, Spelling

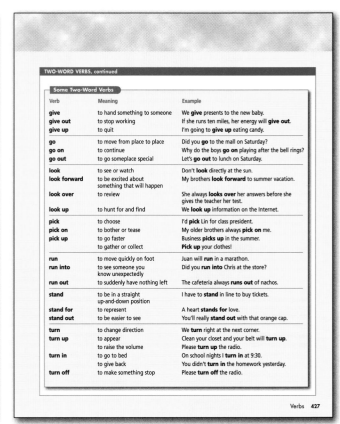

page 427

TWO-WORD VERBS, continued

Some Two-Word Verbs

Verb	Meaning	Example
give	to hand something to someone	We **give** presents to the new baby.
give out	to stop working	If she runs ten miles, her energy will **give out**.
give up	to quit	I'm going to **give up** eating candy.
go	to move from place to place	Did you **go** to the mall on Saturday?
go on	to continue	Why do the boys **go on** playing after the bell rings?
go out	to go someplace special	Let's **go out** to lunch on Saturday.
look	to see or watch	Don't **look** directly at the sun.
look forward	to be excited about something that will happen	My brothers **look forward** to summer vacation.
look over	to review	She always **looks over** her answers before she gives the teacher her test.
look up	to hunt for and find	We **look up** information on the Internet.
pick	to choose	I'd **pick** Lin for class president.
pick on	to bother or tease	My older brothers always **pick on** me.
pick up	to go faster	Business **picks up** in the summer.
	to gather or collect	**Pick up** your clothes!
run	to move quickly on foot	Juan will **run** in a marathon.
run into	to see someone you know unexpectedly	Did you **run into** Chris at the store?
run out	to suddenly have nothing left	The cafeteria always **runs out** of nachos.
stand	to be in a straight up-and-down position	I have to **stand** in line to buy tickets.
stand for	to represent	A heart **stands for** love.
stand out	to be easier to see	You'll really **stand out** with that orange cap.
turn	to change direction	We **turn** right at the next corner.
turn up	to appear	Clean your closet and your belt will **turn up**.
	to raise the volume	Please **turn up** the radio.
turn in	to go to bed	On school nights I **turn in** at 9:30.
	to give back	You didn't **turn in** the homework yesterday.
turn off	to make something stop	Please **turn off** the radio.

Verbs 427

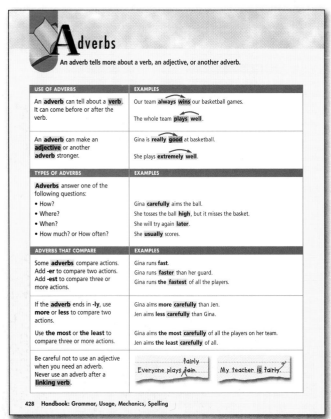

page 428

Adverbs
An adverb tells more about a verb, an adjective, or another adverb.

USE OF ADVERBS	EXAMPLES
An **adverb** can tell about a **verb**. It can come before or after the verb.	Our team **always wins** our basketball games. The whole team **plays well**.
An **adverb** can make an **adjective** or another **adverb** stronger.	Gina is **really good** at basketball. She plays **extremely well**.

TYPES OF ADVERBS	EXAMPLES
Adverbs answer one of the following questions: • How? • Where? • When? • How much? or How often?	Gina **carefully** aims the ball. She tosses the ball **high**, but it misses the basket. She will try again **later**. She **usually** scores.

ADVERBS THAT COMPARE	EXAMPLES
Some **adverbs** compare actions. Add **-er** to compare two actions. Add **-est** to compare three or more actions.	Gina runs **fast**. Gina runs **faster** than her guard. Gina runs the **fastest** of all the players.
If the **adverb** ends in **-ly**, use **more** or **less** to compare two actions. Use **the most** or **the least** to compare three or more actions.	Gina aims **more carefully** than Jen. Jen aims **less carefully** than Gina. Gina aims the **most carefully** of all the players on her team. Jen aims the **least carefully** of all.
Be careful not to use an adjective when you need an adverb. Never use an adverb after a **linking verb**.	Everyone plays fair. (fairly) / My teacher is fairly.

428 Handbook: Grammar, Usage, Mechanics, Spelling

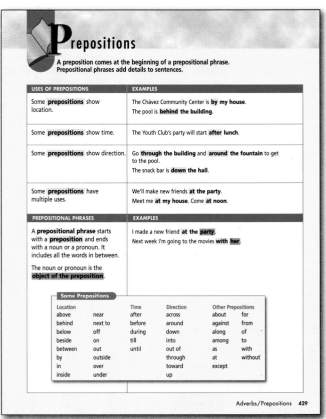

page 429

Prepositions
A preposition comes at the beginning of a prepositional phrase. Prepositional phrases add details to sentences.

USES OF PREPOSITIONS	EXAMPLES
Some **prepositions** show location.	The Chávez Community Center is **by** my house. The pool is **behind** the building.
Some **prepositions** show time.	The Youth Club's party will start **after** lunch.
Some **prepositions** show direction.	Go **through** the building and **around** the fountain to get to the pool. The snack bar is **down** the hall.
Some **prepositions** have multiple uses.	We'll make new friends **at** the party. Meet me **at** my house. Come **at** noon.

PREPOSITIONAL PHRASES	EXAMPLES
A **prepositional phrase** starts with a **preposition** and ends with a noun or a pronoun. It includes all the words in between. The noun or pronoun is the **object of the preposition**.	I made a new friend **at the party**. Next week I'm going to the movies **with her**.

Some Prepositions

Location		Time	Direction	Other Prepositions	
above	near	after	across	about	for
behind	next to	before	around	against	from
below	off	during	down	along	of
beside	on	till	into	among	to
between	out	until	out of	as	with
by	outside		through	at	without
in	over		toward	except	
inside	under		up		

Adverbs/Prepositions 429

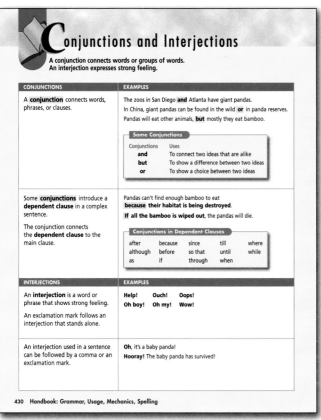

Conjunctions and Interjections

A conjunction connects words or groups of words.
An interjection expresses strong feeling.

CONJUNCTIONS	EXAMPLES
A **conjunction** connects words, phrases, or clauses.	The zoos in San Diego **and** Atlanta have giant pandas. In China, giant pandas can be found in the wild **or** in panda reserves. Pandas will eat other animals, **but** mostly they eat bamboo. **Some Conjunctions** Conjunctions — Uses **and** — To connect two ideas that are alike **but** — To show a difference between two ideas **or** — To show a choice between two ideas
Some **conjunctions** introduce a **dependent clause** in a complex sentence. The conjunction connects the **dependent clause** to the main clause.	Pandas can't find enough bamboo to eat **because their habitat is being destroyed**. **If all the bamboo is wiped out**, the pandas will die. **Conjunctions in Dependent Clauses** after — because — since — till — where although — before — so that — until — while as — if — through — when

INTERJECTIONS	EXAMPLES
An **interjection** is a word or phrase that shows strong feeling. An exclamation mark follows an interjection that stands alone.	**Help! Ouch! Oops!** **Oh boy! Oh my! Wow!**
An interjection used in a sentence can be followed by a comma or an exclamation mark.	**Oh**, it's a baby panda! **Hooray!** The baby panda has survived!

430   Handbook: Grammar, Usage, Mechanics, Spelling

page 430

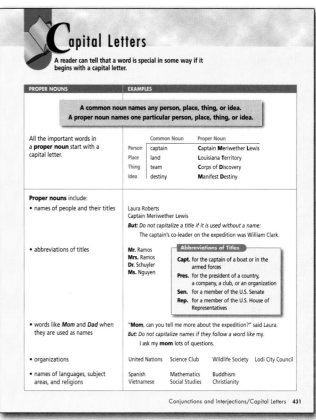

Capital Letters

A reader can tell that a word is special in some way if it begins with a capital letter.

PROPER NOUNS	EXAMPLES
A common noun names any person, place, thing, or idea. **A proper noun** names one particular person, place, thing, or idea.	

		Common Noun	Proper Noun
All the important words in a **proper noun** start with a capital letter.	Person	captain	**Captain** Meriwether Lewis
	Place	land	**Louisiana Territory**
	Thing	team	**Corps of Discovery**
	Idea	destiny	**Manifest Destiny**

Proper nouns include:	
• names of people and their titles	Laura Roberts Captain Meriwether Lewis ***But:*** *Do not capitalize a title if it is used without a name:* The captain's co-leader on the expedition was William Clark.
• abbreviations of titles	**Mr.** Ramos **Mrs.** Ramos **Dr.** Schuyler **Ms.** Nguyen **Abbreviations of Titles** **Capt.** for the captain of a boat or in the armed forces **Pres.** for the president of a country, a company, a club, or an organization **Sen.** for a member of the U.S. Senate **Rep.** for a member of the U.S. House of Representatives
• words like *Mom* and *Dad* when they are used as names	"**Mom**, can you tell me more about the expedition?" said Laura. ***But:*** *Do not capitalize names if they follow a word like* my. I ask my **mom** lots of questions.
• organizations	United Nations Science Club Wildlife Society Lodi City Council
• names of languages, subject areas, and religions	Spanish Mathematics Buddhism Vietnamese Social Studies Christianity

page 431

Capital Letters, *continued*

PROPER NOUNS, continued	EXAMPLES
• names of geographic places	**Cities and States** Dallas, Texas Miami, Florida St. Louis, Missouri **Streets and Roads** King Boulevard Main Avenue First Street **Bodies of Water** Yellowstone River Pacific Ocean Great Salt Lake Gulf of Mexico	**Countries** Iran Ecuador Cambodia **Landforms** Rocky Mountains Sahara Desert Grand Canyon **Buildings, Ships, and Monuments** Empire State Building *Titanic* Statue of Liberty	**Continents** Asia South America Africa **Public Spaces** Hemisfair Plaza Central Park Muir Camp **Planets and Heavenly Bodies** Earth Jupiter Milky Way

• abbreviations of geographic places	**Words Used in Addresses**			
	Avenue Ave. Boulevard Blvd. Court Ct. Drive Dr. East E.	Highway Hwy. Lane Ln. North N. Place Pl. Road Rd.	South S. Square Sq. Street St. West W.	

Abbreviations for State Names in Mailing Addresses

Alabama	AL	Hawaii	HI	Massachusetts	MA	New Mexico	NM	South Dakota	SD
Alaska	AK	Idaho	ID	Michigan	MI	New York	NY	Tennessee	TN
Arizona	AZ	Illinois	IL	Minnesota	MN	North Carolina	NC	Texas	TX
Arkansas	AR	Indiana	IN	Mississippi	MS	North Dakota	ND	Utah	UT
California	CA	Iowa	IA	Missouri	MO	Ohio	OH	Vermont	VT
Colorado	CO	Kansas	KS	Montana	MT	Oklahoma	OK	Virginia	VA
Connecticut	CT	Kentucky	KY	Nebraska	NE	Oregon	OR	Washington	WA
Delaware	DE	Louisiana	LA	Nevada	NV	Pennsylvania	PA	West Virginia	WV
Florida	FL	Maine	ME	New Hampshire	NH	Rhode Island	RI	Wisconsin	WI
Georgia	GA	Maryland	MD	New Jersey	NJ	South Carolina	SC	Wyoming	WY

• months, days, special days and holidays	January February March April May June	July August September October November December	Sunday Monday Tuesday Wednesday Thursday Friday Saturday	New Year's Day Mother's Day Thanksgiving Hanukkah Kwanzaa

432   Handbook: Grammar, Usage, Mechanics, Spelling

page 432

PROPER ADJECTIVES	EXAMPLES
A **proper adjective** is formed from a **proper noun**. Capitalize proper adjectives.	Napoleon Bonaparte was from **Europe**. He was a **European** leader in the 1800s. Napoleon ruled the country of **France**. He was the **French** emperor.

IN LETTERS	EXAMPLES

Capitalize the first word used in the **greeting** or in the **closing** of a letter.
 	
Street, city, and state names in the address, as well as their abbreviations, are also capitalized.
	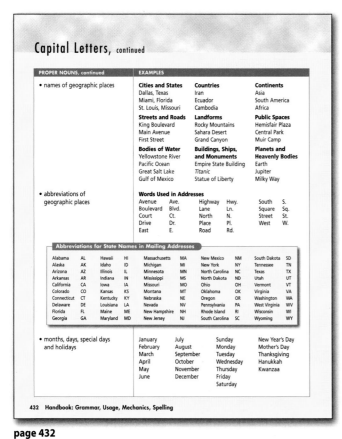Dear Kim,
	   I wish you could explore the Academy of Natural Sciences with me. I've learned so much about the flora and fauna that Lewis and Clark found. The museum even has some of the original samples! I'll tell you about it when I get home. See you soon.
	   Your friend,
	   Jamal
	
	Kim Messina
	10250 W. Fourth St.
	Las Vegas, NV 89015

IN TITLES AND QUOTATIONS	EXAMPLES
Capitalize the **first word** in a **direct quotation**.	Clark said, "**There** is great joy in camp." "**We** are in view of the ocean," he said "**It's** the Pacific Ocean," he added. "**We** are finally here."
All important words in a **title** begin with a capital letter. Short words like *a, an, the, in, at, of, and* and *for* are not capitalized unless they are the first or last word in the title.	**book:** *The Longest Journey* **poem:** "Leaves of Grass" **magazine:** *Flora and Fauna of Arizona* **newspaper:** *The Denver Post* **song:** "The Star-Spangled Banner" **game:** Exploration! **TV series:** "Bonanza" **movie:** *The Lion King*

page 433

Handbook: Grammar, Usage, Mechanics, Spelling

page 434

Punctuation Marks

Punctuation marks make words and sentences easier to understand.

PERIOD	EXAMPLES
Use a **period**:	
• at the end of a statement or a polite command	Georgia read the paper to her mom.
	Tell me if there are any interesting articles.
• after an abbreviation	There's a new restaurant on Stone St. near our house.
	It opens at 10 a.m. today.
	But: *Do not use a period in an acronym:*
	National Aeronautics and Space Administration **NASA**
	Do not use a period in the abbreviation of a state name written in a mailing address:
	Massachusetts **MA** Illinois **IL** Texas **TX**
	California **CA** Florida **FL** Virginia **VA**
• after an initial	The owner is J.J. Malone.
• to separate dollars and cents. The period is the decimal point.	The article says lunch today costs only $1.50.
• in an Internet address. The period is called a dot.	The restaurant has a Web site at www.jjmalone.org.

QUESTION MARK	EXAMPLES
Use a **question mark**:	
• at the end of a question	What kind of food do they serve?
• after a question that comes at the end of a statement	The food is good, isn't it?
	But: *Use a period after an indirect question. In an indirect question, you tell about a question you asked.*
	I asked how good the food could be for only $1.50.

434   Handbook: Grammar, Usage, Mechanics, Spelling

page 435

EXCLAMATION MARK	EXAMPLES
Use an **exclamation mark**:	
• after an interjection	Wow!
• at the end of a sentence to show that you feel strongly about something	One-fifty is a really good price!

COMMA	EXAMPLES
Use a **comma**:	
• to separate three or more items in a series	Articles about the school, a big sale, and a new movie were also in the newspaper.
	The school will buy a new bus, 10 computers, and books for the library.
• when you write a number with four or more digits	There was $500,000 in the school budget.
• before the **conjunction** in a compound sentence	The school could buy books, or it could buy a sound system.
	All the teachers discussed it, and they decided to buy books.
• before a question at the end of a statement	We need science books, don't we?
• to set off the name of a person someone is talking to	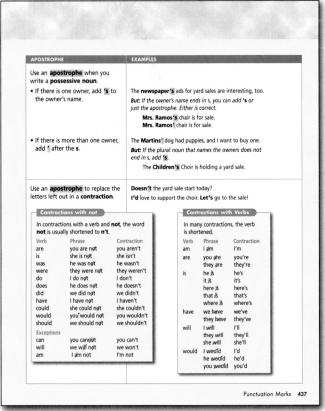 Georgia, does the article say why the school is buying a new bus? Just a minute, Mom, let me look.
• between two or more adjectives that tell about the same noun	The old, rusty school bus is broken.
• after a long **introductory phrase**	**In the last few months,** the bus had to be fixed six times.
• after an **introductory clause**	**Because the bus is old,** it keeps breaking down.
• before someone's exact words	Mr. Ivanovich said, "It is time for a new bus!"
• after someone's exact words if the sentence continues	"I agree," said the principal.

Punctuation Marks   435

page 436

Punctuation Marks, continued

COMMA, continued	EXAMPLES
Use a **comma** in these places in a letter:	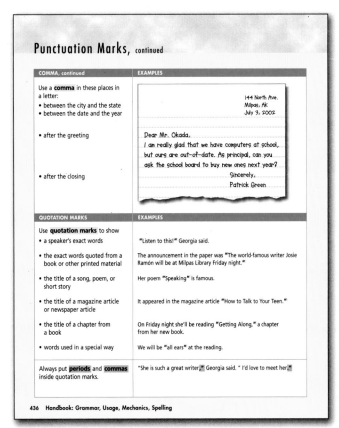
• between the city and the state	144 North Ave.
• between the date and the year	Milpas, AK
	July 3, 2002
• after the greeting	Dear Mr. Okada,
	I am really glad that we have computers at school, but ours are out-of-date. As principal, can you ask the school board to buy new ones next year?
• after the closing	Sincerely,
	Patrick Green

QUOTATION MARKS	EXAMPLES
Use **quotation marks** to show	
• a speaker's exact words	"Listen to this!" Georgia said.
• the exact words quoted from a book or other printed material	The announcement in the paper was "The world-famous writer Josie Ramón will be at Milpas Library Friday night."
• the title of a song, poem, or short story	Her poem "Speaking" is famous.
• the title of a magazine article or newspaper article	It appeared in the magazine article "How to Talk to Your Teen."
• the title of a chapter from a book	On Friday night she'll be reading "Getting Along," a chapter from her new book.
• words used in a special way	We will be "all ears" at the reading.
Always put **periods** and **commas** inside quotation marks.	"She is such a great writer," Georgia said. " I'd love to meet her."

436   Handbook: Grammar, Usage, Mechanics, Spelling

page 437

APOSTROPHE	EXAMPLES
Use an **apostrophe** when you write a **possessive noun**.	
• If there is one owner, add **'s** to the owner's name.	The **newspaper's** ads for yard sales are interesting, too.
	But: *If the owner's name ends in s, you can add* **'s** *or just the apostrophe. Either is correct.*
	Mrs. Ramos's chair is for sale.
	Mrs. Ramos' chair is for sale.
• If there is more than one owner, add **'** after the s.	The **Martins'** dog had puppies, and I want to buy one.
	But: *If the plural noun that names the owners does not end in s, add* **'s**.
	The **Children's** Choir is holding a yard sale.
Use an **apostrophe** to replace the letters left out in a **contraction**.	**Doesn't** the yard sale start today?
	I'd love to support the choir. **Let's** go to the sale!

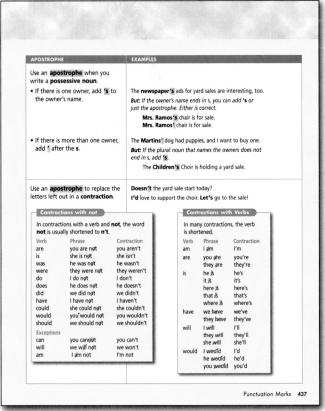

Contractions with *not*

In contractions with a verb and **not**, the word **not** is usually shortened to **n't**.

Verb	Phrase	Contraction
are	you are not	you aren't
is	she is not	she isn't
was	he was not	he wasn't
were	they were not	they weren't
do	I do not	I don't
does	he does not	he doesn't
did	we did not	we didn't
have	I have not	I haven't
could	she could not	she couldn't
would	you would not	you wouldn't
should	we should not	we shouldn't
Exceptions		
can	you cannot	you can't
will	we will not	we won't
am	I am not	I'm not

Contractions with Verbs

In many contractions, the verb is shortened.

Verb	Phrase	Contraction
am	I am	I'm
are	you are	you're
	they are	they're
is	he is	he's
	it is	it's
	here is	here's
	that is	that's
	where is	where's
have	we have	we've
	they have	they've
will	I will	I'll
	they will	they'll
	she will	she'll
would	I would	I'd
	he would	he'd
	you would	you'd

Punctuation Marks   437

Handbook: Grammar, Usage, Mechanics, Spelling

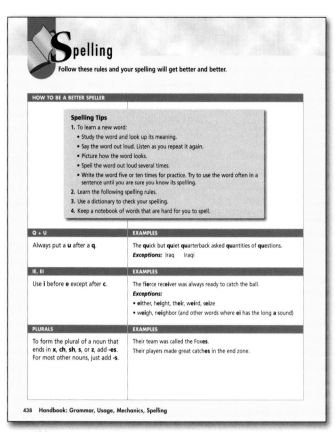

Spelling

Follow these rules and your spelling will get better and better.

HOW TO BE A BETTER SPELLER

Spelling Tips

1. To learn a new word:
   - Study the word and look up its meaning.
   - Say the word out loud. Listen as you repeat it again.
   - Picture how the word looks.
   - Spell the word out loud several times.
   - Write the word five or ten times for practice. Try to use the word often in a sentence until you are sure you know its spelling.
2. Learn the following spelling rules.
3. Use a dictionary to check your spelling.
4. Keep a notebook of words that are hard for you to spell.

Q + U	EXAMPLES
Always put a **u** after a **q**.	The **qu**ick but **qu**iet **qu**arterback asked **qu**antities of **qu**estions. *Exceptions:* Iraq Iraqi

IE, EI	EXAMPLES
Use **i** before **e** except after **c**.	The f**ie**rce rec**ei**ver was always ready to catch the ball. *Exceptions:* • **ei**ther, h**ei**ght, th**ei**r, w**ei**rd, s**ei**ze • w**ei**gh, n**ei**ghbor (and other words where **ei** has the long **a** sound)

PLURALS	EXAMPLES
To form the plural of a noun that ends in **x**, **ch**, **sh**, **s**, or **z**, add **-es**. For most other nouns, just add **-s**.	Their team was called the Fox**es**. Their players made great catc**hes** in the end zone.

438   Handbook: Grammar, Usage, Mechanics, Spelling

page 438

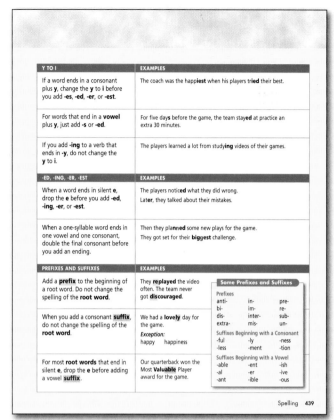

Y TO I	EXAMPLES
If a word ends in a consonant plus **y**, change the **y** to **i** before you add **-es**, **-ed**, **-er**, or **-est**.	The coach was the happ**iest** when his players tr**ied** their best.
For words that end in a **vowel** plus **y**, just add **-s** or **-ed**.	For five day**s** before the game, the team stay**ed** at practice an extra 30 minutes.
If you add **-ing** to a verb that ends in **-y**, do not change the **y** to **i**.	The players learned a lot from study**ing** videos of their games.

-ED, -ING, -ER, -EST	EXAMPLES
When a word ends in silent **e**, drop the **e** before you add **-ed**, **-ing**, **-er**, or **-est**.	The players notic**ed** what they did wrong. Later, they talked about their mistakes.
When a one-syllable word ends in one vowel and one consonant, double the final consonant before you add an ending.	Then they plan**ned** some new plays for the game. They got set for their big**gest** challenge.

PREFIXES AND SUFFIXES	EXAMPLES
Add a **prefix** to the beginning of a root word. Do not change the spelling of the **root word**.	They **replayed** the video often. The team never got **discouraged**.
When you add a consonant **suffix**, do not change the spelling of the **root word**.	We had a **lovely** day for the game. *Exception:* happy happiness
For most **root words** that end in silent **e**, drop the **e** before adding a vowel **suffix**.	Our quarterback won the Most **Valuable** Player award for the game.

Some Prefixes and Suffixes

Prefixes
anti-	in-	pre-
bi-	im-	re-
dis-	inter-	sub-
extra-	mis-	un-

Suffixes Beginning with a Consonant
-ful	-ly	-ness
-less	-ment	-tion

Suffixes Beginning with a Vowel
-able	-ent	-ish
-al	-er	-ive
-ant	-ible	-ous

Spelling   439

page 439

Glossary of Literary Terms

page 440

Glossary of Literary Terms

Action/Reaction Action/reaction tells how one event makes another event happen.
See also **Characterization**

Advertisement An advertisement is a notice of something for sale. It uses persuasive techniques.
See also **Persuasion**

Alliteration Alliteration is the repetition of beginning consonant sounds. An example from "Outside and In" is

Sometimes people tell me,
"You are graceful on the stage!"
"Your voice is smooth and silky."

Article An article is a short piece of nonfiction writing that often appears in newspapers and magazines.
Examples: **"Many People, Many Intelligences,"**
"When Disaster Strikes"

Autobiography An autobiography is a story that a person writes about his or her own life.
Example: **"My Best Friend"**

Biography A biography is the story of a person's life that another person writes.

Cause and Effect A cause is an event that makes another event (the effect) happen.

Character A character is a person or animal in a story. Characters can be real or imaginary.
See also **Characterization; Character Traits**

Characterization Characterization is the way a character is brought to life. It includes descriptions of how a character looks, acts, and thinks.
See also **Character Traits; Motive; Point of View**

Character Sketch A character sketch is a short description of a person.
See also **Characterization; Character Traits**

Character Traits Character traits tell what someone is like.
See also **Character; Characterization**

Climax The climax is the most important event in a story. In "A Mountain Rescue," the climax happens when Rudi lowers his clothes-rope into the crevasse.
See also **Plot**

Conflict and Resolution Conflict describes a character's problem. Resolution tells if the problem is solved.
See also **Plot**

Description A description tells about a person, place, or thing. Many descriptions use sensory words to tell how things look, sound, feel, smell, and taste. An example from "My Best Friend" is

. . . we'd sit on the bottom step of Isabel's front porch with our bare feet on the ground. We'd draw pictures in the dirt while we talked and rub them out with our hands. Or we'd rake the cool, damp dirt on top of our feet and pack it down tight, then slide our feet out, leaving a little cave we called a frog house. And all the time, we'd be just talking.

440 Glossary of Literary Terms

page 441

Dialogue Dialogue is what characters say to one another. Most writing shows dialogue in quotation marks. Plays do not.

Diary A diary is a personal book written about the author's life as it happens. It describes events, thoughts, and feelings.

Essay An essay is short piece of nonfiction writing that informs, entertains, or persuades.
Example: **"Common Ground"**

Exaggeration Exaggeration is saying that something is larger or more important than it really is.

Fable A fable is a short story that teaches a lesson about life. Many fables have animals as characters.
Examples: **"The Mouse and the Lion"**
and **"The Monkey and the Camel,"**
from **"The Qualities of Friendship"**

Fantasy Fantasy is writing about imaginary characters and events. Fairy tales, science fiction, and fables are examples of fantasy.
See also **Science Fiction**

Fiction Fiction is writing that an author makes up. Biographical, historical, and realistic fiction are based on real life. Other fiction comes from the author's imagination. Fiction includes novels and short stories.
Example: **"A Mountain Rescue"**

Figurative Language Writers use figurative language to say something in an imaginative way. Imagery, metaphor, personification, and simile are examples of figurative language.
See also **Exaggeration; Imagery; Metaphor; Personification; Simile**

Folk Tale A folk tale is a very old story that has been told and retold for many years. Most folks tales were told for many generations before people wrote them.
Example: **"Owl," from "Unwinding the Magic Thread"**

Free Verse Free verse is poetry that does not rhyme or have a regular rhythm. Free verse can sound like ordinary speech.
Examples: **"Discovery,"**
"Adobe," from "Together, We Dream"
See also **Poetry; Rhyme; Rhythm**

Genre Genre is a type of literature. The four main genres are fiction, nonfiction, poetry, and drama.

Goal and Outcome A goal is something that a character wants to do or have. The outcome tells if the character met the goal.
See also **Plot**

Historical Fiction Historical fiction is a story based on real people or events. Writers add details that could have happened.

History History is a record of events that happened in the past.

How-to Article A how-to article gives step-by-step directions. It tells how to make or do something.

Imagery Imagery is language that helps create pictures in readers' minds. It is sometimes called sensory language because it tells how things look, sound, taste, smell, and feel.
See also **Figurative Language**

Glossary of Literary Terms 441

page 442

Glossary of Literary Terms, continued

Interview In an interview, one person asks questions of another person.
Example: **"Could I Ask You A Question?"**

Journal A journal is a personal record. It may include descriptions of events, stories, poems, sketches, reflections, essays, and other interesting information. It is like a diary.

Legend A legend is a story about a person or event in the past. The characters can be real or imaginary. Legends often exaggerate things about a character or an event.

Letter A letter is a message that one person gives to another. Friendly letters and business letters are two examples.

Memoir A memoir is a story someone writes about a personal memory.

Metaphor A metaphor compares two things by saying that they are the same thing. These are metaphors from "When I Taste Salt":

She is a hero
and a goddess
and a mermaid

Meter Meter is the pattern of stressed and unstressed syllables in a poem.
See also **Rhythm**

Motive A motive is the reason a character says, thinks, or does something. In "Owl," Owl runs away because he thinks his face is ugly.
See also **Characterization**

Myth A myth is a very old story that explains something about the world. Myths are usually about gods, goddesses, and other superhuman characters.
Examples: **"Echo and Narcissus," "How the Ox Star Fell from Heaven"**

Narrative Poetry Narrative poetry is poetry that tells a story. It has characters, a setting, and a plot. It can also have rhythm and rhyme.
See also **Poetry**

Nonfiction Nonfiction is writing that tells about real people, places, and events.
Examples: **"Grandfather's Nose," "Many People, Many Intelligences," "My Best Friend"**

Onomatopoeia Onomatopoeia is the use of words that imitate sounds. *Buzz*, the sound a bee makes; *hiss*, the sound a snake makes; and *gurgle*, the sound a stream makes are examples of onomatopoeia.

Pantomime Pantomime is the use of gestures, body movements, and facial expressions to tell an idea. Words are not used in pantomime.

Personal Narrative A personal narrative is nonfiction written from the first-person point of view.
Example: **"Art Smart"**
See also **Point of View**

Personification Writers use personification when they give human characteristics to animals, things, or ideas. Examples are found in "The Mouse and The Lion" and in "The Monkey and The Camel."

442 Glossary of Literary Terms

page 443

Persuasion Writers use persuasion when they want their readers to act or think a certain way. Persuasion is used in advertisements, editorials, sermons, and political speeches. For example, in "Evergreen, Everblue," Raffi uses the voices of nature to persuade the reader to help protect the planet.

Photo Essay A photo-essay is nonfiction that includes photographs and captions. The photographs and words are both important sources of information.
Example: **"Teamwork"**

Play A play is a story that is performed by actors. The story is told through the actors' words and actions.
Example: **"Earthquake at Dawn"**

Plot The plot is the sequence of events that happen in a story, a play, or a narrative poem. Plot usually has four parts: problem or conflict, complication, climax, and resolution.
See also **Climax; Conflict and Resolution; Problem and Solution**

Poetry Poetry is writing that tells ideas in few words. Poets choose words and phrases that are usually very imaginative. Many poems are written in sections called stanzas and use rhythm and rhyme.
Examples: **"We Could Be Friends," "Everybody Says"**
See also **Rhyme; Rhythm; Stanza**

Point of View Point of view describes how a story is told. In the first-person point of view, the narrator is a character in the story and uses words such as *I*, *me*, and *we*. In the third-person point of view, the narrator is not in the story and uses words such as *he*, *she*, and *they*.
Example of first-person point of view: **"My Best Friend"**
Example of third-person point of view: **"A Mountain Rescue"**

Problem and Solution A problem is something that a character has to deal with. A solution is how the character deals with the problem.
See also **Plot**

Realistic Fiction Realistic fiction tells about imaginary characters who could be real and imaginary events that could happen.
Example: **"A Mountain Rescue"**

Repetition Repetition is saying the same thing several times. For example, in the poem "Everybody Says," the phrase "everybody says" is repeated three times.

Report A report is nonfiction writing that tells facts. Reports are different from essays because they do not include opinions.

Rhyme Rhyme is the repetition of sounds at the ends of words. Rhyme adds to the rhythm and musical quality of poetry.
Examples: **"Just Me," "We Could Be Friends"**

Rhymed Verse Rhymed verse is poetry that rhymes.
See also **Rhyme**

Glossary of Literary Terms 443

Glossary of Literary Terms/Key Vocabulary

Glossary of Literary Terms, continued

Rhyme Scheme Rhyme scheme is the pattern of rhyming words in a poem.

See also Rhyme

Rhythm Rhythm is a musical quality created by the repetition of stressed and unstressed syllables.

Science Fiction Science fiction is a fantasy story about real or imaginary science. It often takes place in the future.

Sensory Language *See Imagery*

Setting The setting is the place and the time a story happens. For example, the setting of "Earthquake at Dawn," is San Francisco, California, in the year 1906.

Short Story A short story is short fiction that has a single problem and a simple plot.

Simile A simile compares two things by using the words *like, as,* or *than.* An example from "Together We Dream" is

adobes. . .like some big chocolate bars

Stanza A stanza is a group of lines in a poem. Stanzas are separated by spaces.

Examples in "We Could Be Friends"

Story A story is fiction writing that has a setting, characters, and a plot.

Style Style is a special way of writing. It includes choice of words, tone, sentence length, and use of imagery and dialogue.

See also Word Choice

Tall Tale A tall tale is a funny story made up of exaggerated characters and events. Tall tales are not true.

Example: "Pecos Bill," from "The Art of the Tall Tale"

See also Exaggeration

Theme A theme is a main idea. It is the message a piece of writing has. For example, the theme of "The Monkey and the Camel" is that not everyone can do everything well.

Word Choice Word choice is the kinds of words and language the writer uses to tell his or her ideas. Word choice is a part of an author's style.

See also Style

444 Glossary of Literary Terms

Glossary of Key Vocabulary

Many words have more than one meaning. The definitions in this glossary are for the words as they are introduced in the selections in this book.

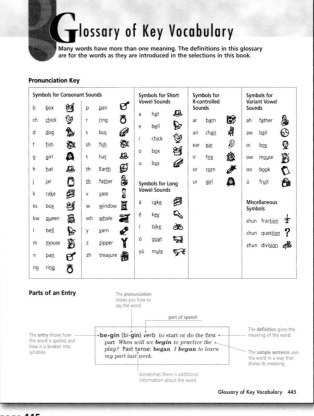

Pronunciation Key

Symbols for Consonant Sounds			Symbols for Short Vowel Sounds	Symbols for R-controlled Sounds	Symbols for Variant Vowel Sounds
b box	p pan		a hat	ar barn	ah father
ch chick	r ring		e bell	air chair	aw ball
d dog	s bus		i chick	ear ear	oi boy
f fish	sh fish		o box	ir fire	ow mouse
g girl	t hat		u bus	or corn	oo book
h hat	th Earth			ur girl	ū fruit
j jar	th father		**Symbols for Long Vowel Sounds**		
k cake	v vase		ā cake		**Miscellaneous Symbols**
ks box	w window		ē key		shun fraction
kw queen	wh whale		ī bike		chun question
l bell	y yarn		ō goat		zhun division
m mouse	z zipper		yū mule		
n pan	zh treasure				
ng ring					

Parts of an Entry

The pronunciation shows you how to say the word.

The entry shows how the word is spelled and how it is broken into syllables.

part of speech

be·gin (bi-**gin**) *verb* to start or do the first part *When will we begin to practice the play?* Past tense: **began** *I began to learn my part last week.*

The **definition** gives the meaning of the word.

The sample sentence uses the word in a way that shows its meaning.

Sometimes there is additional information about the word.

Glossary of Key Vocabulary 445

---

absolute truth / climb

A

absolute truth When something is completely true, it is the **absolute truth**. *Some people lied, but she told the absolute truth.*

ac·cept (ak-**sept**) *verb* When you **accept** something, you like it the way it is. *She learned to accept her friends' ideas.*

a·dapt (u-**dapt**) *verb* When you **adapt** to something new, you change to get used to it. *Juan learned to adapt to his new school.*

a·do·be (u-**dō**-bē) *noun* An **adobe** is a brick made of mud and straw that dries in the sun. *They put one adobe on top of another to build the house.*

a·dor·a·ble (u-**dor**-u-bul) *adjective* Something is **adorable** when it is pretty and delightful. *The new baby is adorable.*

adobes

ad·vise (ad-**vīz**) *verb* You **advise** someone when you tell what you think he or she should do. *Our parents advise us to stay away from strangers.*

aid (ād) *noun* Money, food, and supplies for people who need help is called **aid**. *The class sent aid to the flood victims.*

an·ces·tor (an-ses-tur) *noun* An **ancestor** is a family member who lived before you. *Marie likes to hear stories about her favorite ancestor, her great-aunt.*

an·swer (an-sur) *verb* You **answer** when you say or do something after you hear a question or a statement. *Please answer my question at once.*

at·ten·dant (u-ten-dunt) *noun* An **attendant** is someone who serves another person. *A flight attendant serves meals on planes.*

au·di·ence (aw-dē-uns) *noun* An **audience** is a group of people who watch and listen to a performance. *The audience clapped at the end of the show.*

B

bar (bar) *noun* A **bar** is a solid object that is longer than it is wide. *We used an iron bar to keep the door closed.*

be·liev·a·ble (bi-lē-vu-bul) *adjective* A **believable** event could really happen. *Her story seemed strange, but I thought it was believable.*

ben·e·fit (ben-u-fit) *verb* When you **benefit** from something, you are helped by it. *You will benefit from good food and exercise.*

best friend A **best friend** is the friend you like the most. *Kathy and her best friend do many things together.*

bless·ing (bles-ing) *noun* A **blessing** is something good that brings happiness. *After a long, dry summer, the rain was a blessing.*

blind (blīnd) *adjective* A **blind** person is someone who cannot see. *Blind people use other senses because they cannot see.*

brain power Your **brain power** helps you think, feel, learn, remember, and move. *People use their brain power to help them do many different things.*

brave (brāv) *adjective* A **brave** person does not show fear in a difficult situation. *The brave fireman saved the child from the burning building.*

C

care for People can **care for** each other by loving and helping each other. *My grandparents care for me in many ways.*

cause (kaws) *noun* A **cause** is something that makes something else happen. *The heavy rain was the cause of the flood.*

char·ac·ter (kair-ik-tur) *noun* Your **character** is what you are really like. *Kim has a shy, sweet character.*

climb (klīm) *verb* When you **climb**, you move yourself up with your hands and feet. *Bill tried to climb to the top of the tree.*

446 Glossary of Key Vocabulary

---

combination / echo

com·bi·na·tion (kom-bi-nā-shun) *noun* A **combination** is a mix or a blend. *Peanut butter and jelly make a good combination for a sandwich.*

com·mand (ku-mand) *noun* A **command** is an order; it tells what to do. *The trainer gave the command to stop.*

com·mon (kom-un) *adjective* **1.** If something is **common**, it may be ordinary or average. *Our dog is no special kind, he's just a common dog.* **2.** If something is **common**, it may be shared. *Our common interest in art brought us together.*

common ground Land shared by everyone is **common ground**. *The park is common ground that we all can use.*

com·mons (kom-uns) *noun* A **commons** is a piece of land that is shared by the whole town. *Our commons is used for many different events throughout the year.*

com·mu·ni·ty (ku-myū-ni-tē) *noun* A **community** is a group of people who live in the same place. *Everyone in the community helped to build a new playground.*

co·op·er·ate (kō-op-u-rāt) *verb* You **cooperate** when you work together. *If we cooperate, we will finish our work very quickly.*

co·op·er·a·tion (kō-op-u-rā-shun) *noun* Working together is **cooperation**. *Cooperation can help us do things we cannot do alone.*

count on When you **count on** someone, you need that person to help you. *We can count on Joan to take good care of our dog while we are away.*

crazy about When you are **crazy about** something, you really love it. *Pablo and I are crazy about funny movies.*

crop (krop) *noun* A **crop** is a field of plants that farmers grow. *Rice is an important crop that is grown in many countries.*

crop

crystal clean When something is **crystal clean**, it is clear and pure. *We took a long drink of the crystal clean water.*

cul·ture (kul-chur) *noun* People's **culture** includes their art, customs, beliefs, food, music, and clothing. *He wanted to learn about the culture of Japan.*

D

dam·age (dam-ij) *noun* Harm and destruction are kinds of **damage**. *Heavy rain caused damage to the bridge.*

dance (dans) **1.** *noun* A **dance** is a party where people move to music. *We had fun at the school dance.* **2.** *verb* When you **dance**, you move your body to music. *She likes to dance with a partner or all alone.*

de·cide (di-sīd) *verb* When you **decide**, you make up your mind about something. *We will decide what to do about the problem next week.*

ded·i·cate (ded-i-kāt) *verb* When you **dedicate** your work to someone, you make it for that person. *She will dedicate the book she wrote to her older sister.*

depend on You **depend on** things or people that you need. *The team members depend on the coach for training.*

dis·cov·er (dis-kuv-ur) *verb* When you **discover** something, you learn about it for the first time. *I discover new things about science every day.*

dis·re·spect·ful (dis-ri-spekt-ful) *adjective* You are **disrespectful** when you are rude and impolite. *It is disrespectful to laugh when someone makes a mistake.*

E

earth/Earth (urth) *noun* **1.** The ground or dirt is **earth**. *When she works in her garden, she likes the smell of fresh earth.* **2.** The planet we live on is called **Earth**. *The astronauts saw Earth from the moon.*

ech·o (ek-ō) *noun* You hear an **echo** when you hear the same sound repeated many times in a row. *You can hear the echo of your voice when you yell in a cave.*

Glossary of Key Vocabulary 447

Glossary of Key Vocabulary

ed•u•ca•tion (ej-u-**kā**-shun) *noun* You get an **education** when you learn. *We go to school to get an **education**.*

ef•fect (i-**fekt**) *noun* An **effect** is something that happens because of something that happened earlier. *The flood was the **effect** of the heavy rain.*

en•joy (en-**joi**) *verb* When you **enjoy** something, you like it. *I always **enjoy** parties with my friends.*

en•tire (en-**tīr**) *adjective* Something is **entire** when it is complete or whole. *Nana's **entire** family was with her on her 100th birthday.*

ep•i•dem•ic (ep-u-**dem**-ik) *noun* An **epidemic** is a sickness or disease that spreads quickly. *Everyone in town was sick during the flu **epidemic**.*

e•vac•u•ee (i-**vak**-yū-ē) *noun* A person who must move away from a disaster is called an **evacuee**. *One **evacuee** saved her belongings from the flood.*

eve•ry•bod•y (**ev**-rē-bod-ē) *pronoun* Everyone or every person is **everybody**. ***Everybody** in my class wanted to visit the museum.*

every chance we got When we did something **every chance we got**, we did it whenever we could. *We went to the beach **every chance we got**.*

ex•ag•ge•rat•ed (eg-**zaj**-u-rā-tid) *adjective* Something is **exaggerated** when it is bigger and wilder than the truth. *Jim's **exaggerated** story about a giant fish made us laugh.*

ex•press (ek-**spres**) *verb* You **express** when you show or tell something. *Her art was a way to **express** her feelings.*

ex•pres•sion (ek-**spresh**-un) *noun* Your **expression** is the way you make your face look. Smiling is an **expression** that shows happiness. *Her frown was an **expression** of sadness.*

F

fa•mil•iar (fu-**mil**-yur) *adjective* Things you know well are **familiar**. *She is **familiar** with the rules of the game because she plays it every day.*

family resemblance People in some families look like each other. They have a **family resemblance**. *He and his brother have a strong **family resemblance**.*

fea•ture (**fē**-chur) *noun* A **feature** is part of your face. *Her best **feature** is her smile.*

feel (fēl) *verb* When we **feel**, we can be happy, sad, scared, and so on. *I **feel** excited when our team wins a game.* Past tense: **felt** *We **felt** sorry for the team that lost the game.*

felt (felt) *verb* the past tense of **feel**

figure out When you **figure out** something, you learn how to do it. *He was able to **figure out** how to fix the bicycle.*

for•est (**for**-ist) *noun* A **forest** is a large area with many trees. *There are more than fifteen kinds of trees in our **forest**.*

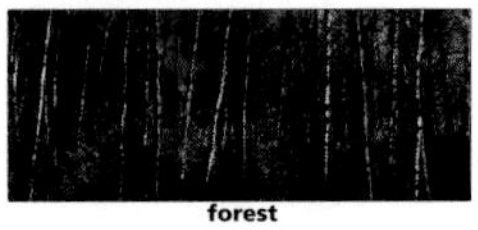

forest

fossil fuel A **fossil fuel** is a source of energy found in the earth. Coal, oil, and natural gas are **fossil fuels**. *Gas is a **fossil fuel** that is used for cooking, heating, and running cars.*

full attention You give your **full attention** when you watch and listen carefully. *The students gave the teacher their **full attention**.*

G

gath•er (**ga<u>th</u>**-ur) *verb* **1.** When people **gather**, they come together. *We will **gather** at the park for lunch.* **2.** When you **gather** something, you collect it. *The farmers will **gather** the crops in September.*

gene (jēn) *noun* A **gene** is the part of a cell that tells your body how to form and grow. *The baby has the **gene** for blue eyes.*

page 448

ge•net•ics (ju-**net**-iks) *noun* The science of **genetics** studies genes and how they are passed from parent to child. ***Genetics** studies why we are the way we are.*

ges•ture (**jes**-chur) *noun* A **gesture** is a movement you make with your hands and arms. *She raised her hand as a **gesture** that she wanted to speak.*

go out of my way When I choose to take a longer way, I **go out of my way**. *I **go out of my way** because I like to walk through the park.*

go over You **go over** to a place when you visit. *She will **go over** to her aunt's house tomorrow.*

goof around When friends **goof around**, they play together and have fun. *After they finish their homework, they can **goof around**.*

guide dog A **guide dog** is trained to help a person who cannot see. *The **guide dog** led the blind woman down the street.*

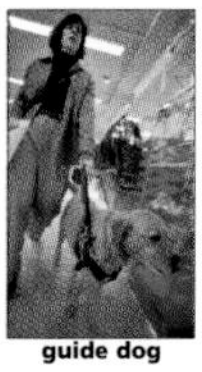

guide dog

H

had our lives all planned out We knew what we wanted to do in the future; we **had our lives all planned out**.

harvest time At **harvest time**, farmers pick and gather their crops. *Many workers picked apples at **harvest time**.*

hold on When you **hold on** to something, you do not let go of it. *He tried to **hold on** to the ball, but he dropped it.*

hu•mor (**hyū**-mur) *noun* When something makes you laugh, it has **humor**. *He adds **humor** to his stories to make them funny.*

I

I (ī) *pronoun* If you are the person speaking or writing, you call yourself **I**. ***I** am the only one who knows what **I** am thinking.* Plural: **we** ***We** all know what **we** think about it.*

identical twins Two babies born at the same time are called **twins**. **Identical twins** have the same genetic information. *Sometimes we call the **identical twins** by the wrong names because they look exactly alike.*

i•den•ti•ty (ī-**den**-ti-tē) *noun* Your **identity** is who you are. *Carlos hid his **identity** by wearing a costume and mask.*

im•age (**im**-ij) *noun* If you are the **image** of someone, you look a lot like him or her. *Everyone said she was the **image** of her mother.*

im•prove (im-**prüv**) *verb* When you **improve**, you get better at something. *She tried to **improve** her grades by studying more.*

in•her•it (in-**hair**-it) *verb* When you **inherit** something, you get it from your parents or ancestors. *Mother hoped the new baby would **inherit** her green eyes.*

in•sist (in-**sist**) *verb* When you **insist** on something, you will not change your mind. *I **insist** that you take the last piece of cake.*

in•struc•tor (in-**struk**-tur) *noun* An **instructor** is a teacher. *The **instructor** helped the students understand the lesson.*

in•tel•li•gence (in-**tel**-i-juns) *noun* The ability to think, understand, learn, and express yourself is called **intelligence**. *His **intelligence** made school seem easy.*

in•tel•li•gent (in-**tel**-i-junt) *adjective* You are **intelligent** if you are smart. ***Intelligent** people often get good grades.*

in•ven•tive•ness (in-**ven**-tiv-nis) *noun* The ability to think up new things is called **inventiveness**. *His creative project showed his **inventiveness**.*

ir•re•spon•si•ble (ear-i-**spon**-su-bul) *adjective* People who are **irresponsible** do not do what they say they will do. *I am **irresponsible** when I forget to feed the dog.*

ir•ri•ta•ble (**ear**-i-tu-bul) *adjective* You are **irritable** when you get upset easily. *The hot weather made Tam tired and **irritable**.*

page 449

is•land (**ī**-lund) *noun* An **island** is land that has water on all sides. *She needed a boat to get to the **island**.*

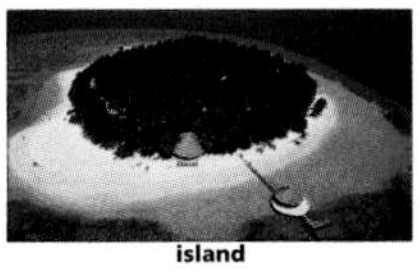

island

J

jeal•ous (**jel**-us) *adjective* A **jealous** person wants what someone else has. *Scott was **jealous** of Sophia because she had a new bike.*

K

kind•ness (**kīnd**-nis) *noun* A **kindness** is something good that you do or say. *She showed her **kindness** by helping me carry the big box.*

L

la•bor (**lā**-bur) *verb* You **labor** when you work hard. *We will **labor** in the garden all summer.*

lay•er (**lā**-ur) *noun* A **layer** is one thickness of something. *We put a **layer** of frosting on the cake.*

la•zy (**lā**-zē) *adjective* A **lazy** person does not want to work or do anything. *I was **lazy** and didn't do my homework.*

lead•er (**lē**-dur) *noun* The **leader** of a group tells the others what to do. *The President is the **leader** of the United States.*

life (līf) *noun* **1.** Something that has **life** is alive. *He saved her **life** after the accident.* **2. Life** can also mean living things. *The ocean is full of sea **life**.*

log•ic (**loj**-ik) *noun* When something has **logic**, it makes sense. *We agreed with her because there was **logic** in what she said.*

look just like When you **look just like** a person, you look the same as the person. *Everyone says I **look just like** my sister.*

low•er (**lō**-ur) *verb* When you **lower** something, you move it downward. *If you **lower** the window, you will keep the cold air out.*

M

me (mē) *pronoun* *I* and **me** mean the person speaking or writing. *I want you to give **me** the answer.* Plural: **us** *Our parents gave **us** gifts.*

mem•ber (**mem**-bur) *noun* A **member** is someone who is part of a group. *Wilma is a **member** of the math team.*

mer•its (**mair**-itz) *noun* Someone's good points are called **merits**. *Kindness and honesty are some of her **merits**.*

miss (mis) *verb* When you **miss** something, you feel sad because it is not there. *I **miss** my sister when she goes away to school.*

my (mī) *adjective* **My** tells that something belongs to the speaker or writer. *I carry **my** books to school.*

my•self (mī-**self**) *pronoun* **Myself** is used with *I* or *me*, or to make a statement stronger. *I fixed my bike **myself**.*

N

na•tion (**nā**-shun) *noun* People who live in one country form a **nation**. *Our **nation** is the United States of America.*

natural resource A **resource** is something people use. A **natural resource** comes from the Earth. *Water is an important **natural resource**.*

O

op•ti•mis•tic (op-ti-**mis**-tik) *adjective* You are **optimistic** when you are cheerful and hopeful. *Joe was **optimistic** about passing the test because he studied hard.*

out•land•ish (owt-**lan**-dish) *adjective* Something is **outlandish** if it is very strange or odd. *He wore his most **outlandish** clothes to the costume party.*

page 450

P

part•ner (**part**-nur) *noun* A **partner** is a person or animal who works with you. *She chose Kim to be her **partner** in the game.*

peas•ant (**pez**-unt) *noun* A **peasant** is a very poor person who works on the land. *The **peasant** worked hard but made little money.*

per•son•al•i•ty (pur-su-**nal**-u-tē) *noun* Your **personality** is the way you act or what you are like. *Everyone likes Felipe because he has a friendly **personality**.*

pine (pīn) *verb* When you **pine** for something, you feel sad and sick because you want it. *When I'm away from home, I **pine** for my mom's good cooking.*

pi•o•neer (pī-u-**near**) *noun* The first person to go someplace new or do something new is a **pioneer**. *An astronaut is a **pioneer** in space.*

plan (plan) *verb* You **plan** when you think about how to do something before you do it. *We **plan** where to go before we leave.*

plan•et (**plan**-it) *noun* A **planet** is any one of the large objects in space that travel around the sun. *The **planet** we live on is called Earth.*

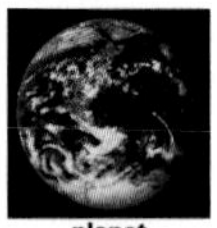

planet

plas•ter (**plas**-tur) *verb* When you **plaster** a wall, you cover it with material to protect it. *The room will look better after we **plaster** and paint the walls.*

plow (plow) *noun* A **plow** is a large tool that opens the earth for planting. *After the **plow** turns over the dirt, we can plant the seeds.*

por•trait (**por**-trit) *noun* A **portrait** is a picture of a person. *She painted a **portrait** of her father.*

pos•i•tive (**poz**-u-tiv) *adjective* You are **positive** when you are sure that things will work out well. *The baker was **positive** that his cake would be delicious.*

pres•ent (**prez**-unt) *adjective* **Present** means at this time. *We need a new classroom because our **present** one is too small.*

proud (prowd) *adjective* You feel **proud** when you are happy about something you did well. *I was **proud** of the good grades I got this year.*

pull (pool) *verb* When you **pull** something, you move it toward yourself. *We used a rope to **pull** the cart up the hill.*

R

rain forest A **rain forest** is an area covered by trees that gets at least 100 inches of rain each year. *Trees in a **rain forest** may grow as tall as 200 feet.*

re•al•i•ty (rē-**al**-u-tē) *noun* The way things really are is called **reality**. *She woke from her dream to face **reality**.*

re•cov•er•y (ri-**kuv**-ur-ē) *noun* When something gets back to normal after a problem, it is called **recovery**. *The town's **recovery** from the tornado took months.*

re•la•tion•ship (ri-**lā**-shun-ship) *noun* A **relationship** is how people connect with each other. Families and friends have **relationships**. *Joanna has a close **relationship** with her sister.*

rel•a•tive (**rel**-u-tiv) *noun* A **relative** is a person in your family. *Carlos met a new **relative** at the wedding.*

relief worker A **relief worker** is someone who helps people after a disaster. *A **relief worker** helped us after the fire.*

re•move (ri-**müv**) *verb* You **remove** something when you take it away. *Mom asked us to **remove** our toys from the living room.*

re•peat (ri-**pēt**) *verb* When you **repeat** something, you say it again. *He asked her to **repeat** the word because he didn't hear it clearly.*

re•quire (ri-**kwīr**) *verb* When you **require** something, you need it. *Beautiful gardens **require** a lot of work.*

page 451

Glossary of Key Vocabulary

rescue worker A **rescue worker** tries to save people in emergencies. *The rescue worker found the lost boy.*

re·spond (ri-**spond**) *verb* When you answer back, you **respond**. *When the teacher asks a question, we try to respond with the correct answer.*

restore power When you **restore power**, you get the electricity to work again. *We hope they will restore power soon so that our lights turn on.*

rise (rīz) *verb* When things begin to **rise**, they start to get up. *Farmers often rise before the sun is up.* Past tense: **rose** *We rose from our seats and clapped at the end of the play.*

rose (rōz) the past tense of **rise**

ru·ins (rū-unz) *noun* Fallen buildings, damaged roads, and bridges that cannot be fixed are called **ruins**. *After the earthquake, we looked through the ruins of our town.*

ruins

S

salt (sawlt) **1.** *noun* **Salt** is a natural product that adds flavor to food. *I added a little salt to my soup.* **2.** *verb* You can **salt** food to add flavor. *I salt my popcorn and add butter.*

sep·a·rate (**sep**-ur-it) *adjective* When something is **separate**, it is by itself. *The nurse put the sick child in a separate room.*

sew·er (**sū**-ur) *noun* A **sewer** is an underground tunnel that carries wastes from houses and buildings. *The sewer took the wastes to the ocean.*

shel·ter (**shel**-tur) *noun* People can stay in a **shelter** when they have no home. *The family lived in the shelter until their house was repaired.*

short·com·ings (**short**-kum-ingz) *noun* Someone's bad points are called **shortcomings**. *Laziness is one of Ted's shortcomings.*

show off When you **show off**, you show others how well you can do something. People **show off** to get attention. *She tried to show off by skating backwards.*

si·lence (**sī**-luns) *noun* When everything is quiet, there is **silence**. *Some students like to study in silence.*

sit·u·a·tion (sich-ū-ā-shun) *noun* A **situation** is something that happens. *When Alex lost his money, he was in a bad situation.*

skill (skil) *noun* A **skill** is the ability to do something well. *Learning a new skill takes a lot of practice.*

skirt (skurt) **1.** *noun* A **skirt** is a piece of women's clothing that hangs from the waist. *She wore a bright blue skirt.* **2.** *verb* When you **skirt** something, you go along its edge. *I will skirt the lake on my way home.*

solve problems When you **solve problems**, you find answers. *Teachers and parents can help us solve problems.*

source of The **source of** something is the place or thing it comes from. *The library is a good source of information.*

source of power A **source of power** is something energy comes from. *Running water is a source of power.*

stop to worry When you **stop to worry** about something, you take time to think about it. *He didn't stop to worry about being late for dinner.*

strange (strānj) *adjective* Something is **strange** when it is different from what people are used to. *Claire did not want to eat the strange food.*

stream (strēm) *noun* A **stream** is a small river of moving water. *The stream led us to a large river.*

strug·gle (**strug**-ul) *verb* When you **struggle**, you try hard to do something. *We had to struggle through the deep snow to get to school.*

sun·down (**sun**-down) *noun* Evening begins at **sundown**, when the sun goes down. *It gets dark very quickly after sundown.*

sun·up (**sun**-up) *noun* Morning begins at **sunup**, when the sun comes up. *The farmer starts his work at sunup.*

sup·plies (su-**plīz**) *noun* Materials that people need are called **supplies**. *The supplies we took to go camping included food, water, and raincoats.*

sup·port (su-**port**) *noun* Strength and encouragement are examples of **support**. *A good friend always gives you support.*

supposed to be The way things are **supposed to be** is how they should be. *He was supposed to be home before dark.*

sur·vi·vor (sur-**vī**-vur) *noun* Someone who is still alive after a disaster is called a **survivor**. *One survivor of the flood was a tiny baby.*

sus·tain (su-**stān**) *verb* When you **sustain** something, you keep it going. *We can sustain the forest by planting new trees.*

T

take care of When you **take care of** something, you give it your time and attention. *Juan has to take care of his sister when his mother goes to work.*

take good care When you **take good care** of someone, you give that person special attention. *Doctors take good care of people who are sick.*

tal·ent (**tal**-unt) *noun* When you have **talent** for something, you do it well. *She has musical talent and plays the guitar very well.*

talk and talk When people **talk and talk**, they talk for a long time. *Richard and I can talk and talk for hours.*

taste (tāst) **1.** *noun* A **taste** of something is a small amount of it. *The cook took just a taste of his special dish.* **2.** *verb* You **taste** something when you put it in your mouth. *I wanted to taste all the different foods at the fair.*

team (tēm) *noun* A **team** is a group that works together. *Each player on the soccer team did her best.*

tend (tend) *verb* When you **tend** something, you take care of it. *I tend the horses every day after school.*

tent city A **tent** is a shelter made of cloth. A **tent city** is a large area with many tents. *After the hurricane, many people lived in a tent city until their houses were safe.*

tent city

ter·ri·fied (**tair**-u-fid) *adjective* When you are **terrified**, you feel very scared. *She was terrified of being left alone in the dark.*

that was all there was to it When you were sure of how something would be, you could have said "**that was all there was to it**." *He would win the prize, and that was all there was to it.*

thick (thik) *adjective* When something is **thick**, it is big and solid. **Thick** is the opposite of thin. *The thick walls of our house kept us safe during the storm.*

threat·ened (**thret**-und) *adjective* If you are **threatened**, you are warned that something bad may happen. *The threatened man ran from the growling dog.*

tight·en (**tīt**-un) *verb* When you **tighten** the way you hold something, you grab it harder. *She had to tighten her hold on the bags so that they would not fall.*

took pity If you **took pity** on someone, you felt sorry for that person. *We took pity on her and helped her find the money she lost.*

tra·di·tion (tru-**dish**-un) *noun* A **tradition** is an action or a behavior that has been done for many years. *It is a tradition in my family to give gifts at the new year.*

train·ing (**trā**-ning) *noun* When you get **training**, someone teaches you how to do something. *Tim had years of training before he could skate well.*

trait (trāt) *noun* A **trait** is a person's way of looking or being. *Kindness is an excellent trait.*

trap (trap) *noun* A **trap** is used to catch animals. *I caught a mouse in a trap.*

U

u·nique (yū-**nēk**) *adjective* Something is **unique** if it is the only one of its kind. *You are unique because there is no one else just like you.*

u·nit·ed (yū-**nī**-tid) *adjective* When people are **united**, they act together for common purposes. *They were united in working to stop pollution.*

up to me When something is **up to me**, I am the one who should do something. *It's up to me to do my homework and get ready for school.*

us (us) *pronoun* the plural of **me**

V

val·ley (**val**-ē) *noun* A **valley** is the land between hills or mountains. *They walked through the valley and saw beautiful mountains on each side.*

valley

vil·lage (**vil**-ij) *noun* A **village** is a small community. *Anna knows the name of every person who lives in her village.*

vil·lag·er (**vil**-i-jur) *noun* A **villager** is a person who lives in a village. *The villager had a garden and kept chickens in his yard.*

W

wa·ter (**waw**-tur) **1.** *noun* Living things need **water**. *I was thirsty, so I drank some water.* **2.** *verb* You **water** plants to help them grow. *I water the garden every day.*

wave (wāv) **1.** *noun* In the ocean, water comes to the shore in a **wave**. *The wave crashed against the rocks.* **2.** *verb* You **wave** when you move your hand back and forth. *I wave to my friends when I see them.*

we (wē) *pronoun* the plural of **I**

weath·ered (**weth**-urd) *adjective* Something is **weathered** when it is changed by wind, sun, and rain. *The weathered house has peeling paint.*

weep (wēp) *verb* When you **weep**, you cry. *She tried not to weep when she left her home.* Past tense: **wept** *He wept when his dog died.*

weight (wāt) *noun* A **weight** is something heavy. *She used a stone as a weight to keep the papers from blowing away.*

wept (wept) *verb* the past tense of **weep**

wood nymph In Greek myths, a **wood nymph** is a spirit that lives in the forest and looks like a beautiful young woman. *The wood nymph ran behind a tree.*

wreck·age (**rek**-ij) *noun* What is left after things are destroyed or ruined is **wreckage**. *After the storm, they walked through the wreckage of the town.*

page 452

page 453

page 454

Staff Development

Meeting the Multi-Level Challenge

English learners entering middle school come from a variety of backgrounds. Some bring a solid educational foundation from their native country. In their home language, they have developed academic skills that are on a par with their native English-speaking peers. Some of these students may be literate in languages such as Arabic, Russian, Chinese, or in other non-Roman alphabet scripts. Even with the challenge of a new written code to crack, these students already bring many of the skills and experiences that will help them succeed in a structured academic setting. They will be able to build on their academic foundation and draw upon an established repertoire of learning strategies as they approach the challenge of learning English and new academic content in English.

Other English learners come with a patchwork of academic and life experiences. War, epidemics, natural disasters, or economic conditions may have caused students and their families to relocate within their home country or in other countries even before arriving in the U.S. School attendance may have been sporadic, with acquisition of skills and content more random than systematic. Such students may also be affected by the emotional aftermath of violence or trauma. Limited academic experiences and the lack of formal literacy skills create special challenges for these students and their teachers. However, the depth of their life experiences can also enrich learning for both peers and teachers.

Between these ends of the spectrum are English learners with every possible constellation of academic and life experiences. The goal of **High Point** is to ensure that each of these students succeeds in becoming a fluent speaker of English and moves into the academic mainstream at a level comparable to fluent English-speaking peers. How is it possible to meet this range of diverse needs?

> *High Point* **offers standards-based instruction with specialized strategies for English learners.**

One key part of the solution is to use standards-based instruction as the medium for learning English. The language arts, mathematics, science, and social studies content of **High Point** is aligned to national and state curriculum standards, ensuring that students gain important experience with key grade-level concepts, vocabulary, and themes as they progress towards fluency in English.

Another key part of ensuring success for all English learners is to tailor the instruction to students' stages of language acquisition. Language acquisition is a process that moves learners through predictable stages of language development on the path toward native-like fluency. However, the way individuals progress through these stages varies widely depending on many factors, including academic background, life experiences, learning styles, and other aspects of individual development. Progress along the pathway toward fluency is not always signalled by forward movement alone. Rather, a student who shows a growth spurt in acquiring new vocabulary, for example, may exhibit less control in using it grammatically. Such spurts and lags in language development are highly individual, and are a normal part of the language acquisition process. For this reason, it is important to identify where each student stands on the language acquisition continuum, and to then use the instructional strategies and techniques that will be most effective in creating continuing language growth and development.

High Point offers differentiated instruction for students across the stages of language acquisition. These differentiated instructional strategies and techniques are embedded throughout the **Teacher's Guide** (see the Multi-Level Strategies features), and are summarized on page T367 to help you target individual students with the most effective language development strategies for their stages of English acquisition.

The Stages of Language Acquisition

High Point incorporates instructional strategies and techniques to help English learners move through the stages of language development.

STAGES AND BEHAVIORS	TEACHING STRATEGIES
BEGINNING	**BEGINNING**
Students with limited formal schooling: • have a language acquisition profile that is similar to Early Beginning students • need lots of age-appropriate oral-to-print and emergent literacy experiences • understand new concepts best when they are previewed in their home language	**Students with limited formal schooling benefit when teachers:** • implement an intensive individualized or small-group emergent literacy program • include them in group activities by using strategies for Beginning students • pair students with a "buddy" with the same home language
Early Beginning students: • need to gain familiarity with the sounds, rhythm, and patterns of English • understand simple messages presented with contextual support (gestures, role-play, etc.) • respond non-verbally by pointing, gesturing, nodding, or drawing • begin to respond with yes/no or one- or two-word answers • read simple language that has already been experienced orally • write labels, patterned sentences, one- or two-word responses	**Beginning students benefit when teachers:** • provide abundant opportunities for active listening, utilizing props, visuals, and real objects • avoid forcing students to speak before they are ready • model memorable language with songs, raps, and poems • pair or group students with more proficient learners • activate prior knowledge, build background, and use visuals before reading activities • ask yes/no, either/or, and Who? What? Where? questions; have students complete sentences with one- or two-word responses • expose students to a variety of understandable texts • have students label/manipulate pictures and real objects • provide writing frames and models
Advanced Beginning students: • understand "chunks" or gist of language, and the gist of group reading by relying on picture clues, titles, and summaries • repeat and recite memorable language; use routine expressions independently • respond with phrases, fragments, and simple subject/verb-based structures • respond to literature with structured support • read familiar, patterned text; read Language Experience texts • write patterned text, short captions; complete simple cloze sentences	
INTERMEDIATE	**INTERMEDIATE**
Early Intermediate students: • understand more details in spoken English • respond using longer phrases or sentences with increasing grammatical accuracy • respond using newly-acquired receptive vocabulary to form messages in English • read material independently following oral previews or experiences with print • respond to literature by explaining, describing, comparing, and retelling • write from models for a variety of purposes	**Intermediate students benefit when teachers:** • have students describe personal experiences, objects, etc. • structure group discussion • structure research projects and guide use of reference material for research • provide opportunities to create oral and written narratives • focus on communication in meaningful contexts where students express themselves in speech and print for a wide range of purposes and audiences • ask open-ended questions; model, expand, restate, and enrich student language • use graphic organizers or storyboards for retelling or role-plays • provide content-area texts, trade books, newspapers, magazines, etc., to promote conceptual development • respond genuinely to student writing and hold conferences that highlight student strengths and progress
Advanced Intermediate students: • participate more fully in discussions, including those with academic content • understand and respond with increasing levels of accuracy and correctness • respond with connected discourse, using more extensive vocabulary • respond with higher-order language (persuade, evaluate, etc.) • read and comprehend a wider range of narrative genre and content texts • read, write, and discuss content-area concepts in greater depth • write connected narrative and expository texts	
ADVANCED	**ADVANCED**
Early Advanced students: • understand non-literal, idiomatic, everyday, and academic language • respond with connected discourse, extensive vocabulary, and decreasing grammatical errors • read a wider range of narrative and expository texts with increasing comprehension, including self-selected material • write using more standard forms with increased depth and breadth of topics and purposes and more creative and analytical writing	**Advanced students benefit when teachers:** • structure group discussion • guide use of reference material for research • facilitate more advanced literature studies • provide for meaningful writing experiences in a variety of modes and forms (fiction, research, penpals, etc.) • publish student-authored stories, newsletters, bulletins, etc. • encourage drama, art, music, and other forms of creative expression to represent meaning and increase students' sense of aesthetics • continue on-going language development through integrated language arts and content-area activities
Advanced/Transitioning students: • respond using varied grammatical structures and vocabulary comparable to native English speakers of the same age • read and write a range of grade-level texts in a variety of subjects • use a repertoire of language-learning strategies to self-monitor, correct, and further develop English language skills	

Good Teaching Practices for English Learners

The **High Point** Teacher's Editions incorporate these instructional strategies to address the varying needs of English learners and to maximize growth in language and concept development.

SET STUDENTS UP FOR SUCCESS!

In **High Point** students acquire English as they learn key grade-level curriculum. To allow students to maximize language learning while processing complex and abstract ideas, each unit begins in a way that sets students up for success:

- **Hands-On Experiences** Each unit is launched with a quick experiential activity that makes the theme of the unit concrete and explicit. For example, in a Community unit, individual students view a visual and list elements that they observe, then repeat the process with a group. This illustrates the powerful dynamics of a community, and the benefits and challenges of working together.

- **Unit Mind Map** As students debrief the Unit Launch activity, they begin to generate key vocabulary that is recycled and developed as the unit progresses. The Unit Mind Map provides an open-ended structure for collecting unit vocabulary, empowering students to take ownership of their learning while providing a structure to facilitate the processing of higher-order vocabulary.

- **Guiding Questions** Each unit explores two related themes. Guiding questions introduced at the outset of each theme establish some of the key ideas to explore through literature, language arts, and content activities. These questions give students an overview of the exploration they are about to undertake and serve as touchstones while the unit progresses. This process helps make learning objectives—and their mastery—visible to students, further empowering them as learners.

The **High Point** program is structured so that key ideas, vocabulary, and content are reviewed, revisited, and expanded at various points within and across courses. This spiraling helps students connect new learning to familiar material and provides an expanding contextual base to help students assimilate new language and concepts with increasing facility.

BUILD BACKGROUND AND ACTIVATE PRIOR KNOWLEDGE

All English learners—even those with limited or no formal schooling—have enough life experience and knowledge to acquire the complex concepts appropriate for middle school students. However, many students do not have a strong enough command of English to rely on spoken or written language alone to grasp new concepts. Here are two crucial strategies that build context for new concepts:

- **Activate Prior Knowledge** Before you introduce new concepts, review familiar, related concepts that help build context. When you invite students to share their experiences, it helps build a common knowledge base. For newly-arrived students, a quick preview in the home language is often the most effective way to ensure that students grasp a complex new concept. If you cannot provide this support, enlist the help of students, volunteers, or bilingual instructional assistants.

- **Build Background** When students have no prior experience with new concepts, common experiential activities, such as the Unit Launch experiences, will help build the concepts and vocabulary that allow students to grasp complex new concepts.

MAKE IT MEANINGFUL!

Imagine listening to a radio newscast in an unfamiliar language. How much do you think you would really comprehend? Help your students get as much meaning as possible from the language they experience:

- **Use Visuals** A picture is worth a thousand words—in any language! In addition to the visuals included in **High Point**, you may wish to begin a picture file with images from magazines, Internet downloads, and content-area books. Although you may not consider yourself artistic, you'll be pleasantly surprised to see how much a simple sketch on the chalkboard can convey to your students! Real objects that students can hold and manipulate also help anchor new vocabulary and concepts in memory.

- **Use Graphic Organizers** Graphic organizers are concrete visuals that help students see the relationship between words and ideas. (See "Graphic Organizers" on pages T336–T337 for a variety of formats.) Quick sketches added to graphic organizers enhance the comprehensibility of these visuals for Beginners.

- **Body Language** Get creative with facial expressions, gestures, pantomime, and role-plays and see how much information you can convey!

- **Restate, Repeat, Reduce Speed** Once you become aware of these simple modifications, you can make your language more comprehensible and build new vocabulary. Incorporate familiar vocabulary and structures into your speech. After using a familiar word, pause and restate using a new expression. This paraphrasing helps link the meaning of new vocabulary to familiar terms. You should also be aware of the length, speed, and complexity of your speech, and modify it to fit your students' needs.

ENCOURAGE INTERACTION

When students learn through an interactive approach, lessons become more memorable and meaningful. Vocabulary and language patterns become anchored in memory, especially for kinesthetic learners.

- **Cooperative Learning** Cooperative learning activities provide a structure that allows students with varying levels of proficiency to participate meaningfully in group projects. These projects offer authentic communication for a wide range of meaningful purposes— from dealing with the logistics of choosing roles, to identifying resources and gathering information, to presenting findings. (See "Cooperative Learning Strategies" on pages T370–T371 for detailed descriptions.)

- **Interactive Writing** Dialogue journals provide a low-risk context for written student/teacher or peer exchanges. (See "Using Journals and Logs" on page T372 for details on journals, including dialogue journals.)

CREATE MIXED GROUPINGS

If your class includes students at various levels of English proficiency, use heterogeneous groupings to turn this challenge to your advantage. When students at differing proficiency levels work together, they all must stretch their communication skills in order to accomplish their goals. This also builds a positive, cooperative learning environment.

> In an interactive approach, lessons are more memorable and meaningful.

LOOK AT LEARNING STRATEGIES

When students understand the strategies that help build language, they are empowered to support their own learning process.

- **Build Metacognitive Awareness** Be sure to familiarize students with the "Strategies for Learning Language" in the Handbook (see page T335). Encourage students to identify and share strategies they use successfully.

- **Reflect in Writing** Reflection logs or journals, learning logs, and peer- or self-evaluation all provide excellent opportunities for students to focus on the role of learning strategies in language development. (See "Using Journals and Logs" on page T372 for details.)

- **Capitalize on Cognates** Students' home languages can provide helpful information for building context and meaning. As you preview literature, encourage students to look for home-language cognates, and to see how much they already know! (See "English–Spanish Cognates" on page T373 for a list of some cognates in the literature selections.)

SEND LEARNING HOME

The *High Point Newsletters* (available in seven languages; see the **Teacher's Resource Book**) allow you to extend learning into students' homes, where families can participate in exploring unit themes in their home language.

CONNECT TO CULTURE

High Point reflects a wide range of cultural traditions. Extend this inclusive approach in your classroom by welcoming students' contributions about the cultural traditions they know best. When students respect each others' linguistic and cultural backgrounds, they will all feel more secure as they learn the language and culture of the United States. A comfortable, non-threatening classroom environment helps all learners achieve at optimum levels.

Cooperative Learning Strategies

High Point's cooperative learning activities involve students of varying language proficiencies in content-rich activities.

STRUCTURE & GRAPHIC	DESCRIPTION	BENEFITS & PURPOSES
ROLES FOR COOPERATIVE GROUPS Supervisor (1) Reporter (4) Recorder (2) Checker (3)	• Form groups according to the number of topics or aspects to be studied. • Assign roles, such as: Facilitator Reporter Researcher Materials Monitor Illustrator Scribe (recorder) • Assign task or project. • Allow time for project completion. • Have groups present their projects.	• When used with heterogeneous groups, roles can be assigned based on language abilities. • Roles can be assigned according to skills or strengths of individuals or to stretch students' skills and abilities. • Assigning roles teaches cooperation and coordination skills. • Assigning roles enhances organizational skills of the group toward task completion.
CORNERS 1's 3's 2's 4's	• Corners of the classroom are designated for focused discussion of four aspects of a topic. • Students individually think and write about the topic for a short time. • Students group into the corner of their choice and discuss the topic. • At least one student from each corner shares about the corner discussion.	• By "voting" with their feet, students literally take a position about a topic. • Focused discussion develops deeper thought about a topic. • Students experience many valid points of view about a topic.
FISHBOWL	• One-half of the class sits in a close circle, facing inward; the other half of the class sits in a larger circle around them. • Students on the inside discuss a topic while those outside listen for new information and/or evaluate the discussion according to pre-established criteria. • Groups reverse positions.	• Focused listening enhances knowledge acquisition and listening skills. • Peer evaluation supports development of specific discussion skills. • Identification of criteria for evaluation promotes self-monitoring.
INSIDE-OUTSIDE CIRCLE	• Students stand in concentric circles facing each other. • Students in the outside circle ask questions; those inside answer. • On a signal, students rotate to create new partnerships. • On another signal, students trade inside/outside roles.	• Talking one-on-one with a variety of partners gives risk-free practice in speaking skills. • Interactions can be structured to focus on specific speaking skills. • Students practice both speaking and active listening.
JIGSAW Expert Group 1 — A's Expert Group 2 — B's Expert Group 3 — C's Expert Group 4 — D's	• Group students evenly into "expert" groups. • Expert groups study one topic or aspect of a topic in depth. • Regroup students so that each new group has at least one member from each expert group. • Experts report on their study. Other students learn from the experts.	• Becoming an expert provides in-depth understanding in one aspect of study. • Learning from peers provides breadth of understanding of over-arching concepts.

STRUCTURE & GRAPHIC	DESCRIPTION	BENEFITS & PURPOSES
NUMBERED HEADS	• Students number off within each group. • Teacher prompts or gives a directive. • Students think individually about the topic. • Groups discuss the topic so that any member of the group can report for the group. • Teacher calls a number and the student from each group with that number reports for the group.	• Group discussion of topics provides each student with language and concept understanding. • Random recitation provides an opportunity for evaluation of both individual and group progress.
ROUNDTABLE	• Seat students around a table in groups of four. • Teacher asks a question with many possible answers. • Each student around the table answers the question a different way.	• Encouraging elaboration creates appreciation for diversity of opinion and thought. • Eliciting multiple answers enhances language fluency.
TEAM WORD WEBBING	• Provide each team with a single large piece of paper. Give each student a different colored marker. • Teacher assigns a topic for a word web. • Each student adds to the part of the web nearest to him/her. • On a signal, students rotate the paper and each student adds to the nearest part again.	• Individual input to a group product ensures participation by all students. • Shifting points of view support both broad and in-depth understanding of concepts.
THINK, PAIR, SHARE	• Students think about a topic suggested by the teacher. • Pairs discuss the topic. • Students individually share information with the class.	• The opportunity for self-talk during individual think time allows the student to formulate thoughts before speaking. • Discussion with a partner reduces performance anxiety and enhances understanding.
THREE-STEP INTERVIEW	• Students form pairs. • Student A interviews student B about a topic. • Partners reverse roles. • Student A shares with the class information from student B; then B shares information from student A.	• Interviewing supports language acquisition by providing scripts for expression. • Responding provides opportunities for structured self-expression.

Using Journals and Logs

*Activities in **High Point** promote the use of journals and logs—
essential tools for English learners.*

Self-expression is essential not only to second-language fluency, but also to the development of critical thinking. Journals and logs are, therefore, essential tools in the ESL classroom. There are many different forms and structures for these writing exercises. Some are impersonal and highly structured to promote a specific kind of thinking; others are free-form and more personal to promote fluency. Some include interactions with the teacher and/or peers; others are primarily for personal use.

Journals and logs enhance language instruction because they:

- engage students in non-threatening development of ideas and language
- provide records of students' thoughts, organization of ideas, language concepts, and reflections
- inspire students to see themselves as writers who set personal goals and self-monitor progress
- provide data for assessment of language development
- serve as a warehouse of ideas for future writing

TYPES OF JOURNALS AND LOGS

Dialogue Journal

Purpose: To focus the student's attention on targeted skills and provide modeling of conventions of English through a written conversation between a student and teacher or peers.

How to Use: Set up pages in two columns.
- Assign free writing or focus attention on a particular idea.
- Invite students to write in one column.
- Respond or invite peer response to the student's writing in the other.
- Use as a Reading Journal to discuss specific selections or as a free-form dialogue about topics of student interest.

Reflection Log or Journal

Purpose: To support development of specific critical thinking skills and to record information for use in follow-up activities.

How to Use: Set a focus for reflection such as identifying main ideas, defining an issue, developing solutions, or applying ideas to personal life.
- Ask students to record their reflections.
- Use as one-time exercises or invite students to continue adding thoughts to their journals as they study a complex topic.

Double- or Multiple-Entry Journal

Purpose: To structure responses for specific kinds of critical thinking.

How to Use: Set up pages in two columns.
- Ask students to title the columns for specific text features or information such as cause and effect, problem and solution, quotation and paraphrase, or literal meaning and interpretation.
- Invite students to respond with entries in each column.
- Expand the number of columns to focus on more than two aspects such as character/plot/setting or word/context/hypothesis/verification.

Learning Log

Purpose: To elicit prior knowledge about a topic, provide a framework for new learning, and intrinsically motivate students toward further study.

How to Use: Set up three columns on a page.
- Have students brainstorm what they already know about a topic in one column.
- Invite students to record questions they hope to answer during study in the second column.
- Encourage students to record answers to their questions during and following study of the topic in the third column.
- Encourage students to record new questions for further research.

Note-Taking Log

Purpose: To promote note-taking efficiency and language fluency and to support recall of information and vocabulary for future assignments.

How to Use: Assign a topic, language structure, or thinking focus for the activity.
- Invite students to take notes about the assigned focus.
- Expand to create a double-entry journal with one column for taking notes from the text and the other for recording the thoughts, questions, and reflections on the text.

Response Journal

Purpose: To provide a low-risk environment for self-expression through written personal responses to literature.

How to Use: Focus attention on a particular aspect of reading about a topic.
- Invite students to record personal thoughts.
- Encourage students to use entries to support evaluation of literature or other critical thinking activities.

English–Spanish Cognates

When you call attention to these cognates, Spanish speakers will see how many English words they already know!

UNIT 1: IDENTITY

Discovery
character	carácter
personality	personalidad
intelligent	inteligente
optimistic	optimista
positive	positivo
irresponsible	irresponsable
merits	méritos

Could I Ask You a Question?
adapt	adaptar
situations	situaciones
culture	cultura
computer	computadora

Many People, Many Intelligences
intelligence	inteligencia
actors	actores
different	diferente
musical	musical
instrument	instrumento
maps	mapas
distance	distancia
angles	ángulos

Art Smart
art	arte
simple	simple
curves	curvas
quiet	quieto
express	expresar
colors	colores
bamboo	bambú
China	China
artists	artistas
George	Jorge
Indian	indio
exotic	exótico
Spanish	español
Italian	italiano
Portuguese	portugués
family	familia
accept	aceptar
decide	decidir

UNIT 2: COOPERATION

Teamwork
cooperate	cooperar
animals	animales
uniforms	uniformes
depend	depender
nations	naciones
problems	problemas

Together, We Dream
adobes	adobes
families	familias
require	requerir
attention	atención
lemon	limón
tomatoes	tomates
reality	realidad

A Dog You Can Count On
instructors	instructores
personality	personalidad
person	persona
especially	especialmente
barriers	barreras
elevators	elevadores
offices	oficinas
banks	bancos

A Mountain Rescue
mountain	montaña
desperately	desesperadamente
silence	silencio
glacier	glaciar
obviously	obviamente

UNIT 3: RELATIONSHIPS

The Qualities of Friendship

The Mouse and the Lion
qualities	cualidades
fables	fábulas
important	importante
lion	león
escape	escapar

The Monkey and the Camel
desert	desierto
camel	camello
directions	direcciones

My Best Friend
music	música
piano	piano
students	estudiantes
pronounce	pronunciar
syllable	sílaba

False Cognate:
college: *not* colegio, *but* universidad

Honoring Our Ancestors
pioneer	pionero
famous	famoso
pilot	piloto
delicious	delicioso
educated	educada
dedicate	dedicar

theory	teoría
magical	mágico

False Cognates:
parents: *not* parientes, *but* padres
support: *not* soportar, *but* apoyar

Grandfather's Nose
article	artículo
science	ciencia
genetics	genética
characteristics	características
genes	genes
human	humano
identical	idénticos
complete	completo
embryo	embrión
exactly	exactamente
combinations	combinaciones
fertilized	fertilizado

False Cognate:
relatives: *not* relativos, *but* parientes

UNIT 4: COMMUNITY

Common Ground
natural	natural
argument	argumento
future	futuro
generations	generaciones
parks	parques
reserves	reservas
gas	gas
distances	distancias
visit	visitar
fossil	fósil

Protecting Our Planet
planet	planeta
crystal	cristal
communities	comunidades
destruction	destrucción
united	unidos
nations	naciones

Earthquake at Dawn
photographer	fotógrafo
epidemic	epidemia
serious	serio
basically	básicamente
authorized	autorizado
committing	cometiendo
crime	crimen
illegal	ilegal
canaries	canarios
horrible	horrible

When Disaster Strikes
disaster	desastre
concrete	concreto
hurricane	huracán
electricity	electricidad
destruction	destrucción
medicine	medicina
repair	reparar
volunteers	voluntarios
President	presidente
helicopter	helicóptero

UNIT 5: TRADITIONS

Echo and Narcissus
echo	eco
exception	excepción
enchanted	encantado
vision	visión

The Art of the Tall Tale
exaggerated	exagerado
cause	causa
effect	efecto
fraction	fracción
logic	lógica
insists	insiste
absolute	absoluta
festival	festival
gallons	galones
coyote	coyote
tornado	tornado
nectar	néctar

Unwinding the Magic Thread
comment	comentar
events	eventos
talents	talentos
compete	competir
decide	decidir
expressions	expresiones
invite	invitar
honor	honor
accompany	acompañar
accident	accidente

When I Taste Salt
salt	sal
Cuban	cubanas
invitation	invitación
timid	tímida
silence	silencio

False Cognate:
memory: *not* memoria, *but* recuerdo

High Point Scope and Sequence

Language Development and Communication

SOCIAL AND ACADEMIC LANGUAGE FUNCTIONS	THE BASICS	A	B	C
Listen actively	•	•	•	•
Repeat spoken language	•			
Express social courtesies	•			
Ask and answer questions	•	•	•	
Use the telephone	•	•		
Conduct a transaction	•	•		
Demonstrate non-verbal communication	•	•	•	•
Adjust communication to the occasion or audience (formal/informal)		•	•	•
Express likes and dislikes	•	•	•	•
Express feelings, needs, opinions, intentions	•	•	•	•
Give and carry out commands	•	•	•	•
Describe people, places, things, events	•	•	•	•
Listen to a preview of a selection	•	•		
Listen to a selection	•	•	•	•
Recite	•	•	•	•
Read a selection	•	•	•	•
Give/Follow directions	•	•	•	•
Role-play	•	•	•	•
Dramatize	•	•	•	•
Ask for/Give information	•	•	•	•
Make comparisons	•	•	•	•
Engage in discussion	•	•	•	•
Persuade		•	•	•
Retell a story	•	•	•	•
Tell an original story		•	•	•
Define and explain		•	•	•
Clarify		•	•	•
Verify or confirm information		•	•	•
Justify		•	•	•
Elaborate		•	•	•
Negotiate		•	•	•
Write	•	•	•	•

LANGUAGE PATTERNS AND STRUCTURES	THE BASICS	A	B	C
Statements	•	•		
Statements with *There is/are/was/were* and *Here is/are/was/were*	•	•		
Statements with infinitives	•	•	•	
Questions/Exclamations/Commands	•	•	•	
Negative sentences	•	•	•	
Complete sentences		•	•	•
Compound sentences		•	•	•
Complex sentences		•	•	•
Relative clauses			•	•
Compound-complex sentences				•
Conditional sentences			•	•
Pronouns and pronoun agreement	•	•	•	•

LANGUAGE PATTERNS AND STRUCTURES, continued	THE BASICS	A	B	C
Demonstrative pronouns	•	•		
Indefinite pronouns			•	•
Adjectives	•	•	•	•
Adjectives that compare		•	•	•
Modals (*can, could, would, might, must*, etc.)	•	•	•	•
Present tense verbs	•	•	•	•
Past tense verbs	•	•	•	•
Future tense verbs	•	•	•	•
Present perfect tense verbs			•	•
Past perfect tense verbs			•	•
Future perfect tense verbs			•	•
Progressive forms of verbs	•	•	•	•
Two-word verbs			•	•
Active/passive voice			•	•
Gerunds			•	•
Contractions	•	•	•	
Adverbs	•	•	•	
Adverbs that compare		•	•	•
Prepositions	•	•	•	

Concepts and Vocabulary

EVERYDAY CONCEPTS AND VOCABULARY	THE BASICS	A	B	C
Greetings and other social courtesies	•	•		
Personal information (name, address, etc.)	•	•		
Categories: Clothing, Food, School, etc.	•	•		
ACADEMIC CONCEPTS AND VOCABULARY				
In Language Arts and Literature	•	•	•	•
In Science, Social Studies, Mathematics	•	•	•	•
In Fine Arts: Music, Art, Drama		•	•	•
VOCABULARY STRATEGIES				
Relate words	•	•	•	•
Structural clues	•	•	•	•
Compound words	•	•		
Prefixes and suffixes	•	•	•	•
Latin and Greek roots			•	•
Context clues	•	•	•	•
Multiple-meaning words	•	•	•	•
Idioms	•	•	•	•
Figurative language			•	•
Analogies			•	•
Denotation and connotation			•	•
Locate and use definitions		•	•	•
Locate word origins			•	•

Reading

LEARNING TO READ

	THE BASICS	A	B	C
Use concepts of print (directionality, etc.)	●			
Recognize high-frequency words	●	●		
Develop phonemic awareness	●			
Associate sounds and symbols	●			
Blend sounds to decode words	●			
Recognize word families	●	●	●	●
Use word patterns to decode words	●			
Use letter patterns to decode words	●			
Identify root words and inflectional endings	●	●	●	
Identify root words and affixes	●	●	●	●
Recognize Greek and Latin roots			●	●
Divide words into syllables	●			
Identify syllable types	●			
Read multisyllabic words	●	●	●	●
Build reading fluency	●	●	●	●

READING STRATEGIES

	THE BASICS	A	B	C
Pre-Reading Strategies	●	●	●	●
Activate prior knowledge/Relate to personal experience	●	●	●	●
Preview	●	●	●	●
Build background	●	●	●	●
Predict	●	●	●	●
Set a purpose for reading	●	●	●	●
Relate reading rate to purpose		●	●	●
Skim		●	●	●
Scan			●	●
Use graphic organizers to prepare for reading	●	●	●	●
Self-Monitoring Strategies	●	●	●	●
Ask questions	●	●	●	●
Clarify	●	●	●	●
Visualize	●	●	●	●
Paraphrase		●	●	●
Use visuals	●	●	●	●
Relate to personal knowledge or experience	●	●	●	●
Compare selection to other texts with similar theme, genres, or text structures	●	●	●	●
Make, confirm, and revise predictions	●	●	●	●
Adjust purposes for reading		●	●	●
Confirm word meaning	●	●	●	●
Use punctuation clues	●	●		
Use signal words	●	●		
Corrective Strategies	●	●	●	●
Reread	●	●	●	●
Read on	●	●	●	●
Search for new clues		●	●	●
Adjust reading rate	●	●	●	●
Reduce the amount of text read at one time		●	●	●
Use reference aids (glossary, dictionary, etc.)		●	●	●

READING STRATEGIES, continued

	THE BASICS	A	B	C
Comprehension Strategies (See also Comprehension)	●	●	●	●
Review	●	●	●	●
Connect new information to known	●	●	●	●
Use text structures	●	●	●	●
Use text and graphic features	●	●	●	●
Use graphic organizers to relate ideas	●	●	●	●
Retell	●			
Use SQ3R			●	●
Summarize	●	●	●	●

COMPREHENSION

	THE BASICS	A	B	C
Follow directions	●	●	●	●
Identify details	●	●	●	●
Classify	●	●	●	●
Identify character's traits, feelings, point of view, motive	●	●	●	●
Identify sequence	●	●	●	●
Identify steps in a process	●	●	●	●
Identify or relate cause and effect	●	●	●	●
Identify or relate main idea and details	●	●	●	●
Identify or relate problem and solution	●	●	●	●
Identify or relate goal and outcome	●	●	●	●
Make comparisons	●	●	●	●
Make an inference	●	●	●	●
Draw conclusions	●	●	●	●
Summarize	●	●	●	●
Form generalizations			●	●
Identify author's purpose		●	●	●
Identify author's biases and point of view		●	●	●
Identify author's assumptions and beliefs			●	●
Analyze story elements	●	●	●	●
Analyze information	●	●	●	●
Distinguish between facts and opinions	●	●	●	●
Recognize missing information				●
Identify fallacies of logic				●
Identify multiple levels of meaning			●	●
Distinguish between fantasy and reality	●	●	●	●
Distinguish between relevant and irrelevant information			●	●
Distinguish between important and unimportant information		●	●	●
Distinguish between apparent message and hidden agenda			●	●
Form opinions	●	●	●	●
Make judgments or decisions	●	●	●	●
Support judgments	●	●	●	●
Identify propaganda			●	●
Evaluate information		●	●	●
Synthesize information			●	●
Recognize how personal background and viewpoint influence interpretation of a selection		●	●	●

Literary Analysis and Appreciation

RECOGNIZE GENRES	THE BASICS	A	B	C
Article	●	●	●	●
Autobiography		●	●	●
Biographical fiction			●	●
Biography	●	●	●	●
Character Sketch		●	●	●
Description	●	●	●	●
Diary/Journal	●	●	●	●
Documentary				●
Drama		●	●	●
Essay	●	●	●	●
Fable		●	●	●
Family portrait/Self-portrait		●	●	
Fantasy		●	●	●
Fiction	●	●	●	●
Folk tale/Legend	●	●	●	●
Historical account	●			
Historical fiction	●	●	●	●
How-to article	●	●	●	●
Interview	●	●	●	●
Memoir/Personal narrative	●	●	●	●
Myth	●	●	●	●
Nonfiction	●	●	●	●
News article/Newscast	●	●	●	●
Persuasive essay		●	●	●
Photo or art essay	●	●	●	●
Play		●	●	●
Poetry	●	●	●	●
Rhymed verse	●	●	●	●
Free verse	●	●	●	●
Proverb/Saying		●	●	●
Quotation		●	●	●
Realistic fiction	●	●	●	●
Report	●	●	●	●
Science article	●	●	●	●
Science fiction		●	●	●
Song/Chant	●	●	●	●
Speech			●	●
Short Story			●	●
Tall tale	●	●		

RECOGNIZE LITERARY DEVICES	THE BASICS	A	B	C
Alliteration		●	●	●
Allusion				●
Analogy				●
Assonance and consonance			●	●
Characterization	●	●	●	●
Compressed language				●
Description		●	●	●

RECOGNIZE LITERARY DEVICES, continued	THE BASICS	A	B	C
Dialect				●
Dialogue		●	●	●
Figurative language		●	●	●
Hyperbole/Exaggeration		●	●	●
Imagery/Sensory language		●	●	●
Simile		●	●	●
Metaphor		●	●	●
Personification			●	●
Irony				●
Mood and tone		●	●	●
Narrator's Point of view		●	●	●
Onomatopoeia			●	●
Plot development	●	●	●	●
Goal and outcome or Problem and solution	●	●	●	●
Conflict/Complications/Climax/Resolution		●	●	●
Rising and falling action			●	●
Flashback			●	●
Foreshadowing			●	●
Suspense				●
Repetition		●	●	●
Rhyme	●	●	●	●
Rhyme scheme			●	●
Rhythm/meter		●	●	●
Setting	●	●	●	●
Style		●	●	●
Symbolism			●	●
Theme		●	●	●
Word choice		●	●	●

RESPOND TO LITERATURE	THE BASICS	A	B	C
Interpret literature	●	●	●	●
Apply literature to personal life	●	●	●	●
Identify questions of personal importance and answer them through literature	●	●	●	●
Develop personal preferences in reading	●	●	●	●
Recognize how literature expands and enriches personal viewpoints and experiences	●	●	●	●
Recognize that literature may elicit a variety of valid responses	●	●	●	●

EVALUATE LITERATURE	THE BASICS	A	B	C
Evaluate the impact of literary devices, medium, or genre on meaning or quality		●	●	●
Evaluate the impact of the author's background, qualifications, biases, or point of view on meaning		●	●	●
Evaluate the impact of culture, time period, customs, or outlooks on meaning		●	●	●
Evaluate the literary quality of a selection		●	●	●
Compare literature on a variety of points (theme, genre, point of view, etc.)		●	●	●
Recognize the defining characteristics of classical literature (timelessness, universality of themes, etc.)			●	●

Cognitive Academic Skills

LEARNING STRATEGIES

LEVELS	THE BASICS	A	B	C
Strategies for Language Learning	●	●	●	●
Listen to and imitate others	●	●	●	●
Recite songs and poems	●	●	●	●
Use gestures and mime to get across an idea	●	●	●	●
Explore alternate ways of saying things	●	●	●	●
Test hypotheses about language	●	●	●	●
Ask for help, feedback, and clarification	●	●	●	●
Use visuals to construct meaning	●	●	●	●
Compare nonverbal and verbal cues	●	●	●	●
Compare and contrast elements of language and identify patterns in language	●	●	●	●
Incorporate language "chunks"	●			●
Use reference aids to verify language/spelling		●	●	●
Practice new language (repeating, etc.)	●			●
Analyze situations to determine appropriate language use (formal/informal)		●	●	●
Self-monitor language use and self-assess	●	●	●	●
Strategies for Reading *See page T331*	●	●	●	●
Strategies for Listening, Speaking, Viewing, Representing, Writing	●	●	●	●
Activate prior knowledge	●	●	●	●
Relate to personal knowledge or experience	●	●	●	●
Predict	●	●	●	●
Ask questions	●	●	●	●
Clarify		●	●	●
Visualize		●	●	●
Paraphrase		●	●	●
Connect new information to known	●	●	●	●
Review	●	●	●	●
Make comparisons	●	●	●	●
Use graphic organizers	●	●	●	●
Interact with peers	●	●	●	●
Plan and set goals	●	●	●	●
Brainstorm	●	●	●	●
Generate and organize ideas	●	●	●	●
Gather information	●	●	●	●
Make observations	●	●	●	●
Take notes	●	●	●	●
Outline		●	●	●
Summarize	●	●	●	●
Self-monitor and self-assess	●	●	●	●

STRATEGIES FOR TAKING TESTS

	THE BASICS	A	B	C
Read directions carefully		●	●	●
Plan time for each item/section		●	●	●
Clarify vocabulary in passages/questions		●	●	●
Use typographic clues to meaning		●	●	●
Reread passages to clarify information		●	●	●
Note test format and select appropriate strategies		●	●	●
Mark answers and check for legibility		●	●	●

CRITICAL THINKING

LEVELS	THE BASICS	A	B	C
Classify	●	●	●	●
Relate events in a sequence	●	●	●	●
Relate steps in a process	●	●	●	●
Relate cause and effect	●	●	●	●
Relate main ideas and details	●	●	●	●
Relate problem and solution	●	●	●	●
Relate goal and outcome	●	●	●	●
Formulate questions	●	●	●	●
Formulate hypotheses		●	●	●
Clarify information		●	●	●
Make comparisons	●	●	●	●
Make inferences		●	●	●
Draw conclusions		●	●	●
Summarize	●	●	●	●
Form generalizations		●	●	●
Analyze information	●	●	●	●
Form opinions	●	●	●	●
Make judgments or decisions	●	●	●	●
Evaluate information		●	●	●
Synthesize information			●	●
Generate ideas	●	●	●	●
Solve problems	●	●	●	●

RESEARCH SKILLS

	THE BASICS	A	B	C
Use the research process	●	●	●	●
Locate resources (library, computerized card catalog, *Reader's Guide*, etc.)	●	●	●	●
Gather information	●	●	●	●
Use alphabetical order		●		
Survey/Skim and scan/Look up key words		●	●	●
Use print resources	●	●	●	●
almanac			●	●
atlas, globe	●	●	●	●
books	●	●	●	●
dictionary		●	●	●
thesaurus			●	●
encyclopedia		●	●	●
magazines and newspapers		●	●	●
Use electronic resources: CD-ROM, electronic encyclopedia, the Internet		●	●	●
Use audio-visual resources	●	●	●	●
Use graphic aids (charts, time line, etc.)	●	●	●	●
Conduct observations, surveys, experiments, and interviews	●	●	●	●
Take notes	●	●	●	●
Organize and synthesize information from multiple sources		●	●	●
Generate new research questions			●	●
Write a research report		●	●	●
Cite sources			●	●

Listening, Speaking, Viewing, and Representing

LEVELS	THE BASICS	A	B	C
LISTENING AND SPEAKING				
Listen actively	●	●	●	●
Listen for information	●	●	●	●
Listen critically to determine purpose and message		●	●	●
Listen to a poem or song	●	●	●	●
Listen to a selection	●	●	●	●
Listen and speak effectively in a discussion	●	●	●	●
Listen and speak effectively in a peer conference		●	●	●
Listen and speak effectively to work with a partner or on a team	●	●	●	●
Speak at an appropriate rate and volume		●	●	●
Make eye contact		●	●	●
Use language and tone appropriate to the audience, purpose, and occasion		●	●	●
Give and follow directions or commands	●	●	●	●
Express feelings, needs, ideas, and opinions	●	●	●	●
Describe	●	●	●	●
Ask and answer questions	●	●	●	●
Conduct an interview	●	●	●	●
Recite	●	●	●	●
Read aloud	●	●	●	●
Role-play or dramatize	●	●	●	●
Retell a story	●	●	●	●
Tell a story		●	●	●
Inform or explain	●	●	●	●
Give an oral report		●	●	●
Give a speech		●	●	●
Persuade		●	●	●
Participate in a debate		●	●	●
Demonstrate non-verbal communication	●	●	●	●
REPRESENTING IDEAS AND INFORMATION				
Create graphic organizers	●	●	●	●
Create illustrations or photographs	●	●	●	●
Create posters and other visual displays	●	●	●	●
Create a map	●	●	●	●
Create a multimedia presentation		●	●	●
VIEWING				
Respond to a visual image	●	●	●	●
Interpret a visual image	●	●	●	●
Identify visual symbols	●	●	●	●
View critically to determine purpose and message		●	●	●
Recognize various types of mass media		●	●	●
Compare and evaluate media		●	●	●

Writing

LEVELS	THE BASICS	A	B	C
HANDWRITING				
Letter formation and spacing	●			
Left-to-right directionality	●			
WRITING PURPOSES, MODES, AND FORMS				
Write for a variety of purposes and audiences	●	●	●	●
Choose the mode and form of writing that works best for the topic, audience, and purpose		●	●	●
Write in a variety of modes	●	●	●	●
Narrative	●	●	●	●
Expository	●	●	●	●
Descriptive	●	●	●	●
Expressive	●	●	●	●
Persuasive		●	●	●
Write in a variety of forms	●	●	●	●
Biography	●	●	●	●
Character sketch		●	●	●
Critique		●	●	●
Description	●	●	●	●
Diary/Journal entry	●			
E-mail/ Internet page		●	●	●
Essay		●	●	●
Fact sheet	●	●	●	●
Letter	●	●	●	●
Magazine/News article/Newscast		●	●	●
Myth			●	
Paragraph	●	●	●	●
Personal narrative/ Self-portrait/ Memoir	●	●	●	●
Persuasive essay		●	●	●
Play				●
Poem/Rhyme/Song	●	●	●	●
Poster	●	●	●	●
Quickwrite		●	●	●
Report	●	●	●	●
Sentences	●	●	●	●
Speech		●	●	●
Story		●	●	●
Summary		●	●	●
WRITING PROCESS				
Prewriting	●	●	●	●
Analyze published and student models		●	●	●
Brainstorm and collect ideas	●	●	●	●
Choose a topic	●	●	●	●
Plan writing with an FATP Chart (**F**orm, **A**udience, **T**opic, **P**urpose)		●	●	●
Organize ideas	●	●	●	●

Writing, continued

WRITING PROCESS, continued	THE BASICS	A	B	C
Drafting	•	•	•	•
Write to communicate ideas	•	•	•	•
Use writing techniques appropriate to the purpose, audience, and form		•	•	•
Use appropriate organizing structures	•	•	•	•
logical order	•	•	•	•
sequential order	•	•	•	•
spatial order		•	•	•
to make comparisons	•	•	•	•
to show causes and effects		•	•	•
to show goals and outcomes	•	•	•	•
to show problems and solutions	•	•	•	•
to show thesis and supporting arguments		•	•	•
Revising	•	•	•	•
Evaluate the draft	•	•	•	•
Participate in peer-conferencing		•	•	•
Add, elaborate, delete, combine, and rearrange the text to improve the draft	•	•	•	•
Editing and Proofreading	•	•	•	•
Check the revised copy for correct conventions of written English and make corrections	•	•	•	•
Use reference materials (dictionary, etc.)		•	•	•
Publishing	•	•	•	•
Create the final version of the work and prepare it for publication, using visuals or multimedia to complement or extend meaning	•	•	•	•
Reflect and Evaluate		•	•	•
Use rubrics to evaluate the work		•	•	•
Use evaluations to set goals as a writer		•	•	•
WRITER'S CRAFT				
Introductions that catch the reader's interest		•	•	•
Effective conclusions		•	•	•
Word choice: colorful, specific, precise words; vocabulary appropriate for the audience, etc.	•	•	•	•
Effective sentences		•	•	•
Combine sentences		•	•	•
Break up run-on sentences		•	•	•
Sentence variety		•	•	•
Effective paragraphs	•	•	•	•
Topic sentence and supporting details	•	•	•	•
Transition words			•	•
Consistent verb tense and point of view			•	•
Show, don't tell		•	•	•
Include important or interesting information		•	•	•
Exclude unnecessary details		•	•	•
Elaborate		•	•	•
Use visual and organizational aids	•	•	•	•
Develop a personal voice or style			•	•
Constantly evaluate the writing		•	•	•
Keep a writing portfolio	•	•	•	•

Grammar, Usage, Mechanics, Spelling

SENTENCES	THE BASICS	A	B	C
Sentence types	•	•	•	•
Negative sentences	•	•	•	•
Conditional sentences			•	•
Sentence structures	•	•	•	•
Phrases			•	•
Clauses			•	•
Simple sentences	•	•	•	•
Compound sentences			•	•
Complex sentences			•	•
Compound-complex sentences				•
Properly placed clauses and modifiers			•	•
Subjects and predicates			•	•
Complete subject			•	•
Simple subject			•	•
Understood subject (*you*)			•	•
It as the subject (*It* is raining)			•	•
Compound subject			•	•
Complete predicate			•	•
Simple predicate (verb)			•	•
Compound predicate			•	•
Complete sentences/Fragments			•	•
Subject–verb agreement	•	•	•	•
PARTS OF SPEECH				
Nouns	•	•	•	•
Common and proper	•	•	•	•
Count and noncount	•	•	•	•
Plurals	•	•	•	•
Possessive	•	•	•	•
Articles		•	•	•
Pronouns	•	•	•	•
Subject	•	•	•	•
Object	•	•	•	•
Possessive	•	•	•	•
Reflexive		•	•	•
Indefinite		•	•	•
Demonstrative	•	•	•	•
Relative			•	•
Adjectives	•	•	•	•
Adjectives that compare		•	•	•
Verbs	•	•	•	•
Action	•	•	•	•
Linking	•	•	•	•
Modals (*can, could, would, might, must*, etc.)	•	•	•	•
Helping	•	•	•	•
Transitive and intransitive verbs		•	•	•

Grammar, Usage, Mechanics, Spelling, continued

LEVELS	THE BASICS	A	B	C
PARTS OF SPEECH, continued				
Verb tenses	●	●	●	○
Present tense	●	●	●	
Habitual present tense	●	●	●	
Past tense (regular and irregular)	●	●	●	
Future tense	●	●	●	
Present perfect tense		●	●	○
Past perfect tense		●	●	○
Future perfect tense		●	●	○
Progressive forms of verbs	●	●	○	
Two-word verbs		●	●	○
Active/passive verbs		●	●	○
Gerunds				○
Participial phrases				○
Contractions		●	●	
Adverbs	●	●	●	
Adverbs that compare		●	●	○
Prepositions and prepositional phrases	●	●	●	○
Conjunctions		●	●	○
Interjections		●	●	○
CAPITALIZATION				
First word of a sentence	●	●		
Pronoun I	●	●		
Proper nouns	●	●	●	○
Abbreviations of proper nouns	●	●	●	○
Proper adjectives	●	●	●	○
In letters		●	●	○
In titles		●	●	○
In direct quotations		●	●	○
PUNCTUATION				
Period	●	●	●	○
Question mark	●	●	●	○
Exclamation mark	●	●	●	○
Comma		●	●	○
Apostrophe	●	●	●	○
Quotation marks		●	●	○
Colon		●	●	○
Semicolon		●	●	○
Dash		●	●	○
Hyphen		●	●	○
Italics		●	●	○
Underline			●	○
Parentheses			●	○
SPELLING				
Use spelling strategies	●	●	●	○
Memorize reliable rules	●	●	●	○

Technology/Media

LEVELS	THE BASICS	A	B	C
TECHNOLOGICAL LITERACY				
Identify forms, purposes and functions of technology		●	●	○
Operate a computer		●	●	○
Operate audio and visual recording devices		●	●	○
USING TECHNOLOGY				
Use e-mail		●	●	○
Use audio, video, and electronic media to generate ideas, gather information, conduct interviews, etc., during the writing process	●	●	●	○
Use word-processing software		●	●	○
Use desktop publishing or multiple media to publish work		●	●	○
Use the Internet and other technology to locate resources		●	●	○
Evaluate quality and reliability of information from electronic resources		●	●	○
Make databases and spreadsheets			●	○
MEDIA STUDY AND MULTIMEDIA PRESENTATIONS				
Evaluate and select media for presentations (based on message, purpose, audience)		●	●	○
Design and create multimedia presentations		●	●	○
Compare print, visual, and electronic media			●	○
Explain how the use of different media affects the message			●	○

Cultural Perspectives

LEVELS	THE BASICS	A	B	C
MULTICULTURAL AWARENESS AND APPRECIATION				
Connect personal experiences and ideas with those of others	●	●	●	○
Compare oral traditions, folk tales, and literature across regions and cultures	●	●	●	○
Read and conduct research to increase knowledge of many cultures		●	●	○
Understand that language and literature are the primary means by which culture is transmitted			●	○
Recognize universal themes that cross cultures		●	●	○
Appreciate the diversity of cultures and generations	●	●	●	○
Appreciate and share aspects of the home, U.S., and world culture	●	●	●	○
History	●	●	●	○
Language	●	●	●	○
Folklore and literature	●	●	●	○
Symbols	●	●	●	○
Holidays, customs, and traditions	●	●	●	○
Political systems and government	●	●	●	○
Media		●	●	○

Audio Scripts for Building Language and Vocabulary

ANNA MODORSKY page T22

Narrator: *Look at the picture on page 22 as you listen to this interview. Claudia Gómez—a reporter—is talking to Anna Modorsky, a middle school student.*

Claudia: Anna, imagine yourself ten years from now. What will you be doing?

Anna: In ten years, I want to be in college.

Claudia: What will you study?

Anna: I'm not sure what I'll study. I really like animals, so I might study something about animals. Maybe I will study to be a doctor who takes care of animals.

Claudia: Do you want to be a veterinarian?

Anna: Yes, that's right, a vet.

Claudia: Do you like science? Veterinarians need to study lots of science.

Anna: Science is one of my favorite classes.

Claudia: Well, that's lucky. What about your trumpet? Will you still be playing that?

Anna: Maybe I can play in a band. Right now, I'm in the school band, and I really like it. I hope I am still playing my trumpet in ten years. I'll probably play a lot better!

Claudia: I bet! When did you start playing the trumpet?

Anna: Last year, in fifth grade.

Claudia: So, in ten years, you will probably play very well. What else do you want to do?

Anna: Well, I really enjoy sports. I play tennis and I'm on a baseball team now. Maybe I can be on a team in college.

Claudia: Do you like to be so busy?

Anna: Yes, I guess I do like to keep busy.

Claudia: Well, I'm sure in ten years your life will be busy and interesting, just like it is now! Thanks for talking to me, Anna. I've really enjoyed it.

Anna: Thank you, Ms. Gómez. It was fun.

A BARN RAISING page T70

Narrator: *Look at the picture on page 70 in your book. Now listen to this description of how Amish men build a barn.*

Voice: A Barn Raising

In Pennsylvania, Amish men work together to build a barn. A carpenter uses tools to measure and cut wood. A man hammers boards together. A boy carries nails. When pieces for a wall are all nailed together, two teams get ready to lift the wall. A leader gives directions. The leader says to lift. Some men lift the wall with their hands. Other men use long boards to help push the wall up. Other workers stop to watch the wall go up.

Over on the grass, women get lunch ready. A woman and a girl carry jars of fruits and vegetables from the house. This food came from their summer garden. Another woman puts the food out on plates. Soon, a girl runs to tell the men that it is time to stop working. Lunch is ready!

MAKING TAMALES page T80

Narrator: *Look at the picture on page 80 in your book. Now listen to a description of how this family makes tamales.*

Voice: Making Tamales

When this family makes tamales, everyone helps. First, the corn husks are put into a pot of water. This makes them soft. Two sisters help Grandfather. They take the soft corn husks from the pot. Grandfather puts the husks into a bowl. The next step is to spread cornmeal dough on the husks. Mother and a cousin each hold their husks over a bowl. They spread the dough with a spoon. An aunt and uncle work on the table. They also spread the dough with their spoons. The next step is to add the meat and sauce to the tamales. Then it is time to roll and fold the corn husks. Finally, Grandmother puts the rolled and folded tamales into a big pot. This is the last step before cooking. After the tamales cook, Grandmother will take them from the pot. Then the family will enjoy a delicious treat!

BEN page T126

Narrator: *Read the friendship proverbs on page 126. Then listen to a short story about Ben, a good friend.*

Voice: We had a big project to do over Winter break. We had to write a research report for Social Studies. When I was ready to start working on it, I looked for the teacher's instructions for the project. I couldn't find them in my notebook or in any of my papers. I was so upset. I didn't know how I would be able to do the work without the instructions.

Then I remembered that my friend Ben is in my Social Studies class. I called him on the phone to see if he had the directions for the assignment. He said he was going to the library the next day to start his research. He invited me to go with him. I felt so happy that I had called him. I stopped worrying so much.

The next day at the library, I made a copy of Ben's directions. We worked together to find the books we needed for our research. My friend really helped me solve my problem! That made me feel good!

Audio Scripts for Building Language and Vocabulary, continued

KING SOLOMON AND THE SMELL OF BREAD page T294

Narrator: *Look at the picture on page 294 as you listen to the story, "King Solomon and the Smell of Bread." The story is from the Jewish tradition as told by a student, Sarah Ross.*

Voice: A long, long time ago, in the city of Jerusalem, there lived a king named Solomon. King Solomon was known for his great wisdom, and people came from near and far to have him solve their problems.

In the same city there was a bakery which was known for its delicious bread. People would line up each day to buy the bread—and sometimes just to smell it. You see, one day the baker saw a poor woman dressed in rags standing by the open door to the bakery.

"What are you doing standing there?" asked the baker.

"I'm just smelling your bread. It smells so wonderful!" said the poor woman.

"Of course this bread smells wonderful. I bake it! I'm afraid that you can't just smell my bread for free! If you are going to smell my bread, you are going to have to pay me!"

The poor woman refused to pay, so the baker dragged her to King Solomon's court. In the court were many people waiting to have King Solomon hear their cases. When it was his turn, the baker said, "I caught this woman smelling my bread, and when I told her she must pay me, she refused. I have come here to get my payment!"

All the people in the court began to laugh, as no one had ever heard anything so ridiculous. King Solomon raised his hand and all grew quiet, so quiet you could hear a pin drop!

King Solomon looked at the woman and asked, "Have you been smelling this baker's bread?"

"Yes, I have, but I meant no harm. Do I really have to pay for smelling the bread?" the poor woman asked.

"By the law of our land, you must pay. Have you any money?"

"Well, I have a little," said the woman. She reached into her pocket and as she took out her money purse, the coins jingled softly.

"There you are," King Solomon said to the baker, "you have been paid in full. For the smell of your bread, you have been paid with the sound of this poor woman's coins."

THE BOY WHO LOOKED FOR THE WIND page T306

Narrator: *Look at the pictures on page 306 as you listen to the beginning of the story, "The Boy Who Looked for the Wind."*

Voice: Once there was a boy who went looking for the wind. He traveled far until he came to a grassy meadow. There he saw a fox. "Have you seen the wind?" he asked the fox.

"I have heard the wind," answered the fox. "I have heard it blowing through the long grass, but I have never seen the wind."

"I have to find the wind," said the boy.

"I cannot tell you where it is," said the fox, "but, here, take this grass. It may help you find it."

The boy took the handful of grass and traveled on. Soon he saw a bluebird singing on a fence. "Have you seen the wind?" he asked the bluebird.

"I have felt the wind," answered the bluebird. "I have felt it beneath my wings, but I have never seen the wind."

"I have to find the wind," said the boy.

"I can't tell you where it is," said the bluebird, "but here is a feather. It may help you find it."

The boy took the feather and traveled on.

Index

Program Features and Resources

Index, continued

Reading and Learning Strategies, Critical Thinking, and Comprehension

Index, continued

Literary Concepts

Listening and Speaking

Technology and Media

Research Skills

Instructional Strategies

Acknowledgments, continued

Francisco X. Alarcón: "Collective Dream," "Adobes," and "Family Garden." Text copyright © 1999 by Francisco X. Alarcón. Used with permission of the author. All rights reserved.

J. Paul Getty Museum: *Echo and Narcissus* by Antonia Barber. Copyright © 1998 by Antonia Barber. Reprinted with permission of the J. Paul Getty Museum.

Harcourt, Inc.: Excerpt from *A Guide Dog Puppy Grows Up* by Caroline Arnold. Text copyright © 1991 by Caroline Arnold, reprinted with permission of Harcourt, Inc.

HarperCollins Publishers: "A Boy and a Man" from *Banner in the Sky* by James Ramsey Ullman. Copyright © 1954 by James Ramsey Ullman. *Teamwork* by Ann Morris. Copyright © 1999 by Ann Morris. "My Best Friend" from *Childtimes* by Lessie Jones Little and Eloise Greenfield. Copyright © 1979 by Eloise Greenfield and Lessie Jones Little. All used by permission of HarperCollins Publishers.

Henry Holt: p13, ("Liberty" by Robert Silvers, reprinted with permission of the publisher, © Robert Silvers).

Margaret Hillert: "Just Me" by Margaret Hillert. Used by permission of the author who controls all rights.

Homeland Publishing (CAPAC). A division of Troubadour Records Ltd.: "Evergreen, Everblue," "One Light, One Sun," "Big Beautiful Planet," and "Clean Rain" from *Evergreen, Everblue* by Raffi. "Evergreen, Everblue" words and music by Raffi, copyright © 1990; "One Light, One Sun" words and music by Raffi, copyright © 1985; "Big Beautiful Planet" words and music by Raffi, copyright © 1982; "Clean Rain" words and music by Raffi, copyright © 1990. All rights reserved. Used by permission.

Limousine Music Co. & The Last Music Co: "Family Tree" from *Family Tree* by Tom Chapin. Copyright © 1988 by John Forster & Tom Chapin. Limousine Music Co. & The Last Music Co. (ASCAP).

Myra Cohn Livingston: "We Could Be Friends" from *The Way Things Are and Other Poems* by Myra Cohn Livingston. Copyright © 1974 by Myra Cohn Livingston. Used by permission of Marian Reiner.

NASA/JPL/Caltech: "Mars Network." Courtesy of NASA/JPL/Caltech.

Dorothy Hinshaw Patent: Selected excerpts from *Grandfather's Nose* by Dorothy Hinshaw Patent. Text copyright © 1989 by Dorothy Hinshaw Patent.

Penguin Putnam: "Everybody Says" from *Here, There and Everywhere* by Dorothy Aldis. Copyright 1927, 1928, copyright renewed © 1955, 1956 by Dorothy Aldis. Used by permission of G.P. Putnam's Sons, a division of Penguin Putnam Inc.

Scholastic: Selected excerpts from *Common Ground* by Molly Bang. Published by The Blue Sky Press, an imprint of Scholastic Inc. Copyright © 1997 by Molly Bang. Reprinted by permission.

Mike Thaler: Question and answer from *Earth Mirth* by Mike Thaler. Used by permission of the author.

Burton Watson: "Peasant Song" from *Ancient China* by Edward H. Schafer. Used by permission of Burton Watson, translator.

Albert Whitman & Company: *How the Ox Star Fell from Heaven* retold and illustrated by Lily Toy Hong. Text and illustrations copyright © 1991 by Lily Toy Hong. Adaptation reprinted by permission of Albert Whitman & Company.

Diane Wolkstein: "Introduction" and "Owl" from *The Magic Orange Tree and Other Haitian Folktales* by Diane Wolkstein. Schocken, copyright © 1997 by Diane Wolkstein.

World Almanac Group: "Looking for Life Elsewhere in the Universe" from *World Almanac for Kids*. Reprinted with permission from *The World Almanac for Kids 1998*. Copyright © 1997 World Almanac Education Group. All rights reserved.

Photographs:

Michael Aki: ppT172, T175 (Michael Aki family photos courtesy of Michael Aki.).

American Foundation for the Blind: pT92 (photograph of Helen Keller courtesy of American Foundation for the Blind.).

Animal Animals/Earth Scenes: ppT190–T191, T220 (rain forest, Doug Wechsler).

AP/Wide World Photos: p75 (rowers, David J. Phillip) pT227 (seismograph, Francesco Belini) pT244 (Taiwan earthquake, Pat Roque) pT248 (sandbaggers, Beth A. Keiser) pT449 (guide dog, Christopher Barth).

Art Resource: p3, pT66b, pT66 (Ringling Bros. Astounding Feat of Ernest Clark Circus Poster 1910, Scala/Art Resource, NY), p18 (telescope, Scala/Art Resource, NY), pT133 (Aesop by Domingo Velazquez, Scala/Art Resource, NY), ppT152–T153 (La Familia by Jose Clemente Orozco, Schalwijk/Art Resource, NY © SOMAAP 2000), pT264 (Ad Marginem by Paul Klee, Giraudon/Art Resource, NY © 2000 Artist Rights Society [ARS], New York/VG Bild-Kunst, Bonn), pT272 (Athena, Nimatallah/ Art Resource, NY) pT273 (Peracles, Scala/Art Resource, NY), pT284 (ruling class, Giraudon/ Art Resource, NY), pT285 (emperor, Giraudon/ Art Resource, NY, scholars, Erich Lessing/Art Resource, NY, knights, Victoria & Albert Museum, London/Art Resource, NY).

Artville: pT40 (coins).

The Bridgeman Art Library: p3, pT262b, pT262, pT333 (Ulysses and the Sirens, Musee du Bardo, Tuni, Tunisia).

Brigham Young University: ppT226, T228, T237 (photograph of San Francisco City Hall 1906 courtesy of L. Tom Perry Special Collections, Harold B. Lee Library, Brigham Young University, Provo, Utah.).

Children's Book Press: pT80("Making Tamales" and cooking pot reprinted with permission of the publisher, Children's Book Press, San Francisco, CA. Copyright © 1990 by Carmen Lomas Garza. All rights reserved.)

Comstock: ppT72–T73, T77 (rafters).

Contact Press: ppT222–T223 (earthquake damage, Alon Reininger).

Corbis: p18 (Jules Verne), pT16 (chessboard), pT21 (George Washington Carver, Bettman/ CORBIS), pT26 (Miami coast, Robert Landau), pT27 (El Morro, Neil Rabinowitz, waterfall, Richard Bickel; coquí frog, Kevin Schafer), pT32 (Caesar Chavez, Ted Streshinsky), pT90 (granite), pT91 (climbers, Warren Morgan), pT102 (crevasse rescue, Joel W. Rogers; rescue inset, Lowell Georgia), pT144 (storefront, Bettman/ CORBIS), pT146 (Jelly Roll Morton), pT212 (tulips), pT7, pT222, ppT262a–T262b, ppT262–T263 (rock texture), pT231 (man watching fires, Bettman/CORBIS), pT233 (San Francisco Earthquake, Bettman/ CORBIS), pT262 (Parthenon) pT272 (Acropolis, Doric Column, Bettman/CORBIS) pT278 (emperor, Pierre Colombel) pT448 (forest) pT451 (planet) p T452 (ruins, John Dakers) pT453 (tent city, Janez Skok).

Corel: p18 (Mayan ruin).

Digital Stock: p3, pT6, pT16, ppT188a–T188b, pT209, pT211, pT215, pT261 (Earth) pT18 (beach) pT210 (girl, boy, man and woman) pT214 (tidal wave) pT224 (roadway) pT238, ppT242–T243, pT250 (lightning) pT265 (sunset) pT447 (crop).

Doménico Fabrizi: ppT321–T323 (Olas en el Malecón).

Dorling Kindersley: pT285 (peasant plowing statuette, courtesy of the British Museum).

DoubleClick Studios: pT17 (soda can) pT140 (autograph book) ppT142–T143, pT149 (teacups).

Estefan Enterprises: pT32 (photograph of Gloria Estefan, courtesy of Estefan Enterprises, Inc.

FPG International, LLC: pT15 (hand w/key, VCG) ppT32–T33 (Albert Einstein) pT70 (Amish women, David S. Strickler) pT79 (ants carrying leaves).

George Contorakes: ppT24–T25, T29 (Téssely Estévez) pT26 (Estévez family) pT28 (Téssely at computer, Gilbert Socas).

Liz Garza Williams: pp4–5 (children, background), ppT10–T11 (girl at mirror/ graduation girl) pT15 (boy w/notebook) pT16, pT18 (boy's eye) pT16 (boys reading)

pT17 (at science fair, dropping trash, refusing food) pT18 (boy w/ribbon and boy recycling) pT22 (bedroom, girl & interviewer) ppT36–T37, pT42 (kids in theater) pT38 (playwright, girl painting, actors talking) pT94, T95, T99 (boy & dog) pT96 (trainer w/dog, trainer w/boy) pT97 (trainer, boy & dog, boy & dog, boy & dog) pT98 (boy & dog on obstacle course, elevator, boy & dog on stairs) ppT137–T139 (boy w/baseball and boy w/basketball) pT143 (tablecloth) pT145 (frog houses, feet in mud) pT147, pT180 (girl walking) ppT167–T168 (girl & portraits) pT170 (ears) pT287 (rice, millet, soy beans)

Rubin Guzman: pT32, (Sandra Cisneros)

HarperCollins Publishers: ppT143–T144, T148 (Lessie Jones Little and Eloise Greenfield courtesy of Eloise Greenfield and HarperCollins Publishers.).

Henry Holt: pT188b, pT188 ("Seeing the World Through Pictures" reprinted with permission from the publisher, Henry Holt, Copyright © 1997 by Robert Silvers.).

Robert Hsiang: ppT32, T46, T47, pT49 (Nancy Hom painting self portrait)

The Image Bank: pT13 (boy with pig, Jay Silverman) pT40 (women farmers, Ken Huang) pT450 (island, Guido Alberto Rossi)

Index Stock: p27 (football players), pT446 (adobes, James Lemass)

Liaison Agency, Inc.: pp T68–T69 (basketball team, Gamma Liaison, J.O. Barcelone Pool)

Major League Baseball Photos: pT32 (Sammy Sosa, David Durochik)

MapArt: pT15 (globe map) pT244 (Taiwan map) pT246 (Dominican Republic map)

NASA: p19 (chimp)

Off the Wall: pT124 (sunflower frame)

Patrick Tregenza: pT3, pT5, ppT122a–T122b, ppT122–T123 (boy's head), pT294 (storyteller)

PGA Tour: pT40 (Tiger Woods)

PhotoDisc: p11 (gymnast), p22 (hawk, snake, frog, grasshopper, plants), pT10 (clouds), pT22 (leopard, ferret, lizard, CMCD, giraffe, Jack Hollingsworth), pT40 (measuring tape, C. Borland/PhotoLink), pT46–T47, pT52 (palette, C Squared Studios), ppT55–T56 (girl on mountain, Louise Oldroyd/Life File), pT68 (basketball), pT120 (newspaper), pT146 (piano keys, Alan Pappe), pT174 (scientist, Keith Brofsky), pT192 (burning rainforest, Kim Steele), pT210 (orchids, PhotoLink), pT211 (sunset at lake, Jeremy Woodhouse), pT212 (trees, pond, PhotoLink), pT213 (buffalo drinking, Alan and Sandy Carey, pulp mill, PhotoLink, sewer, S. Meltzer/ PhotoLink), pT214 (crops, C.Borland/ PhotoLink, burned land, D. Normark/PhotoLink, log pile, Kent Knudson/ PhotoLink), pT215 (planting tree, S. Wankel/PhotoLink, girl recycling), pT220 (boy and girl, CMCD), pT260 (record player), ppT238, T245, T247, T249 (droplet, PhotoLink), pT332 (lightning on mountain, Bruce Heineman), pT454 (valley)

PhotoEdit: pT40 (cashier, Michael Newman), pT63 (Tera, Tera and Ricky, Myrleen Ferguson), pT119 (girl, David Young-Wolff), pT224 (damage, cracked street, Jonathan Nourok), pT227 (bridge, Mark Richards), pT348 (family, Spencer Grant), pT351 (boy holding basketball, Michael Newman)

Photo Researchers: ppT124–T125 (best friends, Richard T. Nowitz), pT285 (peasant, Robert E. Murowchick, 1984)

Sea World: pT22 ("Back from the Brink" poster © 1999 SeaWorld, Inc. All rights reserved.

Sarita Chávez Silverman: ppT5, T122-T123, T187 (family photos courtesy of Sarita Chávez Silverman.).

Siede Preis: p13 (flag)

Stockbyte: pT67 (clown hat), pT153 (family)

The Stock Market: p6 (books and cap), pT16 (scientist, Pete Saloutus) pT19 (talking, LWA/Dunn Tardiff) pT41(3 girls, John Henley) pT151 (child & adult, Lance Nelson) pT170 (DNA model, William Schick, molecular model, Jean Miele) pT291 (modern China, David Ball)

Acknowledgments, continued

Superstock: pT44 (Vendredi I, Auguste Herbin © 2000 Artist Rights Society (ARS) New York/ ADAGP Paris) pT90 (mountain climbers)

Stone: COVER (Gateway Arch, St. Louis, MO © Stone Images/Donovan Reese), p7, p10, T2 (Pyramid of Cheffren, Giza, Egypt © Stone Images/Michel Setboun; Gateway Arch, St. Louis, MO © Stone Images/Donovan Reese; Monument Valley, AZ © Stone Images/David Muench; Central Bank of China, Hong Kong © Stone Images/Michel Setboun) ppT14–T17, pT19 (roadway, Stuart McClymont) pT40 (carpenter, Don Smetzer) pT73 (field workers in Vietnam, Oliver Benn) pT74 (men carrying basket, Alan Le Garsmeur) ppT172–T173, pT177 (double helix, Paul Morrell) pT174 (family, Lawrence Migdale) pT176 (different kids, Robert Mort) pT215 (oil spill, Ben Osborne) pT278 (planting rice, Yann Layma)

UN/DPI: pT76 (United Nations)

University of Arizona: ppT292–T293 (Storyteller statue by Helen Sands, courtesy of the Arizona State Museum, University of Arizona.)

Woodfin Camp & Associates: pT70 (barn raising, Paul Solomon) pT73 (dancers, Ken Heyman) pT74 (firefighters, Mike Yamashita; kids playing ball, spill clean-up, A. Ramey), pp T74, T288 (cows plowing, Ken Heyman) pT75 (women quilting, cod fishermen, Eastcott/Momatuik, bee keeper, Timothey Eagan) pT76 (family dinner, Ken Heyman) pT238 (sandbaggers, Eastcott/ Momatuik).

Author and Illustrator Photos:

pT32 (Nadja Halilbegovich, © J. Kevin Wolfe), pT41 (Joanne Ryder); pT47 (Margaret Hillert); pT76 (Ann Morris); pT87 (Francisco Alarcón, © Francisco Dominguez); pT98 (Caroline Arnold, © Arthur Arnold); pT110 (James Ramsey Ulman); pT139 (Myra Cohn Livingston); pT169 (Dorothy Aldis); pT176 (Dorothy Hinshaw Patent); pT202 (Molly Bang); pT216 (Raffi, courtesy of Troubadour Press.); pT237 (Kristina Gregory); pT249 (Richie Chevat); pT273 (Antonia Barber); pT285 (Lily Toy Hong); pT297, T298 Chuck Larkin); ppT309–T310, pT317 (Diane Wolkstein); pT323 (Carmen Agra Deedy).

Illustrations:

Rick Allen: ppT308–T309, ppT312–T316, pT318 (Unwinding the Magic Thread), **Michael Aki and Michael Bergen:** ppT208–T215, pT217 (Protecting Our Planet), **Fian Arroyo:** ppT296–T297, ppT300–T303, pT326 (Pecos Bill), **Molly Bang:** ppT194–T203, pT254 (Common Ground), **Norm Bendell:** pT206 (garden cartoon), **Centre Georges Pompidou:** ppT70-71 (detail), pT139 (*Rhythm, Joie de Vivre*, Robert Delauney, © L & M SERVICES B.V. Amsterdam 200315/Photo Phillippe Migeat/Centre Georges Pompidou), **Chi Chung:** ppT280–T285 (How the Ox Star Fell From Heaven) pT294 (King Solomon), **David Diaz: p3,** pT3, pT5, ppT8a–T8b, ppT8–T9, pT65 (A Very Unique You) pT304 (Tell an Original Story), **Rita Elsner:** ppT229–T230, ppT234–T235 (Earthquake at Dawn), **Morissa Geller:** pT13 (Transparency 2), pT60 (Transparency 16), pT71 (Transparency 21), pT93 (Transparency 27), pT104 (Transparency 31), **Merilee Heyer:** p24 (Character Map drawings), **Chris Higgins:** ppT116, T260 ("Show What You Did," "It's Cool" © Chris Higgins Proof Positive/ Farrowlyne Associates, Inc); **Sandra Holzman:** pT228 (Earthquake at Dawn cover), **Kathleen Kinkopf:** pp14–17, 20 (Amir), ppT82–T88 (Together We Dream), **JoAnn E. Kitchel:** pT126 ("Friendship"), **Bill Maughan:** ppT104–T109, T111 (A Mountain Rescue), **Paul Mirocha:** pT227 (The Making of an Earthquake), pT246 (Hurricane diagram), pT272 (maps of Ancient Greece), pT284 (maps of Ancient China), **David Moreno:** pT266 ("Mount Olympus Rap"), **Barbara Johansen Newman:** pT12 (girl), **John Patrick:** ppT128–T134 (The Qualities of Friendship), **Joel Spector:** ppT268–T273, pT276 (Echo and Narcissus), **Carol Zaloom:** pT154 (banyan tree)

The High Point Development Team

Hampton-Brown extends special thanks to the following individuals and companies who contributed so much to the creation of this series.

Editorial: Susan Blackaby, Janine Boylan, Bonnie Brook, Shirleyann Costigan, Mary Cutler, Phyllis Edwards, Ramiro Ferrey, Cris Phillips-Georg, Fredrick Ignacio, Barbara Linde, Dawn Liseth, Daphne Liu, Sherry Long, Jacalyn Mahler, Marlyn Mangus, S. Michele McFadden, Debbi Neel, Wilma Ramírez, Michael Ryall, Sarita Chávez Silverman, Sharon Ursino, Andreya Valabek, Alison Wells, Virginia Yeater, Lynn Yokoe, Brown Publishing Network, Ink, Inc., and Learning Design Associates, Inc.

Design and Production: Lisa Baehr, Marcia Bateman Walker, Andrea Carter, Darius Detwiler, Jeri Gibson, Lauren Grace, Debbie Saxton, Curtis Spitler, Alicia Sternberg, Jennifer Summers, Debbie Wright Swisher, Margaret Tisdale, Andrea Erin Thompson, Donna Turner, Alex von Dallwitz, JR Walker, Teri Wilson, Adpartner, Art Stopper, Bill Smith Studios, Chaos Factory & Associates, Ray Godfrey, Hooten Design, Proof Positive/Farrowlyne Associates, and Rose Sheifer.

Permissions: Barbara Mathewson